THE
COMPLETE
D·I·Y
MANUAL

THE
COMPLETE
D·I·Y
MANUAL

MIKE LAWRENCE

BLITZ EDITIONS

CONTENTS

INTRODUCTION

DIY has become increasingly popular over the last two decades, and the reasons are obvious. For many of us, our homes are our greatest asset, so making it a pleasing, comfortable, warm, good-looking and weatherproof place to live in – and keeping it that way – is important both for our well-being and our finances!

Nowadays there are a great many new tools and materials available to make life easier for the amateur DIY enthusiast. But tools alone will not tile the roof or re-plumb the washing machine – first of all, you need knowledge of how things work, and the confidence to tackle a job. Both these things are easy to acquire: your confidence will grow with each job you complete to your satisfaction, and you can get all the basic facts you need by reading this book.

The Complete DIY Manual is the perfect guide to help you ensure your property is in top-notch condition. It has clear, step-by-step instructions, easy-to-follow explanations and hundreds of full-colour photographs and illustrations, which I am confident will inspire you to try out and succeed at any number of DIY jobs. From decorating to plumbing and from flooring to tiling, this book is the first step in teaching you how to maintain and improve your home.

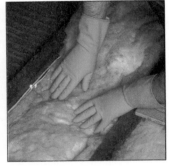

SECTION 1

. . . .

DECORATING

. . . .

TECHNIQUES

. . . .

PAINTING WOOD

Painting is the most popular way of decorating and protecting much of the wood in our homes. As with so many do-it-yourself jobs, getting a good finish depends on your skill. Here's how to paint wood perfectly.

Wood is used extensively in every part of our homes — from roof trusses to skirting boards. Structural timber is usually left rough and unfinished, while joinery — windows, doors, staircases, architraves and so on — is usually decorated in some way. Wood has just one drawback; as a natural material it's prone to deterioration and even decay unless it's protected. Painting wood is one way of combining decoration and protection, and the popularity of paint is a testimony to its effectiveness. Properly applied and well looked after, it gives wood a highly attractive appearance and also provides excellent protection against dampness, dirt, mould, insect attack, and general wear and tear.

Of course, paint isn't the only finish you can choose for wood. If its colour and grain pattern are worth displaying, you can use

PREPARING WOOD FOR PAINT

1 *Before you can apply the paint you must fill any cracks or holes with wood filler (applied with a filling knife) and leave to dry.*

2 *Sand down the filled areas using medium-grade glasspaper. Wrap the abrasive around a sanding block or wood offcut so it's easier to use.*

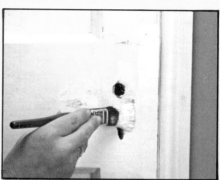

3 *Where paint has been chipped off, sand down the area and apply an ordinary wood primer to the bare wood using a small paintbrush.*

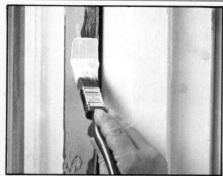

4 *When the surface of the wood is smooth, apply undercoat (as the maker recommends) and leave to dry before you put on the top coat.*

PREPARING PAINT

1 Remove the lid from the paint can using the edge of a knife as a lever – don't use a screwdriver or you'll damage the lip of the lid.

2 Stir the paint (if recommended by the maker) using an offcut of wood, with a turning, lifting motion, or use an electric drill attachment.

3 Decant some paint into a paint kettle, which you'll find easier to carry than a heavy can. Top up the kettle from the can as you work.

4 To load the brush, dip the bristles into the paint to one-third of their length and wipe off excess on a string tied across the kettle rim.

---

oils, stains or varnishes to enhance its looks and also to protect it. But as most of the wood used in our houses is chosen more for performance and price rather than looks, bland and uninteresting softwoods are generally the order of the day for everything from windows and door frames to staircases, skirting boards and door architraves. And painting them offers a number of distinct advantages.

Firstly, paint covers a multitude of sins — knots and other blemishes in the wood surface, poorly-made joints patched up with filler, dents and scratches caused by the rough and tumble of everyday life — and does it in almost every colour of the spectrum. Secondly, paint provides a surface that's hard-wearing and easy to keep clean — an important point for many interior surfaces in the home. And thirdly, paint is easy to apply ... and to keep on applying. In fact, redecorating existing paintwork accounts for the greater part of all paint bought.

What woods can be painted?
In theory you can paint any wood under the sun. In practice, paint (solvent-based or emulsion, see *Ready Reference*), is usually applied only to softwoods — spruce (whitewood), European redwood (deal), pine and the like — and to man-made boards such as plywood, blockboard, hardboard and chipboard. Hardwoods and boards finished with hardwood veneers can be painted, but are usually given a clear or tinted finish to enhance their attractive colour and grain pattern.

Paint systems
If you're decorating new wood, there's more to it than putting on a coat of your chosen paint. It would just soak in where the wood was porous and give a very uneven colour — certainly without the smooth gloss finish expected. It wouldn't stick to the wood very well, nor would it form the continuous surface film needed for full protection. All in all, not very satisfactory. So what is needed is a paint system which consists of built-up layers, each one designed to serve a particular purpose.

The first in the system is a primer (sometimes called a primer/sealer) which stops the paint soaking into porous areas and provides a good key between the bare wood and the paint film. Next, you want another 'layer' — the undercoat — to help build up the paint film and at the same time to obliterate the colour of the primer, so that the top coat which you apply last of all is perfectly smooth and uniform in colour. With some paints — emulsions and non-drip glosses — an undercoat is not always used and instead several coats of primer or two

HOW TO APPLY PAINT

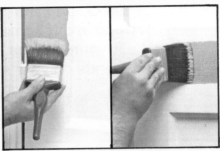

1 Apply the paint along the grain; with non-drip paint (left) you can apply a thicker coat in one go without further spreading (brushing out).

4 Now you must 'lay off' the paint with very light brush strokes along the grain to give a smooth finish that's free from brush marks.

---

top coats are applied with the same result.

The general rule to obey when choosing primer, undercoat and top coat is to stick with the same base types in one paint system, particularly out of doors and on surfaces subjected to heavy wear and tear (staircases and skirting boards, for example). On other indoor woodwork you can combine primers and top coats of different types.

If the wood you are painting has been treated with a preservative to prevent decay (likely only on exterior woodwork) an ordinary primer won't take well. Instead use an aluminium wood primer — not to be confused with aluminium paint — which is recommended for use on all hardwoods too. Oily woods such as teak must be degreased with white spirit and allowed to dry before the primer is applied.

As far as man-made boards are concerned, chipboard is best primed with a solvent-based wood primer to seal its comparatively porous surface. Hardboard is even more porous, and here a stabilising primer (a product more usually used on absorbent or powdery masonry surfaces) is the best product to use. Plywood and blockboard should be primed as for softwood. There's one other

2 *Still working with the grain and without reloading the brush, paint another strip alongside the first one and blend the two together.*

3 *Reload the brush and apply strokes back and forth across the grain over the area you've just painted to ensure full, even coverage.*

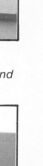

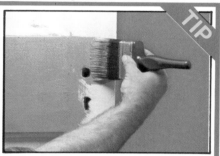

5 *Paint an area adjoining the first in the same way, blending the two sections together by about 50mm (2in) and laying off as before.*

6 *Brush towards edges, not parallel with them or onto them, as the paint will be scraped onto the adjacent face, forming a ridge.*

TIP

WHAT CAN GO WRONG WITH PAINT

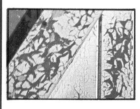

Left: Lifting and flaking occurs if paint is applied over a surface that is damp or powdery.

Right: Crazing is caused when paint is applied over a previous coat that was not completely dry.

Left: Blistering occurs when damp or resin is trapped beneath the paint film and is drawn out by heat.

Right: Cratering results from rain or condensation droplets falling onto the wet paint surface.

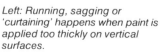

Left: Running, sagging or 'curtaining' happens when paint is applied too thickly on vertical surfaces.

Right: Wrinkling or shrivelling can occur on horizontal surfaces if paint is applied too thickly.

ESTIMATING YOUR NEEDS

Large areas – in all cases coverage per litre depends on the wood's porosity and the painter's technique:
Wood primer 9-15 sq metres (95-160 sq ft)
Aluminium primer 16 sq metres (170 sq ft)
Primer/undercoat 11 sq metres (120 sq ft)
Undercoat 11 sq metres (120 sq ft)
Runny gloss or satin 17 sq metres (180 sq ft)
Non-drip gloss or satin 13 sq metres (140 sq ft)
Runny emulsions 15 sq metres (160 sq ft)
Non-drip emulsions 12 sq metres (130 sq ft)

Small areas – add up all the lengths of wood to be painted. One sq metre is equivalent to:
● 16m (52 ft) of glazing bars
● 10-13m (33-43 ft) of window frame
● 6m (20 ft) of sill
● 10m (33 ft) of narrow skirting
● 3-6m (10-20 ft) of deep skirting

CHOOSING BRUSHES

The best brushes have a generous filling of long bristles and are an even, tapered shape. Cheaper brushes have short, thin bristles and big wooden filler strips to pack them out. The ideal sizes for wood are:
● 25mm (1in) or 50mm (2in) for panel doors, skirtings
● 50mm (2in) or 75mm (3in) for flush doors, skirting, large areas
● 25mm (1in) cutting-in brush for window glazing bars
● 12mm (½in), 25mm (1in) or cheap paintbox brush for spot priming, applying knotting

Alternative to brushes
Paint pads are more widely used on walls than on woodwork, but the crevice or sash paint pad will do the same job as a cutting-in brush. It should be cleaned with white spirit or hot water and washing-up liquid (paint solvents might dissolve the adhesive between the mohair pile and foam).

TIP: PREPARING A BRUSH

Before using a new (or stored) brush work the bristles against the palm of your hand to remove dust and loose hairs.

thing you need to know. If the wood you want to paint has knots in it you should brush a special sealer called knotting over them to stop the resin oozing up through the paint film and spoiling its looks. If the knots are 'live' — exuding sticky yellowish resin — use a blow-torch to draw out the resin and scrape it off before applying knotting.

Paint on paint

You'll often want to paint wood that has already been painted. How you tackle this depends on the state of the existing paint-work. If it's flaking off and is in generally poor condition, you will have to remove the entire paint system — primer, undercoat and top coat — by burning off with a blow-torch,

applying a chemical paint stripper or rubbing with an abrasive. You then treat the stripped wood as already described for new wood.

Where the paintwork is in good condition, you simply have to clean it and sand it down lightly to provide a key for the new paint and to remove any small bits that got stuck in the surface when it was last painted. Then you can apply fresh top coat over the surface; the paint system is already there. You may, of course, need two top coats if you add a light colour to a dark one to stop the colour beneath from showing through.

If the paintwork is basically sound but needs localised attention, you can scrape or sand these damaged areas back to bare wood and 'spot-treat' them with primer and

undercoat to bring the patch up to the level of the surrounding paintwork, ready for a final top coat over the entire surface.

Painting large areas

Though the same principle applies to wood as it does to any other large surface area — ie, you divide it into manageable sections and complete one before moving on to another — if you're using an oil-based gloss paint you have to make sure that the completed area hasn't dried to such an extent that you cannot blend in the new. On the rare occasion that you might want to paint a whole wall of wood you should make the section no wider than a couple of brush widths and work from ceiling to floor.

With emulsions there isn't the same problem for although they are quick drying the nature of the paint is such that brush marks don't show.

You might think that a wide brush is the best for a large area but the constant flexing action of the wrist in moving the brush up and down will tire you out fast. Holding a brush is an art in itself and aches are the first indication that you're doing it wrongly. A thin brush should be held by the handle like a pencil, while a wider brush should be held with the fingers and thumb gripping the brush just above the bristles.

You'll find a variety of paint brushes on sale — some are designed to be 'throwaway' (good if you only have one or two jobs to do), others will stand you in good stead for years. But remember before using a new brush to brush the bristles back and forth against the palm of your hand — this is called 'flirting' and will dislodge any dust or loose hairs that could spoil your paintwork.

It is wise to decant the paint to save you moving a heavy can from place to place — a paint kettle which resembles a small bucket is made for the purpose. Plastic ones are easier to keep clean than metal ones.

Never be tempted to dip the bristles too far into the paint and always scrape off excess from both sides. Paint has the habit of building up inside the brush and if this happens on overhead work, you risk it running down the handle and onto your arm.

Painting small areas

These tend to be the fiddly woodwork on windows, around doors and lengths of stairs or skirting boards — and the hardest bit about all of them is working out how much paint you'll need (see *Ready Reference*).

Special shaped or narrow brushes can make painting these areas easier — for example, they prevent you 'straddling' angles in wood (like you find on mouldings) which damages the bristles in the middle of the brush. With windows and panelled doors you should also follow an order of working to

ORDER OF PAINTING

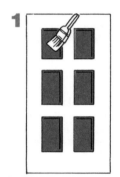 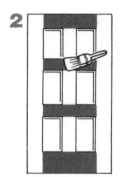 

Panel doors: *tackle any mouldings first, then the recessed panels, horizontal members, vertical members and lastly the edges.*

 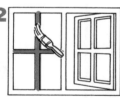 

Casement windows: *start with any glazing bars, then paint the opening casement itself (the hinge edge is the only one which should match the inside); lastly paint the frame.*

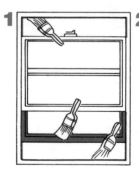 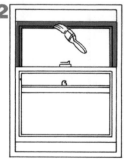 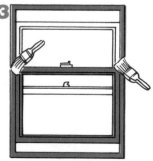

Sash windows: *paint the inside top and bottom and a little way up and down the sides of the frame first. Then paint the bottom of the outer sash. Move the sashes and do the rest of the outer sash, the inner sash and finally the frame.*

avoid causing overlap marks on the parts you've already painted.

Fiddly or not, they are the jobs you have to do first if you are putting up wallcoverings (if you're painting a room, the walls should be done before the woodwork) so that the drops can be placed against finished edges. If you want to touch up the paint without changing the wallpaper, it's best to use a paint shield.

Getting ready to paint

Ideally, before painting doors and windows you should remove all the 'furniture' — handles, fingerplates, keyholes, hooks etc — so you can move the brush freely without interruption. You should also take time to read the manufacturer's instructions on the can. If, for example, they tell you to stir the paint, then stir it for this is the only way of distributing the particles which have settled.

If you open a can of non-drip paint and find a layer of solvent on the top, you should stir it in, then leave it to become jelly-like again before painting.

All your brushes should be dry — this is something to remember if you are painting over several days and have put them to soak overnight in white spirit or a proprietary brush cleaner. If you don't get rid of all the traces of the liquid it will mess up your paint-work. They should be rinsed, then brushed on newspaper till the strokes leave no sign.

Cleaning up

When you've finished painting clean your brushes thoroughly, concentrating on the roots where paint accumulates and will harden. They should be hung up, bristles down, till dry, then wrapped in aluminium foil for storage. Don't ever store them damp for they can be ruined by mildew.

If there's only a small amount of paint left, you can either decant it for storage into a dark glass screw-topped jar so you can use it to touch up damaged spots — it's important to choose a suitable sized jar so there's very little air space. Air and dust are both potential paint spoilers and there are two ways to keep them out if you're storing the can. Either put a circle of aluminium foil over the paint surface before putting the lid on securely, or — and this is the best way if the lid is distorted — put on the lid and then invert the can to spread the paint round the inner rim to form an airtight seal. Set it back the right way for storage.

If despite these safeguards a skin forms on the paint (usually over months of storage) you have to cut round the edge of it with a sharp knife and carefully lift it off.

PAINTING WINDOWS

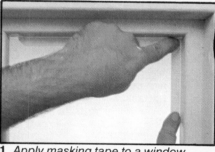

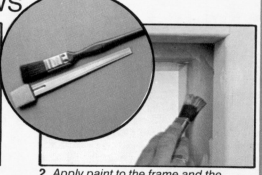

1 *Apply masking tape to a window pane to prevent paint getting onto the glass – leave 3mm (1/8in) of glass exposed so the paint forms a seal.*

2 *Apply paint to the frame and the glazing bars using a small brush, or (inset) a cutting-in brush or a sash paint pad.*

3 *Apply the paint along the grain; remove the tape when the paint is almost dry – if it dries completely you might peel it off with the tape.*

4 *An alternative way of keeping paint off the glass is to use a paint shield or offcut of plywood but, again, leave a paint margin on the glass.*

PAINTING WALLS AND CEILINGS

The quickest and cheapest way to transform a room is to paint the walls and ceiling. But, for a successful result, you have to prepare the surfaces properly and use the correct painting techniques.

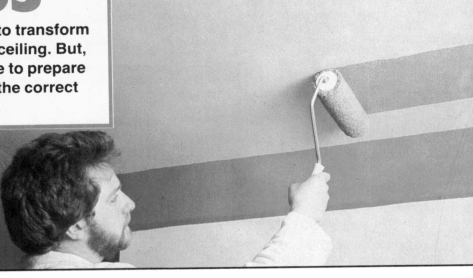

P aint is the most popular material used to protect and decorate walls and ceilings in the home. Whereas many people hesitate before hanging wallpaper or sticking more permanent wall and ceiling coverings in place, few would worry about wielding a paint brush for the first time.

One of the chief advantages of painting a room is that it doesn't take much time; large areas can be given two or even three coats of emulsion paint in a day. The paints now available are hardwearing and totally unlike earlier distemper and water paints. They are easy to apply by brush, roller or pad and can be safely washed at frequent intervals to keep them looking fresh.

Any drawbacks are usually caused by faults in the wall or ceiling surface, rather than by the paints. A standard paint alone cannot cover up defects in the same way that some other wallcoverings can, so a surface which is to be painted usually needs more careful preparation than one which is to be papered.

The majority of walls and ceilings are plastered and this type of surface, when in sound condition, is ideal as a base for emulsion and other paints. But it is not the only surface finish you are likely to come across.

Previous occupiers of the house may well have covered the walls with a decorative paper and even painted on top of that. At the very worst there may be several layers of paper and paint, making it very difficult to achieve a smooth paint surface. In this situation it is invariably better to strip the surface completely down to the plaster and to start again from scratch.

This does not mean that no paper should be overpainted. Certain types such as plain white relief wallcoverings and woodchips are intended to be so treated, and actually look 'softer' after one or two redecorations. In short, most wall or ceiling surfaces you are likely to encounter will be paintable. All you have to do is select the right paint for the job and get the surface into as good a condition as possible.

Choosing paints
Vinyl emulsion paints are the most commonly used types of paint for painting walls and ceilings. They are easy to apply and come in a wide range of colours. You will usually have a choice of three finishes: matt, silk, or gloss.

There are also textured paints which are increasing in popularity, particularly for ceiling use. These are vinyl emulsion paints with added 'body' so they can be applied more thickly and then given a decorative textured finish.

Oil-based eggshell paints can be used where a more durable surface is needed or where you want to use the same colour on both walls and woodwork. Resin-based gloss paint is used occasionally also on walls and ceilings, particularly in humid rooms like kitchens and bathrooms.

You should choose paint carefully. The fact that one make is half the price of another may indicate that it has only half the covering power and you would therefore need to apply two coats of the cheaper paint. Also, if you're using white paint, you may find that one brand is noticeably 'whiter' than another.

Tools and equipment
Few specialised tools are needed for wall and ceiling paintwork. If you are content to work with only a brush you will require two sizes: one larger one for the bulk of the work, and a smaller brush for working into corners. It is worth decanting quantities of paint into a paint kettle which is easier to carry around than large heavy cans.

Rollers make the job of painting large areas of wall or ceiling much quicker and also help to achieve a better finish. But you will still need a small brush for working into corners and for dealing with coving, cornices etc.

To prepare a new fibre roller for painting, soak it in soapy water for 2 to 3 hours to get rid of any loose bits of fibre, then roll it out on the wall to dry it off. One point to remember: if you intend using silk vinyl emulsion paint, it's best not to use a roller as this tends to show up as a stippled effect on the silk surface.

Large paint pads will also enable you to cover big expanses of wall or ceiling very quickly. You can use a brush or a small paint pad for work in corners.

Apart from these paint application tools you'll need a variety of other items for preparing the surfaces so they're ready for the paint. The walls must be cleaned, so you'll need washing-down equipment: sponges, cloths, detergent, and a bucket or two of water.

You'll need filler for cracks and a filling knife about 75mm (3in) wide. When any filler is dry it will need to be sanded down, so have some glasspaper ready for wrapping round a cork sanding block. A scraper will also be needed if old wallpaper has to be stripped from the walls.

Finally, because of the height of the walls and ceiling, you'll need access equipment, such as a stepladder, to enable you to reach them safely and comfortably.

Preparing the surface
No painting will be successful until the

PAINTING THE CEILING WITH A ROLLER

1 Use a brush to paint a strip about 50mm wide round the outside edge of the ceiling; a roller cannot reach right into angles or corners.

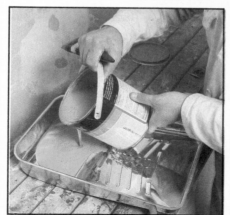

2 Pour paint into the roller tray; don't put in too much at a time or you risk overloading the roller and splashing paint out of the tray.

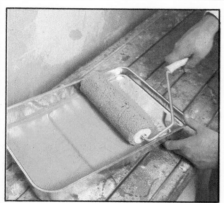

3 Dip the roller in and pull it back so there is paint at the shallow end of the tray. Push the roller back and forth in the paint at the shallow end.

4 Run the roller over the ceiling so there is a band of paint next to the strip of paint you have brushed along the edge of the ceiling.

5 Reverse the roller's direction so you join up the two strips of paint into one band. Then finish off by running the roller over the band.

6 Now start the next section by running the roller alongside the completed band. Work your way round the ceiling in bands.

Ready Reference

LINING WALL SURFACES

You can use lining paper to do the same job for paint as it does for wallpapers, covering minor cracks and defects on the wall or ceiling and providing a smooth surface for painting.

TIP: SEAL STRONG COLOURS

Wallcoverings with strong colourings, and particularly those tinted with metallic inks, will almost certainly show through the new paint. To prevent this they should be stripped off, or sealed with special aluminium spirit-based sealer.

FILLING HAIRLINE CRACKS

You may not be able to push enough filler into hairline cracks to ensure a good bond:
● it is often better to open the crack up further with the edge of an old chisel or screwdriver so the filler can penetrate more deeply and key better to both sides of the crack
● when using a textured vinyl paint there is no need to fill hairline cracks, but cracks wider than 1mm ($\frac{1}{32}$in) should be filled.

DEALING WITH FITTINGS

Protect electrical fittings so paint or water can't enter them during cleaning and decorating:
● ideally, power to these fittings should be cut off and the fittings removed
● if items cannot be removed, use masking tape to protect them.

SELECTING PAINTS

When choosing paints, remember that:
● emulsion paints are quicker to apply, dry more quickly and lack the smell of resin- or oil-based paints. They are also cheaper and can be easily cleaned off painting equipment with water
● non-drip paints are best for ceilings and cover more thickly than runny ones, cutting down on the number of coats
● a silk or gloss finish will tend to highlight surface irregularities more than a matt finish
● textured paints are suitable for use on surfaces which are in poor condition since they will cover defects which a standard emulsion paint cannot.

For more information see pages 9–13.

PAINTING THE WALL WITH A BRUSH

1 *Use a small brush to cut in at the wall and ceiling join and in corners. With a larger brush paint the wall in bands. First, brush across the wall.*

2 *Move the brush across the wall in the opposite direction. The bands of paint should be about 1m wide and you should be working downwards.*

3 *When you are working at the top of the wall your next strokes should be downwards to complete the area you have covered with crossways strokes.*

4 *At the bottom two-thirds of the wall continue working in crossways strokes, but this time finish off each section by brushing upwards.*

USING PAINT PADS

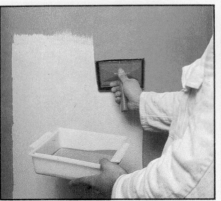

1 *Thin the paint a little (with water for emulsions, turps for oil-based ones). Cut in with a small brush or pad and use a larger pad to paint in bands.*

2 *For precise work you can use a small pad like this. Ensure that you cover areas you don't want painted with masking tape.*

---

surface beneath has been properly prepared. Unless wallpaper is of a type intended for painting it is usually better to strip it off, and walls which have been stripped of their previous wallcoverings need a thorough washing to remove all traces of old paste. Make sure the floor is protected against debris by covering it with a dust sheet or sheets of old newspaper. Emulsion-painted walls also need washing to remove surface dirt. In both cases, use warm water with a little household detergent added. Then rinse with clean water.

If you decide to leave the wallpaper on the walls you will have to wash it down before you paint. Take care to avoid overwetting the paper, particularly at joins. When the surface is dry, check the seams; if any have lifted, stick them down with a ready-mixed paste.

Ceilings should be washed in small areas at a time and rinsed thoroughly before you

move onto another section systematically.

If the surfaces are left in perfect condition, they can be painted as soon as they are dry.

It's possible that walls or ceilings may have been painted with distemper, which may only become apparent after you have removed the existing wallcovering. Unless it is the washable type, you will have to remove it completely since emulsion paint will not adhere well to it. Use hot water, detergent and a scrubbing brush to soften and get rid of the coating; this is hard work, but you could use a steam stripper to speed up the process.

With all the surface cleaned, the next job is to fill any cracks and repair defects such a as indentations caused perhaps by knocks or the blade of a carelessly handled wallpaper scraper (see *Ready Reference*).

Whenever a filler has been used it should be sanded down flush with the wall surface,

once dry, and the resulting dust should be brushed away.

If the plaster is in bad condition and obviously covered in cracks you should consider covering it completely with liningpaper, woodchip or other relief wallcovering before painting it. The paper will provide a good base for redecoration, and will save a great deal of preparation time. However, this can only be done if the plaster itself is still bonded securely to the wall. If it is coming away in chunks or sounds hollow behind the cracks, then the wall should be replastered

Cracks which have developed round door and window frames are best filled with a flexible sealant, which will be unaffected by movement of the frames. Acrylic-based sealants are available for this purpose and they can be easily overpainted.

After all the preparation work has been

PAINTING PROCEDURE

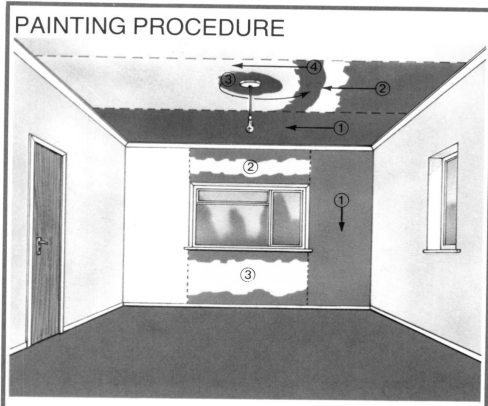

Paint the ceiling first in 1m-wide bands (1 & 2). Paint round a ceiling rose (3), then complete the rest of that band (4). On walls work downwards (1). At a window, paint along the top band (2) and repeat the process at the bottom (3). Work from right to left unless you are left-handed.

completed, have a good clear-up in the room so that when you begin painting you do not stir up dust and have to work around numerous bits and pieces scattered over the floor space.

Re-lay dust sheets and set up your access equipment before even opening the first can of paint. Make sure your brushes or rollers are clean and ready for use.

Painting sequences

If possible, do all your painting in daylight hours. Artificial light is less easy to work by and can lead to small areas being missed.

Painting is always done from the highest point downwards, so ceilings are the first areas to be tackled. The whole ceiling will be painted in bands across the room no wider than you can easily reach without stretching on your stepladder or platform. This generally means that at any one time you will probably be painting a band no wider than 1m and less than 2m long unless you are using scaffolding boards to support you.

You start at the edges first and then work into the main body of the room.

Linking one section to another is seldom difficult with emulsion paint and is simply a matter of blending the paint from the new section back into the previous one.

Walls are treated similarly, starting at the top and working downwards in sections about 1m wide, cutting in at the ceiling and at return walls.

Painting tips

The number of coats required will depend on the previous colour and condition of the surface and the type of paint. If another coat has to be applied, be sure that the previous one is fully dry first. With modern vinyl emulsion paint it may be that because the paint is water-based it will cause the paper underneath to swell and bubble; however, you shouldn't worry about this because as the water in the paint dries out the paper and paste behind the paint surface will begin to flatten again.

If the paper is badly hung with a lack of adhesive at the edge, seams may lift as the paint dries. They will have to be stuck down in the same way as if they had lifted during washing. Careful preparation would prevent this problem anyway.

STAINING AND VARNISHING WOOD

If you want to decorate and protect the woodwork around your home without obliterating its grain pattern with paint, wood stains and varnishes offer a wide choice of finishes. Here's how to get the best results.

When it comes to giving wood a clear finish, you can choose from a variety of traditional and modern materials, including oils, wax, French polish and different types of varnish. Some are suitable for exterior use, others for interior use only. The degree of skill you need to apply them varies; some are quite simple to use, whereas others, like French polish, require special techniques acquired only by patient practice. The type of wood may affect your choice of finish; for example, open-textured woods like teak, iroko and afrormosia are best treated with an oil finish – they don't take varnishes well.

.You may decide to change the colour of the wood before you finish it. You can use a varnish which incorporates a colour or apply a wood stain and then coat the wood with clear varnish or another clear finish.

If you don't wish to change the colour of the wood, but want to restore it to its natural colour – for example, where the wood has been slightly darkened by the action of a paint stripper – you can use a proprietary colour restorer.

Types of varnish and stains
Clear varnishes are like paint without the pigment. They contain a resin carried in a drying oil or spirit and it is the resin which gives a hard protective finish to wood. Traditionally, the resins used were like copal, natural and obtained from various tropical trees, but in modern varnishes they are synthetic, for example alkyd or polyurethane.

While other varnishes are available, by far the easiest to obtain and most widely used are those containing polyurethane resin. Polyurethane varnish is available in gloss, satin or matt finishes and for interior or exterior use. A non-drip variety is particularly suitable for vertical surfaces, ceilings and hard-to-get-at areas.

There are polyurethane varnishes which have added pigments and are known as coloured sealers. It's quicker to use one of these rather than to apply a wood-stain followed by a clear finish but you won't get the same depth of colour, and if the coloured varnish chips in use, timber of a different colour will show through.

Wood stains are colouring pigments suspended in water, oil or spirits. Some come ready-mixed; others in powder form to be mixed up. Oil-based stains tend to be more difficult to obtain and are not as widely used as the other two types.

Preparing the surface
Before staining, bleaching, varnishing or using other types of finish you should ensure that the surface is clean, dry, smooth and free from any old paint or varnish.

To smooth down a flat surface you can use glasspaper wrapped around a sanding block. On small curves and fiddly bits wrap small strips of abrasive round a pencil. For larger curves use a sanding glove which you can make yourself (see *Ready Reference*).

A powered sander is a boon on large surfaces; use an orbital sander rather than the disc type which is tricky to use without causing scratches across the grain.

Besides getting rid of shallow scratches, sanding will also get rid of cigarette burns and similar marks on the wood surface. However, make sure you don't sand for too long in one place or you will leave a depression that will show up after finishing.

Large cracks and dents can be filled with wax (from a crayon of a suitable colour, for instance) or with a proprietary wood

18

filler. But since stains don't hide fillers in the same way as paint would, you may decide not to carry out such treatment and to leave the blemishes for an authentic 'old wood' look. If you do decide to use a filler, don't try to smooth it flat as you apply it with the knife or you'll risk spreading it round – it tends to show up in the nearby grain if it is rubbed in when wet.

Finally, you should make sure the surface is dust-free by wiping it with a clean, dry cloth or a fine brush. It's a good idea, too, to wipe it with a cloth soaked in turpentine to remove any greasy fingermarks you may have left while preparing the surface.

Bleaching wood

One of the snags with staining wood is that you cannot make the surface lighter; you can only make it darker. A light-coloured stain on a darkish piece of wood just won't work. The way round this problem is to bleach the wood before you start sealing it – and for this proprietary wood bleaches are available at most hardware stores.

Some bleaches are applied in one stage and others in two stages. The wood is washed with a neutralizing agent afterwards so the bleach doesn't carry on working when the finish is applied. Follow the manufacturer's instructions when applying the bleach, particularly concerning the time you should allow for each stage of the treatment. Usually, bleach is applied with a sponge or brush; make sure you use a white fibre brush or the dye in the brush may come out onto the wood.

Staining wood

You can apply the stain with a brush or a folded lint-free rag. Aim to get the colour you want in one coat; a second coat can be applied if needed to get a darker finish, but too many coats will result in the stain lying on the surface, lengthening the time it takes for the subsequent coat of varnish to dry and even preventing it from bonding properly to the surface. With water-based types, if overlaps show when the first coat dries you can add about 20 per cent more water to a mixed-up solution of stain and apply a second coat over the whole surface, brushing it out well.

After the stain has dried (usually about 24 hours after application), you should rub the surface thoroughly with a dry cloth to remove excess stain.

Filling the grain

It's not necessary to fill the grain of softwoods, but for a good finish on open-grained hardwoods like oak, mahogany and walnut you will have to apply a grain filler

BLEACHING WOOD

1 In a two-stage bleaching process, apply the first solution liberally and leave it to work for the recommended time – usually 10 to 20 minutes.

2 Brush on the second solution, leaving it to work. If the wood is very dark or stained, reapply both solutions. If a crust forms, wipe it off with a damp rag.

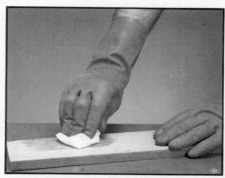

3 Wash the wood with a solution of acetic acid (white vinegar) and water to neutralise the bleach. Allow it to dry completely before staining it.

STAINING WOOD

1 Shake the can well and then pour the stain into a dish wide enough for you to dip in a cloth pad. Avoid plastic dishes; some stains may attack them.

2 Apply the stain liberally using a cloth pad. If you apply it too sparingly you run the risk of getting light and dark areas instead of even coverage.

3 For greater grain contrast, wipe over each strip with a rag after allowing a minute or so for penetration. Leave to dry for 24 hours before varnishing.

VARNISHING WOOD

1 *After you've made sure the surface is clean and dry, use a clean cloth pad to apply the first coat. Rub it well into the wood along the grain.*

2 *Leave the first coat to dry and then brush on the next coat. Make sure the brush is really clean, with no paint particles or loose bristles to mar the finish.*

3 *When brushing, it is important to work with the grain and brush out fully. On a narrow surface like a shelf upright, first apply the varnish in one stroke.*

4 *Then work the brush out towards the edges of the upright, working first to one edge and then to the other, using gentle but firm strokes.*

5 *To complete coating the upright, again move the brush in one upward stroke. This technique will ensure that there are no ugly 'runs' at the edges.*

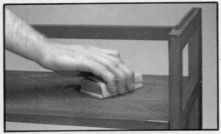

6 *Leave each coat to dry for the recommended time (approx 12 hours) before re-coating. Rub down between coats with flour-grade glass paper.*

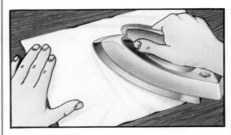
to the wood surface before using varnish.

There are various proprietary fillers available in either a paste or liquid form; choose one to match the wood or stain you are using. Follow the manufacturer's instructions for applying it; normally, you work the filler over the wood with a brush or cloth, wipe off the excess and then sand the surface lightly down with fine glasspaper.

Varnishing wood
Polyurethane varnish is easy to apply; you simply brush it on, taking care to work with the grain of the wood. Follow the manufacturer's instructions as to the number of coats you should apply and the time

allowed between each coat – at least 12 hours. You should sand down the surface lightly with flour-grade glasspaper between coats to provide a key for the next coat, and remove any dust that's accumulated during application with a damp cloth.

As with paints, it's advisable to stir the contents of any can of varnish that's been stored for a while. This ensures an even distribution of the solvents so that the varnish dries evenly when it is applied. Although the varnish will be touch-dry in about 4 hours, it may take as long as 7 days before the surface reaches full hardness – so avoid standing anything on the newly-decorated surface for a week or so.

PAPERING WALLS
the basics

No other wall covering can quite so dramatically alter the look and feeling of a room as wallpaper. Correctly hung paper makes the walls sharp and fresh, and to achieve this finish there are important things to know. What do you do if the walls are out of true? Where's the best place to start? How do you prevent bubbles and creases? The answers are here.

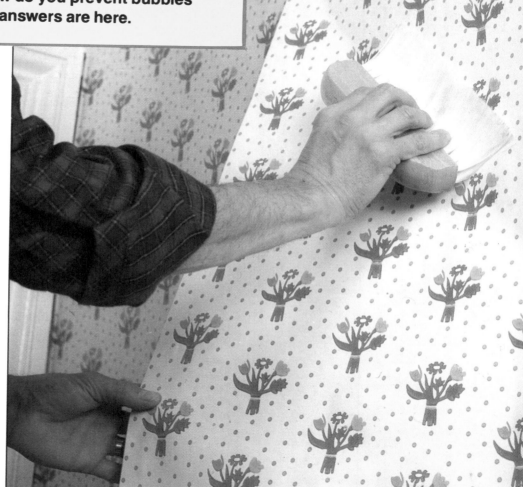

Wallpapering isn't so much an art, it's more a matter of attention to detail. And perhaps the first mistake that's made by many people is expecting too much of their walls. Rarely are walls perfectly flat, perfectly vertical and at right angles to each other. So the first and most crucial part of hanging wallpaper is to prepare the walls properly. Obviously you can't change their basic character – if they're not entirely flat or vertical, you're stuck with them – but you can make sure that the surface is suitably prepared so that the new paper will stick.

This means that any old wallpaper really should come off before you do anything else. Papering on top of old wall coverings won't *always* lead to disaster, but it will quite often simply because the new adhesive will tend to loosen the old. The result will be bubbles at best and peeling at worst.

Adhesives
Always use the correct adhesive for the wallcovering and follow the manufacturers instructions for mixing. Using the wrong paste can result in the paper not sticking, mould growth or discoloration of the paper.

A cellulose-based adhesive is used for all standard wallcoverings. There are two types, ordinary and heavy-duty which relates to the weight of the paper being hung. Heavy-duty pastes are for heavyweight wallcoverings. Certain brands of paste are suitable for all types of wallcoverings – less water being used for mixing when hanging heavy papers.

Since vinyls and washable wallcoverings are impervious, mould could attack the paste unless it contains a fungicide. Fungicidal paste is also needed if the wall has previously been treated against mould or if there is any sign of damp.

Some wallcoverings (like polyethylene foam, some hessians and foils) require a specially thick adhesive which is pasted onto the wall. Follow manufacturers' instructions.

Ready-pasted papers are exactly that and require no extra adhesive – although it's useful to have a tube of latex glue handy for finishing off corners and joints which mightn't

have stuck. (The same applies to all washable wallpapers).

Glue *size* (a watered down adhesive) is brushed over the walls before papering to seal them and prevent the paste from soaking in to the wall. It also ensures all-over adhesion and makes sliding the paper into place easier.

Although size can be bought, most wallpaper pastes will make size when mixed with the amount of water stated in the instructions.

If you buy a proprietary size and the wallcovering you are using needs an adhesive containing ∙ fungicide, make sure that the size you buy also contains a

fungicide. Use an old brush to apply and a damp cloth to clean off any that runs on to paintwork. It can be difficult to remove after it has dried. Sizing can be done several days or an hour before.

Where to begin
The traditional rule is to start next to the window and work away from it, but that is really a hangover from the days when paper was overlapped and shadows showed up joins. Today, papers butt up, so light isn't the problem. But as inaccuracies can occur with slight loss of pattern, you have to be able to make this as inconspicuous as possible. In

21

STRIPPING OLD WALLPAPER

Never hang new coverings over existing wallpaper – the old may lift and bring the new with it.

Ordinary wallpaper:
● use hot water with washing-up liquid or proprietary wallpaper stripper to soak the surface
● scrape off old paper in strips with broad-bladed scraper, re-soaking stubborn areas; wash surface down to remove bits

Washable or painted wallpaper:
● always score surface coating with serrated scraper before soaking and scraping
● for large areas a steam stripper (from hire shops) is a real time-saver

Vinyl wallcovering:
● lift corner of vinyl coating at skirting board level and peel away from backing paper by pulling steadily up and away
● then soak and scrape off backing paper

WHERE TO START

Room with a chimney breast: start at its centre and work outward to each end of the chimney wall, then on down the two side walls towards the door. Any loss of pattern will be least noticed in the short lengths hung over the door.

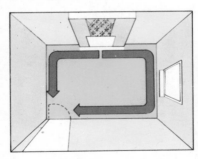

Room without a chimney breast: start at one corner of the room – ideally near the door – and work around continuously until you return to your starting point.

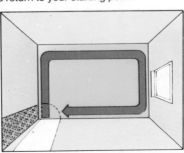

an average room, the corner nearest the door is the best starting point. Any loss of pattern will then end up behind you as you enter the room. In a room with a chimney breast, hang the first drop in the centre and work outwards from both sides of the drop.

Problem areas in a house (window reveals, recesses, arches, dormers) are dealt with on pages 26-29.

Measuring and cutting

Measure the height of the wall you want to paper using a steel tape measure and cut a piece of paper from the roll to this length, allowing an extra 50mm (2in) top and bottom for trimming. This allowance is needed for pattern matching, and to ensure a neat finish at skirting board and ceiling.

Lay the first drop — that's the name given to each length of paper — pattern side up on the table and unroll the paper from which the

second drop is to be cut next to it. Move this along until the patterns match, then cut the second drop using the other end of the first as a guide. Subsequent lengths of paper are cut in exactly the same way, with each matching the drop that preceded it.

Remember some wallpapers have patterns that are a straight match across the width, while others have what is called a drop pattern that rises as it extends across the width. With drop match papers the second length will begin half a pattern repeat further along the roll. Length 3 will match length 1, length 4 will match length 2 and so on.

For things to run smoothly, you should establish a work routine when paper hanging. Cut all the wall drops first (so you only have to measure once) and cut bits for papering above windows and doors as you come to them. If you paste say 3 drops, the first will have had its required soaking time

HOW TO CUT AND PASTE

1 Mark the pasting table with lines at 150mm (6in) and 300mm (1ft) intervals. Measure wall drop and use guidelines to cut your first length.

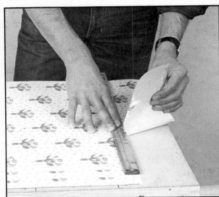

2 Use the first length as a guide for the other drops, matching the pattern carefully. Tear off the waste against a wooden rule.

3 Lay all the drops pattern down, overhanging the far edge of the table. Pull the first drop to the near edge and paste it from centre to edges.

4 Fold pasted end, paste the rest and fold in. Now fold up the whole drop and leave it to soak. The top of the longer fold always goes to the top of the wall.

PAPER HANGING TECHNIQUES

1 Place chosen pattern on ceiling line with waste above. Align side edge with vertical and turn waste onto adjacent wall. Brush up to ceiling first, then corners and edges, and then down. Open out short fold last.

2 Mark cutting line for waste at ceiling and skirting board with a pencil — ends of scissors won't fit creases neatly and can give a thick line which causes you to cut the paper inaccurately and will give an uneven look at ceiling and skirting.

3 To cut waste, pull short length of paper away from wall so pencil line catches the light. Cut using full length of blades — hurried, short cuts can make the edges jagged. Brush paper back on wall so that it is perfectly flat.

4 Reduce waste on adjacent wall to 6mm (¼in) to lessen bulk when paper overlaps from other direction.

5 Continue along wall matching the pattern horizontally. Press drop onto wall so long edges butt.

6 As each drop is hung, brush up first, then to edges and finally down to remove any trapped air.

7 To turn a corner, measure between hung paper and corner at the top, middle and bottom of wall. Add 6mm (¼in) to widest width, then use this measurement to cut the pasted and folded drop into two. Set aside offcut for new wall.

8 Hang drop to complete wall, brushing the waste round the corner. Find the new vertical and mark the line the width of offcut from the corner. Check this measurement at the top, middle and bottom of wall. If the same, hang offcut.

9 If corner is out of true, offcut and wall measurements will differ. To disguise pattern loss, hang the offcut so waste laps onto completed wall. Brush into corner, run pencil down crease line and cut waste.

(with medium weight paper) by the time the third is pasted and folded and is ready to be hung. With heavy papers paste, fold and soak 6 drops at a time as extra soaking time is needed.

Avoiding bubbles
The purpose behind soaking time (apart from making paper supple enough to handle) is to give it time to expand to its natural limit. On the width this can be 6mm-12mm (¼in-½in) and the average wall-size drop will gain 24mm (1in) on the length – this explains why you have more to cut as waste than you started with.

If you haven't given paper the time it needs, it will expand on the walls – but its spread will be contained by adjoining drops and so you get bubbles in the central part.

Soak medium weight papers for 3-4 minutes, heavy weights for about 10. Ready-pasted papers don't need too long a soaking, but to ensure they get wet all over, roll drops loosely and press into water till they are completely covered.

Pasting and soaking
Position the paper with its top edge at the right-hand end of the table (or at the other end if you're left handed). Paste it carefully to ensure that all parts, the edges especially, are well covered. Work from the centre outwards in herring-bone style using the width of the brush to cover the drop in sweeps, first to the nearest edge, then the other – excess paste here will go onto second drop, not the table. Cover two-thirds of the drop, then fold the top edge in so paste is to paste. Move the drop along the table and paste the remainder, folding bottom edge in paste to paste. Because the first folded part is longer than the other, this will remind you which is the

top. Fold the drop up and put aside to soak while you paste the others.

This technique will give you a manageable parcel of paper to hang no matter what length the drop – but always remember to make the first fold longer – this is the one offered to the ceiling line. If in doubt mark the top edge lightly with a pencil cross.

Hanging pasted paper
Wallpaper must be hung absolutely vertical if it is to look right, so always work to a vertical line (see *Ready Reference).*

Position your step ladder as close as possible to where you want to work, and climb it with the first length of paper under or over your arm. Open out the long fold and offer the top edge up, placing the pattern as you want it at the ceiling with waste above. Align the side edge of the drop with your vertical guide line, allowing the other side edge to turn onto the adjacent wall if starting at a corner. Smooth the paper onto the wall with the paperhanging brush, using the bristle ends to form a crease between wall and ceiling, and at corners. When brushing paper into place, always work up first then to the join, then to the side edge, then down. This will remove trapped air.

As soon as the paper is holding in place, work down the wall, brushing the rest of the drop in position, opening out the bottom fold when you reach it. Again use the bristle ends to form a good crease where paper meets the skirting board.

The next step is to trim off the waste paper at the top and bottom. Run a lead pencil along the crease between the ceiling or skirting and the wall — the blades or points of scissors wil make a line that's too thick for accurate cutting. Gently peel paper away from the wall and cut carefully along the line with your scissors. Finally brush the paper back in place.

Hanging the second drop is done as the

Estimator

Most wallpaper is sold in rolls 10.05m (11yds) long and 530mm (21in) wide. Calculate rolls needed by measuring perimeter of the room and height from skirting board to ceiling.

WALLS	Distance around the room (doors and windows included)										
Height from skirting	10m 33'	11m 36'	12m 39'	13m 43'	14m 46'	15m 49'	16m 52'	17m 56'	18m 59'	19m 62'	20m 66'
2.15–2.30m (7'–7'6")	5	5	5	6	6	7	7	8	8	9	9
2.30–2.45m (7'6"–8')	5	5	6	6	7	7	8	8	9	9	10
2.45–2.60m (8'–8'6")	5	6	6	7	7	8	9	9	10	10	11

The number of rolls needed can be greatly affected by the frequency of pattern repeat. With a large pattern repeat, buy an extra roll first except that you have to butt it up against the edge of the first length, matching the pattern across the two. The secret here is not to try and do it all in one go. Get the paper onto the wall at the right place at the ceiling join but just a little way away from the first length. Now press against the paper with the palms of your hands and slide it into place. Using well-soaked paper on a wall that's been sized makes this easy, but if you're using a thin wallpaper press gently as it could tear. Butt the paper up after pattern matching and brush into place.

When trimming waste from drops other than the first, cut from where the lengths butt to ensure even ceiling and skirting lines.

Hanging ready-pasted wallpaper
With these you won't need pasting table, bucket and pasting brush but you will need a special light plastic trough made for the purpose. Put it below where the first drop is to be hung and fill with water – covering the floor with layers of newspaper will soak up accidental spillages. Don't try to lift the trough; slide it along the floor as the work progresses.

Cut each drop so patterns are matching, then roll the first one loosely from the bottom up with the pattern inside. Place it in the trough and press it down so water can reach all the parts covered with paste. Leave for the required soaking time (check manufacturers' instructions but, it's usually between 30 seconds and 2 minutes), then pick the drop up by the two top corners and take it to the ceiling line. Press onto the wall using an absorbent sponge to mop up and push out air bubbles. Press firmly on the edges with the sponge or a seam roller, then trim waste.

COPING WITH WALL FITTINGS ... AND CREASES

Few walls present a perfectly clear surface for paperhanging. Almost all will contain such small obstacles as light switches and power points, while some may carry wall-mounted fittings such as curtain tracks and adjustable shelving. Small obstacles can be papered round with some careful trimming, but larger obstacles are best taken down from the wall and replaced when you have finished decorating. That way you will get a really professional finish.

Creases can also spoil the look of your work. If they occur, take steps to remove them before the paste dries. Here's how.

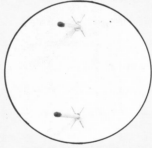

1 Use matchsticks, pushed head out into wall plugs, to show where wall fittings have been taken down.

2 Brush paper firmly over match heads so they pierce it. With hanging complete remove matches and replace fittings.

1 To cut round light switches, mark centre of plate, insert scissor tips and cut out towards plate corners.

2 Crease tongues of paper against edges of plate, lift away from wall, trim along line and brush back into place.

3 With washable and vinyl papers push a strip of rigid plastic against plate edges and trim with a sharp knife.

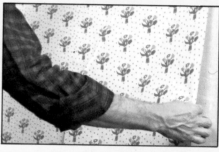

1 Creases are a common fault where the wall is out of true or if you haven't brushed the paper out properly.

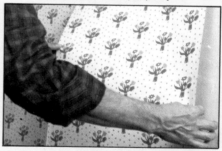

2 To remove the crease, peel the paper from the wall to a point above the crease – to the ceiling if necessary.

3 Brush the paper back into position – across towards the butt join, then to the other edge and down to the bottom.

25

WALLPAPERING AWKWARD AREAS

The techniques for papering round tricky areas like corners and reveals are quite basic. But care and patience is required if you are going to get really professional results from your paperhanging.

Although the major part of wallpapering, hanging straight lengths is fairly quick and straightforward. The tricky areas – corners, doorways and so on – which call for careful measuring, cutting and pattern matching are the bits that slow the job down. There's no worse eye-sore than a lop-sided pattern at a corner; but if you use the right techniques you can avoid this problem.

You have to accept in advance that the continuity of a pattern will be lost in corners and similar places; even a professional decorator can't avoid this. However, he has the ability to match the pattern as closely as possible so that the discontinuity is not noticeable, and this is what you have to emulate.

Things would, of course, be a lot simpler if all corners were perfectly square, but this is rarely the case. When you wallpaper a room for the first time you are likely to discover that all those angles that appeared to be true are anything but.

You can, however, help to overcome the problem of careful pattern matching at corners by choosing a paper with the right design (see *Ready Reference*). The most difficult of the lot to hang are those with a regular small and simple repeat motif. The loss of pattern continuity will be easy to spot if even slight errors are made. The same is often true of large, repeat designs. With either of these types, a lot more time will be involved and it could well take a couple of hours to hang a few strips around a single window reveal.

Sloping ceiling lines are another problem area and certain patterns will show it up clearly. You can understand the nuisance of a sloping ceiling by imagining a pattern with, say, regular rows of horizontal roses. Although the first length on the wall may be hung correctly to leave a neat row of roses along the ceiling line the trouble is that as subsequent lengths are hung and the pattern is matched, you will see less and less of that top row of roses as the ceiling slopes down. And, conversely, if the ceiling line slopes upwards, you will start to see a new row of roses appearing above. So, despite the fact that each length has been hung

vertically, the sloping ceiling will make the job look thoroughly unsightly.

Internal and external corners

Before you begin papering round a corner, you must hang the last full length before the corner. Your corner measurement will be done from one edge of this length. You can use a steel tape or boxwood rule to measure the gap to the corner (see *Ready Reference*) and then cut the piece required to fill it, plus a margin which is carried round onto the new wall. Since it's likely that the walls will be out of square and that the margin taken round the corner will not be exactly equal all the way down, it's obvious you would have a terrible job hanging the matching offcut strip to give a neat butt join.

For this reason you must hang the matching offcut which goes on the 'new' wall to a true vertical and then brush it over the margin you've turned onto this wall. You should aim to match the pattern at the corner as closely as possible. Since the paper overlaps, the match will not be perfect, but this is unavoidable and will not, in any case be noticeable as the overlap is tucked into or round the corner out of sight (see *Ready Reference*).

Papering round window reveals

Unless you intend to paper just one or two walls in a room you will eventually have to cope with papering round a window. Pattern matching is the problem here, but you should find cutting the paper to fit above and

below a window is not too difficult provided you work in a logical order (see box opposite). But you may have to be prepared for lots of scissor work when you cut out strips of paper for the two sides and top of the reveal to ensure the pattern matches the paper on the facing wall. (It's worth getting into the habit of marking some sort of code on the back of each piece of paper before it's cut up so you will be able to find matching pieces quickly.)

Make sure that you don't end up with a seam on the edge of the reveal, where it will be exposed to knocks and liable to lift. Before you begin work on the window wall, take a roll of wallcovering and estimate how many widths will fit between the window and the nearest corner. If it looks as though you will be left with a join within about 25mm (1in) of the window opening you should alter your starting point slightly so that, when you come to the window, the seam will have moved away from the edge of the reveal.

Where the lengths of paper are positioned on the window wall obviously depends on the position of the window, its size and the width of the wallpaper. But the ideal situation occurs when the last full length before you reach the window leaves a width of wall, plus window reveal, that measures just less than the width of the wallpaper. You can then hang the next length so its upper part goes on the wall above the window, the lower part on the wall below it and (after making two scissor cuts) turn the middle part to cover the side of the window reveal. The edge of

PAPERING ROUND A WINDOW

Top: Fill the narrow gap left on the underside of the reveal with a small offcut.
Above: The papering sequence; piece 7 fills the gap left on the reveal by piece 6.

the middle part can then be creased and trimmed so it fits neatly up against the window frame.

Go on to hang short lengths of wallpaper above the window, cutting them so their lower parts can be taken on to the underside of the top window reveal, and again trim them so they fit neatly up against the window frame. When you reach a point where the reveal on the opposite side of the window is less than the width of the wallpaper away from the last edge hung, you should stop and repeat the papering process below the window between the sill and skirting board, trimming as you go.

You can then hang the next full length in the same way as the one you hung on the first side of the window. You should, first, however, hang a plumbline over the pieces in place above the top and bottom of the window then hang the full length to the plumbline, trimming any slight overlap on the new length if necessary. (By doing this, you will ensure that the lengths to be hung on the rest of the wall will be truly vertical.)

Often, however, the position of the last full length at the window will fall so that the paper does not cover the reveal at the side of the window, and in this case you will have to cut matching strips to fill the gap. Similarly, you

will have to cut strips to fill the gaps on the underside of the reveal at the top of the window.

Dormer windows
In attics and loft rooms there will be sloping ceilings and dormer windows with which you will have to contend. If you decide to paper rather than paint the sloping ceiling, then you treat it in the same way as you would a vertical wall; there are no unusual problems involved, other than the peculiar working angle. Remember, too, that if you choose the wrong type of paper the irregular pattern-matching could give unfortunate results.

Paper the wall alongside the window and then round the window itself, moving on to the wall below the other side of the sloping ceiling (see step-by-step photographs). Finally, you can paper the dormer cheeks.

Chimney breasts and fireplace surrounds
Special rules apply to chimney breasts. For a start, since they are a focal point in the room, any pattern must be centralised. The design of the paper will affect where you begin to hang the wallpaper. Where one length of paper contains a complete motif, you can simply measure and mark off the central point of the chimney breast and use a

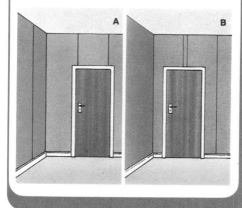

PAPERING AN INTERNAL CORNER

1 *Hang the last full length before the corner. Then measure the gap (see Ready Reference) to determine the width to be cut from the next length.*

2 *Cut from the next length a piece which will overlap 12mm (1/2in) round the corner. Then paste and fix it in position so it fills the corner gap.*

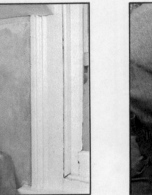

3 *Measure the width of the matching offcut strip of paper and use a plumbline to mark a guideline on the wall this distance from the corner.*

4 *Hang the offcut so its cut edge overlaps the matching edge of the first corner piece and its 'good' edge aligns with the vertical guideline.*

FLUSH WINDOWS

1 *Fix the last full length of paper before the window and pull the excess across. Cut round the sill and fix the paper beneath it.*

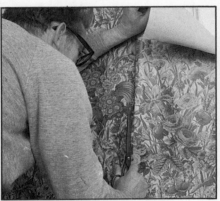

2 *You can then trim off the excess paper which runs alongside the window. Now press and brush the pasted paper into position.*

3 *Work along the wall underneath the window, fixing, creasing and trimming as you go. Afterwards you can fix the paper on the other side of the window.*

plumbline at this point to help you draw a vertical line down the centre. You can then begin hanging the wallpaper by aligning the first length with this line.

On the other hand, if it is the type of paper where two lengths, when aligned, form a motif, you will first have to estimate the number of widths which will fit across the chimney breast and then draw a line as a guide for hanging the first length of paper so the combined motif will, in fact, be centralised.

Your order of work should be from the centre (or near centre) outwards and you will then have to turn the paper round the corners at the sides so you form an overlap join with the paper which will be applied to the sides of the chimney breast. Follow the usual techniques for measuring and papering round external corners, remembering in particular not too take too much paper round the corner.

When it comes to fireplace surrounds, there are so many varying kinds of mantelshelfs and surrounds that only general guidance can be given. Usually the technique is to brush the paper down on to the top part of the wall and then cut it to fit along the back edge of the mantelshelf. You can then cut the lower half to fit the contours of the surround. If it's a complicated outline then you'll have to gradually work downwards, using a small pair of sharp scissors, pressing the paper into each shape, withdrawing it to snip along the crease line, then brushing it back into place.

If there is only a small distance between the edge of the mantelshelf and the corner, it's a lot easier if you hang the paper down to the shelf and then make a neat, horizontal cut line in the paper. You can then hang the lower half separately and join the two halves to disguise the cut line.

PAPERING ROUND A DORMER

1 Where the dormer cheek meets the junction of the wall and ceiling, draw a line at right angles to the wall on the ceiling by the dormer cheek.

2 Draw a vertical line at right angles to the first line on the dormer cheek. You can then fix the first length of paper in place on the dormer cheek.

3 Work along towards the window, trimming as you go. Gently tear along the overlap to feather its edge so you won't get a bulky join later.

4 At the window, crease along the side of the frame by running the edge of the scissors along it. You can then carefully trim along the creased line.

5 Return to the small gap which needs to be filled at the narrow end of the dormer cheek; fix this piece in position, crease and trim.

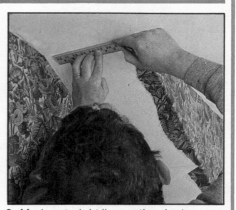

6 Mark a straight line on the sloping ceiling to serve as a guideline for fixing the first length of paper on the underside of the dormer cheek.

7 Cut a piece of paper so it reaches from the point you have marked up to the window and brush it into position ensuring that it covers the feathered edges of the overlap.

8 At the junction of the wall and ceiling you will have to cut round awkward angles. You can then go ahead and brush the paper into its final position.

9 Finally, you can brush the strip of paper which fills the gap between the wall and the underside of the dormer cheek into position to finish off the dormer area neatly.

PAPERING CEILINGS

One way to cover up a ceiling with cracks or other imperfections is to use lining paper or a textured wallcovering and then paint over it. But a good alternative is to make a special feature of the ceiling by using decorative paper.

Papering ceilings can be a rather daunting prospect, even to the experienced home decorator. In fact, once you have mastered the basic technique of paperhanging, ceilings are quite straightforward and you are likely to be presented with far fewer problems than on walls. There will be no windows, few (if any) corners and not so many obstacles with which you have to deal.

If you intend to paint the ceiling it's usually best to hang a lining paper or a textured paper like woodchip first to hide the inevitable blemishes of a plaster ceiling. Or you might decide to choose a fine decorative paper and make a feature of the ceiling with it. Most of the papers that are suitable for walls can also be used for ceilings.

But before you opt for papering, it makes sense to consider the alternative: if the sole objective is to get a textured surface which will cover up cracks and bumps, you can do it just as well with a textured paint. Using a woodchip paper would only make sense if you were skilled at papering and wanted to save money; in any case, you'll still have to paint it. However, if you want a smooth ceiling or a decorative surface of distinction then papering is for you.

The equipment you'll need
You will need the same equipment as for papering walls, with the addition of a safe working platform that spans the width of the room (see *Ready Reference*). You should check with your supplier that the paper of your choice is suitable for ceilings (some heavier types may not be) and ask him to provide a suitably strong adhesive, including fungicide if it is a washable vinyl paper. Such papers are extremely suitable for high humidity environments like bathrooms and kitchens.

Preparing the surface
The surface to which you fix the paper must be clean and sound. This means washing down existing paintwork with detergent or sugar soap and then sanding it with a fine abrasive paper or pad to provide a key for the adhesive. Distempered ceilings, often found in old houses, must be scrubbed to remove the distemper, or the paper will not stick.

If the ceiling has been papered before, you should remove the old paper completely. If you try to hang another paper over it there will be blobs and bubbles where the dampness of the new paper separates the old paper from the plaster. Any surface which is at all porous, such as bare plaster, will tend to absorb moisture from the pasted paper at too fast a rate for a successful adhesion. Such surfaces should be sized by brushing them over with a proprietary size, or a diluted version of the actual paste you're going to use. Let the size dry before proceeding.

New plasterboard, often used in modern construction, needs painting with a primer/sealer before decoration. It is also wise to fix a layer of lining paper before your main decorative paper if you are hanging heavy-weight or fabric wallcoverings.

Decorating perfectionists always recommend using lining paper anyway, whatever the surface. There is no doubt it does improve the final appearance, particularly on older surfaces or with thinner papers. Lining paper comes in different thicknesses or 'weights' and you should consult your supplier about a suitable grade.

One last preparation tip: don't leave cracks and dents in ceilings for the paper to cover. Fill them and sand them smooth, particularly at joins between plasterboards, and at the wall/ceiling angle. Think of your paper as a surface that needs a good smooth base, and not as a cover-up for a hideous old mess.

Planning the job
Consult the estimator panel opposite to gauge the approximate number of rolls you will need; also think about the pattern of your intended paper. Can you cope with a complex drop pattern on a ceiling, or would you be better off with a straight match? A bold paper that looks fine on walls might be a bit overpowering above your head. Is your ceiling good enough for a plainish paper or do you need texture to draw the eye away from the ravages of time that appear in all old lath-and-plaster ceilings?

Modern papers are designed for the strips to be butted against each other, not over-lapped. This means the traditional pattern of working away from, but parallel to, the main source of natural light is not essential. You will generally find it easier working across the narrowest dimension of the room. Well-applied paper will tend not to show the joins too much anyway, particularly if the pattern draws the eye.

All ceiling papering starts from a line which is strung or marked across the ceiling 10mm (⅜in) less than the width of the paper away from the wall. The 10mm (⅜in) on the length of paper which runs next to the wall allows for the walls being out of square and its overlap is trimmed off at the wall and ceiling junction. You can chalk a line and snap it against the ceiling between two tacks to make a mark, or just pin it temporarily in place and butt the first strip of paper against it.

MARKING UP AND PASTING

1 Measure in from the width of the paper minus 10mm (³/₈in), to allow for an overlap at the wall, and mark this distance on the ceiling.

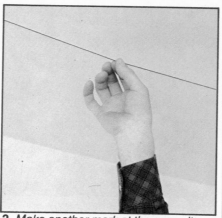

2 Make another mark at the opposite end, the same distance from the wall. Use a chalked line to link the marks, then snap the line onto the ceiling.

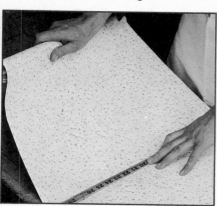

3 Cut or tear the lengths of paper. You should allow 100mm (4in) excess on each piece to give an overlap of 50mm (2in) for trimming at each end.

4 Apply paste to the back of the paper and fold it into concertina folds as you go. Paste enough lengths to allow adequate soaking time.

5 Take the last fold in the length to meet the first, short, fold so the edges meet without paste getting on the front of the paper.

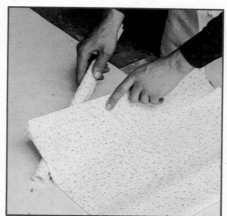

6 Slip a spare roll of paper under the folded-up length; this will serve as a support for the paper so you can carry and hold it easily.

Ready Reference

ESTIMATOR

Distance around room	Number of rolls 10.05m x 530mm (33ft x 21in)
10-12m (33-39ft)	2
12-14m (39-46ft)	3
14-18m (46-59ft)	4
18-20m (59-66ft)	5
20-22m (66-72ft)	6

TIP: WHISK YOUR PASTE
To speed up the process of mixing paste, use a kitchen whisk to beat up the mix.

A SAFE WORKING PLATFORM
Set up two stepladders and a solid plank, at a height where you can comfortably touch the ceiling with the palm of your hand.

TIP: HAVE TOOLS TO HAND
Have the necessary tools with you (in the pocket of an apron or overall) when you're on the working platform to save you scrambling up and down more than you need.

PREVENT WASTAGE
If you are pattern matching, paper in the direction which will save long bits of waste paper left over after cutting the lengths.

LINING PAPER
If you are hanging lining paper, remember that it should be hung at right angles to the paper which goes over it.

PAPERING TECHNIQUE
With the concertina-folded paper supported by the spare roll held in your left hand (if you are right-handed; vice versa if you are left-handed) pull one fold out taut and then brush it into place, working outwards from the centre to avoid trapped air bubbles. Repeat with the other folds.

TIP: TRIM ROSES NEATLY
Don't be tempted to remove the cover of a ceiling rose to trim the paper round it; inaccurate cutting may mean there are gaps when the cover is replaced.
Instead:
● trim round the fitting with the cover in place leaving a slight overlap (see step-by-step photographs)
● remove the cover and press the overlap into place.

FINAL TRIMMING
When the last piece of paper has been hung you may need to spend some time on final trimming if the walls and ceiling do not meet squarely and evenly.
For further information see pages 21-29.

HANGING STRAIGHT LENGTHS

1 *Hang the first length on the 'room' side of the chalk line, not next to the wall. Brush the paper into place gently but firmly.*

2 *Brush the ends carefully into the angles where walls and ceiling meet, and trim. Then hang the next length alongside the wall.*

3 *The lengths should be butt-jointed. Use a seam roller to ensure well-stuck edges by running it gently over the length of the seam.*

4 *Trim off the overlap at the ends and side (if necessary) of each length of paper. Use a scraper as a guide for the knife for accurate cutting.*

5 *Wipe off any excess adhesive where the overlap has been before it dries, or it will leave ugly marks on the wall surface.*

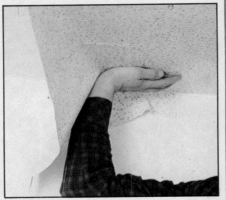

6 *You can now go ahead and hang the next length on the other side of the first piece hung. Continue until you have covered the entire ceiling.*

It makes sense to get all the lengths measured and cut out in advance, and pasted up in batches of twos or threes (depending on your speed of working) to give adequate soaking time for the type of paper you are hanging; check the manufacturer's instructions on this point. Cut all the strips, including those which will be trimmed for chimney breasts, to full room dimensions plus 100mm (4in) excess for trimming.

The concertina fold
The secret of successful ceiling papering is the correct folding technique, as you paste, so that the paper can be transferred to and laid out against the ceiling surface in a smooth manner. Each fold of the concertina should be 300mm (1ft) wide approximately, apart from the first, which can be shorter (see step-by-step photographs). It's worth practising folding with dry paper first.

Hanging the paper
Assemble the working platform securely at the correct height across the whole length of the room, beneath the area where the first strip is to be pasted. Before you get up there with a fold of wet, pasted paper, make sure you have the tools you will need to hand.

The last-to-be-pasted section of each length is first to go on the ceiling; tease off this first section and brush it into place. Continue to unfold the concertina in sections, brushing it down as you go and checking it is straight against the guideline.

Trimming and seam rolling
When you trim, you should make sure the paper butts exactly up to covings, but allow a 5-10mm (¼-⅜in) overlap down to the surface of the walls you intend to paper later. Except with embossed papers, you should roll the butt joints between strips with a seam roller.

Light fittings or shades should always be removed, leaving just the flex hanging down. Turn the power off, to ensure safety.

If a chimney breast falls parallel to the run of the paper, you will need your scissors handy to take out an approximate piece as you work along the platform. It's worth anticipating this before you get up there; mark a rough line on the paper at the approximate position of the chimney breast. Cut out the chimney breast piece, leaving an excess of about 15mm (⅝in) for detailed trimming when the whole strip is in place.

If the strip ends at a chimney breast there are less problems. Remove any vast unwanted sections as you work and trim to fit later. External corners are dealt with by making a V-cut so that one flap of the paper can be folded down the inside alcove edge of the chimney breast (or trimmed there if you are working to a coving).

PAPERING ROUND OBSTACLES

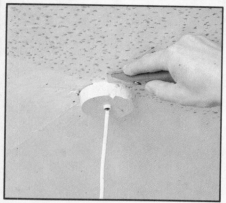

1 If there is a ceiling rose, use a knife or scissors to make a little slit in the paper so it fits round the rose; don't cut too deep.

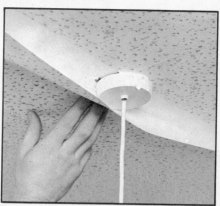

2 Hang the next length so it butts up against the previous one; at the rose take the paper over the top of the obstacle.

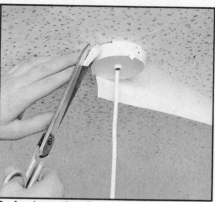

3 Again, make slits in the paper so it fits round the rose; this will allow you to brush the rest of the length of paper in place.

4 When the paper is in place, trim round the rose. Place the edge of a scraper between the knife and ceiling so there's a slight overlap.

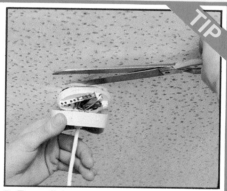

5 Turn off the power, remove the rose cover and press the overlap into place. When the cover is replaced it will conceal the cut edges completely.

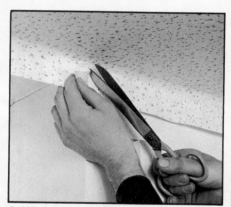

6 Where the paper meets an alcove, make a slit in the paper in line with one corner of the alcove and then in line with the other.

7 You can then brush the paper into place in the normal fashion so it fits neatly into the gap between the two corners. Trim the overlap along the wall leading to the alcove.

8 Fix the next length so it butts up against the previous one. Adhesive may ooze out when seams are rolled; so long as the paper is colourfast you can remove it with a damp sponge.

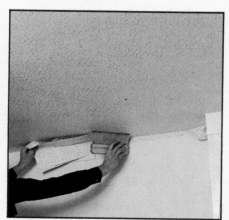

9 Measure up and cut the last narrow piece, allowing for an overlap of about 25mm (1in) at the wall and ceiling junction. Paste and brush it into place; trim to complete the job.

CERAMIC TILES for small areas

Ceramic tiles are easy-clean, hygienic and hard wearing. By starting with a small area in your home where these qualities are needed – like splashbacks or worktops – you'll not only grasp the basics but also gain confidence to tackle bigger things.

M odern ceramic tiles are thin slabs of clay, decorated on one side with coloured glazes. These are baked on to give the tile a hard, glassy surface resistant to water, heat and almost all household chemicals. The clay from which tiles are made, which is known as the biscuit, varies and you need to know the differences before you choose the tile to use. The thinnest ones with a pale coloured biscuit are good on all vertical surfaces (including doors where extra weight puts stress on the hinges).

If the biscuit is reddish/brown it has been high baked (vitrified). The thicker and darker coloured it is the more strength the tile has — floor tiles, for example, are usually big in size as well as thick in biscuit.

Work surfaces need tiles that are strong to withstand weights of heavy pots, while splashbacks and bathroom surfaces can take lighter, thinner ones.

Types of tiles
Within each range of tiles there are usually three types. *Spacer* tiles have small projections on each edge called lugs which butt up to the neighbouring tile and provide the correct space for grouting (with these it is very hard to vary the width of the grouting). *Border* tiles are squared off on all sides but are glazed on two adjacent edges – these give a neat finish to outer corners and top or side edges. *Universal* or *Continental* tiles have no lugs and are square on all edges. All three can be used successfully in small areas, but do remember that if tiles do not have lugs you have to include grouting space in your calculations – the thinnest tiles need to be spaced by nothing more than torn-up pieces of cardboard, while 6mm (¼in) tiles can be spaced with either matchsticks or proprietary plastic tile spacers.

Tiles are sold by the sq metre, sq yd, boxed in 25s or 50s, or can be bought individually. Boxed tiles usually advise on adhesive and grout needed for specific areas. When buying, if there's no written information available always check that the tile is suitable.

How to plan the layout
When tiling small areas you don't have much space to manoeuvre. The idea in all tiling is to create a symmetrical effect, using whole tiles or, if any have to be cut, making them equal.

Knowing about the different sizes of tiles helps in the planning. For example, if you know the width and height or depth of the surface you intend to tile, you can divide this by the known size of tiles until you find the one that gives the right number of whole tiles. Remember that the width of grouting has to be added to the measurement with non-lugged tiles – and except with the very thinnest tiles this can be slightly widened if it saves cutting a tile.

If you're prepared to incorporate cut tiles into the planning remember:
● on the width of the tiled area, place equal cut tiles at each end
● on the height, place cut tiles at the top edge
● on the depth (eg, window-recesses) put cut tiles at back edge
● frame a fitting by placing cut tiles at each side and the top

A mix of patterned or textured with plain tiles is best done first on metricated graph paper. This will help you see where you want the pattern to fall.

Fixings should be made in the grouting lines where possible. Some tile ranges have soap dishes, towel rails etc attached to tiles so they can be incorporated in a scheme, but if these don't suit your purposes, you can drill the tiles to screw in your own fitting

A working plan
All tiles should be fixed level and square so it's important to establish the horizontal and vertical with a spirit level. Draw in the lines with pencil. If you plan to tile where there is no support (eg, on either side of a basin or sink) lightly pin a length of 50 x 25mm (2 x 1in) timber below the tiling line – the batten will prevent the tiles slipping.

On doors you may have to consider adding a timber surround to keep the tiles secure as they will be subjected to movement (also see section on *Adhesives* below).

Adhesives and grouting
The choice of both of these depends on where the tiles are to be fixed. In a watery situation (eg, a shower cubicle or a steamy kitchen) it is important to use a waterproof variety of both, even though you might have

HOW TO HANG TILES

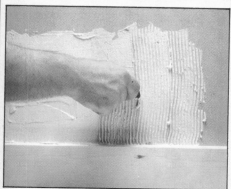

1 Spread ceramic tile adhesive to cover 1 sq metre, then 'comb' with notched spreader. To support tiles where no other support exists, pin a horizontal timber batten to the wall.

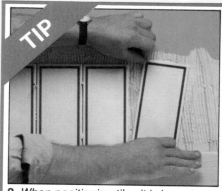

TIP

2 When positioning tiles it is important to twist them slightly to bed them. Don't slide them as this forces adhesive between joints.

3 Form even grouting spaces between tiles without lugs with pieces of matchstick. Or you can use torn-up cardboard from the tile packaging or similar if you want only a narrow grouting space.

4 Remove matchsticks or card after all tiles are hung, and grout 12-24 hours later. Press grout into the spaces using a small sponge or squeegee, making sure no voids are left in either vertical or horizontal spaces.

5 After 10 minutes, wipe off excess grouting with soft cloth. Use fine dowelling (sand the end to round it) to even up and smooth the lines. Fill any voids that appear with fresh grout to prevent water penetration.

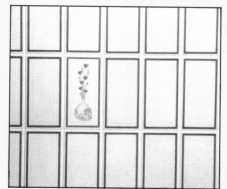

6 When grouting is dry, polish the tiles with a soft cloth so the area is smooth. All the surface needs now is an occasional wipe-down although non-waterproof grout may tend to discolour as time goes by.

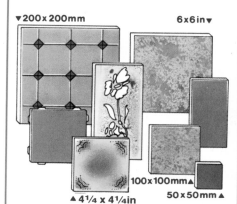

to wait for 4-5 days before exposing the tile surface to use.

All ceramic tile adhesives are like thin putty and can be bought ready mixed in tubs or in powder form to be made up with water. They are what is known as thin-bed adhesives in that they are designed to be applied in a thin layer on a flat even surface. The spread is controlled by a notched comb (usually provided by the manufacturer but cheap to buy where you bought the tiles) to make furrows of a specified depth. When the tiles are pressed on with a slight twist, the adhesive evenly grips the back of the biscuit.

Special latex-based adhesives (usually, two-part products which have to be mixed before using) have much more flexibility and are good for tiles where there is any movement (eg, on doors).

Spread the adhesive on an area no more than 1 sq metre (1 sq yd) at a time, or it will lose its gripping power before you have time to place the tiles. If you remove a tile, before refixing comb the adhesive again.

Grout gives the final finish to the tiled area, filling the spaces between the tiles and preventing moisture getting behind them and affecting the adhesive. Grouting can be done 12-24 hours after the last tile has been pressed into place. Grout can be standard or waterproof (with added acrylic), and both are like a cellulose filler when made up.

If you only make up one lot of grouting, you can colour it with special grouting tints – but remember that it's hard to make other batches match the colour. Waterproof grouting cannot always take these tints.

Press grout between the tiles with a sponge or squeegee and wipe off excess with a damp sponge. Even up the grouting by drawing a pencil-like piece of wood (eg dowelling) along each row first vertically, then horizontally. Do this within 10 minutes of grouting so it is not completely dry.

Leave the tiles for 24 hours before polishing with a clean dry cloth. Wash clean only if a slight bloom remains.

Tiles should never be fixed with tight joints for any movement of the wall or fittings will cause the tiles to crack. Similarly where tiles meet baths, basins, sinks etc, flexibility is needed – and grout that dries rigid cannot provide it. These gaps must be filled with a silicone rubber sealant

Techniques with tiles

To cut tiles, lightly score the glaze with a tile cutter to break the surface. Place the tile glazed side up with the scored line over matchsticks and firmly but gently press the tile down on each side. If using a pencil press on one side, hold the other. Smooth the cut edge with a file. Very small adjustments are best done by filing the edge of the whole tile.

CUTTING AND SHAPING TILES

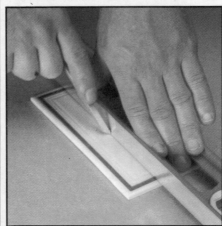

1 *Before a tile will break, the glaze must be scored — on the edges as well as surface. Use a carbide-tipped cutter against a straight-edge.*

2 *Another type of cutter has 'jaws' which clasp the tile during breaking. (It also has a small 'wheel' for scoring through the glaze on the tile).*

5 *Edges of broken tiles need to be smoothed off — use a special tile file mounted on wood, a wood file or rub against rough concrete.*

6 *To cut an awkward shape, make a card template. Place it on the tile and score glaze on the surface and edges with the tile cutter.*

To remove a narrow strip of tile, score the line heavily by drawing the tile cutter across the tile more firmly several times in the same place. Then use pincers to 'nibble' the waste away in small pieces and smooth the edge. Glaze on broken tiles is as sharp as glass, so be careful not to cut yourself.

Templates for awkwardly shaped tiles are not difficult to make. Cut the shape in card, place on a tile and score a line freehand with the tile cutter. Any straight score marks can be deepened afterwards, using a straight edge for support. Then nibble away the waste with pincers. If there's a large amount to be cut away, score the waste part to divide it into sections, then nibble away. A good tip is to do this on a soft or padded surface so the tile doesn't break in the wrong place.

Suitable surfaces

The ideal surface for tiling is one that's perfectly flat, dry and firm. Small irregularities will be covered up, but any major hollows, bumps or flaking, need to be made good.

Plastered walls and asbestos cement sheets: perfect for tiling, but wait a month after any new plastering to allow the wall to dry out completely. Unless surface has been previously painted, apply a coat of plaster primer to prevent the liquid in the tile adhesive from being absorbed too quickly.

Plasterboard: again, ideal for tiling as long as it's firmly fixed and adjacent boards cannot shift. (If they did the joins would probably crack). To prepare the surface, remove all dust, wipe down with white spirit

3 No special tools are needed with other tile-breaking methods. For medium thick tiles use a pencil, for thin tiles use matchsticks.

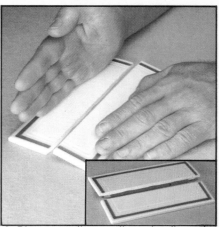

4 Place pencil centrally under tile and score line, hold one side and press firmly on other. With thin tiles, press lightly both sides.

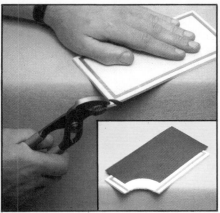

7 On a soft surface, use pincers to take tiny nibbles out of the tile. If you're over enthusiastic you'll break off more than you intended.

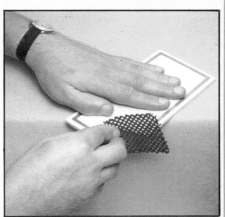

8 Once the waste has been slowly but surely nibbled away, smooth up the edge. Files are also useful when a whole tile needs a slight trimming.

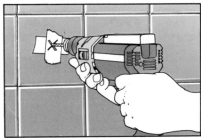

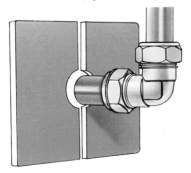

For tiling large areas see pages 38-42.

o remove grease, then treat with primer.

Paint: old emulsion-paint needs to be cleaned thoroughly with sugar soap or detergent to remove all traces of dust and grease. Gloss paint needs to be cleaned thoroughly; remove any flaking paint then roughen up whole surface with a coarse abrasive to provide a good key for the adhesive.

Wallpaper: DO NOT tile directly onto wallpaper, as this can be pulled away from the wall by the adhesive. Strip it off completely.

Wood and Chipboard: perfect for tiling as long as it is flat and adjacent boards cannot shift. Treat with an ordinary wood primer.

Laminates: joins and small, minor blemishes in the surface can be covered up so long as the entire sheet is soundly fixed and absolutely flat. Its smooth face must be

roughened with course abrasive to provide a key for the tile adhesive.

Old ceramic tiles: the thin biscuit ceramic tiles are excellent for tiling over as they add little to the wall's thickness and won't protrude beyond existing fittings. Loose and cracked tiles will have to be removed. Scrape out the grouting surrounding the tile using an old, thin screwdriver or something similar, then, beginning in the centre and working outwards, remove the tile using a club hammer and cold chisel.

Small sections or mis-shapen pieces (as around a new fixture) can be built up level with neighbouring tiles with cellulose filler.

The area should then be sealed with plaster primer or emulsion paint to finish the surface.

TOOLS FOR TILING

Tile cutter: essential for scoring glaze of tiles before breaking them. Score only once (the second time you may waver from the line and cause an uneven break).

Pincers: these are used for nibbling away small portions of tile, after scoring a line with the cutter. Ordinary pincers are fine for most jobs, but special tile nibblers are available.

Special cutter: combines a cutting edge (usually a small cutting wheel) with jaws which snap the tile along the scored line.

Tile file: an abrasive mesh, used as a file to 'shave' off small amounts.

TIP: TO DRILL A TILE

● make a cross of masking tape and mark the point where you want the hole
● drill after adhesive and grouting have set using lowest speed or a hand drill with masonry bit — too much speed at the start will craze the tile
● once through the glaze, drill in the normal way

TIP: TO TILE ROUND A PIPE

● cut tile into two along line corresponding with centre point of pipe; offer up each half to the pipe
● mark freehand semi-circles on tile to match edge of pipe; score line with tile cutter and nibble away waste with pincers

CERAMIC TILING WALL TO WALL

Ceramic tiles are an ideal decorating material for they make a room look good for years and require virtually no maintenance. But covering several walls with tiles is a large-scale job which needs a methodical and careful approach if you are to achieve the best results.

The all-in-one look that wall-to-wall tiling can give has to be planned carefully to avoid expensive and time consuming mistakes. How to do this may depend on whether you want to include special patterns in the design, but following certain rules will give a desirable symmetry to the look.

One of the hardest tasks will probably be choosing the tiles for there's a vast array of shapes, sizes and colours available. Having picked out the ones you want though, don't buy until you've done the planning – for the plans of each wall should tell you whether the pattern will work in the room or would be lost in the cutting or amid the fittings.

Plans on paper also give you an instant method of working out how many tiles to buy (counting each cut one as a whole, and adding 2-5% for unintended breakage) including the number which will need to be border (two glazed edges) or mitred (on square or rectangular universal tiles) for the top row of half-tiled walls or external corners. Buy all the tiles at once, but do check each carton to make sure there's no variation in the colour (this can occur during the firing of different batches).

Planning on paper

The best possible way to start planning for a large expanse of tiling is not on the wall, but on paper. Graph paper is ideal, particularly if you intend including a mix of plain and patterned tiles, or a large motif that needs building up. Of course, advance planning is also essential if you're tiling round major features like windows, doors, mirrors, shower cubicles and so on.

You need separate pieces of graph paper for each wall you intend tiling. Allow the large (1cm) squares on the paper to represent your tiles — one for a square tile of any size, two for a rectangular tile; this will give you a scale to work to. Now mark up sheets of greaseproof paper with your actual wall sizes using the scale dictated by the tile size on the graph paper. Measure and outline on the see-through paper the exact position and in-scale dimensions of all fixtures and fittings (see planning pictures on opposite page).

At this stage, the objective is to decide how to achieve the best symmetrical layout for your tiles — the 'ideal' is to have either whole or equal-size cut tiles on each side of a fixture.

First you have to mark in the central guide lines. For instance, on *walls with a window* draw a line from the sill centre to the floor, and from the centre of the top of the window to the ceiling. If there are *two windows* also draw in the central line from floor to ceiling between them. Mark the centre point above a *door* to the ceiling and also indicate the horizontal line at the top of the door. In the same way draw in a central line from the top of a *basin or vanity unit* to the ceiling.

For all these lines use a coloured pen for you have to be aware of them when deciding where whole tiles should be positioned. But they're only the starting point — other potential problems have to be looked at too.

Place the see-through paper over the tile sizes on the graph paper so you can see how the tiles will fall in relation to the guide lines. Now take into account the following important points:

● The first row above the lowest level — either the floor, the skirting board or a wall-to-wall fitting — should be whole tiles. If necessary, change this to prevent a thin strip being cut at the ceiling.

● Check where tiles come in relation to fittings. If very thin strips (less than 38mm/1½in) or narrow 'L' shapes would need to be cut, move the top sheet slightly up, down, left or right till the tiles are of a cuttable size — areas to watch are around windows, doors and where one wall meets another.

Placing patterns

When you are satisfied that you have a symmetrical and workable arrangement you can tape the top sheet in the right position on the graph paper, then start to plan where you're going to position your patterned tiles. Use pencil this time in case you change your mind and want to make adjustments. These are the points to watch:

● Don't place single motif patterns at internal corners where they would have to be cut — you won't find it easy to match up the remaining piece on the adjacent wall.

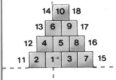
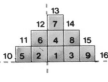
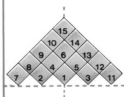

● If the pattern builds up vertically and horizontally over four or more tiles, 'centre' the pattern on the wall so that cuts are equal at both ends. If pattern loss can't be avoided with designs of this type at least it can be kept to internal corners.

● Whole tiles should be used on both faces of external corners.

Now butt each of the wall plans up to the other to make sure that the patterns relate both vertically and horizontally.

Planning on the wall

When there are no complicated tiling patterns involved and walls are free of interruptions such as windows, it's often easier to do the planning directly on the wall itself. Here, the simple objective is to place the tiles symmetrically between the corners. And to do this, all you need is a tiling gauge which you can make.

A tiling gauge is like a long ruler, except that it's marked off in tile widths. Use a long, straight piece of timber ideally about 25mm square (1in square) and remember to include the grouting gap between tiles as you rule off the gauge. If you're using rectangular tiles, mark the widths on one side, the lengths on the other.

Holding the gauge against the walls —

first vertically, then horizontally — tells you instantly where the whole tiles will fit in and where cut tiles will be needed. But first you must find the centre of each wall. Measure the width — doing this at three places will also tell you if the corners are vertical (hang a plumb line or use a spirit level to make absolutely sure) — and halve it to find the centre point. Use the tiling gauge to mark this vertical centre line with a pencil, then hold the gauge against it. Move it up or down until you have at least a whole tile's width above the floor or skirting board — this can be adjusted slightly if it avoids a thin piece of tile at ceiling height — then mark off the tile widths on the vertical line itself.

Now hold the tiling gauge horizontally, and move it to left or right of the vertical line if thin pieces of tile would have to be cut near windows or fittings, or to make cut tiles at both ends of the wall equal. Following this adjustment, mark the wall and draw in a new vertical line if necessary. The wall can now be marked horizontally with tile widths. Keeping to the same horizontal, mark up adjacent walls in the same way.

At corners, whether internal or external, don't assume they're either square, vertical or even. An internal corner is the worst place to start your tiling for this very reason, but it

doesn't matter if you position cut tiles there. On external corners use the tiling gauge to work inwards in whole tile widths.

You can also use the tiling gauge to check that your graph plan is accurate, and make any necessary adjustments.

Putting up battens

Once you have determined that your plan is correct, fix a length of perfectly straight 50mm x 25mm (2in x 1in) battening across the full width of the wall — use a spirit level to ensure that the batten is horizontal. Use masonry nails to fix it in place but do not drive them fully home as they will have to be removed later. If using screws the wall should be plugged. The batten provides the base for your tiling and it's important that its position is correct.

If more than one wall is being tiled, continue to fix battens around the room at the same height, using the spirit level to check the horizontal. The last one you fix should tie up perfectly with the first. If there are gaps, at the door for example, check that the level either side is the same, by using a straight-edge and spirit level to bridge the gap.

Once the horizontal battens are fixed, fix a vertical batten to give yourself the starting point for the first tile. Use a spirit level or plumb line to make sure it's positioned accurately.

Fixing tiles

Begin tiling from the horizontal base upwards, checking as you work that the tiles are going up accurately both vertically and horizontally. Work on an area of approximately 1 sq metre (1 sq yd) at a time, spreading the adhesive and fixing all the whole tiles using card or matchsticks as spacers as necessary. Make sure no excess adhesive is left on the surface of the tiles.

Next, deal with any tiles that need to be cut. You may find the gap into which they fit is too narrow to operate the adhesive spreader properly. In this case spread the adhesive onto the back of the tiles.

When all the tiling above the base batten has been completed wait for 8-12 hours, before removing the battens, and completing the tiling. Take care when removing the base batten that the tiles above are not disturbed — the adhesive is unlikely to be fully set.

Dealing with corners

Your original planning should have indicated how many border or mitred tiles you will need for tiling external corners or for the top line of tiles on a half-tiled wall. You will find external corners, those which project into the room, in virtually all tiling situations — around boxed-in pipework , or around a window or door reveal, or in an L-shaped room.

Where you are using universal tiles at an

PLANNING TILE LAYOUT ON PAPER

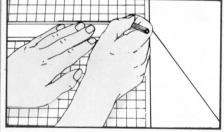

1 *On graph paper with large (eg, 1cm) squares, let each square represent one whole square tile. Strengthen the grid lines with coloured pen if necessary.*

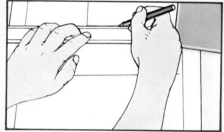

2 *On tracing paper, draw the outline of each wall to be tiled, and mark in doors and windows. Use the scale 1cm = the actual tile size (eg, 150mm).*

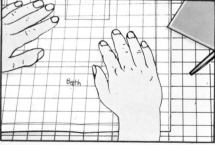

3 *Place greaseproof over graph paper and move it around till you get the most manageable size cut tiles, especially near fixtures, ceiling and floor.*

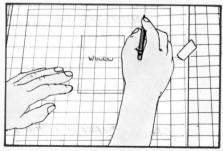

4 *Tape the top sheet in place, then mark the pattern in with pencil. Do each wall the same so that the alignment of the horizontal is correct.*

Ready Reference

TACKLING TILING PROBLEMS

Whenever a fitting, a door or window interrupts the clean run of a wall, it becomes the focal point of the wall. So you have to plan for symmetry *round* the features. Here are some guidelines:

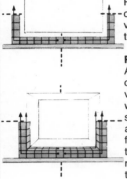

Wall with 1 window
Plan the tiling from a centre-line drawn vertically through the window.

Recessed windows
Again work from a centre-line drawn vertically through window. But make sure that whole tiles are placed at the front of the sill and the sides of the reveals. Place cut tiles closest to the window frame.

Wall with two windows
Unless the space between the two windows is exactly equal to a number of whole tiles, plan your tiling to start from a centre-line drawn between the two.

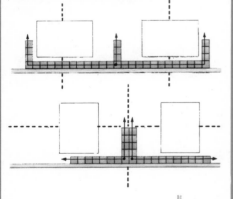

Wall with door
If the door is placed fairly centrally in the wall, plan your tiling from a centre-line drawn vertically through the door. If, however, the door is very close to a side wall, the large expanse of wall is a more prominent focal point. So plan the tiling to start one tile's width from the frame. If the frame is not exactly vertical, you'll be able to cut tiles to fit in the remaining space.

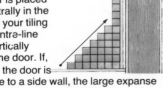

---

external corner, start at the corner with a whole tile — it should project by the depth of the mitre so that the mitre on the other face neatly butts up against it with a fine space for grouting in between.

With window reveals the correct method is to tile up the wall to sill level, cutting tiles if necessary. Fit whole tiles either side of the reveal, then again cut tiles to fill the space between those whole ones and the window frame. Attach whole border or mitred tiles to the sill so they butt up against the wall tiles. If using square-edged tiles the ones on the sill should cover the edges of those on the wall so the grouting line is not on the sill surface. If the sill is narrower than a whole tile, cut the excess from the back — not the front. If the sill is deeper than a whole tile, put cut tiles near the window with the cut edge against the frame. Continually check the accurate lining up of tiles with a spirit level.

Some vertical external corners are not as precisely straight and vertical as they should be and this can lead to problems of tile alignment. The use of a thick-bed adhesive will help to straighten out some irregularities where a corner goes inwards (a thin-bed helps where the wall leans outwards). Buying a 'flexible' adhesive will give you both qualities. As a general rule it is

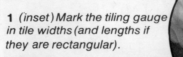
1 *(inset) Mark the tiling gauge in tile widths (and lengths if they are rectangular).*

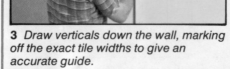
3 *Draw verticals down the wall, marking off the exact tile widths to give an accurate guide.*

5 *Place horizontal batten at least a tile's width above floor or a fitting using masonry nails or screws.*

PLANNING ON THE WALL

2 *Use a plumb line to check that the wall is vertical.*

4 *Check each horizontal with a spirit level, then mark tile positions from floor to ceiling.*

6 *Fix vertical batten and begin to tile where the battens meet. Spread adhesive to cover 1 sq metre (1 sq yd).*

MAKE YOUR OWN TILE BREAKER

1 *Use a timber offcut wider than the tile as the base. Use 3mm (¹/₈in) ply for the top and sides.*

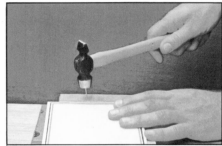

2 *Stack ply strips on both sides till the same height as the tile, then pin. Nail on the top piece.*

3 *The breaking part needs to be as wide and deep as the tile, with the opening on the top a half tile long.*

4 *Score the glaze on the top and edges with a carbide-tipped cutter. Put the tile into the main part.*

5 *Slip on the breaking part so the score line is between the two. Hold one side while you press the other.*

6 *The tile breaks cleanly. This aid costs nothing and will save you time when tiling a large expanse.*

TILING CORNERS

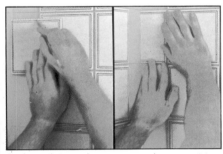

1 *At an internal corner, mark amount to be cut at top and bottom. Break the tile, then fit in position.*

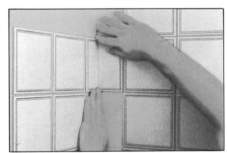

2 *File the remainder until it fits the adjacent area with enough space left for a fine line of grout.*

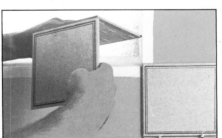

3 *On a window sill, use a whole tile at the front and make sure that it overlaps the one on the wall-face underneath.*

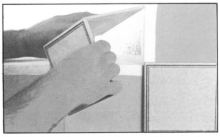

4 *Mitred edges of universal tiles and glazed edges of border tiles give a better finish to external corners.*

better to concentrate on lining up your border or mitred tiles perfectly vertically with only minute 'steps' between tiles, then bedding spacer or ordinary tiles behind to correspond with the line. Don't forget that if you do have to create a very slight stepped effect, you can reduce the uneven effect between the corner tiles and others by pressing in extra grouting later.

Internal corners seldom cause serious problems as cut tiles can be shaped to suit fluctuations from the truly vertical. Don't assume when cutting tiles for a corner that all will be the same size — the chances are that they will vary considerably and should be measured and cut individually. Another point: don't butt tiles up against each other so they touch — leave space for the grouting which will give the necessary flexibility should there be any wall movement.

Tiling around electrical fittings

When tiling around electrical fittings it is better to disconnect the electricity and remove the wall plate completely so that you can tile right up to the edge of the wall box. This is much neater and easier than trying to cut tiles to fit around the perimeter of the plate. Cut tiles as described in the illustration on pages 36 and 37 and fit them in the normal way with the plate being replaced on top, completely covering the cut edges of the tiles. This same principle applies to anything easily removable. The fewer objects you have to tile around the better, so before starting any tiling get to work with a screwdriver.

You have the greatest control over the end result if at the planning stage you work out where you want to place fittings such as towel rails and soap dishes, shelves and the like. Some tile ranges offer them attached so it's only a matter of fitting them in as you put the tiles up.

Tiling non-rigid surfaces

On surfaces which are not totally rigid or which are subject to movement, vibration or the odd shock, tiles should not be attached using adhesive which dries hard as most standard and waterproof types do. Instead use adhesives which retain some flexibility. These may be cement-based types with a latex rubber content, or acrylic adhesives. You may have to surround a non-rigid surface with wooden lipping to protect the tiles.

TILING AROUND FIXTURES

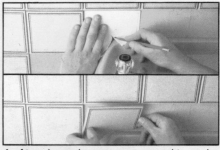

1 At awkward corners use card to make a tile-size template. Place it on the tile and score the shape, then gently nibble out the waste with pincers — the smaller the bits the better.

2 Where basins, baths, kitchen sinks or laundry tubs meet tiles, seal the join with silicone caulking to keep out water. Caulking comes in various colours to match fixtures.

3 After the adhesive has had time to set, the tiles are grouted both to protect them and to enhance their shape and colour.
Accessories can be bought already attached to tiles, can be screw mounted after drilling the tile, or if lightweight can be stuck on to tiles with adhesive pads.

Jem Grischotti   Basin: Royal Doulton Ashford in Whisky; beige Colourseal   Taps: Folkard Bolding

Ready Reference

CHECK FREQUENTLY
● the vertical (with a plumb line)
● the horizontal (with spirit level)
● that tiles don't project beyond each other

TIP: MAKING TEMPLATES
Cut the card tile-size then make diagonal snips into the edge to be shaped. These pieces will be forced out of the way and an accurate cutting line can be drawn.

ADHESIVE AND GROUT
You need 1 litre of adhesive and 0.25kg of grout per sq metre (a little less for 1 sq yd), but for large areas buy in bulk: adhesive comes in 2½, 5 and 10 litre buckets; grout in 1.5 and 3.5kg packs.

WHEN GROUTING
● don't press mixture in with your fingers (it can abrade and irritate your skin)
● do wear light flexible gloves
● don't leave excess on tiles till dry
● do grout or caulk between tiles and window or door frames
● don't forget to grout edges of universal tiles if run finishes halfway up the wall
● use an old toothbrush to get grout into awkward places

TIP: GROUTING WALLS
On a large expanse, it's less tiring to use a rubber float to push grout between tiles — work upwards, then across; remove excess diagonally.

TILING SHOWERS
● use water resistant or waterproof adhesive and grout
● tile at least 1 row above shower head
● on ceiling use large drawing or upholstery pins to hold tiles till adhesive dries
● do floor and ceiling before walls
● don't expose tiles to water for 1 week

For more information on tiling see pages 34-37.

EXTERIOR PAINTING: basics & tools

The main reason for decorating the outside of your house is to protect it from the elements. But paint can also transform the appearance of your house and increase its value, so it's a job worth doing well.

The outside of your house is under continuous attack from rain, frost, heat and light from the sun, dirt and pollution. Properly applied paint or varnish is the best way of protecting the fabric of the house, and it should last for about five or six years before it needs renewing. If the outside hasn't been touched for several years it's probably looking rather shabby by now and you should start to think about repainting.

Modern paints come in a very wide range of colours and are very easy to apply. A little time spent preparing and painting your house now can transform a drab old building into a desirable residence; and increase the value of the house with very little outlay.

The main parts of the house that have to be painted are the woodwork, metalwork, and possibly the walls. Plastic gutters and pipes do not need to be painted. It's up to you whether you paint the walls or not. Brick, pebbledash, stone and rendering can all be left in their natural state, but if the walls are in need of repair or are porous, stained and dirty, a good coat of paint will both protect the surface and brighten up the house.

The first thing to do is to take a long, critical look at your house to assess what needs to be done. Search for any defects that may affect the final paintwork. A common fault on older houses is leaking gutters. These can leave unsightly stains on the wall or cause woodwork to rot. They can be easily sealed or can even be completely replaced with new gutters. Other common faults are flaking and peeling paint, rotten window sills and cracked rendering. The illustrations on pages 44 and 45 show many defects that need repairing. It's unlikely you'll find all these faults on one house, but you'll probably find a few. It is very important that you remedy every fault you find before you begin to paint or the paint won't be able to do its job and your house will only deteriorate further. This preparation will usually be the most time consuming part of the decoration and will often be quite hard work. But it has to be done if you want your new paintwork to last. For details on how to prepare each different type of surface – wood, metal, brick, render etc – see pages 48-52.

When to paint

Outside painting should only be done in dry weather and after at least two days without rain, fog or frost. The ideal time is late summer when the wood has had a good time to dry out and the weather is usually quite settled. Even a small amount of moisture trapped under a new paint film will vaporise, causing blisters and peeling. For the same reason you should wait an hour after sunrise to let the dew dry out, and stop work an hour before sunset. On the other hand, don't paint under the full glare of a hot sun as this will dry out the surface too quickly, leaving relatively soft paint underneath which may cause wrinkling as it dries in turn. The ideal practice is to follow the sun, and only paint when it has dried one part of the house and passed on to another. Unfortunately this advice is often difficult to follow in practice as some walls may never see the sun, so you'll have to look for the best compromise.

What to paint first

There is a logical sequence of painting which holds for nearly all houses. In general it's best to start at the top and do larger areas before smaller ones. So if you're going to paint the whole of your house try to follow this order: do the fascia boards and barge boards first, followed by the gutters. The rendering (if any) comes next, then the windows and doors and finally the downpipes. The reason for doing it in this order is that splashes of paint dropped onto a wall beneath a fascia or gutter, even if wiped off immediately, will leave a mark; but subsequent painting of the wall will cover them up. Also, since windows and doors are smaller in area than the rendering, it will be easier to 'cut in' (that is, leave a finer edge) when painting them, so giving a much neater finish.

You will need to follow this sequence three times in all, first to do the preparation, then to apply primers or under coats, and finally to paint on the top coat. If this sounds like far too much work to do all at once there's no reason why you shouldn't split it up and do just a part each year. You could, for instance, do the walls this year, the woodwork next year and the gutters and downpipes the year after. It may even be better to do it this way, spread over several years, as you'll be more aware of the condition of the paintwork and will be able to touch up bits and make small repairs as you go along, when the first signs of wear show. (But remember that this will restrict you to using the same colour as you have at present. It's going to look odd if you change the colour only gradually.)

COMMON SURFACE DEFECTS

Before painting your house, give it a thorough going over to find out where any faults and defects may lie. You're certainly not likely to find all the faults shown here, but the drawings do point out the problem areas. All faults must be put right before you start to paint, otherwise you are likely to achieve a poor result and will waste much time and money in the effort.

Decorative woodwork like this, as well as fascias and barge boards, are very exposed. Scrape off loose paint and fill holes.

Over the years, rendering can crack and come loose. Clean and fill all holes and sterilise mould and algae growth.

The bottom edge of a garage door may start to rot and break up. You'll have to replace it with new pieces or a whole new rail.

Small holes in asbestos or iron roofs can be repaired, but extensive damage may mean replacing parts of the roof.

Old flashing can crack and tiles can come loose, letting damp inside. Renew flashing and replace tiles.

Weatherboards are sometimes painted only on the surface and if rain gets in they will warp and rot, and paint will flake off.

Any cracks and blisters in paint will let in water, and metal will start to rust. All rust must be removed and the metal primed.

44

TESTING A PAINTED SURFACE

1 Try this easy way of testing your paint surface to see if it's suitable for repainting. First, score a double cross in the paint with a sharp knife.

2 Stick a piece of adhesive tape over the length of the cross cuts and press it down firmly. Then pull the tape away from the surface slowly.

3 If the tape is clean, the paint surface is sound and safe for painting. If flakes of paint are pulled off you must strip off the old paint first.

A blocked gutter can overflow, joints can leak and iron gutters can rust – causing damp patches and stains on the wall.

Old, dry putty can fall out and must be replaced; knots should be stripped and treated; rotten wood must be cut out and holes filled.

The white deposit (efflorescence) is caused by damp; it should be brushed off and the source of damp treated.

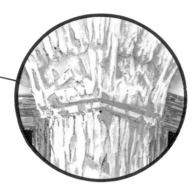

Flaking paint on render should be scraped off and the render brushed down. Fill holes and, if the surface is powdery, apply a stabiliser.

WORKING SAFELY AT HEIGHT

Ladders are an easy and convenient way of reaching heights, but since most domestic accidents involve ladders, it's worth taking time to secure them safely.

Always lean the ladder at a safe angle so that for every 4m of height, the base is 1m from the wall. Always tie it securely at the top or bottom to stop it slipping, and overlap an extension ladder by at least three rungs.

You'll need a roof ladder if you want to paint or repair the chimney or the dividing wall between two roofs. If your house has overhanging eaves, use a ladder stay to hold the ladder away from the wall.

Right: if you have a wide clear area round your house a tower platform is the safest way of getting up high. Make sure it stands perfectly level.

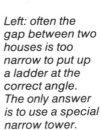

Left: often the gap between two houses is too narrow to put up a ladder at the correct angle. The only answer is to use a special narrow tower.

Special brackets fit on a pair of ladders to provide a long working platform which is useful for reaching the area over a bay window. A third ladder is needed to gain access to the platform.

Tower platforms can be assembled in a cantilevered structure to bridge an outbuilding or a bay window. Protect the roof with sacking and blocks of wood, or use sandbags if the roof is very steep.

Working in safety

To paint the outside of your house in comfort and safety you need the right tools and equipment. There's nothing worse than balancing dangerously on a makeshift working platform with a paint pot in one hand, trying to reach into an awkward corner with the other. But as long as you follow a few simple rules you should be able to work easily and safely. Always work from a step-ladder or an extension ladder and make sure it stands on a firm and level surface. If the ground is uneven, push wedges under a board until the board is level then stand the ladder on this. You'll have to put down a board on soft ground too. If you're working on grass there's a danger of the board slipping, so drive in two stakes on either side of the ladder and rope the ladder to these. On a slippery surface put down some canvas or sacking, and put a board on soft ground. Don't use plastic sheeting as a dust sheet, because the ladder could slip on it.

If you're working high up it's best to tie the ladder to something solid at the top. Don't tie it to the gutter or downpipe as these are not designed to take the extra weight and wouldn't support a ladder if it started to slip. The best way is to fix big screw eyes into sound woodwork such as a window sill, fascia or barge boards and tie the ladder to these. Or, if convenient, you can tie the ladder to the centre mullion of an open window. If there's no sound woodwork, it's advisable to drill and plug the wall to take the screw eyes. Fix them at intervals of about 2m (6ft) and leave them in place when you've finished so they're ready the next time you have to decorate.

Be sure to position the ladder square against the wall so it won't wobble, and lean it at the correct safe angle of 4 to 1, that is, for every 4m of height the bottom should be 1m out from the wall.

When you're working on a ladder don't lean out too far as it's all too easy to loose your balance. Never work from the very top of a step ladder as you'll have nothing to hold on to. A paint kettle, to hold your paint, is an essential piece of equipment as you can hook it on to a rung of the ladder, leaving both hands free.

A safer alternative to a ladder or step-ladder is a tower platform. These can be hired from most DIY shops. The tower comes as a set of tubular steel or aluminium alloy interlocking sections which you build up to the required height. The platform comprises stout boards or prefabricated platform sections. A handrail fits around the top and there is plenty of room for tools and paint. The towers can be extended over bay windows or round chimneys so you can reach all parts of the house in safety. If you have a wide, flat area around your house, choose a tower with locking castors so you can move it along more easily.

THE TOOLS YOU'LL NEED

It saves a lot of time and trouble to have the right tools to hand before you start any job. The tools shown here are the ones you'll need to prepare and paint the outside of your house – the walls, metalwork and the woodwork. Some large items (not shown here) which you'll also need are a dust sheet, a large bucket and a ladder or tower platform.

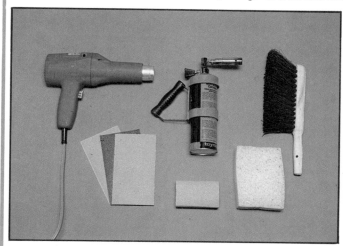

1 Hot air electric stripper for stripping unsound paintwork.
2 Gas blow lamp may be preferred as it saves trailing wires about.
3 A selection of fine, medium and coarse grades of sandpaper for woodwork, and emery paper for metal.
4 Sanding block to hold sandpaper.
5 Sponge for washing down woodwork.
6 Stiff brush for removing dust from masonry.

1 Small trowel for repointing brickwork and repairing holes.
2 Combination shavehook for scraping paint from mouldings.
3 Scraper for flat areas of woodwork.
4 Filling knife for filling holes and cracks.
5 Narrow filling knife for tricky areas round window frames.
6 Putty knife for re-puttying windows.
7 Wire brush for removing rust and paint from metal.

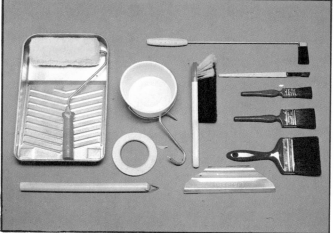

1,2 Long pile roller with extension handle and tray for large areas of masonry.
3 Paint kettle and hook to hold the paint when working on a ladder.
4,5 Masking tape and shield protect areas you want unpainted.
6 Banister brush for painting rough textured surfaces.
7,8,9,10 A selection of brushes for wood and metalwork.
11 Wide brush for smooth surfaces.

EXTERIOR PAINTING: preparation & making good

Properly preparing the outside of your house means that the paint will last much longer.

If your house is in good order and has been decorated regularly, then the paintwork may need no more than a quick wash down and a light sanding before it's ready for re-painting. But if your house is in a rather worse state than this, take some time now to make a really good job of the preparation and you'll have a much easier time in the future. The preparation may seem rather time-consuming, but don't be tempted to miss out any of the steps. Properly applied, paint will protect your house for several years, but it won't stick to an unsound surface.

The most convenient order of working is to start at the top of the house and work down, and to do all the preparation before you start to paint so that the dust and grit won't fall on wet paint. See pages 46-47 for hints on how to work safely on ladders.

Gutters and downpipes

Gutters manage to trap a surprising quantity of dirt and old leaves, so clear this out first. It's a good idea to check that the gutter is at a regular slope towards the nearest downpipe. You can easily check this by pouring a bucket of water into one end and seeing if it all drains away. If puddles form, you'll need to unscrew some of the gutter brackets and adjust the level of the gutter until the water flows away freely. Check all the joints for leaks and if you do find any, seal them with a mastic compound applied with a gun.

Plastic gutters need little maintenance, and they don't need painting. But if you want to change their colour, simply clean them thoroughly and wipe them over with a rag dipped in white spirit or turps to remove any grease spots before starting to paint. There's no need for a primer or undercoat, but you may need two top coats for even coverge.

Metal gutters and pipes need more attention as all rust has to be removed. Scrape off flaking paint first, then use a wire brush and emery paper to remove the rust. A wire brush attachment on an electric drill would make the cleaning easier (but wear a mask and goggles while using one). You can buy an anti-rust chemical from paint shops which is useful for badly rusted metalwork. It works by turning iron oxide (rust) into phosphate of iron which is inert and can be painted over. In any case, prime all bare metal immediately with either a red lead primer or a zinc chromate metal primer. Metal primers contain a rust-inhibitor which protects the metal against further corrosion, so don't miss them out. If the gutters and pipes are in good condition with no sign of rust, simply wash them down and sand the surface lightly to key it ready for repainting.

Fascias and barge boards

Fascias and barge boards run along the top of a wall just below the roof. Fascias support the guttering below pitched roofs and edge flat ones, while barge boards are fitted beneath the roof tiles on gable ends. Because they are so high up, don't worry too much about their appearance; the main consideration is protection as they are in such an exposed position. Clean out well behind the gutters as damp leaves or even bird's nests can be lodged there. Then, using a wide scraper, remove all loose flaking paint, sand down the whole board surface and prime the bare patches. Fill holes and cracks with an exterior-grade filler or water-proof stopping and smooth it level while still damp using a filler knife. You can prime the filler when it's dry.

Walls

The main surface materials and finishes used on the outside of your house are brick, stone, wood and render.

Walls of brick and stone, especially when weathered, have a beauty all of their own and don't really need painting. But the surface can become cracked and dirty and a coat of paint will cover up repairs that don't match the original surface, and protect the wall from further damage. Examine the pointing and, if it has deteriorated, rake out the damaged parts and re-point with fresh mortar. Use a mixture of about 1 part cement to 4 parts of fine sand, or buy a bag of ready-mixed mortar. Use a small trowel and try to match the profile of the original pointing. Don't worry about hairline cracks as these will easily be covered by the paint.

The white crystalline deposit which sometimes appears on brickwork is known as efflorescence. It is caused by water-soluble salts in the brick being brought to the surface, and should be brushed off with a dry brush. Don't try to wash it off as this will only make it worse.

The main types of render are plain, roughcast and pebbledash. Plain render can be applied to give a smooth finish or a textured 'Tyrolean' finish, for example. Roughcast consists of pebbles mixed with mortar before application, and with pebbledash the pebbles are thrown on while the mortar is still wet. Pebbledash deteriorates more quickly than the other types of render as, over the years, differences in rates of expansion between each pebble and the surrounding mortar may result in small surface cracks causing the pebbles to become loose and fall out. Paint will bind in the pebbles and protect small cracks.

PREPARING THE WALLS

1 *Before painting an exterior wall, brush it down well to remove any loose material. Start at the top and use a fairly stiff brush.*

2 *Kill mould and algae with a solution of 1 part bleach to 4 parts water. Leave for two days, then wash down and brush off.*

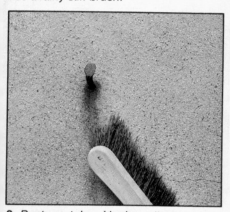

3 *Rusty metal and leaky gutters can easily cause stains, so cure the leaks and clean and prime all metal first. Sterilise the stain and brush down.*

4 *Holes in the wall are often created when old downpipe brackets are removed. Brush them out well and damp the surface with a little water.*

5 *Fill the hole with a sand and cement mixture using a small trowel. Small bags of ready-mixed mortar are ideal for jobs of this size.*

6 *If the wall is powdery or highly porous, or if a cement-based paint has been used previously, seal the surface with a stabilising primer.*

PREPARING THE WOODWORK

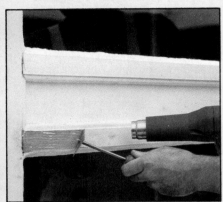

1 Start preparing the woodwork by scraping off all the loose flaking paint. Large areas of unsound paint are better if stripped completely.

2 Sand and prime all the bare wood, taking care to work the primer well into cracks and any exposed end grain, then leave the surface to dry.

3 Where joints have opened up, scrape off the paint and rake out the gap with a knife or shavehook. Clean out all the loose debris.

4 Small cracks can be filled with putty, but use exterior-grade filler or waterproof stopping for larger cracks and holes.

5 Gaps often appear between the window frame and the wall. Fill these with a mastic compound to provide a continuous water-tight seal.

6 Make sure the drip groove underneath the window sill is clear of paint, then thoroughly sand down the whole of the window frame.

REPLACING OLD PUTTY

1 Old, damaged putty must be raked out. Scrape old paint from the glass, and clean the glass with methylated spirit to remove any grease spots.

2 Work the putty in your hands until it has an even consistency. If it's too oily, roll it on newspaper first. Press it firmly into the gap.

3 Smooth the new putty level with the old using a putty knife, then run a soft brush over it to make a water-tight seal with the glass.

TREATING KNOTS

1 *Active knots like this ooze out a sticky resin which quickly breaks through the paint surface, leaving a sticky and unsightly mess.*

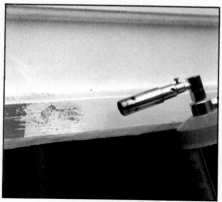

2 *The paint must first be stripped off to expose the knot. Use any method of stripping, and scrape the paint off with a shavehook or scraper.*

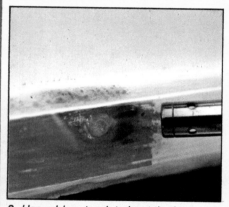

3 *Use a blow-torch to heat the knot until the resin bubbles out. Scrape off the resin and repeat until no more of it appears.*

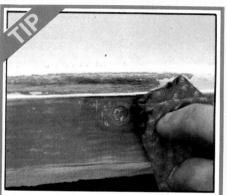

4 *Sand the knot with fine glasspaper, then wipe over the area with knotting applied with a soft cloth. Prime the wood when it has dried.*

When repairing any of these surfaces, try and achieve the same finish as the original, or as near as you can, so that when it's repainted the repair won't be too noticeable. Stop up cracks with mortar, using a mix of 1 part cement to 5 parts sand. Chip away very wide cracks until you reach a firm edge, then undercut this to provide a good key for the new mortar. Dampen the surface, then stop up with a trowel. Use a float if the surface is plain, or texture the surface to match the surrounding area. Where the rendering is pebble-dash, throw on pebbles with a small trowel while the mortar is still wet, then press them into the mortar lightly with a flat piece of wood.

Mould and stains

If there's any sign of mould or algae on the wall, treat this next. Mix up a solution of 1 part household bleach to 4 parts water and paint this on the affected area. Be generous with the solution and cover the area well. Leave for 48 hours for the bleach to kill off all the growth, then wash off thoroughly and brush down with a stiff brush.

Rusty gutters, pipes and metal fittings can all cause stains if rusty water drips down the wall. So cure any leaks first and clean and prime all metal to ensure there's no trace of rust. Mould and algae thrive on damp walls; even if you can't actually see any growth on a damp patch, there may be some spores lurking there, so you should make absolutely sure that you sterilise all stains with the bleach solution just to make sure.

Dusty or chalky walls

All walls, whether dusty or not, should be brushed down thoroughly to remove any loose material. But if, after brushing, the wall is still dusty or chalky, if a cement-based paint was used previously to decorate it, or if the wall is porous, you'll have to brush on a stabilising solution. This will bind together loose particles to allow the paint to stick, and it will seal a porous surface and stop paint

from being sucked in too much. The stabiliser also helps to waterproof the wall and you can paint it on as an extra layer of protection whether it's really necessary or not. Most stabilisers are colourless, but off-white stabiliser/primers are available and this would be a good choice if you were planning to paint your house in a light colour, as it could save one coat of the finishing colour. These off-white stabilisers, however, are not recommended for use on surfaces painted with a cement-based paint.

Stabilisers must be painted on a dry wall and should be left to dry for 24 hours before painting on the top coat. Don't paint if rain is expected. Clean your brush in white spirit or turps as soon as you stop work.

Timber cladding

If the cladding or weatherboarding is bare and you want to leave the natural wood surface showing, it should be treated with a water-repellent wood preservative to give protection against damp penetration and decay. The preservative is available clear or pigmented with various colours.

If the wood has been varnished, scrape off the old varnish and sand down well, following the grain of the wood. Fill cracks and holes with plastic wood or a tinted stopper to match the colour of the wood.

If you wish to paint the surface you'll have to wait a year or so for the water-repellent agents in the preservative to disperse before priming with an aluminium wood primer.

Woodwork

If the paintwork on the windows is in good condition all you need do is give them a wash and a light sanding in preparation for repainting. If the paint is cracked and flaking, a little more preparation is needed. Do the sticky-tape test shown on page 53 to check if the paint surface needs stripping. Occasional chipped or blistered portions can be scraped off and cut back to a firm edge. As long as the edge is feathered smooth with glasspaper, it shouldn't show too much. If previous coatings are too thick for this treatment, build up the surface with outdoor grade hard stopping until it is just proud of the surrounding paint, then sand level when it's dry. Don't allow the stopping to extend too far over the edge of the damage or it'll be difficult to sand smooth.

There comes a time, however, when the condition of the old coating has become so bad that complete stripping is advisable.

A blow-torch or an electric hot air stripper are the quickest tools to use. Start at the bottom softening the paint, and follow up immediately with a scraper. Hold the scraper at an angle so the hot paint doesn't fall on your hand, and don't hold it above the flame or it may become too hot to hold. Try not to concentrate the flame too long on one part or you're likely to scorch the wood.

PREPARING METAL

1 Metal pipes and gutters are often in a very bad state of repair and need a lot of preparation. Scrape off all the old flaking paint first.

2 Brush well with a wire brush to remove all traces of rust. Badly rusted pipes should be treated with an anti-rust chemical.

3 Hold a board or a piece of card behind the pipe to keep paint off the wall, and paint on a metal primer, covering every bit of bare metal.

4 A small paint pad on a long handle is a useful tool for painting behind pipes, especially when they are very close to the wall.

New doors and windows

New wooden windows and doors may already have a coat of pink primer applied at the factory, but it's best not to rely on this for complete protection. Knots, for instance, will rarely have been properly treated, and the primer film will have been damaged here and there in transit. So sand down the whole surface, treat any knots with knotting compound and apply another coat of wood primer overall. It may be advisable to paint doors while they're lying flat; certainly it's vital to paint the top and bottom edges before you hang them in place. It's very important to paint the bottom as rain and snow can easily penetrate unpainted wood causing it to swell and rot. Paint also protects the wood against attack from woodworm.

Metal and plastic windows

Metal doors and windows should be treated in the same way as metal pipes and gutters. So sand them down and make sure all rust is removed before priming. Aluminium frames can be left unpainted, but if you do want to paint them you must first remove any surface oxidation which shows as a fine white deposit. Use a scraper or wire brush, but go very gently and try not to scratch the surface. Prime with a zinc chromate primer. Plastic window frames should not be painted.

Galvanised iron and asbestos

You're likely to find galvanised iron used as corrugated iron roofing, gutters and down-pipes. The zinc coating on galvanised iron is to some extent 'sacrificial', so that if a small patch becomes damaged, the surrounding zinc will, in time, spread over to cover the damage. But this weakens the coating and an application of paint will prolong its life. If the galvanising is new and bright, simply clean it with a rag dipped in white spirit or turps to remove any grease, and apply a calcium plumbate primer. If it's old and grey looking, first remove any existing paint by rubbing lightly with a wire brush, trying not to scratch the surface. Then clean with white spirit or turps and apply zinc chromate primer.

Asbestos is often used for guttering, fascia boards, as walls on out-houses and as corrugated sheeting for roofs. Asbestos is a very dangerous material and for this reason great care should be taken when dealing with it. It'll probably need cleaning before painting and the only safe way is to wet it thoroughly first and scrub it down with a scrubbing brush. Be sure to wear rubber gloves and a face mask. Leave it to dry, then prime it with a stabilizing primer, an alkali resisting primer, or simply a coat of thinned down emulsion paint. Asbestos is very porous, so always paint both sides of an asbestos sheet to prevent damp penetrating from the back.

---

though this rarely matters on exterior woodwork which will be over-painted again. Always be extremely careful when using a blowtorch, and keep a bucket of water or sand nearby in case something does catch fire. A chemical paint stripper is the best method to use near glass in case the glass cracks under the heat of a blow-torch.

Knots, putty and holes

Check the woodwork for any live knots which are oozing out resin. If you find any, strip off the paint over them and then play a blowtorch or electric hot air stripper over them to burn out the resin. Sand lightly and treat with knotting, then prime when dry.

You should also check the putty fillet round each pane of glass, and if any has disintegrated, rake it out with an old knife. Then sand and prime the wood and bed in new putty using a putty knife. Use linseed oil putty on wood and metal glazing or all purpose putty on metal-framed windows. Smooth the putty with a damp cloth and leave it for about a week before painting.

Rake out any cracks in the wood and cut back wood which is starting to rot. If a large amount of wood is rotten – usually along the bottom edge of a sash window – a larger repair will be needed. Once the window has been repaired, prime the bare wood, working the primer well into cracks and end grain as this is where the weather gets in.

Small cracks can be filled with putty, but larger ones should be filled with exterior grade hard stopping or filler. Sand level when dry and spot-prime. Gaps between the window frame and wall should be filled with a flexible, waterproof, mastic compound applied with a special gun.

Finally, sand down the whole of the woodwork to make it ready for repainting.

EXTERIOR PAINTING: completing the job

Here we show you the best way to give a professional look to your home.

If you have completed all the cleaning, repairs and preparation on the outside of your house, and if the weather has been dry for the past couple of days and looks settled for a while, you are now ready to start painting. Tackle the painting in more or less the same order as the preparation, starting at the top and working downwards.

Gutters, fascias and barge boards

If you have plastic gutters and want to paint them, simply apply a thin coat of gloss paint to the outside surface. This is the only case outside where paint is used purely for decoration rather than protection. Iron gutters can be painted on the inside with a bituminous paint as this will provide a waterproof coating and protect the iron. Paint the outside of gutters and downpipes with the usual gloss paint system. You'll need a small paint pad or crevice brush to get into the narrow gaps at the back of gutters and pipes. Protect the fascia with a piece of board held behind the guttering. Don't miss out these awkward bits as this is where the rust will start up again. You can use bitumen paint on the inside of asbestos gutters too, but it's best to use emulsion paint rather than solvent-based gloss ones on the outside. Asbestos is porous and needs to be able to 'breathe'. Gloss paint would trap moisture within the asbestos, and this would eventually cause the paint to blister.

Fascias and barge boards are so exposed that it's best to give them an extra coat of gloss. You'll need your crevice brush or paint pad again to paint behind the gutters.

Walls

There is a wide range of paints available for exterior walls, including types containing fillers or bridging cracks. As for tools, a 100mm (4in) brush is the easiest size to handle; anything larger would put too much strain on the wrist. An alternative is a long-pile roller which has the advantage of being much quicker to use – about three times quicker than a brush. An extra long-pile roller is needed for rough-cast or pebbledash; choose one with a pile 2mm (1¼in) deep, or use a banister brush instead. Use a cheap disposable brush or

A large plastic bucket or paint kettle is essential when working up a ladder. Stir the paint thoroughly first, then pour some into the bucket until it's about one third full. If you're using a roller, use a special roller tray with a large paint reservoir, or else stand a short plank in the bucket (see step-by-step photographs, page 55) to allow you to load the roller evenly.

Hook the bucket or tray onto a rung of the ladder with an S-hook to leave both hands free. Lay a dust sheet below to catch any drips and you're ready to start.

Application

Start at the top of the wall and paint a strip across the house. Work from right to left if you're right-handed, and left to right if you're left-handed.

Use a brush to cut in under the eaves of fascia boards and to paint round obstacles, then fill in the larger areas with a brush or roller. Paint an area only as large as you can comfortably manage and don't lean out too far, your hips should remain between the ladder's stiles at all times.

If you have an awkward area which is too far away to reach, push a broom handle into the hollow handle of the roller, or buy a special extension handle. Protect pipes by wrapping them in newspaper, and mask any other items you don't want to paint. Leave an uneven edge at the bottom of each patch so the join won't be too noticeable, then move the ladder to the left (or right) and paint another strip alongside the first. The principle is always to keep working to the longest wet edge so the joins won't show. When you've done the top series of strips, lower the ladder and paint another series across the middle. Lower the ladder again or work from the ground to do

HOW MUCH MASONRY PAINT?

The spreading power of masonry paints varies according to the porosity and texture of the surface. Roughcast, for instance could take twice as much paint as smooth render. These spreading rates are usually given on the side of the paint tin but in general the coverage is:
● smooth surfaces – 6 to 10m² (65 to 110sq ft) per litre
● lightly textured surfaces – 4 to 6m² (44 to 65sq ft) per litre
● pebbledash, roughcast and Tyrolean – 3 to 4m² (33 to 44sq ft) per litre

CALCULATING THE AREA

To estimate the area of a house wall, simply measure out its length and multiply by the eaves height. Only allow for window area if this is over one fifth of total wall area.

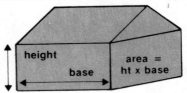

● if you don't know the height, measure the length of the lowest whole section of a downpipe and multiply this by the number of sections making up the complete pipe drop
● for triangular areas, measure the base of the triangle, multiply by the height and divide the answer by two.

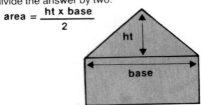

TIP: CLEANING BRICKWORK

Paint splashes from previous careless work can be removed with a chemical paint remover. The paste type is best as it won't run down the wall. This will only strip off the surface paint, however, and some will have soaked into the brick. You may be able to remove this with a wire brush, but if not, apply a poultice of whiting and ammonia kept in position with a piece of polythene taped down at the edges. This will leave a light patch which can be disguised by rubbing with a piece of old, dirty, broken brick. By the time the brick dust has been washed out by rain, natural weathering will have evened out the tone.

another series along the bottom. Working across the house like this means you have to alter the ladder height the least number of times.

Woodwork

You can choose either a non-drip gloss or a runny gloss for the exterior woodwork. The non-drip jelly paints combine the properties of undercoat and finishing coat so a separate undercoat is not required. But this single coat won't be as long lasting as the undercoat-plus-runny-gloss system and you'll have to apply two or three coats to build up a thick enough paint film to give adequate outside protection. Inside, however, one coat of non-drip paint would be quite sufficient.

The sequences of painting all jointed woodwork – windows, doors and frames – is determined by the method of construction. In nearly all cases the rails (horizontal bars) are tenoned into mortises cut into the stiles (uprights). Therefore, you should paint the rails and cross bars first, then deal with the stiles. By painting in this way, any overlaps of paint from the rails and bars are covered up and leave a neater finish. An even edge on the glass is best achieved freehand, but if you doubt the steadiness of your touch, use a paint guard or masking tape. Bring the paint onto the glass for up to 3mm (⅛in) to protect the edge of the putty. If you are using masking tape, remove it shortly after painting round each pane; the paint may be peeled off if it is left to harden completely before the tape is removed.

When a visitor calls at your house, he'll stand face to face with your front door and have nothing to do but examine it while he awaits your answer. So it's here you should put in your best work. Remove all the door furniture such as knobs, knockers, locks, keyhole covers and letterbox. Prepare the woodwork carefully, and wipe it down with a tackrag (a soft cloth impregnated with a sticky varnish) to collect any remaining dust. Tackrags are obtainable from any good paint shop. Use a perfectly clean brush, preferably one that has been used before so that no loose bristles will come adrift. Wedge the door ajar and cover the floor with a dust cloth or old newspapers. Use paint which doesn't need straining, and pour about 50mm (2in) into a small container or paint kettle.

All coats of paint should follow the grain of the wood. Don't attempt to cross-hatch – that is, apply a primer in one direction, undercoat at right angles and finishing coat in the direction of the primer. If you do, you'll get a criss-cross effect which produces a poor finish.

Deal with the door frame first (the top, then the sides) so that any splashes can be

wiped off an unpainted surface immediately. Then do the door itself. Don't put too thick a coat on the inner edge of the door frame because although gloss paint dries fairly quickly, it won't oxidise (i.e., thoroughly harden) for about a week. So in that period, when you close the door, paint may 'set-off' from the frame onto the door, producing a vertical streak an inch or so from the door's edge. A good idea to prevent this is to insert a thin strip of polythene sheeting round the door's edge after the paint has become touch dry, and leave it until the paint has thoroughly hardened.

If you want to apply two finishing coats, wait at least 12 hours but not more than a week between coats. There's no need to sand down between coats because the solvent used in modern gloss paints is strong enough to dissolve the surface of the previous coat and so to ensure a firm bond between the two layers.

Weatherboards

Weatherboards and timber cladding can be left in their natural state as long as you treat them with a wood preservative, and you can use wood stains to enhance or change their colour. If you prefer a glossy finish, use a suitable external varnish such as an oil-resin varnish (marine varnish), rather than a one-pack polyurethane varnish which can prove brittle and difficult to over-coat in future. If you wish to paint the wood you'll have to apply one coat of wood primer, followed by an undercoat and two finishing coats of gloss.

Galvanised iron and asbestos

Because it is waterproof, bituminous paint is best for galvanised or asbestos roofs. In addition to the customary black it can be obtained in shades of red, green or brown to simulate or match tiles. These colours are more expensive than black and may have to be ordered specially from a builders' merchant. Bitumen soon loses its gloss and its surface tends to craze under a hot sun. But that doesn't matter as roofs are not usually visible.

Paint the walls of asbestos outhouses with outdoor-grade emulsion in a colour to match the rest of the house. Thin the first coat to allow for the porosity of the asbestos and follow this with a normal second coat. Apply emulsion on the interior surface as well to minimise moisture absorption. Galvanised iron on vertical surfaces should be painted with gloss paint.

When painting corrugated surfaces, give the high parts a preliminary touch-up with paint, leave it to dry and then paint the whole lot. If you apply paint all over in one go it will tend to flow from high to low parts, giving an uneven coating.

PAINTING WALLS

1 A roller is much quicker to use than a brush, but make sure you have a large enough bucket to dip the roller in. Fill this about ⅓ full.

2 Cut a short plank of wood to the same width as the roller and put it in the bucket so you can load the roller evenly by pressing against it.

3 When painting the house wall, start at the top right hand corner (if you are right-handed) and use a brush to cut in round the edges.

4 Using the roller, cover a strip on your right-hand side. Don't lean over too far and only make the strip as long as you can easily manage.

5 Move the ladder to the left and paint another strip by the first, without overlapping too much. Touch in round obstacles with a brush.

6 Using the brush again, carefully paint round the window. Try to leave a neat edge with the woodwork and wipe off any splashes with a damp cloth.

7 Continue painting a strip at a time from right to left, then lower the ladder and paint a further series of strips until the wall is covered.

8 Protect pipes by wrapping old newspaper round them and securing it with adhesive tape. Use a brush to paint the wall behind the pipes.

9 Be very careful when painting the bottom edge of the wall, and don't load the brush too thickly or paint will run onto the path.

HOW MUCH GLOSS PAINT?

The coverage of a litre of gloss paint depends on several factors, including the smoothness of the surface and whether it is interrupted by edges and mouldings. Also, a lot depends on the painter's technique. However, as a general guide, for one litre of paint:
● runny gloss covers 17m² (180sq ft)
● non-drip gloss covers 13m² (140sq ft).

CALCULATING AREAS

It would be very difficult to calculate the area of every bit of wood and metal you wanted to paint. But you need to make a rough estimate so you'll know how much paint to buy. The following examples are intended as a rough guide and they should give you an idea of how much paint you'll need, assuming you're using **runny gloss** and you give everything **two coats of paint.** If you're using non-drip gloss you'll have to buy about 25% more paint:
● a panelled front door will take ⅓ litre (½ pint)
● a flush door will take about ⅕ litre (⅓ pint)

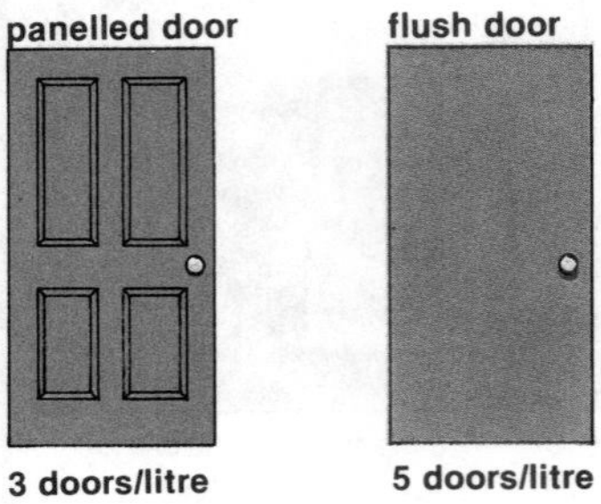

panelled door   **flush door**

3 doors/litre   **5 doors/litre**

● a sash window, about 2x1m (6ft 6in x 3ft 3in) with an ornate frame will take about ⅙ litre (¼ pint)
● a modern picture window of the same size with a plain frame will take only ⅛ litre (⅕ pint)

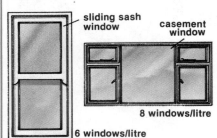

sliding sash window   **casement window**

8 windows/litre

6 windows/litre

● to find the area of a downpipe, simply measure round the pipe and multiply by the height, then add a little for clips and brackets. For two coats of paint, one litre will cover 18m (60ft) of 150mm (6in) diameter pipe and 27m (90ft) of 100mm (4in) pipe.

PAINTING WINDOWS

1 Start to apply undercoat at the top of the window. Prop the window open, tape up the stay and paint the frame rebates first.

2 Paint the rebates on open casements next. If you get paint on the inside surface, wipe it off immediately with a cloth dipped in white spirit or turps.

3 Close the window slightly and paint the area along the hinged edge. You may need to use a narrow brush (called a fitch) to reach this part.

4 A neat paint line on the glass is best achieved free-hand, but if you find this too difficult, use a paint shield or apply masking tape.

5 The general order of painting is to do the cross bars (rails) first, followed by the uprights (stiles) and then the window sill.

6 When the undercoat is dry, sand it down with a fine grade glasspaper, then apply the top coat in the same order as the undercoat.

SECTION 2

FLOORING

TECHNIQUES

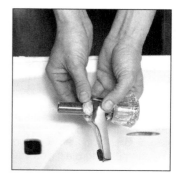

LAYING CERAMIC FLOOR TILES

You can lay ceramic tiles to provide a floor surface which is particularly resistant to wear and tear. If you follow a few basic rules you shouldn't find it too difficult a task and you could at the same time turn the floor into a decorative feature.

Ceramic floor tiles provide a floor-covering which is attractive, extremely hard-wearing and easy to maintain and keep clean. The wide variety of tiles available means you should easily find a pattern which suits your colour scheme.

Floor tiles are usually thicker than ceramic wall tiles (they are generally at least 9mm/⅜in thick), very much stronger and have a tough hardwearing surface to withstand knocks as well as wear from the passage of feet.

The backs of the tiles have a brownish appearance caused by the extra firing – done at a higher temperature than for wall tiles, which are often almost white on the back.

Types of tiles

Square tiles are commonest, in sizes from 150 x 150mm (6 x 6in) to 250 x 250mm (10 x 10in). Besides square tiles you can choose oblong ones in several sizes, hexagons or other interlocking shapes. Surfaces are usually glazed but are seldom as shiny as those of wall tiles or scratch marks would inevitably become apparent as grit was trampled in. So most floor tiles are semi-glazed; others have a matt, or unglazed finish.

Patterned ceramic tiles are quite frequently designed in such a way that several tiles can be laid next to one another to complete a larger design. The commonest is built up by laying four identical tiles in a square, each tile being turned at 90° to its neighbours. The full impact will only be achieved if a sufficiently large area of floor is being tiled.

Patterned and plain tiles can also successfully be intermixed to create unusual designs, but it is essential that the tiles are all supplied by the same manufacturer, and ideally come from compatible ranges, to ensure uniformity of thickness and size.

Some manufacturers supply floor tiles designed to co-ordinate with wall tiles, and in addition make matching panels to act as skirtings between wall and floor tiles.

Types of adhesives

There are several types of adhesives for laying floor tiles. Some come ready-mixed, others in powder form to be mixed with water. A number are waterproof and where the floor will be subjected to frequent soakings (as, for example, in a shower cubicle) or heavy condensation you will need to use one which is water-resistant. Usually the adhesive does not become waterproof until it has set completely, which means that you can clean tools with water and do not require a special cleaner.

On a solid floor with underfloor heating you should use an adhesive which is also heat-resistant or the adhesive will fail and the tiles will lift necessitating continual re-fixing.

A cement-based floor tile adhesive is suitable for use on good, level concrete whereas a suspended wooden sub-floor will need an adhesive with some degree of flexibility built in. Combined cement/rubber adhesives are available for this purpose but even these should not be used on suspended wooden floors which are subject to a lot of movement – you will have to add a covering of man-made boards to provide a more stable surface before fixing the tiles.

Manufacturers' instructions give guidance as to the type of adhesive suited to a particular situation and you should study these carefully before making your choice. You should also follow their recommendations as to the thickness of adhesive bed required; most resin-based ready-mixed adhesives are used as thin beds (3 to 6mm/⅛ to ¼in), while cement-based powder adhesives may be laid up to 12mm (½in) thick. Usually a spreader is supplied with the adhesive to make applying it a straightforward job.

Planning

As when tiling a wall, it is well worth planning your layout on paper first, particularly if you intend using a complicated design. For rectangular or square tiles make a scale drawing on graph paper; for hexagons or other specially-shaped tiles, draw the shapes to scale on tracing paper, to act as an overlay to a scale floor plan of the room. From your scale drawings you can see if the layout you have in mind is going to work. It will help you set out an attractive design and it will also enable you to work out the number of tiles you will require.

Mark on your plan the position of fixtures such as a WC, wash or sink stand, cupboards or pipes to indicate where cutting will be required – where necessary adjust your plan so you will not have to cut pieces which are too narrow for convenient cutting.

Similarly, your layout should be designed so you avoid having to cut narrow pieces of tile to

MARKING UP

1 Choose the corner at which you wish to start tiling, and use a tiling gauge to find out how many whole tiles will fit alongside one wall.

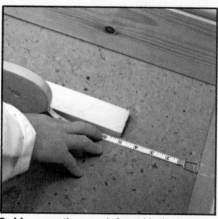

2 Measure the gap left and halve it to give the width of the cut pieces for each end. Allow one less whole tile in the row to avoid very narrow cut pieces.

3 Measure in the width of one cut piece, plus grouting gaps, from the adjacent wall. Mark a line to show where one edge of the first whole tile will be placed.

4 Repeat the measuring process along the adjacent wall to establish the position of the other edge of the first whole tile. Mark this line on the floor too.

5 Lay a batten on the line drawn in **4** and nail it to the floor alongside the first wall to act as a guide for laying the first complete row of tiles.

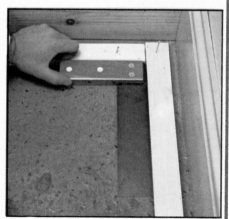

6 Pin a second batten alongside the other wall, its edge on the line drawn in **3**, and check that the two battens are at right angles to each other.

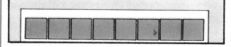

LAYING TILES

1 *In the corner framed by the two battens, spread enough tiling adhesive with a notched spreader to cover an area of about 1 sq m (10 sq ft).*

2 *Lay the first tile in position in the angle between the two battens, pushing it tightly up against them, and bed it into place with firm hand pressure.*

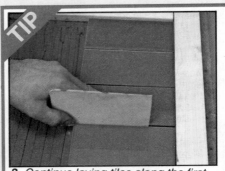

3 *Continue laying tiles along the first row, butting them against the batten to keep the edge straight. Use a cardboard spacer to create even gaps.*

4 *Lay tiles until you have reached the edge of the adhesive, using the spacer as before. Carry on area by area until all whole tiles are laid.*

fit around the perimeter of the room. Floor tiles, being so much tougher, are less easy to cut than wall tiles and attempting to obtain narrow strips is likely to cost you several broken tiles.

Where you are not using a complicated design you can plan your layout directly on the floor. For this you will need a tiling gauge (see *Ready Reference*).

Preparing the floor surface

Surfaces to be tiled should be dry, flat, stable, clean and free from grease, dirt and unsound material. A flat, dry, level concrete floor can be tiled without special preparation. If, however, there are small depressions in the concrete these should be filled with a mortar mix of 3 parts sharp sand and 1 part cement. A more uneven floor should be screeded with a proprietary brand of self-levelling flooring compound.

The screed should be left for two weeks to allow it to dry thoroughly before fixing tiles. If the floor is a new concrete one, it should be left for a minimum of four weeks to allow all moisture . to disperse before you begin covering it with tiles.

Existing ceramic floor tiles, quarry tiles or terrazzo surfaces can be tiled over. They should be checked to ensure that there are no loose or hollow-sounding areas. Any defective sections must be made good before you lay new tiles on top.

You can tile on suspended wooden floors, but it is important that the floor should be made as rigid and firm as possible. To achieve this, cover the floorboards with a layer of water-resistant resin-bonded plywood at least 12mm (½in) thick. Alternatively, you can use chipboard of the same thickness.

Before laying tiles over timber floors cover the surface thoroughly with a priming coat – either a special priming agent from the adhesive manufacturer, or else diluted PVA building adhesive.

Finding the starting point

The first whole tile you lay will determine where all the other tiles are laid, so it is important that you get this positioning correct. Choose the corner in which you wish to start tiling and, laying your tile gauge parallel to one of the walls, measure how many whole tiles will fit along that side of the room. There will almost certainly be a gap left over. Measure this gap, and divide the answer by two to find the width of the cut tiles that will fill the gap at each end of the row. (These should be of equal size.)

If these cut tiles turn out to be less than one quarter of a tile-width across (and therefore tricky to cut), reduce the number of whole tiles in the row by one. The effect of this is to increase the width of each cut tile by half a tile – much easier to cut.

Return to the corner and with your tile gauge parallel to the wall along which you have been measuring, move it so the end of the gauge is the width of one cut tile away from the adjacent wall. Mark this position off on the floor – it indicates where one edge of the first whole tile in that row will fall.

Repeat this same measuring process along the adjacent wall to establish the positioning of the row at right angles to the one you've just set out; you will then be able to mark off where the other edge of this same first tile will fall, and so fix its position precisely. Once that is done, every other tile's position is fixed right across the floor.

You can then place this first tile in position. Mark off and cut the boundary tiles between it and the corner. Remember to allow for the width of the grouting gap when measuring each cut tile.

Each cut tile should be measured individually because the wall may not be perfectly straight. You may then go ahead with laying whole tiles, starting from your original corner.

Laying tiles

In the corner area spread adhesive evenly on the floor over an area of about 1 sq m (11 sq ft) – it is important to work on only a small area at a time, otherwise the adhesive may have begun to dry out by the time you reach it. With a gentle, twisting motion, place the first tile in the corner, and use light hand pressure to bed it firmly in the adhesive. Place the second tile alongside the first, using the same gentle pressure, and placing spacers of cardboard or hardboard between the tiles if they don't have spacer lugs. Continue laying tiles, building up a rectangular area, until you have reached the edge of the adhesive bed.

Use a spirit level to check that the tiles are level; if any are too low, lever them off the bed as quickly as possible with a wide-bladed trowel, add adhesive and re-set them, pressing them down gently.

With the first square metre of tiles laid, you can spread another layer of adhesive over a further area, and lay the next area of tiles.

As you lay the tiles, it is worth checking every now and again that adequate contact with the adhesive is being made and that there are no voids beneath the tiles – any gaps or

FITTING BORDER TILES

1 Mark the width of each border tile in turn, using the spacer to allow for the necessary grouting gap. Kneel on a board so you don't disturb the whole tiles.

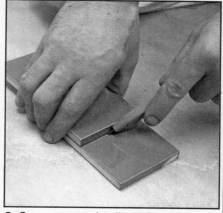

2 Score across the tile surface at the mark with a tile cutter. Press firmly so its tip cuts the glaze cleanly; scoring again may cause a ragged edge.

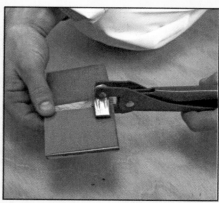

3 Use a tile breaker with V-shaped jaws to break the tile along the scored line. Floor tiles are usually too thick to break over a straight-edge.

4 Butter adhesive onto the back of the cut piece, and press it into position. Use the spacer to form an even grouting gap at either side of the cut piece.

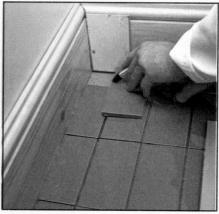

5 Finally mark and cut the piece of tile to fit in the corner of the room, lay it and leave the newly-tiled floor for 24 hours to allow the adhesive to set.

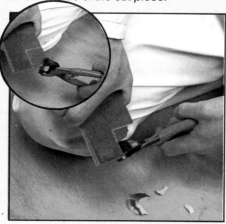

6 To cut an L-shaped piece of tile, score the surface carefully and nibble away the waste with tile pincers. Work from the corner (inset) in to the score lines.

Ready Reference

TIP: CUTTING FLOOR TILES

Because of the high-baked clay back, floor tiles can be hard to snap by hand. Save time and breakages by buying a tile cutter with angled jaws, or hire a special floor tile cutter from a tool hire shop.

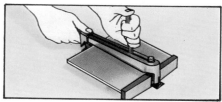

TIP: ALLOW 48 HOURS SETTING

● don't walk on the floor for at least 48 hours after tiling
● where access is essential, lay plywood or chipboard sheets over the tiles to spread the load
● avoid washing the floor until the grout and adhesive have set completely (1 to 2 weeks).

DON'T FORGET DOORS

Tiling will raise the floor level. Remove inward-opening doors from their hinges before starting tiling or they will not open when tiling reaches the doorway.

● measure the depth of tile plus adhesive laid
● plane the door bottom down by this amount
● fit a sloping hardwood strip across the door threshold

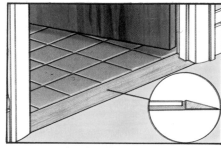

TIP: TILES FOR WET AREAS

Unglazed tiles are less slippery than glazed but ones with a textured surface reduce the chance of accidents in bath and shower rooms.

GROUTING TILES

1 When the adhesive has set, you can grout the joints. Use a sponge or a rubber squeegee to force the grout into all the gaps.

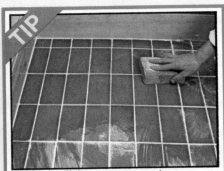

2 Wipe off the excess grout as you work with a damp sponge; if you allow it to set hard it will be very difficult to remove later.

3 Use a piece of thin dowel with a rounded end to smooth off the joints. Don't be tempted to use a finger as grout could irritate your skin.

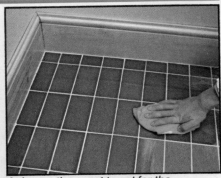

4 Leave the grout to set for the recommended time, and then polish the surface all over with a clean, dry cloth to remove the last traces of grout.

PREPARING FLOOR

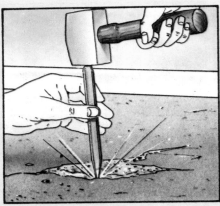

Clean out the small depressions and cracks to be filled with a club hammer and chisel. Beware of flying chippings.

Use a trowel to fill in the depressions with mortar and to level off to provide a suitable surface for the tiles.

---

hollows under the tiles will become weak points later on.

You can proceed with the tiling in 1 sq m sections until all the tiles are in place, then leave them for at least 24 hours. The tiles must not be walked on during this time so that any risk of them being knocked out of place or bedded too deeply is avoided. If you have to walk on the tiles, lay a sheet of plywood or chipboard over them first to spread the load. When 24 hours – or longer; check the manufacturer's instructions – are up, you can remove the spacers. Check with the adhesive manufacturer's instructions to see whether you need to allow extra time after this before you begin grouting.

Cutting tiles

You will have to cut each tile individually since you will almost certainly find variations around the room. Place the tile which is going to be cut against the wall and on top of the adjacent whole tile. Mark it off for cutting.

Using a straight edge as a guide, score the tile surface and edges with a scribing tool. You *can* use a hand tile cutter to cut and break the

tile along the scoreline; but its probably worthwhile hiring a special floor tile cutter to make the job easier.

To cut a tile to give an L-shape you will need to use tile nips to nibble away at the waste area. You can use a tile file, carborundum stone or coarse glasspaper to smooth off the rough edge. For curved shapes (eg, to fit round a WC pedestal), you will need to make a template and again use tile nips to nibble away at the tile.

Grouting the tiles

Mix the grout according to the manufacturer's instructions; make up only a small amount at a time and, as with adhesive, work in areas of 1 sq metre (11 sq ft). Apply it with the straight edge of a rubber float, or a sponge or squeegee, making sure the joints are properly filled. Pack the grout firmly into the joints and smooth off using a small rounded stick – don't try using a finger as the grout is likely to irritate your skin.

It's best to remove excess grout (and adhesive) as soon as possible. If it sets it will be difficult to remove.

Filling cracks and hollows

If you have a concrete floor which is flat, dry and level you can go ahead and lay tiles without further preparation. Often, however, the floor is not level or there are cracks and small hollows on the surface. Indentations should be filled with mortar (a 3:1 sand:cement mix is suitable) mixed to a creamy but not too runny consistency. For mortar with a good bond add some PVA bonding solution to the mix. Cut back the holes to a clean shape and brush out any loose material so it doesn't mix in with the mortar making it difficult to get a smooth surface. You can also coat the holes with a PVA bonding solution to help the mortar adhere.

SURFACES FOR TILING

1

2

3

4

Levelling a concrete floor

A concrete floor which is out of true can be levelled using a self-levelling flooring compound so it is suitable for tiling. For the compound to form a smooth, even surface it should only be applied to a floor which is clean and free from dust, oil, grit or grease so you should first sweep the floor and then scrub it thoroughly (1). You may find you have to use a proprietary cleaner to remove stubborn greasy patches. The compound comes in powder form and you will have to mix it up according to the manufacturer's instructions so it forms a runny paste (2).

If you try covering the entire floor in one operation, it's likely the compound will set into large pools which are difficult to join up. It's better to work in small areas; you can delineate your working area by forming a bay using timber battens. Pour the compound onto the floor (3) and then spread it out as evenly as possible using a steel float (4), any marks from the float will disappear quickly. The compound will set within a couple of hours. If you want extra thickness you can apply a second coat once the first is hard.

5

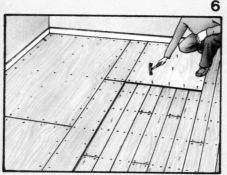

6

7

Laying plywood over a timber floor

A floor which is subject to movement will disrupt tiles laid over it so if you intend tiling over a suspended wooden floor you will first have to make the surface as firm as possible by covering it with a layer of man-made boards. Water-resistant resin-bonded plywood is a suitable material as it will resist penetration by the damp adhesive you will be spreading over it and you will avoid the problem of rotting boards. The boards should be at least 12mm (½in) thick. To prepare the floor to take the plywood you should punch any protruding nails below the surface (5) at the same time checking that the floorboards are firmly secured. You can then go ahead and fix the sheets of plywood to the floor (6) using nails spaced at 225mm (9in) intervals across the middle of the sheets and at 150mm (6in) intervals round their perimeter. You will have to cut the boards to shape round any recess or alcove(7), and where there is a pipe run, fix narrow strips of plywood over the pipes to make access to them easier. Make sure you stagger the joints; this will prevent any floor movement causing the tiles to break up in a run across the floor.

LAYING QUARRY TILES

Quarry tiles will provide a highly attractive natural-looking floor surface in kitchens, bathrooms, hallways and other areas which receive hard wear. They can also be used outdoors – as a patio surface, for example.

Glazed ceramic floor tiles are ideal as a floorcovering in kitchens, bathrooms, utility areas and WCs, but, whether plain or patterned, they are also expensive. This is where unglazed ceramic tiles, commonly known as quarry tiles, compare well. Like glazed tiles, quarry tiles are hardwearing and easy to clean but they are cheaper and, if you want really good value for money, they're well worth considering. They come in subtle shades of brown, red or yellow and will fit in with almost any décor, whether modern or traditional.

Buying quarry tiles

You'll first have to decide on the type of tiles you want (see *Ready Reference*) and their size. Where thickness is concerned, it's worth asking your supplier for advice. Obviously, the thicker the tile, the more hardwearing it is likely to be, but, in practice, few domestic situations warrant anything more than the thinnest of the range. There's also the question of shape: in addition to ordinary square-edged tiles, you'll find RE and REX tiles – with one and two rounded edges respectively – for use on steps (none of these, by the way, has spacer lugs). And, to complete the job, most manufacturers offer a range of skirting tiles, including those for straight runs, internal and external corners, plus stop ends. You can use these in place of timber skirtings and they are ideal in situations where water is likely to be splashed around, providing protection against moisture penetration.

Measuring up

For a rough estimate of how many tiles you need, measure the length and width of the area to be tiled using the size of a whole tile plus the width of a joint as your unit of measurement. Round each dimension up to the next whole number then multiply the two together to find the number of tiles required to cover the whole floor area.

If the area you're going to tile is an awkward shape, perhaps because of sanitary fittings, built-in units and so on, it's better to work out the number of tiles you need accurately with the aid of a floor plan drawn to scale on graph paper, so long as it's not too large. The floor will look best if the tiles are arranged symmetrically, so remember this when you are drawing in the position of each tile. Add up the number of tiles, counting each cut tile as a whole tile.

Preparing the surface

Your aim should be to provide a surface which is sound, stable and free from anything likely to stop the tiles sticking, such as dirt, grease dust, polish and moisture.

With bare concrete you will usually only need to give it a thorough clean, though if the surface is at all powdery you will also have to treat it with a stabilising solution. You may need to give highly polished concrete additional attention, depending on the type of adhesive you intend using. With some adhesives you have to roughen the surface to provide a key. This is not an easy task and you may decide that it's worth looking for an alternative fixing product.

Suspended timber floors require rather more preparation. You should begin by checking that the floor shows no sign of movement when walked on, as any problem of this kind will be increased by the weight of the tiled surface. Loose boards should be refixed with screws and, while you're about it, you should punch all nail heads well below the surface. Overall 'springing' of the floorboards caused by sagging joists presents rather more of a problem for the simple reason that the cure involves virtually rebuilding the floor. In this case it may be better to give up the idea of tiling the floor.

Assuming the floor is sound, the next step is to ensure that the underfloor space is adequately ventilated: in other words that there are sufficient airbricks. You can then level off the surface of the floor with a covering of exterior-grade plywood sheets (see *Ready Reference*). If you intend using adhesive to fix the tiles, check with the manufacturer's instructions to see whether the plywood has to be treated with a special primer before you apply the adhesive.

If you can do so without too much trouble, you should lift existing vinyl sheet or tile floorcoverings and treat the floor surface beneath as already described. You can generally afford to leave existing floor tiles in place. Remove any damaged sections, together with those which have come loose, then fill in any deep depressions that result with mortar. The tiling adhesive should be able to accommodate minor lumps and bumps in the floor. Finish by thoroughly cleaning the floor, making sure you remove all trace of dirt, grease and polish. (Certain tiling adhesives are unsuitable for use over plastic floorcoverings so remember to check for this with the adhesive manufacturer's instructions.)

Depending on the thickness of the floorcovering formed by the tiles plus adhesive or mortar, you may have to remove and refix the skirting boards. If you do remove them, you will have to make good the wall where they were fixed in place, whether you intend to replace them with skirting tiles or to replace the original skirtings when the tiling is finished.

LAYING THE TILES

1 Establish a starting point for the first whole tile and temporarily nail the guide battens in place. Check they are square using a set-square.

2 Use a tiling gauge to work out the position of a third batten, four tiles in from one fixed batten, and temporarily nail it in position.

3 With a spirit level check that the battens are level. If they are not you will have to pack them up (see Ready Reference).

4 Use a trowel to spread a layer of mortar in the bay formed by the battens; aim to get the mortar coverage as even as possible.

5 Draw a notched dragging board over the battens so the mortar is smoothed down to the correct distance below the battens.

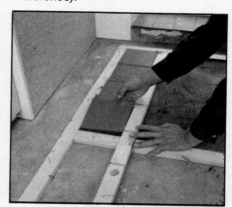

6 Using your tiling gauge as a guide, bed the tiles by hand, making sure you leave the correct grouting gap between them.

7 When you've bedded 16 tiles by hand you can go over them again with a block of wood, tamping them down into the mortar bed. Check they're evenly laid with a spirit level.

8 With the first 16 tiles in place, remove the third batten and fix it in place so it forms another bay for fixing the next area of tiles. Fix all the whole tiles in this way.

9 When a section of tiles is laid securely, you can cut tiles for the border areas and fix these in place. Make sure you don't disturb the whole tiles when you are doing this.

TILE TYPES

There are two types of quarry tiles produced by different methods of manufacture:
● those which are smooth and uniform in size, like ordinary ceramic tiles
● those which are rougher in texture; tiles sold as the same size and shade may in fact vary slightly from each other, particularly in terms of thickness and also in colour. This type may be vitrified or only partly vitrified, with the former being slightly harder and more impervious.

TILE SIZES

Quarry tiles for floors range in size between 75 and 150mm (3 and 6in) square with thicknesses ranging from 12 to 30mm (1/2 to 1 1/4in).

TIP: ALLOW FOR BREAKAGES

After counting up how many tiles you will need, be on the safe side and remember to add an extra 5 to 10 per cent to allow for any breakages when you are cutting and laying the tiles.

TIP: LET CONCRETE CURE

If you intend laying quarry tiles on a new concrete floor, wait at least 30 days after the new concrete has been laid before you go ahead and fix the tiles over the new concrete surface.

LEVELLING A TIMBER FLOOR

To provide a level surface on a timber sub-floor lay sheets of exterior-grade plywood. When fixing them remember to:
● stagger the joints between the sheets so any floor movement won't cause the sheets to move in a continuous line and break up the floorcovering
● use galvanised screws rather than nails to secure the sheets, driving them in at roughly 300mm (1ft) centres across the face of each sheet and roughly 230mm (9 1/2in) apart round the edges (with nails, you run the risk of them pulling out if the plywood warps)
● take special care there is no change in level across the joins between sheets; if need be, reduce the spacing of the screws round the edges to 150mm (6in) or even 100mm (4in) to prevent this.

TIP: KEEP LAYOUT SIMPLE

Quarry tiles for floors are difficult to cut so it's best to avoid the need for awkwardly shaped or very narrow cut tiles. If you are using tiles which vary slightly in size you will not be able to work with 100 per cent accuracy, so ensure that small errors don't lead to big problems by going for the simplest layout you can.

CUTTING TILES

1 Score deeply along the cutting line with a tile cutter. If the tile has ribs on the underside, score in the same direction as the ribs.

2 To help the tile break cleanly, hold it carefully and use a pin hammer to tap the tile sharply on its underside just beneath the scored line.

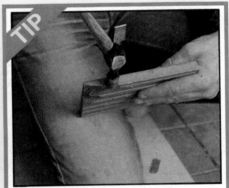

3 To cut an L-shape, score the shape onto the tile and then tap away at the back of the waste with a hammer so it's thinner and easier to remove.

4 Use tile nips or pincers to nibble away at the waste, taking out small pieces at a time so you don't risk breaking the tile.

Laying the tiles

Whether you are going to lay the tiles on a mortar bed or adhesive you will first need to mark up a tiling gauge. You can make up a gauge rod from a 50x25mm (2x1in) timber batten. Lay a row of tiles on the floor, spacing them the correct distance apart, and then transfer the tile positions on to each batten with a pen or pencil.

It's best to begin tiling next to a long, straight wall, preferably the wall furthest from the door. As when laying glazed floor tiles you will have to establish a right-angled starting point for the first whole tile (see pages 58-63). Temporarily nail timber battens in place to indicate the starting point and to serve as a guide for the rest of the tiling. Where you are laying the tiles on mortar which is simply used as an adhesive, the battens' thickness should equal twice the thickness of the tiles; where the mortar is to double as a screed, their thickness should equal the thickness of the screed (usually 50mm/2in) plus the thickness of a tile.

Then, if you are tiling on mortar, use the gauge rod to work out the position of another batten four tiles in from one of the battens already in place, and temporarily nail this batten in position. You now have a 'bay' formed by the three battens and it is within such bays that you work across the floor, spreading the mortar and bedding the tiles area by area.

If you are using adhesive, once you have fixed battens to indicate your starting point and to serve as guidelines for the rest of the tiling, you can begin to apply the adhesive, spreading on enough to cover about 1sq m (1sq yd) of floor area at a time. If you are laying the tiles on a 3mm (1/8in) thick bed of adhesive you simply pour some adhesive onto the floor, spread it out as evenly as possible to the required thickness with a trowel or steel float

TILING A SKIRTING

1 When the skirting board has been removed you can proceed to butter the back of the skirting tiles with mortar; aim for an even coverage.

2 Press the skirting tiles carefully into place, leaving a grouting gap between them and making sure they align with the tiles on the floor.

3 Where necessary, you will have to fill in the gap between the skirting tiles and the rest of the tiles with narrow pieces of cut tile.

TILING A STEP

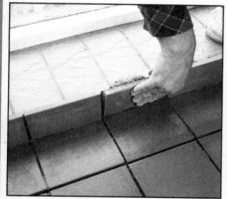

1 Start by covering the riser. Cut the tiles so they will reach 13mm (1/2in) above the top of the step, then butter their backs and press them into place.

2 Then spread a layer of mortar onto the step tread so it just reaches the top of the riser tiles. Smooth the mortar so it's even and level.

3 You can then go ahead and fix the lipping tiles on the tread to form a neat nosing at the front of the step. Fill in with cut tiles at the back.

and then lightly rub the surface with a serrated scraper.

If you are applying a 6mm (1/4in) bed of adhesive you could apply it in areas delineated by timber bays as when using mortar. However, it is easier to lay a 3mm (1/8in) thick bed as described and then to butter the necessary additional adhesive onto the back of each tile just as you are about to lay it. Alternatively, apply the entire 6mm (1/4in) of adhesive to the tile.

Once the adhesive is down you can press the first square metre of tiles firmly into place. Take care that the whole of each tile is firmly in contact with the adhesive and that there are no gaps or pockets of trapped air. Once two or three tiles are down, use a spirit

level to check that they finish flush with each other, then repeat this test as each subsequent tile is pressed in place. When you have covered one square metre, clean off any adhesive that has strayed on to the surface of the tiles before moving on to put down more adhesive and tiles. It's important to do this before the adhesive sets.

When you are fixing tiles in mortar it's best to work in sections when you are laying the cut tiles. Otherwise you risk disturbing the whole tiles which are already laid.

If you wish, instead of bedding the tiles in a dry, crumbly mortar (see *Ready Reference*) you can use a mix like this as the base and then spread a runnier mix over the top in which to bed the tiles.

Cutting tiles

Quarry tiles are cut in much the same way as any other type of ceramic tile. You score the surface with a tile cutter, or where you are cutting an L-shaped piece you nibble away at the waste with pincers or tile nips. Having said that, it's worth remembering that these floor tiles are thick and it's best to take care to score deeply into the tile. If you tap the underside of the tile sharply with a hammer just beneath the cut line it will break more easily. Nibbling away at waste with pincers may still prove troublesome and in some cases it could be worth resorting to the use of a cold chisel and hammer to chip off the tile to the shape you want. You will have to work with care, resting the tile on a firm bed of newspaper for

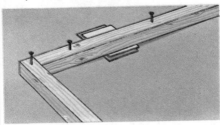
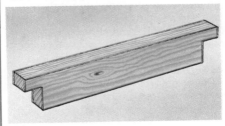
support, to stop the tile from cracking. Alternatively, you can thin the waste part of the tile to make it easier to nibble it away.

Tiled skirting

According to the traditional method of tiling, tiled skirtings are always laid before the floor is tiled. However, you may find it easier to get a neat result, matching the skirting's joins with those between the floor tiles, if you fix them after tiling the floor; this is perfectly acceptable. In this case, make sure you leave the correct gap between the floor tiles and walls to take the skirting tiles.

If you are working with tiling adhesive, use this to fix the skirting tiles to the wall in exactly the same way as when you are fixing tiles to the floor. If you are using mortar, apply this to the wall using a steel float, aiming for a continuous bed roughly 6mm (¼in) thick. Alternatively, you can butter the back of each tile with mortar, taking care that the whole of the back surface is covered.

Finishing off

Where the tiles have been laid on adhesive, leave them at least 12 hours before you grout them. Where you have laid them on a mortar bed this 'waiting time' should be increased to 24 hours.

In both cases it's worth reducing the risk of disturbing the tiles if you have to walk on them by spreading your weight on 'crawl boards' roughly 900x600mm (3x2ft) made from chipboard or some equally rigid sheet material.

The grouting is done in much the same way as when you are grouting other ceramic floor or wall tiles, in that you rub the grout over the tiles so it fills the joints and then clean off the excess. Do make sure that you are using a grout which is designed for floors and that you don't remove too much grout when cleaning off (see step-by-step photographs). Most grouts which are suitable for use with floor tiles are cement-based and are likely to irritate the skin, so avoid unnecessary contact with the grout by wearing gloves. Remember you can buy coloured grout or add colour to a standard type of grout if you want to match the colour of the tiles or set them off in coloured grout which provides a striking contrast.

After grouting you should leave the floor for a day or two to harden and then wash it thoroughly using water and detergent. You can finish off by applying a proprietary tile sealer or, if you like, floor polish, but tiles which have been laid outdoors must never be polished.

A word of warning: do be careful when you are carrying out this first floor wash. Take care that you don't use too much water. The floor, in particular the grout and adhesive, will not be up to a heavy soaking for at least a fortnight.

GROUTING TILES

1 *Leave the tiles for at least 12 hours without disturbing them and then spread grout over the surface with a sponge or plastic spreader.*

2 *To remove the excess grout, first rub a cloth diagonally across the joins, taking away as much of the excess as possible.*

3 *Then, with most of the hard rubbing done, work along the joins with the cloth to neaten the finish. This saves you removing too much grout from within the joins.*

LAYING CORK TILES

Cork tiles will provide you with a floor surface which is warm, wears well and is quiet to walk on. In addition, they are the easiest of tiles to lay.

You can use cork floor tiles in bathrooms, kitchens, dining rooms and children's rooms; anywhere, in fact, where any other resilient floorcovering (eg, vinyl sheet or tiles, or thermoplastic tiles) could be used. They are warmer and quieter than most other floorcoverings and tend not to 'draw the feet', unlike, for example, ceramic tiles, which are very tiring if you have to stand round on them for long periods. They will look particularly elegant if they are softened with rugs or rush matting and blend equally well with modern or traditional style furniture and décor.

Ordinary cork tiles are made from granulated cork, compressed and baked into blocks; the natural resins in the grain bond the particles together, though sometimes synthetic resins are added to improve wearing and other qualities. The tiles are cut from these blocks so they are mm (1/4in) or more thick. 'Patterned' cork tiles (see below) are made by alternating wafer-thin cork veneers with thicker layers of insulating cork and sealing with a protective PVC surface.

Types of tiles

Cork tiles have an attractive natural look; usually they are a rich honey-gold, although there are some darker browns and smoky tones. Dyed cork tiles are available in many different colours ranging from subtle shades to strident primary colours. There are also 'patterned' tiles which have an interesting textured, rather than a heavily patterned look; these come in natural colours as well as red, soft green and rich dark smoky brown: the colour tends to 'glow' through the top surface of cork. One design gives a subtle miniature checkerboard effect. Other tiles come with designs (such as geometric patterns) imprinted on them.

For floors that are likely to get the occasional flood or where spills and 'accidents' are inevitable, such as in kitchens, bathrooms and children's rooms, it wiser to use pre-sealed types of tiles (see Ready Reference). The cheaper seal-it-yourself types are, however, perfectly adequate for living rooms, bedsitting rooms and halls.

Preparing the surface

As with other types of tiles and resilient floor-coverings the subfloor surface on which you lay cork tiles must be smooth, clean and free from lumps, bumps, protruding nails, tacks or screws. Where floorboards are uneven, it's best to cover them up with flooring-grade chipboard, plywood or flooring quality hardboard, either nailed or screwed down securely. Remember to stagger the sheets of chipboard or other material to avoid continuous joins. Then, if there is any floor movement it will not disturb the tiles fixed on top and cause them to lift or be moved out of alignment.

There must also be adequate ventilation underneath a wooden subfloor. Poor ventilation can cause condensation which could lead to the rotting of the floorboards and the floorcovering above them. If the floor is laid at ground level, or directly to joists or battens on ground level concrete, you should protect the cork from moisture penetration by covering the timber with bituminous felt paper before laying hardboard or plywood. The paper should be fixed with bituminous adhesive; and you should allow a 50mm (2in) overlap at joins and edges.

Solid subfloors, such as concrete or cement and sand screeds, should be thoroughly dry. Make sure the floor incorporates an effective damp-proof membrane before laying the tiles: this can

ESTABLISHING THE STARTING POINT

1 Find the centre points of two opposite walls. Stretch a string line between them, chalk it and snap a line across the floor.

2 Repeat the procedure, but this time between the other two walls. Where the two lines intersect is the exact centre of the floor.

3 Dry-lay a row of tiles along the longest line from the centre point to one wall. Adjust the other line if necessary (see Ready Reference).

4 Lay a row of tiles along the other line from the centre point and again adjust to avoid wastage or very narrow strips at the edges.

is irregularly shaped, divide it into rectangles and measure each one separately. If you take these measurements to your supplier, he should be able to help you calculate the quantity of tiles you will require. Or, as many tiles are sold ready-boxed with a guide to quantities printed on the box, you can study the guide to work out the number of tiles you'll need.

If you plan to buy tiles of contrasting colours, and to form a border pattern, or to lay them so you get a checkerboard effect, you should plan out the design on squared paper first. Divide up the floor area so each square represents a tile, and colour the squares in different colours to represent the different colours of the tiles so you can judge the effect. You can then calculate the quantity needed by reference to your plan.

Laying tiles
Whichever type of tile you are laying, it is best to work at room temperature, so don't switch off the central heating. Leave the tiles in the room overnight to condition them.

Make sure you have enough tiles and adhesive on the spot; you don't want to have to stop work halfway through the job and go out and buy extra. Collect together the necessary tools: measure, chalk and string, pencils and ruler or straight edge, notched trowel or spreader, sharp knife, cloth and white spirit. If you are using the seal-later type of tile you will need a sander and brush or roller plus sealer.

As with other types of tiles, cork tiles look best if they are centred on the middle of the room and any narrow or awkwardly shaped tiles come at the edges. So you'll have to establish your starting point (see *Ready Reference*) at the centre of the room. You can then begin laying whole tiles, working from the centre outwards. It's best to work on a quarter of the floor at a time; when all four quarters of whole tiles are laid, you can cut and fix the border tiles. If you are using adhesive, you may have to spread only about one square metre (1 square yard) at a time before it is ready to take the tiles. In other cases it will be best to cover a large area with adhesive, so you don't have to wait too long to bed the tiles, increasing the length of time it will take to complete the job. Since the length of time needed before the adhesive is ready to take the tiles does vary depending on the type of adhesive, you should follow the manufacturer's instructions.

If tiles have to be cut to fit round obstacles such as door architraves, WC bases, or wash stands you can use a scribing block to mark the outline you require. Make up a paper template or use a special tracing tool (which has little needles which retract to fit the shape) if the shape is particularly complicated.

be in polythene sheet form, a cold-poured bitumen solution, or a hot pitch or bitumen solution. If the subfloor is porous or flaky and tends to be very dusty, you can use a latex floor-levelling compound to cover it. This is also practical for very uneven floors. The solution is poured on, left to find its own level and then allowed to dry out before the final floorcovering is laid.

Other floors, such as quarry or ceramic tiles, can have cork laid on top, but they have to be degreased, dewaxed and keyed by rubbing them with wire wool; once again, a floor-levelling compound may be necessary. With flagstones laid directly on the ground there could be damp or condensation problems; it may be best to take up the existing floor and re-lay it.

Alternatively, the floor could be covered with a layer of rock asphalt at least 16mm (⅝in) thick but you will need to call in prof-

essional help for this. (Always seek expert advice if you are worried about the state of the sub-floor: the expense incurred will be worth it to get successful results when you are laying the final floorcovering.)

If there is already a linoleum, vinyl sheet, tile or other resilient floorcovering on the floor, you are advised to take this up, then resurface or rescreed it if necessary; alternatively, use a floor-levelling damp-resistant latex powder mix, or an epoxy surface membrane. If it is not possible to remove the old floorcovering, you should use a proprietary floor cleaner to degrease and dewax it and then key the surface by rubbing over it with wire wool.

Planning
Measure the room, at floor level, using a steel tape or wooden measure; don't use a cloth tape as these stretch in use. If the room

LAYING WHOLE TILES

1 Use a notched spreader to apply adhesive to a quarter of the floor area, using the marked lines as a guide to the area to be covered.

2 Place the first whole tile in the centre right angle which has been coated with adhesive. Check that it aligns with the guidelines.

3 Lay a row of tiles following the guidelines, treading each tile down gently but firmly to make sure it is securely bedded.

4 Work across the floor until that quarter is covered with whole tiles. Then lay tiles on the other quarters of the floor area.

Ready Reference

MARKING OUT

For a balanced look, aim to cut your edge tiles to equal size on both sides of the room. To do this, establish the centre point of the floor, using chalked string lines (see step-by-step photographs, page 582):
● if, when you've dry-laid a row of tiles from the centre point out to the wall, a gap remains of more than half a tile-width at the wall end (A), adjust your chalked line half a tile-width off-centre (B); this will save undue wastage later when you are cutting the perimeter tiles.

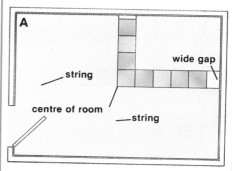

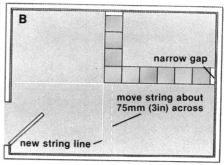

● if, however, by moving the chalked line you are left with very narrow perimeter strips (less than 75mm/3in wide) leave the centre of the floor as your starting point; there will be wastage but narrow cut perimeter tiles won't look very good and should be avoided if possible
● when marking out, avoid narrow strips at door thresholds where they will be subjected to a lot of wear
● adjust your starting point so you don't end up with narrow strips round a feature of the room, such as a chimney breast.

CHECK UNSEALED TILES

Be sure to lay unsealed tiles the right way up. They have a smooth top surface and a bottom surface which is rougher to provide a key for the adhesive. You can judge which surface is which by running your fingers over the tile.

For some awkard shapes (eg, fitting tiles round an L-shape or in an alcove) you can mark out the pieces to be cut by placing a whole tile or tile offcut up against the skirting and the tiles which are already in place and draw the required shape on it. Cork tiles are very simple to cut: all you need is a sharp knife and a straight edge to guide it; there is no risk of breakages as there may be with other tiles which are more difficult to cut, such as ceramic types.

Sealing tiles

If your tiles are the seal-after-laying type, you will have to sand the floor carefully, using a powered sander, to ensure the surface and joins are smooth. Dust carefully; you can wipe the tiles with a slightly damp cloth to remove excess dust but take care not to saturate the tiles. Leave them to dry and then seal them, using a brush or roller to apply the sealer.

If you attach your applicator to a long handle, you can avoid bending or crawling on all fours; work from the furthermost corner, backwards to the door. Leave each coat to dry thoroughly, before applying the next one. There will always be more than one coat of sealer but the exact number will depend on the type of wear to which the floor will be subjected (see *Ready Reference*).

Ideally, you should leave the sealer to dry for a few days before you walk on the floor, but if you have to use the room, seal half the room at a time. Cover the unsealed part with brown paper so it can be walked on without damaging or marking the cork. When the sealed part is completely dry, you can seal the other half.

Don't wash a new cork floor for at least 48 hours after laying and sealing; ideally it should be left for at least five days. It's worth

LAYING BORDER TILES

1 To cut border tiles accurately to size, place the whole tile to be cut exactly on top of the last whole tile in a particular row.

2 Place a second tile over it, this time butting it up against the skirting. Use its edge as a guide to scribe a line on the first tile.

3 Remove the tile to be cut and make a deeper mark. The tile should then break through cleanly when gentle pressure is applied.

4 Place the cut border tile in position against the skirting. You may need to apply extra adhesive to its back to ensure secure fixing.

TILING AN L-SHAPE

1 As when cutting other border tiles, use a tile as a guide to scribe the outline of one side of the L onto the tile to be cut.

2 Move the tile to be cut and the guide tile to the other side of the L and use the same method to scribe its outline for cutting.

3 Remove the loose tiles, cut through the back of the tile along the scribed lines and then fix the tile in position so it aligns with the whole tiles.

putting up with grubby marks for a few days rather than running the risk of moisture penetrating the flooring and reducing its useful life.

Care and maintenance

Once pre-sealed tiles are laid, or the unsealed type has been properly sealed, it will probably be unnecessary to do more than wipe over the floor with a damp mop or cloth to keep it clean. To remove grease or dirt, add a few drops of liquid detergent to the washing water; wipe over again with a cloth rinsed in clean water to remove any traces of detergent. If there are some particularly stubborn marks, made, for instance, by rubber-soled shoes, or paint or varnish spots, you should be able to remove them by rubbing gently with a little white spirit on a damp cloth.

An important point to remember when you

are cleaning your cork floor is that you must take care not to overdampen the floor or the tiles may lift. Also, never use strong abrasive cleaners as these can damage the PVC wear layer.

If you like a fairly glossy surface or are worried about scratches on the floor, you can use an emulsion wax polish on top of the sealed tiles. However, never use a wax floor polish as the surface could become too slippery.

Sometimes a tile can become damaged. If the area which needs repair is small (a cigarette burn hole, for instance) you can fill it with shavings from a cork out of a bottle and reseal the tile. For more extensive damage, you should remove the tile carefully and replace it with a spare one; reseal if this tile is an unsealed type with the number of coats of sealer required to give it adequate protection.

LAYING TILES IN AN ALCOVE

1 *Place a tile over the fixed tiles with its corner butting up against the skirting and make a mark on the 'wrong' side at the correct distance.*

2 *Repeat this procedure, this time to make a mark on the adjacent edge. Transfer the marks to the front of the tile and draw a line between them.*

3 *Cut along the drawn line to give the required shape and then place the cut tile in position so it aligns properly with the whole tiles.*

4 *Use the same techniques to cut the next tile. If there is a pipe against the wall, butt the tile up to it and mark where it's to be cut.*

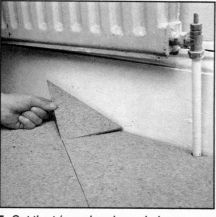

5 *Cut the triangular-shaped piece required to fill the gap between the two larger shaped pieces and fix this in position so that it butts right up against the skirting.*

6 *To complete the job, cut the corner piece to shape and fix it in place. For economy, you can cut these smaller shaped pieces from any tiled offcuts which you may have available.*

Ready Reference

TIP: STORE TILES FLAT

If you take tiles out of their box, weight them down to keep them flat when you are storing them.

FIXING TILES

Fixing methods and adhesives vary. Some adhesives should be applied to both the back of the tiles and floor, others to the floor only; follow the manufacturer's instructions. Remember:
● pre-sealed tiles are always fixed with adhesive
● unsealed tiles are often fixed by driving in 5 headless pins, one at each corner and one in the centre, a technique which may be combined with adhesive (the pin holes can be filled, if necessary, and will then be covered up by the sealer).

REMOVE EXCESS ADHESIVE

As you lay the tiles, wipe off any adhesive from the front of the tiles with a soft cloth which has been dipped in white spirit.

CUTTING ROUND PIPES

To cut a tile so it fits round a pipe, make a cardboard template of the shape required and trace the shape onto the tile. Then cut a slit from the hole made for the pipe to the skirting board; this line will be almost invisible when the tile is fixed in place.

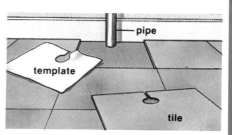

SEAL TILES PROPERLY

Cork is porous and fairly absorbent, so proper sealing is essential; if the tiles get wet, they swell and lift and have to be trimmed and re-stuck. For unsealed tiles, several coats of sealer will be necessary for real protection:
● in areas of ordinary wear, apply two or three coats of sealer
● in heavy wear areas you will need to apply 4 or 5 coats.

TRIM DOORS

To allow doors to open freely after the cork floor has been laid you may have to trim along the bottom of the door to give adequate clearance.

For more information see pages 58-63 and 83-87.

LAYING VINYL FLOOR TILES

Vinyl tiles are supple, easy to handle and don't take much time to lay. They come in many colours and designs so you should have no trouble finding tiles with the look you want.

Vinyl tiles are ideal for use on kitchen and bathroom floors because they are waterproof and resistant to oil, grease and most domestic chemicals. They have the advantage over vinyl sheet flooring in that they are easier to handle, and also, if you make any mistakes when cutting, they will be confined to individual tiles. So if you have a room where you will have to carry out quite a lot of intricate cutting to make the floorcovering fit round obstacles or awkwardly shaped areas, it would be well worth considering laying tiles rather than sheet material.

The tiles come in a wide variety of patterns and colours, with a smooth gloss finish or a range of sculptured and embossed designs. They can be bought with or without a cushioned backing. Cushioned tiles are softer and warmer underfoot, but more expensive than uncushioned tiles. However, even among tiles without a cushioned backing there is a wide variation in price. The cost of a tile is usually a fair indication of its quality, so, in general, the dearer the tile the longer it will last. However you don't need to be greatly concerned about this: even the cheapest tiles can have a life of twenty years in average domestic use, and long before then you will probably wish to remove or cover up the tiles. (On average floorcoverings are changed every seven years.) So your choice of tiles will probably be based simply on the fact that you like the colour or pattern and feel it will fit in well with the rest of the decorative scheme in the room.

Preparing the surface

The floor surface on which you intend to lay vinyl tiles should be free of dust and dirt, so you should go over it first of all with a vacuum cleaner. Then check that the subfloor is in sound condition.

If it is a timber floor you will have to repair any damaged boards, and if the floor has been treated in whole or in part with stains and polishes these will stop the tile adhesive from adhering properly, and will have to be removed with a proprietary floor cleaner. There may be gaps between the boards and they could possibly be warped and curling at the edges. You can cure these faults by

lining the floor with hardboard without adding much to the cost of the job or the time it takes to do it. First inspect the floor; punch home any protruding nails and countersink any screws. Replace missing nails. Where a board squeaks because it is loose, screws will hold it in place more securely than nails.

Hardboard sheets 1220mm (4ft) square will be a manageable size for this type of work. To condition them, brush water at the rate of ½ litre (2/3 pint) per 1220mm (4ft) square sheet onto the reverse side of the sheets. Then leave them for 48 hours stacked flat back to back in the room where they will be laid so they will become accustomed to its conditions. When fixed they will dry out further and tighten up to present a perfectly flat subfloor.

You can begin fixing the hardboard in one corner of the room. It's not necessary to scribe it to fit irregularities at the walls; small gaps here and there at the edges of the boards will not affect the final look of the floor.

Fix the sheets in place with hardboard pins at 150mm (6in) intervals round the edges and 225mm (9in) apart across the middle of the sheets. Begin nailing in the centre of a convenient edge and work sideways and forwards so the sheet is smoothed down in place. On a floor where there are water pipes below, use pins of a length which will not come out on the underside of the floorboards.

The sheets should normally be fixed with their smooth side down so the adhesive will grip more securely; also the pin heads will be concealed in the mesh.

Nail down the first sheet and work along the wall. When you come to the end of a row of sheets, you will have to cut a sheet to fit. Don't throw the waste away; use it to start the next row so the joins between sheets will not coincide. When you come to the far side of the room you will have to cut the sheets to width. Again, don't worry about scribing them to fit the exact contours of the wall.

On a solid floor, check to see if there are any holes or cracks and whether it is truly level and smooth. Fill in holes and small cracks with a sand/cement mortar. Large cracks could indicate a structural fault and, if in doubt, you should call in an expert. To level an uneven floor, use a self-levelling compound, applying it according to the manufacturer's instructions.

When dealing with a direct-to-earth floor you will have to establish whether it is dry or not. There's no point in attempting to lay the tiles on a damp floor: you will get problems with adhesion and in time the tiles themselves will curl and lift.

One difficulty is that dampness in a floor is not always immediately apparent, especially if there is no floorcovering. (If the floor has a sheet covering you should lift up a corner of the covering and inspect beneath for any signs of damp.) A slight amount of damp can rise up through floors of quarry tiles or concrete and evaporate in a room without being noticed.

To test for damp you can heat up a plate of metal over a gas ring or blowlamp, or heat a brick in the oven for about an hour, then

LAYING SELF-ADHESIVE TILES

1 Sponge primer over the floor and leave it to dry for 24 hours. It will help the tiles to form a secure bond when they are fixed in place.

2 Snap two chalk lines which bisect at the floor's centre. Dry-lay a row of tiles along one line to find out the width of the cut border tiles.

3 Adjust the first (centre) tile if the cut tiles will be too narrow. Fix the tiles in place by peeling off the backing and pressing them down.

4 With the first row in place, continue fixing the tiles, working in sections, until all the whole tiles are laid. You can then lay the cut border tiles.

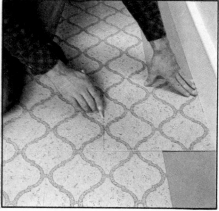

5 Place a tile over the last whole tile in a row and another one over it butted against the wall to use as a guide to mark the cutting line.

6 Leave the backing paper on when cutting the tile with a sharp knife. Remove the paper and press the cut border tile in place.

Ready Reference

TILE SIZES
Vinyl tiles are sold in packs sufficient to cover 1 square metre (1 square yard). The most common size tile is 300mm (12in) square.

FIXING TILES
Some tiles are self-adhesive; you simply pull off a backing paper, then press the tile down in place. Others require adhesive; this should be special vinyl flooring adhesive.

TIP: MAKE A TRAMMEL
A simple device called a trammel can help you find the centre of a room. Take a batten about 900mm (3ft) long and drive a pin through the batten near each end.

FINDING THE CENTRE OF THE ROOM
In an irregularly-shaped room you can find the room's centre in this way:
● strike a chalk line to form a base line, parallel to and 75mm (3in) away from the wall with the door
● place the centre of your trammel on the centre of the base line (A) and use the trammel to mark points B and C on the chalk line
● with one pin of the trammel placed in turn on points B and C, scribe two arcs, meeting at D
● strike a chalk line through points A and D to the wall opposite (this line will be truly at right angles to the base)
● find the centre of the line through A and D to give the centre point of the room (E), then draw a line across and at right angles to it using the same technique.

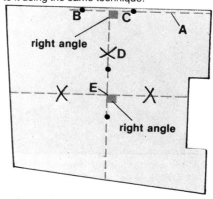

TILING AN L-SHAPE

1 At an external corner, place the tile to be cut over the last whole tile in one of the rows of tiles which adjoin at the corner.

2 Place another tile over the tile to be cut, but butted up against the skirting and use it as a guide to mark the cutting line.

3 Place the tile to be cut over the last whole tile in the other row leading to the corner. Use another tile as a guide for marking off.

4 Cut the tile along the marked lines with the backing paper on. Test if the cut tile fits, then peel off the paper and fix it in place.

TILING ROUND AN ARCHITRAVE

1 Make a template of the area round the architrave. Always test a template out: put it in place before using it on the tile to be cut.

2 When the template fits, use it to mark out the required shape on the tile. Cut the tile, remove the backing paper and press it in place.

place it on the floor. If a damp patch appears on the floor or moisture gathers underneath the metal or brick this indicates that damp is present. Another test is to place a sheet of glass on the floor, seal its edges with putty, then leave it for a couple of days. If moisture appears underneath it is again a sign of damp. These methods are, however, rather hit-and-miss and you may feel it's worth calling in an expert to give a true diagnosis.

Curing a damp floor is a major undertaking which may involve digging up the existing floor and laying a new one. If this has to be done, proper precautions must be taken to prevent damp.

Existing sheet floorcoverings should be removed before you start laying vinyl tiles. You can, however, lay them over existing vinyl tiles provided these are in sound condition and are securely fixed. If they are not, you will have to remove them before you fix the new tiles. To lever them up, use a paint scraper, or even a garden spade (the long handle will give you plenty of leverage).

Marking up

You should start laying tiles from the middle of the floor. To find the centre of a room which is a reasonably regular shape you should take one wall and, ignoring any bays, alcoves or projections, measure and mark its centre. Go to the wall opposite and do the same. Between these two centre points you should snap a chalked line. Snap a second chalk line from the middle of the other two walls: the point where the lines meet is the centre of the floor.

If you are going to tile an irregularly-shaped room you should strike a chalk line, to form a base line, parallel to and 75mm (3in) away from a wall which has a doorway in it. You can then strike a line at right angles to the base line and stretching to the wall on the other side. The centre of this line will be the centre point of the room; draw a line through this centre point parallel to the base line. (Instead of using a large square to help you draw the lines at true right angles, you can use what's known as a trammel; see *Ready Reference*.)

Laying the tiles

When you come to lay the tiles, the first one is all-important. There are four possible positions for it. It can go centrally on the centre point; neatly inside one of the angles where the centre lines cross; centrally on one line and butting up to the second, or centrally on the second line and butting up to the first.

You should choose the position that gives you the widest border of cut tiles round the room. Very narrow cut strips at the edges will tend to give an unbalanced look, especially if you are laying the tiles in a dual colour or chequerboard pattern. So set out the tiles dry

TILING ROUND A WC

1 Butt a paper template, which is the same size as a tile, against the base of the WC and mark off the shape of the WC on the template.

2 Cut the template to shape, then test to see if it fits exactly round the WC base and between the base and the whole laid tiles.

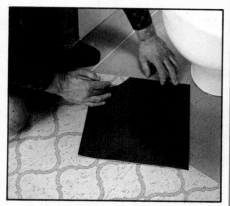

3 Place the template over a whole loose tile (check the tile is the right way round for pattern matching) and mark off the cutting line.

4 Use a sharp knife to cut the tile to shape following the marked line. You can then remove the backing paper and fix the tile.

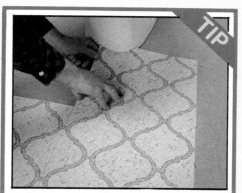

5 Aim to get the tile position right first time. Tiles can be taken up and restuck, but will lose some of their adhesive in the process.

6 Continue to make templates and fix shaped tiles round the curved WC base. You can then fix the cut border tiles next to the walls.

(that is, not stuck down) to find out which position for the first tile gives you borders with the largest cut tiles. In a regularly-shaped room this will be quite straightforward; a couple of dry runs should make things clear. In an awkwardly shaped room, especially if it has a lot of alcoves or projections, you will have to make several of these practice runs. When you've decided on your final starting position, draw round the outline of the first tile to be placed.

When you've stuck down your first tile you can begin laying the rest. If you are laying tiles which require adhesive, you should apply this to as large an area as you can cope with in one go; possibly a square metre (square yard). Butt all the tiles accurately up against each other, and check that they are precisely aligned. Then apply firm hand (or foot) pressure to bed them firmly in place.

It's normal practice to stick down all the full tiles, known as the 'field', leaving a border of cut tiles to be fitted round the edges.

If you are laying self-adhesive tiles, you simply peel off the backing paper and press each tile into place. Where you have to cut tiles, don't peel off the backing until the cutting-to-size is completed. Should a tile be misplaced, lift it quickly and relay it correctly; the adhesive 'grabs' quickly and later attempts to lift the tile will probably tear it.

Cutting tiles

Vinyl tiles can be quite easily cut using a sharp knife and a straightedge. For an intricate shape make a template first.

Border tiles can be marked up for cutting in the usual way; that is, you take the tile to be cut, place it on the last complete tile in the row, place another tile over the first one but jammed hard against the wall and use this tile as a guide for marking off the cutting line

on the first tile (see step-by-step photographs). The main thing wrong with this method is that it can leave a narrow border in which it is difficult to apply adhesive, with the consequent risk that the border tiles will not adhere properly.

Another method, which avoids this problem, is to lay the field except for the last full tile in each row. Then take a tile and place it against the last full tile in the field. Place another tile on top of the first one and jammed against the wall. Use this second tile as a guide to cut through the first (and it will itself become the last full tile fixed in the relevant row).

The two tiles can temporarily be placed on top of the field, adjacent to the position they will occupy, while you cut the rest of the border. When you come to stick the border tiles down you will have plenty of room in which to wield your adhesive spreader and ensure adequate coverage.

LAYING WOOD MOSAIC FLOORS

Hardwood flooring comes in a variety of types and timbers. It can provide you with a particularly elegant floor without your having to spend a great deal of money.

If you want a wooden floor and have decided that sanding and sealing existing floorboards would be inappropriate, you can simply lay hardwood flooring over the floorboards or, for that matter, over a solid concrete floor. Wood flooring is available in several varieties of hardwoods: oak, teak, iroko, beech, sapele, mahogany, maple and walnut, for example. It can be particularly decorative in terms of grain, figure or colour and with a few rugs scattered over it, a hardwood floor can add real elegance to a room. In addition to its decorative qualities the flooring will be hardwearing, durable and easy to clean and maintain.

Another factor in its favour is cost: you can get an attractive hardwood floor for less than the price of a good quality carpet with underlay. And, besides lasting longer, the timber will stand up better to spills and dirt.

Choosing the flooring

The type of hardwood flooring which is most widely available is mosaic flooring, which comes in panel form (see *Ready Reference*). Normally, mosaics are the most flexible of the various types of flooring and therefore the easiest to lay, though those joined by wire and glued together at the edges are more rigid. If you decide to use mosaic panels, you might choose to have types made from different timber on the same floor, building them up into a pattern.

Traditional solid timber parquet blocks are still available, though most manufacturers and importers restrict themselves to supplying the professional floor layer. One or two varieties are, however, available on the DIY market. The problem with blocks is their rigidity, so that it's all too easy to end up with some that have edges sticking up over which people, especially young children or elderly people, might trip. Furthermore, there's the problem of setting out the patterns. Traditional herringbone can be tricky and the trouble with brick bond is that any expansion of the blocks due to moisture absorption from the atmosphere will be in the same direction. Also, since the blocks must go on a flat, rigid floor you must be painstaking with your preparation.

The advantages of block flooring are that the blocks are usually a high quality material which will last a lifetime and you can choose your own pattern (mosaics, on the other hand, always come in basket-weave form).

Wood strip floorings can be laid on top of existing timber or concrete floors; some varieties can also be fixed direct to joists and so can take the place of floorboards. The latter types are therefore particularly worth considering if you are faced with renewing a timber floor or having a house custom-built for you. Laminated strips are always prefinished, so if you want to avoid having to sand the floor and finish it you might choose this type of flooring. Mosaic panels and solid strips are sometimes pre-finished, sometimes not. Unfinished types are less expensive to buy than their pre-finished counterparts, but you will have to sand and finish them.

When buying the flooring remember to allow about five per cent extra for wastage when you are cutting to fit or to remove any defect. Also, if you have underfloor heating you should check with your supplier that the type of flooring you have in mind is one which will not be affected by the heating.

Preparation

The floor must be in sound condition and as level as possible before you lay hardwood flooring over it. One point to remember here is that the more level the sub-floor is before you lay the new flooring, the less sanding you will have to do when finishing.

On a timber floor you will have to punch home protruding nails or countersink screws; knots should be planed down. You may also have to remove any accumulated polish or stains; this is particularly important if you are using adhesive to fix the flooring or it will not stick properly. Instead of going to this trouble, however, you could cover the floor with sheets of hardboard or plywood to ensure a clean level surface. Condition hardboard first, before you lay it, by brushing water into its mesh side and then stack it flat, with the sheets back to back, and leave it in the room where you're going to use it for 48 hours.

It's worth using relatively small sheets of hardboard, say 1220mm x 1220mm (4ft x 4ft) because these are easier to handle than large sheets. Start laying the hardboard in one corner of the room. You don't have to take too much trouble and aim for an absolutely perfect fit; there's no need, for example, to scribe the hardboard so it exactly follows the outline of the skirting. If you are going to use adhesive to fix the hardwood flooring, lay the hardboard mesh side up to help the adhesive to grip properly. Fix the sheets by nailing them at 100mm (4in) centres round the edges and 150mm (6in) centres in the middle. Begin in the middle of one and work forwards and sideways so that the sheet will lie truly flat. When you come to the end of a row, use the

LAYING AND CUTTING PANELS

1 *Snap a chalked line alongside a straight wall. It should be the width of a panel, plus 12mm (¹/₂in) to allow a gap for expansion, away from the wall.*

2 *Using the chalked line as a guide, spread on the adhesive with a notched spreader. When working, protect your hands and clothing from the adhesive.*

3 *Lay the first row of panels along the wall, 12mm (¹/₂in) away from it. Butt the panels against each other, making sure they are aligned.*

4 *Continue spreading adhesive and laying the panels; check they're in straight rows. When the whole ones are laid you can lay the cut border panels.*

5 *To mark off a panel to be cut, place it over the last full panel in a row. Place another one over it 12mm (¹/₂in) away from the wall to use as a guide.*

6 *When you have marked the cutting line you can go ahead and cut the panel. Use a tenon saw and work with the panel face side up.*

offcut from the sheet you've cut to size to start the next row so the joins in the sheets won't coincide; this helps to prevent any movement of the floor occurring in a continuous line down the joins and disturbing the flooring above.

With solid floors there could be a damp problem. If, after you've tested for damp (for example, by heating a metal plate, placing it on the floor and seeing if moisture forms underneath), you are in any doubt at all about the condition of the floor, you should take precautions against damp by laying a damp-proof membrane. The exception to this rule is where you are going to use bituminous adhesive to stick the flooring down, since the adhesive itself will prevent moisture from penetrating the flooring. If you are going to fix the flooring to battens set into or placed on the floor, make sure you use battens which have been preservative-treated.

The other question to consider with a solid floor is how level it is. If it is uneven you should level it using a self-levelling screeding compound (see pages 58-63).

Apart from the state of the floor you will also have to examine the door. Your new floor might stop the door from opening properly. Test for this by placing a piece of flooring under the door. If necessary, you will have to take the door down, trim the required amount carefully off the bottom and then re-hang the door.

You should also condition the flooring. Buy it at least a week before you intend laying it, then unpack it and leave it in the room where it will be laid so it can adjust to the atmosphere; stack it so the air can circulate freely around it.

Setting out

You can start laying mosaic panels, strips and wood blocks alongside the longest uninterrupted wall in a room. You should check first that the position in which you intend to lay your first row won't mean you have to cut very narrow pieces to fit on the other side of the room by dry-laying a row of panels across the room. In the case of strips and blocks it would be easier to work this out on a scale drawing of the floor. Also, check by dry-laying a row of panels alongside the wall that there won't be very narrow cut pieces at the ends of the rows. If necessary, adjust your starting point, then snap a chalked line down the room to serve as a guide when you are fixing the first row. A tip here: if you want, instead of snapping a chalked line you can make a mark at each end of the room in the relevant position, drive in a nail at each mark and then tie a length of string so it's tightly stretched between them. Unlike a chalked line this can't be prematurely rubbed out.

If you are laying wood blocks in an intricate pattern, you would be better off starting from

TYPES OF WOOD FLOORING

There are different types of hardwood flooring available. They include:

● mosaic flooring which consists of thin fingers of wood (generally only 8mm/⁵⁄₁₆in thick) fixed together in a series of squares on a panel to form a basket-weave pattern and stuck to a backing pad of bituminous felt. (Some are, however, wired together and glued at the edges; some are also tongued-and-grooved.) Usually there are 5 fingers per square and 16 squares per panel

● traditional parquet wood blocks which can be laid in different patterns. They must be laid on a flat, rigid base and are usually laid on a solid floor though they can be fixed to suspended timber floors. They are stuck down and are sometimes interlocked by tongues and grooves

● strip flooring, ie, a series of strips rather like very narrow short floorboards. They may be solid and thin (9.5mm/³⁄₈in) or quite thick (19 to 23mm/³⁄₄ to ⁷⁄₈in). Other types are laminated, either coming in pieces designed to look like a solid strip of wood or having a veneer which is split up into strips. They are longer than wood blocks and are usually laid side by side in straight runs. They can be 'secret nailed' to wood floors, joists or battens or glued together along the tongued-and-grooved joints and laid 'floating' on solid floors.

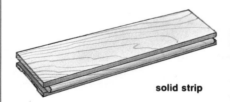

solid strip

FLOORING PATTERNS

Apart from the figure and colour of the wood, the patterns in which wood block flooring is arranged are also a source of interest. Arrangements include various types of basket-weave patterns, brick bond and herringbone patterns.

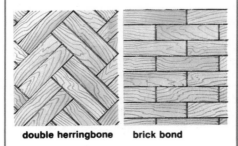

double herringbone   **brick bond**

LAYING PANELS IN AN ALCOVE

1 At the corner leading into the alcove, place the panel to be cut to fit round it on the last full panel in one of the rows which meet at the corner.

2 Place another panel over the panel to be cut, 12mm (¹⁄₂in) away from the wall and use this as a guide to mark off one side of the required L-shape.

3 Repeat this procedure at the end of the other row of panels leading to the corner, to mark off the other side of the L-shape on the panel to be cut.

4 Cut the panel, spread on adhesive and lay the L-shaped panel. Take care to wipe off any adhesive from the front of the panels before it dries.

5 You can now fit the cut border panels at the back of the alcove. Mark them up for cutting in the usual manner before spreading the adhesive.

6 Lay the cut panels so they align with the full-size panels, and make sure there is an expansion gap of 12mm (¹⁄₂in) between them and the wall.

FIXING MOULDING

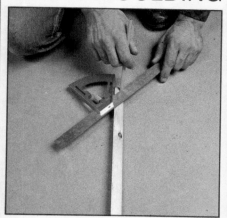

1 Use a combination square to mark off 45° angles on lengths of moulding which will meet at a corner. When cut they should form a neat mitre join.

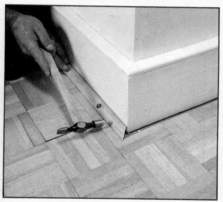

2 Use the moulding to cover the gap left for expansion round the perimeter of the room. Fix it by driving panel pins through it into the skirting.

3 At a corner, nail two lengths of moulding so they form a mitre join. You can seal the moulding later at the same time as you are sealing the floor.

DOORWAYS

1 Where a panel will have to be cut to shape to fit round an architrave, trace the outline of the architrave from a template onto the block.

2 Cut the panel to the required shape; a jigsaw is ideal for this sort of work. You don't need to allow for an expansion gap in the doorway.

3 To finish off the job, fix a length of moulding so it fits just over the edge of the shaped panel and covers the expansion gap along the wall.

the middle of the room, as the effect will be much neater this way.

For a herringbone pattern you should first mark a line or stretch string tightly between the mid-points of two opposite walls. Then, starting at the centre of that line, dry-lay the blocks at an angle of 45° to the line. Once the rows on each side of it are in place the rest are positioned automatically. With other patterns, begin from the middle, setting out your blocks dry first to make sure you get the edge cuts equal and not too small. To prevent them from moving during the setting out, you can pin the odd one here and there on a timber floor.

Laying and cutting flooring

Having worked out your starting point and set up guidelines to help you get it straight, you can go ahead and lay the flooring. If you are using a bitumen-based adhesive, spread it on the floor so it covers an area only slightly larger than the piece of flooring you are laying, then very carefully place the flooring in position. This type of adhesive is very messy to work with and you should aim to avoid getting any on the face of the flooring as it can be difficult to remove; if any does adhere to the flooring surface, scrape it off immediately before it has a chance to set. Also, it's worth wearing gloves when you're applying it and clothes that you don't mind getting possibly permanently marked.

To get tongued-and-grooved boards to slot together fully, you can knock them in using an offcut to protect the exposed tongue. Secret nailing (see *Ready Reference*) will provide a professional-looking fixing. If you're laying strip flooring over joists you should make sure than no two joints between strips are within 150mm (6in) of each other, in any direction to ensure a sound and stable floor surface. (Before you begin laying the flooring check also that the joists are in reasonable condition; you might need to add a splint to an uneven joist to provide adequate support for the flooring.)

In some cases, it is recommended that besides allowing a gap for expansion round the perimeter of the flooring that you leave small gaps (of about 1mm) between the individual units of flooring. Check with the manufacturer's instructions.

The normal procedure is to lay all the whole pieces of flooring first, however you happen to be fixing them, and then to fill in with the cut pieces at the borders. Cutting should be done with a fine-toothed saw; check that it's sharp before you start cutting. Where you have to cut out an intricate shape, for example to fit round an architrave or a WC, a jig saw will make the job much easier and will reduce the risk of splintering the wood so it has to be recut, thus lessening the likelihood of wastage. Make a template of the area where

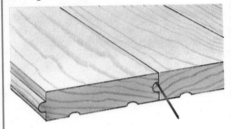

intricate cutting will be required, and test the
template by placing it on the floor in the
relevant position before you trace its outline
onto the flooring. It makes more sense to
remake an inaccurate template than to waste
flooring by cutting it to the wrong shape.

If you are using cork strips (see *Ready
Reference*) to fill in the gaps you've left for
expansion at the perimeter of the room, you
may find that some of the intricate cutting
which would otherwise be required will not
be needed. Round a fluted architrave in a
doorway, for example, you can simply cut
the flooring as if it were a square corner and
then fill in with the flexible cork strip.

Finishing the floor

If you have laid flooring which is not pre-
finished, you will have to give it a sanding
first to smooth it over. In fact, one of the
advantages of using an unfinished type of
flooring is that sanding may in any event be
necessary to remove the odd high spot here
and there.

You can tackle the floor in a small room by
hand or with a portable powered orbital
sander, but on larger rooms you'll need a
heavy-duty floor sander (which you can hire)
and an edging sander for the borders. Since
these sanders are powerful you should take
care when using them; many of the wooden
flooring materials have thin surface veneers
and you run the risk of going right through
them. It's best to use only a fine abrasive belt
for this reason.

Seal off the room in which you're using the
sanders, and wear a dust mask because they
generate an enormous amount of dust.
Remember too to wear ear protectors as
they're also very noisy to work with. Sharp
edges or nail heads can rip the abrasive belt,
causing bits to fly around; this can be
dangerous so make sure you've punched
home nails and removed splinters from the
flooring before you start.

Aim to be very careful not to scratch the
floor surface. To avoid this you should always
sand along the grain, never across it. Even
when you're using the edge sander, move it
along the grain only. In patterns where the
grain is going in all directions (such as
basket-weave) the trick is to approach such
patterns at a 45° angle.

Finally, you'll have to seal the floor. Floor
sealers come in matt and gloss versions and
you will need two or three coats, according
to how fine a finish you want. For a good-
looking result, it's worth sanding each coat
(except the final one) lightly with very fine
glasspaper to provide a key for the following
coat. If you do this, wipe the floor surface
with a cloth moistened with white spirit to
pick up any dust. If you wish, you can apply a
little polish to the flooring once the sealer is
properly dry.

SEALING

1 *Sand the floor to provide a clean,
even surface, removing any high spots
between the panels. To make the job go
more quickly, use an orbital sander.*

2 *Remove dust arising from the
sanding, and then brush on a thin
coat of special wood flooring sealer
over the panels (and the moulding).*

3 *For a good finish, wait until the
sealer dries, then buff it gently with
worn, fine sandpaper or steel wool to
provide a key for the second coat.*

LAYING SHEET VINYL

Vinyl provides a tough, easy-to-clean floor surface which is ideal in kitchens, laundries and other areas of the house where floors are likely to be subjected to heavy wear or spillages. It's also straightforward to lay.

Vinyl flooring was developed in the 1960s and revolutionised the smooth (and resilient) flooring market. At first it was a thin and rather unyielding material. But it was something which could be laid fairly easily by the DIY enthusiast; and this was a breakthrough because its predecessor, linoleum, had had to be professionally laid. Since then, vinyl flooring has been greatly improved and there are now several different types available.

Types of vinyl
The cheapest type of vinyl is known as a 'flexible print' and has a clear wear layer on top, with the printed pattern sandwiched between this and the backing. Then there are the cushioned vinyls, which are more bouncy underfoot and have a soft inner bubbly layer between the wear layer and the backing. They are often embossed to give them a texture, which is particularly successful when the embossing enhances the design, as with simulated cork or ceramic tile patterns. Finally, the most expensive type is solid flexible vinyl, made by suspending coloured vinyl chips in transparent vinyl to create colour and design which goes right through the material and consequently wears longer.

All three types come in a wide variety of colours and designs ranging from geometric and floral patterns to simulated cork, wood block, parquet, ceramic tiles, slate and brick. Some ranges include special glossy no-polish surfaces. Also, there is a special 'lay-flat' type which does not have to be stuck down, except on very heavy wear areas or at doorways. Some vinyls can be folded without cracking, but as with carpets, a good guide to durability is price: the more expensive the flooring, the longer-lasting it is likely to be.

Buying vinyl
To work out the amount of vinyl you'll need, measure up the floor using a metal tape; note down the measurements and then double-check them. Draw a scale plan of the room on squared paper, marking in all the obstacles, door openings and so on.

Take the measurements and plan to your supplier, who will help you to work out quantities. Remember to allow for walls which are not quite true and for trimming the overlap (see *Ready Reference*).

Whatever the type, vinyl is available in standard sheet widths (see *Ready Reference* again). Choose one in a wide width for use on a floor where you do not want to have a seam. (A wide sheet can be difficult to lay so make sure you have someone to help you – If you are going to lay sheets of a narrower width which will have to be joined, remember to allow for pattern matching when buying.

Check the manufacturer's instructions for fixing and order the correct adhesive and other sundries. Make sure you get the right amount; there is nothing worse than running out of adhesive halfway through the job.

A roll of vinyl is usually 30 to 40m (100 to 130ft) long and the retailer will cut off the length you want, re-rolling it for you. Take the roll of vinyl home and leave it, loosely rolled, in the room where it is to be laid for about 48 hours. This will allow it to become acclimatised and it should then be easier to lay. Do not stand it on edge as this can crack the material and take care not to damage the ends when you are transporting or storing the roll.

Preparing the sub-floor
Vinyl must be laid on a sound, reasonably smooth and even sub-floor if the best results

Ready Reference

SHEET SIZES
Sheet vinyl usually comes in three different widths: 2m (6ft 6in), 3m (9ft 9in) and 4m (13ft).

SUITABLE SURFACES
Vinyl can be laid over concrete, wood or tiles. Don't attempt to lay it over old vinyl, linoleum or cork; these should be removed or covered with hardboard.

PREPARING A WOOD FLOOR
To prepare a bumpy wood floor for laying vinyl, cover it with 900mm x 1200mm (3 x 4ft) sheets of flooring underlay hardboard. Stagger the joints between sheets.

When using hardboard, place the shiny side down as the rough side provides a better grip for the vinyl.

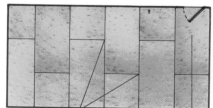

staggered joints   hardboard

LAYING HARDBOARD SHEETS

1 Fix sheets of hardboard, rough side up, by nailing them to the old floor surface. The nails should be spaced about 100-150mm apart.

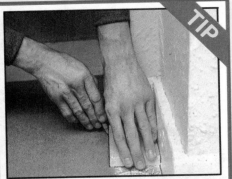

2 Where part of the wall protrudes, use a scribing block to provide a guide when marking off the contour of the wall on the hardboard.

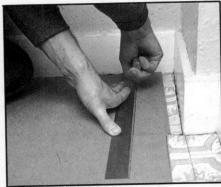

3 Cut along the line you have marked on the hardboard, using a sharp knife and a straight edge to guide the knife.

FITTING AND FIXING VINYL

1 Lay the flooring out fully across the room; with a large width such as this you will probably need help to get it roughly into position.

2 Make diagonal cuts at each corner, taking care not to cut too deep, to make accurate positioning much easier.

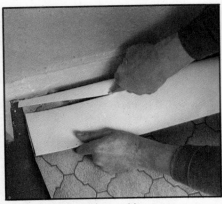

3 With the vinyl in position, use a sharp knife to trim off the excess, starting at the longest straight wall. Remember to allow an overlap.

5 With the excess trimmed away from the longest straight wall and the adjacent wall, pull back the vinyl and spread adhesive on the floor.

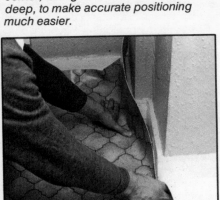

6 Push the vinyl down onto the adhesive making sure it is firmly stuck down. Smooth out the surface as you go so there are no air bubbles.

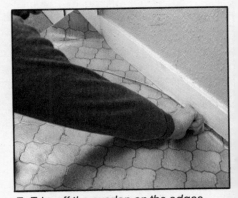

7 Trim off the overlap on the edges where the vinyl has been stuck down. Continue fitting, fixing and trimming round the rest of the room.

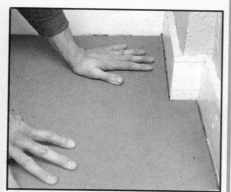

4 *After you have cut out the required shape, push the hardboard into place, making sure it butts up against the bottom edge of the skirting.*

4 *At a doorway, cut into the corners (see Ready Reference) and again trim off the excess, allowing for an overlap for later, final trimming.*

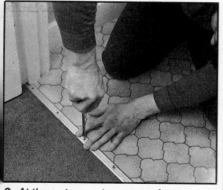

8 *At the entrance to a room, fasten down the fixed vinyl with a threshold strip to cover the join between the vinyl and the carpet.*

are to be achieved and the flooring is to give adequate wear. The floor must also be free from dirt, polish, nibs of plaster or splashes of paint, but above all it must be damp proof, so deal with this first.

In an old property with no damp-proof course (dpc), it may be necessary to install one or to have some other form of damp-proofing carried out. The floor may have to be rescreeded or old floorboards taken up and replaced. But whatever is needed must be done before laying the new flooring. A cover-up job will never be satisfactory and the new material will start to perish from the back.

Remember that screeding a floor will raise its level and so doors will almost certainly have to be taken off their hinges and trimmed at the bottom to accommodate the new floor level.

Where the existing floor covering does not provide a suitable surface for laying vinyl you will have to remove it. You can remove old vinyl by stripping it off from the backing, then soaking any remaining material in cold water, washing-up liquid and household ammonia before scraping it off with a paint scraper.

With a wooden sub-floor you should remove any protruding tacks, nails or screws, or punch them down level with the floor. Any rough or protruding boards should be planed smooth and wide gaps between boards filled with fillets of wood; small holes or gaps can be filled with plastic wood. If the floor is very bumpy it can be covered with man-made boards.

Fitting seamed lengths

Measure for the first length of vinyl along the longest unobstructed wall unless this brings a seam into the wrong position (see *Ready Reference*). After measuring you can cut the first length from the roll. Butt the edge of the vinyl right up to the skirting at one end of the room, tucking the overlap underneath the skirting if possible so you don't have to trim this edge. Then cut the material off across the width, allowing for an overlap at the other end, at doorways and obstacles.

To fit the first doorway you will have to cut slits at the door jambs and then ease the vinyl round the door recess and supports, cutting off a little at a time until you get a perfect fit. Next, either tuck the overlap of the vinyl under the skirting which runs along the length of the room if you can, or trim along the wall or skirting, allowing for a good (but not too tight) fit. Smooth down the flooring as you work along its length and then cut the vinyl to fit at the other end.

If the wall is uneven you will have to 'scribe' its contour onto the vinyl. You pull the vinyl slightly away from the wall and then run a wooden block, in conjunction with a pencil,

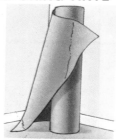
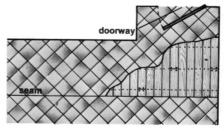

LAYING VINYL IN A RECESS

1 *With the vinyl fixed in place at the straightest edges of the room, deal with awkward areas like a recess. First trim at the corners.*

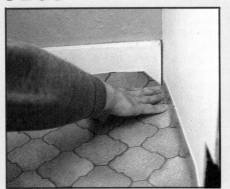

2 *Turn back the vinyl and spread a band of adhesive round the edges of the recess. You can then push the floorcovering firmly into position.*

3 *To complete the job, use a sharp knife to trim off the overlap. Again, make sure there are no bubbles by smoothing the vinyl down.*

along the wall so its profile is marked on the vinyl. To cut along this line you can use a knife and straight edge (with the straight edge on the vinyl which will be used), or if the line is very wobbly, use scissors.

With the first length fitted, you can then place the next length of vinyl parallel to the first, matching the pattern exactly, and cut off the required length, again allowing for extra overlap at the ends and sides. Some people cut all the required lengths first before fitting, but if the room is not perfectly square and several widths are being used, there could be a mismatch.

If the two sheets overlap, the excess will have to be trimmed away. Place one on top of the other, aligning the design carefully, and cut through the two sheets together at the overlap, using a knife and straight edge. Remove the trimmings and then adjust the second sheet to fit doors, skirtings and so on, trimming where necessary.

Where there are more than two sheets, repeat the fitting procedure, making sure the pattern matches.

If you are renewing the skirting, to get a perfect fit you can fit the material first and put the skirting on after the vinyl is laid. Remember, though, that this may make it difficult to take up the floorcovering when you need (or want) to change it.

Fitting extra-wide flooring

The technique is largely the same as for fitting strips of vinyl except there will not be any seams to stick, or pattern matching to do. You should start by laying the flooring out fully – you will probably need help for this – and try to find a long straight wall against which the first edge can be laid. Then make diagonal cuts at each corner to allow the flooring to be positioned roughly, with the

excess material 'climbing up' the skirting board or wall. Trim away the excess, leaving a 50 to 75mm (2 to 3in) overlap all round. Scribe the first wall, if necessary, then trim and ease the flooring back into its exact position. Deal with corners, projections, and obstacles as you work your way round the room, leaving the same overlap; finally trim to a perfect fit.

Fixing vinyl

How you fix vinyl will depend on the type; always follow the manufacturer's instructions. As vinyl can shrink it's wise to stick it down immediately before or after trimming it. To stick the edges you should first turn them back and apply a 75mm (3in) wide band of adhesive to the sub-floor, using a serrated scraper in a criss-cross motion, and then press the vinyl into position immediately. This will usually be at doorways, round the edges of the room, or round obstacles. Where heavy equipment will be pulled across the floor regularly (a washing machine for example) it is worth sticking down the entire area.

At the seams, you should make the width of the spread adhesive generous – 150 to 200mm (6 to 8in). Again, turn back the edges, apply the band of adhesive to the sub-floor and press the vinyl back into position immediately. Wipe away any adhesive which seeps through the seam or round the edges of the vinyl immediately, as this can discolour the flooring if it hardens.

At the entrance to rooms, particularly in heavy traffic areas, or if you have used the 'lay-flat' type of vinyl, you can fasten down the vinyl with a ready-made threshold strip. These come in metal, wood or plastic and are also used to cover joins between two different materials, such as vinyl and carpet.

Cleaning and maintenance

Once you have laid your floor you will need to look after it. Always wipe up any spills immediately, particularly hot fat and grease. It is also wise to protect the surface from indentation by putting heavy pieces of furniture on a piece of hardboard, or standing legs and castors in castor cups.

Some of the more expensive vinyls have a built-in gloss, so they do not need polishing. This type can be mopped with a damp cloth.

Never use a harsh abrasive cleaner on any type of vinyl floor as this could damage the surface layer. The glossy surface should not wear away, but if it does become dull in heavy traffic areas, it can be recoated with a special paint-on liquid provided by the manufacturer.

The less glossy vinyls will need regular sweeping or vacuuming and mopping. It also makes sense to use a clear acrylic polish, applied very sparingly according to the manufacturer's instructions and then buffed gently. Wash occasionally with warm water and a mild liquid detergent, and don't apply lots of coats of polish, or you will get a thick discoloured build-up, which spoils the look of the floor; 2-4 coats over a 12-month period is plenty. Always let the floor dry thoroughly before walking on it, after it has been washed or polished.

Once several coats of polish have built up you will have to strip off the polish and start again. To do this, add a cupful of household ammonia to a bucket of cold water, to which a little washing-up liquid has been added. Scrub the floor with this, taking care not to saturate it too much. When the old surface begins to break down, wipe it with an old soft cloth, rinse thoroughly with warm, clear water and dry before applying a new protective coating.

CUTTING ROUND OBSTACLES

The best way to get a neat floor when fitting vinyl round obstacles such as bathroom fittings is to make a template of paper or cardboard which is slightly larger (by about 25mm/1in) than the obstacle. Place one sheet of paper up against the basin pedestal, WC base or whatever, and tear it round so you have half the obstacle's shape on it. Then repeat the procedure with another sheet of paper for the other half.

Fit the template round the obstacle and use a scribing block and pencil to give the exact profile. Then lay the pattern over the flooring and use the block and pencil to reverse the procedure and transfer the exact outline onto the vinyl by running it round the inside of the line. You can then cut and fit; you will have to make a slit in the edge of the vinyl in some cases to get a snug fit at the skirting. Carefully trim away any excess material round the obstacle once the flooring is placed in position. Fix the vinyl according to the manufacturers' instructions.

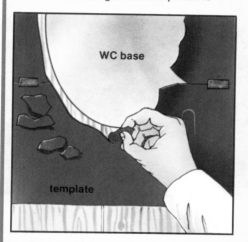

Making a template

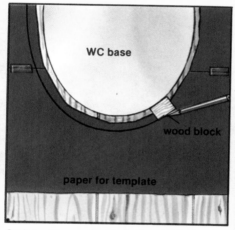

Scribing the contour onto the template

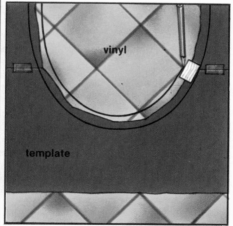

Scribing the contour onto the vinyl

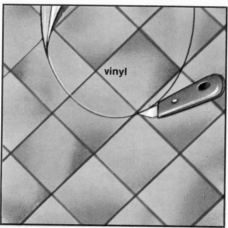

Cutting the vinyl

Ready Reference

FITTING CORNERS
To fit vinyl:
- at internal corners, gently push the vinyl into the corner and cut away the excess, diagonally across the corner, until it fits. Cut a little at a time and pare the edge carefully
- at external corners, press the vinyl into the corner, pull up the excess and cut to allow the vinyl to fall into place round the corner; then trim the excess.

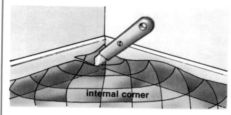

FIXING METHODS
Sheet vinyl can be fixed either by sticking it down all over or only at the edges and seams. Check the manufacturer's instructions.

'Lay-flat' vinyls do not have to be stuck down but they must be firmly fixed at doorways by glueing, or another method. Double-sided tape may be used to secure seams.

TIP: SMOOTH OUT BUMPS
If there are any bumps in the vinyl after you have laid it fill a pillowcase with sand and drag this round the floor to iron them out.

TIP: HIDING GAPS
If you have an unsightly gap between the skirting and the floor, because the walls are very uneven or your vinyl has shrunk, you can pin painted quadrant beading to the skirting round the room to hide the gap.

If you wipe up spills at once you should not get any stains on vinyl flooring, but sometimes they become marked from tar or grit trodden into the house; some types of shoe can leave black scuff marks, and cigarette burns are not unknown.

If normal cleaning doesn't remove marks rub them very gently with a very fine grade wire wool, used dry. Take care not to rub too much of the surface layer away. Wipe with a damp cloth, and reseal/polish the area if necessary. Some grease marks can be removed with white vinegar, others with petrol or lighter fuel. Always, however, wipe the area immediately with clean water.

Any badly discoloured or damaged area may have to be patched, so save any offcuts of sufficient size for this purpose.

LAYING FOAM-BACKED CARPET

Having wall-to-wall carpet is most people's idea of floorcovering luxury. You can even lay it yourself if you choose the right type of carpet.

Carpet is warm and luxurious underfoot, a good insulator, which is particularly important in flats and upstairs rooms, and still something of a status symbol when fitted in every room – particularly in the bathroom. Modern methods of weaving carpets, and the development of new synthetic fibres, have made some forms of carpeting relatively inexpensive, but it is silly to buy carpet just because it is the conventional thing to have; or for its luxurious image and status.

Consider whether it is a practical proposition for your home. Carpets in bathrooms where there are young children splashing about, (or where the lavatory is situated in the same room) may not be a wise choice. Carpets in kitchens (even the special 'utility' area type) are not always practical at the cooking/washing up end of the room, (although the eating end can be carpeted to co-ordinate with a more easycare surface at the 'business' end of the room). In family rooms, childrens' bedrooms and playrooms, halls and dining rooms, a washable surface may be the answer, softened with large cotton rugs (these can be cleaned in a washing machine), a carpet square or rush matting. But for the sitting room, master bedroom, stairs and corridors, there is really no substitute for carpet.

Choosing carpets
So how do you decide exactly which type of carpet to buy? Of course, you will start by looking for a colour or pattern you like, but a trip to a local carpet specialist or department store can often result in complete confusion once you have seen the range. As a general guide, you should choose the best quality (and consequently the most expensive) you can afford for heavy 'traffic' areas such as hallways, stairs, landings and main living rooms. You can then select the lighter weights and cheaper grades for the rooms which get less wear, like bedrooms, bathrooms and so on.

The carpet industry has produced a labelling system which divides the carpets into categories. In each case the label gives details of how the carpet is made, what fibres have been used and how durable it is likely to be.

This is quite a useful guide, but you should also ask for advice from the salesman. Here are some of the terms it helps to know.

Carpet weaves
The traditional types of carpet are known as Axminster and Wilton, terms which refer to the way they are woven.

An **Axminster** carpet is usually patterned and has an extensive choice of colours within the design. The backing is jute or hessian, sometimes strengthened by polypropylene. Different fibres and blends of fibres are used, but an Axminster is frequently woven in an 80 per cent wool and 20 per cent nylon mixture, and also from acrylic fibres, which resemble wool in appearance and feel.

Axminsters come in many different widths, up to 5m (16½ft) wide. They also come with bound and finished edges, known as carpet 'squares', although they are not necessarily square in shape. This type of carpet can be turned round within a room to even out the wear.

A **Wilton** carpet is usually plain or two-tone, although there are some patterned Wiltons made with a restricted number of colours. The carpet is generally close-textures with a velvet, looped, twist-and-loop, or a mixed cut-and-loop pile (called sculptured or carved). Any yarn not used on the face of the carpet is woven into the backing, to add to the thickness, and the backing is usually jute or hessian.

Different fibres and blends of fibres can be used in the construction, but Wiltons are usually made with 100 per cent wool pile, the 80/20 blend (as Axminster) or from an acrylic fibre.

Wilton carpet is woven in widths from 700mm (27in) to 2m (6ft 6in), which are then seamed together when the carpet is to be fully fitted; 3.75m (12ft) widths are also available in some ranges and can be bound to form a carpet 'square'.

Tufted carpets are a more modern type which has been developed during the last 25 years. Tufted carpets come in many different fibre mixtures including wool and wool blends. Widths vary from 1m (3ft) to 5m (16½ft). The tufts are 'needled' into a ready-woven backing and anchored by adhesive; when the main backing is hessian, this can be given a coat of latex to secure the tufts. Foam backing can then be stuck to the main backing; a high-quality foam-backed tufted carpet does not need an underlay.

Bonded carpets are made face-to-face, with the carpet pile held between two specially-treated woven backings. The carpet is then 'sliced' down the middle at the finishing stage, and becomes two carpets. The pile can be cut to different lengths to give a carpet with a texture ranging from a shaggy pile to a velvety velour. Fibres can be wool, wool blends or several different synthetics, and the carpet is usually plain. Widths are as for Axminster carpets.

Needlefelt or needleloom carpet is not really woven. A fibrous material is needled into a strong backing to create a looped ribbed pile or one which looks like dense felt. The fibres used are normally synthetic and the carpet has a rather harsh texture. The backing can be resin-coated hessian or foam, and the surface can be printed or plain. Various widths are available.

Broadloom or body?
These are terms used to describe the width of carpet. **Broadloom** carpets are 1.8m (6ft) or more wide, and are the practical choice for fitted carpets in all but the smallest rooms. **Body** carpets are usually 700 to 900mm (27 to 35in) wide, and are intended for use on stairs and in corridors, although they can be seamed together to cover larger areas.

Carpet fibres
All the carpets previously mentioned can be made in several different types of fibre or different blends, which creates still more confusion.

Acrylic fibres are the synthetic fibres most similar to wool. They have long-lasting qualities, and good resistance to flattening, but are not quite so springy as wool. They tend to soil more easily than a natural fibre, but they can be treated to resist staining and to be anti-static. Acrylic fibres come under many brand names, such as Courtelle and Acrilan.

Nylon is a hardwearing fibre, which has a characteristic shiny look. It soils easily, and can look flat and sad if it is the only fibre used in the carpet construction, but when added to other fibres it increases the durability con-

siderably. Nylon is frequently used in an 80/20 mix with wool.

Polyester is a soft fibre, used to create fluffy light-duty carpets. It is not very hard-wearing and does become flattened easily, but it can be blended with other fibres.

Polypropylene is a fairly tough fibre, which is often used to create 'cord' effect carpet. It does not absorb liquid, so it is often used for carpet tiles and carpets for kitchen and utility rooms.

Viscose rayon is not used very much these days, and has poor wearing and soiling qualities, but it can be used as part of a blend of fibres quite successfully.

Wool is the traditional carpet fibre, and no real substitute for it has yet been found. Wool is warm, hard-wearing, resilient and does not soil easily; from the safety point of view it also resists the spread of flame. It is used alone, or blended with other fibres. The most widely-used blend, 80 per cent wool and 20 per cent nylon, gives the best performance.

Other carpet types
Apart from the different methods of carpet making, and the various blends of fibres, you will find there are many other words in the carpet salesman's vocabulary, which loosely cover what might be called carpet styles, or types.

Cord carpets, for example, come in several styles. Originally the only type was a haircord, which was made from natural animal fibres, and was very hardwearing. This is now very expensive and is not frequently used, but there are some blends of animal hair with synthetic fibres available, and some much cheaper cords which are not particularly hard-

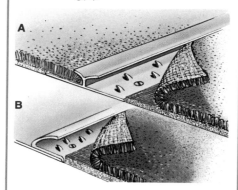
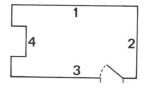
PREPARING THE FLOOR

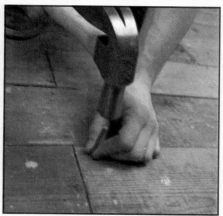

1 *Lift old floorcoverings completely, and remove all traces of underlay. Nail down any loose boards securely with 38mm (1½in) nails.*

2 *Use a nail punch and hammer to ensure that all the nail heads are flush with, or driven below, the surface of the boards.*

wearing. Other types of cord carpet include the Berbers, which have a looped pile and look homespun. Originally these were made from un-dyed, coarsely-woven wool, by Berber tribesmen. Now they are made in many different fibres, including blends of wool and synthetic fibres. These are often called Berber-style.

Hardtwist is a curly, crush-resistant pile, which is sometimes called twist pile. This is frequently found in high-quality Wiltons, in wool or wool blends, but may also be found in all-synthetic carpets.

Shag pile carpets have a long pile, which can be plain or kinked and with a richly textured shaggy surface. The pile needs raking if it is very long, to maintain its appearance, and it is not a practical carpet to choose for areas which get a lot of wear, on stairs, or in halls for example.

Shadow pile is another fairly new development in carpet style. The pile is dyed so it has contrasting colour or tone, usually darker at the base, lightening towards the tip. The pile is usually shiny (synthetic fibres) and when the carpet is walked on the dark tones show as 'shadows'.

Sculptured pile is usually made by combining a looped and cut pile to form a self-coloured pattern, although sometimes different colours can be used. Fibres can be natural, synthetic or a mixture of both.

Printed carpets are another fairly recent development. The carpet is woven and then a design is printed on the surface via computer-controlled dye injection systems. They often resemble Axminsters in colour and design, but on closer examination you can see the pattern does not go right through to the backing. The fibres used in this range are usually synthetic, and the pile is frequently very close and sometimes looped or corded.

Planning and estimating

As with any other floorcovering, start your planning by taking accurate measurements of the room at ground level with a steel tape or yardstick. If possible, work out a scale plan on squared paper, marking in the recesses, corners, angles, projections and so on. Take this with you when you shop for carpet, so the salesman can work out exactly how much you need. It is usual to multiply the room measurements to get square yards or square metres, and you will find most carpeting is sold by the square yard or metre, although some types are still sold by the linear yard or metre.

With the more expensive types of carpet with hessian backing, it is wise to call in an expert to lay the carpet for you, unless you have had a great deal of experience laying other types of carpet and floorcovering. Otherwise you risk marring an expensive carpet if you make a cut in the wrong place; what's

LAYING THE LINING

1 *Unroll the lining down the length of the room. Smooth out the strip and staple down both sides 50mm (2in) in from the edge.*

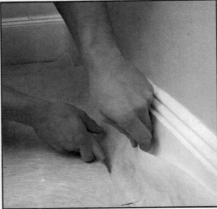

2 *Using a sharp handyman's knife, cut off a strip of the lining 38mm (1½in) wide between the line of staples and the skirting board.*

3 *To fit the lining into an alcove, lay the strip up against the face of the chimney breast and make a cut with your knife in line with its corner.*

4 *Staple down the cut end of the length as before, after ensuring that it is perfectly flat. Then cut off the border strip next to the skirting board.*

5 *Continue covering the rest of the floor with the lining, overlapping each succeeding strip with the previous one by about 25mm (1in).*

6 *Stick double-sided self-adhesive tape down all round the edge of the room where you have cut off the strip of lining. Do not remove the release paper.*

POSITIONING THE CARPET

1 Unroll the carpet parallel with the longest wall, and position it so that there is an overlap at the skirting board all round the room.

2 Roughly trim off the excess carpet with a sharp handyman's knife to leave a 75mm (3in) overlap all round; cut through the foam backing behind.

3 At fireplaces gauge the depth of the alcoves using your cutting knife as a guide. Add 75mm (3in) to allow for the final trimming.

4 Cut into the alcove as you did with the lining. Make the first cut parallel with the side of the chimney breast and allow the tongue to fall into place.

5 Cut across the end of the tongue of carpet that fits into the alcove, taking care not to cut into the pile underneath the tongue.

6 At the corner of the chimney breast, make a diagonal cut on the underside of the carpet, and trim across the face of the chimney breast.

Ready Reference

CUTTING IN AT DOORWAYS
At doorways carpet should extend to a point under the centre of the door. To get an accurate fit round architraves and door stops, start making release cuts in the overlap at one side of the door opening, until the tongue falls neatly into the door opening. Then trim it to fit neatly under the threshold strip (see *Ready Reference*, page 89).

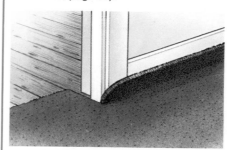

COPING WITH BAY WINDOWS
It's often easier to cope with odd-shaped bay windows by trimming the two flanking walls first. Then
● pull the carpet down the room until its edge is across the 'mouth' of the bay

● measure the depth of the bay, and cut a strip of wood to match this measurement
● use it to trace off the profile on the carpet, marking the line with chalk

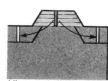

● trim along the marked line and slide the carpet back into place against the wall containing the bay.

FITTING ROUND PIPEWORK
Where pipes to radiators come up through the floor, you will have to cut the carpet to fit neatly round them. To do this
● make an incision in the edge of the carpet, parallel with one edge of the pipe
● measure the distance between wall and pipe, and cut out a small circle in the carpet at this distance from the edge
● fit the carpet round the pipe.

FITTING ANGLES

1 To fit the carpet tightly into an angle, press your thumb firmly down into the corner as shown.

2 Pull up the corner, keeping your thumb in place, and make an incision just beyond the end of your thumb.

3 Cut cleanly across the corner in line with the incision, and press the carpet back in position.

TAPING SEAMS

1 Carefully trim the edges of the two pieces to be joined, and check that they butt neatly together.

2 Cut a piece of carpet tape to the length of the join, peel off the release paper and bed one carpet edge on it.

3 Position the other piece of carpet over the tape, and press it down firmly right along the join.

FINAL TRIMMING

1 Press the carpet tightly into the base of the skirting board with the back of an old knife or a pair of scissors.

2 Turn back the carpet and cut off the excess, using the score mark made by the knife back as a guide.

3 Peel off the release paper from the border tape and press the carpet firmly into place.

more, it will wear out prematurely unless it is tensioned correctly during installation. This involves fitting special toothed gripper strips all round the perimeter of the room, and hooking the carpet on to the teeth once it has been pulled taut across the room.

The foam-backed types are, however, easier to lay yourself, because tensioning is not necessary.

If you are having the carpet professionally laid, ask for a written estimate and check carefully to see whether the price includes underlay or not, and if not, how much extra this will be. With an expensive carpet it may be wise to get several quotes from different firms. Some firms quote a price for carpet 'laid', but again check to see whether underlay is included in the price.

There are several different types of underlay – at different prices. The cheapest is the conventional brown felt, but there are also rubber and synthetic foams, including one on a coarse hessian backing. Foam-backed carpets definitely do not need underlay.

Laying carpet

It is usual to plan and lay carpet so the seams (if any) come in the least obvious place and where the 'traffic' is lightest. When the carpet has to be seamed, both pieces must be laid so the pile is going in the same direction, otherwise the colour would appear slightly different on each side of the seam. The floor

should be clean, level and free from dust and debris. Punch down any nail heads that are proud of the floor surface, and nail down any loose boards. If the boards are very uneven, cover them with sheets of hardboard pinned down at 230mm (9in) intervals to disguise the ridges. Otherwise simply lay stout brown paper or nylon lining to prevent dust from blowing up between floorboards.

Never lay a new carpet down on top of an existing one; the worn areas will quickly transfer themselves to the new carpet. It is not wise to use old underfelt either.

Do not lay a carpet with a latex backing, or a latex underlay, in rooms which have underfloor central heating, as you could find it gives off an unpleasant smell.

LAYING CARPET TILES

Like fitted carpet, carpet tiles can provide warmth and softness underfoot, but they don't require anything like the same sort of skill to lay them.

Carpet tiles are small squares of carpet which you can lay side by side to create a fitted carpet look. You could of course choose to lay ordinary fitted carpet but carpet tiles have advantages that make them well worth considering. For example, since the majority are loose-laid (carpet tiles which require sticking down are available, but only in heavy 'contract' ranges for industrial and commercial use), laying carpet tiles is extremely simple. You certainly won't need to call in a professional carpet fitter for the job. You don't even need an underlay. What's more, they are just as easy to take up again (though some may stick to the floor beneath in heavy traffic areas) which means that, normally, you can remove badly-stained examples for cleaning or else simply move the tiles around to even out wear.

You can also remove the tiles completely if you are redecorating the room, though it's worth pointing out here that you may have a little trouble in achieving the same neat fit as you had before as the tiles may have spread with use. And finally there is the financial aspect. Although not exactly cheap, allowing for the savings you will make on fitting them, carpet tiles tend to be a good deal less expensive than fitted carpet.

What's available
In spite of their advantages, carpet tiles are not very widely available so you should expect to do a fair amount of shopping around before you find exactly what you want.

Basically, the choice is between carpet tiles designed specifically for heavy-duty areas where looks and feel aren't terribly important, and those designed as a straightforward carpet substitute. In the former category, you'll find versions that look rather like needlecord, as well as quite a few very rugged examples made by embedding synthetic fibres, which are often quite coarse in texture, in a fibrous reinforced base. In the second category, you can expect the tiles to have a proper pile, though quality varies considerably with price. At the lower end of the price scale the 'pile' may amount to nothing more than synthetic fibres embedded vertically in a rubber backing. If you pay a

little more you will begin to be offered tiles that approach the quality of normal carpet, with a more luxurious feel.

Calculating quantities
If you simply want to create a plain fitted carpet look, measure the length and breadth of the room using the length of a tile as your unit of measurement. Round each dimension up to the nearest whole number and multiply them together to get the total number of tiles.

If you intend to create a pattern, you will have to work out the quantities of each colour more carefully. It's best to draw up a scale floor plan of the room; then, on this draw a grid to represent the positions of the individual tiles. Colour in the grid to produce the design you want and count up the number of tiles required. Count cut tiles as whole tiles.

Preparation
As with most floorings, the surface on which the tiles are laid must be clean, level and free from damp. So take special care over preparation, levelling concrete floors with a self-levelling compound and floorboards with sheets of hardboard or plywood (see pages 62-63 for more information).

Setting out
Although with carpet tiles which have a thick pile the joins between tiles should in theory be invisible, they nearly always show to some extent in practice, so it's worth going to the trouble of laying the tiles carefully and symmetrically.

This is done in exactly the same way as for vinyl and cork floor tiles (see pages 69 to 77).You simply stretch a chalk string line between the mid-points of opposite walls and snap it down onto the floor to leave a cross at the centre of the room.

Then lay two rows of tiles in an L-shape, starting at the cross and lining up the edges of the tiles with the chalk lines, working out towards the walls until cut tiles are needed to fill the gaps. If your first layout means that you would have cut tiles which are too narrow (see *Ready Reference*), restrike the guidelines in a slightly different position, up to half the length of a tile away from the first set of lines, and try again. Keep trying until you have achieved the layout required.

Laying and cutting tiles
Once you've found a suitable arrangement you can begin laying the whole tiles, starting with one which goes in the angle of the guidelines where they meet at the centre of the room (see step-by-step photographs).

You will eventually have to cut tiles to fill the gaps at the edges. Most tiles can be cut with ordinary scissors; scissors with contoured plastic handles are best, allowing you to apply the pressure needed to cut thick tiles without too much discomfort. Alternatively, you can use a sharp knife. The only thing you have to watch, apart from the obvious need to cut a straight, true line is that when cutting tiles which have a pile, you don't shave off the pile at the edge of the piece you want to use. Although the cut

LAYING THE FLOORING

1 Snap chalk lines which cross at the room's midpoint. Adjust this point if it means you'll have narrow cut tiles. Use the lines to get the tiles straight.

2 At a doorway, nail down a threshold strip. This will give you something to work against when the tile edge is pressed into it.

3 Lay the whole tiles. When you reach the outer edge, take the tile which will fill the edge gap and nick it slightly at either end to mark where to cut it.

5 The cut tile is now ready to be fitted in place. If it's the right size it should stay in place in much the same way that a complete tile does.

6 It's best if you work in a quarter of the floor area at a time. Check that the tiles are straight as you work and cut them to fit at the perimeter.

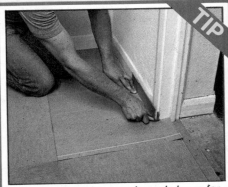

7 Where there is an awkward shape for the tiles to be fitted round, such as the base of a WC or an architrave, make a cardboard template of the shaped area.

9 Fit the shaped tile in the same way as you would any other, butting it against adjacent tiles and, in this case, press it under the threshold strip.

10 When cutting a tile to fit round the angle formed by an alcove, nick on the back on two adjacent sides to indicate where it should be cut.

11 Cut the tile to the required shape and then lay it in place. Here, another tile will have to be cut to fill the gap near the alcove back wall.

4 *Still working on the back of the tile, join up the nicks with a sharp knife using a straightedge to guide you. Then slice right through the tile.*

8 *Place the template on the back of the tile to be cut and trace round it with a pencil. You can then cut out the shape with a sharp knife.*

12 *Vacuum the flooring to remove surplus lint. The tiles shown here have been laid with the pile directions at right angles for a chequerboard look.*

edge will be up against the wall, the bald line sometimes spreads and can look quite unsightly after a short time.

To work out where you make the cut you can, with tiles which have no pile, use the same trick as you would with cork, vinyl or ceramic tiles. That is, you lay the tile to be cut over the whole tile which will be its neighbour, then lay another whole tile on top with its edge butted against the wall to serve as a guide to mark the cutting line on the tile to be cut. The snag with this method is that because there is a certain amount of 'give' in the tiles, it tends not to be very accurate.

A more sensible approach, therefore, is simply to measure the width of the cut tile required. To allow for the fact that the walls may not be exactly straight or out of square, take three readings, one at each end and one in the middle of the gap to be filled and transfer these measurements to the back of the tile you are going to cut using a very soft pencil. Don't use a felt-tipped pen, on rubber-backed tiles in particular, the ink may not dry, with the result that it transfers itself to the pile of the tile you are cutting via the scissor blades, or it may stain tiles you have already laid when you throw aside the offcut. If you feel fairly confident you can, in fact, cut down on the measuring and marking part of the process when it comes to cutting tiles. You can take the tile to be cut, and with its back side facing you, place it so it butts against the wall and exactly over the gap to be filled. then make nicks on the back with a sharp knife to indicate where it should be cut and, finally, cut it to size (see step-by-step photographs).

Finishing off

With all the tiles in place, it's worth leaving them for a few days to settle down under normal use. If they spread it may be necessary to re-trim the edges around the walls.

You can then carefully lift the tiles round the edge of the room and re-lay them, sticking them down with a single strip of heavy duty double-sided sticky tape, positioned close to the edge of the tiles which faces into the room. If you have been unable to avoid narrow cut tiles you should use 'tramlines' of adhesive tape, with an extra line of tape running close to the wall. Sticking down tiles on the perimeter is not essential but it helps to stabilise the tile arrangement and prevents further movement. On very large floors in heavy traffic areas it may even be desirable to fix perhaps one in three rows of whole tiles right across the floor.

You should fit ordinary carpet threshold strip to protect the edges of the tiles at doorways and eliminate the risk of them lifting and forming a ridge which you could trip over. Do remember to vacuum the floor thoroughly to remove any surplus lint.

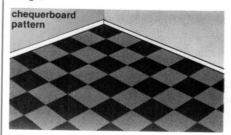
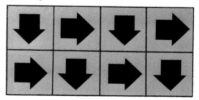

LAYING CARPET ON STAIRS

Carpet provides an attractive covering for stairs, and will cut down considerably on noise levels in the home. Fitting a stair carpet is relatively straightforward providing you use the right techniques.

If you intend to fit a stair carpet you will first have to make sure that the carpet you have in mind is a suitable type. Since stairways are subjected to a lot of use, the carpet must be durable and hardwearing. The label on the carpet may help you make your choice; for example, carpets suitable for light wear only may be labelled as 'not recommended for stairs'. On the other hand, some ranges will be labelled as being specifically suited for use on stairs and others as being suitable for the whole house, including stairs. If the staircase is very heavily used and you require the carpet to last a long time, you will have to go for one of the toughest quality.

Foam-backed carpets are generally unsuitable for stairs; the cheaper light-weight ones tend not to be sufficiently durable and the heavier ones can be too inflexible to fit properly. You should also avoid carpets with a long pile which could impede movement and make the edges of the treads more difficult to locate. Again, some carpet patterns may obscure the outline of the treads or make people feel dizzy. Carpets with these kinds of patterns can be a safety risk, especially where elderly people will be using the stairs.

After you have chosen the carpet you must decide either to call in a professional to lay it or to go ahead and lay it yourself. The complexity of the job is a factor to take into account here; for example, if you want to cover a spiral staircase with a carpet fitted 'edge to edge', that is across the complete width of the stairs, it would normally be advisable to have a professional installation. A straight flight is likely to cause less problems, particularly if you intend to have a carpet runner which simply runs down the centre of the stairs and doesn't cover the complete width.

Measuring up
You will then have to work out how much carpet you'll need. The amount will be affected by the way you intend fitting the carpet: that is, edge-to-edge or as a carpet runner. If you have decided on an edge-to-edge fitting and the staircase is a regular width all the way up, you may find that this measurement coincides with one of the regular widths in which carpet is supplied. If the staircase is narrower than a regular width, you can buy the regular width, trim the carpet to size and seal the cut edge. Where the staircase is a width which is going to waste a great deal of carpet in trimming you might decide to buy broadloom carpet and cut it into strips to match the stair width.

To calculate the length of stair carpet required you should add the height of all the risers to the depth of all the treads and then add on an additional 38mm (1½in) for each step to allow for the space taken by the underlay. Where there are curved nosings at the edges of the treads you will also have to allow for these – add 50mm (2in) for each nosing. Where you are using a carpet runner you can add on an extra 500mm (20in) to the length so you can reposition the carpet later to even out wear (see *Ready Reference*).

On a curved staircase measuring up is more complicated. You will have to calculate the bends separately, taking the largest dimensions of the winder treads which go round the corners.

As well as the quantity of carpet, you will also have to work out how much underlay to order. The underlay is cut in strips, with a separate piece used for each step. Order an amount of underlay which will ensure that each strip is big enough to cover the treads and lap round the nosing so it can be secured to the riser beneath. Check with your supplier about a suitable type of underlay to use with the carpet you have chosen (remember that the better the quality the more wear and sound insulation it will give).

The preparation
As when you are fitting carpet on a floor, the stair surface must be in a suitable state; both treads and risers should be flat, smooth and dry. Check that they are in sound condition. You might find it necessary to nail down loose treads, or perhaps remove and replace any faulty treads or risers.

Unless you happen to have bought one of the few types of foam-backed carpet which are suitable for stairways you will have to fit an underlay before you go ahead and lay the carpet. And before you do this, if you are using the tackless gripper system, you will have to nail the gripper strips to the treads and risers. Fix the grippers to the back of each tread and the bottom of each riser so the pins face into the angle. The gap between the grippers on tread and riser should be

FIXING THE GRIPPER AND UNDERLAY

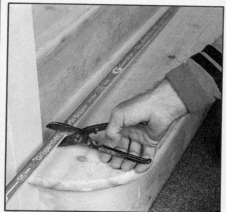

1 Use tinsnips to cut the gripper to size; its width should match that of the tread, measured where the tread meets the riser.

2 Fix the gripper strips to the treads by driving in the nails with a hammer; check that the gripper's teeth are not flattened as you do this.

3 Fix the gripper to the risers; there should be a gap of 15 to 18mm (5/8 to 3/4in) between the gripper strips on the tread and riser.

4 On a landing, nail the gripper strips in place so the gully between the strip and wall is just less than the carpet thickness.

5 Place a strip of underlay in position on the landing and then trim it so it reaches the edges of the gripper strips.

6 Trim the underlay on the landing so it just reaches down to the edge of the gripper strip fixed to the first riser beneath the landing.

7 Use a staple gun to fix the underlay securely in place on the landing and then to fix it above the gripper strip on the riser beneath.

8 Work down the stairs, continuing to cut strips of underlay to size and fixing them in place between the gripper strips.

9 Where there is a bullnose tread at the bottom of the stairs you will have to cut the underlay so it fits the shape of the curved tread.

TIP: CENTRE THE CARPET

Before you lay a carpet runner which does not completely cover the width of the treads, mark out the positions of the carpet edges to help you get the borders equal.

FIXING METHODS

There are three ways of fixing stair carpet. They are:

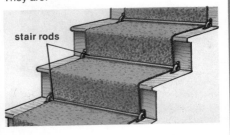

stair rods

● using stair rods which are anchored with side clips; this is the simplest method and the rods form part of the stair decoration.

tacks

● tacking the carpet down with special carpet tacks

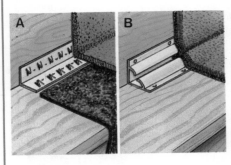

A   B

● using tackless gripper strips or right-angled metal stair grippers (A) (a pinless type is available for foam-backed carpet (B)).

TIP: CHECK PILE DIRECTION

Always make sure the pile of the carpet is facing *down* the stairs to prevent uneven shading and to ensure longer wear. If you move a carpet runner, never be tempted to reverse the pile direction.

---

equal to about twice the thickness of the carpet, to allow the carpet to be tucked down between the grippers. If you are using special right-angled stair grippers, you don't have to worry about a gap. Where you are fixing a carpet runner you should cut the gripper strips 38mm (1½in) shorter than the width of the carpet so the method of fixing won't be obvious when the carpet is finally fixed in place.

You will have to cut the underlay into strips so there is a separate piece for each step. If you are fitting a carpet runner the width of the underlay should be about 38mm (1½in) less than the width of the carpet so it won't be visible under the carpet edges. Where you are using gripper strips, each piece of underlay should just reach the edges of the gripper strips on the tread above it and the riser below it. If you are using tacks to fix the carpet, each piece of underlay can be slightly longer, but you must allow enough room (ie, stair uncovered by underlay) to drive in the tacks which secure the carpet. The underlay can be tacked down, or, to make the job go more quickly, you can use a staple gun to staple it in place. If you are using a carpet runner, you should make sure the underlay is centrally placed (measure and mark off its position before you attempt to secure it). At the same time as you mark off the position of the underlay you can mark the position of the carpet runner so it too will eventually be centrally placed. Care taken at this stage will save you spoiling the look of the stairs later.

Where you are fitting edge-to-edge carpet, treat a landing as you would a floor; that is, cover it with underlay, except that the underlay should lap down over the edge of the landing onto the first riser beneath it. Where you will be fixing the carpet with gripper strips this overlap should reach to just above the gripper strip which you have fixed in place on the top riser.

Laying the carpet

Of the various methods you can use to secure the carpet in place, stair rods provide the simplest one and the tackless gripper system the most difficult (but it also gives the most 'professional' look). Don't forget that if you are using a foam-backed carpet, you can use stair rods instead of special right-angled grippers to hold it in place. You may already have stair rods holding an old stair carpet which you want to replace: these can be removed and used again. Or you may choose to buy new ones; they come in a range of types, including simple streamlined ones and more ornate versions, so you should be able to choose a variety which gives you the look you want for your staircase. Remember that it is simple to move a carpet if you have used stair rods to secure it and that they are the easiest of the various fixing methods to

take up and re-fix. So do bear this in mind.

With the next method, tacking, you should start at the top tread. First, centre the carpet if it is a runner and allow an extra 13mm (½in) for turning under where the carpet meets the top riser. This riser will be covered by the carpet which laps down from the landing. Turn the allowance under and tack the carpet down in one corner, then stretch it so it fits smoothly across the tread and tack it down at intervals of about 100mm (4in) across the riser. Then continue down the stairs, tacking it at the edges in the angles formed by the treads and risers. Make sure it's firmly stretched over the nosings as you go. To complete the job, drive in more tacks at 100mm (4in) intervals across the risers at the angles between treads and risers and, where you have made an allowance for moving the carpet at the bottom, tack up the sides of the folded-under carpet on the bottom step.

For an invisible fixing you will have to use the tackless gripper system. You can use a bolster to stretch and fit the carpet over the gripper strips (see step-by-step photographs) and in this case you should again begin work from the top downwards. But, if you prefer, you can instead use a knee-kicker to get the tension you want, in which case you will be working from the bottom step upwards. With the roll of carpet resting further up, push the carpet into the gully on the first (bottom) step so it is tightly held. Then roll the carpet further up the stairs and, using the knee-kicker on the second tread to pull the carpet tight, push the carpet into the gully between this tread and the second riser. Continue in this way, pulling the carpet tight (but not too tight) as you go, until you reach the top of the stairs.

Left-over carpet at the top and bottom can be tucked into the top and bottom risers and tacked firmly down. Sometimes it is tucked under another carpet at the top and bottom of the stairs; sometimes it continues to meet another carpet, and at other times it is finished with a binder bar. It all depends on the existing arrangements at the top and bottom of the staircase.

On stairs with winders where you are fitting edge-to-edge carpet, you will have to cut separate pieces for each step (see *Ready Reference*). To help you get the shape right it's worth making a paper template of each winder and using this as a guide when you are cutting the carpet.

Where you have cut the carpet to width from a wider measure you will have to seal it at the edges before you lay it. Otherwise the backing will fray, tufts will work loose from the edges and the appearance of the carpet will be spoiled. To seal the edges, run strips of latex adhesive along the underside and allow it to dry before you go ahead and fix the carpet.

FITTING THE CARPET

1 Cut the carpet so it fits the landing and overlaps onto the riser beneath. Stretch and fix it in place using a knee-kicker.

2 With the carpet hooked in place on the gripper at one side of the landing, use a bolster to push the overlap down into the gully.

3 On the other side of the landing, where the carpet and the balustrade meet, cut into the overlap so you can fit the carpet round the corner.

4 Fix the rest of the carpet on the landing and then use a bolster to press the carpet down onto the gripper strip on the riser beneath.

5 With the carpet loosely secured, go over it again with the bolster, this time tapping it with a hammer to fix the carpet firmly in position.

6 Trim off the overlap with a sharp knife to expose the gripper strip fixed to the tread below the riser where the carpet is secured.

7 Again use a bolster to push the carpet down onto the gripper on the tread; go over it again, tapping the bolster with a hammer.

8 Unroll the length of carpet down the stairs and press the folds securely in place onto the gripper strips with your bolster.

9 Finish a straight flight by trimming the carpet off at floor level; with a bullnose tread, cut it off below the last-but-one riser.

COPING WITH HALF-LANDINGS

Where the staircase changes direction at a half landing, treat it as two sets of stairs when you are laying carpet, whether you are fitting carpet edge-to-edge or using a runner.

WINDING STAIRS

Where you are laying carpet on winding stairs, you can use one of two methods to fit the carpet to the winders:

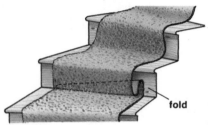

fold

● where there is a carpet runner, leave the gripper strips off the risers of the winders and take up the slack with a series of folds which you can tack in place using 40mm (1½in) non-rusting tacks.

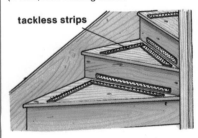

tackless strips

● where you are fitting carpet edge-to-edge, use a separate piece of carpet for each winder. Fix additional gripper strips to the sides of the treads

MOVING CARPET RUNNERS

You can move a carpet runner to equalise wear if you allow an extra 500mm (20in) when first laying it. Tack the carpet at the top and bottom with the extra 500mm tucked under the bottom step, to act as an underlay. Move the carpet (*before* signs of wear become obvious) as follows:
● start from the top and remove the tacks carefully so you don't damage the carpet
● gently ease the carpet off the grippers (or remove tacks or stair rods), move it and then fit it back on to them
● as you move the carpet up, insert strips of underlay on the bottom tread and riser.

For more information see pages 88-92.

CARPETING A BULLNOSE TREAD

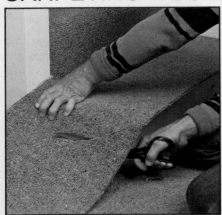

1 *If you have a bullnose tread at the foot of the flight, lay a piece of carpet across it and cut it 50mm (2in) bigger than the curve all round.*

3 *Then cut up to the edge of your thumb with shears to get the correct depth of the zig-zag cut. Cut in this way right round the curve.*

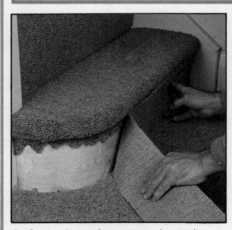

5 *Cut a piece of carpet to size so it fits along the exposed riser under the bullnose tread; then press it round the curve.*

2 *Make zig-zag cuts in the overlap where it fits round the curve. First of all press the carpet under the edge of the tread with your thumb.*

4 *Use a hammer to fix carpet tacks along and under the edge of the bottom tread to hold the carpet neatly and securely in place.*

6 *Nail the width of carpet in place at the sides of the riser and along the top; don't nail along the bottom, where tacks would be visible.*

STRIPPING TIMBER FLOORS

Sanding wooden floorboards is dusty, time-consuming work, but it's not difficult. You'll find the effort well worthwhile when the boards are transformed into an attractive floor surface.

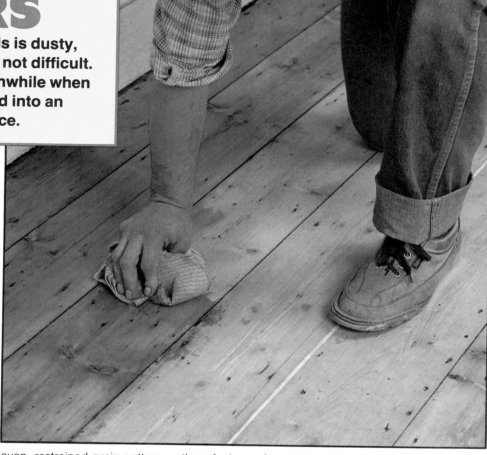

Using floorcoverings can be expensive, particularly if you have to deal with passages, stairs or landings as well as main rooms. As an alternative you could decide to leave a wooden floor uncovered after treatment to make it an attractive surface in its own right. Since timber is one of the most versatile flooring materials there is, it will fit in with most styles of decor, whether modern or traditional. It's extremely hardwearing and easy to look after. And, just as important, it has a warmth you don't get with most modern floorings of comparable durability.

You can, if you wish, lay a completely new timber floor surface from scratch, finishing it off with stains or varnish to bring out the natural beauty of the wood. But the chances are that you won't need to go to this trouble and expense. You may well already have a wooden floor which is covered up. The old floorboards may not look that good when you first expose them but if you sand them smooth – taking off the uneven top layers engrained with dirt – you'll be surprised how beautiful they can become: especially after they've been coated with varnish to make the grain pattern clear.

Checking out the floor

Of course, ordinary floorboards are not intended to be displayed, so you cannot guarantee good results. A particularly unattractive, inferior grade of timber may have been used. Or the boards may have been badly laid or badly looked after. The only way to find out is to lift any floorcovering and see for yourself. You can make a preliminary survey simply by lifting a corner of the floorcovering; but to be absolutely sure the whole floor should be exposed.

When you lift the existing floorcovering, take care to remove any fixing nails and the remains of flooring adhesive. Many flooring adhesives are soluble in white spirit (turps) or petrol. But obviously, if you're using petrol you must ensure the room is adequately ventilated. Don't smoke while you're doing the work.

The look of the timber grain is important, but here much depends on personal taste. Some people like wooden floors to have

even, restrained grain patterns; others feel that, unless the pattern is striking and irregular, the floor doesn't look like real wood. It's up to you, but do allow for the fact that any grain pattern will become slightly more pronounced once the boards have been sanded and sealed.

You should also see if the floorboards have been stained, and if so, whether or not the staining covers the entire floor: it was once popular to stain the edges and cover the central unstained portion with a carpet or linoleum square. If the staining has been carried out over the whole of the floor area there shouldn't be any problem with sanding and sealing later. Thoroughly sand a trial area by hand to get an idea of the finished result. If you don't like the way the floor looks, you can try restaining it experimentally; alternatively try to lighten or remove the existing wood stain with a proprietary wood bleach. Border staining can be more of a problem because of the need to match the border with the unstained part of the floor. Again, experimenting with stains and bleaches is the only answer; make sure you sand the test area first. If, when later you come to tackle the job in earnest, you give the floor its main sanding

after staining, there is a risk that the old and new stains will respond in rather different ways.

Preparing the surface

When you've got a good idea of what the final result will look like, you can turn your attention to the physical state of the floor. Are there lots of large gaps, wider than 2 or 3mm (up to 1/8in) between boards? If there are, the finished floor may well turn out to be excessively draughty so you will have to fill the gaps before sanding. To maintain the floor's 'natural' look involves tailoring a fillet of timber for each gap and you may well decide, as a result, that a wooden floor simply isn't worth the effort. Watch out, too, for signs of excessive localised wear resulting in dips and ridges that no amount of sanding will remove. And, finally, check for signs of woodworm. This must be treated, but, remember, woodworm treatment will not restore the appearance of the affected wood.

If, at this stage, things don't look too promising, there are three remedies to consider which may provide you with the solution you require.

The first is a cure for gaps. All you do is lift every single board and re-lay them closer together: not difficult but very hard work. Next there is the remedy for boards disfigured by wear or woodworm, and you can also use it to overcome the problems associated with stained boards. Again, all you do is lift and re-lay the boards, but this time, you re-lay them with what used to be the underside uppermost. This is also very hard work, and there is a possibility that the underside of the boards may look no better; a good builder should have laid the boards with the worse side face down when the house was built.

Because of the amount of work involved with both of these solutions it's best to consider them as a last resort. You could instead adopt the third remedy: give up the idea of sanding the existing boards and cover them with new ones. Such 'non-structural' boards are available in a variety of hardwoods and softwoods, so the results can be very rewarding indeed in that you will end up with a very attractively coloured and grained floor surface. However, this type of floor is likely to prove very expensive and rather tricky to lay. The actual techniques involved will be covered in a later article.

If, on the other hand, you check the boards and discover that they are suitable for sanding, you should fill any gaps and make sure there are no protruding nails or screws. These should be driven well below the surface otherwise there could be dire consequences when you are sanding (see *Ready Reference*). Giving screws an extra half a turn should do the trick; otherwise unscrew them, drill out a deeper countersink and replace them. For nails which cause you a problem you will need a nail punch (if you don't have one you can use an old blunt nail instead) to drive the offending nails home so they can't cause any further nuisance.

Sanding the floor

Sanding floorboards is in essence, no different to sanding any piece of natural timber. You must work your way through coarse, medium and then fine grades of abrasive until you achieve the desired finish. It's simply that you are working on a larger scale than usual.

However, this question of scale does create a few complications. First, there will be a great deal of dust flying about, and a lot of noise, so you must protect yourself with the appropriate safety equipment (see *Ready Reference*). You must also take steps to stop the dust being trodden all round your home. Second, the job will be far too large for sanding by hand and, in any case, the average DIY power sander wouldn't be up to the task. What you need are two special floor sanders, and these you will have to hire. (See below for tips on hiring).

The first sander looks a bit like a lawn mower, but is in fact a giant belt sander and its role is to tackle the bulk of the floor. It has a revolving rubber-covered drum set on a wheeled frame which can be tilted backwards to lift the drum from the floor. You wrap a sheet of abrasive round the drum to provide the sanding surface. There is a bag attached to the sander into which a fan blows the wood dust and particles produced by the sanding process. The second sander is a sort of heavy duty orbital sander, and it is used to tackle the parts the main sander cannot reach. It works on the same principle as the large sander (you attach an abrasive sheet to a rubber pad) but, being small and lighter, it's easier to manoeuvre.

You won't be able to rely entirely on these labour-saving devices, though. After machine sanding there will be small unsanded patches left, usually at the edges of the floor and these

will have to be sanded by hand or scraped with a shave hook or some other form of scraper.

The need to hire equipment raises a further complication: careful planning is needed to keep the cost to a minimum. As always, the best way to start is by shopping around the hire shops in your area to find the best price. In particular, look for firms that give discounts for extended periods of hire (for example, one where the weekly rate is cheaper than say, four or five days at the day rate) and find out how much flexibility there is in allowing you to switch rates should you decide to keep the sanders for a day or two longer than originally anticipated. This is important because, although it's only sensible to keep the period of hire to a minimum by doing all the preparation (punching nail heads below the surface and so on) before you pick up the equipment, and returning it as soon as you've finished, floor sanding is physically very demanding, and may well take longer than you think.

Check up, too, on the cost of the abrasives. If there is a marked difference in price between two shops, it may be due to the fact that, while one offers ordinary glasspaper, the other offers a more modern synthetic paper which will last longer and clog less readily, and so works out cheaper than it appears. You will also encounter differences in the way abrasives are provided. For example, some shops will give a refund for any abrasive you don't use. A point to remember here is that as it's difficult to estimate exactly how much abrasive you will need it's wise to take an amount which appears surplus to requirements. If you take this precaution you will avoid the annoying situation where you have to down tools and buy extra abrasive.

PREPARING THE FLOOR

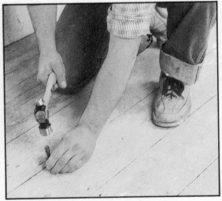

1 *Go over the entire floor, punching all nail heads well below the surface. If screws have been used, check they're adequately countersunk.*

2 *Cut thin fillets of wood to fill gaps between the boards; hammer them in, protecting the edges of the fillets with a block of softwood.*

3 *Plane the fillets flush with the surrounding surface, taking off a little at a time to prevent chipping and splintering.*

ORDER OF WORK

After you have checked that the floor is in a suitable condition for sanding, with gaps filled and no protruding nails or screws, you should adopt the procedure indicated below when using the large and small sanding machines. The arrows indicate in which direction the sander should be moved.

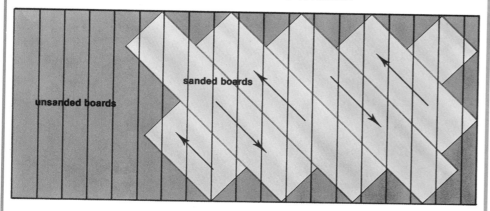

1 Use the large sander in a diagonal direction across the boards in order to flatten them out and remove thoroughly the top dirt-engrained layer.

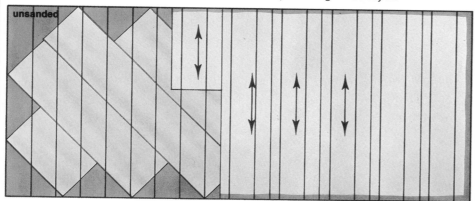

2 Work in strips along the boards. Work down a strip, then with the machine on, move back along the strip. Switch off when you reach your starting point.

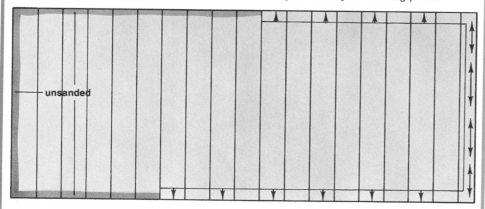

3 When the floor has been sanded as in (2), with first coarse, then medium and fine abrasives, you can use the small sander on the perimeter of the floor.

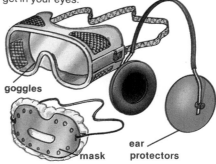

SANDING AND SEALING THE BOARDS

1 Fit a large floor sander with a coarse grade of abrasive; the paper is locked into a slot in the revolving drum of the machine.

2 You can now start sanding the floor by running the sander diagonally across the floorboards to remove the rough and dirty surface layer.

3 Continue sanding the floor in this way until the bulk of the floor area has been treated; the sander will flatten out any warped boards.

4 Sand a strip down the length of the room. Work in the same direction as the boards and allow the sander to pull you along.

5 Sand this strip again, dragging the sander backwards. Repeat for the rest of the floor. Afterwards, sand using medium then fine grades of paper.

TIP

6 Use a small sander to sand round the perimeter using progressively finer grades of paper. Work in the direction of the grain.

7 You can use a shave hook to scrape stubborn areas at the edges. Other areas that the machines have missed will have to be sanded by hand.

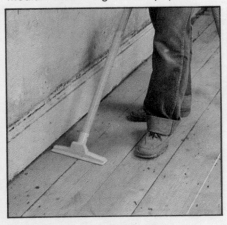

8 Allow the dust to settle, then vacuum the floor clean, paying particular attention to the gaps between the floor and skirting.

9 To reduce the amount of sealant needed, apply polyurethane varnish, diluted with white spirit on a clean cloth to prime the boards.

Finally, you should make sure that the shop from which you hire the equipment will give you adequate tuition on how to use and clean the sanders. If you damage them through misuse, or return them dirty, you will have to pay more.

Finishing the floor

Having dealt with the sanding, the final thing you have to consider is how to finish the floor: that is, add to its decorative quality and protect the boards from scratches and other types of wear.

If you feel that the boards are too dark to leave as they are after sanding you can apply bleach to lighten them. Use a proprietary wood bleach and follow the manufacturer's instructions for applying it. The fumes from the bleach can be at the least unpleasant and at worst dangerous, so make sure you keep the windows open and wear a protective face mask.

You may want to change the colour of the boards, as well as lighten them. You could use coloured polyurethane varnish for this, but as the surface of the floor becomes subject to wear, so the colour may become thin in some places, highlighting the wear more strongly than you would wish. So it's better to use wood stains which colour the timber itself and then seal with clear polyurethane varnish. Again apply the stain according to the manufacturer's instructions as to the number of coats needed. Work in the direction of the grain when you are applying the stain. Stains come in a variety of colours and allow you to go in for different attractive decorative effects.

Polyurethane varnish is by far the best choice for sealing the floor, simply because it is so hardwearing and easy to look after. You should choose a brand that is available in large cans rather than in the small tins you are probably familiar with. You'll need a lot to give the floor the two or three coats it requires, and buying such a large amount in small cans can work out very expensive. It's up to you whether you choose a polyurethane giving a high gloss, a satin look or a matt finish; it all depends on the style of the room as a whole. However, it's worth bearing in mind that a very high gloss will show marks more readily and may make the floor rather slippery.

Care and maintenance

To look its best, a wooden floor should be kept free of dust; regular vacuuming will attend to this. If you like a shiny look you can polish it with a proprietary floor polish. Dirty marks can be removed with a damp cloth or mop; more stubborn marks may require treatment with a proprietary cleaner. Where the finish or floorboard has been slightly damaged, such as by a cigarette burn, you will have to sand down the affected area until the signs of damage are removed and then apply polyurethane to reseal it. If there is more extensive damage you will have to remove the affected floorboards, replace them (or use them with the undamaged side face up), sand to provide a smooth surface and reseal.

Take care when you are moving bits of furniture about that they don't scratch the surface (see *Ready Reference*). There's not much point in spending the time and energy it takes to get an attractive varnished wooden floor surface only to spoil it in a few careless minutes.

Ready Reference

TIP: KEEP MOVING
If the sander is left running when standing still, it will gouge deep chunks out of the floor, so don't let it linger in one spot. Instead:
● sand down the length of the boards, letting the sander pull you across the room
● when you reach the far end, drag the sander back over the strip you have just sanded, switching off only when you reach your starting position
● repeat this procedure for the next strip, and continue in strips across the floor.

TIP: VACUUM FREQUENTLY
It's worth vacuuming the floor several times during sanding. This will enable you to see any bits you have missed which require further attention and will prevent the sander from becoming clogged up.

USE THE RIGHT ABRASIVE
For a truly smooth finish you should first sand with a coarse paper to remove the roughest bits, then use a medium paper and finish off with a fine grade paper.

FINISHING EDGES
After machine sanding, there will be small unsanded patches left, usually at the edges and in the corners. Sand these by hand, or scrape them with a shavehook.

ALLOW VARNISH TO DRY
If you are to provide an effective seal you must allow the varnish to dry thoroughly before applying the next coat. Similarly, if you remove dust by wiping over with a damp cloth in between coats, allow the floor to dry before continuing.

TIP: AVOID SCRATCHING
While polyurethane provides a hardy surface which will resist a lot of wear and tear, you should avoid dragging heavy furniture over it as this is liable to mark the surface. Move such items on cloth pads.

FINISHING THE FLOOR

10 *Follow the priming with at least two, preferably three, coats of polyurethane varnish applied with a brush, working with the grain.*

11 *Allow each coat to dry, then rub lightly down with medium glasspaper to provide a key for the next. Use a damp cloth to remove dust.*

SECTION 3

WOODWORKING

TECHNIQUES

SIMPLE JOINTS

It's often thought that only elaborate joints give good results in woodwork. It isn't true. There are simple ways to join timber, and one of the simplest is the butt joint. It's easy to make, can be used on natural timber or man-made boards, and it's neat. What's more, given the right adhesive and the right reinforcement, a butt joint can also be strong enough for most purposes.

The great thing about butt joints is their simplicity. You can use them on any kind of timber or man-made board, provided it isn't too thin – not under 6mm (¼in). The only problem you will run into is where you are joining chipboard. A special technique is needed here to get the screws to grip, as is explained later.

Although it is possible to simply glue two pieces of wood together, unless you add some kind of reinforcement the result won't be very strong. So in most cases, the joint should be strengthened with either screws or nails. The question is which? As a rule of thumb, screws will give you a stronger joint than nails. The exception is where you are screwing into the endgrain of natural timber. Here, the screwthread chews up the timber to such an extent that it has almost no fixing value at all. Nails in this case are a much better bet.

Choosing the right adhesive

Even if you are screwing or nailing the joint together, it ought to be glued as well. A PVA woodworking adhesive will do the trick in most jobs, providing a strong and easily achieved fixing. This type of adhesive will not, however, stand up well to either extreme heat or to moisture; the sort of conditions you'll meet outdoors, or in a kitchen, for example. A urea formaldehyde is the glue to use in this sort of situation. It isn't as convenient – it comes as a powder that you have to mix with water – but your joints will hold.

Choosing the right joint

There are no hard and fast rules about choosing the best joint for a particular job. It's really just a case of finding a joint that is neat enough for what you're making, and strong enough not to fall apart the first time it is used. And as far as strength is concerned, the various kinds of butt joint work equally well.

Marking timber

Butt joints are the simplest of all joints – there's no complicated chiselling or marking out to worry about – but if the joint is to be both strong and neat you do need to be able

to saw wood to length leaving the end perfectly square.

The first important thing here is the accuracy of your marking out. Examine the piece of wood you want to cut and choose a side and an edge that are particularly flat and smooth. They're called the face edge and face side.

Next, measure up and press the point of a sharp knife into the face side where you intend to make the cut. Slide a try-square up to the knife, making sure that its stock – the handle – is pressed firmly against the face edge. Then use the knife to score a line across the surface of the timber. Carry this line round all four sides of the wood, always making sure that the try-square's stock is held against either the face edge or the face side. If you wish, you can run over the knife line with a pencil to make it easier to see – it's best to sharpen the lead into a chisel shape.

Why not use a pencil for marking out in the first place? There are two reasons. The first is that a knife gives a thinner and therefore more accurate line than even the sharpest pencil. The second is that the knife will cut through the surface layer of the wood, helping the saw to leave a clean, sharp edge.

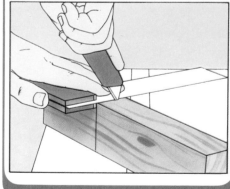

Sawing square

One of the most useful – and easiest to make – aids to sawing is a bench hook. It'll help you to grip the wood you want to cut, and to protect the surface on which you are working. You can make one up quite easily, by gluing and screwing together pieces of scrap timber (see *Ready Reference*).

You also need the ability to control the saw, and there are three tips that will help you here. Always point your index finger along the saw blade to stop it flapping from side to side as you work. And always stand in such a way that you are comfortable, well balanced, and can get your head directly above the saw so you can see what you are cutting. You should also turn slightly sideways on. This stops your elbow brushing against your body as you draw the saw back – a fault that is often the reason for sawing wavy lines.

Starting the cut

Position the piece of wood to be cut on the bench hook and hold it firmly against the block furthest from you. Start the cut by drawing the saw backwards two or three times over the far edge to create a notch, steadying the blade by 'cocking' the thumb of your left hand. Make sure that you position the saw so that the whole of this notch is on the waste side of the line. You can now begin to saw properly using your arm with sort of piston action, but keep your left (or right as the case may be) hand away from the saw.

As the cut deepens gradually reduce the angle of the saw until it is horizontal. At this point you can continue sawing through until you start cutting into the bench hook. Alternatively, you may find it easier to angle the saw towards you and make a sloping cut down the edge nearest to you. With that done, you can saw through the remaining waste holding the saw horizontally, using the two angled cuts to keep the saw on course.

Whichever method you choose, don't try to force the saw through the wood – if that seems necessary, then the saw is probably blunt. Save your muscle power for the forward stroke – but concentrate mainly on sawing accurately to your marked line.

Cleaning up cut ends

Once you have cut the wood to length, clean up the end with glasspaper. A good tip is to lay the abrasive flat on a table and work the end of the wood over it with a series of circular strokes, making sure that you keep the wood vertical so you don't sand the end out of square. If the piece of wood is too unmanageable, wrap the glasspaper round a square piece of scrap wood instead and sand the end of the wood by moving the block to and fro – it'll help in keeping the end square.

DOVETAIL NAILING

This is a simple way of strengthening any butt joint. All you do is grip the upright piece in a vice or the jaws of a portable work-bench, and glue the horizontal piece on top if it – supporting it with scrap wood to hold the joint square – and then drive in the nails dovetail fashion. If you were to drive the nails in square, there would be more risk that the joint would pull apart. Putting them in at an angle really does add strength.

The only difficulty is that the wood may split. To prevent this, use oval brads rather than round nails, making sure that their thickest part points along the grain. If that doesn't do the trick, try blunting the point of each nail by driving it into the side of an old hammer. This creates a burr of metal on the point which will cut through the wood fibres rather than parting them.

Once the nails are driven home, punch their heads below the surface using a nail punch, or a large blunt nail. Fill the resulting dents with wood stopping (better on wood than ordinary cellulose filler) and sand smooth.

1 *Drive nails at angle: first leans to left; next to right, and so on.*

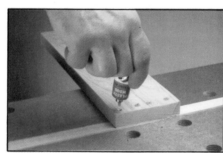
3 *Fill resulting dents with stopping compound to cover up nail heads.*

THE OVERLAP

This is the simplest of all and is one you can use on relatively thin timber. The example shown is for a T-joint, but the method is the same if you want to make an X-joint.

Bring the two pieces of wood together as they will be when joined, and use a pencil to mark the position of the topmost piece on the one underneath. To reinforce the joint, countersunk screws are best, so mark their positions on the top piece of wood, and drill clearance holes the same diameter as the screw's shank – the unthreaded part – right the way through. The screws should be arranged like the spots on a dice (two screws are shown here, but on a larger joint where more strength is needed five would be better) to help stop the joint twisting out of square. Enlarge the mouths of these holes with a countersink bit to accommodate the screw heads, and clean up any splinters where the drill breaks through the underside of the wood.

Bring the two pieces of wood together again using a piece of scrap wood to keep the top piece level. Then make pilot holes in the lower piece using either a bradawl or a small drill, boring through the clearance holes to make sure they are correctly positioned. Make sure the pilot holes are drilled absolutely vertically, or the screws could pull the joint out of shape. Finally, apply a thin coating of adhesive to both the surfaces to be joined (follow the adhesive manufacturer's instructions), position the pieces of wood accurately and, without moving them again, drive home the screws.

3 *Reassemble joint and bore pilot holes in bottom piece with bradawl.*

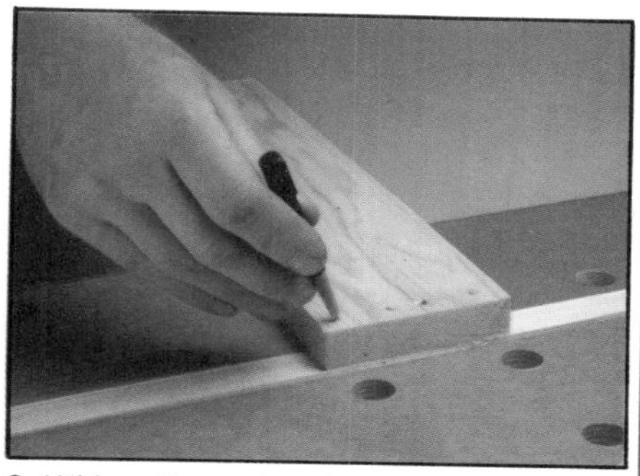

2 *With nail punch or large blunt nail, hammer nail heads below surface.*

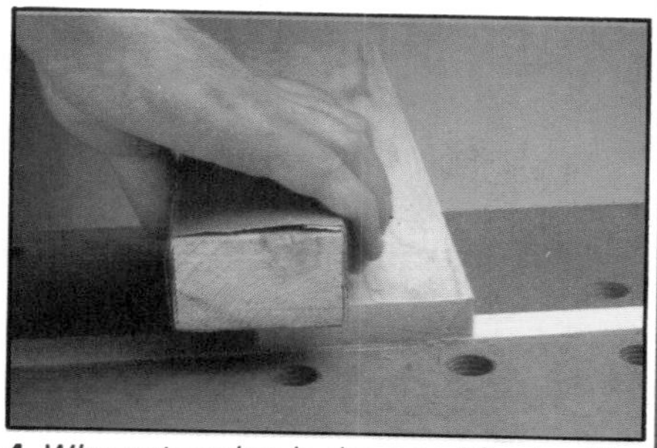

4 *When stopping is dry, sand flush with surface of surrounding timber.*

CORRUGATED TIMBER CONNECTORS

Another simple way of holding a butt joint together is to use ordinary corrugated timber connectors. Simply glue the two pieces of wood together, and hammer the connectors in across the joint. Note that they are driven in dovetail fashion – the fixing is stronger that way.

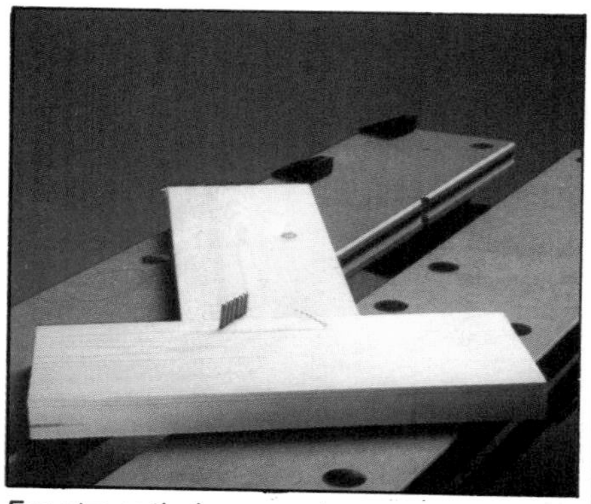

For strength, hammer in connectors diagonally rather than straight.

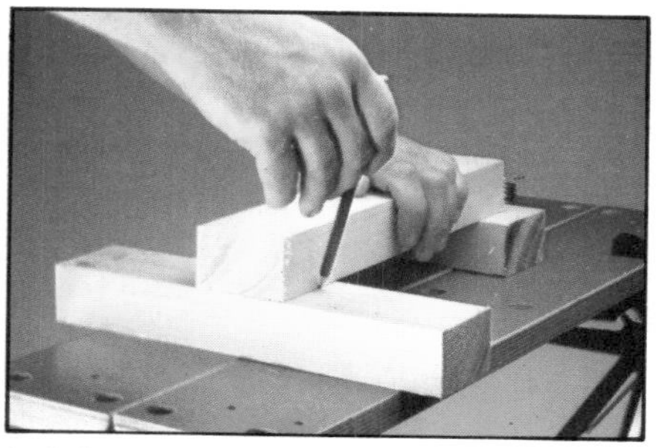

1 *Bring pieces squarely together. Mark position of each on the other.*

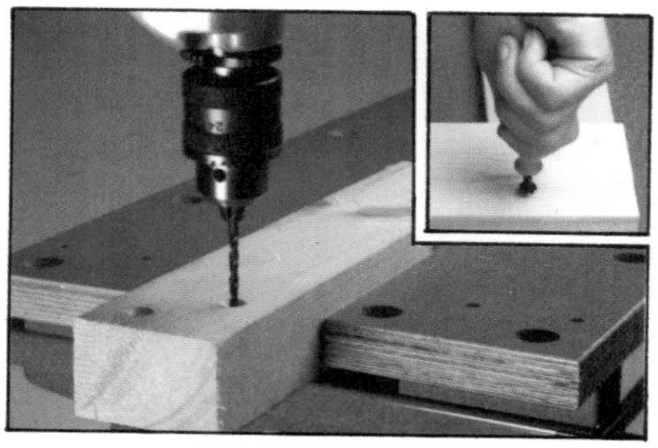

2 *Drill and countersink (inset) clearance holes for screws in uppermost piece.*

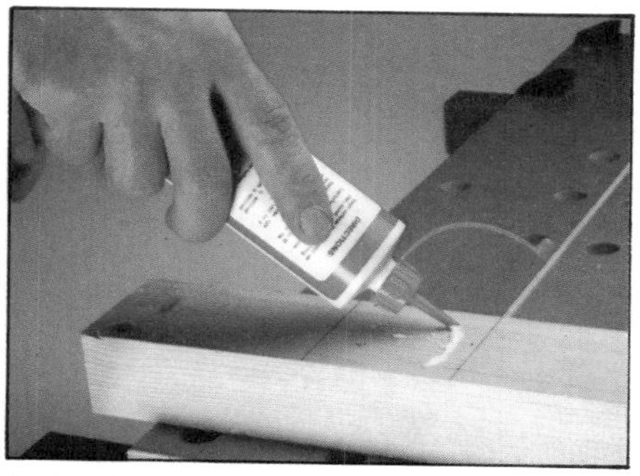

4 *Apply woodworking adhesive to both pieces and press them together*

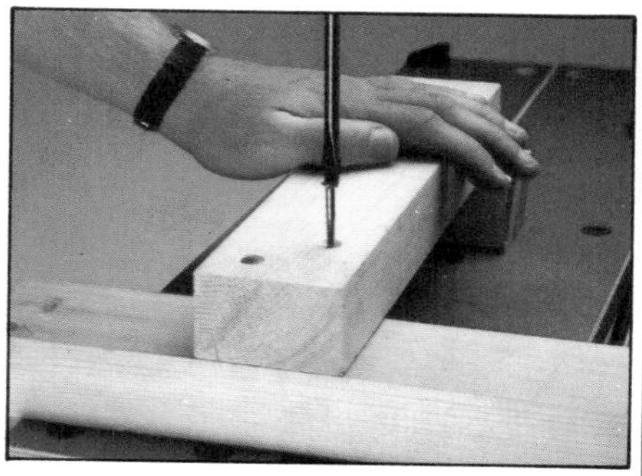

5 *Carefully drive in screws. If they're tight, remove and lubricate with soap.*

Ready Reference

MAKING YOUR OWN BENCH HOOK

This a very useful sawing aid to help grip the wood when cutting. Hook one end over the edge of the workbench and hold the wood against the other end. Make it up from off-cuts and replace when it becomes worn.

You need:

- a piece of 12mm (1/2in) plywood measuring about 250 x 225mm (10 x 9in)
- two pieces of 50 x 25mm (2 x 1in) planed softwood, each about 175mm (7in) long. Glue and screw them together as shown in the sketch. Use the bench hook the other way up if you're left-handed.

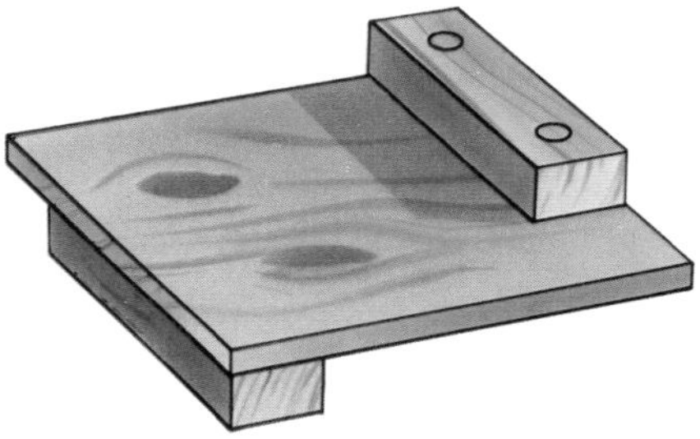

TIP: SAWING STRAIGHT

- hold wood firmly against bench hook and start cut on waste side of cutting line with two or three backward cuts
- decrease angle of the saw blade as cut progresses
- complete cut with saw horizontal, cutting into your bench hook slightly

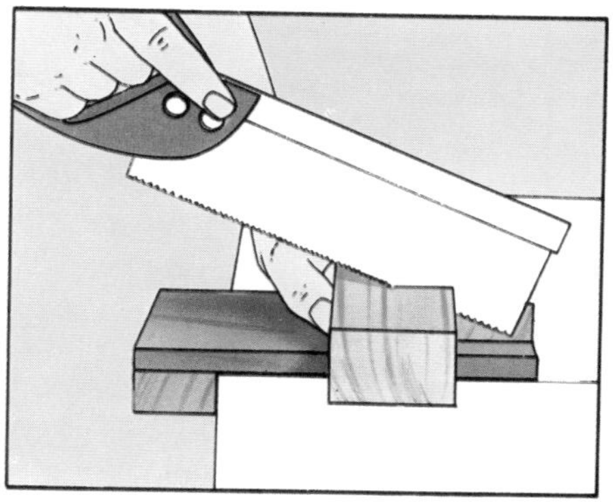

TIP: TO SMOOTH CUT END

- rub with a circular motion on glasspaper held flat on the workbench, so you don't round off the corners
- on large pieces of wood, wrap glasspaper round a block of wood and rub this across the cut end

FIXING INTO CHIPBOARD

Because neither nails nor screws hold well in chipboard, how do you hold a butt joint together? The answer is that you do use screws, but to help them grip, you drive them into a chipboard plug. Chipboard plugs are a bit like ordinary wall plugs. In fact, you can use ordinary plugs, but you have to be careful to position the plug so that any expanding jaws open across the board's width and not across the thickness where they could cause the board to break up.

The initial stages of the job are exactly the same as for the overlap joint – marking out, drilling the clearance holes, and so on. The difference is that instead of boring pilot holes in the second piece of wood, you drill holes large enough to take the chipboard plugs. Pop the plugs into the holes, glue the joint together and drive home the screws.

Incidentally, if you can't use any sort of plug at all – for example, when screwing into the face of the chipboard – the only way to get the screw to hold properly is to dip it in a little woodworking adhesive before you drive it home.

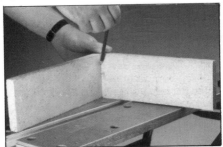

1 Bring pieces together and mark position of overlap with a pencil.

2 Drill and countersink clearance holes in overlapping piece.

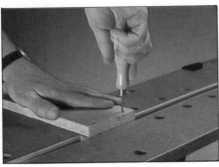

3 Mark screw positions through holes onto end of second piece.

4 Drill chipboard to take plugs, then glue and screw joint together.

REINFORCING BLOCKS

The joints described so far are fairly robust, but if a lot of strength is needed it's worth reinforcing the joint with some sort of block. The simplest is a square piece of timber.

First drill and countersink clearance holes through the block and glue and screw it to one of the pieces you want to join so that it's flush with the end. To complete the joint, glue the second piece in position, and drive screws through into that. You can arrange for the block to end up inside the angle or outside it. Choose whichever looks best and is easiest to achieve.

With the block inside the angle, you'll have a neat joint and the screw heads won't be openly on display. However, in most cases it means screwing through a thick piece of wood (the block) into a thin piece (one of the bits you want to join), so it's not as strong as it might be. If greater strength is needed work the other way round, driving the screws through the pieces to be joined, into the block. You can neaten the result to a certain extent by using a triangular rather than a square block.

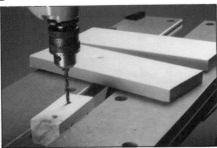

1 Drill and countersink clearance holes through reinforcing block.

2 Glue and screw block in place level with end of one piece of wood.

3 Glue second piece in place and drive screws into it through block.

4 In some cases this joint looks better with block outside angle.

JOINTING BLOCKS

Made from plastic, these are just sophisticated versions of the wooden blocks you can make yourself, and they're used in similar situations. Their only real advantage is that they tend to give a neater result when you're working with veneered or melamine covered chipboard, but only because they come in the right colours. There are basically two kinds to choose from.

The simplest is just a hollow triangular 'block' that comes with a snap-on cover to hide the screws. More complicated versions come in two parts. You screw one half of the block to each piece of wood, and then screw the two halves together using the machine screw provided. It's essential here that both halves of the block are positioned accurately, and since the blocks vary from brand to brand in the details of their design, you should follow the manufacturer's instructions on this point.

1 Screw half of block to one piece of wood and mark position on other.

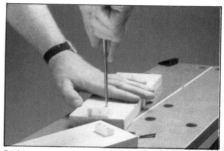

2 Next, screw second half of block in place on second piece of timber.

3 Finally, connect both halves of block using built-in machine screw.

4 Treat blocks that come in one piece as wooden reinforcing blocks.

ANGLE IRONS

If still greater strength is needed, use either an angle iron or a corner repair bracket to reinforce the joint. These are really just pieces of metal pre-drilled to take screws and shaped to do the same job as a reinforcing block (the angle irons) or to be screwed to the face of the two pieces of timber across the joint (the flat T-shaped and L-shaped corner repair brackets).

In either case, bring together the pieces of wood to be joined, position the bracket, and mark the screw holes. Drill clearance and pilot holes for all the screws, then screw the bracket to one of the pieces before glueing the joint together and screwing the bracket to the second piece. They don't look very attractive, so use where appearance isn't important, ie, at the back of a joint, or where the joint is going to be concealed in some other way.

1 Corner joints strengthened with plywood and an angle repair iron.

2 T-joints can be simply made with angle irons or repair brackets.

SKEW NAILING

There'll be some situations where you cannot get at the end of the wood to use dovetail nailing. Here you must use skew nailing instead. This means glueing the two pieces securely together and then driving a nail into the upright piece of wood at an angle so it also penetrates the horizontal piece. Put a couple of nails into each side of the upright so that they cross. To stop the upright moving, clamp a block of wood behind it or wedge it against something solid.

Stop movement while driving nails with scrap wood block and G-cramp.

HALVING JOINTS & simple mitres

Getting joints to fit snugly is one of the major objectives in carpentry, and nothing introduces the techniques so well as the halving joint. As for the perfect finish, that's the role of the mitre.

There are many situations in woodwork when you need a joint that's fast and simple, but also neat and strong. And this is where halving joints come into their own. Despite their simplicity, they're very effective joints because the two pieces of wood are cut so they interlock together, either face to face or edge to edge, making the joint as strong as — if not stronger than — the timber itself. They are used almost exclusively for building frameworks, joining the rails (side pieces) either at a corner or in a cross absolutely flush. You end up with a frame that's neat enough to be on show and sturdy enough to need no reinforcement.

Mitre joints, though not strictly speaking considered halving joints as there's no interlocking, are halved to make up a perfect 90° angle. In this section, only the simple mitre is dealt with — the more complicated forms (eg, mitred secret dovetails) are covered in another section.

Strength of joints

There are three things that affect the strength of a halving joint — the size of the timber, the quality of the timber, and any reinforcement you add.

The size of timber is important because it governs the amount of adhesive in the joint; the greater the areas glued together, the stronger the joint will be. Usually problems only arise when you are trying to join thin pieces of timber together — it's almost impossible to get the joint to stay rigid. Regarding timber quality, hardwoods rarely present a problem, but with softwoods, splitting can occur which will seriously weaken the joint. You should, therefore, reject timber containing knots, cracks and other potential weak spots.

In many cases, the correct adhesive is all the reinforcement you need — use a good quality PVA woodworking adhesive, or, if the joint will be subjected to heat or moisture, a urea formaldehyde woodworking adhesive. If still greater strength is required — this is more likely on corner halving joints than on cross halvings — you should drive screws through the overlaps, or, for a more natural look, drill a hole right through and glue in a length of dowel. Both the dowels and screws are set like the spots on a dice to stop the joint twisting.

Butt joints (see pages 107-111) have to be reinforced in some way to have strength, but with mitred butt joints this would defeat the decorative aim. Because of this, they are normally reserved for situations where strength is not required – picture frames and decorative edgings, such as door architraves for example.

Marking corner halving joints

Having sawn the ends of the two pieces of wood to be joined perfectly square (see pages 107-111 for more details), place one on top of the other, and mark the width of the top piece on the one below. Carry this mark right round the timber using a knife and a try-square, then repeat the process, this time with the bottom piece on top.

Next divide the thickness of the timber in two. You need a single-tooth marking gauge for this: it consists of a wooden shaft with a sharp metal pin called a spur near one end, and a block of wood (the stock) which can be moved along the shaft and be fixed at any point with the aid of a thumbscrew.

Position the stock so that the distance between it and the spur is roughly half the timber's thickness, and place it against one edge of the wood. Use the spur to dent the surface of the timber, then repeat with the stock against the other edge. If the dents co-incide, the gauge is set correctly. If they don't, reset the gauge. Don't try to make small adjustments by undoing the thumbscrew and moving the stock — you'll go on for ever trying to make it accurate. Instead, with the screw reasonably tight, tap one end of the shaft sharply on a hard surface. Depending which end you tap and how hard you tap it, the setting will increase or decrease by the merest fraction.

With the setting right, wedge one end of the timber into the angle of a bench hook, place the stock of the gauge firmly against the timber's edge and holding it there, score the wood from the width line to the end. You'll find this easier if, rather than digging the spur right into the wood, you merely drag it across the surface. Score identical lines on the other side and the end.

Use a pencil to shade the areas on each piece of wood that will form the waste (the top of one, the bottom of the other), then grip the first piece upright in a vice. The lower down you can get it the better. If you can't get it low, back it with a piece of scrap wood to reduce vibration. Using a tenon saw, carefully saw down until you reach the width line — the first one you marked. The golden rule of sawing any kind of joint is to saw on the waste side of the marked line (it's *always* better to saw or chisel off too little rather than too much since you can always take off a little more but you can never put it back). And remember that the closer the fit, the

MAKING A CORNER HALVING JOINT

1 First mark the width of each piece of wood on the other. Then, using a knife and square, continue these width lines round all four sides of each piece.

2 To mark the thickness line, set a marking gauge to half the thickness of the wood and, holding the stock firmly against one edge, scribe the line.

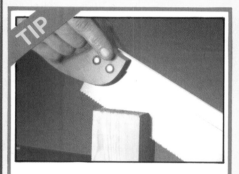

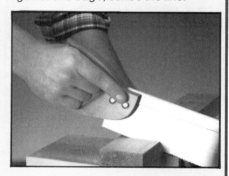

3 It's easier to start sawing at an angle, then gradually bring the saw to the horizontal. Keep the wood gripped firmly in the vice until you're finished.

4 Transfer the wood to a bench hook and cut down along the width line to remove the waste wood. Be sure to cut on the waste side of the guide line.

5 Smooth both parts to be joined with glasspaper and apply adhesive. Clamp together with a G-cramp until dry, protecting the wood with scrap timber.

6 When the adhesive has set, drill holes for reinforcing wood screws or dowels. If using screws, countersink the hole to take the screw head.

stronger the joint will end up. Basically, it should fit like a hand in a glove.

Remove the wood from the vice, put it on a bench hook and cut down along the width line to release the waste wood. Again make sure you cut on the waste side of the line and be prepared to make final adjusments with a chisel. Treat the second piece of wood in exactly the same way, then bring the two together and check the fit.

You can use either a chisel or a piece of glasspaper to take off any unevenness in the timber, although it'll be quicker to use a chisel to clear out the edges so that the corners are absolutely square. When the pieces finally fit neatly, spread adhesive on both faces of the joint and hold them in place with a G-cramp (protecting the wood's surface with scrap timber) until the glue has set. Remove the cramp, and add any re-

Ready Reference

WHERE TO USE HALVING JOINTS

Halving joints are usually used for making frameworks. Here you can see which joint to use where, and how each one is assembled.

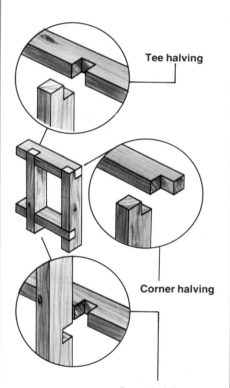

Tee halving

Corner halving

Cross halving

TOOLS FOR HALVING JOINTS

For measuring and marking: use a *handyman's knife* rather than a pencil for marking; use a *marking gauge* on each face of the joint – it'll be more accurate than using a tape measure; a *try-square* ensures accurate squaring off.
For cutting: use a *tenon saw* and a broad-blade *chisel* (25mm/1in) for cutting out cross halvings.

TIP: LABELLING JOINT PARTS

Avoid mixing up the pairs of joints by labelling the two parts with a letter and a number as soon as you cut them.

MAKING A CROSS HALVING JOINT

1 *First mark out the waste area to be removed, then cut down the width lines with a tenon saw.*

2 *Hold the timber in a vice or against a bench hook and remove the waste by chiselling at a slight upward angle.*

3 *Do the same on the other side until there's a 'pyramid' of waste in the middle. Gradually flatten this.*

4 *When nearing the thickness line, hold the cutting edge at an angle to the wood grain. Trim fibres in the corners.*

The next step is to turn the wood round and slope the other edge to leave a sort of pyramid of waste. With that done, pushing the chisel through the wood rather than hitting it, gradually flatten off the pyramid until you have brought it level with the half-way lines. You'll get a neater finish here if, in the final stages, you work with the chisel's blade flat but at an angle to the grain of the wood. Finally, again pushing the chisel, remove any ragged fibres lodged in the angles of the housing.

Once you've sawn and chiselled out the housing in the second piece of wood, the next step is to try fitting the two together. Don't try forcing them if they don't quite fit — you're in danger of splitting the wood. Instead, carefully chisel off a fraction more wood, bit by bit, until you can fit the pieces together without undue force. If, on the other hand, you've cut the housing too wide so the fit is very loose, you'll have to add some re-inforcement like screws or dowels, and fill in the gaps with a wood filler, stopping or a mixture of fine sawdust and PVA adhesive. It's not worth trying to add a wedge unless the gap is very wide (over 6mm/¼in) because the result can be very messy.

Making a mitre joint
With wood that's square or rectangular in section, the first job is to make sure that both pieces are absolutely squarely cut. Use the try-square to check this — if they're not, it's better to cut another piece of wood than attempt to make adjustments. Next, place one piece on top of the other to form a right angle. Mark an internal and external corner on both, then take them apart and carry the marks across the edge with a knife and try square. Join up the marks on each piece of wood — this will give sawing lines at 45°. Mark the waste side of each with a pencil.

Wood that is raised on one side (eg, mouldings for picture frames) cannot be marked in the same way as the pieces won't sit flat on each other. The easiest way is to mark the

inforcing screws or dowels that may be needed, drilling pilot holes first.

Making cross halving joints
The difference between cross halving joints and corner halving joints is that you cannot remove the waste using only a saw. You have to make a 'housing' and for this you need a chisel (see Housing Joints on pages 120-123 for more details).

Saw down the width lines to the halfway mark and make additional saw cuts in between to break up the waste — these can be the same width as the chisel blade to make chipping out easier. Grip the work in a vice, or on a bench hook, and now use the chisel to remove the waste. This is done in four stages. Guiding the chisel blade bevel uppermost with one hand and striking the handle with the palm of your other hand — for this job your hand is better than a mallet — reduce the edge of the timber nearest to you to a shallow slope ending a fraction above the halfway line. Don't try to remove all the wood in one go or it will split. Remove just a sliver at a time.

MAKING MITRES

1 *With square or rectangular wood, cut ends absolutely square and stack to form a right angle. Then mark the inner and outer corners on both pieces.*

2 *Carry lines down each edge with knife and try square, and score a line between corner marks to create an angle of 45°. Shade waste in pencil.*

3 *Press the wood against the bench hook and keep the saw at a shallow angle. Cut the diagonal, using the line on the edge to keep the saw vertical.*

THE SIMPLE MITRE

1 *The ends of two battens are cut to 45° and, when fixed together, make a 90° angle in this simplest of mitre joints, ideal for picture framing.*

2 *With thick timber frames, use corrugated steel fasteners driven into the back of mitre joints, where they will not be seen from the front.*

3 *Another method of strengthening a fairly thick mitre joint from behind is to pin triangles of plywood across the corner, out of sight.*

4 *Ready-made angle brackets with pre-drilled, countersunk screw holes make a quick, rigid and hidden fixing for two mitred battens in a frame.*

point of the mitre (the corner point) and then to use a simple *mitre block* to cut the angle. A mitre block not only helps you support the piece of wood (like a bench hook) but also has saw cuts at 45° in the back face to guide the saw. Then you only have to line up the mitre point on the wood with the saw now set at the correct angle. You can make a mitre block yourself — see *Ready Reference*.

Mitre aids

There are other devices available to help you cut mitres accurately. A proprietary *jointing jig*, for example, guides the saw either at right angles or at 45°; a *mitre box* is like a mitre block but has an extra side so that the whole length of the saw is kept in line.

Without these devices, getting the angles right isn't easy — but if necessary you can use a bench hook, driving in two nails so the wood is held against the block and the line of cutting is free of the bench hook. This is not as easy as using one of the other methods. Mark the wood so you know the sawing line, then place it in the mitre block, box or jig, to line up with the appropriate groove to guide the saw. If the wood you are cutting is very thin, put some blocks of scrap wood under the device to bring it up to a reasonable height. Insert a tenon saw into the guide slot and, holding it level, saw away.

There are only two things that can go

wrong. If the block is old, the 'guide' cut may have widened, resulting in an inaccurate cut. A larger tenon saw may help, but really the only answer is to hold the saw as steady as possible. The other common error when cutting mouldings and the like is to cut two mitres the same — that is two right-handed or left-handed angles, instead of one of each. This can be avoided by always marking the waste on the wood, and checking that the saw is in the correct guide slot before you begin.

Clean up the cut ends with glasspaper, taking care not to alter the angle, and glue and cramp the joint together. For frames, special mitre cramps are available, but you again make up your own. From scrap wood, cut four L-shaped blocks, and drill a hole at an angle through the point of each L. Feed a single piece of string through the holes of all four blocks, position the blocks at the corners of the frame and tie the string into a continuous loop. To tighten up, twist the string around a stick, and keep twisting the stick to draw the blocks together. You can then wedge the stick against the frame to stop it untwisting until the adhesive has set.

There are three ways to strengthen mitres — with timber connectors, plywood triangles or metal angle repair irons. For frames they should be fitted from behind, either by glueing, or glueing and pinning (see the photographs above).

MAKING A MITRE BLOCK

Mitre blocks and boxes already have 45° angle cuts made as a saw guide. Rather than buying one, you can make one that's used in the same way as a bench hook. You'll need:
● a piece of 19mm (¾in) plywood measuring about 250 x 150mm (10 x 6in)
● a 250mm (10in) length of 50 x 50mm (2 x 2in) softwood – or hardwood such as beech if available
● a 250mm (10in) length of 50 x 25mm (2 x 1in) softwood.

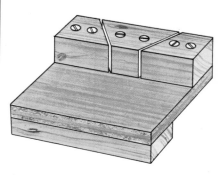

Glue and screw together as shown in the diagrams, then
● use a combination square, or make a template by folding a square piece of paper in half diagonally, as a guide for the 45° angle saw cuts
● square the lines down both faces of the block, and cut the slots with a tenon saw.

MAKING A MITRE CRAMP

You can make a simple cramp for small mitred frames from 4 L-shaped softwood blocks. Drill holes through one leg of each block, thread string through holes and tie tightly to hold blocks against frame corners.

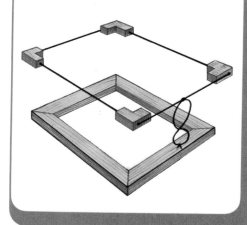

MAKING JOINTS WITH DOWELS

Called wood pins or pegs, dowels are lengths of hardwood with an important role to play in simple carpentry. They can be a decorative part of joints made with them, or be there for strength alone. Few tools are needed but the secret of success lies in using them accurately.

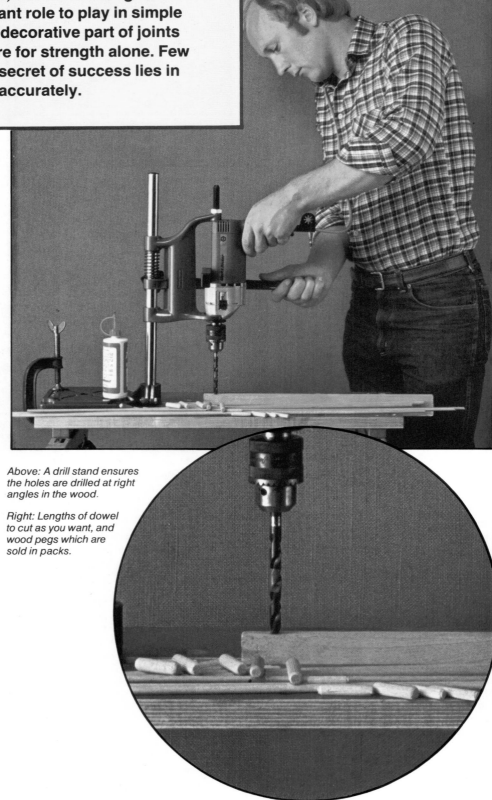

There are two basic ways in which you can use dowels in woodworking joints. You can drive a dowel through such joints as a half lap instead of using a nail or screw, or you can use them to make joints in their own right by drilling holes in one piece of wood, glueing in dowels, and then slotting these into corresponding holes in the second piece.

The dowel joint proper is used mostly in furniture making where it provides a neat joint of great strength without intricate cutting and without the need for unsightly reinforcement. Dowels can also be used to repair furniture.

In any joint, the size of the dowel is very important. Use a small one in a big joint and it won't have sufficient strength; use one that's too large and the holes you drill to accommodate it will weaken the wood. Ideally you should choose dowels which are no more than one third the thickness of the timber into which they will be fixed.

The thickness of the wood must be considered, too, for the dowels must have sufficient space between them and at each side otherwise when they're hit home or pushed into their corresponding holes the wood will split. So follow the carpenter's 'one third rule' and mark the width as well as the thickness into three (ie, a 9mm/⅜in dowel will need at least the same amount on both sides of it). And don't forget that planed wood can be up to 5mm less all round than the dimensions you ordered, and three into this size might not give you enough room for a successful joint.

Types of joints

There are different types of dowel joint. The simplest and easiest to make is the *through* dowel joint in which the dowel peg passes right through one piece of timber and into the other, sometimes passing through this as well if it's thin enough. Because in either case the ends of the dowels show, they are often used as a decorative feature of the article you're making.

If you don't want the ends of the dowels to be seen, you must make a *stopped* joint. In

Above: A drill stand ensures the holes are drilled at right angles in the wood.

Right: Lengths of dowel to cut as you want, and wood pegs which are sold in packs.

JOINTS MADE WITH DOWELS

The through dowel joint ready for assembly. The dowels are firmly embedded in one piece and will pass right through the other.

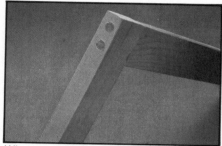

When assembled the through joint shows up the dowels. Cut them a little longer so after cramping they can be planed flush with the wood.

The stopped joint has dowels in one piece which will go into the other far enough to ensure rigidity but won't be seen on the other side.

A close fit for the finished stopped joint. When drilling the holes they should be slightly deeper than the dowel to hold any excess adhesive.

Mitred dowel joints can be tricky to make as you can't use the 'pin' method (see next page) for marking up because of the 45° angle.

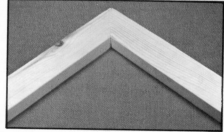

The hidden strength in this joint is the two different lengths of dowel. Very effective for frames where you don't want reinforcement to be seen.

A halving or half lap joint made at a corner can either be glued and screwed or, if it will be on show, made secure with dowels which fit into holes placed like spots on a dice.

The completed dowelled halving joint gives one overall look of wood. The same effect can be achieved by topping countersunk screws with dowel pellets cut from an offcut of the wood.

Jem Grischotti

MARKING UP

1 With wood that's rectangular or square in section, use a marking gauge to make the central line on the edge where the dowels will go.

2 Divide this central line into three, then draw two lines at right angles.

TIP

3 Lightly tap small panel pins into the wood at the two centre points. Snip off their heads leaving about 3mm (¹/₈in) protruding.

4 Holding the second piece of timber firmly against a bench hook or edge of the try-square, press the pins in to mark the drill positions (inset).

Leave the pins slightly proud of the surface and snip off their heads with pliers. Bring the two pieces of wood together in the correct joint position, and the heads of the pins will mark where the holes are to be bored in the second piece of timber. Remove the pins with pincers before drilling.

Where you are joining two horizontal rails to an upright at a corner, you should stagger the holes, otherwise the dowels will clash inside the upright.

Cutting holes

Holes for the dowels can be made either with a hand drill or an electric drill. In each case, obviously, the bit used must match the diameter of the dowel. The main difficulty is that you must ensure the bit is truly at right angles to the timber you are drilling, or a dowel that protrudes from one hole will not fit snugly into the hole in the matching timber.

You can use an electric drill held in a drill stand to guarantee that the bit is truly at right angles to the timber. Or where the timber is too large for this you can use a dowelling jig to ensure accuracy. Where you are cutting a through dowel joint, you can avoid this problem by cramping both pieces of wood together in a vice and boring through both.

For stopped joints, the hole you bore should be slightly deeper than the depth to which the dowel penetrates, to leave a small reservoir for any excess glue that is not squeezed out along the groove. A depth gauge ensures this. Various types for both hand and electric drills are available but you can improvise by making your own. Either stick a bit of tape on the bit's shank, carefully positioned so that the distance between its lower edge and the end of the drill exactly equals the depth of the hole required. Or you can take a length of timber – 25mm (1in) or 38mm (1½in) square according to the diameter of the dowel – and bore a hole right through its length. Cut this timber to length so that when it is slipped onto the bit's shank, the part of the bit left protruding will cut a hole of the right depth. In both cases you should take your measurement to the cutting end of the drill only – not to any threaded or shaped lead-in point.

For a stopped dowel joint, drill holes so the dowels will penetrate each piece of timber by between one-half and two-thirds of the timber's thickness.

Fixing and finishing dowels

Always check first that the joint is a good fit and is accurately square before applying PVA adhesive. You can then squirt adhesive into the holes, but since you risk applying too much this way, it is better to brush the

---

this the peg doesn't go right through either piece of timber. This is perhaps the most common dowel joint.

Joint shapes

Dowels can be used to make joints of various types, including L-joints, T-joints and X-joints between rails or boards, and three-way joints between rails and posts, as in furniture-making. They can also be used to reinforce edge-to-edge joints between boards, for example when making a drawer.

Cutting dowels

Cut dowels to length with a fine-toothed tenon saw, holding the dowels in a bench hook or a vice. For through joints, cut one dowel slightly longer than the combined thicknesses of the timbers, so that the ends can be trimmed flush after the joint is assembled. For stopped joints, cut the dowels slightly shorter than the combined depths of the holes into which they fit, and lightly chamfer the ends using glasspaper, a chisel or a proprietary dowel sharpener (which works just like a pencil sharpener).

Dowels need a shallow groove cut in their sides to allow excess adhesive to squeeze out as the joints are assembled. With much

practice you can do this with a chisel or tenon saw (having cramped it lengthways in a workbench), but it is probably easier to buy grooved dowel in the first place – in lengths you cut to size yourself, or for small jobs as pre-packed pegs. If buying pegs make sure you choose ones that correspond with the bit size for your drill.

Marking hole positions

First, use a try-square to check that the meeting faces or ends of the timber to be joined are cut perfectly square and are of the same thickness. You can then mark the positions for the dowel holes. Set a marking gauge to half the width of the timber, and mark a line down the middle of the end of one length of timber. Determine exactly where on this line the centre of the holes will be – the ideal is that they should be from 25mm (1in) to 50mm (2in) apart and never nearer than 19mm (³/₄in) from the edges. Using a try-square, draw lines across the gauge line to mark the exact centres of the holes.

To mark matching holes in corresponding positions on the second piece of timber use the following method to ensure accuracy. Drive small panel pins into the first piece at the positions you've marked for the holes.

DRILLING HOLES

1 *To ensure that holes will be in exactly opposite positions on a through joint, drill both pieces of wood at the same time.*

2 *The depths you have to go to for a dowel joint can be marked on the bit with a piece of tape, allowing a little extra at both ends for glue.*

3 *Another way of making sure you don't go too deep is by making a depth gauge from a scrap of timber. Or you can buy a proprietary gauge.*

4 *A dowelling jig has holes for different sized bits. When you cramp it over the wood use spare timber to prevent the screw marking the wood.*

adhesive onto the dowel before tapping it into place with a mallet — you can use a hammer but you should protect the dowel with a block of wood. You should also apply adhesive to the meeting faces of the timber.

The glued joints should be cramped until the adhesive has set.

With through joints and halving joints, you now saw off the bulk of the protruding dowel and use a block plane to trim the end flush. You can use an ordinary plane for this, but it must be set for a very fine cut. Smooth off any remaining roughness with glasspaper.

If using dowel pellets, hit them into place over the countersunk screws (with the ones you've cut yourself make sure the grain follows that of the wood). Plane off excess after the adhesive has dried.

MAKING THE JOINT

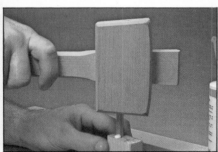

1 *First check that the dowel fits snugly, but not too tightly. Then apply adhesive and gently tap it into place with a mallet.*

2 *After cramping to allow the adhesive to set, finish off a through joint by planing away the excess along the side of the wood.*

Dowelling jig: Buck & Ryan *Jem Grischotti* *Block plane: Stanley Tools* *Jem Grischotti*

RULES FOR DRILLING HOLES
● make them the same diameter as the dowels
● they should be a little deeper than the dowel's length
● slightly countersink these where the pieces of wood meet

TIP: DOWELLING JIG
With a drill use a dowelling jig so the holes will be straight and square.

WHAT CAN GO WRONG?
The most common problems are:
● the dowels being too tight. Forcing the joint together causes the wood to split – so always check the fit first
● the joint being forced out of alignment because the holes were drilled out of line with one another – always check the alignment before finally applying the adhesive

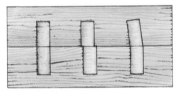

MITRED DOWEL JOINTS
● use a mitre box for accuracy
● place mitred pieces together in a cramp and mark them at the same time
● the dowel at the outer corner should be shorter than the one at the inner corner

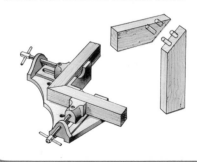

HOUSING JOINTS

If you're putting together a bookcase or installing shelves in any other sort of furniture, then housing joints are the ones to use for attaching the shelves to the uprights. Here's how to make them.

Housing joints are very useful in constructing drawers, door frames and partition walls, among other things: but they're indispensable for fixing shelves neatly into uprights. The joint gets its name because the end of the shelf fits into a square-bottomed channel or 'housing' across the upright. A basic housing joint is as simple as that, and very easy to cut and assemble. What's more, it's ideal for supporting the weight of a shelf and its contents – it resists twisting, and it looks much more professional than the metal brackets or other fittings which can do the same job.

Such fittings are readily available and often easy to use, but if your design is modern, they'll tend to spoil its clean lines; and if it's traditional, they'll naturally be inappropriate. They will never give the unobtrusive and craftsmanlike finish which you can obtain from carefully designed and made housing joints.

Types of housing joint

There are a few variations, and each has its own purpose. A 'stopped' housing joint is completely invisible; you can't see the connection between shelf and upright at all, because (unlike the basic 'through' housing joint) its housing stops about 20mm (¾in) short of the front of the upright. You can also cut out a step in the front of the shelf to allow it to fit flush with the upright just as in a through housing joint, and so get the best of both worlds.

A 'barefaced' housing joint is a little more complicated. You still slot the shelf into the upright – but this time you also cut away a step or 'rebate' across the end of the shelf to form a sort of tongue (with one 'bare face'). So the housing into which it fits has to be correspondingly narrower than the shelf thickness. This type of joint is used at corners, where you can't cut an ordinary housing; and its stepped shape helps to keep the structure rigid. It can also be used with the rebate in the upright where you want unbroken woodgrain across the top surface of the horizontal.

Strongest of all is the dovetail housing

joint. For this one, the housing has sloping (undercut) sides, and the end of the shelf is shaped to fit – which means it can't be pulled out sideways. This is an attraction where you expect furniture to come in for rough treatment, (eg, being dragged across the floor). However, it's tricky to cut without power-tool assistance, and in practice the do-it-yourselfer will seldom find it really necessary.

It's worth saying here that even the best-made housing joint is only as strong as the shelf. If you're planning shelf storage, you have to think about what the shelf is made of, its thickness, its length and how much weight you want it to carry. A thin shelf bends easily, and it's unwise to try to span a gap of more than 1,200mm (4ft), at the very most, without some support in the middle. Even then, a full load of books will cause sagging.

Making a housing joint

Even with hand tools, housing joints are among the easiest to cut. For a basic through housing joint, you don't need to touch the shelf at all. You just mark out the position of the housing in the upright, cut down the housing sides with a tenon saw, and pare

away the waste with a chisel and wooden mallet (see page 114 for details). The only difficulty, as in all carpentry, is to make sure that your marking, sawing and chiselling are always careful and accurate.

A stopped housing takes a little longer to cut, but only because you need to hollow out its stopped end first, to make sawing easier. You may also need to remove a small notch or 'shoulder' from the shelf, which is easily done with a tenon saw and perhaps a chisel too.

For a barefaced housing joint, the housing is cut in the same way as a basic housing. Cutting the rebate in the shelf is another job for tenon saw and chisel.

Using power tools

A power router is an integral tool with a chuck that accepts a wide range of special bits for cutting grooves and mouldings quickly and accurately. It saves a lot of time when making housing joints, and eliminates both sawing and chiselling. Or you can use a circular saw, setting it for a very shallow cut and running it across the upright where you want the housing to be – first clamping on a batten to act as a guide. Because the saw-

BASIC HOUSING JOINT

1 *Use your knife and try-square to square a mark across the inner face of the upright where the top of the shelf is to go.*

2 *Measure up the full shelf thickness with a carpenter's rule or a flexible tape measure. As always, try for absolute accuracy.*

3 *Mark this distance on the upright, working down from the first line to give the housing width; square the mark across in pencil only.*

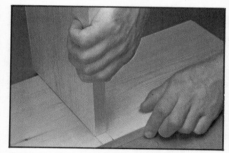

4 *Place the shelf between the two lines to check them. If necessary, re-draw the second. When that's right, go over it with knife and try-square.*

5 *Use a rule to set your marking gauge to ⅓ the thickness of the upright, which is the usual depth of a housing for a strong and rigid joint.*

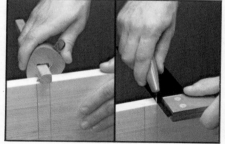

6 *With the gauge, mark the housing depth on the upright's edges. Then use a knife to square the marks for the housing sides to depth across the edges.*

7 *When cutting the sides to depth, cramp on a batten to prevent the saw from wandering sideways.*

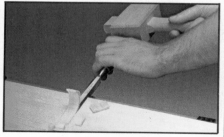

8 *Remove the waste with a chisel, working from both ends on long housings. Pare along the sides if necessary to clean them up.*

Jem Grischotti

Ready Reference

WHICH HOUSING GOES WHERE

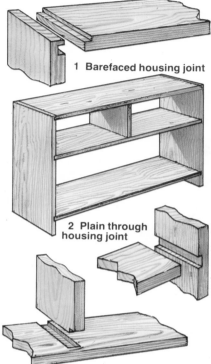

1 **Barefaced housing joint**

2 **Plain through housing joint**

3 **Stopped housing joint with shoulder**

THE TOOLS YOU'LL NEED

A tenon saw: for cutting the sides of housings, rebates and shoulders.
A bevel-edged chisel: the same width as the housing, plus a wooden mallet.
A hand router: is useful for smoothing the bottom of the housing.
Marking gauge, knife, pencil and try-square: for accurate setting-out.

POWER TOOL OPTIONS

A power router: ideal for cutting all types of housing quickly and easily.

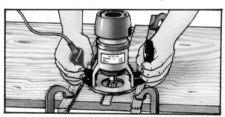

A circular saw will cut an ordinary housing very well – but you'll need to make several passes with it across the timber to cut the housing.

STOPPED HOUSING WITH SHOULDER

1 After marking out the housing on the upright (except on the front edge), mark where it stops, about 19-25mm (³/₄-1in) inside the front edge.

2 With the marking gauge still at the same setting, mark the shoulder depth across the shelf end and a little way down each of its faces.

3 Set the gauge to ¹/₃ the thickness of the upright, and mark the housing depth on its back edge only. Bring the side marks down to meet it.

4 Use the same setting to mark the shoulder width on the front edge and both faces of the shelf, meeting the marks you've made for the depth.

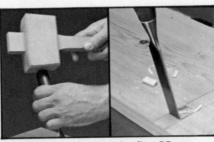

5 Roughly chisel out the first 25mm (1in) or so of the stopped end of the housing – across the grain and up to the sides, then back towards the end.

6 Cut the sides of the housing with a tenon saw. You'll need to use short careful strokes so as not to bang against its inner end.

7 Clear out the housing with a mallet and chisel, inching forwards at an angle if the chisel won't reach all the way in when held flat.

8 Saw down into the front edge of the shelf until you reach the marked depth of the shoulder, being careful not to overshoot.

9 Chisel into the endgrain to remove the waste and complete the shoulder; or you can use a saw – but again, don't cut too deep.

blade is narrower than the housing you're cutting out, you'll need to make several parallel, overlapping cuts.

Putting it together

When you assemble the joint before glueing, to see if it fits, you may think that it's too tight and you need to pare away wood from the housing or the shelf.

But be sure not to overdo this – and be careful where you remove it from. A shaving off the wrong place can allow the end of the shelf to rise or fall so that it's no longer level.

If, on the other hand, the joint turns out to be very loose, you'll need thin slivers of wood or veneer to pack it out.

For maximum tightness, strength and squareness, a housing joint should really be glued, then cramped together while the adhesive sets. Where a shelf or shelves fit between a pair of uprights, as usually happens, your best plan is to glue and cramp the whole structure up at once, so as to get it all square in one go. Use sash cramps (long bars of steel with two adjustable jaws) and simply place the structure between them, with the shelf running along their length, and blocks of scrap wood positioned on the outside of the uprights to protect them from the pressure of the jaws. You'll probably have to borrow or hire the sash-cramps. When using them, you need to

check the structure constantly for squareness, as cramping, unless done correctly, can cause distortion.

You can always reinforce a housing joint by nailing through the outside of the upright and into the endgrain of the shelf, concealing the heads by punching them in and plugging the holes with wood filler.

On the whole, screws are best avoided, since they grip badly in endgrain; but for a chipboard shelf you can use special chipboard screws – or ordinary wood screws each driven into a special plastic plug, or 'bush', which is pressed into a pre-drilled hole in the end of the shelf. You can disguise screwheads with plastic covers.

Jem Grischotti

BAREFACED HOUSING JOINT

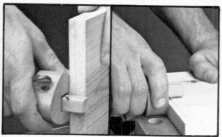

1 At ⅓ the shelf thickness, mark the rebate depth along its end and across its edges; likewise mark across the upright's edges and inner face.

2 At ⅓ the upright thickness (very likely the same as the shelf thickness), mark your rebate width across the top face and both edges of the shelf.

3 Saw out the rebate depth across the shelf with a tenon saw, using careful strokes to keep it the right side of the line.

4 Chisel out the rebate width along the endgrain. You'll get a more accurate result if you do it in several goes rather than all at once.

5 Measure the full shelf thickness and set your marking gauge to that measurement by holding it against the rule.

6 Pressing the gauge against the end of the upright, mark across its face and edges where the bottom of the shelf will be positioned.

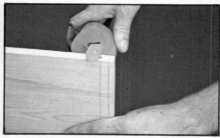

7 Mark the depth of the housing on the back edge of the upright, only ⅓ of the way across: any further and you'll weaken the joint.

8 Cut the housing just like the basic one, taking care not to break off the end. After glueing, nail through into the tongue for extra rigidity.

Jem Grischotti

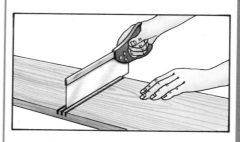

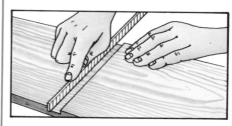
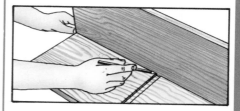
123

SHELVING: THE BASICS

There are lots of ways of putting up shelves. Some systems are fixed, others adjustable – the choice is yours. Here's how both types work, and how to get the best from each.

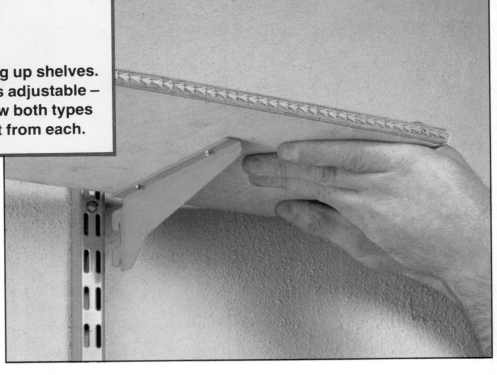

Deciding how much shelving you'll need is always tricky – because, the more shelves you have, the more you'll find to go on them! So it's always wise to add an extra 10 per cent to the specification when you start planning.

Think carefully about what you want to store and display, and try to categorise it by size and weight. The size part is fairly easy. Concentrate first on the depth (from front to back) and length; a collection of paperback books, for instance, might need 3.5m (10ft) of 150mm (6in) deep shelves. Having the shelves a bit deeper than you really need is always worthwhile, and if you add 10 per cent the length should look after itself.

Next, the heights in each grouping will tell you roughly how far apart the shelves must be. Most paperbacks are 175mm (7in) high – allow an extra 25mm (1in) for easy access and removal.

Finally, weight. The trouble here is that, even if you weigh what you'll be storing, you can't translate the result into shelf, bracket and fixing materials or sizes. Instead, think in terms of light, moderately heavy and very heavy. Items such as the TV and stereo, while not especially weighty, are best treated as very heavy, because it would be nothing short of disastrous if a shelf did give way under them!

Shelf design

Where you put the shelves affects the amount of storage you can gain, how you build them, and the overall look of the room itself. This last may not be important in a workshop, for instance, but in a living room, where the shelves may well be the focal point, a bad decision can be serious.

The obvious spot for shelving is against a continuous wall. This offers most scope to arrange the shelves in an interesting and attractive way. An alcove is another possibility. Shelving here is neat, and easily erected; it is a very good way of using an otherwise awkward bit of space. A corner has similar advantages if you make triangular shelves to fit – though they're really only suitable for displaying plants or favourite ornaments.

Planning it out

If appearance matters and you're putting up a lot of shelves, a good way to plan is by making a scale drawing of the whole scheme to see how it looks. Then check for detail. If your TV has an indoor aerial, make sure you have room to adjust it. With stereo systems, ensure the shelf is deep enough to take all the wiring spaghetti at the back. And do think about the heights of the shelves from the floor (see *Ready Reference*).

Finally, make sure you provide adequate support for the shelves and the weight they'll be carrying. There is no very precise method of gauging this, but you won't go wrong if you remember that for most household storage a shelf needs support at least every 750mm (30in) along its length. This will usually be enough even with chipboard, which is the weakest of shelving materials. But bowing may still be a problem, so for items in the 'very heavy' category it's advisable to increase the number of supports by reducing the space between them.

Which material?

Chipboard is usually the most economical material, and if properly supported is strong enough for most shelving. It can be fairly attractive, too, since you can choose a type with a decorative wood veneer or plastic finish. These come in a variety of widths – most of them designed with shelving in mind.

Natural timber, though more costly and sometimes prone to warping, is an obvious alternative. You may have difficulty obtaining some timber in boards over 225mm (9in) wide, but narrower widths are readily available. For wider shelves, another way is to make up the shelf width from narrower pieces. An easy method is to leave gaps between the lengths and brace them with others which run from front to back on the underside, forming a slatted shelf.

Blockboard, plywood and medium-density fibreboard are also worth considering for use as shelving. All three are stronger than chipboard and have a more attractive surface which can be painted or varnished without trouble. However, in the thicknesses you need – at least 12mm (1½in) – plywood is relatively expensive, blockboard is cheaper, and chipboard cheaper still. All these man-made boards need to have their edges disguised to give a clean finish. An easy yet effective way to do this is just to glue and pin on strips of timber moulding or 'beading'. Also remember that the cheapest way to buy any of these boards is in large sheets (approximately 2.4m x 1.2m/8ft x 4ft), so it's most economical to plan your shelves in lengths and widths that can be cut from a standard size sheet.

Shelves needn't be solid, though. If you want them extra-thick, for appearance or strength, you can make them up from a timber frame covered with a thin sheet material. Hardboard is cheap, but thin plywood gives a more attractive edge; alternatively use a timber edging strip.

BRACKET SHELVING

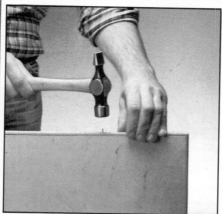

1 *If your shelves are of man-made board, a good way to give them neat edges is to pin on decorative 'beading', mitred at the corners.*

2 *Begin by screwing the shorter arm of the bracket to the shelf. Position it squarely and in such a way that the shelf will lie snugly against the wall.*

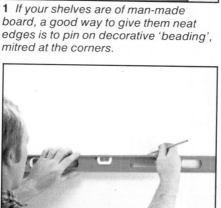

3 *Using a spirit level as a guide, mark a pencil line along the wall at the height where you want the top of the shelf to be positioned.*

4 *Hold the shelf, complete with brackets, against this line, and mark with a pencil through the screw holes in the brackets, so you know where to drill.*

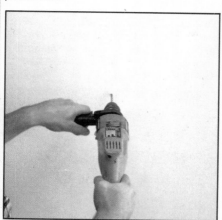

5 *Drill holes in the wall with a power drill, using a masonry bit if necessary, and being sure to keep the drill straight. Then insert plastic plugs.*

6 *Hold the shelf in position, insert one screw in each bracket and tighten it halfway; then insert the others and tighten the whole lot up.*

Ready Reference

PLANNING SHELVES

When you design storage, plan ahead and think about *how* you're going to use it.

Height. Keep everyday items well within reach. That means between 750 and 1500mm (30 and 60in) off the ground.
Depth. Shelves that are deepest (from front to back) should be lower, so you can see and reach to the back.
Spacing. An inch or two over the actual height of the objects means you can get your hand in more easily.

HOW TO SPACE BRACKETS

Space brackets according to the shelf thickness. Heavy loads (left) need closer brackets than light loads (right).

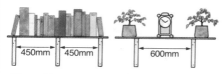

12mm (½in) chipboard

12mm (½in) plywood
19mm (¾in) chipboard

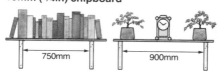

19mm (¾in) plywood

ADJUSTABLE SHELVING

1 *Metal uprights come in a range of sizes, but occasionally they may need shortening. If so, you can easily cut them down with a hacksaw.*

2 *After using your level to mark the height for the tops of the uprights, measure along it and mark out the spacings between them.*

3 *Hold each of the uprights with its top at the right height, and mark through it onto the wall for the position of the uppermost screw hole only.*

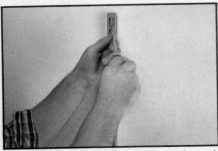

4 *Remove the upright, drill the hole and plug it if necessary. Then replace the upright, and fit the screw – but don't tighten it completely.*

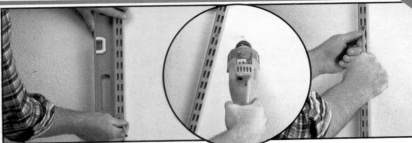
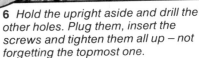

TIP

5 *With the upright loose, hold a level against it and adjust it till it's vertical. Then mark through it for the other screw positions.*

6 *Hold the upright aside and drill the other holes. Plug them, insert the screws and tighten them all up – not forgetting the topmost one.*

7 *Now you can screw the bracket to the shelf, aligning it correctly and taking particular care over how it lines up at the back edge.*

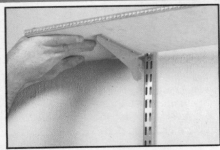

8 *One type of adjustable system uses brackets with lugs at the back. It's easiest to let these lugs project behind the shelf when screwing on brackets.*

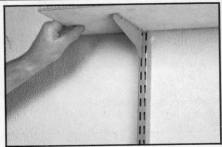

9 *The lugs simply hook into the slots in the uprights. Changing the shelf height is just a matter of unhooking them and moving them up or down.*

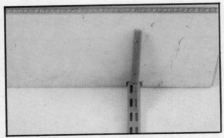

10 *If you want the back edge of the shelf right against the wall, notch it with a tenon saw and chisel to fit round the upright. Inset the bracket on the shelf.*

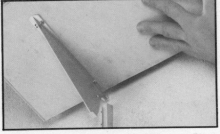

11 *The channel system is different. First of all, you engage the bracket's upper lug in the channel and slide it down, keeping the lower one clear.*

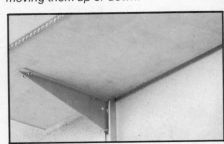

12 *When you reach the position you want, level the shelf and the bracket, so as to slide its lower lug into one of the pairs of slots down the upright.*

Fixing shelves

The simplest method of fixing shelves is directly to the wall, using brackets. L-shaped metal brackets of various sizes and designs are available everywhere – some plain and functional, some with attractive lacquered or enamelled finishes. It's just a question of choosing ones about 25mm (1in) less than the shelf depth, spacing them the right distance apart and screwing them to both shelf and wall.

If you're filling up your shelves with books, the support brackets won't be seen. But if you're using the shelves for ornaments, the brackets will be visible, so choose a style that blends. Alternatively, you can make up your own brackets from two pieces of timber butt-jointed into an L shape and braced with a diagonal strut or triangular block.

The fixing technique is the same either way. First you draw a line on the wall where the shelf is to go, using a spirit level. Next, fix the brackets to the shelf and put the whole assembly up against the line. Mark on to the wall through the pre-drilled screw holes in the brackets; then take the shelf away and drill holes in the wall, filling each with a plastic plug. Lastly, drive in one screw through each bracket; then insert the rest and tighten them all up.

Because the accuracy of this method relies largely on your ability to hold the shelf level against your line, you may find it easier to work the other way round. By fixing the brackets to the wall along the guide line, you can then drop the shelf into place and screw up into it through the brackets. This works, but you must position the brackets with great care, and avoid squeezing them out of position as you screw them into the wall. That isn't always easy. For one thing, many brackets don't have arms which meet at a neat right angle. They curve slightly, which makes it hard to align the top of the shelf-bearing arm with the line on the wall.

Making a firm fixing

Remember that the strength of all brackets depends partly on the length of their arms (particularly the one fixed to the wall) and partly on the strength of your fixing into the wall. The longer the wall arm in proportion to the shelf arm, the better; but it's also important to use adequate screws – 38mm (1½in) No 8s or 10s should do – and to plug the wall properly. In a hollow partition wall you really must make sure you secure the brackets to the wall's wooden framework and not just to the cladding. Even if you use plasterboard plugs or similar devices for the fixing, a lot of weight on the shelf will cause the brackets to come away from the cladding and possibly damage the wall.

Of course, there is a limit to how much weight the brackets themselves will take.

Under very wide shelves they may bend. With shelves that have heavy items regularly taken off and dumped back on, and shelves used as desk-tops, worktops and the like, the movement can eventually work the fixings loose. In such cases it's best to opt for what's called a cantilevered shelf bracket. Part of this is set into the masonry to give a very strong fixing indeed. Details of its installation vary from brand to brand, but you should get instructions when you buy.

Alcove shelving

All proprietary brackets are expensive. However, for alcove shelving there's a much cheaper alternative, and that is to use battens screwed to the wall. All you do is fix a 50 x 25mm (2 x 1in) piece of softwood along the back of the alcove, using screws driven into plastic plugs at roughly 450mm (18in) centres. Then screw similar ones to the side walls, making sure that they line up with the first. In both cases, getting the battens absolutely level is vital. In fact, it's best to start by drawing guidelines using a spirit level as a straight edge.

A front 'rail' is advisable where the shelf spans a wide alcove and has to carry a lot of weight. But there's a limit to what you can do. With a 50 x 25mm (2 x 1in) front rail and battens, all on edge, 1.5m (5ft) is the safe maximum width.

A front rail has another advantage because, as well as giving man-made boards a respectably thick and natural look, it also hides the ends of the side battens. So does stopping them short of the shelf's front edge and cutting the ends at an angle.

The shelf can be screwed or even just nailed to the battens to complete the job.

Movable shelves

Unfortunately, both brackets and battens have one big drawback: once they're fixed, they're permanent. So you might consider an adjustable shelving system which gives you the chance to move shelves up and down. Such systems consist of uprights, screwed to the wall, and brackets which slot into them at almost any point down the length.

There are two main types. In one, brackets locate in vertical slots in the uprights. The other has a continuous channel down each upright. You can slide brackets along it and lock them at any point along the way, where they stay put largely because of the weight of the shelf. With both types, brackets come in standard sizes suitable for shelf widths, and there's a choice of upright lengths to fulfil most needs.

Many proprietary shelving systems of this sort include a number of accessories to make them more versatile. These include book ends, shelf clips and even light fittings.

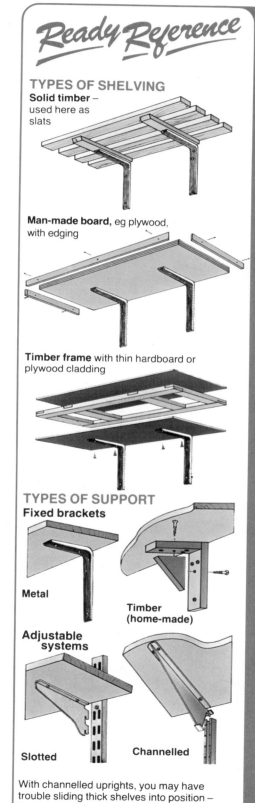

Ready Reference

TYPES OF SHELVING

Solid timber – used here as slats

Man-made board, eg plywood, with edging

Timber frame with thin hardboard or plywood cladding

TYPES OF SUPPORT
Fixed brackets

Metal

Timber (home-made)

Adjustable systems

Slotted

Channelled

With channelled uprights, you may have trouble sliding thick shelves into position – but you can always position the brackets first and screw the shelves to them afterwards, or not at all.

BUILDING CUPBOARDS IN ALCOVES

Built-in cupboards save you money because you use your walls instead of side, back and top panels. Fitting them neatly and snugly is just a matter of knowing the right methods.

Making freestanding storage furniture that's rigid and stable – even fairly simple box-type pieces – calls for accuracy, plus a certain amount of basic woodworking ability and design sense. It's certainly worth taking the trouble to acquire these. But you may be unsure of your skills, especially when it comes to large items – or perhaps you just don't want to take chances.

The answer is built-in units. These are almost sure to be structurally sound because they're anchored to the walls – and often to the floor and ceiling too. They don't usually require any joints more complex than halvings (see pages 112-115). And, of course, fitting storage facilites into alcoves and odd corners is an excellent way to make the most of available space.

But any built-in cupboard does face a disadvantage. The walls of your room will probably not be flat or true. Although (at least in modern homes) the masonry itself will be vertical, and walls will be square with one another, it's impossible to apply plaster to a uniform thickness over an entire wall, so there will be variations. This means you'll have to take some trouble to make your cupboard fit.

Working in an alcove
Let's suppose you're building a cupboard in an alcove – the most obvious place, and a very sensible one. What you need to know first is the alcove's width at its narrowest.

This is very hard to find accurately with a tape measure, because it's flexible and the casing gets in the way. Instead you can use 'pinch rods'. Improvise these from a couple of pieces of square-sectioned timber – say 25x25mm (1x1in) or 38x38mm (1½x1½in). Each should be longer than half the width of the alcove. Hold them together horizontally inside the alcove, and slide them until the end of each one meets a side wall.

Now move them up and down the alcove until you've found its narrowest part, and tilt them till you're sure they're level – that is, when they show the shortest width yet still have both ends touching the walls.

Then, grasping them tightly, draw a pencil line across both, so that you can re-assemble them in the correct position. Take them down from the wall and measure their combined length.

Making a frame
Your next job is to make a simple rectangular frame, to the overall width you've just measured. This consists of two cross pieces, plus two uprights which can be any height you choose – possibly dictated by the height of ready-made doors (such as louvre doors) if you plan to fit them.

You can use square or rectangular timber for the frame, making the corners with halving joints, glued together and then screwed from the inside. Keep checking the frame for squareness as you assemble it. To ensure it stays square during the rest of the job, tack battens of thin timber diagonally across two opposite corners.

Place the frame in the alcove where you want it, and fix it by drilling and screwing through the frame sides into wall plugs. Alternatively, if the frame is made of rectangular timber such as 50x25mm (2x1in), you can screw vertical battens to the wall at either side and fix the frame to them, with timber strips or plastic jointing blocks. Use a spirit level to make quite sure it's upright. If it leans forward, the doors will always tend to fall open; if it slopes backwards, they'll be

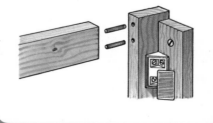

inclined to stay shut. And of course, the frame needs to be set truly horizontal too.

The frame probably won't fit exactly. If it's too wide, you can plane it down; take an equal amount off both sides. On the other hand, there may be gaps. Don't attempt to make the timber follow the contours of the wall if this is so.

If the gaps are narrower than about 5mm (³⁄₁₆in), you can stop them up with filler, which will be disguised with paint. A length of foam plastic draught strip, inset about 3mm (¹⁄₈in) back from the front, and inserted before you screw the frame to the wall, makes an excellent backing for the filler.

If you don't want a painted finish, glue and pin moulding (eg, quadrant) to the front of the frame so it hides the gaps. Hold it in position, mark it as best you can and shape it with a file; then re-position, re-mark and re-shape it till it hugs the wall tightly.

Wider gaps call for the insertion of packing strips of thin timber, plywood or hardboard before adding the moulding.

Supporting the top

If the cupboard doesn't reach to the ceiling, it will need a top. This can be of blockboard or plywood – painted, veneered or covered with plastic laminate if you wish. But, as always, proprietary veneered or laminated chipboard is a cheap and attractive alternative. If you decide on this, bear in mind that it comes in standard widths, with each long edge ready-finished. So, unless you're lipping the front edge yourself in any way, you need to fix the frame at a distance from the back wall that allows you to make use of one of these widths.

Think about the details beforehand: do you want the top to overhang the cupboard doors, or to project even further? The treatment of the front edge is one of the small points which make all the difference to the final appearance of the unit, so it's worth making sure you've got it right from the start. A few of the possibilities are shown in *Ready Reference*. Small decorative mouldings such as triangle, quadrant, astragal, ogee, scotia and even glass bead may come in handy as ways of giving the edge a slightly softer and more interesting look, and getting away from the functional effect of straight lines everywhere.

In any case, allow enough extra width for trimming the top panel to fit the contours of the back wall.

Supported on the frame at the front, the top rests at the back on a corresponding horizontal batten screwed to the wall. This must be at exactly the same height as the top of the frame. You can use a spirit level to achieve this. If your level is too small, place it on top of a straight length of wood.

For a cupboard that rises above eye level,

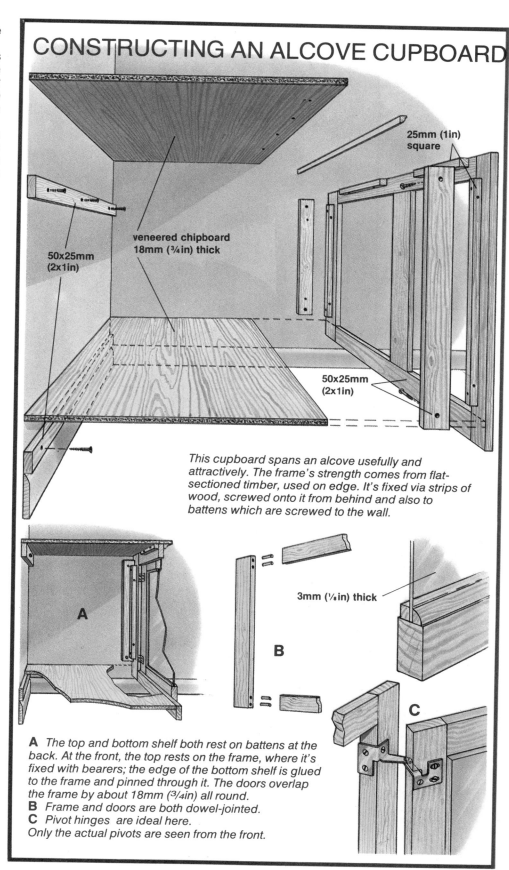

CONSTRUCTING AN ALCOVE CUPBOARD

25mm (1in) square

50x25mm (2x1in)

veneered chipboard 18mm (¾in) thick

50x25mm (2x1in)

This cupboard spans an alcove usefully and attractively. The frame's strength comes from flat-sectioned timber, used on edge. It's fixed via strips of wood, screwed onto it from behind and also to battens which are screwed to the wall.

A

B

3mm (¹⁄₈in) thick

C

A The top and bottom shelf both rest on battens at the back. At the front, the top rests on the frame, where it's fixed with bearers; the edge of the bottom shelf is glued to the frame and pinned through it. The doors overlap the frame by about 18mm (¾in) all round.
B Frame and doors are both dowel-jointed.
C Pivot hinges are ideal here.
Only the actual pivots are seen from the front.

MAKING THE FRAME

1 Cut 'pinch rods' to find the alcove width. Slide them apart till each meets a wall, mark across both, and measure their combined length.

2 Make up a front frame for the cupboard to this width. Use dowels or halving joints; glue them and if possible cramp the frame together.

TIP

3 If the side uprights overlap the cross members, not the other way round, they'll be easier to plane down later if necessary.

4 Cut two battens, and hold one vertically where you want it on the wall, allowing for frame and door thickness. Mark its position.

5 Screw this batten in place, using wall plugs, after making sure that it's not long enough to get in the way of the bottom shelf.

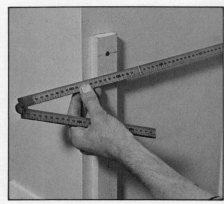

6 Measure its distance from the back wall, so you can position and fix another batten the same distance from the wall at the other side.

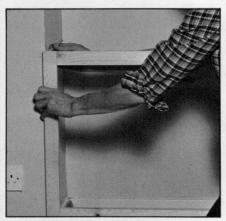

7 Place the frame in position, and mark it if it's too wide. Alternatively, it may need packing out with timber or thin board.

8 If the frame is too wide, plane a bit from both ends. Bevelling each edge inwards across the thickness will give an even easier fit.

9 Glue and screw a fixing block down each side of the frame, insetting it by the thickness of the battens you've fastened to the wall.

COMPLETING THE UNIT

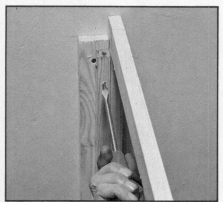

1 Re-position the frame, and glue and screw in the other direction through each fixing block, attaching it to the batten.

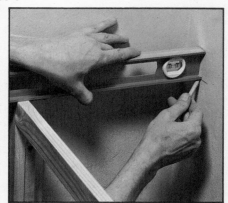

2 Use a level to mark on the back wall, in at least two places, the position of the bearer which will support the cupboard's top.

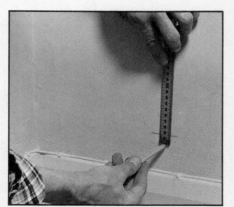

3 After making similar marks for the bottom shelf, add a second mark below each one, to indicate the shelf thickness accurately.

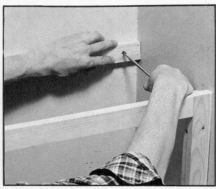

4 Screw the top bearer to the wall, keeping its upper edge against the pencil marks. Screw the bottom bearer against the lower set of marks there.

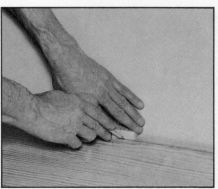

5 After checking the side walls and cutting each shelf to fit at either end, scribe the contours of the wall along its back edge.

6 Fit the top shelf into position. Fasten it to the cross-bearers with plastic jointing blocks, or more strips of wood glued and screwed.

you needn't even use chipboard for the top. Thin plywood or hardboard will do. However, hardboard should never span a greater distance than 450mm (18in) without support. This is bound to mean fitting an extra bearer or two from front to back, halved across the front cross piece and rear batten.

Fitting the top

Next, you need to make the top. First, use pinch rods to see if the alcove is the same width at front and back. If the angles are more or less square and the walls straight, go ahead and cut the top to size. Whatever you do, don't make it any smaller than the space; rather leave it a bit too big, then trim the back edge and one end with a plane, filing or Surforming where necessary to ensure that you have a perfect fit.

If, on the other hand, the end walls are well out of true, you'll have to make angled cuts at either end. Cut pieces of cardboard to fit by trial and error, then use them as templates to mark out the top panel before you saw it.

Lastly, note where the top needs trimming at the back. If the back wall is very bumpy, it's best to scribe the top to fit. That means holding it a bit less than 25mm (1in) from the wall, and placing a small block of 25mm (1in) thick timber there, with one face against the wall. Hold a pencil against it, and move both block and pencil along the top. This will give you a line on the board which follows the contours of the wall, so you can cut along it for a perfect fit.

The top can be held in place by screws driven up through the battens and frame if the timber is square in section, or otherwise through small strips of timber screwed to the inside faces of the frame and battens.

Fitting a bottom panel

A cupboard that stops short of the floor will need a bottom shelf panel, which should be measured and prepared in just the same way as the top. It rests on a batten screwed to the wall at the back, also like the top.

You can position this level with the top of the bottom cross piece in the frame, notching the panel at the front corners so it fits round the uprights and rests on the bottom cross piece. In that case it can act as a doorstop if you cut it short of the front. Or, cutting it even shorter, you can let it rest on a small additional bearer (say 25mm/1in square). This can be screwed to the inside of the cross piece, and positioned so that the panel is flush with the top of the cross piece. For the same result, you can simply glue and pin the front edge of the panel through the cross piece. Either way, you'll need to adjust the height of the rear batten accordingly.

Further possibilities

If you want shelves inside the cupboard, they too can rest on bearers screwed to the

7 *After positioning the bottom shelf, glue and pin into its front edge through the front cross-bearer, to give it extra rigidity.*

8 *A small moulding (eg, a glass bead), glued and pinned below the top overhang, improves its looks. Now add doors to the unit.*

walls at the back and sides. Alternatively, you can make them adjustable, in case your storage requirements change. Just use one of the proprietary systems described in pages 124-127.

If your cupboard reaches to the floor, you'll have to take account of the skirting board. One option is to take it off (for replacement or re-use), complete your cupboard, saw the skirting to length, and re-fix it to any stretches of wall that are visible outside the cupboard – and inside it, too, if you wish. The other possibility, where the skirting isn't too thick, is to scribe and cut away the frame of the cupboard to fit.

Full-height cupboards

An alcove cupboard that reaches to the ceiling as well as the floor presents its own problems. In theory you could build a frame to the correct size, slide it into position, and fix it in the way already described. But, since

it would be the same height as the room itself, it would be difficult to manoeuvre into position. You'd do far better to assemble it all in place.

It pays, however, to be wary. Filling or packing gaps isn't really satisfactory for such a large structure. Place a spirit level vertically against each wall. If either of them is out of true by more than, say, 20mm (¾in) along its length, or if any curves in it are deeper than that, cut the upright member of the frame to a length equal to the height of the alcove at its lowest and scribe it to fit the wall – using a pencil and block of wood while holding the timber precisely vertical. Then cut halving joints in each end.

A bottom frame cross piece is also needed to act as a doorstop, if nothing else. Cut it to length (ie, as long as the alcove's narrowest width), and screw it to the floor, making sure it's truly level. (Incidentally, before driving screws or nails into a floor, you should always try to make sure there are no water or gas pipes underneath. If in doubt, choose screws too short to pass through floorboards.)

Then glue the joints, and screw both uprights to the wall. Cut the top cross piece to the same length as the one on the floor. Joint it to the tops of the uprights, screwing it to a ceiling joist if possible. If you've worked accurately, it will be horizontal, and square to the rest – but do check!

Lastly, fit any intermediate cross pieces. You may need one to help support a shelf, and perhaps act as a doorstop, if you plan to create a small cupboard at the top.

Bottom and top panels aren't necessary in floor-to-ceiling units, but it doesn't cost much – and it makes a neat-looking touch – to fit a cupboard floor of plywood or hardboard.

Adding doors

Doors, or course, are what complete the cupboard. They can be sliding or hinged, and in construction they can be flush – perhaps consisting of single pieces of board – or else panelled. They can even be glazed; louvres are also a popular feature.

All these types can easily be installed in the front frame of the cupboard. For sliding doors, you fit tracks or channels; others can be hinged to the timber uprights, either overlapping them or inset between them. On a wide cupboard, you can always add extra uprights.

Whatever plan you decide on, it's always sensible to sort out the details before you buy any materials or begin work on the project. In both construction and design you'll find it pays dividends to think of the doors as an integral part of the unit.

You'll find more information in CARPENTRY TECHNIQUES 16.

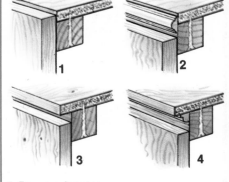

BUILT-IN WARDROBES

Fitted cupboards are not only cheaper than ready-made furniture; they're neater, too. And you can choose from any number of different details to suit your own needs and tastes.

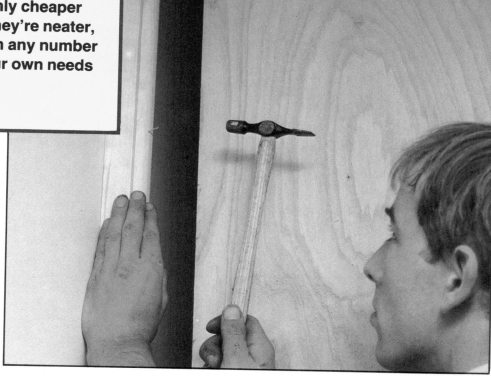

The traditional wardrobe is, of course, a completely freestanding unit with a bottom, a top and four sides. Many people possess one as a hand-me-down, and there are plenty of handsome, well-crafted examples.

However, if you're thinking about providing storage facilities from scratch, movable furniture has at least four important disadvantages when you compare it with built-in pieces.

The first is its cost. Except perhaps for the very cheapest (and shoddiest) off-the-shelf wardrobes, you'll find it cheaper to buy the materials and fit your own units — simply because the walls, floor and ceiling of the room replace (instead of duplicating) some of the panels of the cupboard. This saves space, too; and it means you don't have to devote much thought to the often tricky question of making the cabinet rigid.

The second point is that factory-made furniture won't necessarily fit neatly into the room. A freestanding wardrobe that's too big for an alcove can be a real nuisance, obstructing free movement and even light. This problem, of course, doesn't arise at all when you design your own scheme to fit the room.

And when it comes to style, you needn't simply accept a manufacturer's idea of what constitutes elegance. There's a vast range of alternatives.

Lastly, all ready-made wardrobes create a natural dust-trap above and below. A fitted unit scores here, too, provided you run it right up to the ceiling.

Thoughtful design

So think positively. Aim to build a wardrobe — or a whole set of cupboards — which meets all your requirements.

The first consideration, naturally, is what you're going to store, and how much space it will take up. Think to the future as you do this, so you can make allowances for potential expansion of your storage requirements. When it comes to clothing, your best guide is a close look — tape measure in hand — at all the items likely to be involved. Coats, trousers, and so on must hang clear of the floor; and you need to be sure you provide enough depth from front to back if you're planning to hang your garments sideways.

At the same time, consider the room itself, including existing furnishings (beds, for example), in relation to where you're going to site the cupboard. One obvious place to put it of course, is in an alcove (see pages 128-132), where it will be completely unobtrusive, and construction will be easiest of all. But it can just as well run right across one end of the room. Alternatively, it can start or stop (or both) part of the way along a wall, with the addition of side panels at one or both ends.

Visual effect, as well as convenience, plays a big part here. Even before you think about the details of materials, trim and finish, you know that full-width and full-height fitments will have cleaner (or, if you prefer the word, starker) lines than smaller ones.

They may provide other bonuses, too. Suppose, for example, that you have an unused and unsightly fireplace. There's no reason why you shouldn't build cupboards which run in a continuous line not only across the alcoves on either side, but also in front of the chimney breast, thereby concealing the whole thing. You could fit a fixed panel over the fireplace, but install shallow shelves behind doors in the cupboard area above the mantelpiece. Other items — pipework, perhaps, or even a washbasin or shower cubicle — can be hidden in the same way.

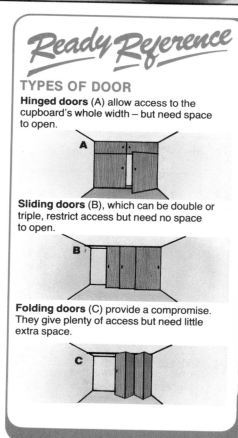

DESIGNING CUPBOARDS

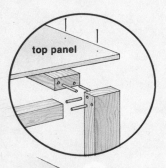

top panel

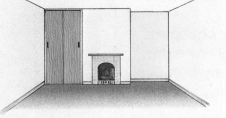

Above: One very natural location is in an alcove. A cupboard here makes use of what can be an awkward corner, while taking up no actual living space.

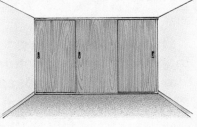

Above: You can also run cupboards right across the room. If appropriate, you can use both alcoves and hide the chimney breast too.

You can choose from many ways to construct fitted cupboards.

Above: Not only can you build the whole frame out from the wall behind, you can also add a panel overhead (top). This is often handy for long-term storage of objects too bulky to fit inside, such as suitcases.

Frame members which aren't fixed to the floor, wall or ceiling will require at least simple jointing.

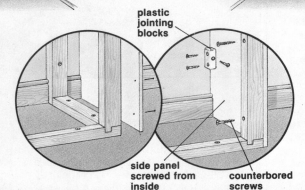

plastic jointing blocks

side panel screwed from inside

counterbored screws

Above: Cupboards needn't run all the way from wall to wall. Stop them short if necessary. Side panels can be fixed from outside (far left) – being either cut from thick board, as shown, or cut from thin plywood and pinned on. More neatly, they can be attached from inside (left), for example with counterbored screws.

PREPARING FOR WARDROBE DOORS

1 Your first job is to locate the joists and decide where to make your fixings. Then check whether the ceiling is level along that line.

TIP

2 If the ceiling isn't flat, you'll need a batten to take up the unevenness. Hold it in position and scribe the ceiling's contours onto it.

3 Plane the upper face of the batten down to the scribed line, so that it will fit snugly into place across the ceiling without any gaps.

Basic construction

One way to approach fitted-cupboard design is to think of a frame, screwed to the walls, floor and ceiling, on which doors are hung.

If you're using timber for this frame, it needs to be wide enough for wall fixing, and also thick enough to take hinges if any. Timber measuring 50x50mm (2x2in) or 75x38mm (3x1½in) is likely to be suitable; for various possible fixing details, see *Building cupboards in alcoves* on pages 128-132. Remember that you'll almost certainly have to scribe the uprights to match the exact shape of the wall for a true fit.

If the cupboard runs from wall to wall and from floor to ceiling, you can get away without cutting corner joints, because all the pieces are fixed in position. If it stops short in either direction, at least one upright or crosspiece will need jointing in (see pages 286-7). Mortise and tenon, bridle, halving and dowel joints are all possibilities. Top panels can be nailed to the frame from above; they can be of any board thick and strong enough to bear what's likely to be stored on them. Side panels – of blockboard, chipboard (plain, veneered or plastic-faced) or plywood – are best screwed from inside for strength and neatness, though you could economise by using 6mm (¼in) plywood, pinned from outside.

Fitting doors

Doors can be hinged, sliding or folding. Hinged doors can of course be lay-on or inset. Lay-on doors are less trouble to fit, because they're unaffected by frames that are out of square; in fact the doors will cover up any misalignment of the frame. Moreover the frame makes separate doorstops unnecessary.

Whichever type of door you are hanging, make sure you take both the cupboard and hinge design fully into account before deciding which hinges to use.

Sliding and folding doors are very popular alternatives. You buy the track and sliding gear as a kit; it will come complete with fixing instructions. On a floor-to-ceiling cupboard, you need a secure ceiling fixing in order to mount the track safely. Cavity fixings into plasterboard (often secure enough in other situations) won't do. If you can't fix through into ceiling joists – and can't take up the floorboards upstairs in order to fit noggins between the joists and fix into those – go for hinged doors instead.

Sliding or folding doors which are fitted on a full-height cupboard can enable you to do without a frame altogether. You simply fasten their track directly onto the ceiling, and allow the doors to slide right from wall to wall. This is probably the easiest system of all to install. If a wall is uneven, fix a strip of timber down it to cover the gaps down the edge of the closed door. If, on the other hand, you're incorporating a side panel, fix that to wall, floor and ceiling via battens or even plastic jointing blocks. (You could hinge a door to it instead.)

Even sliding doors' obvious drawback – that they allow access to only part of the cupboard at any one time – can sometimes be overcome. If you run the unit across a chimney breast as suggested above, the doors from each alcove can slide into the middle and thus out of the way.

When you are hanging sliding or folding doors, follow the track manufacturer's instructions carefully. The principles are just the same whether you're installing them in a doorway or in a cupboard.

STORAGE OPTIONS

You'll need hanging space for both long and short garments. This can either run lengthwise (A), or transversely (B) if necessary – though the latter is less convenient. The arrangement at A also includes drawer space.

Allow for shoes at the bottom. Any space at the top, for long-term storage, can be either inside the cupboard (A) – or outside (B) for really bulky items.

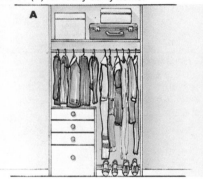

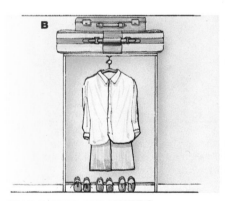

CHOOSING DRAWERS

Drawers for cupboards don't need fronts. You can buy ready-made plastic types, which slide in plastic runners as shown (A). Or you can make up your own with a low front (B). Timber runners could go underneath, as shown.

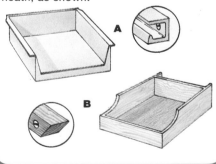

4 *Re-position the batten, and use the spirit level again to check whether its lower face is now true. If not, plane it down a bit further.*

5 *When you've got the alignment right, drill and countersink the batten, drill the ceiling, and finally, screw the batten into position.*

COMPLETING THE CUPBOARD FRONT

1 For sliding doors, screw the track onto the batten. Remember to allow for the depth of any beading to be fitted down the sides – see 9.

2 Cut each side upright to length (to fit under the ceiling batten) and mark on it the height of the skirting-board. Square the mark across the piece.

3 A good way to gauge the skirting-board's thickness is with a combination square; loosen the screw and adjust the square accordingly.

5 Fit the upright against the wall and check it for plumb in both directions. Then, if necessary, scribe and cut it, or else pack out any gaps.

6 Screw both uprights into position. With hinged doors, and often with sliding doors, you'll want to fix a similar batten to the floor as well.

7 Cut the doors to size, allowing for clearance and any overlap. For sliding doors, add wheels or sliders as instructed by the manufacturers.

9 Make adjustments so the doors hang properly. For sliding doors, fit floor guides, and pin beading down each side to hide gaps and exclude dust.

10 Often a pelmet strip (say 12mm/1/2in thick), nailed in position, is useful to hide the track and any ceiling batten when sliding doors have been hung.

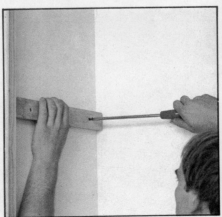

11 If you want an interior shelf, just screw battens to all three walls, ensuring they're level, and place a board on top of them.

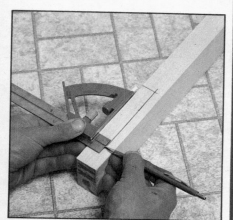

4 Then you can hold a pencil against the square, run both down the side of the upright, and cut away the waste area you've marked out.

8 Hang the doors. Wheels or sliders just hook onto the track; hinges usually require screws. Either way, you'll probably need a helper.

12 Lastly, add door handles, plus whatever finishing treatment you think is appropriate, in order to make your fitted wardrobe complete.

Making doors

The doors' appearance, of course, makes or mars the whole thing. But there's no limit to your choices here. For a start, they can be either full-height, or split at a certain level (available sizes may well decide this particular question for you).

As for materials and finishes, you can use plywood or blockboard, suitably edged, varnished or painted (chipboard is less than ideal because of its weight). You can decorate it with decorative wood mouldings. You can paper it or paste fabric onto it, to match the rest of your decorations. You can use decorative wallboards, ready-made louvred doors, or even mirrored glass. And, in addition to sliding and folding tracks and gear, some firms supply aluminium edging which forms part of the hanging system, and turns sheets of board into handsome doors.

You can even buy complete 'cupboard fronts' – sets of hinged doors already hung in over-large frames, which can be cut down to the height you want. Scribed panels will hide any gaps at floor and ceiling level.

Internal details

Inside the unit, the first necessity is a rail for hanging clothes. Chrome- and brass-plated tubing is readily available; you can fix it either with the special brackets made for the purpose, or in notches cut in the upper edges of wall battens at either end.

At least one shelf, often at high level, is very useful. Use whichever fixing is most appropriate – see the section on Shelving: The Basics, pages 124-127, for more information. Choose the material for thickness according to what it will have to carry.

The occasional drawer, too, is invaluable for storing underclothes, socks and so on. Think out your storage requirements carefully when planning how many you need. Since the drawer will be behind doors anyway, dustproofing isn't vital, and the front is often cut lower than the sides for easy access. You could also consider sliding wire or plastic trays – more commonly found in kitchen units, but also available in versions suitable for wardrobes.

Whatever details you choose, a properly designed fitted unit may well enable you to do away with other storage furniture altogether in a particular room. And of course, there's nothing to prevent you from combining it with open shelving to make a complete 'wall system'. This can provide space for books, ornaments, plants and whatever else you like – as long as the structure is strong enough to support it.

However you design the system, the crucial point is convenience. Try to ensure that each run of shelving gives the space you require at a height that's appropriate for the items concerned.

Ready Reference

FITTING SLIDING DOORS

The commonest type of sliding door gear (A) features wheel units which you fix to the tops of the doors, plus a track which you fix to the ceiling – directly or via a batten. Then you simply hook the wheels onto the track.

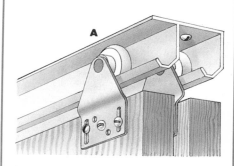

Also available, for lighter duty, are plastic sliders (B) instead of wheels. These too engage in a metal track.

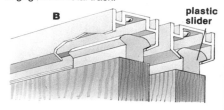

plastic slider

Although heavy-duty gear may have a bottom track too, the usual way of keeping the doors on course is plastic guides screwed to the floor or frame.

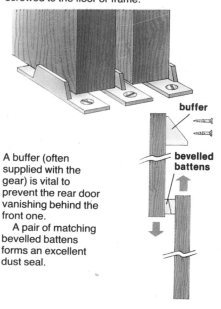

buffer

bevelled battens

A buffer (often supplied with the gear) is vital to prevent the rear door vanishing behind the front one.

A pair of matching bevelled battens forms an excellent dust seal.

BUILDING SHELVING UNITS

Self-supporting shelves, unlike the wall-mounted type, can be moved wherever and whenever you like – without leaving screw holes to be plugged. Here's how to make them rigid and roomy.

A part from their most obvious advantages over built-in units, freestanding units don't have to be tailored to fit any irregularities of walls and alcoves. But, because they aren't fixed in position, you have to devote a bit more time and thought to making them both strong and rigid.

This is often a matter of making a straightforward box, although frame construction is another possibility. Either way it is important to remember that the shelves themselves won't add much stability, particularly if they're adjustable. You need additional stiffening to compensate the tendency for the whole unit to fold up sideways into a diamond shape.

The basic box

Always keep your materials in mind. The options are, of course, solid timber or man-made boards. Plywood is probably the best all-rounder, but it's quite expensive. Chipboard is cheap, and chipboard screws make a strong butt joint. In solid timber and blockboard, you're restricted by the fact that you shouldn't screw or nail into end grain.

Dowels or plastic jointing blocks are good for assembling most of the structure, but dowels are less than ideal for corners, because a dowel joint isn't all that rigid. A timber strip, glued and screwed into both surfaces, can add some necessary reinforcement; but shelf units often rise above eye level, and you'll have to be careful that it's not unsightly as well.

A barefaced housing joint is one remaining possibility – that is, apart from those afforded by power tools. A circular saw or router makes it a lot easier, for example, to cut rebate joints or mitres.

An additional point is that plastic facings such as melamine laminate won't accept glue, so that some form of screw fastening is virtually your only way of fixing other components to them.

Stiffening the unit

The simplest way of making a unit rigid is to pin a back panel to the rear edges of the box and perhaps even to the back edges of the shelves as well.

However, there may be occasions (for example, if the unit is to stand in the middle of a room) when you want a more open, airy look than is possible with this unmodified form of construction. In such cases the answer is to add bracing to the actual box components themselves. Even if you are incorporating a back, the extra stability such bracing provides won't come amiss – especially on large units.

The principle works as follows. Flat boards bend under stress. You can counter this by fixing lengths of reinforcing timber along them, preferably on edge. Every board thus dealt with helps to keep the whole structure stable.

You can even stiffen the open (front) face of the cabinet, by running bracing members across it, provided these are firmly jointed to the cabinet sides – say with dowels, plastic jointing blocks or steel angle repair brackets. A recessed plinth does this job and the type of plinth that's made up separately stabilises the cabinet by stiffening its bottom.

Frequently the neatest way of stiffening the front is to place such reinforcement along the shelves – either underneath them (inset if you like) or fixed to their front edges.

Rectangular-sectioned timber such as 50x25mm (2x1in), or a metal L-section, is ideal here. The procedure has the added advantage of strengthening the shelves, and you can treat intermediate shelves in the same way – not just the top and bottom panels.

Supporting the shelves

You can fix shelves into the unit by any of the methods appropriate for box construction using hand tools. The strongest and most professional of these is to house the shelves into uprights (for further information see pages 120-123).

A stopped housing makes the neater joint here, since it means the front edge of each upright is unbroken by the ends of the shelves, but a through housing is quite adequate. The other invisible fastening for fixed shelves is dowels. Screws will leave plastic caps showing on the outsides of the side panels.

The choice between these methods depends largely on your materials. A plastic-faced upright panel means the dowel joints can't be glued, so you rely even more than usual on the main box for strength. Timber shelves,

A STURDY SHELF UNIT

This unit's top and sides are made of plastic-faced chipboard; the softwood shelves are planed down in the width to match.

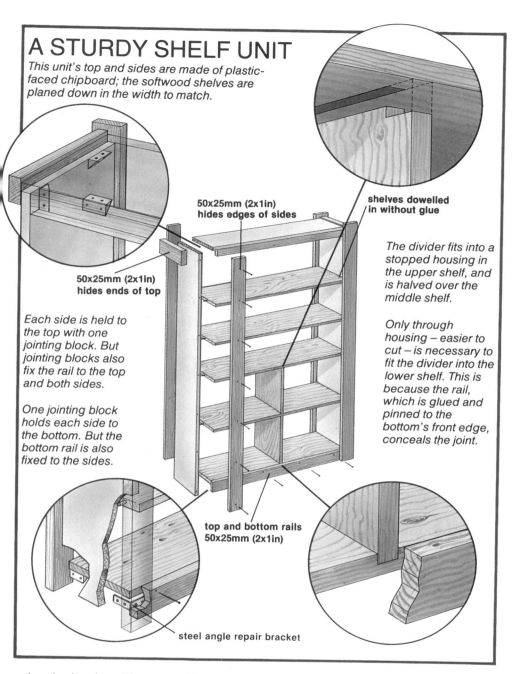

50x25mm (2x1in) hides edges of sides

50x25mm (2x1in) hides ends of top

Each side is held to the top with one jointing block. But jointing blocks also fix the rail to the top and both sides.

One jointing block holds each side to the bottom. But the bottom rail is also fixed to the sides.

steel angle repair bracket

shelves dowelled in without glue

The divider fits into a stopped housing in the upper shelf, and is halved over the middle shelf.

Only through housing – easier to cut – is necessary to fit the divider into the lower shelf. This is because the rail, which is glued and pinned to the bottom's front edge, conceals the joint.

top and bottom rails 50x25mm (2x1in)

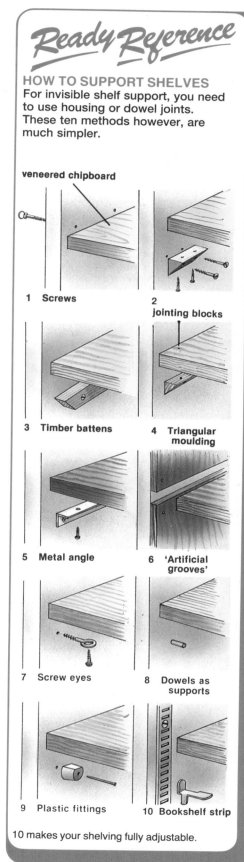

on the other hand, can't be screwed in directly because you'd be going into the end grain.

Plastic jointing blocks are an obvious and fairly unobtrusive possibility. Timber battens, glued and pinned, or screwed and if possible glued, to shelves and uprights are tough; they can also be quite neat if you chamfer their front ends, cut them off at an angle, or hide them with a front rail. A triangular-sectioned timber 'stair rod' moulding, or an L-sectioned strip of steel or aluminium, is neater still.

You can create artificial housings by using pieces of timber or board, the same width as the uprights, pinned and glued to their inside faces, and leaving just enough space for the shelves to fit between them. This means you can make the uprights themselves a bit thinner.

A rather different approach is to let the shelf ends rest on small supports sticking out of the uprights. These might be screw eyes (with screws driven up through them into the undersides of the shelves to fix them in place if necessary); they could be 6mm (¼in) diameter dowels. You can also get several sorts of plastic studs which screw in, nail in or push into drilled holes. Some are specially designed for glass shelves. And sometimes the hole is filled by a bush which

ASSEMBLING THE CARCASE

1 After cutting all the shelves to the same length, mark and cut housings for the divider halfway along the shelves above and below it.

2 Use one of the housings as a guide to mark the position of the halving to be cut in the shelf which the divider crosses.

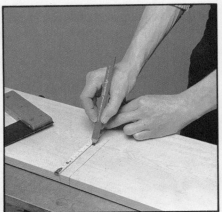

3 Measure halfway across the shelf for the depth of the halving. Then cut the divider to length, and measure and mark it out likewise.

4 Cut the matching halvings in the divider and the shelf it crosses; use a tenon saw across the grain and then a chisel to chop out the waste.

5 Align both uprights exactly and mark on them the height of each shelf (at a point which is halfway across the shelf's thickness).

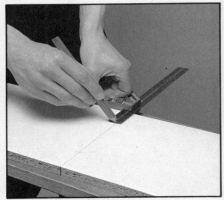

6 Use a combination square at the same setting to mark the exact dowel positions on both the uprights and on all the shelf ends.

7 Drill all the dowel holes, glue the dowels into the shelf ends, and fit all but the top and bottom shelves to the uprights when the adhesive sets.

8 Screw the top and bottom shelves into position with plastic jointing blocks, or any other appropriate jointing technique.

9 Insert the divider into the unit from the back, using scrap wood to prevent damage to its rear edge as you tap it into position.

ADDING REINFORCEMENT

1 Fix a stiffening rail across the top, screwing it to the uprights and the underside of the top shelf with jointing blocks.

2 Glue and pin the plinth rail to the front edge of the bottom shelf (which is cut narrower than the other shelves to allow for this).

3 Use steel angle repair brackets to hold the plinth firmly to the uprights and thus help to keep the whole unit rigid as well.

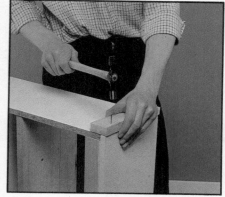

4 Glue and pin lengths of timber, as long as the uprights are wide, to the ends of the top shelf in order to conceal them.

5 Glue and pin further lippings to both long edges of each upright to enhance the unit's appearance and give it extra rigidity.

6 Lastly, fill all nail holes with wood stopping of the appropriate shade, and varnish the timber parts to improve their looks and durability.

will accept a number of different types of stud.

Lastly, there's a very neat way to make the shelves in a freestanding unit fully adjustable. This is to use 'bookshelf strip' – metal strips with continuous rows of slots, into which you clip small metal lugs; the shelves rest on these. The strips (of which you'll need two each side) can be simply screwed to the insides of the uprights, or fitted into vertical grooves if you've got the power tools to cut them.

A home-made version of this system uses removable dowels in vertical rows of regularly spaced drilled holes.

Installing dividers

For the distance you can safely span with various thicknesses of materials, see *Ready Reference* page 125. Really wide shelves may need extra support in the middle. Vertical dividers will provide this, and can also add to looks and usefulness. They're usually housed or dowelled in at top and bottom, and halved over intermediate shelves.

Alternatively, a square- or rectangular-sectioned timber upright, fixed to the front edges of the shelves, will help matters. It can be glued and pinned to the shelves, dowelled in or notched over them.

Frame shelving

If you only think in terms of box construction, you limit the scope of your projects. A shelf unit's sides can just as well be open frames as single slabs. This gives a lighter look, and also avoids the problems of using man-made boards. But you do need to pay even more attention to making the structure rigid. You'll certainly need extra strengthening pieces running from side to side.

Shelves can be supported in most of the ways already mentioned – with the additional possibility of placing them on the cross pieces in the frames themselves. These cross pieces can even be pieces of broomstick – in other words, each upright is in effect a ladder, with the shelves resting on the rungs.

Box modules

In fact, as far as freestanding shelves are concerned, the possibilities are limitless. One more example may help to demonstrate this. There's no reason why you shouldn't make your 'shelving' up as a stack of completely separate open-fronted boxes. They needn't even be the same depth from front to back. Such a system lets you rearrange its shape completely at will. Its main disadvantage is that most of the panels are duplicated, so the cost of materials goes up. But moving house is easy: each box doesn't even need packing!

As long as you make the structure rigid, the choice of design is yours.

PANELLING WALLS WITH TIMBER

Natural timber panelling can transform your walls like no other material, bringing warmth and atmosphere to even the least promising room. Yet the technique of installing it is easily mastered.

Cladding interior walls with natural timber is an age-old decorative technique. Nowadays, it's most popular in the form of narrow boards.

They look extremely attractive and have other advantages too. Panelling is a perfect cover-up for plaster in poor condition, and for lumpy walls often found in older houses. Moreover, it has excellent insulation properties.

If you plan to panel one or more of your walls, go and see what the timber merchant has to offer. Cedar, ramin, mahogany and meranti are all possible woods for the purpose. But by far the most popular is 'knotty pine' — softwood of various species with knots that would be unacceptable in ordinary joinery work. It's available from almost all suppliers. The commonest size is 100 × 12mm (4 × ½in), in lengths up to 3m (about 10ft). Width and thickness, as usual, are nominal: since the timber is planed smooth, these dimensions will actually be smaller.

Most boards used for panelling have a protruding tongue along one edge, and a groove in the other, so that each piece fits into the next. Quite often both outer edges are chamfered, forming attractive V-shaped grooves when the boards are interlocked; hence the name 'TGV' — tongued, grooved and V-jointed.

Boards with concave faces are also obtainable as in 'shiplap', which has one edge rebated to overlap the thin edge of the next board. It's almost always used horizontally. Horizontal cladding creates the optical illusion that the wall is wider than it really is: vertical cladding makes it seem taller.

Battening the wall

All cladding is normally fitted onto 50 × 25mm (2 × 1in) rough sawn softwood battens, which are themselves nailed or screwed to the existing solid wall.

They're unnecessary if the wall is a hollow plasterboard-covered timber-framed type, built with vertical studs and horizontal noggins to which the cladding can be nailed. But be quite sure you're nailing through into the timber frame and not just into its covering, which is usually plasterboard and thus won't hold the nails well.

If cladding the inside of an external wall, you can keep out damp with a vapour barrier such as polythene sheeting. You simply place it under the battens before you fix them to the wall. Even if you don't include a vapour barrier, it's wise to treat the battens and the back of the cladding with wood preservative, in case condensation leads to rot. And the job also offers a unique opportunity to fight heat loss, for you can easily place insulating material between the wall and the cladding.

Buying the timber

If the shop prefers to supply panelling in assorted lengths, it will be cheaper to buy it that way, rather than in the exact dimensions you want; but many suppliers now sell TGV in pre-cut bundles, containing timber in lengths of 1800mm (just under 6ft), 2400mm (8ft) or 3000mm (10ft).

To work out how many lengths of vertical cladding you need, divide the wall width by the board width — remembering that the board's face will be only about 90mm (3½in) wide if it's nominally 100mm (4in).

For horizontal cladding, divide the wall height by the board width. For board length, just measure the wall — though on wide walls you may have to fit boards end-to-end.

Before buying boards always check them — especially knotty pine — for splits, loose knots, discolouration and twisting. Don't be afraid to reject bad ones.

Battens should run at right angles to cladding; in the case of diagonal panelling, either vertically or horizontally. They should be spaced about 600mm (24in) apart, except that the first and last in a row of vertical battens should be at either end of the wall. And you'll always need battens next to doors, windows and other fitments, and under any butt joints between the ends of boards.

Buy your cladding at least two weeks before use, and keep it inside the house. This is because your home will be warmer than the place the timber has been stored. The heat will reduce the amount of moisture in the wood, which will make it shrink. You should therefore give this time to happen *before* you fix the cladding in place; otherwise it will shrink afterwards. That may result in tongues coming out of grooves, which will leave unsightly gaps.

As soon as you get the cladding home, lay it flat on the floor (provided the floor is dry) in small piles, with boards face to face. Leave it for a fortnight, shuffling the boards around every few days. Don't attempt to dry them out artificially, as this will be sure to warp them.

FIXING THE BATTENS

For a professional finish, the wall battens to which the cladding boards are fixed should not follow any undulations in the surface. You can test whether your wall surface is uneven by holding a timber straight edge against it horizontally and vertically; you will then be able to see at a glance where lumps or hollows fall. The examples here are for vertical cladding; the hollows are exaggerated.

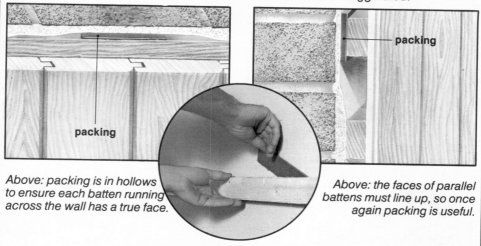

packing

Above: packing is in hollows to ensure each batten running across the wall has a true face.

Above: the faces of parallel battens must line up, so once again packing is useful.

packing

Inset: hardboard is an ideal packing material

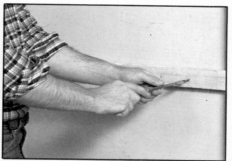

1 Fix battens with No 8 screws, 600mm (2ft) apart and 63mm (2½in) long – long enough to go through the plaster. Masonry nails are an alternative.

2 To form a neat link between the bottom of an existing cornice and the top edge of the cladding, use scotia moulding. Butt the cladding up to it.

Fixing the cladding

If the wall is solid, use masonry nails, or screws in plastic plugs, to fix the battens. Take care not to drive them into cables or pipes; be especially careful round electrical fittings. The important thing is to get the battens at a constant level, both vertically and horizontally. Insert pieces of hardboard, plywood or scrap timber behind them where necessary. On a slightly concave wall, for example, you'll have to pack behind the centres of the battens to get them truly vertical, whereas on a convex wall you'll have to pack behind the top and bottom of each batten.

Then position a piece of cladding as the first in the row – usually against a side wall (against the ceiling for horizontal cladding). If the side wall isn't vertical, or is uneven, you'll have to scribe the board – see overleaf – and then cut to the resulting pencil line.

Place the first board so the tongue is ready to fit into the next piece, and nail the board to the battens. Another method, which avoids you having to conceal the nail heads, is to fix the first board in place on the wall with panel or impact adhesive. This will hold it firmly in place straight away without nailing or cramping. (Note: no other adhesive will achieve this.)

You can nail the next board through its tongue, angling the nails inwards. The heads will be covered by the groove in the following board. Use this 'secret' nailing for all the other boards too, except the last. With cladding other than tongue-and-groove, such as shiplap, there is no tongue; so secret nailing means

Ready Reference

FINISHING TOUCHES

Whatever area of cladding you have been fixing, you will need to finish off the edges where the cladding meets other walls, ceilings, skirting boards and openings.

INTERNAL CORNERS

Finish off with quadrant, triangular or scotia moulding, pinned into the angle.

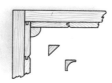

CEILINGS

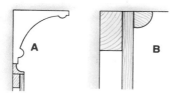

Where there is an existing coving, stop the cladding just below it and fill the gap with scotia moulding (A). Otherwise take the cladding up to ceiling level and finish with quadrant or other beading (B).

EXTERNAL CORNERS

Where the cladding covers both walls, plane off the tongue for a neat overlap, and cover it if you wish with a decorative moulding (C). If only one wall is covered, finish off with a vertical strip of wood pinned to the ends of the horizontal battens (D).

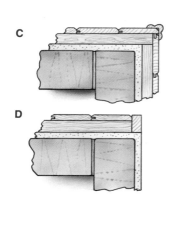

C

D

FIXING THE CLADDING

1 Hold the first board vertically against the side wall – or its skirting, if the cladding goes that far down. Lightly pin the board to the battens.

2 Scribe the board with a pencil pressed against a block of wood 50mm (2in) wide and run down the side wall. The mark follows the wall profile.

3 For a neat result, scribe around the shape of the skirting too. A second pencil can take the place of scrap timber as a guide for this.

6 Then fix the first board to the battens permanently by driving 25mm (1in) panel pins through its face. (On stud partitions you'll need 38mm/1½in pins.)

7 Before nailing each subsequent board, ensure a snug fit by tapping an offcut held against it. Check with a spirit level, and adjust it if necessary.

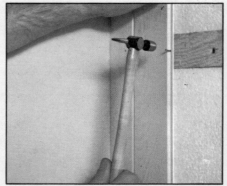

8 Nail at an angle through the board's tongue – but not too near the end, or you'll split the wood. The groove in the next board will cover the pin heads.

placing the nails where the rebated edge of the next board will cover their heads.

Repeat the fitting and nailing process right across the wall, checking that each board is still vertical (or horizontal). When you get to the end, it's unlikely that the last board will fit exactly, so you'll probably have to scribe it.

Even once you've cut it to shape, you may have trouble squeezing it in if you've already nailed all the other boards in position. There are two ways of dealing with this. One is to fit the last three or four boards at the same time, inserting the tongues in the grooves and then springing them into place, before nailing through their faces. The other is to plane or chisel off the back of the groove in the last board, and simply lay the board onto the battens – fixing it either with impact adhesive, or nails.

An external corner (eg, the end of a chimney breast) means planing off the tongue, at least from the last board. If the cladding continues round the corner, give the angle a neat finish by butting the grooved edge of the next board

at right angles against the tip of the last one, perhaps pinning a right angle or 'birdsmouth' (L shaped) softwood moulding on to cover the join. If the cladding ends there, your best bet is to nail a small rectangular-sectioned piece of planed timber (say 32 x 13mm/1¼ x½in) to the ends of the battens so that it covers the edge of the last board as well. This method will also work at a door frame.

At an internal corner, just butt the boards together, or butt the last one against the next wall if the cladding ends there.

A quadrant, triangle or scotia moulding will give added neatness; you can use this along the junction with the ceiling too, or below a ceiling moulding.

Skirtings and other features

If the wall you're panelling has an existing skirting board, it's best left on and used as a batten, nailing the cladding to it. If it's thinner than the other battens, you'll need to pack it out first. So nail on a strip of timber, hardboard or thin ply-

wood, to bring it to the right thickness.

You can also use it as a recessed plinth. This will prevent the bottom of the cladding from being scuffed or damaged. Stop the cladding short of the floor, so that it ends some way up the skirting. Or fix the bottom of the cladding to a batten nailed immediately above the skirting, leaving the whole of the skirting exposed.

Alternatively, you can put new skirting over the cladding. With horizontal cladding, back the skirting with short lengths of board, nailed one to each batten, rather than wasting a whole board behind the skirting. Another form of skirting is a quadrant moulding (nailed to the cladding, not the floorboards, in case of timber movement).

If the old skirting is thicker than the battens you'll have to take it off carefully, or it will prevent you from nailing the cladding flat. If it's an obsolete pattern, removing it has the advantage that you can still match the room's other skirtings, because you can put it back on top of the cladding.

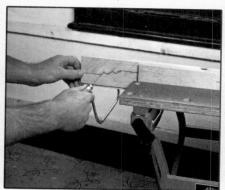

4 Take down the board and cut out the skirting profile with a coping saw or power jigsaw. Then cut along the rest of the board with a rip saw.

5 To prevent heat loss through the wall, place polystyrene insulation board, of the same thickness as the battens, between them.

9 At a window, door or end wall, pin the last board to the second last and use an offcut of cladding to scribe it. Then remove it, cut it to shape and fit it.

10 You'll need to cut short boards for some places, such as under a window. The bottom edge of the cladding can often be nailed to existing skirting.

MORE FINISHING TOUCHES

Finishing off cladding neatly at a doorway, skirting boards and round electrical accessories can be tricky. Here are some solutions.

DOOR FRAMES

Fit cladding up to the door frame, then pin a vertical strip to the ends of the battens and add new door architrave moulding.

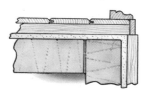

SKIRTING BOARD

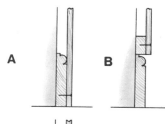

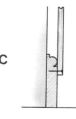

Pin the cladding directly to the skirting at floor level (A) or higher (B), or fix battens just above the skirting board (C).

ELECTRICAL FITTINGS

Pin battens round surface-mounted fittings (D) and cut the cladding to fit flush with the edges of the mounting box (D). The face plate may not be exactly flush with the cladding surface.

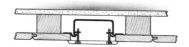

Remove flush fittings, and refix to the cladding with a new box and proprietary fixing lugs (E).

Like skirting, the architrave round doors and windows can either be removed or left. If you remove it, finish the cladding with strips of wood, in the same way as for any external corner where panelling ends; for decoration fit architrave (new, or old if it's in good condition) on top of the boards. If you leave the old architrave, fit battens up against it where necessary, nail the cladding to those, and cover its edge with a right-angle, birdsmouth or rebated moulding, planed to fit.

Electrical sockets also need battens next to them. A surface-mounted box generally needs no further treatment, since its face will end up more or less level with the surface of the cladding.

The simplest way of dealing with a flush-mounted box is to re-fix it to the wall surface, put battening and cladding next to it, and screw the face plate back on to overlap the cladding. If a flush-mounted box is too deep or shallow for this, use it as if the cladding were plaster-board. That is, attach special metal lugs to the sides of the box, so that screwing on the face plate clamps the box to the cladding.

Wall-mounted light fittings can usually be dealt with by re-fixing them onto the cladding, having drilled a hole through it for the wires.

The cladding, of course, will need to be cut round all projecting features.

Surface finishes

As you fix the cladding, punch any visible nail heads below the timber surface. Then, when you've finished, you can fill the holes with a matching-coloured wood filler. Next, sand the entire timber surface with fine grade abrasive paper. An orbital sander will take much of the hard work out of this job.

When you've prepared the surface in this way, you can apply a stain, if you want to give the wood a deeper, richer or brighter colour. Follow this with a clear varnish in a matt, satin or gloss finish according to your taste. For fuller information on finishing natural timber, see pages 18 to 20.

SECURITY DEVICES: WINDOWS

Burglary is a growth industry these days, and windows are particularly vulnerable to attack. But fitting security bolts and latches takes only a few minutes and is a relatively inexpensive job.

Just because you have locks on the outside doors and you are careful to shut all the windows before you go out doesn't mean that your house is safe against a burglar. Such action may deter the thief acting on the spur of the moment, but it won't prevent the committed house-breaker from trying to get in, particularly if he thinks the pickings are worth the risk.

Fortunately there is a wide range of security bolts and locks which you can easily fit to prevent easy access. And the fact that some of these devices are visible from the outside may instantly put off a would-be burglar. You can buy bolts for specific situations – say for a sliding metal frame, a wooden casement window or a sliding sash window. Some can be used in more than one position, but it's important to follow the manufacturer's instructions closely on where to fit them. There are multi-purpose locks which can be fitted in several ways, but these tend to be more expensive.

Of all the window types, louvre windows still present the greatest security risk. Even if they are closed, it is still relatively simple for a burglar to remove some of the glass slats to gain access to your home. One solution is to glue the glass panes into their holders on either side of the frame, but there is the disadvantage that if you accidentally break a slat it becomes difficult to fit another.

The surest method of all is to fit a grille on the inside of the window. This may seem like drastic action. However, if the window is concealed from general view, this may be the only means of keeping a determined thief out unless a burglar alarm is installed.

Fitting a grille could make your home look like a prison. Fortunately, ornamental designs are available to lessen the impact. Normally you have to order the grille to the size of your window. It is installed by being mortared into the surrounding brickwork – inevitably this will cause some damage to the decoration. Some grilles are hinged and incorporate a lock to secure them in position. This enables the grille to be moved aside so that the glass can be cleaned, and, more importantly, in the event of a fire, you are still able to use the window as an escape route.

PROTECTING YOUR HOME

Railings (1), and a locked side gate, will hamper access to the back of the house. Lock a garage side door (2) with a rim lock or padlock. Use anti-vandal paint on a down-pipe (3). Fit grilles behind louvre windows (4) and special locks on sash windows (5).

There are special casement locks for wooden or metal windows (6). The outer doors or a porch (7) should be secured with rack or barrel bolts as well as a rim or mortise lock. At the back of the house fit a sliding door lock to patio doors (8). Likewise, aluminium sliding windows (9) should be locked with a similar device. Hinge bolts, rack bolts or barrel bolts will give added security to a back door (10). Secure any garage window (11).

FITTING A PUSH-LOCK

1 Mark the position of the lock on the fixed and opening sections of the frame. Use the plastic wedge to ensure the lock sits square to the casement.

2 Separate the lock from the backplate and screw the backplate to the casement. This is deep enough to receive the bolt so you don't need to drill a hole.

3 Push the lock over the backplate and position the wedge, then screw the lock against the side of the frame. Cover the screw holes with plastic plugs.

4 A special key is needed to unfasten the lock. Keep it accessible, but out of reach of the window so the frame can be opened quickly in an emergency.

The simplest security devices, particularly from the point of view of fitting, are those which give added support to the latch and stay already attached to the window. Stay bolts, for example, are available in various designs; some just clamp on, others have to be screwed in place (see *Ready Reference*), replacing the existing stay catch entirely. And if you don't want to go to the trouble of replacing the latch with a lockable version you can always fit a cockspur lock underneath the catch instead (see *Ready Reference*).

Fitting the devices

The step-by-step photographs show how different windows can be secured using various security devices. However, there is little point in fitting a bolt if the frames are rotten or unsound, as the bolt can easily be prised off by any burglar using force.

Most devices can simply be screwed into position on the surface of the opening or fixed frame. But some bolts, for example the rack bolt, have to be concealed within the frame itself, like a mortise lock. For added security it's often advisable to fit two bolts, one at the top, the other at the bottom.

When fitting any of these devices it's important that they can't be removed even if the glass is broken or a hand slipped through a fanlight inadvertently left open. So use clutch-head screws which are almost impossible to remove once they have been driven into place. Alternatively, you may have to drill out the heads of Supadriv screws so they can't be taken out. On metal frames you'll first have to drill pilot holes before you can drive in the screws, but do make sure you avoid the glass. On old galvanised frames, prime any holes with a rust inhibitor before driving in the screws, otherwise your fitting can be forced out by a burglar

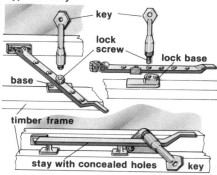
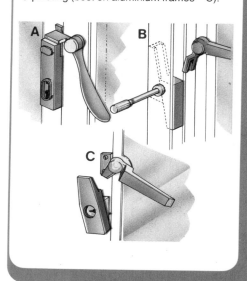

METAL FRAMES

1 Mark and drill fixing holes on the opening frame. Use a depth gauge on the drill bit to prevent overdrilling. Then screw the lock in place.

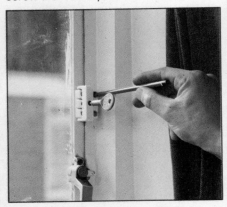

2 Set the locking staple on the fixed frame and close the lock to keep it in place. You can then mark the fixing holes with a pencil.

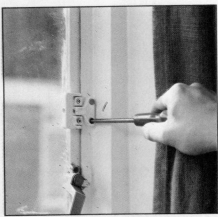

3 Unfasten the bolt and push the locking bar to one side. Drill the fixing holes and screw the staple into place, covering the self-tapping screws with plastic plugs.

SECURING SASH WINDOWS

1 There are various types of acorn stop. For the simplest, drill a hole no more than 75mm (3in) above the bottom rail of the outer sash and fit the backplate.

5 Mark the position of the backplate on the outer sash and use a chisel to cut a recess so the plate will sit flush with the surface of the rail.

9 A special 3-stage sash lock is also available. To fit it, hold the striking plate against the outer frame and mark where the recesses have to be cut.

2 The stop screws into this plate to prevent the sashes sliding past each other: fit two for added security. Some stops can be locked in place.

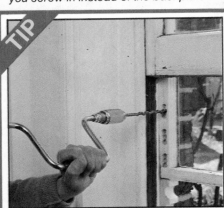

6 Next, screw the backplate into position. With some dual screws there may be a small threaded barrel which you screw in instead of the backplate.

10 It's easier and more accurate to use a brace and bit, rather than an electric drill, to cut the recesses so that the striking plate sits flush.

3 When fitting dual screws, check that the rails of the sashes are thick enough to take the barrels. Site the locks about 100mm (4in) in from the side edges.

4 Drill a 10mm (³/₈in) diameter hole through the inner sash and for 15mm (⁵/₈in) into the outer one. Mark the bit with tape as a guide.

7 Close the frame, then screw the large threaded barrel of the bolt into the inner sash. Make sure you stop when it is flush with the rail surface.

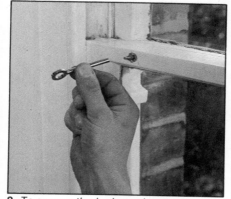

8 To secure the lock you have to screw a bolt through the large barrel on the inner sash and into the locking plate on the outer sash using a key.

11 Use a sharp chisel to square up the edges and clear out the waste in each recess. Then screw the striking plate into position.

12 Screw the locking unit to the top edge of the inner sash with clutch head screws. The locking bar is wound into the striking plate with a special key.

SLIDING WINDOW LOCKS

The clamp-on type has jaws which are opened and closed with a special key. The lock is placed over the track and against the frame of the closed window and is then locked in position.

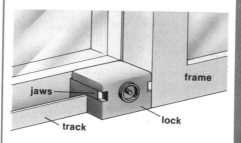

TIP: FIT A DEPTH STOP

When drilling holes in metal (and particularly aluminium) frames, fit the twist drill with a depth stop so there is no risk of drilling into the glass of the window and cracking it, or of breaking the weatherstrip or sealing strip.

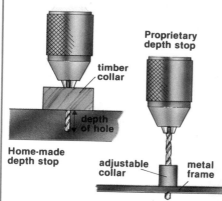

TIP: NARROW STILES

Rack bolts are often too bulky to fit into frames with narrow stiles, but special surface-mounted locks are available. When closed they draw the sash tightly into the frame so the sash can't be levered out. They also help to cut down draughts.

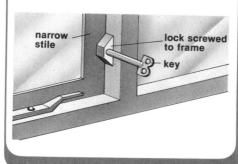

FITTING A RACK BOLT

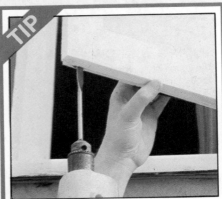

1 Mark and drill the hole in the frame to accommodate the bolt – vertically, if the frame sides are narrow. Repeat the operation for the keyhole.

2 Next screw the bolt into place. You may have to recess it slightly so that the bottom plate doesn't foul the moving frame when it's being closed.

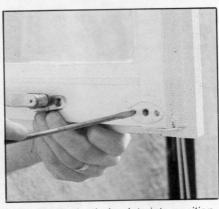

3 Screw the keyhole plate into position. Coat the bolt with chalk, shut the window and then try to close the lock so the bolt marks the frame.

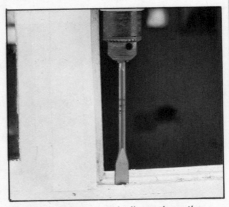

4 This will leave a chalk mark on the fixed frame. You can now drill a hole to receive the bolt. When doing this it's important to keep the drill upright.

5 Screw the backplate over the hole to prevent wear. Again you may first have to recess it so that it doesn't obstruct the frame when it's being closed.

6 For extra security fit two bolts – one at the top, the other at the bottom of the opening edge of the frame. Don't forget to remove the key after locking the bolt.

LOCKING LATCHES

1 Remove the old latch and catch and fill the fixing holes. Sand the newly exposed woodwork, then prime and paint it the same colour as the frame.

2 With the window closed, screw the new latch to the window frame midway between top and bottom. Then position the catch in relation to this.

3 When the latch is in the closed position you can insert a special key and wind the locking bar into the backplate to secure the casement.

SECURITY DEVICES: DOORS

There's little point in going to the time, trouble and expense of fitting security devices to windows if you don't carry out a similar operation on doors.

A door sitting solidly in its frame may appear an impressive barrier to a would-be burglar, but if it's only fitted with a traditional mortise or rimlock then it's far more vulnerable than you may think. Modern locks, admittedly, are hard to pick; however, a burglar isn't going to waste time trying to do this. He wants quick access, and brute force rather than stealth is often his best means of getting in. Consequently, he may try to force open an outside door either by kicking it or by using a crowbar to lever it free. If the door isn't properly protected, it will only take a few seconds before he's inside.

Attacking the weak points

Your main entry/exit door is the most difficult to make secure. The best protection is offered by fitting a standard mortise deadlock into the edge of a substantial door. A rimlock is less resistant to forcing, because it is merely screwed to the face of the door. Check that all fixings – including the hinges – are secure, and that the woodwork is in good condition. Also make sure that the lock cannot be reached by a hand pushed through the letterbox.

For added protection of this door when you're in the house, the simplest device to fit is a door chain. There are various types, but all depend on a secure fixing if they are to be effective. The plate close, into which the chain is hooked, is screwed to the opening edge of the door, and the chain staple is screwed to the fixed frame – see step-by-step photographs overleaf. With aluminium doors, it helps to improve the strength of the fixing if a block of wood can be slipped into the door frame section, perhaps through the letterplate opening or lock cut-out. This will give the self-tapping securing screws more to grip on. Also, fix the chain staple to the timber part of the door frame and not to the aluminium sub-frame.

Security for other doors

The best protection for other doors is given by substantial bolts. These can be surface-mounted, but make sure that the fixings are secure and that they cannot be reached if glass in the door is broken.

Better protection is offered by rack bolts mortised into the door edge at the top and bottom. But it's best not to use these on thin doors as they can weaken the stile. And don't set them into the mortise and tenon joints at the corner of the door as this will also weaken the door structure. As an alternative, you can fit flush or barrel bolts.

Protecting the hinges

The other area frequently forgotten is the hinge side of the door, which is most vulnerable to being kicked in if the door opens outwards. Hinge bolts, however, help prevent this and can be fitted to front doors as well as other external doors. The stud type (see step-by-step photographs) are best set 25mm (1in) inside the top and bottom hinges, but on heavier doors it's best to use the tongue type. The male part is fixed to the edge of the door and a recessed plate is set in the frame.

Patio doors

At one time sliding patio doors had a poor security record, notably because burglars had the audacity to lift the sliding sash clear of the track. This isn't possible with modern designs, which also incorporate a locking device. However, there are purpose-made patio door locks available to give added security (see *Ready Reference*).

Ready Reference

SECURING FRENCH DOORS

Because the doors lock against each other they are awkward to secure. Fit hinge bolts on the outside edges, and rack or barrel bolts which should lock into the top frame and the floor.

PATIO DOOR LOCK

This is screwed to the bottom edge of the inside frame and a bar is pushed into a predrilled hole in the outer one.

PREVENTING FORCED ENTRY

One of the most unpleasant situations anyone can experience is to answer a knock at the door to be faced with someone barging his way in uninvited.

Once the door has been opened, a rim or mortise lock is totally ineffective at keeping an intruder out. But to prevent this happening you can fit one of a variety of door chains so you can identify who is at the door without having to open it more than just ajar.

Most chains can be hooked in position when you are in the house, but there is a type that you can lock in place from the outside to give added protection to the door locks.

Don't forget that you can also fit a door viewer to a solid timber door and this will enable you to see who is on the other side without them seeing you.

1 Set the door chain centrally on the opening edge of the door. First mark the fixing holes of the plate close that has to be attached to the door itself.

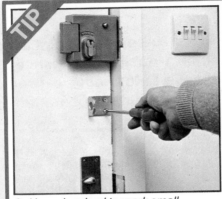

2 Use a bradawl to mark small starting holes in the door and then screw the plate in position. If the timber is soft, resite the plate.

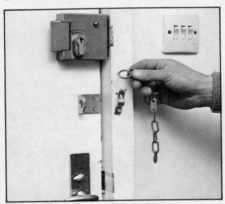

3 Partly drive in the bottom screw of the staple that holds the chain in place on the frame. Slip the chain over the staple and fasten both fixing screws.

4 To make the door secure, slip the tab on the linkage through the slotted ring on the plate close and draw the chain back to lock against the plate.

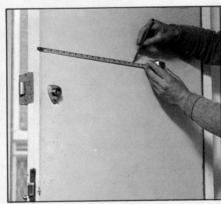

5 A door viewer should be fitted centrally at eye level to a solid timber door. It allows you to see who is on the other side without them seeing you.

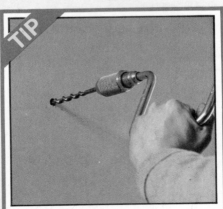

6 Next drill a 12mm (1/2in) hole through the door. If using an electric drill hold a wood block at the back of the hole to prevent splitting.

7 Push the barrel through the hole from the outside of the door so the flange surrounding the lens of the viewer presses tightly against the door.

8 On the inside, screw the eyepiece, which has a swivel cap over the end, to the barrel using a coin. This will hold the viewer firmly in place.

SECURING DOOR EDGES

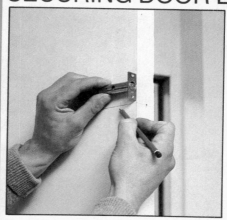

1 Rack bolts for doors have a longer barrel than their window counterparts. First mark the position of the barrel and the keyhole on the edge of the door.

2 Drill the barrel hole and keyhole, then cut a recess so that the plate of the bolt sits flush with the door edge. Check that the barrel hole is deep enough.

3 Screw the bolt and keyhole plate into place. Chalk the end of the bolt, close the door, then use the special key to try to lock the bolt.

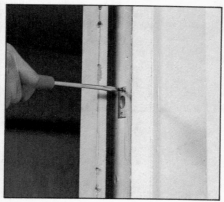

4 Where the bolt makes a chalk mark on the frame, drill a suitably-sized receiver hole. This should be protected by a metal plate recessed into the frame.

5 To fit a stud-type hinge bolt, drill a 10mm (3/8in) diameter hole about 38mm (1 1/2in) into the closing edge of the door. Tape the bit to act as a depth stop.

6 Drive the ribbed part of the bolt into the hole with a hammer. Then partially close the door so that the bolt makes a mark on the door frame.

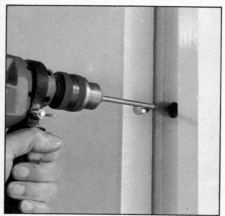

7 Measure how far the stud protrudes from the door edge and then drill a 12mm (1/2in) diameter hole in the door frame to slightly more than this depth.

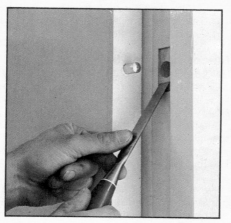

8 This hole in the frame is covered with a mating plate; you will probably have to recess this to ensure that the door can close properly without sticking.

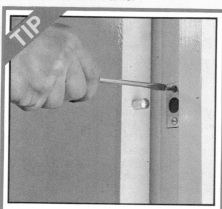

9 Screw the mating plate into the recess, making sure you drive the screws squarely into the countersunk holes so they don't foul the door.

FITTING NEW DOORS AND FRAMES

A smart new door can make all the difference to the appearance of a home. But remember that the quality of the frame is important too – to keep out intruders and bad weather, and to match the style of the door.

Not all doors have frames. Internal doors are generally fitted into 'linings', also known as 'casings'. A lining differs from a frame in being made from wider pieces of timber. These are usually flat, cut at the time of installation to the lengths required, and fitted together in the opening with simple housing or rebate joints.

A frame, on the other hand, is a fairly sophisticated piece of joinery, often in hardwood, which comes ready-made. It's heavier and stronger than a lining, and it's always used for external doorways; as a result, it's specially designed to keep out the weather. Lighter frames are sometimes also found in internal doorways – especially those in thin walls, because the pieces in a frame are narrow and squarish in section, not flat. Rebates are moulded in them to receive the door, and they're usually machined in other ways as well.

Joints, usually mortise-and-tenon, are already cut in the frame components, so that you can't choose your own length and width. In other words, the opening in the wall has to fit the frame you've bought, because you can't make the frame fit the opening. So you need to make sure you buy the right size of frame for the door in the first place.

A door frame may consist of only three pieces – the head, which goes at the top, and the two jambs which go on either side. In that case, for an external doorway you'll have to buy a separate threshold or sill (the part you step on). However, four-piece door frames, which include thresholds, are also available.

Why install a frame?

Strong though it is, an existing door frame isn't invulnerable. Often fully exposed to the elements, it may eventually rot, usually in the bottoms of the jambs. Hard knocks (and even an attack by vandals or burglars) may necessitate replacement, too.

Alternative reasons for installing a new frame may be to improve security, fire protection, weather resistance or appearance. Ask your timber merchant or other joinery supplier about frames with the particular characteristics you're looking for. Yet another reason for fitting a new frame may be because you want a new door, and the old frame is the wrong size or is otherwise unsuitable.

Lastly, you might want to make a new doorway where none existed before (eg, for access to a back yard). This might mean enlarging an existing window opening by removing the brickwork beneath the sill. But if you're making a completely new opening, remember you'll need a lintel to support the wall above, and flashing to stop moisture from penetrating. If in doubt, consult your local Building Inspector.

Removing an old frame

Before putting in your new frame, you may well have to take out an old one. It's worth knowing the quickest way of doing this (see *Ready Reference*).

First, saw through the head in two places, making the cuts slope upwards and inwards, towards the centre of the frame. The middle portion of the head will then come away easily.

Next, saw through the jambs – again at an angle – downwards and outwards. This enables you to pull the lower part of each jamb up and out. Then you have plenty of freedom to work the top corners of the frame away from the brickwork.

Lastly, clean up the opening, removing any loose timber plugs to which the frame

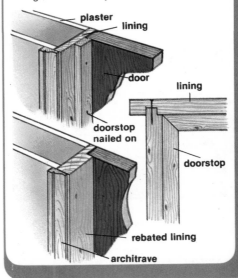

WAYS OF FITTING DOOR FRAMES

External doorways

Here are two ways of fitting a frame into an outside wall. Note that mastic and a dpc are both used to prevent moisture from penetrating.

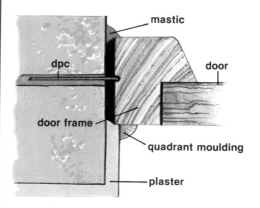

mastic
dpc
door
door frame
quadrant moulding
plaster

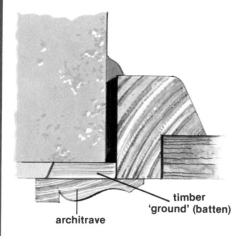

architrave
timber 'ground' (batten)

Internal doorways

A is a common arrangement, B a specially shaped frame, and C a frame narrower than the wall is thick: lengths of wood make up the width.

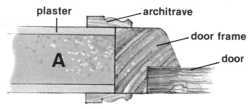

plaster
architrave
door frame
door

A

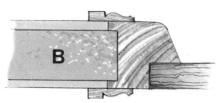

B

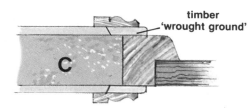

C

timber 'wrought ground'

Fixing frames to walls

Apart from screwing into wall plugs, you can use metal anchors (A), or timber plugs (B), cut as shown and driven into the joints between bricks.

metal anchor

A

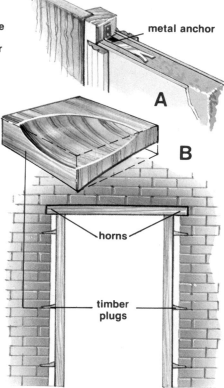

B

horns

timber plugs

Joins between frame and skirting

Usually skirting (nailed to battens fixed to the wall) is butted against the back of the architrave (A).

If the skirting is too thick (B), add a 'plinth block' below the architrave. Chamfer its edges for neatness.

Threshold design

A ready-made hardwood threshold has either a metal water bar, which you bed in mastic as shown, or a rebate which does the same job.

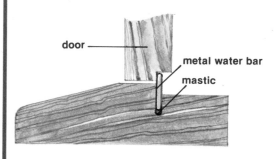

door
metal water bar
mastic

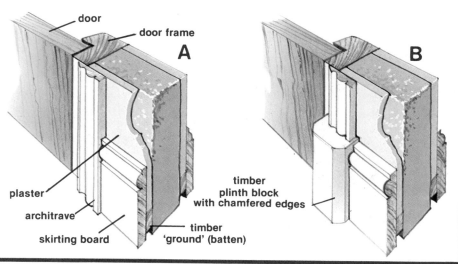

door
door frame
A

B

plaster
architrave
skirting board
timber 'ground' (batten)

timber plinth block with chamfered edges

PREPARING THE DOORS AND FRAME

1 Nail a length of dpc to the underside of the threshold. Then paint over and seal the nail heads with bituminous emulsion.

2 Assemble the joints in the frame, fitting the threshold across the two jambs. Then skew-nail them together to provide reinforcement.

3 Fit the frame into the opening. Prop it up so that it's vertical (check with a level). Ensure the threshold is the right height.

4 Drill holes in the timber and masonry and insert wall plugs into them. Then screw the frame straight onto the wall.

5 Spread a layer of mastic along the bottom of the threshold groove. Then fit the metal bar along the threshold, bedding it into the mastic.

6 After placing the doors in the opening and checking how well they fit, plane them down if necessary for a slight gap all round.

7 Mark along the bottom of the door the width of the rebate you'll need to cut to ensure that the door fits over the water bar.

8 Lightly nail a strip of wood to the door, to act as a guide, before sawing the rebate to depth in the bottom of the door.

9 Chisel out the waste to the same depth to complete the rebate. Alternatively, you can do the whole job with a rebate plane.

FITTING THE DOORS

1 Decide and mark the hinge positions along the inner edge of each door. Heavier doors need three hinges, but two usually suffice.

2 Mark the hinge recesses' depth with a marking gauge, and use a hammer and chisel to cut them. Begin by chopping round the edges.

3 Cut across the grain, then finish the recesses by carefully removing the waste. You need a sharp chisel; don't split the timber.

4 Position the hinge, making sure it's absolutely straight. Use a bradawl to make starting holes for the screws; then drive them home.

5 Position each door in the frame, and prop it up at the right height. Then use the loose leaf of each hinge to mark its recess in the frame.

6 Screw the hinges to the jambs, after chiselling out the recesses as in the door. Half the knuckle's thickness projects beyond the edge.

7 A neat way of fixing glass into a door is to start by laying putty or other suitable sealant in the rebates before you insert the glass.

8 Then lay the panes of glass (ready cut to size) into position, making sure that they are bedded carefully into the putty or sealant.

9 Finally, pin mitred lengths of glass bead all round. Don't glue them, in case you need to remove the glass (eg, after a breakage).

may have been fixed plus, of course, any rubble which may be lying at the bottom.

Removing a doorframe while keeping it intact for subsequent re-use is a trickier business, since at the top corners frames often have 'horns' (these are projections where the head overhangs the jambs at either side; they are built into the brickwork for maximum stability). You'll have to extract these by carefully cutting out the mortar joints from between the bricks around the horns.

To remove the fixings at either side of the frame, carefully cut away any plastering or rendering that conceals the frame edges and run a pad saw fitted with a hacksaw blade down between the jamb and the wall on either side; saw through any obstacles you meet. This will be easy enough if the fixings are nails or screws, but quite hard if they're metal anchors.

Occasionally, steel dowels are also used to fasten a door frame to the floor, projecting down into it from the ends of the jambs. They prevent the jambs from working loose with heavy use. Although they can often be omitted when fitting a new frame, their presence makes it very difficult to remove an old frame in one piece. But it may be possible to chip the floor away round them.

Lastly, place a large flat piece of timber against the edge of the frame, in various positions all round it in turn, and hit it so as to knock the frame out of the opening.

Fixing a new frame

There are three ways of fixing the jambs to the walls on either side. Firstly, you can screw them into plastic or fibre wallplugs; in external doorways, use screws which are rust-proof (eg, stainless steel) or rust-resistant (eg, zinc-plated), not plain steel ones.

Secondly, you can attach the jambs to metal anchors or fixing cramps, cemented into the brick joints. And thirdly, you can nail them to wooden plugs wedged between the bricks.

The first of these methods is probably the simplest, but the second is the strongest, and the last means you can get a secure fixing in brick or blockwork even if there are gaps between the frame and the wall, because you can cut the plugs off to exactly the length you need. The method works as follows.

Assemble the frame and see how it fits the opening. If it's too big, your best plan is to enlarge the opening slightly, by chopping away up to one third of a brick's length from either side of the opening. Then insert the timber plugs, opposite each other, firmly in the brickwork joints – at least three on each side. Drop a plumbline from the top of the opening on one side, and mark its position on each plug there.

Measure the width of the frame (from outside edge to outside edge) and, working from the mark you've already made on one of the plugs, mark that width on the plug opposite. Then drop the plumbline past this and mark its position on the other plugs that side. Lastly, cut off all the plugs at the marks. The plug ends should now give an opening which is exactly the right width for the frame, with its sides vertical and parallel, even if the wall itself has ragged edges.

After that you can insert the frame for final fixing. Although most frames are made of preservative-treated timber, the new frame should also be primed first – and ideally given a complete paint finish of undercoat and top coat on all surfaces which will adjoin brickwork or concrete, to keep out any damp which finds its way through and so prevent rot. However, few people bother with this.

Once the frame is in position, check that the head is level and that one jamb is more or less plumb (vertical). Nail through that jamb into the top plug. Adjust the jamb further till it's exactly plumb, and nail it into the bottom plug. Then repeat the procedure for the other jamb; in addition, before you nail through its bottom end, sight across both jambs to ensure that the frame isn't twisted.

Finish off by nailing into all the intermediate plugs, and punching all the nail heads below the surface of the timber.

This is also the time to mortar the horns, if any, into the brickwork.

Finishing the job

The final stage is to pack timber into any remaining gaps between the frame and the wall. On an internal door frame, you'll need to finish the whole thing with architrave mouldings, which may need to be fixed to timber grounds (see page 18). In an external doorway, a mastic seal between frame and wall on the outside is also essential to keep out the damp.

For protection against driving rain, the threshold of an external door frame will either be rebated (ie, stepped), or will have a metal 'water bar', if not both. The latter rests in a groove along the top of the threshold, into which it needs to be set on a bed of non-setting mastic. The bottom of the door will have to be rebated to fit over it.

If you've bought wisely, the door should fit the frame exactly – but you can always saw and plane off small amounts from the top, bottom or sides if necessary.

Hanging the door is a straightforward matter of marking out and chiselling hinge recesses on the door, screwing the hinges into them, and repeating the procedure on the frame.

Remember, however, that a door must hang quite vertically. The hinges should be exactly above one another; you may have to enlarge or pack out the recesses with thin slivers of wood, or even cardboard.

REMOVING A DOOR FRAME
This procedure is especially appropriate when you're removing a frame from a solid wall:
● start by sawing through the head at an angle in two places; the piece in the middle should then come away easily

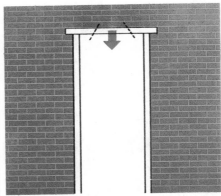

● next, saw through the jambs at an angle, and remove the lower part of each; you may have screws or nails to contend with here. And, if the jambs are fixed to the ground with metal dowels inserted into the end grain, you'll have to pull these free at the same time

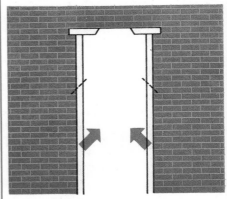

● lastly you can remove each of the top corners from the brickwork or blockwork. Having cut away the rest of the frame first means that you now have freedom to work any 'horns' (projecting ends of the head) loose from the wall.

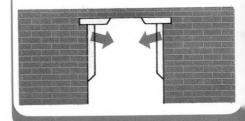

SECTION 4

BUILDING

TECHNIQUES

– OUTDOOR

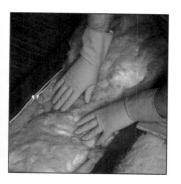

BUILDING A BRICK WALL

There's a lot in bricklaying that you only really pick up with practice. But there are some rules which can guide you every step of the way. Understanding bricks themselves, the right way to mix mortar and how to use the trowel correctly will help you achieve a result to be proud of.

Brickwork is made up of two things: the bricks, and the mortar which forms the joints. Building a wall that's going to last needs careful attention to both, and the first thing is to choose the right bricks for the job.

Know your bricks

There are three groups of clay bricks:

1 <u>Common</u> bricks have no special finish because they are made to be used where they will not be seen or be subjected to major stress or load. They are mostly used in situations where they will be covered by paint, plaster, cladding, rendering etc. They are a relatively inexpensive brick and are usually a rather patchy pink in colour.

2 <u>Facing</u> bricks come in a variety of colours and textures for they are made to be displayed indoors and out. Also called *stocks,* they are capable of bearing heavy loads. If classed as *ordinary quality,* it means they can be used for most projects, but in very exposed conditions outdoors will need to be protected by a damp proof course at ground level (either a course of engineering bricks, see below, or a layer of bituminous felt) or with a coping above to prevent the bricks becoming saturated with rain. Without this protection they are liable to be affected by frost which would cause disintegration. *Special quality* facing bricks are suitable for use in exposed places or where great strength is needed, eg, for paving, retaining walls, garden walls and steps.

3 <u>Engineering</u> bricks are smooth and dense, designed to be used where strength and low water absorption is essential – for example in foundation courses (thus providing a damp proof course for a wall or planter) and load bearing walls.

Another type of bricks completely are the *calcium silicate bricks.* These are flint/lime bricks which are whitish when steam-hardened in an autoclave (they aren't fired like clay), but these are available in many colours because they take pigment well. They absorb moisture easily, so must never be laid with a mortar that doesn't contain a plasticiser. They can be used in just the same way as clay bricks. Like engineering bricks, they are also more regular in shape and vary less in size than ordinary bricks.

Brick types

Bricks also vary in their character as well as their composition: they may be solid, perforated or hollow, but most fall into the solid category. Even bricks with small or large holes in them (these are also known as cellular) are classed as solid so long as the perforations do not exceed 25% of the total volume. The same is true of bricks with a shallow or deep indentation known as a *frog.* As well as making the bricks lighter, perforations and frogs give bricks a better key (ie, the mortar is better able to bond them together).

The actual size of a standard brick is 215mm long, 102.5mm wide and 65mm deep, however, when calculating the number of bricks you will need, add about 10mm to each of these dimensions to allow for the mortar joints, ie 225mm × 113mm × 75mm – this is known as the format size.

Standard 'specials' are also made to co-ordinate with standard bricks. These either provide protection (eg, copings) or add a finishing touch to the top or end of a wall

(eg, single, double or left and right-hand bullnose).

Storing bricks

As all bricks (except engineering bricks) are porous, they should be stacked on a level area away from damp, otherwise long after you've used them the mineral salts inside the clay will stain the surface with an unsightly powdery white deposit (known as *efflorescence*). In the garden, put bricks on planks or a metal sheet and cover them with plastic sheeting. Apart from anything else, bricks which are saturated with water (as opposed to just being wet) are hard to lay and will prevent a satisfactory bond between bricks and mortar.

Mortar for bricklaying

Cement and sand made into mortar with water will set quickly, but is liable to create a crack between the mortar and the brick if it shrinks during drying. The ideal mortar, in fact, doesn't set too quickly, doesn't shrink much and can take up settling movements without cracking. There are two ways of making a mortar like this:

● The first way is by adding hydrated lime to the mix. This makes the mortar more workable and smooth (or 'buttery' as the experts say).

● The second is by adding a plasticiser — a proprietary liquid or powder. Air bubbles are formed which provide spaces for the water to expand into, thus preventing cracks.

● Basic to mortar is cement. This acts as the adhesive, binding the particles of sand together. Ordinary portland cement is the one most commonly used.

● Fine sand is used for mortar to give it its correct strength. Use clean builder's sand (also known as 'soft' sand) which does not contain clay, earth or soluble salts (these can lead to efflorescence).

Buying the materials

Cement is usually sold in 50kg (112lb) bags, although you may also find smaller sizes. Sand is sold by the cu metre (1.1/3 cu yd) and in parts of a cu metre. To give you a sense of scale, a cu metre of sand weighs about 1,500kg (1½ tons) — a very large heap. Both are usually bought from builders merchants, where you can also buy lime or

MIXING MORTAR

1 Unless you're using dry ready-mix (most suitable for small jobs) carefully proportion 1 part cement to 6 parts builders sand.

2 Thoroughly mix the cement into the sand so that you end up with an entirely consistent colour. Turn the mix over at least three times.

3 Adding a little plasticiser to the water (the amount will be specified on the container) will make the mortar easier to work with.

4 Form a crater and pour in half the water. In total you'll need about the same amount of water (by volume) as cement — but add the rest gradually.

5 Mix in the dry mortar from the inside walls of the crater. As the water is absorbed, add a little more. Turn the whole mix over several times.

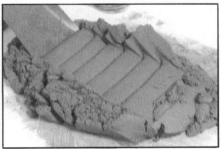

6 The final mix should look like this. Check it by stepping the shovel back — the ridges should be firm and smooth, holding the impression of the shovel.

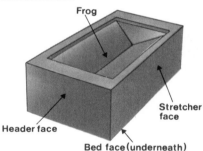
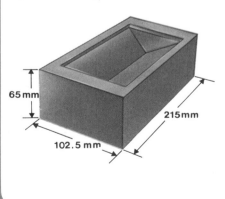

USING THE TROWEL

1 *Use the trowel to chop off a section of mortar (about the same size as the trowel) and separate it from the rest with a clean slicing action.*

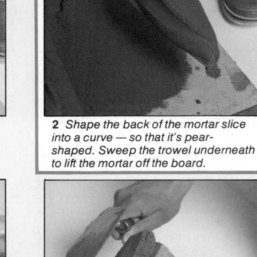

2 *Shape the back of the mortar slice into a curve — so that it's pear-shaped. Sweep the trowel underneath to lift the mortar off the board.*

3 *Slide the trowel sharply backwards to lay the mortar in a 'sausage' shape. Spread it out by stepping the tip of the trowel down the middle.*

4 *When you've laid a brick in position, remove the mortar that squeezes out of the joint by sweeping the trowel upwards with its edge just scraping the brick.*

5 *To create the vertical joints between bricks, you 'butter' one end before you lay it. Scrape the mortar on by sliding the trowel backwards.*

6 *Hold the brick upright and scrape down all four edges. Finally spread out the mortar evenly to a thickness of 10mm-12mm (about ½in).*

proprietary plasticisers. Alternatively you can buy special masonry cement which has a plasticiser already in it and only needs to be mixed with sand and water.

Proprietary plasticisers are available in 5kg containers and you will have more than you need if you're only doing a small job — only a capful or two for each bucket of cement. But always follow manufacturer's instructions for use. Hydrated lime is a powder bought in 25kg bags.

Dry ready-mix mortars are also available with all the necessary ingredients ready mixed — so you just add water. Although more expensive than buying the sand and cement separately, it's a convenient way of buying for small projects. Bags usually come in

10kg, 25kg, 40kg and 50kg sizes. Alternatively, you can buy bags in which the cement is packaged separately from the sand.

Remember that it's always better to have a little more than you need — so be generous in estimating (see *Ready Reference*). Also make sure that any surplus cement or dry-mix is well sealed. This is vital to prevent it going off.

Rules to remember

● When filling the cement bucket (proportions are by volume, not weight), tap it frequently to disperse any trapped air.
● Mortar that has begun to set is no use. Any not used within 2 hours of the wetting of the cement should be discarded – if used it would

dry too quickly and would not give the required strength to the brickwork.
● The sand and cement have to be thoroughly mixed before any water is added. Turn mixture over and over with the shovel until the pile is a consistent colour all through. The same rule applies to dry-mix mortar.
● When mixing in water, make crater on top of the pile, add some water and bring dry materials from sides to centre. Turn over whole pile several times, make another crater and repeat until mixture has a consistency which will hold the impression of the fingers when squeezed, or the impression of the trowel point.
● As builders' sand is rarely dry it is not possible to know how much water will be

eeded to achieve the right consistency. Using a small container such as an empty tin will give you more control than using a bucket – and add water bit by bit.

The vital bricklaying tool

The trowel is the tool which makes the job, and no other tool can be substituted for it. A bricklayer's trowel is heavier and less flexible than any other trowel, and can be used to pick up and smooth down a required amount of mortar. Brick trowels can be bought in various blades sizes (from 225 to 350mm, or 9in to 14in) but the easiest to handle is the 250mm/10in one.

Brick trowels are roughly diamond shaped with a sharp point at the end opposite to the handle. The left side has a straight edge for scooping up mortar; the right side has a slight curve used for cleaning up the edges of bricks and for tapping the brick down into the mortar to level it. These are reversed in left-handed trowels.

Professional bricklayers use the curved edge of the trowel to cut bricks, but a more accurate and cleaner cut can be made with a brick hammer and bolster chisel. The trowel has a wooden handle raised slightly above the diamond, and at an angle to it to prevent you brushing your knuckles on the bricks as you are working. Getting the feel of the trowel and handling it properly is the key to good brickwork.

The trowel must be manipulated so that the mortar is scooped up in what's called a 'pear' or 'sausage' shape (see left) and placed on the bricks. This action is one that needs a lot of practice, for mortar that isn't compact is hard to manoeuvre and won't go where you want it to.

Practice routines

Make up a small amount of mortar (or 1 part of lime to 6 of sand, plus water to make it pliable) and practise combining it with bricks before you undertake a bricklaying project. The bricks can be scraped off within 2 hours (before the mortar sets). You have longer with

BRICK JOINTS

1 *The simplest brick joint is a 'struck' joint — do the vertical joints first, drawing the trowel upwards or downwards with a firm action.*

2 *Next do the horizontal joints — use the full length of the trowel and drawing it firmly backwards with a sliding action.*

Types of pointing

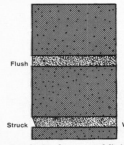

Flush

Struck

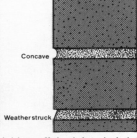

Concave

Weather struck

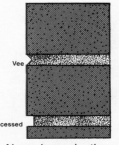

Vee

Recessed

There are lots of ways of finishing off the joints in brickwork. Above is a selection of six of the most common. The flush joint is finished flush with the brick surface, while struck, weatherstruck and vee joints are all formed with the point of the trowel. Concave or rounded pointing is formed by running the edge of a bucket handle or a piece of hose pipe along the joints, while recessed pointing is pressed back with a piece of wood planed to the same size as the brick joints.

LAYING AND LEVELLING

1 Check layout by 'dry laying' the bricks, setting them a finger-width apart. Use string and pegs as a guide, fixing the ends with bricks, as shown.

2 Use your gauge rod — see **8** — to check that a corner is square. Measure 3 marks along one side, 4 along the other; if square, the diagonal will be 5 marks.

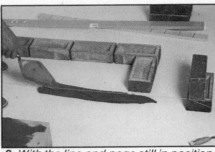

3 With the line and pegs still in position, lay the mortar on the base by drawing the trowel sharply backwards. Lay enough for at least 2 bricks at a time.

4 Tap the first brick into position, using the string as your guide. The mortar should make a joint 10mm (just under ½in) thick.

5 Lay the next 4 or 5 bricks, still following the line, making sure all mortar joints are the same thickness. Carefully scrape off the excess mortar.

6 Use the spirit level to check that the bricks are sitting perfectly level. If one is too high, tap it down. If too low, remove it and add mortar.

7 Each brick for the next course should straddle two on the first course. This creates the 'stretcher bond', evenly distributing the weight of bricks.

8 Check that the courses are rising correctly with a 'gauge rod'. The rod is marked at 75mm intervals — brick height plus a 10mm mortar joint.

9 With string and pegs removed, check each brick with the spirit level as you lay it. Tap the bricks gently with the trowel handle.

10 With each new course, check the corner with the gauge rod. With the first brick correctly positioned, other bricks are aligned with it.

11 Check that the faces of the bricks are vertical and aligned with each other. If not tap bricks back into position with the trowel.

12 Also check diagonally across the face of the bricks. Lay the bricks frog (the indentation in the top of the brick) down only on the final course.

lime mortar. The 'sausage' or 'pear' is the basic shape of mortar lifted onto the trowel. The following sequence is worth practising over and over until it becomes easy to do. Chop down into the mortar and draw a slice of it towards the edge of the board. Move the trowel to and fro, along the length of the slice, pressing the body of the trowel on to the mortar till you have shaped the back of the slice into a curve – the mortar should be smooth and have no cracks.

Now sweep the trowel underneath the curved slice and load it on to the trowel, it will either look like a sausage or a pear, hence the name. Put it back on the spot board, shape it again, then sweep it up ready for placing. This amount of mortar should give you a 10mm thick bed for two stretchers. Hold the trowel parallel to the course, then, as you draw it back towards you, lift and jerk it slightly so the mortar rolls off gradually in a smooth elongated sausage. Press the mortar along the middle with the point of the trowel so a furrow is made in the mortar. When you place a brick on it a small amount of mortar should ooze out.

Joints in brickwork

Bricks are laid with both horizontal and vertical joints to keep the bricks apart. After the excess mortar has been removed from the face of the bricks (and behind), the joints can be finished in various ways – for an attractive effect as well as for protection against the weather. Coloured mortar is a specially prepared dry mix to which only water needs to be added. Pigment can be bought to colour your own mix of mortar but it can be difficult to obtain the same colour for each batch..

Making a cross joint

Sometimes 'buttering' is used to describe the technique of coating the end of a brick with mortar to form the vertical joint. Sweep up enough mortar to cover about a third of the trowel. Now sharply flick the trowel so the mortar lifts up, then falls back onto the trowel, (this squashes out air and makes the mortar 'sticky'). Hold the brick at a slight angle, then scrape the trowel against the bottom edge. Use the trowel point to flatten and level the mortar on the header – it should be 10mm thick.

Cleaning off

The other important trowel action is removing excess mortar from the side of the bricks as you lay them. Cut the mortar off cleanly by firmly lifting the trowel upwards (if you do it horizontally it will smudge the bricks). This leaves a flush joint.

Tricks or bad habits?

Bricklayers will often add a few squirts of washing-up liquid to the water when mixing mortar. This on-site plasticiser, used instead of lime or a proprietary plasticiser, is not added in any precise manner. Although it might make the mortar more pliable it could also weaken it. And how much is a squirt anyway? If you want a pliable mix, buy a proprietary plasticiser additive, or ready-mix with it already added.

● The shovel is frequently used as a measuring stick when mixing mortar, and there's no doubt it's an easy way of proportioning the ingredients. It can, however, give wildly inaccurate results. A mound of powdery cement won't sit on a shovel in the same way as sand will. Measurement should always be by volume. A bucket is ideal for most quantities – although if you're only making a very small amount use a small metal container instead.

● The curved edge of the bricklayer's trowel will effectively cut bricks when wielded by a professional. Apart from doing a great deal of damage to the trowel (the edge of which is needed for the upward sweep required to remove mortar from brickwork), it is easier to cut bricks on a sandy or soft ground with a bolster chisel and a hammer.

Protecting brickwork from damage

As soon as you have finished bricklaying, and you've cleaned off and finished all the joints, it's worth taking a few simple precautions to protect your work until the mortar has set and it is able to take care of itself.

The biggest enemy is rain. A heavy downpour could wash mortar out of freshly-pointed joints – which you would then have to re-point – and stain the face of the brickwork. Such stains are particularly difficult to remove except by hosing and scrubbing. Furthermore, if your brickwork is set on a hard surround – a patio, for example, or alongside a path – rain could splash up from the surface onto your brickwork, again causing staining and erosion of mortar joints at or near ground level.

So on small projects it's a good idea to cover your work, at least for 24 hours or so, until the mortar has had time to set to something like its final hardness. Drape polythene or similar water-proof sheeting over the brickwork, anchoring it on top with several loose bricks, and drawing the sides of the sheeting away from the face of the brickwork before anchoring them at ground level a foot or so away from the wall. In windy weather, lay a continuous line of bricks, or use lengths of timber, to prevent the wind from whipping underneath the sheeting.

Remember that until the mortar has hardened any knocks will displace bricks and break mortar joints. Corners are particularly prone to knocks and accidental collisions. So it's well worth erecting some kind of simple barricade in front of the new work for a day or two.

CORNERS in brickwork

The techniques involved in making a brick wall turn a corner or to finish with a pier require an understanding of bonding and how cut bricks might have to be used to keep a design symmetrical.

Building walls isn't simply a matter of arranging bricks in straight lines. You may have to include corners and, when you come to the end of the wall, it must be finished off properly. The techniques for doing this effectively are relatively easy once you know the basis of brick bonding.

Brick bonds are crucial to bricklaying; simply stacking bricks one above the other without any kind of interlocking would neither distribute the weight of the wall evenly nor provide the wall with any kind of strength, however strong the mortar between the bricks. And because the joints line up they would provide a perfect channel for water to get in and wash out the mortar.

The simplest way of bonding is to overlap the brick, with no vertical joints continuing through adjacent courses. This kind of bonding can create numerous different patterns – some very simple, such as the stretcher bond used to build the brick wall on pages 160-165, others much more complicated and requiring advance planning.

Exactly the same principle applies whether you're building a wall a half-brick thick (a single line of bricks) or one that needs to be one brick thick (two adjacent lines of bricks or one line laid header on). The difference is that instead of only overlapping the bricks lengthways as in a *stretcher bond* you can also overlap them widthways. With the *header bond*, for instance, all of the bricks are arranged header on to the face of the wall — and again the vertical joints only line up in alternate courses. In effect, the bricks overlap by half their width.

With any bonding pattern, there may be a need for cut bricks to maintain the bond. This may happen at the end of a wall built in stretcher bond where half bricks (called ½ bats) are needed in alternate courses. It may also occur where a new wall is being tied in to an existing wall (see below).

Similarly, with a wall built in header bond the ends need two three-quarter bricks (called ¾ bats) laid side by side in alternate courses to maintain the symmetry, the overlap and wall thickness. With other types of bond, the number and variety of cut bricks increases. The *English bond*, for instance, alternates a course of bricks laid stretcher face on with a course header face on to make a one-brick thick wall — and it needs a brick cut in half lengthways (called a queen closer) in each header course or two ¾ bats laid side by side in the stretcher course.

Corners in brickwork

When it comes to turning a corner in brickwork (known as a *quoin*) the importance of correct bonding is even more apparent. Without it, you'd be building two walls which weren't interlocked and so lacking in real strength. In a half-brick thick wall in stretcher bond the corner is easy to make. Instead of cutting ½ bats for alternate courses, a whole brick is placed header face on at right angles to the front face of the wall.

The necessary 'tying in' of bricks with other bonding patterns, however, usually requires additional cut bricks and careful planning. In effect, the bond may change when you turn a corner. In header bond for example, which has alternate courses starting with ¾ bats, ¾ bats must be placed header on as well to create the corner. In English bond the stretcher course on one side of the quoin becomes the header course on the other.

MARKING OUT FOR A CORNER

1 Bricks can be used to hold the string lines on already laid concrete but use profile boards if a trench has to be dug. Check with a builders square that all the lines cross at right angles.

2 Laying the bricks dry is the best way of checking your calculations after setting out is completed, the width of your finger being a good guide to the eventual thickness of the joint.

3 After the first course is laid there are two things to check: the bricks must be horizontal (you can tap down any out of alignment) and their faces must be truly perpendicular.

4 From the first course onwards, the squareness of the corner must be checked so that any adjustments can be made immediately to prevent the wall leaning out (called an overhang).

A bond may also have to be altered if the bricks don't fit the actual length of the wall. When this happens you have to break the bond as close as possible to the centre of the wall. If the length differs by 56mm or less don't use a ¼ bat (this is considered bad building practice) but use ½ and ¾ bats instead, making sure you place them so that no straight joints occur.

The end of the wall

If you're building a wall as a boundary, or enclosing a corner of your garden, it may have to meet existing walls at one or even both ends. In such situations you have to tie in the bricks with the other wall(s), so this may affect your choice of bond for the new wall — it's always better if the new matches the old. It also means you have to match levels, and before you lay your first new brick you have to chip out bricks from alternate courses of the existing wall to provide for 'toothing-in'. Even if you can satisfactorily match the bond pattern, the old bricks may be a different size, so to make a proper connection expect to cut bricks to odd lengths to tooth in. More about this in another section.

If your wall comes to a free-standing end you must create what's called a *stopped end*. This requires careful checking for vertical alignment, and needs to be finished off to make a clean, neat face. But it is important to make sure the end is strong enough — and to do this you actually increase the width by a half brick to create a 'pier'. In effect, instead of cutting a ½ bat to finish off each alternate course, you lay the last brick in alternate courses at right angles to the wall face. By adding a ½ bat next to it you create a squared-off end — a simple pier.

Piers for support

It's not just at the end of a wall that you may need the added strength of a pier. To give a wall extra support, particularly on a long run, you need piers at regular intervals. For instance, walls of half-brick thickness need piers that project by at least half a brick every 1.8m (6ft). To do this in a wall built in stretcher bond, you will have to alter the bonding pattern to accommodate the pier, and add cut bricks to ensure the correct overlapping is maintained. For how to do this see pictures page 95. If the wall is over 12 courses high, a more substantial pier is needed: three bricks are placed header on in the first course, and ¾ bats are used on the pier and either side of the middle stretcher in the second course.

One brick thick walls need piers at less frequent intervals — in fact every 2.8m (9ft) — but the pier has only to project by half a brick (see diagram).

Where piers occur, the foundation must be dug slightly wider at that point (about half a brick wider on both sides and beyond the end of the pier).

Method of building

Planning how you're going to lay the bricks is, of course, only the theoretical side of bricklaying. In practice, to make sure the wall stands completely perpendicular and the corners and ends are vertical it's most important to follow a certain order of work. Lay at least the first course of bricks dry so that you can check the layout and ensure that all the

PROFILE BOARDS

These are placed to give accurate lines when digging the trench for the foundation. Strings attached to nails in the top of the boards define the width of the trench and must cross at perfect right angles where the corner is to be built.

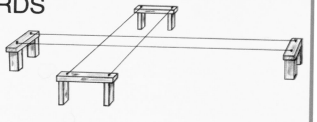

Keith Morris

A BUILDERS SQUARE

Essential for checking that corners are 90°, this is simply three pieces of wood cut in the proportions of 3:4:5 (ie, a right-angled triangle). Nail them together with a half-lap at the right-angled corner and with the longest side nailed on top of the other two sides.

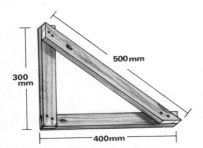

300 mm
500 mm
400mm

WHAT CAN GO WRONG

You can lose the horizontal because you didn't check often enough as the wall was rising. With every course
● use the spirit level
● use the gauge rod
The wall can lean out or in because you didn't check the vertical with the spirit level. Use it when
● racking back
● starting a new course
When laying to a line the last brick won't fit because the vertical joints further back along the course were not the same width. So make sure that in each course
● the joint width remains constant
● vertical joints line up in alternate courses – use the gauge rod for this.

LAYING TO A LINE

When you build up two corners at opposite ends of a wall, the process of laying bricks in between is called 'laying to a line'. To fix the line for each course use
● a bricklayers line and pins

● twine tied around two spare bricks

● triangular profile boards (good for beginners as you can see that the courses are rising evenly).

TURNING A CORNER

1 On each face of the wall check that it is perpendicular by holding the level at an angle. Tap bricks in or out.

2 As each course is laid use the gauge rod to check that the wall is rising evenly, with equal horizontal joints.

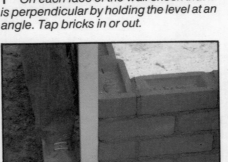

3 Check that the corner is vertical by using the spirit level straight. Hold it steady with your foot.

4 Lay the first course from the corner to the stopped end following a line and cutting bricks as needed.

5 Build up the stopped end so the courses are stepped by the correct overlap. This is called 'racking back'.

6 Raise the line to the next course between the racked corner and stopped end and fill in between.

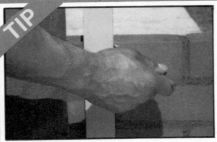

TIP

7 To make sure you get vertical joints in line, mark the position of each one on the whole brick above it.

8 In the next course, align the edge of the brick with the mark. The joints will then be the right width too.

bricks fit in (see page 164). Another big problem is that it is difficult to lay a line of bricks with each vertical join exactly the same width – an inaccuracy of just 1mm in each joint between a line of 10 bricks will mean that the last brick at the corner or end will project over the one underneath by 10mm. The best way to avoid this happening is by 'racking back' – build up each corner or end first, stepping the bricks upwards and checking the vertical each time. When the bricks reach the required height, start filling in. Any slight inaccuracies can be accommodated by the joints in the middle part of the wall where they'll be less noticeable as long as you make sure the bricks overlap each other by as close to half a brick as possible.

Making the corner square

Marking out the corner for the foundations is the first priority – and it's vital that it is square. Using profile boards and strings – explained on pages 181-183 – is the best way to start. Set the boards for each line of the corner about 1 metre (3ft) back from the actual building line (see diagram page 167). The strings must cross at right angles (90°) and to make sure they do, use the 3:4:5 triangle method (see *Ready Reference,* page 168) to make yourself a builder's square. This is a

large set-square made by nailing together three 75mm × 38mm (3in × 1½in) softwood battens cut into lengths of 450mm (18in), 600mm (2ft), and 750mm (2ft 6in) so that the sides are in the ratio 3:4:5.

Laying out the corner

When you have the profile boards in position, dig the foundation trenches – see pages 180-184 – and lay the concrete. Allow it to cure for 5 or 6 days before laying the first course of bricks. This gives it time to harden properly (although it needs about 3 weeks to reach its full strength). The next step is to mark out the actual building lines on the concrete, again using the profile boards and strings (see pages 181-183).

Lay the first course of the entire wall, starting at the corner and working outwards first along one wall line and then along the other. In building a half-brick thick wall in stretcher bond it is easy to turn the corner simply by laying two bricks to make a right angle. Check the angle using the builder's square.

Once the first course is laid, check again with the spirit level to make sure that all the bricks are sitting correctly. Add a little mortar or remove a little from underneath any bricks which are out of true. At the same time, check again that all the bricks follow your building line, and tap them into position if they don't.

A PIER IN STRETCHER BOND

1 *In order to prevent any straight joints you have to break the bond. On the first course place two bricks header on, then place a ½ bat so it spans the joint equally.*

2 *On the second course to get the pattern right you have to lose a quarter from each of the stretchers on either side of the ½ bat. So cut and place two ¾ bats.*

3 *On the pier itself, the second course is not tied on but is merely a stretcher laid across the projecting two headers. This gives a pier the same width as the wall.*

CORNERS AND STOPPED ENDS

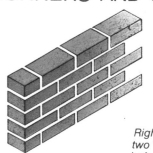

Left: At a stopped end in stretcher bond, the cut side of the ½ bats on alternate courses are hidden by the mortar joints.

Right: In a brick-thick wall in English bond, two ¼ bats or a queen closer are laid before the final header at a stopped end.

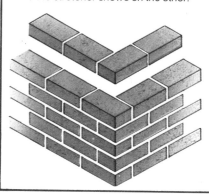

Below: At a corner in a stretcher bond wall, the header face is seen on one side while the stretcher shows on the other.

Below: The arrangement is the same at a corner, but to maintain the bonding the course on the other face becomes stretchers laid side by side.

BRICK CUTS

The most common cut bricks, used in different bonds, are:

¾ bat – cut widthways, ¼ removed

½ bat – brick cut widthways, ½ removed

¼ bat – brick cut widthways, ¾ removed (the same size as a ½ queen closer)

queen closer – brick cut in two lengthways

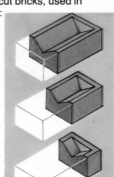

CUTTING BRICKS

Mark cutting line on each face with chalk

Nick the line all round; with hard bricks nick each face at least twice

Place brick bottom up on grass, sand or newspaper. Put bolster on nicked line, give sharp blow with hammer

DON'T use the edge of the trowel to cut bricks because
● it's an expensive tool
● it's rarely accurate

Once this is done you can remove the lines and start building up the ends and corners.

Putting in the piers

If you're going to need piers at any point along the wall, don't forget to plan them in from the beginning. In a half-brick thick stretcher bond wall a pier is tied in by two bricks laid header on in alternate courses. The courses in between are not tied in but consist of a single stretcher laid parallel to the wall for the pier, and a ½ bat and two ¾ bats replacing two stretchers in the face of the wall.

A pier at a stopped end in a half-brick stretcher bond wall is made using a stretcher face at right angles at the end. The course is completed with a ½ bat and on the alternate course two stretchers are used parallel to the wall.

Checking as you build

One of the most useful checking tools you can make yourself is a gauge rod (see pages 160-165) and as you build up the corners and ends check each course with the rod to make sure the horizontal joints are consistent. If you're aiming for a wall of about 12 courses in total, build up the corners and ends to about 6 or 7 courses first before starting to fill in between them.

To step the bricks correctly, lay 3 bricks along the building line for every 5 courses you want to go up – so it's best to start by laying 4 bricks along each side of the corner and in from each end (see photographs 5 and 6 on page 168).

Filling in

Once you've built up corners and ends properly racked back (stepped with the correct overlap), the rest of the wall can be filled in course by course. Although you can lay the bricks normally, checking each time with the level and gauge, a good tip here is to string a line between bricks already laid at each end, then lay the bricks in between to this line. A bricklayer's line and pins (the pins are specially shaped to slip into a mortar joint) is ideal, but a string can be hooked around a brick at the correct height and then anchored under a loose brick to give a start line to follow.

If you over-mortar a brick and it protrudes above the level, gently tap it down with the end of the trowel handle and scrape off the excess mortar squeezed out of the joint. If a brick does not stand high enough, remove it and the mortar underneath, then replace it with fresh mortar.

Getting the last brick into the line can be quite tricky and a good tip is to scrape the mortar onto the end of bricks at each side — then squeeze the brick in.

PIERS

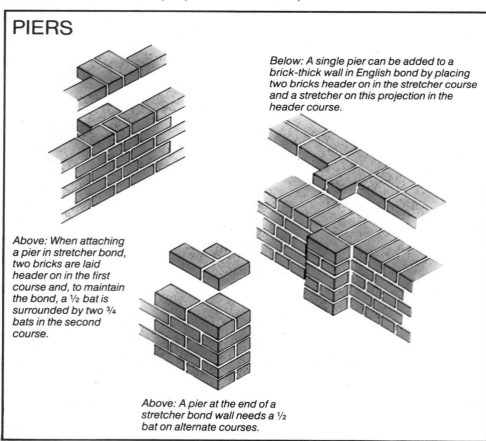

Below: A single pier can be added to a brick-thick wall in English bond by placing two bricks header on in the stretcher course and a stretcher on this projection in the header course.

Above: When attaching a pier in stretcher bond, two bricks are laid header on in the first course and, to maintain the bond, a ½ bat is surrounded by two ¾ bats in the second course.

Above: A pier at the end of a stretcher bond wall needs a ½ bat on alternate courses.

WORKING WITH CONCRETE

One of the most versatile of all building materials, concrete is also one of the easiest to work with. The techniques for laying anything from a garden path to a patio are much the same – once you know the basic rules for mixing up the ingredients, making formwork, laying and levelling.

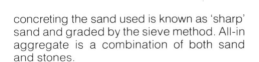

Concrete is made of cement, aggregate and water. Cement itself is quite a complex chemical formed by burning chalk, limestone and clay at high temperatures and then grinding the resulting clinker to a fine powder. Added to the water it becomes an adhesive and coats and binds the aggregate (clean, washed particles of sand, crushed stone or gravel — never brick — for the clays can react against the cement).

The strength or hardness of any concrete simply depends on the proportions of these ingredients. Only a small part of the water you add is used up in the chemical reaction — the rest evaporates.

Ordinary portland cement is used for most concreting work. (The name doesn't refer to the manufacturer or where it is made, it's simply that when invented in the 1820s it was thought to resemble Portland stone.)

Aggregates are graded according to the size of sieve the particles can pass through — anything from 10-20mm. Coarse aggregate has the largest stones (20mm) while fine aggregate, often described as shingle, can be 10-15mm. Sand, the third part of concrete, is also considered aggregate. (The cement holds the sand together and the combination of sand and cement holds the stones together.) In concreting the sand used is known as 'sharp' sand and graded by the sieve method. All-in aggregate is a combination of both sand and stones.

Choosing your mix

Different projects require different mixes of concrete. Three are most commonly used.

Mix A (see ESTIMATOR below and *Ready Reference* overleaf) is a general-purpose mix for surface slabs and bases where you want a minimum thickness of 75mm-100mm (3-4in) of concrete.

Mix B is a stronger mix and is used for light-duty strips and bases up to 75mm (3in) thick – garden paths and the like.

Mix C is a weaker mix useful for garden wall foundations, bedding in slabs and so on, where great strength is not needed.

The amount of water needed depends very much on how wet the sand and stones in the aggregate are. A rough guide is to use about half the amount (by volume) of cement. But add it gradually. Too much will ruin the mix and weaken the concrete.

How concrete works

New concrete hardens by chemical action and you can't stop it once it's started. The slower the set the better and it is important that after laying, exposed surfaces are covered with wet sacks, sand or polythene (and kept wet) for the first 4-6 days. Concrete also gives off heat as it sets — a useful property in very cold weather, although it would still need covering to protect it from frost.

Freshly mixed concrete will begin to set within 1-2 hours — in dry hot weather it will be faster. It takes 3-4 days to become properly hard — you can walk on it at this stage. To reach full strength, however, may take 28 days or more.

How to buy concrete

For small jobs it's best to buy the cement, sand and aggregate dry-mixed together, in

What to buy for mixing concrete

The quantities given here for sand and aggregate are rounded up to the nearest fraction of a cu metre that can be ordered. The mixes are made up by volume (see **Ready Reference**) so some sand and aggregate may be left over.

To make 1 cu metre eg 10m x 1m x 100mm	Cement 50kg bags	Sharp sand plus aggregate	OR	All-in aggregate
MIX A (1:2½:4)	6 bags	½ cu metre + ¾ cu metre		1 cu metre
MIX B (1:2:3)	8 bags	½ cu metre + ¾ cu metre		1 cu metre
MIX C (1:3:6)	4 bags	½ cu metre + ¾ cu metre		1¼ cu metre

GETTING A LEVEL BASE

This is vital to avoid weak, thin spots in the concrete which will crack. These methods work on a reasonably flat site:
● drive 300mm (12in) pegs into the ground at 1 metre (3ft) intervals
● align their tops with batten and spirit level to match the final surface level of the concrete
● dig away soil to required depth, taking care not to disturb pegs. Use amount of peg exposed as your depth guide

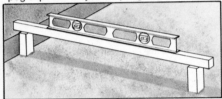

To level top of pegs over longer distances and round corners:
● tie a length of transparent hose between pegs
● fill the hose with water and drive in pegs so their tops match the water levels either end

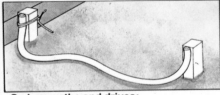

On long paths and drives:
use sighting rods made from sawn softwood – each is the same height (about 1.2 metres/4ft) and has a tee piece exactly at right angles across the top – you'll need three rods, and two helpers. Place rods on pegs and line up tops by adjusting pegs in ground.

FOUNDATIONS FOR CONCRETE

● as a general rule lay rammed hardcore to the same depth as the final concrete
● on soft sub-soil excavate to twice the depth, filling soft pockets carefully with extra hardcore
● on clay, lay concrete quickly before the clay can dry out

See pages 180-184 for more details.

MIXING

1 *Unless you're using dry ready-mix, first spread the cement over the aggregate and gradually mix by heaping into a 'volcano'.*

2 *Add about half the water to start with. Form a crater and mix in from the inside walls. Add the rest of the water gradually — not all at once.*

3 *When the concrete is about the right consistency shovel it into heaps again. Turn it into a new pile 3 times to ensure thorough mixing.*

4 *The finished concrete should look like this. When you draw the shovel back in steps, the ridges should be smooth and firm and not 'slump'.*

either 10kg, 25kg or 50kg bags. All you have to do is add water.

For larger projects, this can work out to be very expensive. Here it is better to buy the materials separately. The cement is normally sold in 50kg (just under 1 cwt) bags, though smaller (again more costly) quantities – 10kg and 25kg – are available. Both sand and aggregate are sold in 50kg bags, but it is more common to buy them loose by the cubic metre or fraction of a cubic metre. The combined or 'all-in' aggregate is available in the same way.

For really large work, however, (patios, long drives and the like) mixing the amount of concrete required by hand is extremely hard work. You could hire a powered mixer, but generally it is more convenient to buy it ready-mixed and have it delivered to the house. Check with the supplier on the minimum amount they are prepared to deliver — for quantities close to that minimum you could find it prohibitively expensive and you should consider sharing a load with a neighbour who is also carrying out building work. With ready-mix remember that you

have to be prepared to lay it fast and if there is no direct access to the site and the concrete can't be tipped directly into your prepared formwork, you must have plenty of able-bodied help with heavy-duty wheelbarrows (you can hire these) standing by.

Dry-mixes have the amounts that made-up concrete will cover printed on the bag. For mix-at-home quantities, see the ESTIMATOR.

How to store materials
Under normal conditions cement will start to harden after about 30 days simply because it'll be absorbing moisture from the air. However, older cement that's still powdery inside can still be used where great strength or a high quality finish is *not* essential – but mix in a higher proportion of cement than usual, ie 1:1:2.

Cement should always be stored under cover and raised well off the ground — on a platform of wood, for example. Stack the bags closely, keep them clear of other materials and cover them to help keep the moisture out. If a bag has been part used, the remainder can be stored for a while inside a well-sealed plastic bag.

Loose sand and aggregate should be piled on a flat, dry and hard area and covered with heavy-duty plastic sheeting. It's most important to avoid the aggregate being contaminated by soil or other foreign materials. Any organic matter would decompose in the concrete leaving 'voids' which weaken it.

Site preparation

This is a major stage before you begin to erect any formwork, mix or lay any concrete. For accurate marking out, use pegs and strings to give yourself guide lines to follow. The area should be dug out and made as level as possible (see *Ready Reference*).

The big question is, how deep should you dig and how thick should you lay the concrete? To some extent this depends on how firm the soil is. For a path or patio a 75-100mm/3-4in thickness of concrete is usually enough — add a layer of hardcore of the same depth if the soil is very soft. If, however, you're building a driveway where there'll be a lot more weight on top, then 125-150mm/5-6in of concrete on top of hardcore would be advisable.

Some soils can lead to unsuccessful concreting. If your site is *clay* for example you have to concrete it as soon as possible after it has been revealed. The reason? Clay dries out quickly and then contracts. Because it will absorb water from the concrete mix, it makes an unreliable base.

Peaty and loamy soils will sink under a heavy load. Use good hardcore (see below) in the prepared area.

Made-up ground is another way of describing land that's been reclaimed. There's no knowing what was used as the in-fill, and it should always be assumed that it has minimal load-bearing capacity. Any concreting here will need good reinforcement such as hardcore, well compacted and the same thickness as the concrete you're laying on top.

Soft pockets

After you've prepared a site for laying a path or patio you could find pockets of soft soil which will cause any concrete to sink.

Large areas of soft pockets or made-up ground need something solid as a base — and this is where hardcore (broken concrete), rubble (broken brick) or a very coarse aggregate is essential. Tamp it into the ground until well consolidated — a must for areas such as drives or structural foundations taking a lot of weight.

If necessary small areas can be reinforced with a steel mesh set into the concrete. For most purposes 7mm diameter rods formed in a mesh of 150mm squares is quite adequate, and this is readily available at most builders' merchants. Rest the rods on small pieces of broken brick before you lay the concrete; make sure that the ends of the rods don't protrude from the area you're concreting, and that the mesh is completely covered.

Creating the work area

Using formwork boards to create a kind of box in which to lay your concrete has two big advantages. Firstly, it contains the concrete neatly, and secondly it gives you levels on either side to guide you in levelling the concrete itself. Although this is the most usual method of containing concrete, a brick

LAYING AND LEVELLING

1 *Shovel the concrete well into the corners and only lay as much as you can finish off in one go. It's important that there are no hollows.*

2 *Roughly level the concrete with your shovel to a height about 6mm/¼in above the sides of the formwork. This will allow for compaction.*

3 *The 'tamping' board fits neatly across the formwork. First use a sawing action to level the mix, then a firm chopping action to compact it.*

4 *With the surface level, tap sides of formwork with hammer. This helps to compact the concrete. Fill in any hollows that result and level off again.*

5 *For an expansion joint use a piece of softboard the same depth as the concrete you're laying. Support it with pegs on one side.*

6 *Finish the concrete off on one side before you start laying on the other. Once the board is supported, hammer the pegs in deeper.*

SETTING UP FORMWORK

You need:
● planks of sawn softwood 25mm (1in) thick and wide enough to match the concrete depth
● pegs of 50 x 50mm (2 x 2in) softwood at least 300mm (12in) long
● a string line to aid setting out

Position formwork along all edges to keep concrete in place until it's set, and provide a working edge for levelling the concrete:
● hammer pegs into the ground at 1 metre (3ft) intervals round the perimeter of the area to be concreted; use foot to hold peg in position

● place formwork against the pegs, aligning the boards accurately against a string line
● check levels between opposite lines of formwork with batten and spirit level, and allow for drainage slope if required
● nail the boards to the pegs

CONCRETE: WHAT TO MIX

MIX A for concrete over 75mm (3in) thick

1 bucket cement	**OR**	1 bucket cement
2½ buckets sharp sand		5 buckets all-in aggregate
4 buckets washed aggregate		

MIX B for concrete less than 75mm (3in) thick

1 bucket cement	**OR**	1 bucket cement
2 buckets sharp sand		3¼ buckets all-in aggregate
3 buckets washed aggregate		

MIX C for rough bedding concrete

1 bucket cement	**OR**	1 bucket cement
3 buckets sharp sand		8 buckets all-in aggregate
6 buckets washed aggregate		

All mixes need about ½ bucket water; exact amounts depend on the dampness of the sand.

FINISHES

1 Using a wooden 'float' gives you a smooth finish. Press the float down firmly as you 'scrub' the surface with circular movements.

2 A brushed finish leaves a much rougher surface by exposing the small stones in the aggregate. Use a stiff brush to create a pattern of straight lines.

3 For a polished finish, use a steel 'float' at a slight angle to the surface, drawing it towards you with a sweeping semi-circular action.

surround can be used just as well — and this has the added advantage of not having to be pulled up. With bricks, however, it's more difficult to establish a completely straight and level line to follow.

For formwork use sawn (unplaned) softwood — it's called carcassing in the trade — for concrete that's to be placed below ground. It should be as wide as the depth of concrete you intend to lay and 25mm (1in) thick. Don't skimp on the thickness for it must be firm and rigid to support the weight of concrete.

Pegs are used to keep the formwork in place. They must be sturdy, not less than 50mm (2in) square and long enough to go well into the ground. Place pegs every 1 metre (3ft) against the *outside* face of the boards.

If building a raised path, formwork will give a finish to the concrete edge so you should use a timber that's planed. Unplaned timber can be used if the formwork is lined with 6mm (¼in) plywood, or if you intend finishing off the edges with more concrete after the formwork has been removed.

If you want to curve a corner in the formwork, use hardboard cut into strips as wide as the concrete is deep. This will need to be supported with pegs at more frequent intervals than softwood boards.

If you have difficulty driving the pegs into the ground (which may happen if you've put down hardcore) use lengths of angle iron instead. Alternatively drive the pegs in further away from the formwork and put timber blocks between the peg and formboard.

Expansion joints

Any large area of concrete needs expansion or movement joints to control cracking. A one-piece slab shouldn't be more than 3 metres (10ft) in any direction without a joint being included; a path should have joints at intervals of 1½ times the width of the path.

The simplest way of doing this is to incorporate a length of flexible plastic movement joint as you're laying the path. The material can be bought at most builders' merchants. Alternatively, use a piece of softboard impregnated with bitumen — it should be the same depth as the concrete and about 12mm (½in) thick.

Drainage slopes

With a wide expanse you should have a gentle slope (1 in 60 is the general rule) so that rainwater can drain away. This is achieved by setting the forms on one side slightly deeper into the ground. To check that the slope is the same all along the formwork, set a small piece of wood (about 12mm/½in for a 1m/3ft wide path) thick on the lower side and use your spirit level to check across to the other side.

To keep the formwork on each side of a path rigid, place a length of softwood across the width at the peg points, but not so that it will make an impression on the concrete. This can be used as a guide for levelling as well.

Whether you are building a concrete path, a base for a shed or garage, a hardstanding for a car or even a large patio, the principle of formwork is the same — only the number of boxes or bays you divide the area into varies. With each stage of the job you should mix only enough concrete to fill one bay or box at a time.

As the concrete starts to dry (after 2 hours) cover the surface with plastic sheeting or damp sacking to stop it drying too quickly.

LAYING CONCRETE BASES

Concrete is the ideal material for laying a slab for a shed, patio or driveway. Once you've mastered the techniques of mixing and casting it, you can provide a hard durable surface that will last for years.

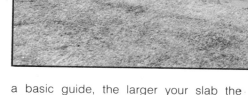

A concrete slab can be a tough, hardwearing base for a variety of uses in your garden, but its success is only as good as the preparation you have put into making it. Concrete consists of stone particles called 'aggregate', bonded together with a Portland cement and water mix (see pages 171-174). You must mix the ingredients very carefully, cast the slab on specially prepared foundations, apply a finishing texture, and allow the concrete to set properly, if your results are to be long-lasting.

Planning a concrete slab

After you've decided exactly where you want to put your square or rectangular slab, you'll have to mark out the ground accurately and prepare the foundations before laying the concrete. But if you're laying a more complex shape or a much larger concrete base, you'd be wise to make some preliminary sketches and transfer them to squared paper, to help in calculating the material required.

Before you start to lay your slab it's sensible to check with your local authority whether you're infringing any bye-laws. One of the main objections they might have is the position of your planned slab in relation to existing drains and pipe runs. As a result of these investigations, you might have to re-route some of these.

Access to the site and the time you'll have available for laying your slab are important considerations, particularly if you're laying a large concrete drive or a garage floor, for example. With work on this scale you should use ready-mixed concrete, which is delivered in bulk ready for casting. If you go for this method, it's vital that you provide access for the lorry and space for the load to be dumped as close as possible to your site. You must have your foundations prepared so that you can cast the mix as soon as it's delivered. Any delay could mean that the mix starts to set rendering it useless.

Calculating the size of slab

Before you can mark out your slab on the ground and prepare its foundations you'll have to work out its dimensions and calculate how much concrete you're going to need. As

a basic guide, the larger your slab the thicker it must be.

For an ordinary garden shed, for instance, you'll need a slab about 75mm (3in) thick, except where the ground is soft clay, when you should increase its depth to 100mm (4in). If your slab is to form the floor of a workshop, or a drive leading to your garage, a thickness of 100mm (4in) is appropriate on ordinary soils, 125mm (5in) on soft clay or other poor sub-soils.

Once you've decided on the dimensions of your slab you can estimate how much concrete you'll need and how you're going to mix it (see *Ready Reference*).

Marking out the slab

Before you start to mark out your slab on the ground, dig out and remove the top-soil, including any grass and the roots of shrubs, from the area you're going to concrete. Allow a margin of a few feet all round your proposed slab for working space.

Use strings stretched between wooden pegs driven into the ground just outside the area you're going to concrete to mark out the shape of your slab (although, for a very small slab it's possible simply to mark it out using planks positioned squarely on the ground – see photographs). Use a builder's square (see *Ready Reference*) to set the corners of your slab accurately. If you're

Ready Reference

SETTING UP FORMWORK

Formwork is needed to mould and retain the concrete while it sets. To set up a frame for a small square or rectangular slab:
● drive 50x50mm (2x2in) softwood pegs 300 (1ft) long into the ground just outside the slab perimeter at 1m (3ft) centres
● nail lengths of sawn softwood 25mm (1in) thick and as wide as the concrete depth to the pegs, making sure they're level and square
● butt joint the corners. Alternatively, make up the formwork to size elsewhere, and then carry it into position

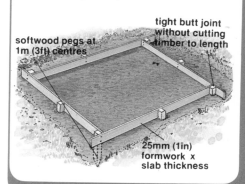

tight butt joint without cutting timber to length

softwood pegs at 1m (3ft) centres

25mm (1in) formwork x slab thickness

175

making strip foundations for a wall, you can use 'profiles' to set the levels (see pages 171-174).

Once you've positioned your string lines you can dig out the sub-soil to roughly the depth of your foundation, taking it about 150mm (6in) beyond the strings to leave space for setting up 'formwork', which moulds and retains the concrete while it's hardening.

Setting the levels

While the base for a shed should be virtually level, a concrete slab patio or garage drive should be laid with a slight slope to allow rainwater to run off quickly. And of course, if the slab is near a wall you'll have to ensure that the fall drains away from it. You must allow for the slope when you're preparing the base. A gradient across the site of about 1 in 60 is about right.

You'll also have to make sure when laying a drive leading to a garage that the drive doesn't drain into the garage. If the ground is naturally sloping in that direction take it to a level below the garage floor and lay a short section of slab sloping away from the garage. Where the two slopes meet you'll have to include a channel leading to a suitable drainage point.

To establish the level of your slab over its entire area hammer 50x25mm (2x1in) softwood pegs into the ground at about 1.5m (5ft) intervals. The first peg must be one that establishes the level of the others, and its called the 'prime datum'. If your slab is to adjoin a wall you can fix the level of this peg at the second course of brickwork below the dpc, (damp-proof course) or some other fixed point of reference.

Drive in some more pegs and check across their tops from the first peg with a spirit level on a straight-edged length of timber to check their level.

You can allow for a drainage fall by placing a wedge of timber called a 'shim' under one end of the straight edge.

Once you've set the datum pegs, measure down them whatever thickness of concrete you'll need for your slab and excavate the ground, or fill in, where necessary.

Fixing the formwork

Wet concrete tends to spread out as it sets and so you'll have to fix a timber frame called 'formwork' at the perimeter of the foundations to retain it and support its edges. It must be strong enough to withstand heavy tamping, which compacts and strengthens the mix. Use straight lengths of stout timber a minimum of 25mm (1in) thick, set on edge and nailed to pegs of 32x32mm (1¼x1¼in) timber driven into the ground at the perimeter of the slab at 1m (3ft) centres. Fix the pegs outside the area that's to be con-

PREPARING THE FOUNDATIONS

1 *You can mark out a small concrete slab on the ground with scaffold boards and pegs at the corners, then start to remove the topsoil or turfs.*

2 *Continue to dig out the topsoil or turfs until you've accurately marked out the shape of your slab. Then dig down to the depth you want the slab.*

3 *To fix formwork around your base butt joint four lengths at the corners. Nail battens at each corner to hold the angle; then saw off the waste.*

4 *Position the formwork within the foundations and check across the top with a long spirit level to ensure that it's level, or sloping for drainage.*

5 *Tamp or roll the base of the foundations firm. If the soil is soft, add some hardcore and compact this into the surface with a sledge hammer.*

6 *Add as much hardcore as you need to give a firm base for the concrete. You may need to add a layer of sand to fill any voids in the surface.*

creted, with their tops flush with, or slightly below, the top edge of the formwork.

You can use your string lines as a guide to positioning the formwork and a builder's square to ensure that the corners are set perfectly at right angles.

The top edge of the formwork must be set so that it's flush with the top of your finished slab; it's best to use timber that's the same thickness as your slab, otherwise you'll have to recess it into the ground. You can use your intermediate datum pegs as reference points when levelling the formwork with a builder's level, making sure you incorporate the drainage falls.

The corners of the formwork must be tightly butt-jointed (see *Ready Reference*) to prevent the wet concrete from seeping through. If you have to join two planks together end to end in order to make the required length you should again use butt joints, but back both planks at the joint with a short section of timber nailed in place and wedged with a peg at this point.

Movement joints

You can cast a slab in one piece if it's no longer than about 3m (10ft) in width or length. But if it's bigger than this, or if its length is greater than twice is width, it's usual to divide the overall slab into 'bays' that are as square as possible – or equal in size – and to include a gap called an 'expansion joint', which prevents the slab from cracking due to expansion or contraction. Fill the gap with a length of softwood 10 to 12mm (3/8in to 1/2in) thick, the depth of the slab, and cut to fit between the formwork at the sides of the slab. Treat the fillet with preservative before fitting it within the slab.

Each bay is cast separately so it's best to back up the jointing timber with a piece of formwork temporarily pegged in place for support. When you've cast and compacted the first bay, remove the formwork behind the jointing timber and cast the second bay, leaving it permanently in place.

Mixing the concrete

If your slab is too small to justify a load of ready-mixed concrete or you wish to lay it in stages over several weekends, you'll need to buy all the ingredients and mix them yourself. To decide on the volumes of cement and aggregates you'll need for your particular slab, you must first decide on the concrete mix proportions to use. *Ready Reference* gives a basic guide to proportioning, which you can relate to your own needs. Following these guidelines and using the example of the car port base given in *Ready Reference*, the volume of concrete you'd need is 1.8m³ (63 cu ft). Materials needed are therefore going to be in the order of: 1.8x6 = 10.8 bags of cement; 1.8x0.5 = 0.9³ of sand;

1.8x0.8 = 1.44m³ of coarse aggregate.

Allow a 10 per cent margin for wastage to the cement to the nearest whole bag and buy 12 bags of cement. Round up quantities of aggregates to the nearest whole or half cubic metre and buy 1m³ (36 cu ft) of sand and 1.5m³ (53 cu ft) of coarse aggregate. Your calculations, though, should always be regarded as a guide only; exact amounts needed for a job will depend on the care you take in storage and handling and on the accuracy with which you prepare the base for the slab.

When you've an idea of the amounts of materials you'll need, you must decide on what method to use to mix them: by hand or by power mixer. Many different types of electric- petrol- and diesel-powered mixers are available for hire, and take much of the hard work out of mixing.

To get the correct consistency of concrete using a mixer, add half the coarse aggregate needed for the batch and half the water first. Then add all the sand and mix for a few minutes. Next you can add the cement and the remainder of the coarse aggregate. Finally add just enough water to achieve a workable mix. Most beginners add too much water; when it's of the right consistency the concrete should fall off the blade of your shovel cleanly without being too sloppy.

If you have to break off your work for a while, add the coarse aggregate and water you'll need for the next batch and leave the mixer running, while you are away, to keep the drum cleam.

For how to mix concrete by hand (although it's really only viable for small jobs), see pages 171-174.

If you're mixing the concrete yourself you can store the aggregates indefinitely on a hard surface covered with a polythene sheet to keep it clean. Cement, however, must be kept dry: moisture in the air can penetrate the paper sacks and cause it to harden. Stack the sacks,under cover if possible, flat on a raised platform of planks on bricks and cover them with polythene.

Using ready-mixed concrete

Ready-mixed concrete is delivered by mixer lorry, usually in minimum loads of 3m³ (105 cu ft). If you need this amount, or more, ready-mixed concrete is worth considering as it takes a lot of hard work out of concreting and enables you to complete fairly large projects quickly.

Your supplier will want to know the volume of concrete you'll need, at what time you want it delivered, what it'll be used for, and how you're going to use it on delivery. This information will enable him to determine an appropriate mix and give you a price. You'd be wise to seek several quotations and try to choose a depot close to your home: much of

MAKING A BUILDER'S SQUARE

Set out square corners accurately with a builder's square, which you can make. To do this:
● nail together three strips of 50x25mm (2x1in) softwood in the proportion of 3:4:5, so that the angle between the two shorter sides is 90°.
A convenient size for the pieces is:
● 450, 600, 750mm (18, 24, 30in) respectively
● make a half-lap joint at the 90° corner and overlap the other two corners.

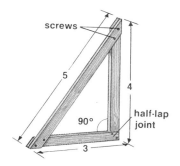

MAKING A TAMPING BEAM

To compact and level a concrete slab you'll need:
● a tamping beam made from a straight-edged length of 175x25mm (7x1in) softwood about 300mm (1ft) longer than the width of the slab
● or, for a very broad slab, a beam of 150x50mm (6x2in) timber with handles bolted on at each end so you can work standing up.

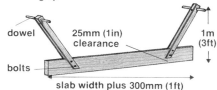

To use a tamping beam:
● lift the beam and drop it to compact the concrete as you work along the slab
● repeat this process a few times
● change to a sawing action, levelling the concrete flush with the top of the formwork.

CURING THE CONCRETE

Curing prevents the slab from drying out too quickly and becoming weak and cracking. To cure your slab:
● cover it with a large sheet of polythene
● weight down the edges – but not on the concrete – with bricks
● sprinkle sand on top to stop the sheet ballooning in the wind
● leave for 3 or 4 days before removing
● don't use the slab for 7 to 10 days.

CASTING THE CONCRETE

1 Lay a path of scaffold boards from the concrete mix to the slab so you can take the mix by wheelbarrow without harming the ground.

2 Spread out the first barrowload of concrete over your foundations, using a shovel to work it into the hardcore and to avoid air bubbles.

3 Continue to tip barrowloads of concrete into your foundations until you've half-filled the area, just proud of the tops of the formwork.

6 Compact the wet concrete by lifting and dropping the tamping beam onto the concrete as you work across the slab. Repeat using a sawing action.

7 When you've filled the entire slab and have tamped the mix thoroughly tap the outside edge of the formwork with a hammer to settle the concrete.

8 You can produce a non-slip finish of fine swirls on your slab by running the back of your shovel over the wet surface.

the cost of the concrete is in its transportation.

To receive your concrete you'd be wise to lay down a large polythene sheet to make clearing up easier afterwards. If you need to transport it any distance from the point of delivery get together as many wheelbarrows – heavy-duty ones, not light garden types – shovels and helpers as you can. It's sensible to lay a pathway of scaffold boards or planks from the pile to your site if you have to cross areas of lawn or go up or down steps.

Laying the concrete

When your formwork has been positioned you can remove the levelling pegs from within the areas, and the string lines from the perimeter, but if you're going to lay the concrete on a hardcore base you should add the ballast at this stage. Compact it well with a sledge hammer, fence post tamper or a garden roller, and leave the levelling pegs in

place until you've set the foundations at the correct level.

When the base is ready, tip in the concrete from a barrow, or by the bucketful: if you're making a big slab you might even be able to get the delivery lorry to tip the mix straight into your prepared base.

Spread the concrete evenly with a garden rake to level it to just above the tops of the formwork. This allows an excess for compacting the mix. When all the concrete has been cast, compact it, using a tamping beam (see *Ready Reference*) made from a straight-edged length of 175x25mm (7x1in) softwood about 300m (1ft) longer than the width of your slab. For very large slabs use 150x50mm (6x2in) timber to make the beam, with handles fitted at each end so that you can work from a standing position rather than crouching (see *Ready Reference*).

Use the beam with a chopping action, lifting

it then dropping it to compact the concrete and force out any air bubbles. Work along the slab in this way and, after a few passes, change to a sawing action, which levels any high spots and fills depressions as you move down the formwork. Continue to tamp until the concrete is even and flush with the top of the formwork.

Finishing the concrete

You can apply a variety of finishes to your concrete slab to suit its purpose. For a garage drive you can simply leave the fairly rough, non-slip, texture created by the tamping beam or you could brush the fresh concrete across its width with a stiff-bristled broom to give a more regular, but still non-slip, finish.

A smoother finish is easier to keep clean for a shed or garage floor, and you can produce this with a wooden float used in a wide, sweeping action. For a more polished effect,

4 *Draw a stout timber tamping beam across the tops of the formwork to spread the concrete roughly and to flatten any high spots.*

5 *Fill any indents left behind after you've drawn the tamping beam over the top with shovelfuls of concrete, then draw the beam across again.*

9 *Run the blade of a steel trowel along the perimeter of the concrete to prevent the edges crumbling when you remove the formwork.*

10 *After about 24 hours, when the concrete has set, remove the formwork by tapping it away from the slab with a hammer.*

you can smooth over the surface with a steel trowel after you've treated it with the wooden float, and once more when the concrete has almost set.

One of the simplest finishes to apply is to go over the surface with the back of a shovel, producing fine swirls.

Curing the concrete

After you've applied the finishing texture to your slab you should 'cure' the concrete by leaving it to set without drying out too quickly, which could cause it to crack.

Although you shouldn't attempt to lay concrete at all during frosty weather (as this can affect the strength of the slab) it's possible that a cold spell will strike when you're least expecting it. If this happens you can protect your freshly cast concrete by insulating it with a quilt of straw sandwiched between two layers of heavy gauge polythene, or you

can shovel a layer of earth, sand or compost on top of your conventional curing sheet, which has the same effect.

Once you've cured the concrete properly, which normally takes about three or four days (ten in winter), you can remove the polythene. It's perfectly alright for you to walk on the slab, and you can even start to build onto it, but be very careful at the edges, which will still be weak and susceptible to chipping.

Don't put the base to full use for about ten days, when you can remove the formwork. To do this, tap it downwards with a hammer in order to release it from the slab, then knock it away from the face of the concrete edges by releasing the nails securing the butt joins at the corners.

Once you've removed the formwork you can fill in the gap it occupies with soil or lay turfs to continue your lawn.

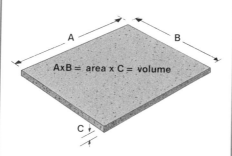

FOUNDATIONS
for garden walls

Even if it's only for a wall to grace the garden, building a solid foundation is a must. But how deep should you dig? How wide? And what's the right thickness of concrete? Here's an easy to follow explanation of why foundations are so important, how they differ and which one to choose.

All walls need foundations to give them stability, and free-standing garden walls are no exception. The foundation is like a platform, helping to spread the weight of the bricks in the wall onto the earth base below.

Most foundations are made of concrete laid in a trench, and for a garden wall where there's no additional weight for it to carry (unlike a structural wall, for example, which may also carry part of the weight of a roof) the concrete itself doesn't need to be very thick – between 100mm (4in) and 150mm (6in) of concrete is quite enough for a wall up to a metre in height. But the thickness of the concrete is not the only thing you have to consider. How deep in the ground you place it is just as important.

For a concrete foundation to provide an effective platform which won't allow the brick wall to crack, it has to be laid on firm 'subsoil'. And you won't find this until you get below the topsoil. The depth of topsoil varies enormously from place to place, so there can be no hard and fast rules about how deep you must dig – but expect anything between 100mm and 300mm (4-12in). Once you're through to the harder subsoil, you've then got to dig out enough for the depth of concrete – at least another 100-150mm (4-6in).

In practice the other big variable is the nature of your soil. Different subsoils have different load-bearing capacities – for instance hard chalky soils can support more weight than clay (see Choosing Your Foundation, page 184), but sandy soil can take less. The weaker the subsoil, the wider you have to build the foundation – consult your local building inspector for advice on soil conditions in your area.

There's another important reason for digging down so deep and that is the effect the weather has on soil. In clay subsoils, for example, a prolonged dry spell will cause the clay near the surface to shrink; then, when it rains, the clay will swell. All this causes considerable movement of the ground and unless a concrete foundation has been laid deep enough it'll crack up under the stress of constant expansion and contraction. To counteract this, the foundation has to be laid *below* the point at which the weather can cause movement. Again, in different soils, this varies from 150mm (6in) to 500mm (20in) or more down, but it's advisable to consult your local building inspector to get a more precise figure for soil conditions in your area.

Foundation design

All foundations have to be designed so that they evenly transfer the weight of the wall above to the earth base below. Because of the way the wall's weight spreads out onto

The weight of a wall spreads at an angle of 45° from its base into the foundation and then on into the subsoil.
This is called the angle of dispersion.

David Pope

MARKING OUT

1 Set the pegs for the profile board outside the line the foundation will follow. First hammer the pegs in, then nail a cross-piece on top.

2 You'll need profile boards at each end of the foundation trench so that you can string guide lines for digging out between the two.

3 Fix nails in the cross-pieces to establish the width of the trench. Normally this is a minimum of 300mm (12in).

4 Tie the line to one of the nails, then string up to the others. Loop the line round each nail and keep it taut. Don't cut the line.

5 The lines now mark the edges of the trench. At a later stage the building line for the wall is marked out in the same way.

6 To give you an accurate line to follow for digging out, sprinkle sand beneath the lines. After this remove the strings, but not the profile boards.

the foundation – called the angle of dispersion – the foundation is built so that it is wider than the wall. In fact this load spreading follows an angle of 45° (see page 180) and means that the width of the foundation on each side of the wall has to be at least equal to the depth of the concrete. This is a simple rule of thumb that will help you decide how wide your foundation has to be for different wall widths. Of course, if you're building on a relatively soft subsoil, your building inspector may recommend that you build a wider foundation. Like a raft floating on water, the bigger it is the more stable it will be.

Once you've dug your trench, you'll be faced with another decision: do you just lay the minimum thickness of concrete or lay enough concrete to fill up the trench so you have fewer bricks to lay? In fact, there can be quite a difference in the amount of work involved. If your trench is 500mm (20in) deep and you only lay a 150mm (6in) depth of concrete, it means that just to get back to ground level you've got to lay some 5 courses of bricks which ultimately won't even be seen. Nevertheless, it makes no difference to the strength of the foundation – it

PREPARING THE TRENCH

1 Once the trench is dug out, check the depth at 1 metre (3ft) intervals. The actual depth depends on the nature of the soil – see page 184.

TIP

2 Hammer in pegs at 600mm intervals down the middle of the trench. These can be adjusted to act as an accurate depth guide for laying the concrete.

3 Use a spirit level to check that the tops of the pegs are level. This marks the top of the foundations, and accuracy is essential.

simply depends on whether you prefer laying more concrete (and it'll be quite a lot more) or more bricks. Engineering bricks are recommended for any work below ground, though any special quality brick will do almost as well.

Marking out

Digging a trench foundation to a depth of about 500mm (20in) is probably the safest rule of thumb to follow if you're building a wall that's going to be more than 5 or 6 courses above ground level. (For smaller walls see Foundations for low brick walls).

And to make sure that the line of the trench is straight and the width constant, you have to mark out accurately. For this you need to set up what are called 'profile boards' at each end of the trench. All you do is string lines between the boards in the position you want for the foundation.

To make profile boards, use lengths of 50mm x 25mm (2in x 1in) timber cut a little wider than your trench. For pegs, use 50mm square (2in square) timber about 600mm (2ft) long. You'll also need nails and string.

Hammer two pegs into the ground at each end of the wall line, and nail the cross-pieces onto them. Next drive nails into the tops of the boards – to mark the outer edges of the foundation – and string lines between them, pegging the string into the ground beyond the profile boards.

These strings are then the guide lines for digging the trench, and can be transferred down to the ground using a spirit level. When the trench is dug and the foundation laid, these same profile boards can be used to create the building lines for the wall – you just add more nails and string up as before.

Constructing the trench

Remove the topsoil and dig a trench according to your marking up. To give you a guide for laying the concrete, you'll need pegs about double the depth of concrete required. These

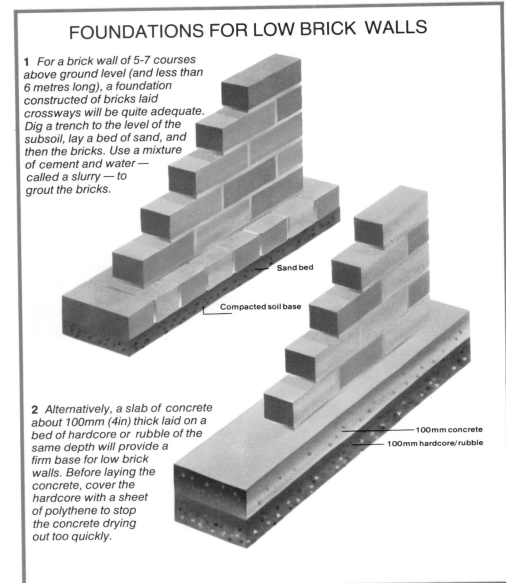

FOUNDATIONS FOR LOW BRICK WALLS

1 *For a brick wall of 5-7 courses above ground level (and less than 6 metres long), a foundation constructed of bricks laid crossways will be quite adequate. Dig a trench to the level of the subsoil, lay a bed of sand, and then the bricks. Use a mixture of cement and water — called a slurry — to grout the bricks.*

Sand bed

Compacted soil base

2 *Alternatively, a slab of concrete about 100mm (4in) thick laid on a bed of hardcore or rubble of the same depth will provide a firm base for low brick walls. Before laying the concrete, cover the hardcore with a sheet of polythene to stop the concrete drying out too quickly.*

100mm concrete
100mm hardcore/rubble

LAYING THE CONCRETE

1 *Fill the trench with concrete to just above the level of the pegs. Make sure it's well compacted before you roughly level it with the shovel.*

2 *Use a large piece of timber as a 'tamping' beam to finally level off so that the tops of the pegs are just visible. The surface doesn't need to be smooth.*

3 *Check the level of the foundation using a spirit level placed across a straight edge. If necessary make adjustments by adding more concrete.*

should have tops cut square and should be driven into the centre of the trench at intervals of 600mm (2ft). The tops should all be precisely levelled using a builders level or a straight-edge and spirit level. Soak the trench with water and allow it to drain before the concrete is poured in. This should then be well 'rodded' (with a broom handle, for example) to ensure that the entire volume of the trench is filled and the concrete is as high as the tops of the pegs (these don't have to be removed and will eventually rot). Use a wooden float or suitable piece of timber to level the surface.. It needn't be perfectly smooth as a fairly rough surface provides a good key for the mortar. Cover the concrete with plastic sheeting or damp sacking and leave for 6 days to 'cure' – longer if the wall is more than 12 courses high. The slower the curing the stronger the concrete, so don't try and build a wall on the foundations too soon.

Concrete foundations

Concrete is ideal for foundations for no other material can take up the precise shape of the subsoil surface at the bottom of the trench and transfer the load so evenly. It should be made up of 1 part cement to 3 parts sand to 6 parts aggregate (see pages 171-174). Be careful to use just enough water to produce a pliable consistency.

Trench foundations can be reinforced with rods or mesh – either will increase the strength of the foundation and whatever is built upon it. Both kinds of reinforcement are actually quite simple to add – you just have to make sure that the steel rods or mesh are bedded in the lower part of the concrete and not exposed at the sides or ends. In some cases, reinforcement is essential – for example, if you're laying a foundation over a drainpipe. For most garden brick walls, however, going to the trouble of reinforcing a foundation just isn't necessary – the weight of the wall doesn't justify it. What is important is that the wall doesn't crack because the ground underneath moves slightly.

Raft or slab foundations

For small walls of 7 courses or less the simplest concrete foundation is a raft or 'slab'. This is cast just below ground level (after the topsoil has been removed) in much the same way as you'd lay a concrete path. First dig out to a depth of about 200mm (8in), then add a layer of compacted broken brick or hardcore to provide drainage. Cover this with light polythene sheeting just before concret-

ing – this will prevent the concrete drying out too quickly because of water being absorbed by the base. Then lay your concrete about 100mm (4in) deep and tamp to a level surface (see pages 181-182). Once the wall is built the concrete foundation can be hidden by soil and grass.

Brick foundations

For low walls under 7 courses high you could even avoid the expense and trouble of mixing concrete altogether, because a foundation strip of bricks laid cross-ways can be perfectly adequate. Lay the bricks on a thin layer of sand which has been well compacted and levelled in a shallow trench. This should be dug to below the level of topsoil – anything between 100mm (4in) to 300mm (12in) below ground level. Grout these together with a 'slurry' – a creamy mixture of cement and water. This is called a 'footing' course and you can lay bricks on top in the usual manner even before the slurry is hard.

Earth retaining walls

Sometimes walls built in the garden may not be free-standing but used to retain earth on one side – for example, as terraces on a sloping site or to enclose flat areas of lawn or

MARKING BUILDING LINES

1 For a half brick thick wall (a single line of bricks) position nails on the profile board 100mm in from each side of the trench and string up between them.

4 A piece of scrap wood held diagonally against the spirit level gives a bit of extra support as you mark down vertically and score the mortar bed with a trowel.

2 These strings give you clear guidelines to follow, but it's usually worth double-checking that the building lines are positioned centrally on the concrete.

5 Lay the bedding mortar for the first course of bricks alongside the marked line. Furrow the mortar with the tip of the trowel.

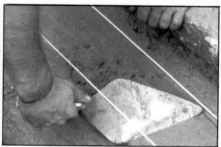

3 Lay a thin bed of mortar directly underneath the building lines and smooth it out with the trowel. This is for marking down from the line.

6 Lay the first three bricks, and then check them with the spirit level. Once the first course is complete, remove the profile lines.

CHOOSING YOUR FOUNDATION

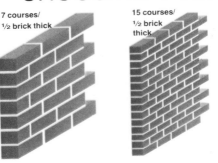

7 courses/
½ brick thick

15 courses/
½ brick thick

7 courses/
1 brick thick

15 courses/
1 brick thick

STRIP FOUNDATIONS

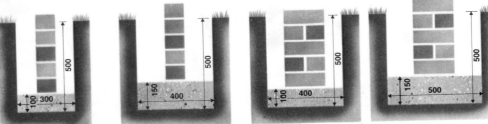

TRENCH FILL FOUNDATIONS

The size of foundation you lay depends on the height and thickness of the wall you intend to build, and on the load-bearing capacity of the subsoil. The chart above gives recommended dimensions for strip and trench-fill foundations for half-brick and one-brick thick walls, below 7 courses or up to 15 courses high, on a typical clay subsoil. On crumbly, loose soils the recommended widths should be doubled. See also Ready Reference.

Ready Reference

PROBLEM SOILS

- clay subsoils are prone to shrink and swell so make the foundation trench at least 500mm deep, and lay the concrete to the width and thickness shown in the chart
- loose, poorly-compacted subsoils need foundations double the normal width to help spread the load of the wall, and should be laid as trench-fill foundations
- if the sides of your trench tend to collapse, use timber to shore them up before pouring in the concrete, or cut them wider than necessary and slope the sides.

TIP:
LET CONCRETE DRY SLOWLY

- first soak the trench with water and allow it to drain away
- cover concrete with damp sacking or plastic sheet
- Allow concrete to 'cure' for at least 6 days before building on it.

UNEXPECTED HAZARDS

- if the trench fills with water it must be drained before you lay the foundation concrete. Water in a small trench can be emptied with a bucket; in a large trench you may have to hire a pump
- if you discover underground pipes as you're digging the trench, dig soil away around them to the required depth. Lay the foundation as normal on either side of the pipes, then 'bridge' them with a short reinforced concrete lintel or, for narrow gaps (300mm/12in or less) lengths of paving slab laid two courses deep.

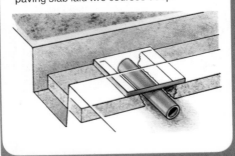

flower beds. In such cases the soil behind the wall is constantly trying to push outwards, completely changing the pattern of stress involved.

The simplest solution is to make the structure strong enough to withstand this extra pressure. With a 4 or 5 course wall this can usually be done by building the wall one brick thick (instead of ½ brick thick) and by providing 'weepholes' at regular intervals to drain excess water. These are made by removing mortar from a number of the vertical joints before it sets.

If you find that the surface of an earth-retaining wall is marked by white crusty deposits – called 'efflorescence', and caused by water carrying salts through the wall from the soil behind – dig away the earth and coat the inner surface of the wall with bituminous emulsion to create a damp barrier.

Building on a slope

It is visually unsettling and structurally undesirable to lay bricks running parallel to a slope. So, to build a wall that 'steps' down a slope, the trench foundations also have to be stepped or 'benched' into the slope. Levelling, pegging, pouring and finishing are all carried out in the same way as with a horizontal trench, but in stepped sections. You'll need form boards to frame the outer edge of each step, but otherwise the width and depth of the foundation is exactly the same as for an ordinary wall. Only the length of each step varies.

SECTION 5

BUILDING

TECHNIQUES

– INDOOR

WORKING WITH PLASTER

Patching small areas of plasterwork is a fairly straightforward job, but sometimes you'll need to replaster a whole wall. Before you can start, you have to learn the basic techniques.

Plaster is used on internal walls to give a smooth, flat surface that you can decorate with paint, wallpaper or tiles. There are two basic types of plaster in common use. One is a mix based on a mineral called gypsum. The other, cement-based plaster, is used mostly as 'rendering' to weatherproof the exterior walls of a house. But it is also employed indoors, especially as part of the treatment of damp walls, or as an 'undercoat' for other plasters. Its disadvantages are a slow drying time and the possibility that mistakes in proportioning of the constituents could result in a weak mix.

Types of plaster

Gypsum-based plasters have largely superseded cement-based plasters. They are quicker-setting and usually available in pre-mixed form, which requires only the addition of clean water to make them workable. Another point in their favour is that they contain lightweight aggregates such as perlite and vermiculite instead of sand, so they're easier to use.

Ready-mixed plaster is usually spread onto the wall in two parts. The first is a backing or 'floating' coat, which is applied fairly thickly – up to 10mm (³⁄₈in) – to take up any unevenness in the wall. The second is a finishing coat, which is spread on thinly – up to 3mm (¹⁄₈in) – and finished to give a smooth, matt surface.

Carlite is the most widely-used lightweight pre-mixed gypsum plaster and it's available in various grades for use on different wall surfaces, depending upon how absorbent they are: the plaster will crack if the wall to which it's applied draws moisture from it too quickly. Common brickwork and most types of lightweight building blocks, for instance, are described as having 'high suction', which means that their absorption rate is rapid. Concrete, engineering bricks, dense building blocks and plasterboard, on the other hand, have 'low suction'.

You can recognise which walls are high- or low-suction by splashing on a little clean water. If it's absorbed immediately, the wall is high-suction, but if it runs off the surface the wall is low-suction. If after this test you're still unsure, you can treat the wall with a coat of PVA bonding agent or adhesive, which, when brushed on, turns all backgrounds into low-suction, and both seals and stabilizes the surface.

For a high-suction background you'll need Carlite Browning plaster for the base coat; for low suction choose Carlite Bonding plaster. Use Bonding where the wall is of a composite nature (containing both high- and low-suction materials). Carlite Finish plaster is used as the final coat on Bonding and Browning plaster.

Preparing the surface

You'll achieve a smooth, flat and long-lasting plastered finish only if you've prepared the background properly. If you're re-plastering an old wall of bricks or blocks, hack off all the old plaster using a club hammer and bolster chisel and examine the mortar joints. If they're soft and crumbly, rake them out and repoint them.

Lightly dampen the wall using an old paintbrush – this is essential if the new finish is to stick properly, and prevents the wall absorbing too much moisture from the plaster. New brick or block walls probably won't need any preparation before you plaster other than light wetting.

Smooth surfaces such as concrete and timber (used as lintels over doors and windows, for example), must be keyed to accept the plaster. You can do this either by nailing expanded metal laths (see *Ready Reference*) or plasterboard to them, applying PVA bonding agent, or by hacking a series of shallow criss-cross lines on the surface with a cold chisel.

Applying the plaster

Plaster is applied to the wall in a series of sections called 'bays'. These need to be marked out. One method is to use timber battens called 'grounds' lightly nailed vertically to the wall. Another method employs 'screeds', which are narrow strips of plaster. These are spread onto the wall

MIXING PLASTER

1 Sprinkle handfuls of dry plaster onto clean water, breaking up any lumps between your fingers. Mix up equal volumes of plaster and water.

2 When the water has soaked into the dry plaster, stir thoroughly using a stout stick until the mix reaches a uniform consistency without any lumps.

3 Test the consistency of the plaster mix: Browning and Bonding plaster should resemble porridge and should be fairly stiff in texture.

4 When the plaster is mixed, tip it from the bucket onto your spot board, which should be positioned close to the wall you're about to work on.

TIP

5 Use the trowel to knead the mixed plaster on the spot board; if the mix is too sloppy sprinkle on more plaster.

6 Temporarily nail 10mm (³⁄₈in) thick softwood battens vertically to the wall at 1m (3ft) spacings to act as grounds (thickness guides) during plastering.

TOOLS FOR PLASTERING

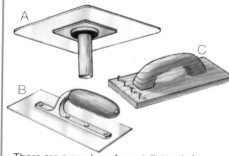

There are a number of specialist tools for plastering but the following are the basic requirements:

● hawk (A) – a 300mm (1ft) wood, aluminium or plastic square with a handle, used to carry plaster to your working area

● plasterer's trowel (B) – the basic tool for applying plaster to the wall; it has a thin rectangular steel blade measuring about 250 x 115mm (10 x 4¹⁄₂in) and a shaped wooden handle

● wood float (C) – generally used to give a flatter finish coat to plaster, it is rectangular in shape. It can be converted to a devilling float for keying surfaces by driving in two or three nails at one end so that their points just protrude

● rule – a planed softwood batten measuring about 75 x 25mm (3 x 1in) and about 1.5m (5ft) long, used to level off the floating coat when applied between screeds, grounds or beads

● water brush – used to dampen the wall and to sprinkle water on the trowel when finishing

● spirit level – for positioning the timber grounds accurately.

MAKING A SPOT BOARD

The spot board is used to hold the mixed plaster near the work area. Make one from a 1m (3ft) sq panel of exterior grade plywood mounted on an old table or tea chest so it's at a convenient height. Make sure it projects over the edge of the stand so you can place the hawk underneath when loading with plaster.

BUYING PLASTER

Large quantities of plaster are sold in 50kg (110lb) bags; smaller amounts for patching are sold in 2.5 to 10kg (5¹⁄₂ to 22lb) bags.

HOW FAR WILL IT GO?

● 10kg (22lb) of Carlite Browning laid 10mm (³⁄₈in) thick will cover about 1.5sq m (1.8sq yd).

● 10kg (22lb) of Carlite Bonding laid 10mm (³⁄₈in) thick will cover about 1.6sq m (1.9sq yd).

● 10kg (22lb) of Carlite Finish will cover about 5sq m (6sq yd).

USING A HAWK AND TROWEL

1 *Hold the hawk under the edge of the spot board and scoop a trowel-load of plaster onto it. Use the trowel to push the plaster into a neat mound.*

2 *With the hawk level, hold the edge of the trowel blade on it at right angles to the face. Push the trowel forward while tilting the hawk towards you.*

3 *When the hawk is vertical push up with the trowel, which should still be at right angles to the hawk face, and scoop off the plaster.*

4 *Return the hawk to the horizontal position and keep the trowel upright with the plaster on top. This whole sequence takes only a few seconds.*

5 *Without hesitating, tip the trowel forwards to return the plaster to the centre of the hawk. Don't drop it from too great a height or it will splash.*

6 *The mound of plaster should keep a roughly rounded shape, if it's of the right consistency. Practise this loading technique several times.*

from floor to ceiling, generally using wood blocks called 'dots' at the top and bottom as thickness guides.

The distance between these markers can vary according to your skill in applying the plaster, but 1m (3ft) is an easily manageable width for the beginner. Screeds and grounds are essentially guides that enable you to apply the backing coat to the correct thickness, and when the plaster's been applied to one bay it's smoothed off level with them using a timber straight edge called a 'rule'.

Expanded metal screed beads for flat surfaces and angle beads for external corners (see *Ready Reference)* serve the same purpose as timber grounds.

Applying a plaster screed to the correct thickness takes some practice and it's much easier to use timber grounds or metal beads.

When you've plastered one bay using timber grounds as guides, leave the plaster until it is partially set; then remove one of the battens, move it along the wall about another 1m (3ft) and refix it.

Plaster this second bay using the edge of the first one as a thickness guide, and rule off the surface carefully. Carry on in this way until you've covered the whole wall.

To ensure the finishing plaster will adhere to the backing coat the latter must be 'keyed' using a tool called a devilling float. This is a wooden or plastic block with nails driven in from the top so that their points just protrude through the base, and it's used to scratch the surface of the backing coat lightly.

Two thin coats of finishing plaster will give a smooth and flat surface. The first coat is applied from bottom to top, working left to right if you're right-handed, right to left other-

wise, and is then ruled off. The second coat is applied straight away and then flattened off to produce a matt finish. When this has been done you return to the starting point and, with the addition of a little water splashed onto the wall, you trowel over the entire surface. When the plaster has hardened, trowel the surface again several times, applying water to the surface as a lubricant to create a smooth, flat finish.

Mixing the plaster
Cleanliness in mixing plaster is of prime importance because any dirt or debris that gets into the mix could affect the setting time and mar the finish. Keep a bucket of water nearby for cleaning the tools and don't use this water for mixing the plaster – use clean, fresh tap water. See the photographs on page 187 for how to mix the plaster.

PRACTISING ON THE WALL

1 Place some plaster on your hawk and move over to the wall you're going to plaster. Repeat the process you've just practised (left, 2 to 6).

2 Take about half the plaster from the hawk. Keeping the trowel horizontal, position yourself near the right-hand timber ground.

3 With the right-hand edge of the trowel resting on the timber ground, tilt the blade up until its face is at about 30° to the wall surface.

4 Push the trowel upwards, keeping an even pressure on its heel, which rests on the timber ground. Decrease the angle of the blade as the plaster is spread.

5 When most of the plaster has been spread, the trowel blade should be parallel with the wall. Press in its lower edge to pinch in the plaster.

6 Spread a second trowel-full of plaster immediately to the left of the first one, taking care not to make the layer thinner by pressing in too hard.

Ready Reference

MIXING PLASTER

When mixing plaster you'll need the following equipment:
- a trough about the size of a galvanized bath for large amounts, or a tea chest lined with polythene
- a 5 gallon (22 litre) bucket for small amounts
- a clean bucket containing clean water for adding to the mix
- a bucket to transfer mixed plaster to the spot board
- a clean shovel for stirring large mixes.

TIP: FIXING GROUNDS

It's important that the timber grounds are fixed truly vertical as they're guides to the thickness of the floating coat. On uneven walls, pad out gaps between the grounds and the wall with wood offcuts to make their faces vertical.

USING METAL BEADS

Expanded metal lath and plaster beads act as a thickness guide for applying plaster to the wall and levelling it off. They're bedded on plaster dabs and remain in the wall when plastering is complete.

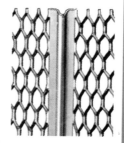

- Screed beads are used instead of timber grounds or plaster screeds.

- Stop beads are used for plastering up to doorways or abutting skirtings

- Angle beads fit over external corners and protect the plaster from chipping.

For plastering plasterboard see pages 201-205.

APPLYING THE FLOATING COAT

1 *After your trial run, scrape the plaster from the wall, clean and dampen the surface, then start plastering at the bottom right of the bay.*

2 *Work your way up the bay, spreading on the plaster in rows. You'll have to rig up a trestle to reach the top of the bay.*

3 *Use a timber batten to rule off the plaster level with the face of the timber grounds. Draw the rule upwards with a side-to-side sawing action.*

TIP

4 *Look for any hollows in the surface and fill them in with more plaster. Then rule off again as before.*

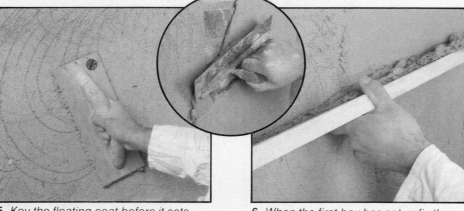

5 *Key the floating coat before it sets with a devilling float. Wet its base and keep it flat to the wall so the nails score shallow marks in the plaster.*

6 *When the first bay has set, refix the right-hand ground 1m (3ft) away. Plaster between this and the raw edge of the first bay (inset), then rule off carefully.*

APPLYING TH

1 *Mix the finishing plaster in a bucket, then transfer it to the spot board and knead as before. It should have the consistency of melting ice-cream.*

5 *Once you've applied the finishing coat of plaster to this area, return to the starting point and apply a second even thinner coat immediately.*

Basic techniques: Floating

Patching small areas of damaged plasterwork is fairly straightforward, but plastering a whole wall calls for a degree of skill in using the various tools that can only be achieved by practice.

When you've mixed the plaster place it on the spot board. If you're right-handed, hold the hawk in your left hand and the trowel in your right (vice versa if left-handed). Grip the trowel so that your index finger is against the front shank, the toe of the trowel pointing left. The knuckles of your right hand should be uppermost. The hawk should rest in the left hand on your thumb and index finger.

To load the hawk, place it under the edge of the spot board, scoop a small amount of plaster onto the hawk and move it away.

Hold the hawk level and place the bottom

FINISHING COAT

2 When the floating coat has hardened – after about two hours – scoop a trowel-load of finishing plaster onto your hawk and move over to the wall.

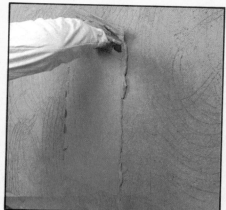

3 Spread half of the amount onto the floating coat, working from bottom to top. Keep the coat very thin. Apply the other half, blending the two.

4 Work from bottom left to top right over an area about 2m (6ft 6in) wide, with broad, sweeping arm movements.

6 Trowel off any ridges or splashes on the finishing coat with light downward strokes; hold the wetted trowel blade at about 30° to the surface of the wall.

7 When the finishing coat has hardened, trowel again using water to lubricate the blade. This polishes the surface and gives a smooth, flat finish.

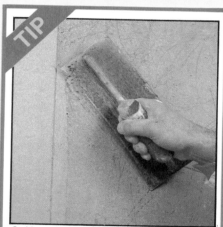

TIP

8 You probably won't be able to complete a whole wall in one go. If you do break off, scribe down the plaster and scrape off to form a neat edge.

edge of the trowel on it, blade at right-angles to the hawk face. As you push the trowel forward against the plaster, tilt the hawk until it's almost vertical, keeping the trowel at right angles to the hawk face. Push the plaster off the hawk and gently slide it all back. Don't drop it from too great a height or too fast as it will splash. Repeat this several times before attempting to spread the plaster onto the wall.

When you're fairly confident, move to the wall and repeat the operation, but only remove half the plaster from the hawk. Keeping the trowel horizontal, place the lower edge hard against the wall at chest height. Open the gap between trowel and wall to about 5mm (¼in), tilt the trowel up until its face is at about 30° to the wall surface and then move the trowel upwards. The gap

is similar to a valve and controls the thickness of plaster applied to the wall. As the material is spread evenly and disappears from under the trowel, decrease the angle between trowel and wall so that you apply the last of the plaster with a pinching movement between the trowel edge and the wall. This prevents the plaster from sliding down. Repeat this until you get the plaster to stay on the wall.

After your 'practice run', scrape the plaster from the wall, and apply a 'floating' coat of backing plaster between the grounds; don't worry about any ridges or hollows at this stage but aim to get coverage of an even thickness all over.

Rule over the plaster and fill in any hollow areas, then rule again. Before the plaster has set, lightly key it with a devilling float.

Basic techniques: Finishing

Carlite plaster sets in less than two hours, so you should apply the finish coat as soon as possible after the floating coat has hardened. Use the hawk and trowel as if applying the floating coat, but take less plaster onto the hawk and apply a very thin coat to the floating coat, working left to right and from bottom to top. Smooth out all ridges to leave the surface as flat as possible. Once you've covered the undercoat, repeat the operation. Lightly sprinkle water onto the face of the trowel using a brush. With the trowel blade at an angle of 25 to 30°, trowel over the finish coat with long straight sweeps to achieve a smooth, flat finish.

Leave the plaster until set, then trowel once more, aided by water and harder pressure, to polish the surface.

PLASTERING ANGLES AND REVEALS

When you're plastering large areas, you'll have to cope with corners sooner or later. Metal angle beads make it easy to get perfect corners every time.

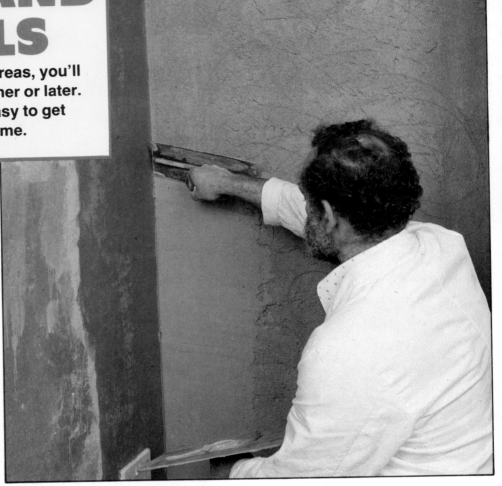

Applying plaster to walls may seem like a daunting task, but you will have seen from the previous section that, provided you practice the right techniques, it's relatively easy to obtain a professional quality finish on both exposed brick and plasterboard surfaces.

In the previous section, plastering was confined to flat, uninterrupted surfaces, but in practice there will be a certain amount of finishing off needed at internal and external corners, and around door and window openings. You will need to learn a few more techniques to deal with these. However, with a few exceptions, the method of applying the plaster, and the tools for doing so, are basically the same as those explained so far.

Internal angles
You are likely to meet two types of internal angle when plastering. The first is where your newly-plastered wall meets an existing hard plaster surface on the adjacent wall, and the second is where both adjacent walls are being plastered simultaneously.

Where you have a hard surface to work to, apply your floating coat to the wall in the normal manner. Then rule the plaster outwards from the corner, using the wooden rules vertically instead of horizontally. Key the plaster well with a devilling float and then cut out the internal angle. This is done by laying the trowel flat against the finished surface so that it is at an angle of 30 to 40° to the vertical and then moving it into the corner until the tip of the toe cuts into the fresh plaster. Move the trowel up and down the angle and then repeat the procedure with the trowel flat against the floated surface and its tip against the hard plaster. This will cut out the corner cleanly. Leave it to harden.

Next, apply the finishing plaster, ruling vertically away from the angle with a feather-edge rule and cut into the corner as before. The second coat of finishing plaster should be trowelled in to form a flat surface. Just before the plaster hardens fully, pass a wooden float up and down the angle.

When you are satisfied that the angle is straight, you can finish it off. To do this, hold your trowel so that its toe is flat against the finished wall with one corner just touching the new plaster at the angle. By moving the trowel down the entire length of the corner you should be able to produce a clean and sharp internal angle.

When plastering two adjacent walls at the same time, the procedure for dealing with the internal angle is basically the same, but extra care is required because there is no hard surface to work from. You can use a special internal angle trowel for finishing off the angle smoothly, but it is probably not worth buying one unless you will be doing a lot of plastering.

External angles
Although it is possible to finish off external corners freehand, considerable skill would be needed; for the do-it-yourselfer there are two simple methods which will produce successful results without too much trouble. Probably the easiest of these is to use a metal angle bead, which has the added advantages of allowing simultaneous plastering of both walls and providing an extremely durable corner. The other method is to use a timber rule to form first one side of the angle and then the other.

The metal angle bead will provide a true, straight arris (corner) that will not chip. It comprises a hollow bead, flanked by two bands of perforated or expanded metal lath. Two versions are available (see *Ready Reference*): one that will take the full thickness of a floating and finishing coat of plaster, and another that is shallower for use with plasterboard. The latter is called a 'thin coat' bead.

The first type of beading is fixed by means of 30mm (1¼in) thick dabs of backing plaster applied at 600mm (2ft) intervals to both sides of the angles. After pressing the bead into place on the dabs, it is trued up and straightened with the aid of a straightedge and plumb line. Then the plaster dabs are allowed to harden before the floating coat is applied. Alternatively, the bead can be bedded in a thin strip of plaster running the full height of the wall as this makes truing up easier. It can even be pinned in place with galvanised nails, trued up and then secured with plaster pressed through the lath on the

FITTING ANGLE BEAD

1 Cut a length of angle bead to fit the height of the corner to be plastered, then spread a screed of Carlite Browning plaster down the angle.

2 Position the length of angle bead on the corner and bed its mesh wings gently in the screed. Don't press hard until you've set the bead correctly.

3 Using a long, straight-edged length of timber and a spirit level, check the plumb of the angle bead, and adjust it if necessary before the plaster sets.

4 When you've accurately positioned the angle bead on the corner, spread plaster over the mesh wings to secure it, then check its alignment again.

Ready Reference

TOOLS AND EQUIPMENT

You'll need the following tools and equipment for plastering angles and reveals:
● metal angle bead of the appropriate type, plus tinsnips and hacksaw for cutting it to length
● a hawk to hold the plaster close to the work
● an angle trowel (A)
● a steel trowel (B) for spreading and smoothing the plaster
● a devilling float (C) for scoring the floating coat
● a floating rule – a planed softwood batten about 75 x 25mm (3 x 1in) and 1.5m (5ft) long, to level the floating coat up to the angle.
● a reveal gauge for gauging the plaster thickness within the reveal, plus a try-square
● a spirit level for positioning angle beads.

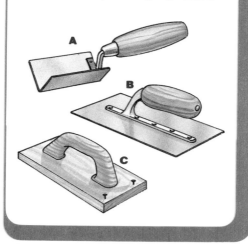

wall surface beneath. Thin coat bead is usually fitted by nailing (with galvanised nails) through the side wings into the wooden batten behind the plasterboard.

Whatever type is being used, the bead can easily be cut to length, using tinsnips to cut through the wings and a hacksaw to cut the nosing.

Once the bead is secure, it may be used as a screed for the floating coat. When this has become sufficiently hard, it should be cut back with a steel trowel to just below the level of the bead nose to allow room for the finishing coat. This coat is applied in the normal way, using the bead as a guide. When the finishing coat has been trowelled off to the angle bead, a sharp, clean and hard arris should be left exposed. The same method is used when applying the finishing coat to thin coat bead.

If you are using a wooden rule as a guide

for plastering an external corner, you should nail it first to one of the walls so that it projects beyond the corner ready to act as a ground for floating the other wall. Once the floating coat has hardened on the first wall, the rule should be removed and nailed to the wall just floated to enable the second wall to be treated in the same way. Once again, you should wait until the floating coat has hardened and then remove the rule.

The next stage is to reposition the rule so that the wall floated in the first instance may be finish-coated. Wait until this coat has hardened, remove the rule once more and refix it to the second wall so you can complete the finishing coat. When this has hardened the rule may be removed.

When you remove the rule after applying the last finishing coat, you will probably find that a slight selvedge will have formed behind the rule. This should be removed by using

the back edge of the laying trowel in a scything action, working away from the angle.

Sometimes you may find this tendency for a selvedge to form will allow you to finish the second wall without the aid of the rule. When you finish up to the rule on the first wall, a slight selvedge will form between the rule and the floating coat on the second wall.

To finish off the plaster angle, a Surform block plane may be used lightly to produce a perfect slightly rounded corner. Alternatively, use a piece of fine abrasive paper. As with internal angles, there is a special trowel for finishing off external angles. Using angle beads or rules means you simply will not need one, however.

Door and window reveals

The narrow strips of wall at door and window openings, which are normally at right angles to the main wall surfaces, are known as

APPLYING A FLOATING COAT

1 When the plaster retaining the bead has set, apply a floating coat between the bead nosing and the original, hard plaster at both sides of the angle:

2 Use a short wooden floating rule to level the backing plaster at each side of the corner. Draw the rule up the angle from bottom to top.

3 Place the trowel flat on the plaster, with one corner against the nosing; draw the trowel down the wall to cut in a margin for the finishing coat.

4 To plaster an area of wall between two corners, set a 'dot' of plaster at the base of the wall; press a small strip of wood in its centre as a thickness guide.

5 Lay one end of your floating rule and spirit level on the dot and the other end on the original plaster surface so that they're truly vertical.

6 Spread on a screed of backing plaster between the dot and the original hard plaster and level it off with your long floating rule to an even thickness.

7 Make another dot and screed at the other side of the area to be plastered. Spread on a floating coat between the two screeds and then rule off the surface.

8 Score the hardening plaster lightly with a 'devilling float', then draw the float down the angle between the original plaster and the freshly-applied coat.

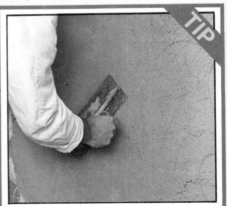

9 Trim off the excess plaster from the angle by running the trowel down the original, hard plaster, with one corner cutting into the fresh plaster.

FINISHING

1 When the backing coat of plaster has set sufficiently, apply the first coat of finishing plaster, spreading it between the nosing and the hard plaster.

2 Apply a second coat of finishing plaster immediately after the first and smooth the surface. Use an angle trowel with a little plaster to smooth internal corners.

3 Trim off the excess ridge of plaster left by the sides of the angle trowel using your steel trowel. Be careful not to disturb the corner itself.

reveals. They may also be found at the sides of a chimney breast or on a plain pier.

Actually forming the corners in these is straightforward, using the methods described previously. However, there are two points which require special attention. These are the depth of the reveal (ie. the distance from the face of the main wall to the window or door frame, or back wall) and the thickness of plaster, or 'margin', at the frame or back wall. It is essential that the depth of the reveal is the same all the way round the opening and that the plaster is the same thickness across the reveal. This will ensure that a uniform amount of frame remains visible.

Setting the depth of the reveal is simple providing the metal angle bead or fixed wooden rule for the arris is the same distance from the top of the door or window frame as it is from the bottom. Make sure, too, that it is vertical when viewed from the front.

When applying the plaster you will need a reveal gauge (see *Ready Reference*) to make sure the plaster is the same thickness all the way round. This may be simply constructed from a piece of wood which should be at least 50mm (2in) longer than the width of the reveal. After installing the metal angle bead (or fixed rule) as for external angles, lay a wooden or plastic set square (which should be long enough to reach from the back of the opening to beyond the main wall) on to the sill or floor. Push one side of its right angle against the horizontal window frame member, or bottom of the door frame, with the adjacent side against the front edge of the metal angle bead or rule. Now lay your reveal gauge on top of the square so that its long edge is in line with the set square edge that runs from the frame to the rule or bead. Using a pencil, mark the window frame end of the gauge opposite the inner edge of the window frame. Drive a nail into the end of the gauge at the pencil mark, leaving approximately 25mm (1in) protruding.

The nail acts as a shoulder when using the gauge as a horizontal rule for the plaster, supporting the inner end of the wood as you run it around the inside of the frame and maintaining an equal distance from the wall. Thus the thickness of the plaster where it meets the frame will be exactly the same all round. Or cut a right-angled notch out of the gauge to form a shoulder.

The gauge is also used to complete the underside of the reveal, although you may need to adjust the nail position if the frame is deeper at the top than down the sides. This is plastered last, after the reveal sides have been floated, and the same technique is used (with the obvious difference that you are working on a horizontal 'ceiling'). Lay on the floating coat firmly, working to the angle bead or batten, and rule off with the reveal gauge before adding the finish coat.

Ready Reference

TYPES OF ANGLE BEAD
There are two basic types of metal angle bead. These are:
● ordinary bead, fixed to masonry walls with dabs of plaster, which takes a floating and finishing coat of plaster (A)
● thin coat bead, nailed over the angle, which takes only a thin plaster finish on plasterboard (B).

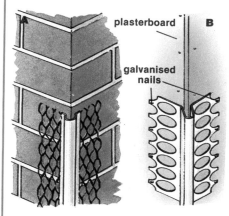

plasterboard

galvanised nails

TIP: JOINING BEADS
Where you have to join two lengths of angle bead, fix the first length to the angle and insert a dowel – a short length of stout wire or a headless galvanised nail – into the nose of the bead. Then position the second length over the dowel and bed it into place.

MAKING A REVEAL GAUGE
To ensure that reveals are plastered squarely and with a uniform thickness of plaster, use a piece of softwood about 75mm (3in) larger than the reveal depth. Lay it in the reveal, against the angle rule or bead, and parallel to the blade of the square, and mark one end to match the margin on the frame. Cut out a notch and use the gauge as a short rule to level the plaster within the reveal.

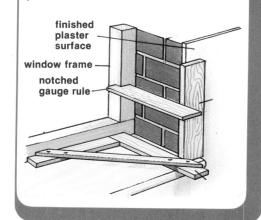

finished plaster surface

window frame

notched gauge rule

BUILDING A STUD PARTITION

Building a partition wall gives you two rooms where you only had one before. Surprisingly, you don't have to be a skilled craftsman. Here's how to build a simple framework.

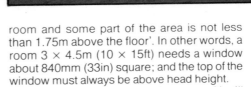

Sometimes, even after the most careful planning and the cleverest space-saving schemes, one room just won't do all the jobs you want it to do. Perhaps you've got a combined kitchen and dining room, but you could really do with one of each. Maybe the house needs a second toilet. Or, try as you may, you can't squeeze everyone into the available bedrooms.

In any of these situations the answer could be to build a timber-framed partition wall. That may sound daunting, but it's not. An ordinary partition — even one that stretches from floor to ceiling and right across the room — needs only simple carpentry and easily obtainable materials. You can even incorporate a door, overhead glazing, or a serving hatch without much extra trouble.

Putting together a partition is simplicity itself. One long piece of wood (the 'head' or 'top plate') is fixed to the ceiling. A second piece (the 'sole plate') is fixed to the floor. Uprights run between them; these are the 'studs', which is why the structure is usually called a 'stud partition'. Between the studs run short horizontal spacers called 'noggins'. That's the framework, and all you do after building it is to nail sheets of cladding, which are usually plasterboard, to it.

The planning stage

A partition wall will make quite a difference to your house, and it needs to be made properly. Here, as so often, thoughtful planning is the key to success.

Be careful, for example, that you do not accidentally create two narrow, gloomy cupboards. Think about lighting in particular. Only in very small rooms such as toilets can you rely solely on artificial light. Elsewhere, you may be able to 'borrow' light through windows in the partition itself. Existing outside windows may take care of the situation — but you should avoid, at all costs, the temptation to site the partition so that one window sheds half its light on each side. It will look terrible, and it's against the law.

Ventilation needs similar attention. A habitable room must either have a mechanical ventilator, or one or more ventilation openings so constructed that 'their total area is not less than one twentieth of the floor area of the

room and some part of the area is not less than 1.75m above the floor'. In other words, a room 3 × 4.5m (10 × 15ft) needs a window about 840mm (33in) square; and the top of the window must always be above head height.

Another point to consider is access. You'll do well to plan the partition so that you don't have to put a new doorway in an existing structural wall. It's far less work and just as effective to include one in the partition.

You must also consider how the ceiling joists run. This is important because you'll have to fix your partition to them, not just into the ceiling plaster. They're probably spaced regularly, but you'll have to find their exact positions by tapping and making small holes, or by removing the floorboards above. If they lie at right angles (or nearly) to the intended line of your partition, there's no problem. If you want the partition to run in the same direction as the joists, think carefully. You'll have to position it directly underneath a joist, fit a new joist and fix it to that, or fit 50 × 50mm (2 × 2in) bridging pieces between existing joists at regular intervals and fix the top plate to them. Moreover, an especially long and/or tall partition may be too heavy for the floorboards alone to support — so you'll have to make similar decisions about the floor joists.

Have a look at the electricity, gas and water supplies, and see that any necessary modifications to these won't be too difficult to make.

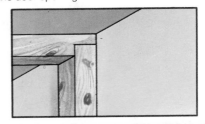

196

And lastly ring the local council. Unless you are converting a house into flats, you don't need planning permission. But you can't be too careful where the Building Regulations are concerned, because they deal with things like fire hazards and proper ventilation. The council should be able to tell you whether your plans conform.

When you've thought about all this and worked out a likely scheme, it's a good idea to sketch it out on paper. If there's a hidden snag, you'll find it staring at you in black and white, and you can deal with it before it causes any trouble.

Constructional details

Something you'll need to decide is how far apart the studs should be. Studs set at '600mm (2ft) centres' (i.e., with their centres that distance apart) give what is really the maximum spacing, and 450mm (18in) will make an even more rigid structure.

You should also measure and take into account the sizes of whatever cladding material you'll be fixing to the wooden framework. Plasterboard, for example, is standardised at 2440 × 1220mm (8 × 4ft) and 3000 × 1220mm (10 × 4ft). You might therefore want to arrange the studs so that there's one every 1220mm (4ft). Putting them at either 600mm (2ft) or 400mm (16in) centres would ensure this.

The door opening, of course, needs to be wider. Take its size from that of the door you plan to use, plus 3mm (⅛in) clearance either side and the thickness of extra 'lining' pieces of, say 100 x 25mm (4 x 1in) wood, fixed round its inside at top and sides. These should be wide enough to cover the edges of the cladding on both sides. A window opening should be lined in the same way (see *Ready Reference,* page 200).

It's unlikely, of course, that you'll be able to fit an exact number of whole sheets of cladding from wall to wall or floor to ceiling. So you'll need to cut some to fit. Besides, the walls and ceiling may not be dead straight or true, so you'll need to mark and cut the edges of the sheets which adjoin them, to make them fit snugly. Luckily, plasterboard is extremely easy to cut.

Noggins need only be placed 1220mm (4ft) above the floor, and again at 2400mm (8ft) if the ceiling is higher — assuming you'll be using 2400 × 1200mm (8 × 4ft) sheets.

Starting work

First, of course, you'll need to buy your timber. This is made easy by the fact that all the pieces (except for door and window linings, which are added later anyway) are the same cross-sectional size. This can be as massive as 100 × 50mm (4 × 2in), but 75 × 50mm (3 × 2in) is quite big enough for most purposes, and 75 × 38mm (3 × 1½in) will

FIXING TOP AND SOLE PLATES

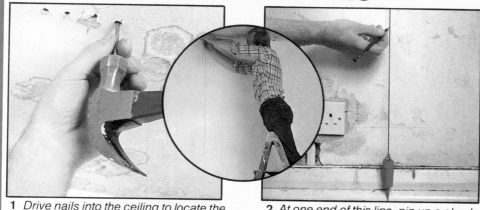

1 *Drive nails into the ceiling to locate the exact centre of the joist (or joists) to which the top plate will be fixed. Mark the new wall's position on the ceiling.*

2 *At one end of this line, pin up a plumbline to mark the exact centre of the top plate (inset). Mark a true vertical line down the side wall to floor level.*

3 *Cut the sole plate to length. Suspend the plumbline further along the ceiling line and position the sole plate using plumbline and wall marks as guides.*

4 *Nail the sole plate in place (inset – use screws and plugs on solid floors). Then cut the top plate to length and drill screw clearance holes through it.*

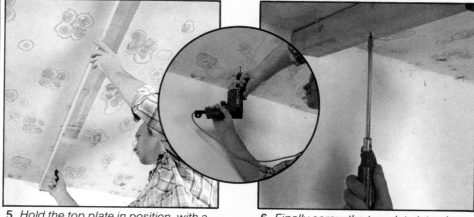

5 *Hold the top plate in position, with a helper or a stud to support it, and mark the screw positions. Drill pilot holes into the joist or joists (inset).*

6 *Finally screw the top plate into place using 90 mm (3½in) screws. Check that it is precisely aligned with the sole plate by suspending the plumbline at each end.*

PUTTING IN THE STUDS

1 Measure the distance between the two plates, add 3 mm (⅛in) and cut the end stud to this length. Drill clearance holes, then mark the wall through them.

2 Drill holes for wall plugs at each point, using a masonry drill. Be sure to drill deep enough to penetrate the masonry beneath. Insert wall plugs.

3 Tap the stud into place – it should be a tight fit – and drive in the fixing screws. The same procedure is used to complete the other end of the framework.

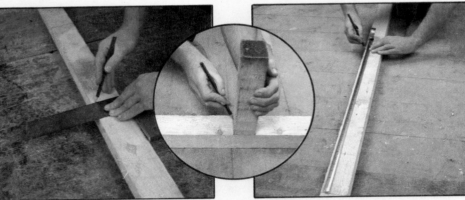

4 Mark the stud position on the sole plate – usually at 610mm (24in) centres. Square a line across the sole plate with a try square at each mark.

5 Hold an offcut of stud timber against each line (inset) and mark the stud width. Leave a wider gap between studs at door openings, allowing for door linings too.

6 Measure and cut each stud as in **1**, tap it into place with its foot on the mark made on the sole plate, and check that it is precisely vertical.

7 Temporarily nail an offcut to the sole plate beside the base of each stud to stop it from moving out of position as you nail it into place.

8 Drive two nails at an angle through one side of each stud into the sole plate. Check that the stud hasn't moved, and then remove the offcut.

9 Drive two more nails down into the other side of each stud, and then repeat the skew-nailing process to nail the top of each stud to the top plate.

PUTTING IN NOGGINS

1 Mark across one edge of the studs, at the desired height, where the tops of the noggins should go. Cut the noggins exactly to length.

2 Nail a steadying block, as for studs, under one end of the noggin; hammer a nail horizontally through the stud into the other end of the noggin.

3 Next skew-nail through the end of the noggin above the steadying block, and down into the side of the stud. Repeat the procedure for each noggin in turn.

4 In some cases you'll also need an upper row of noggins so that you can fix the top edge of the cladding to them. The procedure is exactly the same as before.

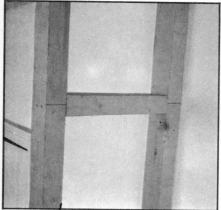

5 Each upper noggin has its centre (not top or bottom) aligned where the top edge of the cladding will come, so further cladding can be nailed to its upper half.

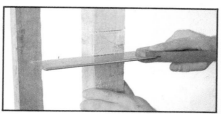

6 The noggin above the door opening needs a firmer fixing. Use a tenon saw and chisel to cut housings (marked with the square and an offcut) across the studs.

sometimes do for the top and sole plates. Buy ordinary softwood: it needn't even be planed smooth — just sawn.

Next, you should cut away the existing skirting board and cut or chip away the ceiling moulding, if any, so that the corners of the framework will fit closely into the angles between wall and floor and between wall and ceiling. Doing this will help to make the structure rigid and secure. However, for a light partition it's often omitted. (You need only cut away to fit the partition round skirting and moulding.)

Then cut the sole and top plates to length. (Keep each as a single piece of timber if at all possible.) Screw the top plate to the ceiling joist or joists, and use a plumbline to position the sole plate directly underneath it. Then nail or screw the sole plate through the floorboards and into the floor joist(s), or screw into a solid floor with the aid of fibre or plastic plugs.

Adding the studs

Now you can start on the studs. You'll have to measure separately for the length of each one, in case floor and ceiling aren't quite parallel. Skew-nailing (see the pictures in steps 2 and 3) is a perfectly adequate way of fixing them for most purposes. You can also buy specially shaped metal connectors which you just nail into place. For an exceptionally sturdy job, cut housings across the plaster with a tenon saw and chisel, and simply fit the ends of the studs into them (see step 6).

The last stage in building the framework is to cut and fix the noggins. Skew-nailing is, once again, the usual way of attaching them. They make better braces if you stagger them slightly, positioning them alternately higher and lower. But if you're going to fix the edges of the cladding to them, they'll have to be in a straight line. Either way, be careful not to make them too long. If you do, you'll probably still be able to squeeze them into position, but they'll bend the studs out of true.

The lintel (the noggin above the door opening) should be housed in the studs at each side for stability. If you are mounting cupboards on the wall, you may find it helpful to fix bearers for them in the same way.

Next, screw the door lining to its frame; the top piece is fitted to the side pieces with either rebate or barefaced housing joints (see pictures 3 and 4 on the next page).

Pipes and cables

The final job before putting on the cladding (though you can do it after cladding one side) is to bore holes in studs and perhaps noggins, and run any essential pipes and cables through them. At the same time remember to nail or screw on blocks on which to mount light switches, power points and any other electrical accessories that you have decided are necessary.

TIPS FOR BETTER PARTITIONS

● To help you align the sole plate, you can nail the end in position before moving the other end round to centre it under the plumbline.

● You'll need at least No 10 screws for fixing to walls and ceiling; that means a 2mm (⁵/₆₄in) diameter pilot hole, and a 5mm (³/₁₆in) clearance hole through the timber.

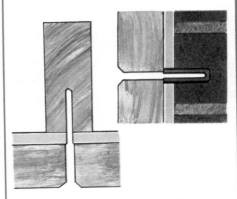

● Studs should always be cut slightly too long, for a really tight fit; you should have to knock them in. But noggins should be just right — any less and they'll be loose; any more and they'll push the studs out of true.

● Door and window linings are made of planed timber, fitted together with rebate or barefaced housing joints, and just wide enough to cover the edges of the cladding either side. The lining is screwed to the framework. You can subsequently fit doorstop or glazing beading to its faces, and architrave mouldings over its edges to cover the join with the cladding. The illustration below shows this in horizontal cross-section.

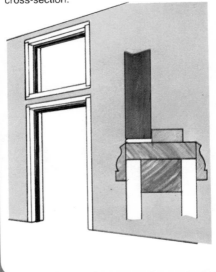

COMPLETING THE FRAME

1 *Measure between the housings, cut the noggin exactly to length, and nail it horizontally through the sides of the studs like the other noggins.*

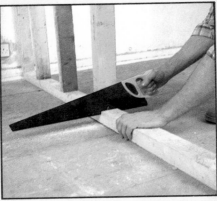

2 *Now that the partition's framework is held straight and rigidly in position, you can cut away part of the sole plate to complete the door opening.*

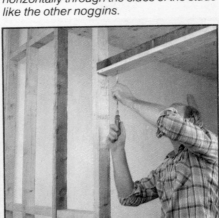

3 *Finish off the door frame by screwing on lining pieces of planed timber. It's best to cut a rebate across each end of the top piece, using a tenon saw and chisel.*

4 *Then you can fit the sides of the frame into the rebates and screw them to the studs. Any windows (eg, over the door) are treated in just the same way.*

5 *Next nail the first piece of cladding to the studs and noggins, after cutting the edge to fit against skirtings, mouldings and uneven walls.*

6 *Holes for pipes and electricity cables should be drilled in studs and noggins before you complete the cladding.*

PLASTERING PLASTERBOARD

A timber stud partition makes a sturdy wall dividing up a room. You can clad it with sheets of plasterboard and finish the surface with a skim coat of plaster so it looks like an integral part of the house's structure.

You can build a timber-frame partition to divide a room into two separate areas using only basic carpentry techniques (see the previous section). In doing so you'll not only add areas of interest in the room but gain some extra space for putting up shelves and storing items.

Your partition can be built from floor to ceiling and wall to wall, or else simply project into the room; you can also incorporate a doorway, serving hatch or glazed areas. Timber studs form the frame of the wall and you can clad it with one of a variety of sheet materials to give a finish which can be easily decorated to match adjacent walls.

Insulating wallboards, which are made of lightweight fibre, can be used to give a surface you can paint or paper. They give good thermal and sound insulation but they're fairly soft and therefore susceptible to knocks.

You can also fix sheets of plywood and hardboard with a natural wood veneer, or with a plastic coating printed on one side to simulate natural wood. Some boards even come with a decorative finish of imitation ceramic tiles. A more expensive, but very attractive, alternative is to go for real timber cladding.

Fireproof boards can also be used to clad your partition where you need some resistance to fire. They're normally used underneath other wallboards.

These materials are adequate if you want a ready-made decorative finish or a surface that you can paint or paper, but if you'd like your partition to look like a solid, integral part of the house, the best treatment is to plaster it to match adjacent walls.

To give your partition a suitable surface for plastering you'll have to nail sheets of plasterboard (see *Ready Reference*). This is a sheet material that consists of a core of gypsum plaster sandwiched between two sheets of heavy-duty paper. There are various grades for use on ceilings or on walls that require insulation but the ones to use for a stud partition are called 'dry lining boards'.

They have a grey side intended for plastering and an ivory-coloured side specially prepared for decorating directly with paint or wallpaper.

Cladding the partition

Plasterboard cladding is nailed to the wooden framework of the partition wall so you'll have to take into account the dimensions of the sheets when spacing out the studs.

The commonest sheet size is 2440 × 1220mm (8 × 4ft), but a number of other sizes are available. Remember to space studs accurately so their centres coincide with joins between adjacent sheets; with 1220mm (4ft) wide sheets the studs should be at 610mm (2ft) centres.

If your house has very high ceilings a 2440mm (8ft) long sheet might not fit exactly from floor to ceiling height so you'll have to add a smaller panel above it. Fix extra noggins (see *Ready Reference*) to coincide with the horizontal joints in the cladding, so you can nail the boards in place.

It's best to stagger these horizontal joints in the cladding, to prevent the likelihood of the surface plaster cracking across the wall, and to stiffen the partition. The way to do this is to fix the first whole sheet at the top of the partition and fill in the gap below with a cut piece, then to fit the second whole sheet at the bottom and clad the gap at the top (see *Ready Reference*). It's a good idea to use the waste piece from the first cut sheet to fill the gap in the second row, to avoid wastage.

Leave cladding around any doorways or

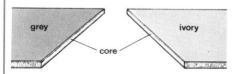

hatch openings until you've fixed all the full-width sheets you can. The best place to start fixing the boards to a half-partition is at the free end. Make sure the first sheet is flush with the end of the partition, parallel with the studs, and that the inner edge runs up the centre of an intermediate stud.

If you're cladding a wall-to-wall partition, however, you can start nailing on the boards at either end. You'll probably have to scribe and cut one edge of the first sheet to butt up with the adjacent wall accurately: few walls are truly vertical (see *Ready Reference*).

Fixing the plasterboard

You'll find that sheets of plasterboard are fairly heavy and cumbersome for one person to lift and the corners are likely to break off if knocked or dropped. When you're carrying a sheet you should grip it at each side at about shoulder height and tilt back the top so that you can walk without kicking it; if you allow it to tilt forward it'll tend to pull you over. You'll probably find it easiest to walk sideways with the board. When you reach the partition, set it down first then lean it against the wall.

To fit your first sheet of plasterboard measure the height of the partition and if it's less than the length of the board, transfer this dimension to one face and subtract about 12mm (½in). Scribe a line against a straight edge across the board using a sharp trimming knife and 'snap' back the waste piece. Run the knife up the opposite side to cut through the paper and free the waste piece.

It's important that the sheet is fixed tightly at the ceiling, so offer it up to the wall, pushing it up with a 12mm (½in) gap at the floor. There's a simple device you can use to lever the plasterboard into position. It's called a 'foot-lifter' and you can make it yourself from a small block of softwood and a thinner strip, which fits on top. It works like a seesaw, levering up the board from the floor so you can make the first fixings at both sides. When you've hammered in a few nails at each side you can remove the footlifter and hammer in the remaining nails.

Use only galvanised plasterboard nails 30mm (1¼in) long, evenly spaced about 150mm (6in) apart and no closer to the edge of the board than 12mm (½in) or there's a danger that the edge might tear away. Don't use ordinary nails that aren't galvanised or they'll rust and stain the plaster finish.

Hammer in the nail so that the head just grips the surface of the paper without tearing or punching its way through. If you don't hammer it in this far the projecting head will be visible on the finished plaster surface; if you knock it in too far so that it punctures the paper any subsequent vibrations will work the plasterboard loose.

Continue along the partition, nailing up whole sheets of plasterboard. If you find that

1 Mark the height of the partition on the plasterboard, less 12mm (½in) for fitting, and scribe across the sheet with a trimming knife.

2 Hold the board against your side and grip the top end. Slap your other hand sharply on the waste piece, pulling it back gently as you do so.

5 You'll probably have to cut a sheet to width at the end of the partition. Measure the space at the top, centre and bottom of the partition.

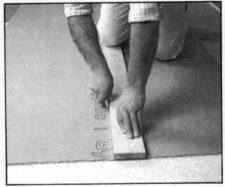

6 If the wall is fairly even, simply transfer your measurements to the board, scribe along the side of a timber straight edge and cut off the waste.

they don't overlap the studs half-way you've made an error in the initial setting-out. This will have a cumulative effect across the wall but you won't have to remove all the boards to remedy the fault: simply cut one sheet to the required width.

Your last sheet of plasterboard will probably be narrower than a full sheet so you'll have to cut it to size. If the adjoining wall is fairly straight and vertical (test this with a spirit level) you can just measure the width of the gap, transfer this to the board and cut off the waste. Fit the board in the same way as the others. But if the wall's untrue you'll have to cut the cladding to fit the profile.

Hold the sheet against the partition, using your footlifter, and butt its edge up to the wall. Make sure that the opposite edge is parallel with the edge of the last fixed sheet or stud. There's a simple trick you can use to scribe the profile of the wall onto the face of the plasterboard: hold a small block of wood and a pencil against the wall and draw it along to

mark the profile of the wall on the face of the board (see *Ready Reference*). Lie the board flat on the floor and carefully cut along the guideline with a sharp knife. Return the board to the wall and butt the cut edge up to the wall. Mark the opposite side where it falls halfway between the last stud. Cut off the waste and nail the sheet in place.

When you've covered one side of the partition you can move to the opposite side and clad that in the same way. Now's the time to add some form of thermal or sound insulation to the cavity between the two skins. You can cut strips of insulating fibreboard or sheets of expanded polystyrene to fit between the studs before you fix the second skin.

Don't forget that now is also the time to lay in any electric wiring or pipe runs that traverse the wall.

Plastering the plasterboard

You can apply a finishing coat of plaster to the partition as soon as you've nailed all the

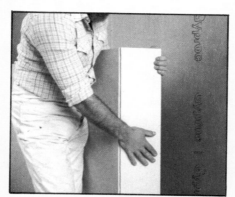

3 *The plaster core within the board should snap cleanly along the line of your cut, but the waste piece will be held by the paper lining at the back.*

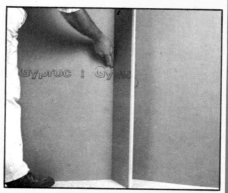

4 *Go around to the other side of the sheet and, with the waste piece bent back, run your knife up the fold in the paper backing to remove it.*

7 *To fit the board tightly into the ceiling angle you'll need a 'footlifter', made from two offcuts of wood, which you use to lever up the sheet.*

8 *You'll now have both hands free to nail the plasterboard to the studs, using 30mm (1¼in) galvanised plasterboard nails 12mm (½in) in from the edge.*

plasterboard sheets in place. When the plaster is set you can then decorate the surface with wallcovering, tiles, or just emulsion paint, to match adjacent walls.

You'll probably find plastering dry lining boards much easier than plastering a wall made of bricks or blocks because you don't need to worry about how absorbent the surface is, as you do on solid masonry; the heavy grey paper used to surface the board is designed to be plastered on directly, and has exactly the right absorbency for the job.

The correct plaster to use on an internal stud partition is a ready-mixed gypsum plaster called Thistle Board Finish. It's usually spread on to the wall in two parts; the first is intended to cover the joints between the boards and the second is a flat, finishing coat.

Using the plasterer's tools

Plastering a large area of wall requires some skill in handling the various tools (see *Ready Reference*) and the only way to acquire this is

to practise. First mix the plaster; you can do this in a 14 litre (3 gallon) bucket. Half-fill the bucket with perfectly clean water – any dirt that gets into the mix could affect the setting time and mar the finish – and add handfuls of plaster until you've almost filled the bucket. Leave the mix to soak until all of the dry plaster has been absorbed by the water, then stir vigorously with a stout stick. The plaster should have a smooth, creamy consistency – like melting ice cream.

The main tools you'll need are a steel trowel to apply the plaster and a hawk to hold the plaster close to the wall. If you're right-handed, hold the hawk in your left hand (resting on your thumb and index finger) and the trowel in your right. Your index finger should be against the shank of the trowel, with the toe of the trowel pointing left. Your knuckles should be uppermost.

It's a good idea to practice loading the trowel and spreading the plaster (see pages 186-191 for instructions) on a spare

Ready Reference

TOOLS AND EQUIPMENT

You'll need the following tools for plastering your stud partition:
● steel trowel for spreading on and smoothing the plaster (A)
● hawk of wood or aluminium to hold small amounts of plaster (B)
● spot board to hold large amounts of plaster

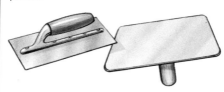

● two 14 litre (3 gallon) plastic buckets – one for mixing plaster, the other to hold clean water for mixing.

WHAT IS A STUD PARTITION?

A timber stud partition consists of:
● a timber sole plate, which runs the length of the partition at floor level
● a timber top plate, which runs the length of the partition at ceiling level
● vertical timber studs at intervals along the partition, their centres coinciding with joins in the plasterboard
● horizontal timber noggins nailed between the studs to strengthen the structure and provide support for the plasterboard cladding.

CLADDING A TALL ROOM

If your house has tall rooms a standard-sized sheet of plasterboard might not fit from floor to ceiling. You'll have to cut a piece to fill the gap. Avoid a continuous line across the partition, which could cause the plaster surface to crack, by staggering the joins. Proceed as follows:
● nail the first full sheet at floor level to the studs and noggins and fill the gap above with a cut piece
● fix the second full sheet at ceiling level and fill the gap below with a cut piece; use the waste from your first cut sheet
● continue across the partition alternating full sheets and cut sheets.

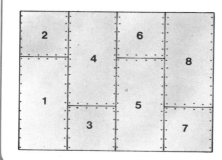

SCRIMMING THE JOINTS

1 *When you've nailed up all of the cladding, cut lengths of narrow tape (called 'scrim') to cover each joint from floor to ceiling.*

2 *Mix up some plaster and take a small amount on your hawk to the partition. Spread a thin 50mm (2in) wide layer along the joint from floor to ceiling.*

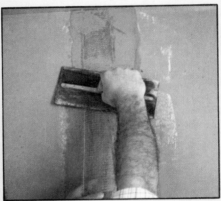

3 *Drape a length of scrim over your trowel and press it into the strip of wet plaster at the top of the partition. Then draw the trowel down the joint.*

4 *When you've laid the first length of scrim, trowel lightly over the surface from the bottom to the top to bed the tape completely in plaster.*

5 *You'll also have to seal any horizontal joints with scrim. Spread on the plaster as before, with your trowel blade held at 30° to the wall.*

6 *Press the scrim into the plaster and trowel it smooth. You mustn't allow an overlap of scrim where a horizontal joint meets a vertical joint.*

sheet of plasterboard until you're confident you can get the plaster to stick before attempting to plaster the partition.

Sealing the joints

Before you can apply the plaster you must seal the joints between the sheets so they won't show through on the finished surface. This is done by embedding a strip of hessian called 'scrim' in a thin layer of plaster covering each joint. Next you apply a thin coat of plaster to the board between the scrimmed joints to make the surface level again. The finishing coat is applied after this to conceal the joints, and you can polish it to a smooth, matt surface.

Scrim is sold by builder's merchants in rolls 100m (330ft) long × 75mm (3in) wide. It's best to cut your scrim to the length of the joints before you mix your plaster. If there are any horizontal joints in your wall you'll have to scrim these also. You mustn't fold or overlap the scrim as double thicknesses will prevent the plaster from sticking properly and will cause unsightly bulges on the finished surface. Where a horizontal joint meets a vertical joint you'll have to butt up the strips.

To stick the scrim to the wall, spread a thin 100mm (4in) wide strip of Thistle Board Finish along the first joint with a steel trowel. Drape one end of the scrim over the top of your trowel and position it on the screed at the top of the wall: you might need a stepladder to reach the top. Keep the trowel blade at about 30° to the surface of the wall and draw it down the joint, feeding the scrim on to the plaster strip with your free hand. Don't press too hard or you'll drag the scrim down the wall and might even tear it. When you've positioned the first strip, pass the trowel lightly over the joint from the bottom upwards to embed it in the plaster. Scrim the second joint in the same way, forming a 'bay' between the two joints. When the plaster has begun to set it'll turn from dark pink to light pink in colour and when this happens you should spread a thin layer of plaster over the bay, working from the bottom left hand side of the wall. This will bring the whole plastered surface to the level of the scrimmed joints. Scrim the remaining joints and plaster the bays between them.

By the time you've applied the first coat of plaster to the entire wall the surface will be set hard enough to acept the second, finishing coat. Apply an even layer of plaster 4mm (just over ⅛in) thick to the entire surface of the wall, again working from the bottom left, but this time make your strokes long, light, and sweeping to avoid ridges in the plaster.

When the finishing coat has almost set, go back over the area with your trowel – without any plaster – to give a smooth finish. When it's completely set, trowel again but splash a little clean water onto the wall from a brush to lubricate the trowel and create a polished and perfectly smooth surface.

PLASTERING THE PARTITION

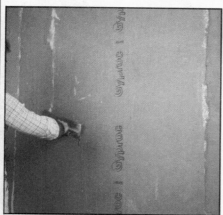

1 Spread on the plaster in the bays between the scrimmed joints. Work from the bottom left, spreading a very thin layer of plaster.

2 You'll have to spread the plaster from the ceiling angle downwards to make a clean, neat edge and to avoid smearing the ceiling with plaster.

3 Complete the bay, applying a very thin coat of plaster, if required, from bottom to top. Try to avoid creating a build-up of plaster over the scrim.

4 Plaster the subsequent bays with a thin coat; by the time you've finished the plaster will have set enough to accept the finishing coat.

5 Spread on the finishing coat over the entire surface of the wall, working with long, sweeping strokes to remove any ridges in the plaster.

6 When the plaster has set trowel over it to polish and flatten the surface. Repeat this several times, lubricating the wall with a little water.

Ready Reference

FITTING TO AN UNEVEN WALL

If the wall which your timber stud partition meets is uneven or not truly vertical you'll have to cut the sheet of plasterboard to fit its profile. To do this:
● lightly tack the plasterboard against the partition, one edge butted up to the uneven wall, the other vertical
● place a small block of wood and a pencil against the wall, resting on the plasterboard
● draw the block and pencil up the angle to mark the profile of the uneven wall on the face of the plasterboard
● lie the board on the floor and cut along the guideline using your trimming knife
● return the board to the partition and butt up the cut edge to the uneven wall
● mark on the other edge of the board the position of the stud centre
● cut off the waste and nail up the board.

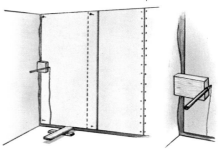

FINISHING HALF-PARTITIONS

To plaster the end of a half-partition:
● nail a plasterboard strip to the end stud
● scrim the external corners
● tack thin battens to the end, projecting over the corners by 3mm (⅛in)
● plaster both faces of the partition using the battens as thickness guides
● remove the battens when the plaster's set. Refix them to the faces of the wall, projecting 3mm (⅛in) over the end
● plaster the end (A)
● or bed 'thin coat metal angle bead' in plaster on each corner and use its 'nose' as a thickness guide (B).

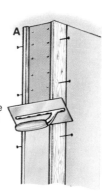

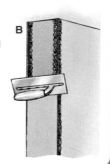

REPLACING AN OLD CEILING

If you've a drab, old ceiling that's badly cracked or sagging you can replace it with a completely new one made of plasterboard, which you can either decorate directly or plaster first.

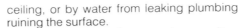

A weak or faulty ceiling is not only unsightly but also, if it should partially collapse, dangerous. So it's wise to check it periodically for signs of deterioration and put right any defects immediately.

If the damage to your ceiling isn't widespread you can sometimes make a 'patch' of plasterboard, which won't be visible after you've redecorated (see *Ready Reference*). However, if the problem's more serious or if you think that the ceiling looks particularly shabby, it's usually better to take it down completely and start again from scratch.

How ceilings are made
The ceilings of your house are probably constructed in one of two ways, depending upon the age of the property and whether any renovation has already been carried out. Older houses usually have ceilings consisting of thin wooden battens called 'laths' nailed to the underside of the joists above, and clad with a thin coat of lime plaster reinforced with hair fibres to give a smooth, flat surface.

Modern ceilings, however, are made in a much simpler way: sheets of plasterboard are nailed to the joists and can be decorated directly or plastered first.

Causes of damage
Damage to your ceiling can be caused in a number of ways; not always due simply to failure of the original structure. If, for example, the joists in your loft are overloaded with your household storage, or you've hammered back loose floorboards in an upstairs room (it's best to screw them back), it's possible that you'll have jarred loose the plaster 'nibs' that secure the plaster to the laths. These nibs were formed when the original plaster was spread on, and consist of a ridge of plaster that's squeezed up between the laths to anchor the whole ceiling in place when set. If the nibs are broken, parts of your ceiling are likely to sag and may even fall away.

Damage might also have been caused by someone in the loft accidentally putting their foot – or dropping something – through the ceiling, or by water from leaking plumbing ruining the surface.

It's not likely that all or part of your ceiling will collapse without warning: usually you'll see signs such as bulges or large cracks appearing. If your loft is directly over the suspect ceiling, you can easily judge how well the plaster is keyed to the laths from above. Alternatively, you can lift a few floorboards in the room above the ceiling to inspect the nibs.

Unless a catastrophe such as a burst water tank occurs, it's rare for a complete plasterboard ceiling to need replacement. But it's quite likely you'll have to put right minor defects caused by accidents in the loft or by the fixing nails working loose.

Knocking down an old lath-and-plaster ceiling is a very messy job, so it's worth anticipating trouble should bulges or cracks appear, by covering the ceiling with sheets of plasterboard.

Making a new ceiling
Before you can put up your new ceiling you'll have to hack off the original lath and plaster surface to reveal the joists. You can then nail up sheets of plasterboard and finish off the surface with a skim of plaster or simply decorate with paper, paint or a textured finish.

There are a number of types and thicknesses of plasterboard and it's important to choose the right one for the job. The standard type is British Gypsum Gyproc wallboard and consists of an aerated gypsum plaster core encased in thick paper liners. One side has a smooth, ivory-coloured surface suitable for direct decoration, and the other face a grey surface, which you fix outermost when you're going to finish the ceiling with a skim coat of plaster.

There's also insulating wallboard, which has a veneer of aluminium foil on the grey face. It's useful for upstairs ceilings when used in conjunction with conventional loft insulation.

Wallboards are available with three different types of edges: squared, bevelled or tapered. The type with a tapered edge is the one to choose for your ceiling because it's designed for smooth, seamless jointing.

There are also two thicknesses of plasterboard: the 9.5mm (⅜in) thickness is used where the ceiling joists are a maximum of 450mm (18in) apart; the 12.7mm (½in) thickness is used for maximum joist spacings of 600mm (2ft).

There are many sizes of board but the most commonly available in builder's merchants are sheets 1800mm (6ft) and 2400mm (8ft) long by 1200mm (4ft) wide. The bigger the sheet you have the fewer the joints you'll have to fill, but you'll find the boards very heavy to lift to the ceiling, so it's probably best to go for the smaller size.

If the joists are widely spaced, you can use a board called Gyproc plank for the repair. It's available in one thickness (19mm/¾in) and one width (600mm/2ft), but in several lengths, the most common being 2400mm (8ft) with an ivory face and tapered edges.

If you're replacing the ceiling of an upstairs room you should use a special board called Gyproc vapour-check wallboard, which has a water vapour-resistant, blue-tinted plastic film bonded to the grey side, leaving the ivory surface exposed for direct decoration. The plastic film stops water vapour from inside the

REMOVING THE OLD CEILING

1 Working from a hop-up or a sturdy testle, start to hack away the old plaster ceiling using the claw of a large claw hammer.

2 When you've removed a section of plaster, prise away the laths. Hack away from you so you don't pull down the ceiling on top of you.

3 Work your way across the room, removing sections of plaster, then the laths. Bag up the plaster and bundle up the laths for disposal.

4 When you've cleared away the old ceiling, work your way along each joist to remove all the lath-fixing nails using a pair of pincers.

building passing into the roof space above.

Where you want to repair and insulate your ceiling in one go, you should use Gyproc thermal board. This consists of standard plasterboard bonded to a backing of expanded polystyrene, with a vapour-check membrane between the two. It has an ivory surface and tapered edges for direct decoration. It comes in several thicknesses ranging from 22 to 65mm ($\frac{7}{8}$ to $2\frac{1}{2}$in); it's 1200mm (4ft) wide and the usual length is 2400mm (8ft).

Handling plasterboard

Carrying sheets of plasterboard is a two-man job in most cases, and you'll probably find it easiest to carry on edge. Store them flat in a dry place, such as your garage or, better still, in the room where you're going to fix them. If this isn't possible, have the boards delivered on the day you want to fix

them. If you're going to collect the boards, don't stack more than two or three sheets at a time on your car roof rack, and use a couple of long lengths of stout timber to support them as they're quite brittle.

If you find the full-size boards too difficult to handle, you can cut them in half, using a sharp trimming knife held against a steel straight edge. Cut through the ivory face with the knife and crack the board over a batten. Fold back the board to form a crease and run your knife blade along the fold.

Removing the old ceiling

There'll be years of accumulated dust and dirt above an old ceiling, so if your loft is directly above, it's worth hiring an industrial vacuum cleaner to clear away as much of the debris as you can.

It's best to wear overalls or old clothes, a dust mask and a pair of stout gloves. You'll

SUPPORTING THE BOARDS

To avoid having to rig up complex working platforms for you and your helpers while you nail up the boards:

● make T-shaped supports from 50x25mm (2x1in) softwood with reinforcing battens (A)

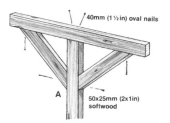

● get your helpers to use the supports at each end of the board to hold it against the joists while you nail it in place from a hop-up (B).

PLASTERING

If you want to plaster the surface of your new plasterboard ceiling:

● fix up the sheets grey-side-down, using plasterboard nails

● spread a thin layer of Thistle Board Finish plaster along the joints, about one arm's length at a time

● embed 75mm (3in) wide hessian scrim in the band of wet plaster using your trowel and leave to set

● spread a 3mm ($\frac{1}{8}$in) thick layer of plaster over the entire surface of the ceiling

● when the plaster has set, trowel over the ceiling without any plaster, to polish the surface. Lubricate your trowel blade with flicks of water from a brush.

FIXING THE NOGGINS

1 *Tidy up the perimeter of the walls; then mark the centre line of each joist on the wall as a guide to nailing up the plasterboard sheets.*

2 *Nail up long 50x50mm (2x2in) noggins parallel with the joists to support the boards; use a batten to set them level with the joists.*

3 *To support the long edges of the boards, fix noggins between the joists. Use a batten marked with the board width to mark their centres.*

4 *Skew-nail 50x50mm (2x2in) noggins between each joist, placed so that the plasterboard will cover half their width.*

need a helper (or helpers) to lift the boards into place and it's a good idea to wear a crash helmet, a hard hat like those worn on building sites, or some sort of padded cap so you can use your head to support the boards while you're driving in the nails.

Clear the room of all furniture, roll back and remove your carpets or other floor-covering and seal the gaps under doors with rolled-up sheets to stop dust blowing into the rest of the house. You'd also be wise to cover the floor with dust sheets or heavy gauge polythene to help you collect the rubble, and open the windows to ensure good ventilation.

Keep lots of old sacks or thick polythene bags handy to carry away the debris. You may also find it useful to keep a house plant spray close to hand to douse the dust.

After that it's just a matter of hacking away the plaster from above with a claw hammer

or a club hammer and bolster chisel. Then you can prise away the laths and extract the nails that are left protruding from the joists.

If you've a central pendant light on your ceiling, or other ceiling-mounted electrical fittings, you'll have to remove these before you start to hack off the plaster. Switch off the electricity supply at the mains and disconnect your fitting leaving only the cable – suitably insulated – hanging down. If you can get into the loft, pull up the flex until you've installed your new ceiling. Otherwise make a hole in the plasterboard and draw the flex through it before fixing the board in place. Locate lights under joists, or nail a batten between adjacent joists, to provide a firm fixing for the rose.

Fixing the plasterboard
With the joists exposed and clear of nails, you should mark their centre points on the

adjacent walls as a helpful guide when positioning the fixing nails.

The board should be fixed with the long paper-covered edges lightly butted together at right angles to the run of the joists, with the grey, foil or polystyrene surface against the joists. The ends of the boards must be located centrally over a joist so you'll probably have to cut them to the correct length.

If the joists are more than 450mm (18in) apart, you'll also have to support the edges of the boards. This means nailing 100 x 50mm (4 x 2in) timber battens called 'noggins' between the joists at these positions. Fix up the noggins by skew nailing (see picture step 4) before you start to nail up the boards.

The noggins will ensure that your new ceiling is set perfectly flat and rigid. However, you can omit noggins if the joists are fairly closely spaced, or if you are using 19mm (¾in) thick Gyproc plank.

Secure the boards to the joists with galvanised plasterboard nails. Use nails 30mm (1¼in) long for 9.5mm (⅜in) thick boards; 40mm (1½in) long for 12.7mm (½in) boards. Thicker boards, such as thermal board, should be fixed with nails that are long enough to sink at least 25mm (1in) into the joists.

To enable you to reach the ceiling you'll need to rig up a platform such as a hop-up or planks between stepladders. Alternatively, you can make T-shaped timber supports (see *Ready Reference*), which will enable your helpers to hold up the boards at each end from floor level.

Drive home the nails firmly without the head fracturing the paper surface; the final hammer blow should leave a slight depression, which you can fill later. Nail each board to every joist and noggin at 150mm (6in) centres, starting at the centre of each board and working outwards. The nails shouldn't be closer than 13mm (½in) from the ends of the boards and 10mm (⅜in) from the edges.

Try to arrange the boards so that the cut edges fit into the internal angles at the sides of the room. When you're forced to have cut edges within the ceiling area, you should stagger the end joints and arrange the boards so that they fall mid-way over a joist, with a 3mm (⅛in) gap between each.

Sealing the joints
If you're going to plaster you new ceiling, you'll have to seal the new joints with hessian scrim (see *Ready Reference* and also page 204) and spread on a skim coat of special Board-Finish plaster. But if you just want to decorate the surface with paint or paper you should seal the joints with a special tape.

You'll need Gyproc joint filler, joint finish

FITTING THE PLASTERBOARD

1 The corners of your walls won't be truly square, so scribe your first plasterboard sheet to fit. Set the angle on a profile gauge.

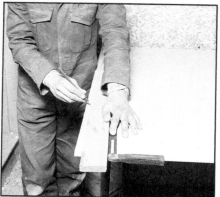

2 Transfer the angle to your first sheet of plasterboard and, using a straight-edge length of timber as a rule, mark the waste and cut it off.

3 Lift up your first plasterboard sheet and position it squarely across the joists with its long inner edge square on the intermediate noggins.

4 Nail the board at 150mm (6in) centres. Once you've made enough fixings to hold the board you and your helper can work simultaneously.

5 Line up a straight-edged length of timber with the centre of each joist, as indicated by the guidelines you drew on the wall, and make intermediate fixings at 150mm (6in) centres.

6 When you've nailed up the first board, lift up the second, butting it lightly against the first, and nail it to the joints and noggins. Continue in this way to complete the ceiling.

and joint tape and, to apply them, a 200mm (8in) jointing applicator, a 50mm (2in) taping knife, and a jointing sponge.

To seal the joints you have to use the applicator to spread an unbroken band of joint filler to fill the taper between the edges of the boards. Next you cut the jointing tape to the exact length of the joint and gradually press it into the filler using your taping knife.

Use the applicator straightaway to spread another band of filler over the tape. Here, you should aim to fill the taper level with the surface of the boards. Inevitably, there'll be some surplus material at the edges of the band of filler and you should wipe this away immediately, using your sponge moistened with water.

After about an hour the filler will have set, though it might not feel dry. Use your applicator to spread a thin film of joint finish over the joint. Dampen the sponge again and carefully 'feather out' the edges of the band of finish to smooth any ridges. Allow this first coat of finish to set then apply a second and feather out the edges.

While the joints are drying you can tackle the nail head depressions by applying a thin coat of joint filler followed by a thin coat of joint finish.

When the joints have dried, there'll be a slight difference in the surface texture between them and the board. You can even this up by spreading a slurry of joint finish over the whole ceiling, or you can apply, by brush or roller, a material called Gyproc drywall top coat. One coat is enough to prepare the ceiling for normal decorating; two coats provide a water vapour-barrier.

If your wall is solid and plastered, there'll be a fairly wide gap of the angle with your new ceiling, which you'll have to fill with plaster. But you can fill the joint between the new ceiling and wall using the basic technique as for flat joints. First, fill any gaps with joint filler, then cut the tape to length. Crease it firmly down the middle, apply a thin band of joint finish to each side of the angle between the ceiling and the wall and press the tape in place.

Run a thin layer of joint finish over the top and feather out the edges with your damp sponge. When this has dried, apply a band of finish to both sides of the angle and feather out the edges.

Finishing the ceiling

When you've filled the joints and have treated the entire surface of your ceiling with slurry of joint finish or drywall top coat you can decorate the ceiling with emulsion paint for a smooth finish, put up woodchip or a relief wallcovering (and again cover with emulsion paint), brush on a textured compound or simply hang a wallpaper with a pattern to match your wallcovering.

FINISHING THE CEILING

1 To conceal the joints between the boards you'll have to seal them. Mix up some joint filler and spread a band along the tape.

2 Cut a length of jointing tape to fit the joint and press it into the filler using the special taping knife to bed it evenly.

3 Again using the applicator, spread another band of filler over the joint, covering the tape. Smooth out any air bubbles trapped underneath.

4 Remove any surplus filler from the edges of the joint with the sponge moistened with a little water, and leave for about one hour to set.

5 While the joint's drying, fill the nail head depressions with filler. Mix up some joint finish and spread it over the joint and then the nail heads.

6 Feather-out the edges of the joint with the sponge so that the surface is flush with the plasterboard. Apply top coat and decorative finish.

SECTION 6

ROOFING

TECHNIQUES

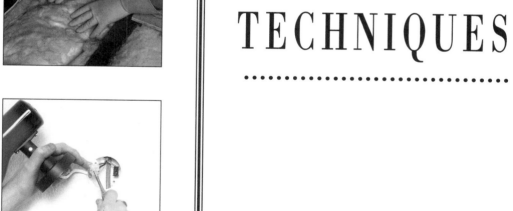

REPLACING ROOF TILES

A tiled roof provides a weatherproof and extremely durable covering for your house. But, occasionally, constant buffeting from the weather takes its toll and individual tiles or areas of tiling require repairing. Here's how to tackle the job.

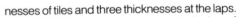

A tiled roof provides a durable, weatherproof covering to your house, even though the individual tiles are surprisingly brittle and can be damaged by the effects of high winds, driving rain and frost. Also they're fixed to the roof structure in rather a crude fashion, so it's not unusual to find cracked, broken or slipped tiles, or even ones that have fallen out completely.

Keep a regular check on the condition of your roof and make good any damage as soon as you notice it, before it has a chance to let water into your home.

Types of tiles
Roof tiles are either made of clay or concrete. They're available in a wide range of shapes, sizes and colours, with a shiny or matt glaze, and in a wide variety of profiles. Matching existing tiles is usually quite easy.

The simplest form of tile, called the 'plain' tile, was traditionally made of clay, although more recently concrete has been used because it's cheaper and more versatile.

The basic tile used on the main part of the roof measures 265x165mm (10½x6½in); it has a slight bevel or sometimes a 'double camber (see *Ready Reference*) which ensures that each tile is bedded down evenly on its neighbours.

There's also a wider 'tile-and-a-half' tile, which you use at the edge, or 'verge', of the roof to maintain the bonding pattern without having to cut tiles. Shorter 'ridge under' and 'eaves under' tiles are made for use at the top and bottom of the roof slope respectively, in addition to numerous half-round and angled tiles to seal the ridge and 'hip' of the roof (for more information see 'Roof construction ' and *Ready Reference*).

Plain tiles are usually simply hooked onto the fixing battens by the two integral 'nibs' under their top edge; they also have two holes below the nibs so they can be nailed to the battens at every third or fourth course to make the structure more secure. The tiles are set out on the roof in a 'double lap' pattern in which each tile overlaps two tiles below it and is itself overlapped by the two tiles above it (see *Ready Reference*). This means that the whole roof is covered by at least two thick-nesses of tiles and three thicknesses at the laps.

The individual tiles in a 'single-lap' roof overlap their neighbours on one side and are overlapped by their neighbours on the other side; the overlap is also a single tile above and below. Used mainly on the roofs of new houses or where a property has been re-roofed, they're usually made of concrete with either flat or ridged profiles. Some incorporate a side or head-and-side locking groove, sometimes held with special clips (see *Ready Reference*).

Reaching the roof
It's vital that you work safely and securely while on the roof. You'll need either a ladder or scaffold tower to reach gutter level and a roof or 'cat' ladder to enable you to move about and work on the roof slope and at its apex.

You must secure your ladder to the house at the top by tying it to a ring bolt at the soffit to prevent the ladder sliding sideways as you climb onto it from the roof ladder. If your house has overhanging eaves you'll have to use a ladder stay to position the ladder out from the wall; but you'll need to secure it as well.

Otherwise like a conventional ladder, a roof ladder has a large hook at the top, which secures it to the ridge of the roof, two wheels for running it up the slope and pressure plates, which spread the load over the fragile surface of the roof. Crawlboards are an alternative to a roof ladder. They usually comprise slot-together sections of slats with footholds at right-angles, a ridge hook, wheels and pressure plates.

Replacing a single plain tile
Because replacement of a single plain tile is easy and cheap it isn't worth attempting to repair a cracked or damaged tile, unless you're merely doing so as a stop-gap until you can obtain a new, matching tile. In which case you can trowel thick mastic into the crack, or cover the tile with a strip of self-adhesive flashing strip, tucking the top under the tile in the course, or row, above. If a piece of tile has broken off you can temporarily stick it back with epoxy putty or glass fibre resin repair paste.

Replacement of damaged tiles is, however, the best solution. To make this task easier you need two small wedges made from off-cuts of softwood about 25mm (1in) thick, 150mm (6in) long and tapering almost to a point. Push the wedges under the sides of the two tiles in the row above the one you're going to replace. The wedges will hold these tiles clear of the damaged one, allowing you to slide the point of a bricklaying trowel underneath, lift its nibs clear of the batten and remove it.

Tiles are usually held at every third or fourth course with nails. If the damaged tile is one of these you may be able to loosen the nails by working the tile from side to side, but if this fails you'll have to pull them free with a pair of pincers, or saw off their heads by

ROOF CONSTRUCTION

The diagram below shows the basic construction of a tiled-and-felted roof. The details (right) illustrate some of the features you may find on your roof; their presence or absence depends on its shape and design.

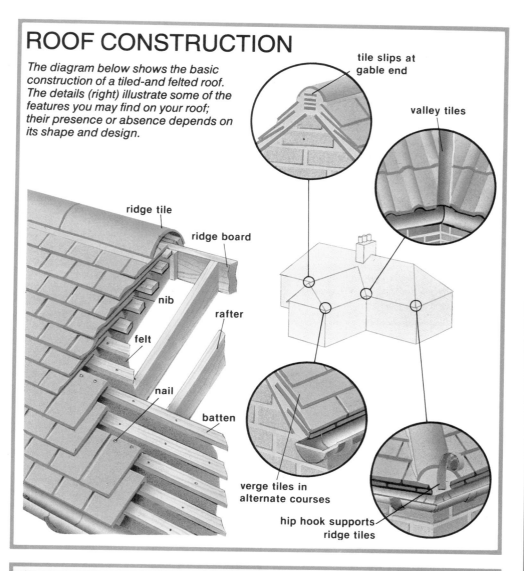

tile slips at gable end

valley tiles

ridge tile

ridge board

nib

rafter

felt

nail

batten

verge tiles in alternate courses

hip hook supports ridge tiles

ERECTING A ROOF LADDER

1 Make sure your access ladder or scaffold tower is secured in place. Haul up the roof ladder and run it gently up the tiles on its wheels.

2 Carefully turn the ladder over so that the hook latches over the ridge. This prevents the ladder slipping back down the roof.

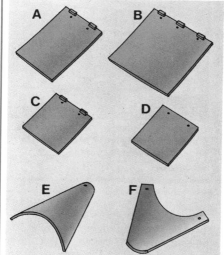
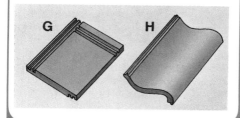

REPLACING A SINGLE TILE

1 *Use wooden wedges to force up the two tiles immediately above the one you're replacing, so it can be lifted clear of the tiling batten.*

2 *You may be able to remove the tile by hand. But, particularly if it has broken awkwardly, you can use a trowel to remove the remaining segment.*

3 *Slide the trowel under the tile until it's virtually touching the batten. Then lift the nibs clear so the tile can be withdrawn.*

4 *Guide a new tile into place with your hand or a trowel so the nibs engage over the back of the batten. Then remove the wooden wedges.*

inserting a hacksaw blade underneath them.

Try to buy a replacement tile of exactly the same size, style and colour as the one that you've removed. Rest the new tile on your trowel and, with the wedges still in place, simply guide the tile upwards until its nibs hook over the batten. When it's correctly positioned, remove the wedges and the job is complete.

Replacing an area of tiles

If a small area of roof is to be renewed, first remove the damaged tiles from the top course within this area and then work down the roof until all the tiles are removed from the defective area, leaving the felt (if present) and battens exposed. You'll probably find a lot of dust and debris on the felt surface, which you can brush away carefully with a hand brush.

Replace the broken tiles with new ones by hooking them over the battens, working upwards course by course from the lowest point. Fit the tiles in the top course using the method previously described for replacing single tiles. Don't forget to secure the tiles at every third or fourth course using 30mm (1¼in) long aluminium alloy roofing nails or galvanised nails.

Replacing interlocking tiles

Single lap interlocking tiles are usually made of concrete and they're widely used on modern houses and on houses that have been re-roofed. Adjacent tiles interlock with one another and it's usual for each course to overlap the one below.

Replacement of defective tiles follows basically the same guidelines as for plain tiled roofs; tiles in the course above are lifted with wedges, which makes it easier for you to lift and remove the damaged tile below. It's usually necessary to tip the tile at an angle so that its nibs clear the batten and the interlocking grooves can be disengaged from the tiles at the side. You may also have to wedge up the overlapping tile in the same course as the one you're replacing.

This type of tile is often nailed at every course and therefore you'll have to remove or cut through the nails. Additionally, interlocking tiles may be held with clips hooked over the interlocking ridge and nailed to the battens: in a case like this you'll have to lever out the clips first. A single replacement tile of this type can be replaced without a clip, but if you're repairing a larger area you should use clips on each one.

Some clay pantiles are simply hung onto the battens and if these tiles become displaced or need replacement it's best to refix them with a patented roof tile clip which hooks over the top edge of the tile and is nailed to the batten. The last tile in the repair, which you can't nail because the surrounding tiles overlap it, can be held with epoxy putty or a gap-filling building adhesive.

Fitting new valley tiles

Valley tiles are frequently found as an alternative to a metal-lined valley at the junction of two roofs (see *Ready Reference*). They can be used on plain and interlocking tile roofs but they can be tricky to replace. They're usually fixed with nails and the adjacent tiles interlock into them. Consequently you may have to remove a larger number of tiles in order to gain access to the fixing. If possible, you can attempt a simple repair using self-adhesive flashing strip tucked well under the tile above.

Sometimes it's possible to replace a single valley tile by following the standard methods of removing tiles described previously; otherwise it's necessary to strip and re-tile the entire area, refixing the valley tiles by working from the eaves up towards the ridge.

Repairing ridge tiles

Ridge tiles, which seal the apex of the roof, are held in place with mortar. It's common for the mortar between the individual ridge tiles to crack and fall out of place, but if the tiles are firmly fixed you can fill narrow cracks easily by injecting a bead of flexible non-setting mastic using a special gun for application. This mastic is available in various colours, including fawn and brown to tone with most roof tiles, so the repair shouldn't be too obtrusive.

Larger gaps can be refilled with mortar, using a one part cement to five parts sharp sand mixture to which you've added some PVA bonding agent to improve its workability. First rake old, loose mortar out of the gaps between the ridge tiles, with a cold chisel, and brush out any dust. Then dampen the

REPLACING AN AREA OF TILES

1 Again you can use wooden wedges to free the damaged tiles to make their removal easier. Work from the top of the damaged area to the bottom.

2 Discard all broken or cracked tiles. You may have to remove some whole tiles to gain access to broken ones; save them for re-use later on.

3 Once all the damaged tiles have been taken down, check the batten for rot and brush away any debris that has accumulated on the roofing felt.

TIP

4 If the repair is in an easily visible place, you could take good tiles from a less noticeable area and re-tile that area with new ones.

5 Start laying the tiles in the bottom course of the repair first and then work upwards. It's a good idea to secure every third or fourth course with galvanised nails.

6 You can reposition the wedges as you work to make fitting the tiles that much easier. The last tile is set in place in the same way a single tile is replaced; then the wedges are removed.

Ready Reference

ROOF TILE LAYOUT
Roof tiles are laid out in either single-lap or double-lap fashion.
- single-lap tiles overlap their neighbours on one side and are overlapped by their neighbours on the other side; similarly the overlap is a single tile above and below (A)
- double-lap tiles overlap two tiles below and are overlapped by the two tiles above; the overlap is double at the side also (B).

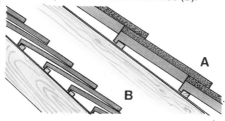

INTERLOCKING TILES
There are several designs of interlocking tiles. Some are nailed to the battens on alternate rows as well as hanging on nibs; others are fixed with tile clips to the battens.

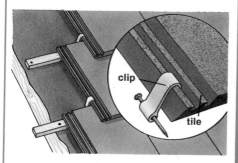

clip

tile

MAKING A BONNET HIP
To make a bonnet hip at the external angle between two roof slopes:
- nail the bonnet hip tiles to the hip rafter from the eaves up to the ridge
- fill the cavity between each tile with mortar to bed them in place
- mortar in tile slips at the last tile cavity

tile slips at gable end

cracks with water, splashed on from a paint brush; this prevents the new mortar from drying out too quickly and cracking. Brush on PVA bonding agent to aid adhesion, allow it to become tacky before trowelling in the new mortar, and smooth it off.

Loose ridge tiles should be removed, and the apex cleared of old mortar, before they are rebedded on fresh mortar. Soak the ridge tiles in water, and dampen the top-most course of roof tiles too, then trowel on mortar in strips at each side of the apex to coincide with the edges of the ridge tiles. Butter the end of the adjacent ridge tile with mortar to seal the two together. It's important to keep most of the underside of the ridge tile free of mortar to leave an air space, which keeps the timber ridge board (to which the rafters are fixed) dry; this also minimises the chance of the ridge tiles cracking. Smooth off the mortar around the edge of the ridge tiles, forming a bevel to ensure good drainage of rainwater.

Seal the open end of the ridge tile at the edge of the roof with pieces of broken tile called 'tile slips' bedded into place in a cement mortar filling (see *Ready Reference*).

Fitting hip tiles

Hip tiles are half-round ridge-type tiles that are fixed along a sloping roof to the eaves. They can be repaired or replaced as described for ridge tiles, except that it's usual to fix a metal bracket called a 'hip hook' (see 'Roof construction') at eaves level as a safety precaution to help prevent dislodged hip tiles from sliding off the roof. The hip hook is simply screwed to the hip rafter using zinc-plated screws. Then the hip tile that covers it is re-bedded on mortar with tile slips to help fill the cavity at the end.

Bonnet hip tiles are also used to weather-proof hips. These are generally fixed with a nail at the top and are bedded in mortar. This mortar can sometimes fall out, in which case you should rake clean the cavity with a cold chisel, dampen the surface with water and then paint on PVA bonding agent before filling in with mortar.

If a single bonnet hip tile is damaged and needs to be replaced, the bedding mortar will be sufficient to hold it. If the entire hip is being renewed, work from the eaves up-wards, setting each tile on bedding mortar and securing it with an aluminium alloy roofing nail at the top.

Re-sealing verges

Traditionally the verges, or edges, of a roof were sealed with mortar pressed into the space between the tiles. If this mortar is slightly cracked you can repair the damage with non-setting mastic. But if larger pieces have fallen away, rake out the mortar, dampen the area and treat with PVA bonding agent.

REPLACING A RIDGE TILE

1 *Gently lift off the loose ridge tile and set it aside. You should be able to re-use it, so be very careful that you do not damage it.*

2 *Use a club hammer and cold chisel to remove the old mortar on each side of the ridge. Work carefully so you don't break any of the roof tiles.*

3 *Dampen the top row of tiles and then lay a fillet of mortar on each side of the ridge. Avoid getting mortar on the ridge timber itself.*

4 *Butter the ends of adjacent ridge tiles with mortar so the old tile can be bedded firmly in place. Again avoid getting mortar on the timber.*

5 *Soak the edges of the ridge tile in water. Press it firmly into its mortar bed, butting it up to its neighbours and checking that it is level.*

6 *Use a trowel to smooth the mortar joints and, if working at the edge of the ridge, pack up the mortar at the end with 'tile slips' – see page 213.*

REPAIRS FOR CHIMNEY STACKS

Perched high on the roof, your chimney is exposed to the worst that the weather can subject it to, so it's no wonder that it soon shows signs of wear and tear. If damage isn't dealt with, rain will penetrate the flue, and perhaps make the chimney unsafe.

A chimney isn't in the most accessible of locations: to reach it you'll need special ladders and even scaffolding. You'd be wise, therefore, to keep a regular check on its condition in case any damage becomes widespread. So that you can readily identify the problem areas it's useful to know just how your chimney is built.

How a chimney is made

A chimney is basically a brickwork or stonework shaft with a central 'flue' that conveys smoke and fumes from an open fireplace or boiler and channels it out of harm's way into the open air.

Traditionally the inside of the flue was rendered in a sand and cement mortar to protect the brickwork but nowadays it is built with clay or terracotta liners, which prevents condensation or corrosive gases damaging the masonry. Where gas or oil-fired central heating has been installed in an old house, the existing flue will probably have been fitted with a flexible aluminium tube or it might have been treated with a self-hardening fluid liner.

The chimney breast is the part of the shaft that's visible in your rooms. It's built into the internal or external walls of the house. The shaft rises through the floors and out of the roof; sometimes a group of chimneys, called a 'stack', rises together. Depending on the layout of the rooms containing a fireplace, the chimney might pass through the roof at the apex, lower down the slope, or at the gable end.

Where the shaft passes through the roof the join is sealed against rain, usually with cement mortar, tile fillets or sheet metal bands known as 'flashings'. The top of the shaft is topped with a cylindrical earthenware pipe or pot, which channels the smoke into the air in a column. The pot is usually set in a sloping mortar bed called 'flaunching', which ensures that rainwater runs off the top and is thrown clear of the stack.

Sometimes the last few courses of bricks at the top of the chimney are built so that they project a little to throw rainwater clear of the stack sides and lessen the risk of water penetration. If the chimney is redundant it may be fitted with a metal or earthenware 'cap', which ventilates the flue – important for prevention of condensation – and keeps out rain.

Signs of damage

Your examination of the chimney should begin indoors: look for signs of dampness on chimney breast walls, and in ceilings around the chimney breast in upper floor rooms, which indicates that water is penetrating the flashings and running down the walls.

Stand away from the house to examine the stack: you'll find it much easier to spot defects if you use a pair of binoculars. Faults to look for include cracked or leaning pots, missing mortar pointing between the bricks, cracked or damaged rendering or pebble-dashing. More seriously there may be cracks or large bulges in the masonry, or even a leaning stack: tell-tale signs that the structure is in a dangerous condition, and could even collapse during high winds.

In addition to making good any defects in the stack you may also feel it's worthwhile sealing off a disused chimney against rain, or even cutting down a tall, disused stack to a lower level for safety.

Access to the chimney

Before you attempt any work on your chimney it's vital to ensure that you carry it out safely. For comparatively simple jobs such as repoint-

Ready Reference

CHIMNEY STRUCTURE

A basic chimney consists of:
● a brickwork or stonework shaft that conveys smoke and fumes from an open fireplace or boiler into the open air.
● cement mortar, tile or sheet metal 'flashings' to seal the join where the chimney passes through the roof (A)
● one or more 'pots' (B) on top of the chimney set in cement flaunching (C)
● top two courses of bricks built out to throw rainwater clear (D).

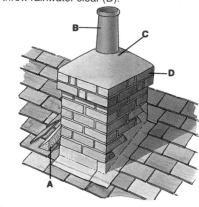

217

ing small areas of brickwork and mending flashings on a stack that's located on the apex of the roof, it may be possible for you to work from a roof ladder (see *Ready Reference*), which hooks over the ridge of the roof: you may be able to reach a chimney built lower down the roof slope or on a gable end by using just a single ladder.

For work on tall chimneys that can't be reached from a roof ladder, and for more major jobs such as replacing or removing the chimney pot, you'll need a secure, flat working platform. If the chimney is at the gable end of the roof it may be possible for you to erect a sectional scaffold tower close to the shaft.

But where the chimney is within the roof area some form of chimney scaffolding is essential for safe working. Specially designed chimney scaffolding sets are available for hire, or you may be able to build a platform around the chimney using conventional scaffolding, which, again, you can hire. In either case you'll need to erect a scaffold tower up to gutter level, position a roof ladder to reach the stack, and lay builder's scaffold boards on the roof around the stack to spread the load of the chimney scaffolding so that it doesn't damage the roof covering.

Dealing with dampness

Dampness high up on a chimney breast wall and on a ceiling close to a chimney stack usually indicates problems with the flashings around the chimney stack, which seal the join between the roof and the base of the stack. You have to go onto the roof to make these repairs; there's nothing you can do about them from the inside.

If the dampness is lower down the chimney breast wall, then the problem could be due to the flue and the fireplace having been completely sealed. In cases like this you should introduce a gentle supply of air into the flue. The most usual way of doing this is to fit either an airbrick or a ventilator grille in the blocked-off fireplace – seal the top with a chimney pot cap.

Renewing the flashings

Flashings may be triangular fillets of cement mortar, although sheet metal flashings made from lead or zinc are much more reliable. At the sides of a chimney it's usual to have 'stepped' metal flashings, which are tucked into the horizontal mortar joints at the base of the stack, and fold onto the roof, where they cover 'soakers' (separate pieces of lead or zinc interleaved between tiles or slates adjacent to the stack).

On roofs that are covered with modern single-lap interlocking tiles, and occasionally with slate and plain tiled roofs, the stepped flashings may simply be beaten down or 'dressed'

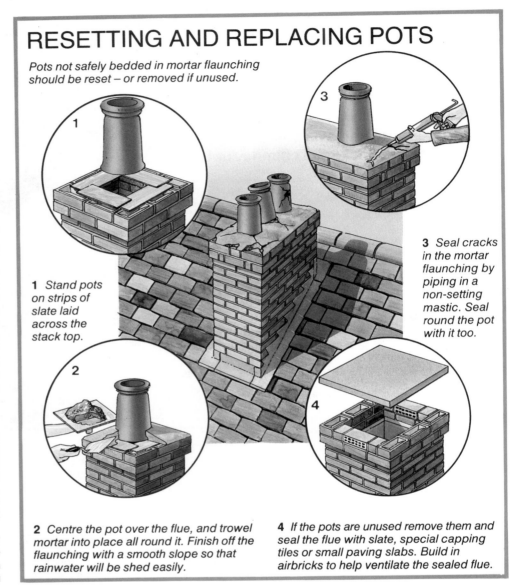

RESETTING AND REPLACING POTS

Pots not safely bedded in mortar flaunching should be reset – or removed if unused.

1 *Stand pots on strips of slate laid across the stack top.*

2 *Centre the pot over the flue, and trowel mortar into place all round it. Finish off the flaunching with a smooth slope so that rainwater will be shed easily.*

3 *Seal cracks in the mortar flaunching by piping in a non-setting mastic. Seal round the pot with it too.*

4 *If the pots are unused remove them and seal the flue with slate, special capping tiles or small paving slabs. Build in airbricks to help ventilate the sealed flue.*

over the adjacent tiles: this is known as 'apron flashing'.

The flashings at the sides of a stack may be either the soaker or apron types, but invariably the flashing at the lower face of the stack is of the apron type. If the chimney isn't built on the apex of the roof, straddling the ridge, the upper side of the stack is weatherproofed with a metal channel and flashing, called a 'back gutter'. If the chimney is built into the ridge it should be fitted with a special 'saddle' flashing.

Each of these flashings can give trouble, often parting from the masonry or roof material and admitting rain. With cement fillet or tiled flashings, it's common for gaps to appear where the fillet moves away from the brickwork. In this case, if the fillet is sound, you can simply inject a bead of non-setting mastic into the crack. This kind of

mastic comes in a cartridge and is applied with a special gun.

But if the fillet is badly cracked or crumbling, chip it away with a club hammer and cold chisel and replace it with a new flashing. You can use either fresh mortar or a metal-faced self-adhesive flashing strip, which is available in rolls. These strips are sold in various widths, 150mm (6in) wide being the most useful, and with an aluminium foil face or a grey finish that resembles lead.

Rolls of flashing are usually supplied with a small tin of primer, which you paint on to ensure good adhesion of the strip to the bricks and tiles; but it's not necessary to use this on slates. The primer is a black bituminous liquid, which you apply in a band to the angle between the brickwork and the roof where the flashing is to go. After the primer has dried you can cut the flashing strip to length,

REMOVING FAULTY FLASHING

1 Inspect the flashing where the chimney shaft passes through the roof. Look for tears in the flashing or gaps at the joins.

2 Remove the defective flashing but leave any soakers in place. Stepped flashing has 'tabs' slotted into the mortar joints, which you can lever out.

3 Rake out the mortar with a pointing chisel where the flashing was slotted, ready for the new mortar. Then brush dust from the joints.

4 Wet the joints, then press in the new mortar using a pointing trowel; in exposed areas like this it's best to make weatherstruck joints.

5 Bevel the pointing at the top and run the trowel along to leave an overhang. Run the trowel along a batten to form a neat 'lip' at the bottom, which throws rainwater clear.

6 The flashing at the lower face of the chimney may have been the apron or mortar fillet type. You can lay a triangular fillet and either bed tiles in it or lay an apron over it.

RENDER AND PEBBLEDASH REPAIRS

To repair hairline cracks in smooth render:
- widen the crack with a chisel so new mortar will adhere
- undercut the edges with a scraper to improve the bond
- brush out debris from the crack
- apply PVA bonding agent
- press a mortar mix of 5 parts sand to 1 part cement into the crack and smooth flush with the surrounding surface.

To repair 'blown' render:
- cut back the damaged section until you reach sound edges
- undercut the edges
- rake out the mortar joints
- brush out dust and debris
- apply PVA bonding agent to the surface
- trowel on a new mortar mix of 1 part cement to 5 of sand to slightly more than the required thickness
- draw a straight-edged timber batten over the patch with a sawing action to remove excess mortar and leave a smooth flat finish.

To repair a pebbledashed area:
- prepare the hole as for smooth render, then throw handfuls of matching pebbles onto the wet mortar and press them into the surface with a wooden float
- if you can't find matching pebbles, you may have to paint the stack to conceal the patch completely.

peel off its backing paper and then press the strip carefully down into position. Roll it down firmly using a wallpaper seam roller. It's best to seal the lower face of the chimney first, followed by the sides and finally the back, or upper part, folding the flashing onto the previously laid strip in each case.

Original metal flashing may be torn, corroded or displaced, and this may allow rainwater to trickle behind and down the wall.

Displaced flashings usually pull away at the top where they're tucked into the horizontal mortar joints in the stack. If this has happened you should rake out the mortar joints and tap the flashing back into place with a hammer. Cut small strips of lead, roll them up and use them as wedges to hold the flashing in place. Spray water into the mortar joints from a house plant sprayer to prepare them to take new mortar, and then repoint the joints using a mix of one part cement to five parts of sharp sand with a little PVA bonding agent added to improve its workability.

The best way you can repair slightly corroded or torn metal flashings is to patch them with pieces of self-adhesive flashing strip. In the case of a leaking back gutter it's best to line it completely with a self-adhesive flashing strip. To ensure good adhesion, key the area to be repaired by rubbing it with medium-grade abrasive paper.

If a flashing is badly corroded the simplest solution is to remove it completely and replace it with self-adhesive flashing strip, which you can apply around the base of the stack without the need for stepping or inserting it into the mortar joints. Leave any soakers in place as this will avoid disturbing the tiles or slates and will give a useful second line of defence.

Fitting a new lead stepped flashing around a chimney is best for the sake of traditional appearance – especially in an old house – and for long-lasting weather-proofing. It's quite a difficult job, but it's possible if you use the original flashings as patterns when you cut the new pieces of lead. Lead in sheet and strip form is available from builders' merchants; the various thicknesses are given code numbers. Number 3 lead (1.25mm thick) is used for soakers, and No 4 lead (1.80mm thick) for cover flashings, apron flashings and back gutters.

Repointing the mortar joints

If the mortar between the bricks in your chimney is missing or crumbling away it's likely that moisture will penetrate, soak into the bricks and, in winter, cause the masonry to crack. You should rake out the joints, dampen them and repoint with a 1:5 cement to sand mixture with PVA adhesive added, copying the pointing profile used originally. The technique is exactly the same as that used for pointing a brick wall (see page 163 for more details about joint profiles).

FITTING SELF-ADHESIVE FLASHING

1 So that new flashing will stick firmly, brush on a wide band of bituminous primer to the angle between the masonry and the roof.

2 Apply the primer all around the chimney. While it's drying, cut a length of flashing for the lower apron seal and peel off its backing.

5 Use a trimming knife to cut the strip at an angle at both corners then fold them onto the bricks at the sides and down onto the tiles.

6 To ensure a perfect seal, press the flashing strip firmly onto the primed areas. Eliminate gaps or air pockets by using a wallpaper seam roller.

Repairing, rendering and pebbledashing

Chimneys are sometimes cement-rendered or pebbledashed to match the house walls. Eventually the surface is likely to crack or even 'blow', when it parts from the masonry in places. You can usually identify blown areas by bulges in the surface which, when tapped with a hammer, will sound hollow and may even shatter. If the damage isn't too bad you can probably make a repair that won't be noticeable (see Ready Reference), at least from ground level.

Damaged flaunching

Minor cracks in mortar flaunching can be repaired with stiff mastic pressed into the cracks. However, when the flaunching is badly damaged it's best to replace it completely. Remove the old flaunching using a club hammer and cold chisel, taking care

that pieces don't fall from the roof on top of anyone: instead, try to collect them in a sturdy bucket and lower them on a rope to a helper at ground level. Take care not to damage or displace the chimney pots. Sometimes the diameter of the pots isn't wide enough to straddle the flues and you'll have to support them on strips of slate bedded in mortar arranged around the perimeter of the flue to restrict the size of the opening. In older houses it's possible that the pots may fall into flues when you remove the flaunchings, so, as a precaution, secure them with rope to the stack to preclude any possibility of an accident while you are at work.

When you've removed the flaunching, check that the brickwork at the top of the stack is secure, and if necessary re-lay loose bricks using a 1:5 cement:sand mortar mix. Dampen the top of the stack and then spread on the new flaunching mortar using a mix of

3 Position the flashing strip in the angle, taking care not to crease it too much or this may enable moisture to penetrate the seal.

4 Press the flashing strip carefully with your fingers into the angle over the primed band, but don't fold it around the corners at this stage.

7 Unroll the flashing and cut off lengths to fit down the sides of the chimney and the back gutter, allowing an extra 25mm (1in) for overlaps.

8 Peel off the paper backing from the flashing and press the side strips into place first, followed by the piece for the back gutter.

Ready Reference

USING A ROOF LADDER

To enable you to reach a chimney that's within the roof slope, or at its apex, you'll need a roof or 'cat' ladder. This is like a conventional ladder but with a large hook (1) at the top for securing it to the ridge of the roof, two wheels (2) for running it up the roof slope, and pressure plates (3) to spread the load over the fragile roof surface.

To fit and use a roof ladder:
● turn the ladder on its back and run it up the roof slope on its wheels
● at the apex, turn the ladder over so that the hook anchors over the ridge
● when climbing, use your hands on the rungs and take one step at a time.

one part cement to four parts sharp sand to which you've added some PVA bonding agent to improve its workability.

The mortar should be thickest around the base of the pots and should slope down to about 20mm (¾in) thick at the edges. The actual maximum thickness of flaunching mortar depends on the size of the stack: 65mm (2½in) close to the pot is about right on a small, single-pot chimney. On very large chimneys with several pots you'll have to pack out the flaunching at the centre with broken bricks to give a sufficient fall to throw rainwater clear of the stack.

Cracked or leaning chimney pots
Leaning pots should be reset in new flaunching mortar, but cracked pots can't be repaired and should be replaced. Before you start work, secure the pots with rope to the stack and then hack off the flaunching.

Pots with a square base are available to fit the flue exactly, but if they're of a diameter that's smaller than the size of the flue opening you'll have to support them on strips of slate as previously described.

Sealing the flue
If the flue is no longer used, it's a good idea to seal it to prevent rain getting in. However, it's vital that you maintain an air supply inside to keep it dry and free from condensation. A simple solution is to clip a metal ventilator cap into the chimney pot. Alternatively a clay type ventilator cap can be set into the pot, bedded in mortar.

A better solution is to remove the pots and replace at least two bricks from opposite sides of the flue with airbricks. Then seal the top of the flue with a paving slab bedded on 1:5 cement to sand mortar mix, or cover it with slates and then spread new flaunching

all over the top of the stack. When the mortar has dried, paint the entire stack with a clear silicone water repellent: this will prevent water from soaking into the stack.

Lowering the chimney stack
A chimney stack that's never likely to be used again can be cut down by several courses, especially if it seems dangerous and would need extensive repairs to make it safe.

Secure scaffolding around the stack is essential for this job and you'll have to lower the stack course by course, transferring all debris to the ground in a sturdy bucket on a rope.

When you reach one or two courses above the flashing level, re-lay the top two courses of bricks, including an airbrick at each side so they overhang the sides of the stack slightly. Not only will this improve the appearance of the stack but also, when the stack is sealed rainwater will be thrown clear.

REPAIRING FELTED ROOFS

A flat roof, although cheaper to produce than a conventional sloping or 'pitched' roof, is susceptible to the prolonged effects of the weather. But you can often make minor repairs, and even replacing the entire surface is not a job beyond the capabilities of the enthusiastic handyman.

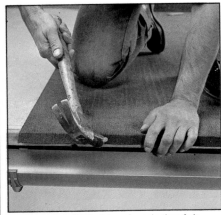

1 *Cut your first strip of underlay felt to length, position it in the centre of the roof and nail an overlap to the batten at the eaves.*

2 *Working along the strip, nail the felt to the decking at 150mm (6in) centres. Use a thin batten to smooth the felt and start the nails.*

3 *Cut your second strip of felt to length then paint a margin of adhesive just over 50mm (2in) wide along one edge of the first strip.*

M ost house roofs are sloping or 'pitched' and are clad with either slates or tiles. But a roof built in this traditional way can be costly. So, to minimise costs, an extension to your home, or a small outbuilding such as a garage or shed, will usually have a flat roof clad with roofing felt, a laminated material consisting of two or three layers of bitumen-impregnated fibres bonded with bitumen. Several layers of felt may be used, and on small buildings they are usually bonded together with cold bitumen emulsion. On larger buildings with flat roofs the layers are often bonded together with asphalt, applied hot.

You may find that your flat roof has a sheet metal covering of zinc or lead, and, although both types usually last much longer than a felt-covered roof, it is possible for you to make minor repairs to them.

A felt-covered roof can be fairly easily damaged so you're more likely to have to make repairs to this type of roof than to any of the others. Although a felt roof is perfectly adequate, it's susceptible to blistering and cracking of the covering. This can allow rain to penetrate and form damp patches on the ceiling and, if undetected, can even lead to the onset of rot in the roof timbers.

Signs of damage

Look inside first for any evidence that the roof is defective. The most obvious signs are damp patches on the ceiling or even drips of water seeping through. But the source of the leak might not be immediately above this point; water can travel quite some distance on top of the ceiling before it finds its way through and down.

Access to the roof

To discover more precisely what's wrong with your roof you'll have to inspect it from above.

You'll probably be able to reach your roof with just a ladder and it's usually perfectly safe to walk on the surface, as long as you wear soft-soled shoes. But, if you suspect that the decking or structural joists are rotten, you'd be wise to spread the load by laying scaffold boards across the roof so that you can walk safely.

Make sure your ladder is secured at the top

by tying it to a ring bolt at the soffit or wall and at the bottom to stakes driven into the ground. It's best to check your roof after particularly hot weather because intense sunlight can cause cracks and bubbles in the felt. Look, also, for pools of water on the surface after long periods of rain, as this could indicate a sagging in the structure of the roof. This sagging is another cause of cracks appearing.

How a flat roof is made

To pinpoint exactly the source of the problem it helps to understand just how a flat felt-covered roof is constructed.

Usually timber joists are set at the top of the walls, spaced at 400 to 450mm (16 to 18in) centres, to span the width of the room. To these are nailed square-edged or tongued-and-grooved softwood planks called 'decking' or, in some cases, sheet materials such as exterior grade plywood, chipboard, pre-felted chipboard or compressed straw-board; you may even find that the roof below is concrete. The very edge of the roof – the verge – might be flat or there may be a ledge, formed by a triangular fillet of wood, which stops rain from 'driving' off the edge.

Even a flat roof must slope slightly towards the front to ensure adequate drainage of rainwater, and this slope is usually provided by lengths of timber called 'firring pieces', which taper towards one end and are fixed on top of each joist.

To ensure that it's truly watertight, this type of roof should have a covering of three layers of roofing felt, the edges of each staggered so they don't coincide. The first underlay felt is usually nailed directly to the decking and the second underlay and the top layer (called the 'capsheet') are bonded in place with cold bitumen or hot asphalt.

The edges of the roof are sealed with strips of felt, called 'welted aprons', which are taken over the verge and usually project beyond the fascia board to throw rain clear.

A flashing strip seals the join between the flat roof and the house wall. It's usually a strip of felt cut specially to shape and it's top edge slots into a mortar joint in the brickwork to keep out rainwater. Internal and external corners on a roof are also felt-covered.

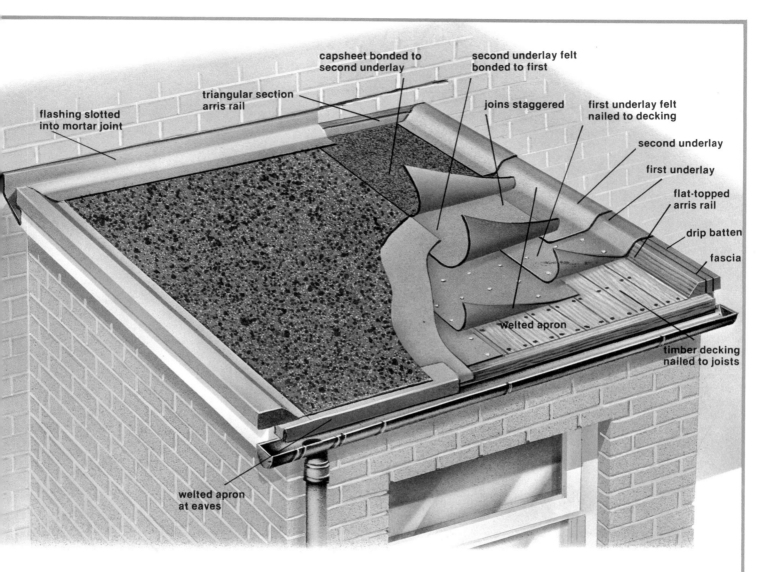

flashing slotted into mortar joint

triangular section arris rail

capsheet bonded to second underlay

second underlay felt bonded to first

joins staggered

first underlay felt nailed to decking

second underlay

first underlay

flat-topped arris rail

drip batten

fascia

welted apron

timber decking nailed to joists

welted apron at eaves

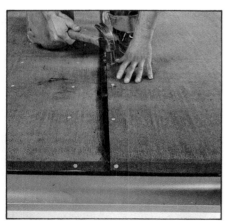

4 Place your second strip of felt on the decking so it overlaps the first by 50mm (2in). Press it onto the adhesive and nail along the overlap.

5 Coat the first underlay with adhesive then bond the second layer to it at one side of the roof. Both layers should overlap the drip battens.

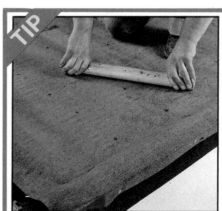

6 Press down the second underlayer using a round-section length of wood or an old rolling pin to smooth out air bubbles. Continue across the roof.

Finally, the entire roof surface is usually covered with chippings of limestone, granite, gravel or calcinated flint bedded in mastic or a special proprietary chipping compound. This surface is intended to reflect sunlight and to further strengthen the felt-covered surface.

Repairing minor faults

You can usually seal small cracks simply by spreading on a bitumen mastic, but bubbles, caused by moisture seeping underneath the felt and then swelling in the heat of the sun, require different treatment. First burst the bubble by making a cross-shaped cut in it with a sharp trimming knife, peel back the four triangular leaves you've formed and allow the moisture to dry out. Then bed the felt back in a cold bitumastic compound. Apply more compound on top of the repair, and then sprinkle a few chippings on top of it, pressing them into the mastic. You can repair small holes in the felt similarly, by sticking down a patch of felt over the hole.

If the roof covering appears sound, yet there's still evidence of dampness, it's likely that the flashing strip has come away from the wall, allowing water to trickle behind. If this has happened, prise it away completely and rake out the mortar joint into which it was slotted, using a pointing chisel. Brush away any dust and debris, dampen the joint with water so the new mortar won't dry out too rapidly and crack, then mortar the flashing strip back in place and repoint the joint.

Repairing large areas

However, if there aren't any obvious signs of localised damage, you will have to suspect extensive failure of the felt covering. You can either apply a waterproofing treatment to the existing roof, or strip off all the felt and re-cover it.

A waterproofing treatment can be given in two ways, depending upon how bad the damage is. The simpler method is to brush off as many of the loose chippings from the roof as you can, along with any other dirt and debris. But remember to bung up the tops of downpipes to make sure no debris causes a blockage. If there's any moss or lichen on the roof you should scrape it off and brush on a proprietary fungicide. Seal any cracks with mastic, then brush on a bitumastic water-proofing liquid with an old broom.

The second method of waterproofing a flat roof involves bedding a special membrane in the waterproofing liquid, applying a further coat of liquid followed by chippings.

But if the condition of the roof is poor it's advisable to remove the felt and replace it.

Estimate how much you'll need, buy it well in advance and then cut it to the required lengths with a sharp trimming knife. Leave it flat for a few days, weighted down, to uncurl, or you could find that it won't stick properly

MAKING WELTED APRONS

Welted aprons protect the eaves and verge of a flat roof from the rain, and throw water clear of the fascia.

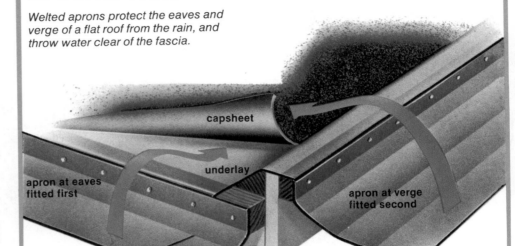

1 *Cut a strip of felt for the apron at the eaves and, with the strip hanging down, nail its top edge to the batten at 50mm (2in) centres.*

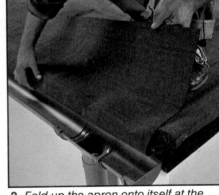

2 *Fold up the apron onto itself at the drip batten, forming a felted ledge just over 50mm (2in) deep. Take it onto the roof and bond it down.*

3 *Paint mastic over the surface of the completed second underlay, plus the top of the apron. Then you can bond the capsheet on top.*

4 *Cut an apron to fit along the verge (join two strips if necessary), nail it to the drip batten then bond it onto the capsheet with felt adhesive.*

FINISHING OFF THE ROOF

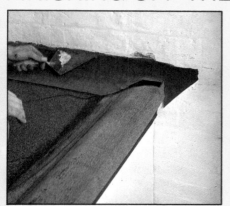

1 *Cut a strip of felt to shape and size for the flashing where the roof adjoins the house wall. Mortar its top edge into a chased-out brick joint.*

2 *Coat the surface of the roof with bitumen adhesive then scatter on handfuls of chippings. You can use your trowel to spread out the gravel.*

and bubbles in the surface might result. When you're cutting the felt to length, ensure that you lay it out parallel to the drainage fall.

Removing the old felt

Start to strip off the old, bonded layers of felt using a tough wallpaper scraper or even a garden spade with a sharp blade. When you reach the last layer you'll need a claw hammer to remove the roofing nails that secure it.

When you've completely stripped the roof of felt, give the decking a thorough sweeping and then inspect the boards for defects. You should replace any boards that are rotten and treat the new wood with preservative; don't use creosote, which is incompatible with bitumen materials used for refelting. Replace any loose or missing nails using 50mm (2in) wire nails, two per board to each joist. Punch all nail heads below the surface to prevent the new felt from snagging on them.

If your decking is plywood or chipboard you can treat it in exactly the same way as the softwood planks. If it's strawboard, the joins between sheets will be sealed with 100mm (4in) wide strips of a special tape; should you damage the tape when you remove the felt you must renew it. After cleaning the strawboard, treat the surface with a special primer, then fix the new felt using 45mm (1¾in) 5-gauge aluminium serrated nails, or bond it to the board with mastic.

Laying new felt

If you've a conventional planked or sheet timber roof, nail the first underlayer of felt to the decking, parallel to the drainage fall, using 20mm (¾in) extra-large-head galvanised clout nails. Start nailing in the centre of the sheet and work outwards, nailing at 150mm (6in) centres. Smooth out the felt as

you go. Overlap the second and subsequent sheets by about 50mm (2in), seal with bitumen mastic and nail along the overlap at 50mm (2in) centres.

The second underlay must be bonded to the first with a bitumen mastic or special proprietary adhesive. You'll find it easier to tackle half a length of felt at a time; lay the strip flat on the roof, roll half of it back and then paint the mastic onto the surface of the first, nailed underlay. Unroll the second underlay onto the mastic and press it into place, making sure there aren't any air pockets trapped underneath. You can tread the strip down if you're careful. Roll back the other half, apply the mastic, then smooth this half into place. Once again, overlap the lengths by about 50mm (2in) and remember to stagger the joints between layers (see *Ready Reference*).

You can fix the top layer of felt, the cap-sheet, in the same way. Cover the edges of the roof with strips of felt called 'welted aprons'.

At the eaves the apron must project so that rainwater will run well clear of the fascia board. The way to do this is to nail a 50x25mm (2x1in) softwood batten to the fascia and take the welted apron onto this.

If you're cutting the aprons from the standard 1m (39in) wide roll of felt you should do so along their length, not across their width, or you'll find it difficult to fold the material. However, it's possible to buy some felt in 250mm (10in) wide rolls.

Finish off the roof by applying a coat of mastic or chipping compound to the entire roof, working in easily manageable sections towards your ladder. Then scatter on hand-fuls of 12mm (½in) chippings. You'll need about 100kg (220lb) of chippings for every 5sq m (6sq yd) of roof.

REPAIRING SLATE ROOFS

Slate provides an excellent weatherproof barrier lasting 50 years or more. Replacing a single slate or repairing a damaged area are straightforward jobs that can be done at a fraction of the cost of a new roof.

Not so long ago, slate used to be one of the main materials used for roofing. As it was commonly available it was relatively cheap, yet it provided a durable barrier against the elements – a well-laid slate roof would last a lifetime. Nowadays, with increasing costs, slate has become expensive and it has largely been superseded by manufactured tiles on new buildings. But there are many roofs still with a slate covering and the more they age the more they are likely to need repairing.

So a little investigation now and again is a worthwhile exercise to see that no damage has occurred. As with a tiled roof (see pages 212-216) it's far better to put any problems right as soon as you find them, as a roof that perpetually leaks can lead to all sorts of other problems.

Checking the roof
Although slate is hardwearing, it does deteriorate with age. From the ground it may look in a good state of repair, but close up there are a number of tell-tale signs to indicate that all is not well. So although you can check for broken, slipped or missing slates from the street, it's far better to get up a ladder and have a closer inspection. If a slate has a flaky or powdery surface, then it isn't doing its job effectively, likewise with hairline cracks and split edges. And if some slates have slipped or fallen from the roof, check to see that the others haven't deteriorated around the nail holes. Slipped tiles could also result from corroded fixing nails – a fault known as 'nail sickness'.

Apart from inspecting the outside, it's also worth looking inside the roof space. Although there is now meant to be a layer of felt between the timber battens and the rafters, when many slate roofs were laid this wasn't the case. So if you can see light coming through, or if you detect rot in the woodwork, you'll know some work on the roof is necessary. Bear in mind that once water penetrates a roof it has a nasty habit of working its way along battens and joists to cause damage in an area you may have thought was problem-free. So make absolutely sure you know where the leak is before

you trace the place on the outside and get up on the roof to carry out the repair.

How slates are fixed
Before launching into the job, you should check to see how the slates are fixed to the roof. The usual way is for them to be nailed at either side to the battens which run at right angles to the rafters. The position of the fixing holes can vary up or down the slate and ideally they should be centre-nailed (see *Ready Reference*) as opposed to head-nailed because there is then less chance of the slate being lifted by the wind. Head-nailing tends to be used for small slates. But whatever method you find, you'll have to copy it when replacing an area of slates.

Replacing a single slate
If you're lucky you may only have to replace a single slate, and this shouldn't be too difficult or expensive to get hold of. While it's important to get a replacement of the same thickness (otherwise the new slate will not bed in correctly with the surrounding ones) you can always cut a larger one down to size (see page 8). Also try to get one of a similar colour to the rest of the roof so the repair isn't conspicuous.

There are now two ways of putting in the new slate: the traditional method which uses a bent metal strip called a 'tingle'; and a proprietary method which uses a specially manufactured fixing bracket.

But regardless of the method you intend using you first have to remove the damaged

slate. And to do this you'll need a specialist tool called a slate ripper (see step-by-step photographs). As it's fairly expensive to buy it's probably best to hire one, because it's not something you'll need very often.

The slate ripper is a flat tool with cutting barbs at the end. To use it you slide it under the centre of the damaged slate and then move it to one side and pull it down so that the barb engages one of the fixing nails. You then have to give the handle a sharp tug or hammer blow to cut through the nail or pull-it out. Repeat the process for the other nail and the slate should then be free to slide out.

What will now be obvious is that the course of slates above the one you've removed masks the fixing batten, so you can't just nail the new slate in place. The traditional fixing method gets round this problem using a tingle – a strip of lead, zinc or aluminium about 200mm (8in) long by 25mm (1in) wide. You have to fix one end of this strip to the batten just visible between the slates of the row below the displaced slate. You can use an aluminium alloy or galvanised clout nail to do this. Then push the replacement slate into position so that it is level with the other slates in the row. You can even use the ripper to guide it into place. Finally, bend the tingle over the lower edge to secure the slate. In fact what you're doing is hooking it in place. A tip worth noting is to double over the end of the clip so that it is less likely to be bent flat by melting snow. Some people prefer to use stronger copper wire for the tingle because it is less conspicuous than the strip material.

REPLACING A SINGLE SLATE

1 Slide the slate ripper under the middle of the damaged slate. Work it to one side, then draw it down so that the barb hooks round the nail.

2 Jerk the ripper down the roof to break the nail fixing. If it won't move, tap the handle sharply with a hammer.

3 Repeat the operation for the other fixing nail, then slide the slate out from under the course above. You can do this by hand or use the ripper.

4 Next fit the lead strip in place. Use a galvanised nail, driven into the batten and positioned between the slates of the course below.

5 If necessary cut the new slate to size, using the old slate as a guide. Then work it into position under the course above.

6 When the slate has been correctly aligned, fold the strip round the bottom edge to prevent the slate from slipping down the roof.

Ready Reference

TEMPORARY REPAIRS
Cracked slates can be repaired temporarily by sticking strips of self-adhesive flashing tape over the surface. Alternatively, use thick roofing repair mastic trowelled over the crack, covered with a strip of aluminium cooking foil or thin roofing felt and then finished with another layer of mastic.

BUYING REPLACEMENT SLATES
You can buy replacement slates from:
- specialist roofing suppliers
- builders' merchants
- demolition sites.

Slates vary in colour depending on where the rock was quarried. Make sure the new ones match the existing roof.

SLATE SIZES
Slates vary in size from 225x150mm (9x6in) to 610x355mm (24x14in). If you can't get the correct size get the next size up and cut it down to size. But only buy tiles the same thickness as the existing ones, or the difference will show up.

TIP: CHECK SLATES
Slates are graded, eg, bests, seconds and thirds. The grading varies from quarry to quarry and refers to the thickness of the slates and not the quality. So regardless of the grade, check for:
- a flaking or powdery surface
- cracks
- poor edges
- broken nail holes.

Don't buy the slates if you notice any of these faults.

FIXING SLATES
Slates are fixed to the roofing battens with two nails made of copper, aluminium alloy or zinc. For most domestic roofing work these need to be 32mm (1¼in) long. Most nail holes are half way down the slate (A); this is centre-nailing. The short slates at the apex and eaves have nail holes at the top; this is head-nailing (B).

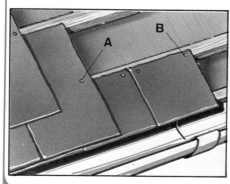

ROOF CONSTRUCTION

Knowing how a slate roof is constructed will alert you to the possible areas where faults can occur, so you'll know what to look for when you make periodic checks.

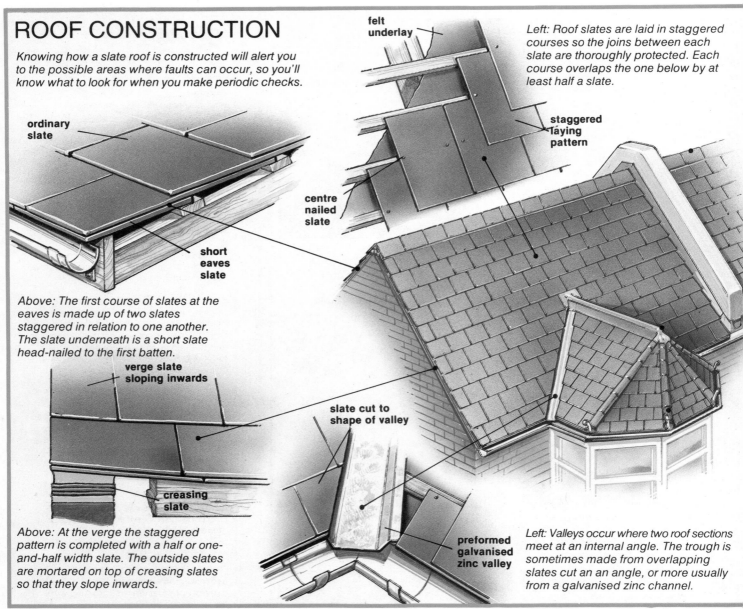

Left: Roof slates are laid in staggered courses so the joins between each slate are thoroughly protected. Each course overlaps the one below by at least half a slate.

ordinary slate

felt underlay

staggered laying pattern

centre nailed slate

short eaves slate

Above: The first course of slates at the eaves is made up of two slates staggered in relation to one another. The slate underneath is a short slate head-nailed to the first batten.

verge slate sloping inwards

slate cut to shape of valley

creasing slate

preformed galvanised zinc valley

Above: At the verge the staggered pattern is completed with a half or one-and-half width slate. The outside slates are mortared on top of creasing slates so that they slope inwards.

Left: Valleys occur where two roof sections meet at an internal angle. The trough is sometimes made from overlapping slates cut an an angle, or more usually from a galvanised zinc channel.

This is where the hidden clip method can come in useful, because it too makes a repair that can't be seen, and it also has several other advantages over the tingle. However, it can only be used on slate roofs attached to battens and not where slates are fixed direct to a boarded roof – one where planks have been nailed over the rafters, and where battens are not used. You have to drill holes in the sides of the slate and fit special clips that will coincide with the top of the batten. You then slide the slate into place and toggles drop down from the clips behind the batten to hold the slate permanently in position. Unlike the tingle, the clips are completely protected from adverse weather and can't be bent straight by the weight of snowfalls and even wind.

Cutting slates

Whether you are replacing only one slate or a larger area, the chances are you may have to cut the replacement slates to size. This could well be the case if you are buying secondhand slates from a demolition site. Cutting isn't as difficult as it may appear. Once you've marked out the size and shape of the slate required, you may find the easiest method is to score deeply over the lines with a tile cutter tool. Then support the slate on a flat timber board and gently tap a wide bolster chisel along the lines until the slate is cut. Alternatively, you can hold the slate over the edge of the timber and chop along the line with a builder's trowel. Once you get to the centre, some people find they can get a neater finish by turning the slate

round and working from the other edge in wards. The effect of this cutting is to create a bevelled edge on the face down side and i is this side which should be laid facing up wards on the roof as the bevels aid drainage

While you should carry out cutting work or the ground, a professional roofer will cut his slates on a chopping iron that he drives into one of the rafters. This means he can work or site on the roof and it allows him to tes the fit of the cut slates that much more easily and quickly.

Recently a new cutting device has beer developed, simply called a slate cutter. It resembles a large pair of scissors with a parro bill. Once you've marked out the cut you jus snip along the line – it results in a good clean edge.

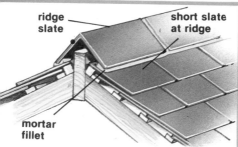

Above: The apex of the roof is often protected by special angled or half-round ridge slates set on mortar fillets.

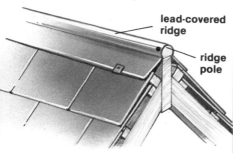

Above: Alternatively, the ridges of some roofs are covered by a lead strip wrapped over a ridge pole.

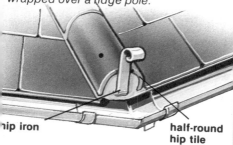

Above: At an outside angle the resulting ridge is protected by half-round or angle hip tiles. A hip iron is fitted at the eaves.

Making holes in slates

If a large area of slates is being repaired it may be necessary to make fixing holes so the lower courses of slates can be nailed into place. You can use an old slate as a template for the exact position of the holes and then drill the slates with a masonry bit. Alternatively, turn the slate face down and hammer a hole through it with a large nail. This has the advantage of splintering the face of the slate so creating a countersunk hole. The head of the fixing nail can then lie flush with the surface of the slate. A professional roofer uses a variation of this method. Instead of a nail he uses the pointed end of a slater's hammer to knock out the hole. Again he does this on site on the chopping iron.

It's a good idea to drill the holes in the slate before you cut it down to size. That way you avoid the risk of shattering it when you drill the holes close to the edge. But wherever possible you should always drill holes at least 25mm (1in) away from any edge.

Re-slating a large area

If a number of slates are damaged, it may be better to remove completely an area of slates and re-lay that section of roof. You may even be able to reuse some of them. Before you start work, decide how many new slates you are likely to need and add on a few to guard against accidental breakages. When you've acquired them you can cut them to the sizes and shapes required, and drill the fixing holes – check whether the existing slates are centre- or head-nailed. If you are working up to a gable end the last slate on alternate courses will have to be one-and-a-half slate widths across to compensate for the staggered laying pattern, so remember to allow for this. However, you could use a half slate to complete the course. The slates here should also rest on a verge or creasing slate so they tilt inwards to prevent water draining off the roof onto the side wall; instead, the water is channelled to the guttering.

When you've got everything prepared on the ground you can start to remove the old slates. Again you can use the ripping tool to free them. Don't throw them to the ground but lower a few at a time gently in a bucket. You can bring the new slates up in the reverse manner.

Start the repair work by laying the bottom course. The slates should be butted together with the bevelled edge side facing up. And they will overlap the course below by about a half, or even as much as two-thirds. You can use 30mm (1¼in) copper, zinc or aluminium alloy nails to keep them in place. Then lay the next course, staggering the joins by half a slate. For the final course, where it isn't possible to nail the slates you'll have to use tingles or special fixing brackets as described earlier.

Ridge and hip slates

Because of the shape of ridge and hip 'slates' it's not possible to make them from slate itself. Usually they are made of clay, but given a finish to blend in with a slate roof. Occasionally, they can become loose and so need to be reseated or replaced – a job virtually identical to that for a tile roof. You may have to use a hammer and bolster chisel to prise the 'slate' off and then clean up the concrete fillets on either side of the ridge. You then have to re-bed the 'slate' on new fillets of mortar. For this you need a mix of one part cement to four parts clean sharp sand, and again a PVA bonding agent improves bonding and workability.

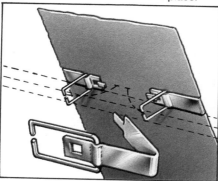
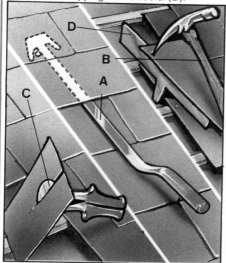

REPAIRING A DAMAGED AREA

1 Remove the area of slates using the same method as for a single slate. Check the battens for rot, and repair or replace any damaged sections.

2 You'll need a short slate at the eaves. Scribing its shape can be done over a batten on the roof or, if you prefer, at ground level.

3 Cut the slates to size using a slate cutter or a club hammer and bolster chisel. Then drill the fixing holes.

4 Alternatively make the holes with a slater's hammer and chopping iron. Tap lots of times, then tap at the back of the hole to knock through.

5 Note that the eaves slates are head-nailed. When they are fixed in position they are completely covered by the course of full slates above.

6 Continue laying the slates, course by course, up the roof. You'll have to lay a slightly wider slate to compensate for any 'out of line' slates.

7 At the verges fix two lead strips in place, one in the normal way and the other at right angles to it. Fold the strips round the slate to secure it.

8 Continue to build up the courses, working towards the top of the area. Remember to lay the slates with the bevel side up to aid drainage.

9 You can't nail the last course into place unless the slate is at the ridge of the roof. So use the same technique as for fitting a single slate.

SECTION 7

ELECTRICAL

TECHNIQUES

Understanding ELECTRICS

In theory, you could do electrical jobs knowing nothing about electricity, given accurate step-by-step instructions. But you can't deal with any part of an electrical installation in isolation — everything is linked. And unless you understand how each part of the system works you have no way of knowing if you are making a mistake. With electricity, ignorance is dangerous.

We're all familiar with lights and power sockets, but how does the electricity reach them so we can use it? In fact, electricity enters your home along one thick cable (the service cable), passes through a large 'service fuse' and into a meter which records the amount you use. Everything up to and including that meter belongs to the electricity board, and is their responsibility. Everything beyond is the householder's property, which is perhaps why installations vary so much.

In a modern installation — one wired in the last 30 years — there are two wires carrying electric current that lead from the meter to what is called the consumer unit. These wires are known as the meter tails — one is termed live, the other neutral.

On the inlet side of the consumer unit there's a switch with which you can turn off the power altogether, but the unit's principal job is to divide up the power and send it round your home through a network of cables.

These cables are organized into circuits. There are circuits for lights, power sockets and so on, each with its own fuse in the consumer unit. The cables themselves run under the floor, above the ceiling and may even be visible on wall surfaces, although more often they are buried within them.

In older installations, instead of a consumer unit there may be individual fuse boxes protecting separate circuits. And each of these fuse boxes will have an isolating switch to cut off power to the circuit it controls. These fuse boxes are connected direct to the meter by

live and neutral meter tails. Alternatively the fuse boxes may be supplied from a distribution board which in turn is connected to the meter.

Sometimes, even with a consumer unit you may find separate fuse boxes. This is normally the result of the system having been extended.

What are circuits?

If you take a battery, and connect a wire to the positive (+) terminal, and another to the negative (−), then bring the free ends of the wires together, electricity will flow from positive to negative along them. That's a circuit. You can build a torch bulb and holder into it to prove it works. Break the circuit by cutting one wire, and the light goes out (the flow of current has stopped), and it will stay out until the cut ends are rejoined. That's a simple switch.

Of course, the circuits in your home are a good deal more complex than that, and their design varies according to whether they supply lights, power sockets or whatever. Even the electricity is different. Instead of flowing in one direction, it goes back and forth 50 times a second — hence its name *alternating current*, or AC for short.

But the principle is the same., Think of 'live' as positive, 'neutral' as negative, and you will see that for any appliance such as an electric fire to work it must have wires connecting it to the live and neutral terminals in the consumer unit. Those wires may be contained in a single cable, but the link must always be there, with switches *en route* to make or break it, and for safety reasons, switches are on the live wire.

What are fuses?

The main service cable has its fuse; the various circuits have theirs in the consumer unit or fuse box and if you remove the back of a flat-pin plug you'll find a fuse in there.

Think of an electric light bulb. It gives out light because electricity passing through the filament (the fine wire just visible inside the bulb) makes it very hot. If you pass enough electricity through any wire, it will also heat up. If that wire happens to be a circuit cable, an appliance flex, or the service cable to the meter, then the consequences would. be serious. So, to protect them, a weak link called a fuse is built into the circuit.

Most fuses are just thin pieces of wire. They can be fitted to rewirable fuse carriers, in which case you can replace them, or they may be in ceramic cartridges, in which case you throw them away and fit another. In any event, the fuse's thickness is described in terms of how much electricity — expressed in amps — is theoretically needed to melt it.

The word 'theoretically' is important because, in fact, fuses aren't particularly accurate or reliable. For this reason, a more sensitive device called a miniature circuit breaker (MCB) may be used instead. It's just a switch that turns off automatically when danger threatens. Once the fault responsible for the overload is put right, you switch on again.

Why cables?

It would be far too complicated to wire a house like a battery and bulb circuit using individual wires. Instead, the copper wires carrying the electricity are encased in PVC insulation to stop them touching and making their circuit in the wrong place — what's called a short circuit — and then bound together in PVC sheathing to form a cable. In this way, the live, neutral and earth wires can be run as one, even though each one is still connected up separately.

Different kinds of cable are used for different jobs. Follow the instructions in this section carefully to select the right one for each job.

Earthing

The purpose of the earth wire within the cable is to make up the earth continuity conductor (ECC). This is an essential safety feature of any electrical installation. Its role is to act as a 'safety valve' in the event of a fault, causing a fuse to blow or an MCB to trip to isolate a faulty circuit or faulty appliance from the mains supply. In doing so it could prevent the risk of fire or someone being electrocuted.

Earth wires are connected to the metal parts of switches, socket outlets, fittings and appliances (and even plumbing) in a really up-to-date system. Electricity will flow along the line of least resistance, so that if by some mishap any of these parts became live (by coming into contact with a live conductor) the earth wire would offer a line of 'less' resistance. In effect the faulty current would travel along the earth wire rather than through a person touching the live metal part. And the extra current passing through one circuit would

be sufficient to blow the fuse or activate the MCB.

Unfortunately this doesn't always happen – so, for added safety, a special device called a residual current device (RCD for short) can be fitted to detect the slightest leakage of current to earth. It shuts off the power within milliseconds – quickly enough to save a life – at the first sign of a fault.

RCD's can be added to an existing system, or included within the consumer unit in a new installation. They usually protect all the circuits in the house and also act as a mains on/off switch.

Ring circuits

For getting electricity to the power points, the most common system of wiring is what's called a 'ring' circuit. Wired in 2.5mm² two-core and earth cable, most homes have one such circuit for each floor of the house.

The two-cores and the earth wire are connected to their terminals in the consumer unit (or fuse box) and then pass through each power socket in turn before returning to their respective terminals in the consumer unit (fuse box). The circuit is protected by a 30A

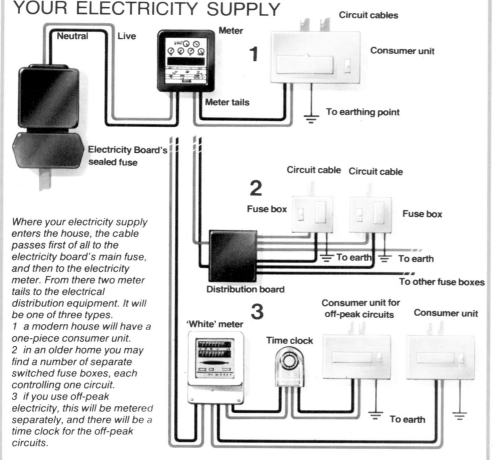

YOUR ELECTRICITY SUPPLY

Neutral   Live   Meter   Circuit cables

1   Consumer unit

Meter tails

To earthing point

Electricity Board's sealed fuse

Where your electricity supply enters the house, the cable passes first of all to the electricity board's main fuse, and then to the electricity meter. From there two meter tails to the electrical distribution equipment. It will be one of three types.
1 a modern house will have a one-piece consumer unit.
2 in an older home you may find a number of separate switched fuse boxes, each controlling one circuit.
3 if you use off-peak electricity, this will be metered separately, and there will be a time clock for the off-peak circuits.

Circuit cable   Circuit cable

2

Fuse box   Fuse box

To earth   To earth

To other fuse boxes

Distribution board

3   Consumer unit for off-peak circuits   Consumer unit

'White' meter   Time clock

To earth

Trevor Lawrence

fuse. The advantage of this system is it allows the cable to cope with more sockets than if it made a one-way trip (as with radial circuits). In fact, you are allowed as many sockets as you like on the ring, so long as the floor area served by the circuit doesn't exceed 100 sq metres (1,080 sq ft). What's more, you can increase the number of sockets by adding 'branch lines' off the ring. These are called 'spurs' and break into the ring via a junction box, a spur connection unit, or an existing socket. You are allo-

wed as many spurs as can feed one single socket, one double socket, or one fixed appliance via a fused connection unit. Until a recent change in the IEE wiring regulations, a spur could feed two single sockets, and you may find such spurs on your existing circuits.

Of course, with all those sockets, there is a risk of overloading the circuit, but in the average family home it's unlikely that you'll have enough sockets in use at any one time. The circuit may carry up to 30 amps of current

which is equivalent to having appliances and portable lamps using 7,200 watts of power all switched on together. It's doubtful that you would want all this on at the same time, but it's wise not to go above this level of power use. If the circuit does overload, the fuse will blow. or the MCB will switch off.

Radial circuits
Unlike ring circuits, radial circuits consist of a single cable that leaves the fuse box and runs to one or more sockets. In older homes in the UK, before ring circuits were introduced, all power circuits were wired as radials. Since homes had (and needed) only a few sockets, individual circuits were usually run to each one from the fuse box. The sockets themselves were rated at 2A, 5A or 15A, and had round holes to accept round-pin plugs. Such circuits will probably have been wired in rubber- or lead-sheathed cables, which deteriorate with age (see pages 20 – 21), and are not able to satisfy the far greater electrical demands of a modern household. It's wise to have such circuits examined by a qualified electrician, and best of all to have them replaced.

Radial circuits are, however, also used in modern wiring systems where a ring circuit could be inappropriate for some reason. There are two types, with different current-carrying capacity.

A 20A radial circuit uses 2.5mm² cable and

A ring circuit originates from a 30A fuseway in the consumer unit. Protection may be by an MCB rather than a rewirable or cartridge fuse.

Spurs are sometimes added when the ring circuit is installed to save on the wiring runs. They are usually connected at a three-terminal junction box.

Socket outlets on a ring circuit take the fused 13A flat-pin plug. They can be one- or two-gang (ie, take one or two plugs); the best have switches.

THE RING CIRCUIT

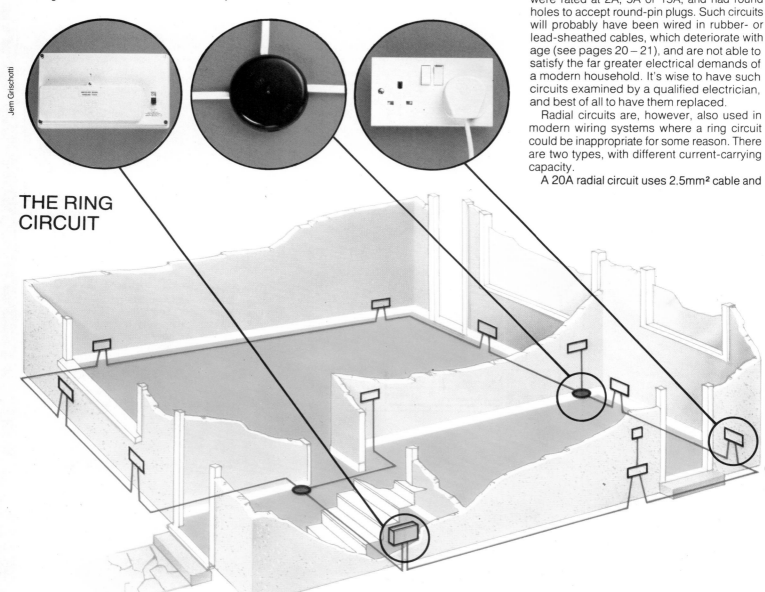

Jem Grischotti

is protected by a 20A fuse (rewirable or cartridge) or an MCB in the consumer unit (or fuse box). It can supply an unlimited number of 13A socket outlets and fixed appliances using 3kW of power or less, providing they are within a floor area not exceeding 20 sq metres (about 215 sq ft).

The other type of circuit is the 30A radial which is wired in 4mm² cable and can feed a floor area of up to 50 sq metres (540 sq ft). It can be protected by a 30A cartridge fuse or MCB, but *not* by a rewirable fuse.

These restrictions on floor area mean that several radial circuits would have to be installed to cover the same area as a ring circuit. This is one of the reasons why the 'ring' is now the most common method of wiring in the UK, but radial circuits can supplement an overworked ring circuit.

Special purpose circuits

In addition to rings and radials, your home may have special circuits which supply only one outlet or appliance. Cookers, immersion heaters, instantaneous showers and the like are wired in this way and each has its own individual fuse. In effect, these circuits are just radials that have had both the cable and fuse sizes 'beefed up' to cope with the often heavy demands of the appliances they supply — for example, a large family-size cooker might need a 45A fuse, and 6mm² or even 10mm² cable.

Because electric night storage heaters all come on together they could overload a ring circuit; consequently each one is supplied by

The various radial power circuits originate from fuseways in a consumer unit or from individual fuse boxes. They are protected by rewirable fuses.

Modern radial circuits have sockets that take 13A flat-pin plugs. Older radials with lead or rubber-sheathed cable take round pin plugs.

Even if you have ring circuit wiring, radial circuits are used for special purposes, such as supplying a cooker. It may also contain a 13A socket outlet.

A fused connection unit sometimes supplies a fixed appliance on a radial circuit. This could be a wall mounted heater or an immersion heater.

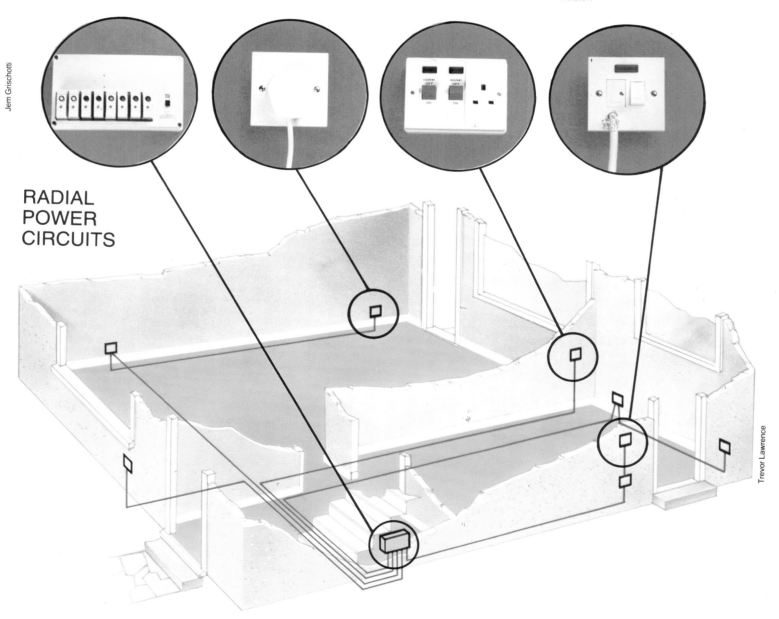

RADIAL POWER CIRCUITS

LIGHTING CIRCUITS

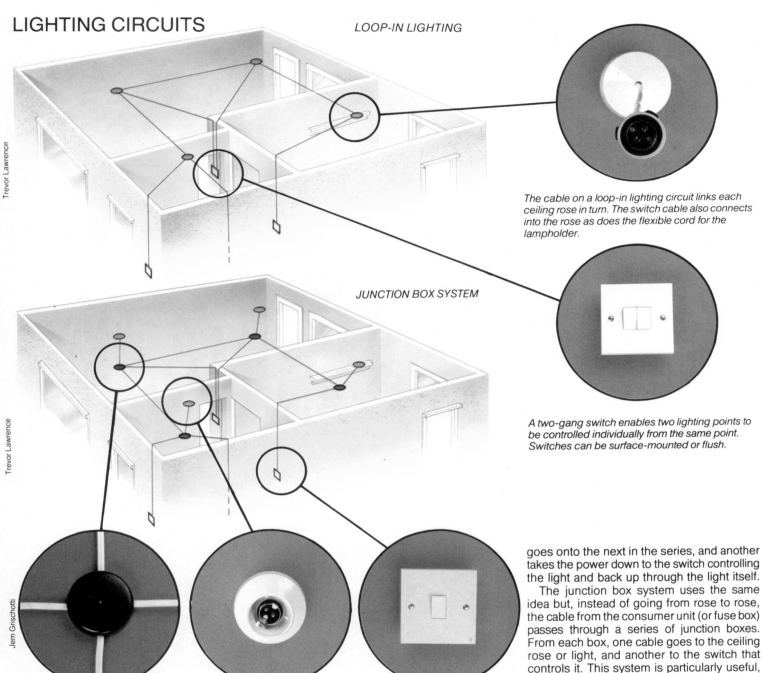

LOOP-IN LIGHTING

The cable on a loop-in lighting circuit links each ceiling rose in turn. The switch cable also connects into the rose as does the flexible cord for the lampholder.

JUNCTION BOX SYSTEM

A two-gang switch enables two lighting points to be controlled individually from the same point. Switches can be surface-mounted or flush.

Trevor Lawrence

Trevor Lawrence

Jem Grischotti

With junction box wiring the main cable runs between four-terminal junction boxes. The other cables go to the lighting point and the switch.

Batten holders are used to fit a light close to the ceiling. In bathrooms, they must have a 'skirt' to prevent contact with metal on the fitting or bulb.

The simplest switch is a one-gang type mounted on a face-plate. They can be either surface mounted or recessed to be flush with the wall.

a separate radial circuit protected by a 20A fuse. The fuses are housed in a separate consumer unit which is linked to a sealed time clock and uses off-peak electricity.

Lighting circuits

Two systems of wiring lighting circuits are in common use, and it is not unusual for an installation to contain a little bit of each. One is called the loop-in system; the other the junction (or joint) box system.

With the loop-in system, a cable (normally 1.0mm² but sometimes 1.5mm²) leaves a 5A fuse in the consumer unit (or fuse box) and is connected to the first in a series of special loop-in ceiling roses. From this rose, one cable goes onto the next in the series, and another takes the power down to the switch controlling the light and back up through the light itself.

The junction box system uses the same idea but, instead of going from rose to rose, the cable from the consumer unit (or fuse box) passes through a series of junction boxes. From each box, one cable goes to the ceiling rose or light, and another to the switch that controls it. This system is particularly useful, for example, when fitting wall lights as there is little space at the back of a wall light fitting for looping-in.

Lighting circuits are rated at 5 amps, which means they can take a load of up to 1,200 watts. In effect, they could supply 12 lampholders containing bulbs of 100w each or smaller. But as you may want to fit bulbs with higher wattages, it is usual for a lighting circuit to supply up to eight outlet points, so separate circuits are required for each floor.

Strictly speaking it's better to arrange the circuits so that there is more than one on each floor — this means that you won't be in total darkness if a fuse in the consumer unit blows.

TRACING ELECTRICAL FAULTS

When the lights go out or an electrical appliance won't work, the reason is often obvious. But when it isn't, it helps to know how to locate the fault and put it right.

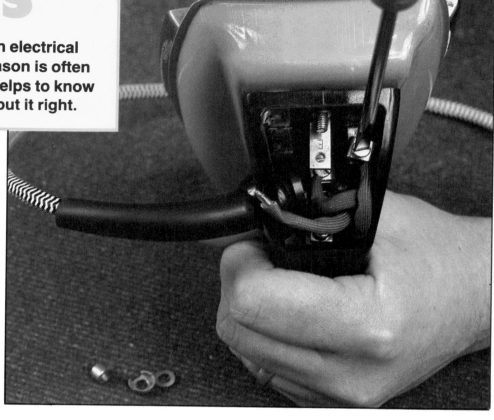

Most people's immediate reaction to something going wrong with their electricity supply is to head for the meter cupboard, muttering darkly about another blown fuse. Fuses do blow occasionally for no immediately obvious reason, but usually there is a problem that needs to be pin-pointed and put right before the power can be restored. It's no use mending a blown fuse, only to find that when the power is restored the fuse blows again because the fault is still present.

Tracing everyday electrical faults is not particularly difficult. You simply have to be methodical in checking the various possible causes, and eliminating options until you find the culprit. More serious faults on the house's fixed wiring system can be more difficult to track down, but again some careful investigation can often locate the source of the trouble, even if professional help has to be called in to put it right.

Safety first

Before you start investigating any electrical faults, remember the cardinal rule and switch off the power at the main switch. When fuses blow, it is all too easy to forget that other parts of the system may still be live and therefore dangerous, and even if you know precisely how your house has been wired up it is foolish to take risks. If the fault appears to be on an electrical appliance, the same rules apply: always switch off the appliance *and* pull out the plug before attempting to investigate. Don't rely on the switch to isolate it; the fault may be in the switch itself.

It's also important to be prepared for things to go wrong with your electrics; even new systems can develop faults, and in fact a modern installation using circuit breakers will detect faults more readily than one with rewireable or cartridge fuses, so giving more regular cause for investigation. Make sure that you keep a small emergency electrical tool kit in an accessible place where it won't get raided for other jobs. It should include two or three screwdrivers, a pair of electricians' pliers, a handyman's knife, spare fuses and fuse wire, PVC insulating tape and a couple of spare light bulbs. Don't forget also a *working* torch.

Check the obvious

When something electrical fails to operate, always check the obvious first – replace the bulb when a light doesn't work, or glance outside to see if everyone in the street has been blacked out by a power cut before panicking that all your fuses have blown. Having satisfied yourself that you may have a genuine fault, start a methodical check of all the possibilities.

A fault can occur in a number of places. It may be on an appliance, within the flex or plug linking it to the mains, on the main circuitry itself or at the fuseboard. Let's start at the appliance end of things. If something went bang as you switched the appliance on, unplug it immediately; the fault is probably on the appliance itself. If it simply stopped working, try plugging it in at another socket; if it goes, there's a fault on the circuit feeding the original socket. If it doesn't go, either the second socket is on the same faulty circuit as the first one (which we'll come to later) or there may be a fault in the link between the appliance and the socket – loose connections where the cores are connected to either the plug or the appliance itself, damaged flex (both these problems are caused by abuse of the flex in use), or a blown fuse in the plug if one is fitted.

Plug and flex connections

The next step is to check the flex connections within the plug and the appliance. The connections at plug terminals are particularly prone to damage if the plug's cord grip or flex anchorage is not doing its job; a tug on the flex can then break the cores, cutting the power and possibly causing a short circuit. If the connections are weak or damaged, disconnect them, cut back the sheathing and insulation and remake the connections. Make sure that the flex is correctly anchored within the body of the plug before replacing the cover.

If the plug contains a fuse, test that it has not blown by using a continuity tester, or by holding it across the open end of a switched-on metal-cased torch – see *Ready Reference*. Replace a blown fuse with a new one of the correct current rating; 3A for appliances rated at 720W or below, 13A for higher-rated appliances (and all colour televisions).

Next, check the flex connections within the appliance itself. Always unplug an appliance before opening it up to gain access to the terminal block, and then remake any doubtful-looking connections by cutting off the end of the flex and stripping back the outer and inner insulation carefully to expose fresh conductor strands. If the flex itself is worn or

Ready Reference

COMMON FAULTS

Many electrical breakdowns in the home are caused by only a few common faults. These include:

- overloading of circuits, causing the circuit fuse to blow or the MCB to trip
- short circuits, where the current by-passes its proper route because of failed insulation or contact between cable or flex cores; the resulting high current flow creates heat and blows the plug fuse (if fitted) and circuit fuse
- earthing faults, where insulation breaks down and allows the metal body of an appliance to become live, causing a shock to the user if the appliance is not properly earthed and blowing a fuse or causing the RCD to trip otherwise.
- poor connections causing overheating that can lead to a fire and to short circuits and earthing faults.

TIP: TESTING FUSES

You can test suspect cartridge fuses (both circuit and plug types) by holding them across the open end of a switched-on metal-cased torch, with one on the casing and the other on the battery. A sound fuse will light the torch.

CHOOSE THE RIGHT FLEX

When fitting new flex to an appliance, it's important to choose the correct type and current rating. The table below will help:

Size (mm²)	Rating amps	watts	Use
0.5	3	720	Light fittings
0.75	6	1440	Small appliances
1.0	10	2400	Larger appliances
1.5	15	3600	
2.5	20	4800	

If you are buying flex for pendant lights, remember that the maximum weight of fitting that each size of twin flex can support is
- 2kg (4½lb) for 0.5mm² flex
- 3kg (6½lb) for 0.75mm² flex
- 5kg (11lb) for larger sizes.

Select circular **three-core PVC-insulated flex** for most appliances, **unkinkable** or **braided flex** for irons, kettles and the like, **two-core flex** for non-metallic lamps and light fittings and for double-insulated appliances, and **heat-resisting flex** for powerful pendant lights and for heater connections.

REWIRING A PLUG

1 Strip the outer sheathing carefully, cut each core 12mm (½in) longer than is necessary to reach its correct terminal and then remove 12mm of core sheathing.

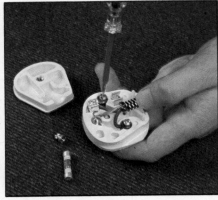

2 Twist the strands of each core neatly and form a loop that will fit round the terminal screw. Connect the cores as shown here and screw down the studs.

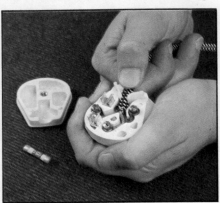

3 Check that the core insulation reaches right to each terminal, and that there are no loose strands visible. Then fit the flex securely in the cord grip.

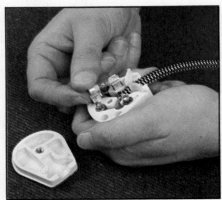

4 Lastly, in a fused plug press in a cartridge fuse of the correct rating for the appliance concerned, and screw the plug top firmly on.

damaged, take this opportunity to fit new flex of the correct type and current rating – see the *Ready Reference* panel (left) and the step-by-step photographs for more details. Make sure you re-use any grommets, heat-resistant sleeving, special captive washers and the like that were fitted to the appliance.

Lastly, check the flex continuity; it is possible that damage to the flex itself has broken one of the cores within the outer sheathing. Again use a continuity tester for this, holding the two probes against opposite ends of each core in turn, or use your metal-cased torch again, touching one core to the case and the other to the battery. Replace the flex if *any* core fails the test; the appliance may still work if the earth core is damaged, but the earthing will be lost and the appliance could become live and dangerous to anyone using it in the event of another fault developing in the future.

Lighting problems

Similar problems to these can also occur on lighting circuits, where the pendant flex linking ceiling roses to lampholders can become disconnected or faulty through accidental damage or old age. If replacing the bulb doesn't work, switch off the power at the mains and examine the condition of the flex carefully.

Look especially for bad or broken connections at the ceiling rose and within the lampholder. You must replace the flex if the core insulation has become brittle, and fit a new lampholder if the plastic is at all discoloured. Both of these problems are caused by heat from the light bulb.

Mending blown fuses

A circuit fuse will blow for two main reasons, overloading and short circuits – see *Ready Reference*. Too many appliances connected to a circuit will demand too much current, and this will melt the fuse. Similarly, a short circuit – where, for example, bare live and neutral flex cores touch – causes a current surge that blows the fuse.

If overloading caused the fuse to blow, the remedy is simple: disconnect all the equipment on the circuit, mend the fuse and avoid using too many high-wattage appliances at the same time in future. If a short circuit was to blame, you will have to hunt for the cause and rectify it before mending the fuse – see photographs on the next page.

When a circuit fuse blows, turn off the main switch and remove fuseholders until you find the one that has blown. Then clean out the remains of the old fuse wire, and fit a new piece of the correct rating for the circuit – 5A for lighting circuits, 15A for circuits to immersion heaters and the like, and 30A for ring circuits. Cut the wire over-long, thread it loosely across or through the ceramic holder and connect it carefully to the terminals. Trim the ends off neatly, replace the fuseholder in the consumer unit and turn on the power again. If the fuse blows again, and you have already checked for possible causes on appliances, flexes and lighting pendants, suspect a circuit fault – see below.

If you have cartridge fuses, all you have to do is find which cartridge has blown by removing the fuseholder and testing the cartridge with a continuity tester or metal-cased torch. A blown cartridge fuse should be replaced by a new one of the same current rating. Again, if the new fuse blows immediately, suspect a circuit fault.

If you have miniature circuit breakers (MCBs) you will not be able to switch the MCB on again if the fault that tripped it off is still present. Otherwise, simply reset it by switching it to ON or pressing in the centre button.

Residual current devices (RCDs)

If you installation has an RCD, it will trip off if an earthing fault occurs – for example, if a live wire or connection comes into contact with earthed metal. Like an MCB, it cannot be switched on again until the fault is rectified – a useful safety point. However, it will not trip off in the event of a short circuit between live and neutral, or when overloading occurs.

The modern high-sensitivity type of RCD, in addition to detecting earth faults, also protects against the danger of electric shocks by tripping off if it detects current flowing to earth through the human body. It can do this quickly enough to prevent the shock from causing death.

Tracing circuit faults

If you have checked appliances, flexes, plug connections and pendant lights, and a fault is still present, it is likely to be in the fixed

REPLACING FLEX

1 To replace damaged flex, remove the appropriate cover plate or panel from the appliance. Make a note of which core goes where before undoing it.

2 Loosen the cord grip within the appliance and withdraw the old flex. Here heat-resisting sleeving has been fitted; save this for re-use.

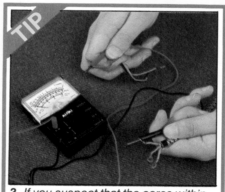

3 If you suspect that the cores within apparently undamaged flex are broken, test each core in turn with a continuity tester.

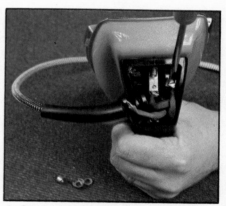

4 Connect in the new flex by reversing the disconnection sequence, re-using grommets, sleeving and washers. Make sure each connection is secure.

wiring. Here, it is possible to track down one or two faults, but you may in the end have to call in a professional electrician.

The likeliest causes of circuit faults are damage to cables (perhaps caused by drilling holes in walls or by nailing down floorboards where cables run), ageing of cables (leading to insulation breakdown, and overheating) and faults at wiring accessories (light switches, socket outlets and so on). Let's look at the last one first, simply because such items are at least easily accessible.

If the cable cores are not properly stripped and connected within the accessory, short circuits or earth faults can develop. To check a suspect accessory such as a socket outlet, isolate the circuit, unscrew the faceplate and examine the terminal connections and the insulation. Ensure that each core is firmly held in its correct terminal, and that each core has insulation right up to the terminal,

so that it cannot touch another core or any bare metal. There is usually enough slack on the mains cable to allow you to trim over-long cores back slightly. Check that the earth core is sleeved in green/yellow PVC, and try not to double over the cable as you ease the faceplate back into position; over-full boxes can lead to short circuits and damage to cable and core insulation ... and more trouble. You can carry out similar checks at light switches and ceiling roses. Any damaged accessories you find should be replaced immediately with new ones.

Damage to cables is relatively easy to cure provided that you can find where the damage is. If you drilled or nailed through a cable, you will of course be able to pin-point it immediately. Cable beneath floorboards can be repaired simply by isolating the circuit, cutting the cable completely at the point of damage and using a three-terminal junction

CHECKLIST FOR ACTION

When something goes wrong with your electrics, use this checklist to identify or eliminate the commonest potential causes of trouble.

Fault 1
Pendant light doesn't work
Action
● replace bulb
● check lighting circuit fuse/MCB
● check flex connections at lampholder and ceiling rose
● check flex continuity.

Fault 2
Electrical appliance doesn't work
Action
● try appliance at another socket
● check plug fuse (if fitted)
● check plug connections
● check connections at appliance's own terminal block
● check flex continuity
● check power circuit fuse/MCB
● isolate appliance if fuses blow again.

Fault 3
Whole circuit is dead
Action
● switch off all lights/disconnect all appliances on circuit
● replace circuit fuse or reset MCB
● switch on lights/plug in appliances one by one and note which blows fuse again
● isolate offending light/appliance, and see Faults 1 and 2 (above)
● check wiring accessories on circuit for causes of short circuits
● replace damaged cable if pierced by nail or drill
● call qualified electrician for help.

Fault 4
Whole system is dead
Action
● check for local power cut
● reset RCD if fitted to system (and see Faults 1, 2 and 3 if RCD cannot be reset)
● call electricity board (main service fuse may have blown).

Fault 5
Electric shock received
Action
● turn off the power supply *or*
● pull person clear immediately but DON'T TOUCH his/her body – grab the clothes or use a wooden stick, length of rubber or leather *(no metal; no moisture)*
● if victim is conscious, call a doctor; don't give brandy or food or wrap in blankets
● if breathing and/or heartbeat has stopped, give artificial respiration and/or heart massage, then CALL AN AMBULANCE

REPAIRING A CIRCUIT FUSE

1 *Switch off the mains and locate the blown fuse. Then remove the remains of the old fuse wire and clean off any charring that has occurred.*

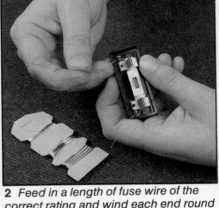

2 *Feed in a length of fuse wire of the correct rating and wind each end round the terminal before tightening up the screw. Don't pull the wire taut.*

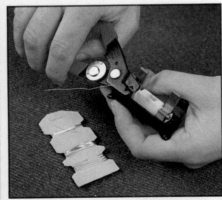

3 *Trim off the unwanted ends of fuse wire neatly with wire strippers, then replace the fuse carrier in the fuse box and restore the power.*

4 *Test a suspect cartridge fuse with a continuity tester or torch (see* Ready Reference*) and replace it by pressing in a new fuse of the correct rating.*

box to link the cut ends. Cable buried in plaster must be cut out and a new length of cable inserted between adjacent accessories to replace the damaged length. Where this would involve a long length of cable (on a run to a remote socket, for example) it is acceptable to use junction boxes in nearby floor or ceiling voids to connect in the new length of cable. You will then have to make good the cutting-out.

Tracking down a break in the cable elsewhere in the installation is a difficult job best left to a qualified electrician. If, however, you find that your house is wired in rubber-sheathed cable and faults are beginning to occur, don't waste time and effort trying to track them down. It is very likely that your house needs rewiring. This will save you time and prevent problems in the long run.

If you are unable to trace an electrical fault after checking all the points already de-scribed, call in a professional electrician who will be able to use specialist test equipment to locate the fault. Do *not* attempt to bypass a fault with a makeshift wiring arrangement, and NEVER use any conducting foreign body such as a nail to restore power to a circuit whose fuse keeps blowing. Such tricks can kill.

Regular maintenance
You will find that a little common-sense maintenance work will help to prevent a lot of minor electrical faults from occurring at all. For example, it's well worth spending a couple of hours every so often checking the condition of the flex on portable appliances (especially those heavily used, such as kettles, irons, hair driers and the like) and the connections within plugs. Also, make a point of replacing immediately any electrical accessory that is in any way damaged.

CEILING LIGHTS AND SWITCHES

Most ceiling lights are positioned centrally in a room to give general lighting. But by adding another light, or changing the position of an existing fitting, you can highlight particular areas and enhance the decoration.

Keith Morris

Putting in a new pendant ceiling light and switch, or changing the position of an existing one, usually presents few problems – even if you have little or no experience of electrical work.

A pendant is the most common ceiling light and consists of a lampholder wired to a length of flexible cord which hangs from a ceiling rose. Another type can be plugged into the ceiling rose – in this case the flexible cord has to have a special fitting which slots into a batten holder.

Know your system

Installing a new ceiling light requires making a simple connection into a nearby lighting circuit either by inserting a junction box or at an existing loop-in rose and then running a cable to a switch. In order to connect into the circuit you'll first need to know how the lights in your house are wired and which lights belong to which circuit. Then you'll be able to work out whether you can actually add another light to the circuit that is nearest to the new light's position.

There are two principal methods of wiring a lighting circuit. In the loop-in method the cable runs from ceiling rose to ceiling rose, stopping at the last one on the circuit, and the switches are wired into the roses. With the junction box system the cable runs to a number of junction boxes each serving a switch and a light. You may well find that both methods have been used in the same circuit to simplify and reduce the cable runs.

It's possible to connect into a nearby rose provided it's a loop-in type. You can check this simply by turning off the power and unscrewing the rose cover. A loop-in rose will have more than one red insulated wire going into the central terminal bank of the three in-line terminal banks. However, it can be quite fiddly to fit another cable, given that the terminal banks are very small, so you might find it easier to insert a junction box in the main circuit. And if there isn't a loop-in rose you'll have to use this method anyway.

Earthing for lighting circuits

Modern lighting circuits are protected by an earth. But if you've got a fairly old system (it's

likely to be based on junction boxes), you might find that it doesn't have one. So when you're extending such a circuit, you're now required to protect the new wiring, light fitting and switch by installing an earth. Consequently, you have to use two-core and earth cable for the extension, which will most probably connect into the existing circuit at a junction box. You then have to run a 1.5mm² earth cable from this point to the main earthing point.

Circuit additions

Usually there's a lighting circuit for each floor of a house and in a single storey dwelling there are likely to be two or more. But it's easy to identify the individual circuits simply by switching on all the lights, turning off the power and taking out a 5A fuse from the consumer unit or switching off an MCB. When you restore the power you'll know that the lights that remain off all belong to the same circuit.

Generally speaking, a lighting circuit serves six to eight fixed lighting points. In fact it can serve up to 12 lampholders provided the total wattage of the bulbs on the circuit doesn't exceed 1,200 watts. This means that unless other lights have previously been added – wall lights for example – there shouldn't be a problem of connecting in another light.

Remember, when adding up the bulb wattages, a bulb of less than 100 watts counts as 100 watts and not its face value.

The place for lights

Apart from bathrooms, where special regulations apply, you can position lights and switches in any place you like inside the house. But bear in mind they are there to fulfil a function, so switches, for example, should be conveniently located – by a door is often the most satisfactory position. Usually they are set on the wall 1.4 metres (4ft 6in) above floor level. But they can be higher or lower to suit your needs.

You mustn't install pendant lights, especially plain pendants with exposed flexible cords, in a bathroom. This is for your safety. Flexes can become frayed, and if, say, you tried to change a bulb while standing in the bath and touched an exposed conductor you could electrocute yourself. Consequently, all light fittings here must be of the close-mounted type and preferably totally enclosed to keep off condensation. If instead you use an open batten lampholder it must be fitted with a protective shield or skirt which makes it impossible for anyone changing the bulb to touch the metal clamp.

A wall-mounted switch must also be out of reach of a person using the bath or shower. In modern small bathrooms, however, this is often impossible. The alternative is to place the switch just outside the room by the door, or to fit a special ceiling switch operated by an insulating cord which doesn't have to be out of reach of the bath or the shower.

LIGHTING BASICS

● Extensions to lighting circuits are usually wired in 1.00mm² two-core and earth PVC-sheathed and insulated cable.
● You can extend from an existing rose only if it is of the loop-in variety with three banks of terminals; such roses can accommodate up to four cables. If you have older roses, extensions must be made via a junction box.

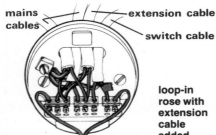

mains cables · extension cable · switch cable

loop-in rose with extension cable added

TOOLS FOR THE JOB

Electrician's pliers have cutting edges on the jaws and insulated handles.
Wire strippers can be adjusted to the diameter of the insulation to be stripped.
Handyman's knife – ideal for cutting back the sheathing of the cable.
Screwdrivers – a small one is best for the terminal fixing screws and a medium sized one for the fixing screws on the rose and switch.

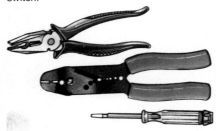

HOW TO STRIP CABLE

● Use handyman's knife to cut sheathing between neutral and earth cores.
● Use wire strippers to remove core insulation.

PREPARING THE CABLE RUN

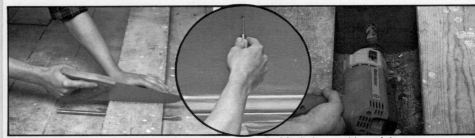

1 *Raise the floorboard above the proposed location of the new light and any others necessary for laying the power supply and switch cables.*

2 *Mark the position of the new rose, then bore a 12mm (1/2in) hole. Where the cable crosses a joist, drill a 16mm (5/8in) hole 50mm (2in) below the top.*

3 *If the new rose can't be screwed to a joist, drill a 12mm (1/2in) hole in a wooden batten to coincide with the hole in the ceiling and fix the batten in position.*

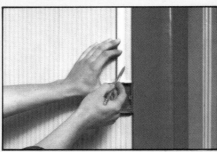

4 *If flush-fitting the switch and chasing in the cable, use a mounting box and a length of conduit to mark their positions on the wall.*

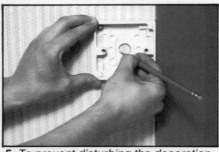

5 *To prevent disturbing the decoration in one room, you can bring the switch cable down the other side of the wall and surface-mount the switch.*

6 *Use a small bolster chisel and club hammer to channel out a groove in the wall to take the switch cable and to chop out the recess for the switch.*

TIP

7 *With cornices, make the channel in the wall first, then drive a long cold chisel gently up the back.*

8 *Fix the conduit in place with old nails, although you can also use clout nails. Drill and plug the fixing holes for the box and screw it into place.*

Mounting box: MK

LAYING THE CABLE

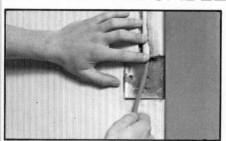

1 *Run the cable from where it joins the existing circuit to the new rose and lay in the switch cable. Allow 200mm (8in) for connections.*

2 *With the switch cable, you might find it easier to pull down the required length and then slide on the conduit before fixing it in place.*

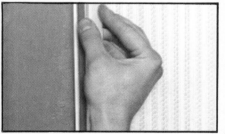

3 *It's not a good idea to leave cable exposed on a wall. When surface-mounting, the cable should be laid in PVC trunking with a clip-on cover.*

4 *If the cable is brought down on the other side of the wall to the switch, you'll need to drill a hole through so the cable enters the back of the box.*

FIXING THE SWITCH

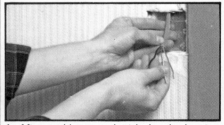

1 *After making good, strip back about 100mm (4in) of sheathing; take off 15mm (⁵⁄₈in) of insulation and bend over the exposed wire; sleeve the earth wire.*

2 *Because the switch is wired into the 'live' of the circuit, the black wire is live and not neutral; mark it as such with red PVC tape.*

3 *Connect the earth wire to the earth terminal of the metal box and the two conductors to the terminals on the back of the faceplate.*

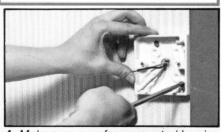

4 *Make sure a surface-mounted box is square before connecting the switch. With a flush fitting squareness can be adjusted when attaching the faceplate.*

Putting in switches

There is a great variety of switches available, but all perform the same function of breaking or completing an electrical circuit so you can turn the light off or on. Modern switches are of the rocker type; a one-gang switch has a single switch on the faceplate; a two-gang switch has two switches on the same faceplate, and so on. Dimmer switches are slightly different in that you can vary the power flowing to the bulb (so reducing or increasing its brightness) by rotating a control knob.

With a new light, you can either connect it into an existing switch position (fitting a two-gang switch in place of a one-gang one, for example) or a new switch. Depending on how you connect into the existing circuit, you'll have to run the switch cable above the ceiling from a rose or a junction box down the wall to where you are going to locate it. If you want to conceal the cable on the down drop you'll have to cut a shallow channel – which will damage the existing decoration. Or, you can surface-mount it in trunking.

Making the connection

Once you've decided where you want to put the light fitting and switch, you then have to decide where it's best to make the connection into the existing circuit.

Wiring runs may require some detective work to find out what each cable is doing – you don't want to connect into a switch cable by mistake. This may mean climbing into the roof space or raising a few floorboards. You'll need to do this anyway to run in the new cables to the required positions. As cable is expensive, it's best to plan your runs to use as little as possible. But when you measure along the proposed route, don't forget to allow about 200mm extra at the switch, rose and junction box for stripping back the conductors and joining in.

Changing the position of a ceiling light is even easier than adding a new one. If after you've turned off the power you undo the existing rose you'll see immediately the type of lighting circuit you are dealing with.

If there is only a black, a red and an earth wire going into it on the fixed wiring side then you have a junction box system. All you have to do is to disconnect the wires from the rose and reconnect them to the respective terminals of a new three-terminal junction box that you'll have to put in directly above the old fitting. You can then lead off another cable from this junction box to the re-positioned ceiling rose. The switch remains unaffected.

If the rose is a loop-in type, you have to carry out a similar modification, but this time the switch wires have to be incorporated in the new junction box, which must be a four-terminal type.

243

FITTING THE NEW ROSE AND LAMPHOLDER

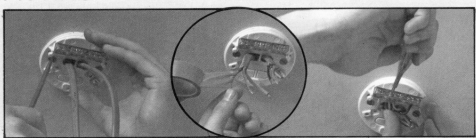
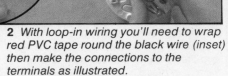

1 Fix the new rose to the ceiling. Strip back 75mm (3in) of sheathing and 8mm (1/3in) of insulation from the conductors, and sleeve the earth wires.

2 With loop-in wiring you'll need to wrap red PVC tape round the black wire (inset) then make the connections to the terminals as illustrated.

3 With junction box wiring, the earth is connected to the earth terminal, the black conductor goes to the neutral bank and the red to the SW terminal.

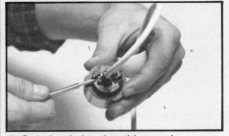

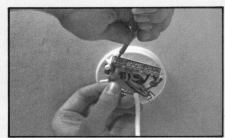

4 Strip back the sheathing and insulation of one end of the flex and connect the blue and brown conductors to the two terminals of the lampholder.

5 Screw on the cap and then slip the rose cover over the flex. Cut the flex to length and prepare the free end for connecting to the rose.

6 At the rose, connect the blue conductor to the terminal on the neutral side and the red to the SW side. Hook the wires over the cord grips.

CONNECTING INTO THE CIRCUIT

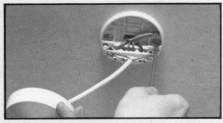
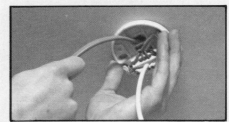

1 When connecting into a loop-in rose, undo the fixing screws and pull the fitting a little way from the ceiling. But keep all the wires in place.

2 Tap out a knockout, then draw down through it about 200mm (8in) of the cable that leads to the new ceiling rose, or else feed the cable up from below.

3 Prepare the cable by stripping back about 75mm (3in) of sheathing and 10mm (3/8in) of insulation from the conductors. Sleeve the earth wire.

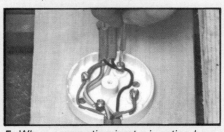

4 Connect the earth to the earth terminal, the black to the neutral terminals and the red to the central in-line terminals.

5 When connecting in at a junction box, use a four-terminal type mounted on a batten. Connect the wires to the terminals as shown.

6 When taking out an old loop-in rose, disconnect the switch and feed cables and connect up the two feed cables as shown in a three-terminal junction box.

TWO-WAY SWITCHING

In a room lit by a single pendant light, controlling that light from a single switch is no great hardship. But if the room contains wall lights it's useful to be able to control them from different parts of the room and that's exactly what two-way switching lets you do.

In most rooms, lights or groups of lights are controlled by just one switch. It's the standard set-up, and electricians call it one-way switching. However, there are situations where a one light, one switch arrangement isn't very convenient.

Take the light over a flight of stairs as an example. Having the light switch at the bottom of the flight is fine if you want to go upstairs. You can turn on the light before you go up without difficulty. But what happens when you reach the top? You can't turn the light off again. And suppose you want to come downstairs and the light is turned off? You can't switch it on without negotiating the stairs in the dark, which rather defeats the object of having a light there at all.

Obviously, what's needed is another switch at the top of the stairs and a system of wiring that allows either switch to turn the light on and off independently of the other. This system is called two-way switching.

Where it can be used

The example of the light above the stairs is such a common one that providing two-way switching for stair lights is now more or less standard procedure. There are, however, many other situations where two-way switching may be useful.

Think of the advantages of having a switch at both ends of a long hallway. And what about rooms with more than one entrance? It makes sense to have a switch beside each of the doors. The same applies to a garage with a side door in addition to the main one.

There are also situations where two-way switching is not vital but still worth considering. For example, where you have installed wall-mounted bedside reading lamps: it is a great advantage when you can control these from the door, as well as from a switch by the bed. You might also want to install a two-way switch for the main bedroom light so you can turn it on and off without getting out of bed.

And don't forget the hall light: in many homes this is one-way switched despite the fact that it often serves as a stair light by illuminating the bottom steps of the staircase. It's all too easy to go upstairs having forgotten to switch it off.

How it works

The key to two-way switching lies in using a special switch at both switching positions.

An ordinary one-way switch has two terminals and when you operate it you either make or break the electrical connection between them. For the current to reach the lightbulb and make it work, it must pass down one of the cores in the switch-drop cable, and back up the other. Making or breaking the link between terminals also makes or breaks the link between the two cores and therefore switches the light on or off.

A two-way switch works in a completely different way. It has three terminals, marked 'Common', L1, and L2, and when you operate it, flicking the switch one way provides a link between L1 and Common; flicking it the other way provides a link between Common and L2. If you link the terminals of two two-way switches in a certain way, then one switch can complete the circuit (and turn the light on) while the other can over-ride it and turn the light off again. The reverse also applies.

So, what is this remarkable wiring arrangement? Well, in its traditional form – the one normally illustrated in text-book wiring diagrams – the switches are linked with a pair of single-core cables called straps. Each joins the L1 terminal in one switch to the L2 terminal in the other. The switch drop from the light is

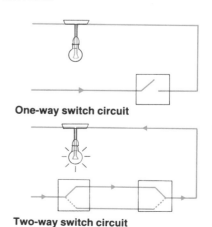

THE THEORY OF TWO-WAY SWITCHING

How a two-way switching circuit works can be seen in the way in which the switches are linked and how the power flows between them.

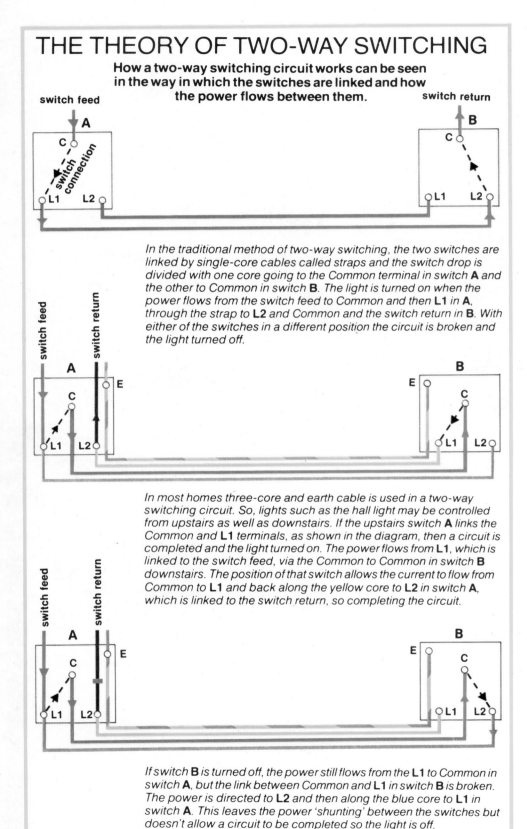

*In the traditional method of two-way switching, the two switches are linked by single-core cables called straps and the switch drop is divided with one core going to the Common terminal in switch **A** and the other to Common in switch **B**. The light is turned on when the power flows from the switch feed to Common and then **L1** in **A**, through the strap to **L2** and Common and the switch return in **B**. With either of the switches in a different position the circuit is broken and the light turned off.*

*In most homes three-core and earth cable is used in a two-way switching circuit. So, lights such as the hall light may be controlled from upstairs as well as downstairs. If the upstairs switch **A** links the Common and **L1** terminals, as shown in the diagram, then a circuit is completed and the light turned on. The power flows from **L1**, which is linked to the switch feed, via the Common to Common in switch **B** downstairs. The position of that switch allows the current to flow from Common to **L1** and back along the yellow core to **L2** in switch **A**, which is linked to the switch return, so completing the circuit.*

*If switch **B** is turned off, the power still flows from the **L1** to Common in switch **A**, but the link between Common and **L1** in switch **B** is broken. The power is directed to **L2** and then along the blue core to **L1** in switch **A**. This leaves the power 'shunting' between the switches but doesn't allow a circuit to be completed so the light is off.*

then divided in two: the first core goes to the Common terminal in one switch, the second to the Common terminal in the other. It's all run in single-core cable, and is designed for use where your home's wiring is run entirely in conduit – as it may well be if you live in a flat.

In most homes, though, the wiring takes the form of multi-cored PVC-sheathed cables, and in this case, a different two-way switching circuit is generally more convenient. What happens is that the switch drop, run in two-core and earth cable, is connected to only one of the two-way switches: one core to L1, the other to L2. This switch is then linked to its partner with three-core and earth cable, a cable which has rather oddly colour-coded wires – one red, one yellow, and one blue. However, this doesn't make the wiring up any more complicated. The yellow and blue cores are connected in the same way as the straps in the traditional system, and the red core is used to link the two Common terminals.

Converting an existing switch

That's the theory, but how does it work in practice? How do you convert an existing one-way switching circuit to two-way switching? You may be surprised at just how simple it is. Using a club hammer and cold chisel, make a hole in the wall to take a one-gang, plaster-depth mounting box at the spot where you want the new switch to go. This should be secured to the wall with a couple of screws and wallplugs.

Then, before running a length of 1.0 or 1.5mm² three-core and earth PVC-sheathed cable to the original switch position, connect up the new switch in order to minimise the time the power has to be switched off at the mains. The red core should go to the Common terminal with the yellow and blue cores acting as strap wires. The running of the cable shouldn't pose any difficulty. The cable is taken up the wall, above the ceiling and back down the wall to the old switch.

Chop a channel in the plaster at the wall sections of the run, insert a length of PVC conduit and pass the cable through that. Above the ceiling, if the cable runs at right angles to the joists, feed it through holes drilled at least 50mm below their top edge.

If the cable runs parallel to the joists, simply rest it on top of the ceiling, unless it is likely to be disturbed – as in a loft, for example. In that case it must be secured to the sides of the joists with cable clips. Turn off the power at the mains before removing the fixing screws. Then, ease the original switch from the wall so you can pass the cable into the mounting box.

With the cable in position, all that remains to be done is connect it up to the new two-way switch at the original switch position. Finally, connect the two cores of the switch drop to terminals L1 and L2, screw the switch securely to its mounting box and restore the power.

New circuits

The same system can also be employed in new work where you require two-way switching. For example, if you are installing a new wall light and want to be able to control it from a switch at the door of the room, as well as from a switch near the light itself, all you need to do is to install a new two-way switch in the normal way (see pages 241-244) and then run a length of three-core and earth cable from this switch to the switch by the door (the one controlling the room's main light). Here, you replace the old one-gang, one-way switch with a two-gang, two-way switch and connect the three-core and earth cable to one gang for two-way switch-

ing. Then connect the switch drop belonging to the room's main light to the other gang, this time connecting it up for one-way switching with one of the cores going to the L2 terminal and the other to the Common.

This method is quite straightforward, but it is not necessarily the most convenient way of setting about the job. Suppose you were installing not one new wall light, but two or more. If they are all to have two-way switches then you'll be involved in a great deal of cable running and, therefore, a great deal of work. After all, for each light you have to run a cable down to the new switch, back up above the ceiling, then back down the wall again to the second switch position.

This extra work can be avoided by using a junction box and a variation on the traditional two-way switching circuit. You run the circuit using three-core and earth PVC-sheathed and insulated cable. Doing this you are using the cable's red core as one half of the switch drop and the yellow and blue cores as straps. Then connect them up, together with the cables to the wall lights and the cable supplying the new circuit with power (taken from a loop-in ceiling rose, or from a junction box inserted into one of your home's main lighting circuits) in a large multi-terminal joint box called an RB4. The step-by-step photographs will explain what is happening but note that only one cable need be run to each wall-light.

INSTALLING A NEW TWO-WAY CIRCUIT

Using an RB4 multi-terminal junction box can save you running extra cable when you install a new two-way circuit with more than one light. Here it has been used to install a bedside lighting circuit, shown diagramatically. Overleaf we show you how the circuit is wired up, step by step.

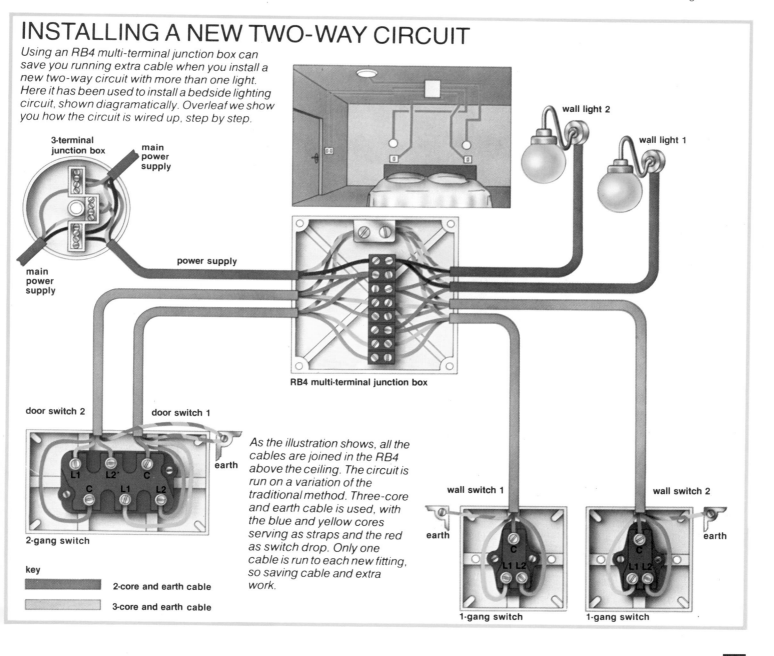

wall light 2

wall light 1

3-terminal junction box

main power supply

power supply

main power supply

RB4 multi-terminal junction box

door switch 2

door switch 1

L1   L2*   C

C   L1   L2

earth

2-gang switch

As the illustration shows, all the cables are joined in the RB4 above the ceiling. The circuit is run on a variation of the traditional method. Three-core and earth cable is used, with the blue and yellow cores serving as straps and the red as switch drop. Only one cable is run to each new fitting, so saving cable and extra work.

wall switch 1

earth

C
L1 L2

1-gang switch

wall switch 2

earth

C
L1 L2

1-gang switch

key

2-core and earth cable

3-core and earth cable

CHANGING THE DOOR SWITCH

1 Turn off the power at the mains and remove the screws in the old switch's faceplate. Ease the switch from the wall until you can disconnect it.

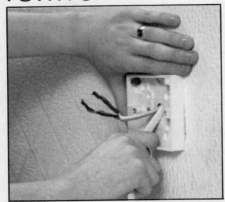

2 Run one three-core and earth cable per light from the RB4 box to the switch mounting box, using an existing conduit to carry it down the wall.

3 For two wall lights, install a three-gang, two-way switch. Use two gangs to connect the three-core cables – yellow to L1, blue to L2 and red to Common.

FITTING THE BEDSIDE SWITCHES

1 Using a club hammer and bolster chisel, chop a channel in the wall from the ceiling down to the new switch position ready for the cable.

2 Mark the exact position of the switch on the wall, then chop out a recess, taking care to ensure that it is deep enough to take the metal mounting box.

3 Before running the cable, insert a length of PVC conduit into the channel; where possible poke it through into the void above the ceiling.

5 Strip the ends of the three-core and earth cable from the RB4 ready for connection, remembering to fit the earth wires with green and yellow sleeving.

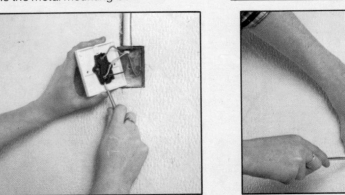

6 Next connect the cable to a one-gang, two-way switch, linking the yellow core to the L1 terminal, the blue core to L2 and the red core to Common.

7 Having connected the earth core to the terminal on the mounting box, screw the new switch securely into place and check that it is level.

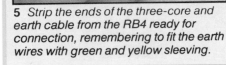

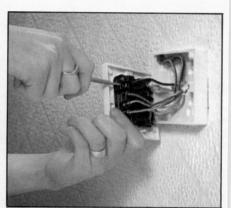

4 *Connect the switch drop from the room's main light to the third gang to give one-way switching. One core goes to L2, the other to Common.*

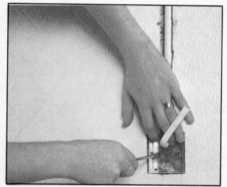

4 *At the second switch position of each light, use screws and wallplugs to fix a one-gang, plaster-depth mounting box in a hole cut into the wall.*

8 *Finally, join up all the cables in the RB4 junction box. It's much easier than it looks and the connections can be seen in detail on page 247.*

Intermediate switching

There is one other kind of two-way switching that could be useful in your home. It's called an intermediate switching circuit and it means that a light or group of lights can be controlled by three or more separate switches. It's easy to install because all you do is introduce one or more additional switches into the circuit between the two two-way switches. This can, of course, be very convenient because you can then control a light from as many positions as you like. For example, you could control a hall light from a switch near the front door, from one near the living room door and from another switch on the landing upstairs.

There are two ways of carrying out the wiring but with both methods a special switch called an intermediate switch is needed. This has four terminals: two marked L1 and two marked L2. To install an intermediate switch in a two-way switching circuit all you do is use the switch to interrupt the three-core and earth cable – or the strap wires in a traditional circuit that has been installed in a flat or where the cables are all run in conduit.

The cores from the L1 terminals and L2 terminals in one two-way switch go to the L1 terminals on one side of the intermediate switch and the L1 and L2 cores from the second two-way switch go to the L2 terminals on the other side. However, with a three-core and earth circuit this leaves a break in the core linking the two-way switches' Common terminals. One way of solving this problem is to join the ends of the two cores with a cable connector. Once the two red cores have been joined the connector unit is then placed in the space behind the intermediate switch. However, it's better to interrupt the three-core and earth cable with a multi-terminal junction box above the ceiling near the intermediate switch position. You need six terminals in the junction box: one for the earth cores, one for both the red cores from the Common terminals and one each for the remaining cores.

At this stage you should introduce two lengths of two-core and earth cable which, by connecting up to the appropriate terminals, are used to extend the yellow and blue cores from each two-way switch. When that's done, run the two two-core and earth cables down to the intermediate switch and connect them up just as if they were the two pairs of yellow and blue cores in the three-core and earth cable. It is worth remembering that if one of the switches in an intermediate circuit is to be cord-operated then it should be one of the end switches. This is because there are no cord-operated intermediate switches available.

TWO-WAY SWITCHING

Two-way switching lets you control a light from two separate switches. The illustration shows the back of a two-way switch with its

three terminals labelled Common, L1 and L2. In any two-way switching circuit, both switches are exactly the same and have equivalent terminals. But wiring up the switches is completely different from connecting up one-way switches.

This is because each two-way switch must be able to control the light independently of the other.

The traditional way of wiring two-way switches as used in flats or all-conduit installations is to use single core to make the connections:

● the L1 and L2 terminals of each switch are linked by single-core cables that are known as straps

● the switch drop cable that provides the power to the circuit is divided with the feed going to one Common terminal and the return going to the other.

More often PVC-sheathed three-core and earth cable, colour coded red, yellow and blue, is used:

● the Common terminals are linked by the red cores, with the yellow and blue cores acting as straps

● the switch drop is then connected to the L1 and L2 terminals of just one of the switches.

CONVERTING A CIRCUIT

To convert an existing one-way switching circuit to two-way switching:
● replace the existing switch with a two-way switch
● run 1.0 or 1.5mm² PVC-sheathed and insulated three-core and earth cable to the new switch position
● connect it to another two-way switch.

This method can also be used to create new two-way switching circuits.

INSTALLING WALL LIGHTS

Ceiling lights are simple and effective, but if you want a lighting scheme that is a little more exciting, more decorative and more versatile, they are not enough. One solution is to fit wall lights. Here's how.

There are two keys to a really successful lighting scheme: variety and versatility. Variety, because having a uniform level of light throughout a room is just plain boring. And versatility because your lighting needs change from one part of the room to another. In a living room, for example, you may prefer the overall lighting level to be fairly low and restful, but you will still need pools of intense light for reading, or perhaps simply to show off decorative feature like pictures, plants or ornaments. That's where wall lights come in. They are very good at creating interesting pools of light.

Choosing a light

With so many wall lights to choose from where do you start? It really depends on what you want the light to do. Few provide a light you can put to practical use. Most are purely decorative.

The traditional wall light is a good example. It normally has a low wattage, candle-shaped lamp, mounted on a wooden base, and concealed behind a pretty parchment shade, so that it spreads a fan of soft light across the wall.

More recent versions take the imitation candelabra and gaslight theme still further, having ornate brass, copper, and aluminium stems, and, instead of shades, translucent bowls in plain, coloured, frosted, smoked, and sculpted glass or plastic. They tend to use more powerful bulbs, and can be made to light the top or bottom of the wall, but the net result is the same. They are for looking at, rather than seeing by.

This is also true of many modern wall light designs. There are, for example, cylindrical fittings open at top and bottom to spread a shaft of light in two directions, either vertically or horizontally.

Still attractive, but producing a more useful light, there are the fully enclosed fittings. 'Opals', for example, create a beautifully soft, even light, and look rather like round, square or rectangular blocks of milky glass or plastic. For those who prefer more ornate lights, sculpted glass versions (they look like cut crystal) are also available. Enclosed fittings are particularly handy

where space is limited — in a hallway, perhaps — and since many are weatherproof, they are an excellent choice for the humid atmosphere of a bathroom or an outside porch.

More useful still are the spotlights. Usually mounted on adjustable arms away from the wall, they can be used to send a strong beam of light almost anywhere — back onto the wall, say, to light a picture, or out into the room to illuminate a desk or sitting area. Their only real snag is that they need careful shading, if they are not to dazzle you. Mounting them on the ceiling may overcome this problem.

And finally, don't forget fluorescent lights. Slimline fluorescent tubes, though inhospitable looking, give off little heat and are easily concealed. Use them to spread a sheet of light over a wall. The light assembly can be mounted on a wooden batten and

shaded by a pelmet or baffle. If you wish, the pelmet can be painted or papered to match the wall. Miniature fluorescents are also handy for lighting pictures and shelves, but whatever the size, be sure to use a 'de luxe' warm white' tube, or the light will look cold and harsh.

Positioning the fitting

Choosing a light is only half the battle. To give of its best it must be carefully positioned. With the exception of enclosed fittings, which stand very well on their own, most need to be arranged at least in pairs, and sometimes even in a group. Traditional wall lights and mock candelabra, for example, tend to look best when arranged symmetrically in pairs — say, on each side of a chimney breast. Spotlights, on the other hand, are often most effective in a cluster.

Of course, there are no hard and fast

CABLE RUNS

1 From a loop-in rose
To install a new wall light you need to run a supply cable from an existing loop-in ceiling rose to a new four-terminal junction box and then run cables to the switch and fitting.

existing loop-in rose · new supply cable · 4-terminal junction box · existing switch cable · new switch cable · new 2-gang switch · new cable to wall light

2 From a nearby circuit
You can also get the power for the wall light by connecting a three-terminal junction box to an existing circuit cable and run cable from this to the new four-terminal junction box.

existing loop-in rose · existing switch cable · 4-terminal junction box · new switch cable · 3-terminal junction box · new 2-gang switch · new cable to wall light · circuit cable

——— existing cable runs
- - - - new cable runs

INSTALLING THE FITTING

1 Mark the position of the BESA box on the wall where the light is to go. Use a through box if the light's switch is to be immediately below the BESA box.

2 With a club hammer and bolster chisel, chop out the hole to take the box, and channels to take cables up to the ceiling and down or across to the switch.

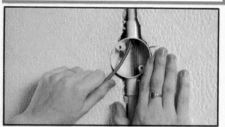

3 Fix the box in place with screws and wall plugs, then run in the cables for the light and switch. Note that the switch cable passes straight through the box.

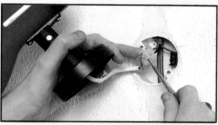

4 Connect the light cable to the light with insulated cable connectors Tuck the earth wire out of the way if it is not needed.

INSTALLING A SWITCH

1 To install a new switch, mark out the position of the switch mounting box (a plaster-depth box) and chop out the hole to receive it.

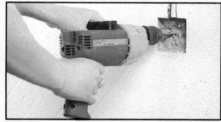

2 Drill and plug the wall, then screw the mounting box in place, checking it is level. Next, feed in the cable coming from the new circuit's junction box.

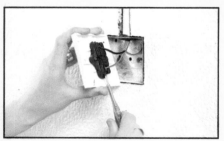

3 Connect the cable to a one-gang one-way switch. Ensure the terminal marked 'TOP' is at the top. Connect the earth wire to the box terminal.

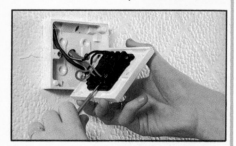

4 If using an existing switch position, insert a new two-gang plate switch. Connect existing cable to one set of terminals, new cable to the other.

POSITIONING WALL LIGHTS
● fix ordinary wall lights about 1.5m (5ft) above floor level
● bedside lights are best set about 1.2m (4ft) above floor level.

WHAT SWITCH TO USE
Use a one-way plate switch for the wall light. Set it on a metal mounting box sunk into the wall or on a plastic box mounted on the surface.
● a separate switch is needed to isolate a wall light from the main circuit even if it has a built-in switch of its own

● alternatively you can use an existing switch position to control an extra wall light by replacing a one-gang switch unit with a two-gang unit.

FITTING THE WALL LIGHT
The wires of the fitting are linked to the circuit cable using insulated cable connectors. These are housed in a BESA box or an architrave box which is sunk into the wall and hidden by the light fitting.

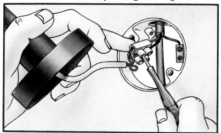

ALTERNATIVES

1 If the light switch is not to be vertically below the light position, use a single entry BESA box instead of a through one, fitting it in the same way.

2 If the light cannot be mounted on a BESA box, connect the wires in an architrave mounting box. Knockouts let this act as a single entry or through box.

LIGHTING CIRCUIT CONNECTIONS

1 Turn off the power at the mains, unscrew the rose and ease it away from the ceiling so you can pull through new 1.0 or 1.5mm² cable.

3 Run the cable to a junction box between the switch and light. Then run one cable to the light, another to the switch position.

2 Connect the cable to the rose's loop-in terminals; the red wire to the centre terminal block, the black to the neutral block, and the earth to the earth block.

4 If you can't connect to the rose, insert a junction box at some point along one of the rose's feed cables. Run cables down to the light and switch as before.

CONNECTING TO A RING CIRCUIT

1 The easiest way to link a lighting spur to the ring circuit is to connect a 2.5mm² cable to the back of a socket. Ensure the socket isn't already on a spur.

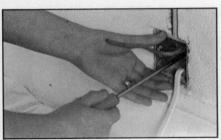

4 Fix the mounting box for the connection unit into the whole, and then run the cable into it from the power socket or three-terminal junction box.

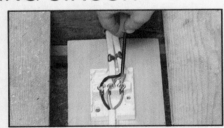

2 Alternatively, cut the ring circuit cables and connect them to a three-terminal junction beneath the floor; then run the spur cable into that.

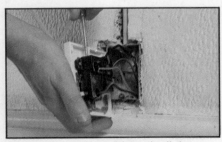

5 Having run the cable to the light position (or four-terminal junction box), fit the connection unit with a 5A fuse and connect it up.

3 Mark the position of the fused connection unit. Cut through the wallpaper with a sharp knife before you chisel out the hole for the mounting box.

6 Finally, fit an architrave box or a stopped BESA box at the light position and install the light as before. Note the cable will now enter from below.

rules. In the end, it's all down to what looks and works best in your particular situation. Try to imagine how the lights will affect the room – not only the lights themselves and their position, but also the direction of the light they will give out.

You ought to pay particular attention to the light's height above the floor. The general rule is to place the light at just below eye level – about 1,500mm (5ft) – but you can vary this as necessary to stop the light getting in your eyes or to help direct it where it's needed. Wall lights used as bedside lamps, for example, should be about 1,220mm (4ft) above the floor and positioned so they can't get knocked as someone walks past them.

Installing the light

If you've read pages 232-236 and 241-244, then you shouldn't experience too much difficulty in fitting the light. But remember electricity can be dangerous if abused, so follow the instructions to the letter. If they don't tie in with your home's existing wiring, or you're unsure about what you're doing, don't take chances – seek expert advice before attempting anything yourself.

The first step is to find a power source, though it is best to leave the connections into the existing circuit until last. That way, you can do almost all the work with your home's electrics working normally; you'll have to turn off the power at the mains only for the few minutes needed to make the final connection.

In most cases, taking a spur off the existing lighting circuit is your best bet. Do check, though, that the wall light will not overload it. Isolate the circuit in question by removing the fuse carrier from the consumer unit, or by turning off its MCB, and add up the total wattage of the bulbs it feeds – those that are now dead, in other words. Bulbs rated at 100W or more count at face value; less powerful bulbs count as 100W. When you've done that, add on the wattage of the new light and make sure the grand total is less than 1,200 watts.

Assuming this is so, there are two ways to break into the circuit. In theory, the simplest is to connect a 1.0 or 1.5mm² two-core and earth cable to a loop-in ceiling rose, and run it to a four-terminal junction box above the ceiling. In practice, it's often hard to fit the extra wires in, so, as an alternative, trace a mains feed cable out of the rose, and connect the junction box into this cable.

Once you've got power to the junction box, wire up the wall light and its switch on the conventional junction box system (see pages 232-236 and 241-244) with one cable going to the light, and another to the switch. The switch can be anywhere convenient, either close to the light or away from it. You can use the switch position by the room's door if

you wish. It's a simple matter to convert the existing one-gang switch there (for ceiling light) to a two-gang switch (for ceiling light and wall light).

Many wall lights have a built-in switch, so you may wonder why a switch is necessary. Although these are fine for everyday use, you ought to be able to isolate the wall light completely so an additional ordinary plate switch is required.

Though fitting a wall light is not complicated there are two problems you may meet. The first is in fixing the light to the wall. Many can be screwed to the holes provided in the BESA box housing connections between light and cable. Failing that, you can fix the light to the wall using screws and wall plugs, and house the connections in a metal architrave mounting box sunk into the wall behind it.

The second problem is earthing. Even if the wall light doesn't need to be earthed, the earth wire in the new cables must be linked to your home's main earthing point at the fuse box or consumer unit. (Never connect earth wires to water or gas pipes.) You can, of course, do this by connecting it to the earth wire in the existing wiring, but, if the existing wiring is old, it may not have an earth wire. In this case, you should run a single sheathed earth core from the new junction box back to the earthing point.

Connecting to a ring circuit

You might find that it's inconvenient or impossible to take power from the lighting circuit – if this is the case you can connect the wall light to a ring circuit. Essentially, what you do is run a spur to the wall light's junction box. You break into the ring either by connecting a 2.5mm² two-core and earth cable to the back of a power socket, or by joining it to a three-terminal junction box and connecting this to the ring circuit cable beneath the floor.

However, there is a snag. The ring circuit fuse has too high a rating for a lighting circuit (remember, these need a 5A fuse). To get round this, you have to run the 2.5mm² cable into a fused connection unit fitted with a 5A fuse, and continue the circuit to a four-terminal junction box and then on to the light and switch junction box with 1.0 or 1.5mm² cable.

Obviously, this involves considerable extra work and expense, but there is a short cut. You can do away with the junction box and separate switch, and instead use a switched fused connection unit to control the wall light. It sounds appealing, but it too has its drawbacks. The connection unit will not match the other light switches in the room, and it needs to be as close as possible to the light – an unnecessarily complex cable run would be needed to control the light from the far side of the room.

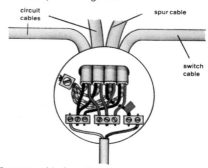
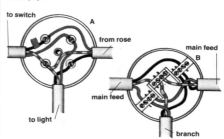

INSTALLING TRACK LIGHTING

Track lighting allows you plenty of scope in lighting your home. It's efficient, versatile and attractive and, what's more, extremely easy to install.

The time is bound to come when you want to alter the lighting in your home. You may want to highlight certain features, such as paintings, or merely provide yourself with extra light. You may want to change your wall lights or depart from the traditional concept of a ceiling rose and pendant light. In all these cases you should think about installing track lighting.

What is track lighting?
Track lighting consists of individual light fittings of various types that are mounted on special tracks fixed to ceilings or walls. This enables you to move the lights into whatever position you like and, in addition, to adjust them so their light is thrown in whichever direction you want.

The track itself is a metal casing, usually square or tubular in cross-section, that contains twin electrical conductors. These live and neutral conductors are bare and extend from one end of the track to the other. They function in much the same way as the conductor rails of an electric railway, with the light fittings instead of the trains picking up electric current from the live rails. The conductors are shielded from touch, while the lights are fitted with special adaptors for making contact with the conductors inside the track and which also serves to hold the lights in place.

Once the track has been fixed in position and the electrical connections made, then the adaptors are placed on to the track and the spotlights moved along to exactly where you want them. You can then lock them into position.

Obtaining the power supply for your track lighting is very simple. You're really faced with two options. On the one hand you can simply connect the 'live' end of the track to the existing ceiling rose, after removing the flex of the original lampholder, or you can run in an entirely new lighting circuit. For track lights mounted on the wall, power can be supplied either by an existing light circuit or the room's socket outlet circuit. The best method, however, is to wire the lights through a fused connection unit, as if it were a wall light linked to the power circuits.

Any number of lights can be fitted onto any one track, provided you don't exceed the track's current rating. With a 10A track, the most suitable for a domestic situation, this will be 2400W and with a 16A track, 4000W. In other words, with a 10A track you could, in theory, fit up to 24 100W spotlights. In practice the limiting factor is more likely to be the circuit wiring. Remember, lighting circuits are actually ratd at 5A which means that each one can take a load of up to 1200W or, in effect, can supply twelve lampholders containing lamps of 100W each or smaller. So when you are adding track lighting to an existing circuit, check that the extra lights won't mean exceeding this figure. If they will, run a spur from a nearby power circuit (via a fused connection unit) instead – see page 256 for more details.

Choosing your lighting track
Lighting track for commercial purposes comes in various standard lengths. The domestic variety usually only comes in two lengths, 1000mm (39in) or 1500mm (59in). Once you've decided on the approximate lengths of track that you'll need, visit your local stockist to see exactly what is available. When making your choice of track, it's a good idea to check what type of light fittings are available

with it and whether they'll meet your requirements. After all, the track itself is usually available in only a few finishes – white, brown, polished brass and polished silver are the commonest – while there are probably over a hundred different types of light fitting available. If you find that you can't get the exact length you require, don't worry; it can easily be cut to size with a hacksaw and if longer lengths are required, special connectors are available. And there are 90° angle connectors for when a track is required to turn a corner.

Choosing the lights
There are so many different types of fitting available that you're bound to find one that will suit the decor of your home and do the job you want it to. The number you fit on any one track will depend largely on what you want to light. As a rule, though, track lighting would prove expensive for just one or two fittings.

Installing the track
There are a number of ways of fixing the track to your ceiling or wall. It can be fixed almost flush to the surface with the help of small clips. Alternatively, you can use a special mounting canopy that will fit conveniently and neatly over an existing ceiling rose or

PREPARING THE CEILING

1 *Switch off the electricity supply at the mains and unscrew the existing ceiling rose cover. You can then remove the old pendant flex and lampholder.*

2 *Site the first surface clip so that the live end of the track will sit close to the power source. Make sure the clip has a secure fixing.*

3 *Measure the position of the second clip: with a 1m (39in) track it should be 600mm (2ft) away; with a 1.5m (39in) track it should be 800mm (32in) away.*

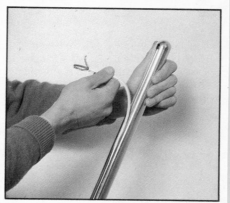

4 *Before fixing the track in place you'll have to free the flex. This is housed in a channel on the top side of the track and can be pulled clear.*

you can use mounting stems, which are merely short rods on backplates. You'll probably find that your lighting track will have a length of special flex already connected to its live end. This is likely to be the same length as the track. An advantage of these mounting methods is that in addition to providing a simple means for fitting the track itself, they help to conceal the track flex – so you won't have to cut it to length. The flex is fitted into a channel on the ceiling face of the track and you may well have to remove the shorter plastic end piece so you can free it. If you're going to use a mounting canopy and obtain power from an existing ceiling rose then the excess flex can be simply tucked into the canopy. Using surface clips will enable you to thread the flex up into the ceiling so that it can be neatly connected to a BESA box or a junction box. Only the mounting stems don't actually conceal the flex. But in their case all

you do is run the flex in its channel and leave only a short section exposed where it runs up to the ceiling rose or BESA box.

Before installing the lighting you'll have to finalise the position for the track on the ceiling or the wall. Ideally you should make sure that the mains outlet of your existing light coincides with the live end of the track. This could mean altering the position of the outlet, or even installing some new wiring, and if this is the case it should be done before you fix up the track.

Mounting track on the ceiling is perfectly straightforward but it will require solid fixings. It's best to use the joists, but if these don't coincide with the fixing holes drilled in the square cross-sectioned track you can easily drill some new holes in it to match your joist spacings. Alternatively, secure a piece of chipboard between the relevant joists and fix the track to this. Most mounting canopies

MOUNTING METHODS

There are three methods of fixing lighting track to a ceiling:

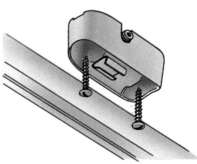

● surface clips – also suitable for use with wall-mounted track

● mounting canopies – designed to fit neatly over an existing ceiling rose and to also conceal any excess flex

● mounting stems – also suitable for use with wall-mounted track.

TIP: USE A COVER PLATE

An existing BESA box and the connections within it can be neatly concealed by a cover plate with the surface clip fixed on top. You might well find that the mains outlet point is not immediately above where you want to position the lighting track. One solution is to use a cover plate and to run the connecting cable to the track in mini-trunking.

MAKING THE CONNECTIONS

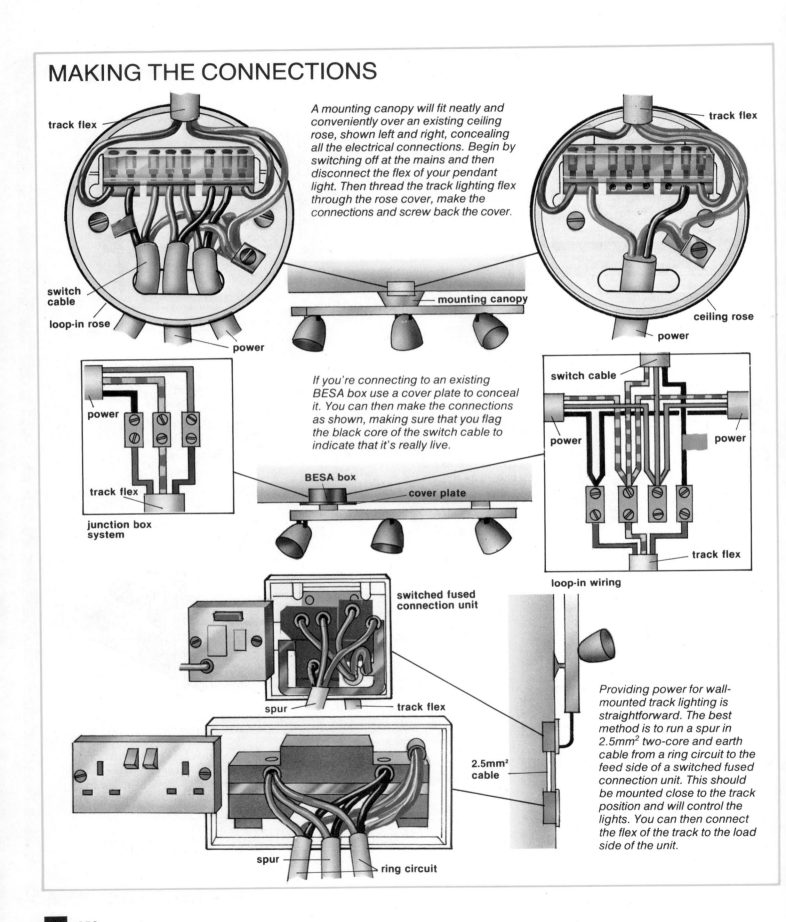

track flex

switch cable

loop-in rose

power

track flex

ceiling rose

power

A mounting canopy will fit neatly and conveniently over an existing ceiling rose, shown left and right, concealing all the electrical connections. Begin by switching off at the mains and then disconnect the flex of your pendant light. Then thread the track lighting flex through the rose cover, make the connections and screw back the cover.

mounting canopy

power

junction box system

track flex

If you're connecting to an existing BESA box use a cover plate to conceal it. You can then make the connections as shown, making sure that you flag the black core of the switch cable to indicate that it's really live.

BESA box

cover plate

switch cable

power

power

track flex

loop-in wiring

switched fused connection unit

spur

track flex

spur

ring circuit

2.5mm² cable

Providing power for wall-mounted track lighting is straightforward. The best method is to run a spur in 2.5mm² two-core and earth cable from a ring circuit to the feed side of a switched fused connection unit. This should be mounted close to the track position and will control the lights. You can then connect the flex of the track to the load side of the unit.

256

INSTALLING THE TRACK AND FITTINGS

1 Offer up the track to the surface clips, making sure that it will be centrally positioned and that the clip grub screws are slackened.

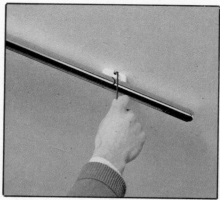

2 When you have the track precisely in position, secure it in place by tightening up the clip grub screws with the hexagonal key provided.

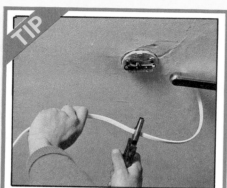

3 Before making the electrical connections, cut the flex to length. If you're using a mounting canopy, you can safely tuck the excess inside.

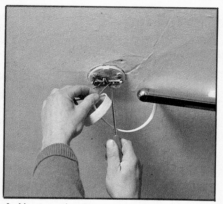

4 Next, make the connections. Link the brown core to the bank of live terminals, the blue core to the neutral bank and the green/yellow core to the earth terminal.

5 Most track lights are stepped on one side so you can't fit them incorrectly. Move the lever through 90° to retract the contacts and fixing levers.

6 Then fix the lights onto the track. Simply hold them in place, reposition the lever and lock the lights in the desired position on the track.

have fixing holes 51mm (2in) apart. In other words, the canopy will be able to fit over an existing rose, and the connection to the circuit can then be completely concealed. However, where the existing rose is old and has different spacings between its fixing holes you'll have to discard it and use an alternative method of connecting to the circuit.

This method involves fixing a BESA box flush with the surface of the ceiling. Inside the BESA box the flying leads of the lighting track are connected to the existing circuit wires with insulated cable connectors. The box itself has two screwed lugs that are spaced at 51mm (2in) centres, so the canopy will fit perfectly in place. If you're using stems, you'll find that the procedure is virtually the same although there could well be slight differences between the various systems currently on the market. Fixing track to walls is much the same as fixing it to the ceiling.

However, you'll probably find that you have to drill and plug the wall to get a really secure fixing, and you'll also have to cut a channel in the plaster to run in the cable unless your track reaches right up to the ceiling and the cable can be concealed within it.

Obtaining power for track lighting

One of the major advantages of track lighting is that it can often be connected to an existing lighting point without any alteration of the circuitry. However, new wiring will be necessary when there is no convenient lighting which can be used to supply the track; where the addition of track lighting is likely to overload the lighting circuit, and where track lighting is to be used in addition to the existing lighting.

If you're going to have to run in a new circuit for the track you should use 1.0mm² two-core and earth cable rated at 5A. This will

be able to supply power for up to 12 spotlights on three or four tracks. The circuit will be the same as an ordinary lighting circuit and you'll probably find it easiest to use junction boxes as each track will need to be controlled by a wall switch. That way you can use BESA boxes in which to make the connections to the track. For further details on running a new circuit see pages 266-269.

Track lighting fixed to the wall will be able to obtain its power supply from the existing lighting point if it is replacing wall lights. However, if you're mounting new lights then you're faced with two options. You can either break into the lighting circuit in the ceiling void above and run cable down to the track or you can break into the socket outlet circuit. In the latter case you should take a spur to a switched fused connection and then run 1.0mm² two-core and earth cable to the track itself.

ADDING A POWER POINT

Electrical equipment is now used more and more in the home, so an extra power socket is always useful. Here's how to fit one.

There's nothing really difficult about installing a new power point. It's easier than putting in a new light as you don't have to worry about a switch cable.

Ever since the early 1950s, the power supply to the sockets has almost always been wired as a ring circuit (see pages 232-236), and it is almost certain that any house rewired since then will have had this system installed. This means that once you've decided where you want the new outlet point – by a shelf in the living room for a hi-fi system, or over a work-top in the kitchen, for example – all you have to do is to run a 'branch' or 'spur' to it from a convenient point on a nearby ring circuit.

The connection could be made at any socket on the ring (unless it already has a spur coming from it), or by using a three-terminal junction box inserted into the cable run. Each spur can have either one single or one double socket connected to it, or else one fused connection unit. Until a recent change in the Wiring Regulations, you were allowed two single sockets on a spur, but this is no longer permitted.

Checking your circuits

Although it's very likely that your house has ring circuits for the power supply, it's important to make sure. A ring circuit serves a number of 13A power outlets, and the sockets themselves take the familiar three-pin plugs with flat pins. But having this type of socket doesn't necessarily mean you've got a ring circuit – a new radial circuit may have been installed with these fittings, or an old radial circuit may simply have been modernised with new socket outlets. Pages 232-236 explain the distinction.

First you've got to check whether you've got a modern consumer unit or separate fuse boxes for each of the circuits. Having a consumer unit is a fair indication that you've got ring circuit wiring, and if two cables are connected to each individual 30A fuseway in the unit this will confirm it. Normally each floor of the house will have a separate ring circuit, protected by a 30A fuse or MCB.

If you have separate fuse boxes, look for the ones with 30A fuses. If they have one supply

cable going into them and two circuit cables coming out, this indicates a ring circuit.

It's easy to identify the sockets on any particular circuit simply by plugging in electrical appliances, such as table lamps, turning off the power and then removing a 30A fuse from the fuse box or consumer unit, or switching off a 30A MCB. When you restore the supply, the equipment that remains off will indicate which sockets are on the circuit.

Dealing with radial circuits

Where a house hasn't got ring circuits, then the power sockets will be supplied by some form of radial circuit. Because there are different types of radial circuit, each governed by separate regulations controlling the number and location of sockets on the circuit, size of cable to be used and the size and type of circuit fuse protecting it, you should only add a spur to an existing radial circuit if you can trace its run to the fuse box and identify its type, and if it has been wired up in modern PVC-sheathed cable throughout.

If you've still got unfused 15A, 5A and 2A round-pin plugs, then this is a sure sign of very old radial circuits, which were installed more than 30 years ago. Rather than extending the system you should seriously consider taking these circuits out and replacing them with ring circuits, as the wiring will almost certainly be nearing the end of its life. You'll then be able to position the new sockets exactly where you want them. If you're in any doubt about the

circuitry in your house you should contact your local electricity authority or a qualified electrician before carrying out any work.

Adding a spur to a ring

Once you've established you're dealing with a ring circuit and what sockets are on it, you'll need to find out if any spurs have already been added. You can't have more spurs than there are socket outlets on the ring itself. But unless the circuit has been heavily modified, it's unlikely that this situation will arise. You'll also need to know where any spurs are located – you don't want to overload an existing branch by mistake.

You can distinguish the sockets on the ring from those on a spur by a combination of inspecting the back of the sockets and tracing some cable runs (see *Ready Reference*). But remember to turn off the power first.

When you've got this information, you can work out whether it's feasible to add to the ring circuit. And you'll have a good idea where the cable runs.

Installing the socket

It's best to install the socket and lay in the cable before making the final join into the ring, since by doing this you reduce the amount of time that the power to the circuit is off.

You can either set the socket flush with the wall or mount it on the surface. The latter is the less messy method, but the fitting stands proud of the wall and so is more conspicuous.

FLUSH FITTING IN A BRICK WALL

1 Decide where you want to position the socket, then pencil round the mounting box as a guide for where to chop out the wall.

2 Drill slightly within the pencil lines to the depth of the mounting box, then work along the lines with a bolster chisel before chopping out the recess.

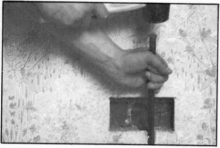

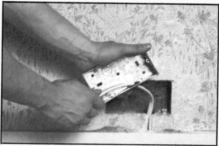

3 Channel a cable run down the back of the skirting using a long, thin cold chisel. Alternatively, use a long masonry bit and an electric drill.

4 Thread the cable up from under the floor, through some PVC conduiting behind the skirting and into the mounting box.

5 Push the box into position, then use a bradawl to mark where the fixing holes are to go in the recess. Remove the box and drill and plug the holes.

6 Set the box back into place and screw it tightly into the recess. Check that it is level, and then make good if necessary with plaster or filler.

Keith Morris

Flush-fixing a socket on a plasterboard wall is a little more involved.

If you choose to surface-mount the socket, all you have to do is to fix a PVC or metal box directly to the wall after you've removed the knockout (and, if metal, use a grommet) where you want the cable to enter. The socket can then be screwed directly to this.

Laying in the cable
Because cable is expensive, it's best to plan the spur so that it uses as little cable as possible. When you channel cable into a wall you'll need to chase out a shallow run, fix the

cable in position with clips, then plaster over it. But the best method of all is to run the cable in oval PVC conduiting. It won't give any more protection against an electric drill, but it'll prevent any possible reaction between the plaster making good and the cable sheathing. Always channel horizontally or vertically, and never diagonally, so it's easier to trace the wiring run when you've completed decorating. You can then avoid the cable when fixing something to the wall.

Normally the cable will drop down to below floor level to connect into the circuit. Rather than remove the skirting to get the cable down

WARNING
The power supply to the sockets will probably be wired as a ring circuit. You can add a spur to this provided the number of spurs doesn't exceed the number of sockets on the ring.

CABLE SIZE
New spurs should be in 2.5mm^2 cable

CHECKING OUT A RING CIRCUIT
These instructions assume that your installation conforms to the Wiring Regulations. If it seems to have been modified in an unauthorised way, get a qualified electrician to check it.

TURN OFF THE POWER SUPPLY. Start by undoing a socket near where you want to install the new socket.

AT A SINGLE SOCKET
One cable entering
Socket is on the end of a spur. There could be another single socket on the branch.
Action: trace cable. If it goes to another single socket and this socket has only two cables going to it, then you have found an intermediate socket on the spur. It it goes to a double socket where there are three cables, then the single socket is the only socket on the spur. It's the same if the cable goes to a junction box.

Two cables entering
Socket could be on the ring, or it could be the intermediate socket on a spur.
Action: You'll need to trace the cable runs. If the cable is the only one going to another single socket, then the socket is on a spur. If the cable makes up one of two cables in another socket then it's on the ring.

Three cables entering
Socket is on the ring with a spur leading from it.
Action: to check which cable is which you'll need to trace the cable runs.

AT A DOUBLE SOCKET
One cable entering
Socket is on a spur. You can't connect a new socket from this.
Two cables entering
Socket is on the ring. You can connect a spur into this.
Three cables entering
Socket is on the ring with a spur leading from it. Checking to see which cable is which is the same as for a single socket with three cables. You can't connect a spur from this socket.

FLUSH FITTING IN A PLASTERBOARD WALL

1 Knock along the cavity wall to locate a stud near where you want the socket. Pierce the wall with a bradawl to locate the centre of the upright.

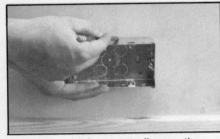

2 Position the box centrally over the stud and pencil round it. Be as accurate as you can because eventually the box should fit neatly in the opening.

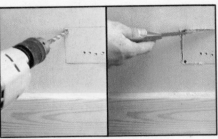

3 Drill the corners of the guidelines. Push a pad saw (or keyhole saw) into one of them and cut along the lines. The plasterboard will come out in one piece.

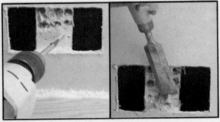

4 Once you've exposed the stud, you'll need to remove some of the wood so the box can be fully recessed. You can do this with a drill and chisel.

5 Use a long drill bit to drill down through the baseplate of the stud partition. Try and keep the drill as upright as possible.

6 Lay the cable from the point where it joins the main circuit and thread it up through the hole in the baseplate and into the box.

7 Set the box in the recess and fix it in place by screwing to the stud. The cable end can now be prepared and connected to the socket terminals.

8 Where there is no stud to fix to, fit special lugs to the box sides. These press against the plasterboard's inner face when the faceplate is attached.

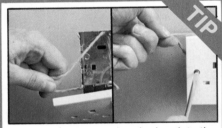

9 Before manoeuvring the box into the recess, thread some string through the front so you can hold it in position.

CONNECTING THE NEW SOCKET

1 Strip back the sheathing of the cable by running a sharp knife down the side of the uninsulated earth. Avoid damaging the other cores.

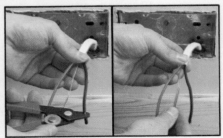

2 Set the wire strippers to the correct gauge and remove about 9mm (³⁄₈in) of insulation from the cores. Sleeve the earth core in green/yellow PVC.

3 Connect the three cores to the relevant terminals of the socket, making sure no exposed core is showing. Then screw the socket into position.

the back you can use a long steel cold chisel to chip out a groove. You'll then have to drill down through the end of the floorboard with a wood bit. Alternatively, you can use a long masonry bit with an electric drill to complete the task.

But if the floor is solid, the ring is usually in the ceiling void above, in which case the branch will drop down from the ceiling. And this will involve a considerable amount of channelling out if you want to install the new socket near floor level.

Stud partition walls also present a few problems. If the socket is near the floor, you should be able to get a long drill bit through the hole you cut for the socket to drill through the baseplate and floorboard. You can then thread the cable through. But if the socket is to be placed higher up the wall, noggings and sound insulation material may prevent the cable being drawn through the cavity. In this case you will probably have to surface-mount the cable.

In fact, surface-mounting is the easiest method of running the cable. All you do is fix special plastic conduit to the wall and lay the cable inside before clipping on the lid. But many people regard this as an ugly solution.

When laying cable under ground floor floorboards you should clip it to the sides of the joists about 50mm (2in) below the surface so that it doesn't droop on the ground. Cable in the ceiling void can rest on the surface.

When you have to cross joists, you'll need to drill 16mm (5/8in) holes about 50mm (2in) below the level of the floorboards. The cable is threaded through them and so is well clear of any floorboard fixing nails.

Connecting into the circuit

If you use a junction box, you'll need one with three terminals inside. You have to connect the live conductors (those with red insulation) of the circuit cable and the spur to one terminal, the neutral conductors (black insulation) to another, and the earth wires to the third. Sleeve the earth wires in green/yellow PVC first.

You might decide that it's easier to connect into the back of an existing socket rather than use a junction box, although this will probably mean some extra channelling on the wall. Space is limited at the back of a socket so it may be difficult to fit the conductors to the relevant terminals. However, this method is ideal if the new socket that you're fitting on one wall is back-to-back with an existing fitting. By carefully drilling through the wall a length of cable can be linked from the old socket into the new.

SOCKET MOUNTINGS

Metal boxes are recessed into the wall and provide a fixing for the socket itself. Knockouts are provided in the back, sides and ends to allow the cable to enter the box. Rubber grommets are fitted round the hole so the cable doesn't chafe against the metal edges.

Elongated screw slots allow box to be levelled when fixed to wall.

Adjustable lugs enable final adjustments to level of faceplate on wall.

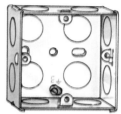

Boxes are usually 35mm deep, but with single-brick walls boxes 25mm deep should be used, along with accessories having deeper-than-usual faceplates.

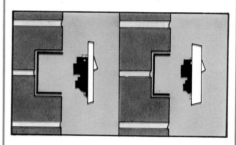

Lugs can be fitted to a metal box so that it can be fitted into stud partition walls.

Surface-mounted boxes (usually white plastic) are 35mm deep, and are simply screwed to the wall surface where required.

TIP: FIT SAFETY PLATES

Safety plates can be fitted to sockets to prevent young children playing with them.

PROBLEMS

● **Crumbly plaster** There's little that can be done other than cutting back to sound area. Position box and socket as required then make good surrounding area.
● **Poor bricks** Because of soft bricks you can quite easily chop out too big a recess for the box. Pack the recess with dabs of mortar or plaster.
● **Cavity Walls** To prevent breaking through into the cavity only chop out a recess big enough to take a shallow box, about 25mm (1in).

CONNECTING INTO THE CIRCUIT

1 *Unscrew a nearby socket to check that it's on the ring – normally there'll be two red, two black and two earth wires. Sometimes the earths are in one sleeve.*

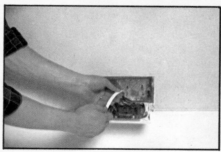

2 *Usually it's easier to push the new cable up into the mounting box from below the floor, although you might prefer to take it the other way.*

3 *Prepare the cores and sleeve the earth of the new cable, then connect them into the appropriate terminals on the back of the socket.*

4 *If installing a junction box use a three-terminal type. Connect the red conductors to one terminal, the blacks to another and the earths to a third.*

Keith Morris

INSTALLING SHAVER SOCKETS

If you want to use an electric shaver you'll have to install a special shaver socket. There are a number of different models available, some of which can be installed in a bathroom.

shaver supply unit from MK Electric

A shaver socket is merely an outlet point designed to accept the kind of two pin plugs that are fitted to electric shavers. You'll find that the two-hole socket is virtually universal and accepts a variety of different plugs, including those fitted to British, Australian, American and European shavers.

Types of shaver sockets
There are two principal types of shaver socket – the shaver supply unit and the shaver socket outlet. In addition, there are some models of shaver striplights, which are designed to fit next to a mirror, that include shaver sockets and there are fused shaver adaptors which are similar to 13A plugs except that they have a shaver socket on their backs.

The *shaver supply unit* is designed specially for safe operation in the bathroom. As such, it's the only socket outlet that's allowed there, which means that the shaver is the only mains-operated, portable appliance that should be used in the bathroom.

The reason why the unit is safe for a bathroom is quite simple: it incorporates an isolating transformer which has the effect of providing an earth-free electricity supply at the outlet. This means that there is no direct link between the appliance or socket and the mains supply, so that if your shaver does go wrong, there is virtually no chance of you getting a shock. And, with a maximum current output of 20W, a shaver supply unit is restricted to use for shavers only. If, for example, you try to fit a shaver plug onto some other sort of portable appliance, such as an electric fire or television, a self-resetting overload device will operate.

The usual voltage of the supply unit is 240V, but dual voltage models are available for use with both 240V and 115V shavers. These usually have a switch enabling you to select which voltage you want, but some models have a three-hole socket and the shaver plug is inserted into the centre hole and one of the others according to the voltage required.

The *shaver socket outlet* is similar to the supply unit and performs the same function. However, there is one major difference:

because it does not incorporate an isolating transformer it cannot be installed in a bathroom or washroom. Most shaver socket outlets, however, do incorporate a self-resetting thermal overload device that limits the current to 0.2A and is protected by a 2A fuse. Some poorer quality units have only a fuse to protect them, so it's a good idea to check that you have the safest model before installing one.

Shaver strip lights, which have a built-in shaver socket, have either miniature fluorescent tubes or tungsten filament strip lamps. There are two main types. The first contains an isolating transformer and is designed for use in bathrooms, while the other has no transformer and is suitable for any other room. Like the shaver supply unit, some models have a three-hole, dual voltage shaver outlet, while others have just a single 240V outlet. Both types have a self-resetting thermal overload device for the shaver socket, while the light itself is controlled by a cord switch.

A shaver adaptor is merely a standard 13A three-pin plug that has a two-hole socket on its back into which a shaver's two-pin plug will fit. Like all shaver socket outlets, the holes are shuttered and as a precaution marked 'shavers only'. These adaptors are

certainly convenient if you're travelling in the UK, but it's not really a good idea to use them as a permanent substitute for a shaver socket as they don't have a thermal overload cut out. And, of course, as no mains socket outlets are allowed in a bathroom, shaver adaptors can't be used there.

Obtaining the power
The best method of obtaining power for your supply unit is to use a non-fused spur from the ring circuit.

You should use 2.5mm² two-core and earth PVC-sheathed cable and link into the nearest socket to the bathroom. Before doing this, however, you must switch off the mains. Then remove the socket from its mounting box to check that it's on the ring circuit.

This is quite easily done. If you're dealing with a single gang socket outlet, one cable entering means that it's on the end of a spur; two cables show that it could be either on the ring or else be an intermediate socket on a spur, and three cables entering the socket indicate that it is on the ring and already has a spur from it. With a double socket, one cable shows it's on a spur and therefore you can't connect a new socket from it, two that it's on the ring and therefore suitable for a spur,

262

FOUR WAYS OF OBTAINING POWER

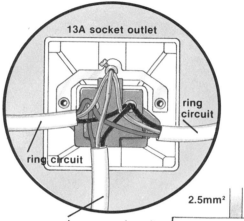

13A socket outlet

ring circuit

ring circuit

shaver supply unit

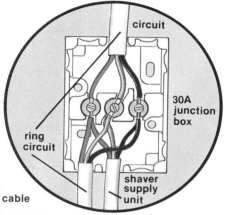

circuit

30A junction box

ring circuit

shaver supply unit

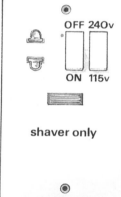

2.5mm² cable

OFF 240v

ON 115v

shaver only

shaver only

200-250v. ac

From a non-fused spur

Above: After switching off at the mains, find the nearest 13A socket to the bathroom and check it's on the ring circuit. Then connect the cores of 2.5mm² two-core and earth cable to their respective terminals and run it to the supply unit or shaver socket.

From a junction box

Below: You can easily supply either type of unit by inserting a junction box into the lighting circuit. The circuit you use depends on the position of the socket, but you need use only 1.0mm² two-core and earth cable to take the power to the socket.

From a 30A junction box

Above: If you can't conveniently run a spur from a socket, insert a junction box into the ring circuit and again use 2.5mm² two-core and earth cable to supply the unit. Lift the floorboards near the socket to gain access to the ring circuit.

From a connection unit

Below: For shaver sockets only, take a spur from a ring circuit and connect the 2.5mm² two-core and earth cable to the 'supply' side of a non-switched connection unit fitted with a 3A fuse. Then run 1.0mm² cable from the 'load' side to the socket.

shaver socket

1.0mm² cable

junction box

fused connection unit

linking cable

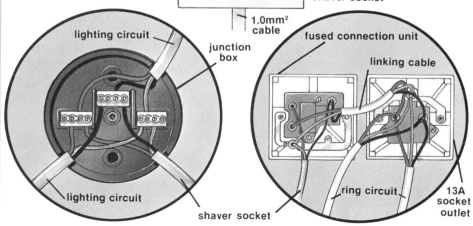

lighting circuit

lighting circuit

shaver socket

ring circuit

13A socket outlet

Ready Reference

BATHROOM ELECTRICS

The bathroom can be one of the most dangerous places for electrics unless you follow the stringent regulations. Remember:
● the only socket allowed in a bathroom is a shaver supply unit
● the only plug that can be used in a bathroom is a shaver plug
● the only portable appliance that can be used in it is an electric shaver
● other than the rocker switches on a shaver supply unit, all switches must be cord switches.

shaver supply unit

13A socket outlet

OFF 240v
ON 115v
shaver only

switch

ceiling switch

13A plug

shaver plug

13A plug

hairdrier and plug

electric shaver and plug

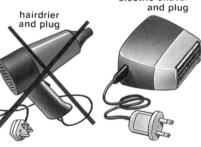

Shaver plugs provide the link between the socket and the shaver.

Sockets will accommodate most types of shaver plugs, including those fitted on Australian, American and European electric shavers.

INSTALLING A SHAVER SUPPLY UNIT

1 *Check your wall is thick enough to take the unit's mounting box. Then mark its position and use a club hammer and chisel to make the hole.*

2 *You can then chop out the chase for the conduit and cable. Drill holes for the mounting box to the back of the recess and insert wall plugs.*

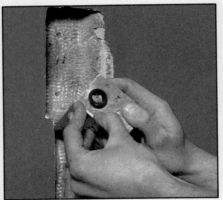

3 *Remove a blank in the base of the mounting box to admit the cable. Remember to fit a grommet to protect the cable from chafing.*

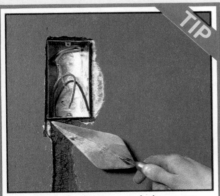

4 *As both the recess and chase are almost 50mm (2in) deep, making good should be done in two stages: use mortar first and then filler.*

5 *You should then connect the cores to their respective terminals. Make sure you add an extra earth core to earth the box and unit completely.*

6 *You can now screw the shaver supply unit to its mounting box. If you wish to, you can repaint or repaper before putting the unit back.*

and three that it's on the ring and already has a spur from it. If you're in any doubt as to which cable is which you'll have to trace the cable runs.

Most terminals should be able to accommodate a third cable core, but if you have any difficulty in running a new cable into the existing socket then it's probably better to lift a floorboard adjacent to the nearest socket and insert a 30A junction box into one of the ring cables. Another alternative is to use a suitable loop-in ceiling rose or junction box in the lighting circuit. In this case you would only have to use 1.0mm² two-core and earth PVC cable.

Whichever way you pick up the power, the cable should run either under the floor or in the ceiling void to a point below or above the unit (for fuller details see pages 274-277). It should then be chased into the wall and run to the unit itself.

Installing a shaver supply unit

Supply units can be either flush or surface-mounted. If you intend to flush – fit the unit in a metal mounting box recessed in the wall you must make sure that your wall is thick enough to take it. When you're sure that it is, you can cut a chase in the wall so that the front edge of the box is flush with the wall surface. If the wall is tiled, it's a good idea to centre the box at the junction of four tiles and cut a section from the corner of each to give a neater finish. You should then drill and plug the necessary holes before fixing the box to the wall with wood screws.

Before you actually fit the box, however, don't forget to remove a blank from one of the knockout holes so you can insert the cable. It's also wise to fit a grommet onto the sharp edges of the holes so the cable can't chafe against them. Having cut a chase for the cable and prepared it (not forgetting to

sleeve the earth in green/yellow PVC), connect the cores to their respective terminals and fit the unit to the box with the screws provided. The procedure for fitting a surface-mounted supply unit is exactly the same except that the plastic mounting box is screwed to the wall surface.

Shaver socket circuit

A shaver socket is supplied from the lighting circuit, so all that's required is to run 1.0mm² two-core and earth PVC cable from either a loop-in ceiling rose or a lighting circuit junction box. Which lighting circuit you choose to extend depends on the position of the shaver socket. But it's worth remembering that an unlimited number of shaver sockets may be supplied from one cable – which means that you can install one in each bedroom merely by looping in and out of each socket in turn. In fact, the back of the socket has

INSTALLING A SHAVER SOCKET

1 *Using a club hammer and cold chisel, cut a recess and chase approximately 30mm (1¼in) deep to take the mounting box and conduit.*

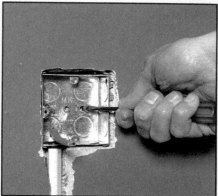

2 *Drill the holes and plug them. Before fixing the box to the wall with wood screws, put a grommet into the knockout hole.*

3 *Do the making good and make the connections. In the case of a shaver socket the earth core is connected directly to the mounting box.*

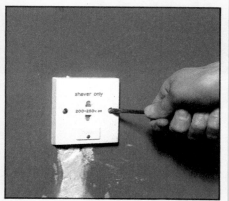

4 *Fix the socket to its mounting box. Remember that you can fit other sockets easily by looping in and out of each one of them.*

extra cable holes expressly for this purpose. The sockets can be fixed at whatever level you find most convenient. If you want to fit one low on the wall, it's best to tap into the circuit supplying the lights in the room below – as the cables are likely to be under the floorboards. But if you want one at a higher level, tap into the lighting circuit in the same room – as the cables will be in the ceiling void or roof space.

You'll have to make sure that you have a ceiling rose with a loop-in system and if you don't, look for a junction box. If you have neither then you'll have to insert a new junction box in the circuit feed cable.

There is another option. This involves replacing the one-gang box of a single 13A socket outlet with a dual mounting box. Using 2.5mm² cable you can then join the original socket to the 'supply' side of a non-switched, fused connection unit (fitted with a

3A fuse to add greater protection). Then run, 1.0mm² cable from the 'load' side of the unit to the shaver socket.

The socket itself is fixed to the wall and connected in much the same way as a conventional 13A single socket outlet (for further details see pages 258-261).

Shaver strip light

A shaver strip light is supplied by 1.0mm² two-core and earth PVC-sheathed cable run from a loop-in ceiling rose or junction box in the lighting circuit or else from a fused connection unit on the ring circuit. It should be fixed either at the side or above a shaving mirror in the bathroom or bedroom. The end of the cable should be prepared in the normal way and then passed simply through the cable entry hole so it can be connected to the live, neutral and earth screws on the terminal block.

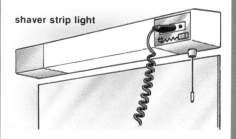

ADDING NEW POWER CIRCUITS

A radial circuit can provide power for individual appliances such as cookers, immersion heaters and freezers, or can give you extra socket outlets for plug-in equipment. It's an easy job to install one.

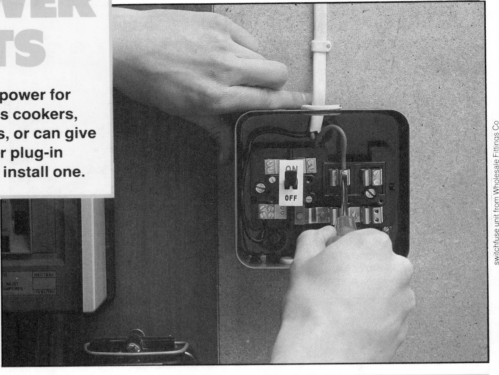

Radial circuits have only one cable running from the consumer unit (fuse box) to the power outlet because the circuit terminates at the last outlet. In this way they differ from the more common ring circuit as their cable doesn't have to return to the consumer unit. Installing one can therefore save you both cable and extra work (see pages 232-236 for more details).

Before ring circuits were introduced the radial circuit was the standard domestic power circuit. There were fewer sockets and electrical appliances to be supplied than nowadays and a number of radial circuits each supplying an individual outlet usually proved adequate. As more and more electrical appliances came on the market, so the ring circuit was developed to cope with the greater current demands in the modern home. Nowadays, the ring circuit is the more common power circuit.

However, a new radial circuit is especially useful when you want to fit extra fixed electrical appliances such as a deep freeze or immersion heater, supply a couple of new sockets or else provide power for an extension to your home. That way you don't have to run spurs from an existing ring circuit and you avoid the possibility of overloading that circuit through heavy demand.

Types of radial circuits

There are two basic types of radial circuit. These are the 'solo' circuit, which provides power to one fixed appliance such as an immersion heater, cooker or freezer, and the power circuit which can help out a ring circuit or provide power to new sockets and appliances. The second type is itself divided into two kinds. The first is the 20A circuit. This uses 2.5mm² cable and can supply an unlimited number of 13A socket outlets (or fixed appliances using up to 3kW of power) – provided they are all within a floor area of 20 sq m (about 215 sq ft). The second type is the 30A radial circuit, which uses 4.0mm² cable and can carry power to a floor area up to 50 sq m (540 sq ft). If you look round your home you will see that these restrictions

POWER SUPPLY FOR RADIAL CIRCUITS.

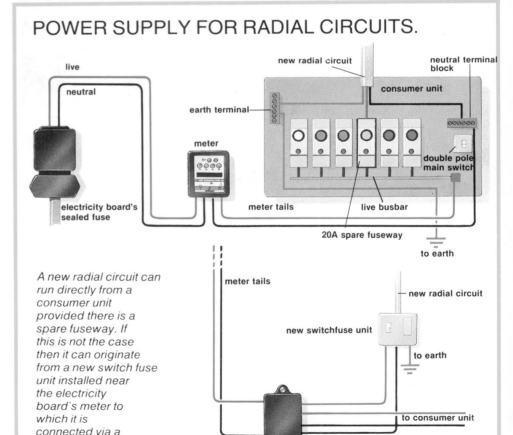

A new radial circuit can run directly from a consumer unit provided there is a spare fuseway. If this is not the case then it can originate from a new switch fuse unit installed near the electricity board's meter to which it is connected via a distribution board.

USING A SPARE FUSEWAY

1 *After you've had the mains supply cut off, remove the consumer unit cover, lift the mounting plate forward and remove the live busbar.*

2 *Slide the units along the busbar to make space for the new MCB or fuse. Remember to arrange the units in the correct current rating sequence.*

3 *Fit the new MCB unit onto the mounting plate, making sure that it's in the right place. Then screw back the live busbar underneath the units.*

4 *Finally refit the mounting plate and connect the cable to the correct terminals. Get the electricity board to reconnect and test the circuit.*

consumer unit and meter from Mk

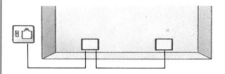
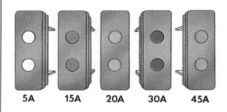
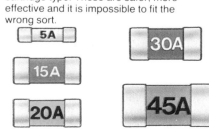
mean that several radial circuits would have to be installed to supply power to all the sockets and appliances supplied by a normal ring circuit. So radial circuits really come into their own when you want to supply power to fixed appliances. And radial circuits can be modified to cope with heavy demand. So, if you want to have a large cooker you will probably have to run a radial circuit that has been 'beefed' up and will use a 45A fuse and 6.0 or 10.0mm² cable.

Obtaining the power

If you want to install a new radial circuit you'll need a circuit fuseway. First check whether you have a spare (unconnected) one in the consumer unit. If so, check its current rating (see below). If not, you'll have to install a new main switch and fuse unit near the consumer unit and connect it separately. If you have to do this then it might be an idea to install one

with two or more fuseways to save work if you are planning any future extension to your domestic wiring. If you decide to do this it is a good idea to blank off the fuseway you are not using or else fit another MCB or fuse unit without connecting it. Whatever you do, before inspecting or working on the consumer unit you must turn off the main switch.

If there is a spare fuseway it may well be sealed off with a blanking plate or else there might be a fuse unit or MCB without any circuit connections. If you use offpeak electricity for heating then you will have two consumer units and it's very important to make sure that you use the correct one. The unit supplying the night storage heaters will be on a restricted time switch and if you connect to that, you will only get power to your circuit at night. Not a very good idea if it is supplying a freezer for example.

USING A NEW SWITCHFUSE UNIT

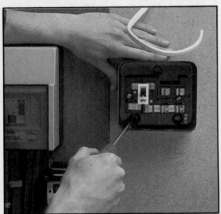

1 The new switchfuse unit should be mounted on a sheet of non-combustible material such as fire-resistant chipboard or asbestos.

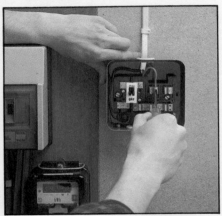

2 Knock out a panel at the top of the new unit and fix a protective grommet before running in the new circuit cable and making the connections.

3 You will have to use extra single core cable (6.0mm^2) to connect the unit to the distribution board as you are allowed only two tails to the meter.

4 Screw on the colour-coded shields for the new MCBs. It's an idea to fit a new unit with a spare fuseway for an extra circuit in the future.

5 Fit the cover over the unit and then slot in the new MCBs or fuse unit. You can fit a blanking plate until you decide to use the spare fuseway.

6 Screw on the smaller shield to protect the new MCBs. Remember, you'll probably have to knock out its lid to allow access to the MCBs.

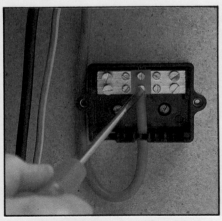

7 Fix the distribution board and then connect the live core from the switchfuse unit and the live meter tail to the live terminal block.

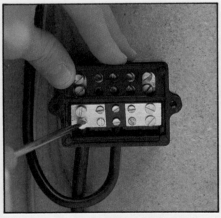

8 Fit the neutral terminal block and base plate which hold the live block in place, and then connect the remaining neutral cores to the block.

9 Connect the earths and then get the electricity board to connect the old meter tails to the distribution board and the new tails to the meter.

Using a spare fuseway

If you are connecting to a spare fuseway, you must check that it has the equivalent current rating to the circuit running from it. Most modern fuses have two spots on their cases to indicate their current rating: white indicates a 5A rating; blue 15A; yellow 20A; red 30A and green 45A. If it's not the correct rating for the circuit you're installing, you'll have to insert a new one. There is the chance that your consumer unit is so old that it could be obsolete. In that case, if you have a spare fuseway in it you will be able to use it only for a new circuit that has the equivalent current rating. Circuit fuses are either the rewirable type or the cartridge type and when buying a new one it is best to get the latter as they are safer and more effective.

The new radial circuit starts at the fuse unit and runs in two-core and earth PVC-sheathed cable, the size of which is determined by the circuit's current rating. A 5A circuit should be run in 1.0mm² cable, 15A in 1.5mm², 20A in 2.5mm² and 30A in 4.0mm², provided that the circuit fuse is a cartridge type or an MCB protects the circuit. Any circuit with a higher rating should be run in 6.0mm² or 10.0mm² cable.

For detailed advice on how to run cable under floors, in ceiling voids and down walls see pages 274-277. Where you are using larger cable for a beefed up circuit, it might be a good idea to measure the length of cable required fairly precisely – this is because the larger the cable, the more expensive it is. Allow sufficient for connecting the cable within the consumer unit and in the mains outlet, and add a little extra for contingencies, for example, hidden obstructions.

The choice of mains outlet depends upon its situation and the appliance supplied. For example, a 13A socket is fine for any appliance up to 3kW, but cannot be used in the bathroom where the only socket permitted is one for a shaver. An immersion heater with a dual element, say, should have a 20A dual switch as its outlet.

Connecting to the spare fuseway

The spare fuseway in the consumer unit will usually be at the end of the row of units and furthest away from the main switch. Units should be placed in the correct rating sequence, with those of the largest current rating (45A) next to the mainswitch, and those of the lowest, (5A) at the other end. The new circuit should be located in sequence, and this might well entail moving the units. With some boxes the fuses slide along a 'top hat' bar after the screws have been released, and in others, the units are simply removed and refixed in their new positions. Turning off the main switch renders all live parts dead, but in some units, where the

mains terminals (to which the meter leads connect) are not recessed, there is still a shock risk even if those main terminals are shrouded. So, in addition to turning off the main switch, it is sometimes advisable to get the electricity board to cut off the mains supply before you work on the consumer unit. Then, when they restore the power, you can ask them to test the new circuit. After you've rearranged the fuse units, thread in the circuit cable and strip off the outer sleeving, leaving about 25mm (1in) within the unit. Trim the cores by stripping off 10mm (⅜in) of insulation, and connect the red core to the fuseway terminal of the new unit and the black to the neutral terminal block. The earth should be sleeved in green and yellow PVC and connected to the earth terminal block. The cable can now be run to the circuit outlet, but remember, it is best to complete all the work at the outlet end of the circuit before connecting up. That way power is off for the shortest possible time and causes least inconvenience.

Unless there is plenty of room on your backing board, you will have to fit a sheet of non-combustible material, such as treated chipboard, to your wall to provide a base for the unit and prevent fire risk.

Installing a switchfuse unit

After choosing a switchfuse unit containing an MCB or cartridge fuse of the same current rating as the new circuit, fix it to the wall using No 8 wood screws with wall plugs. The unit should be sited close to the electricity board's meter so that the meter leads bringing power to the new unit are as short as possible. When the electricity board come to connect the new meter leads they might well require a distribution board to be fitted so that the power coming through the meter can be divided up and fed to both units. For the mains leads use 16mm² single core PVC-sheathed cable – one red and one black. They should be connected to the live and neutral terminals of the unit respectively, and you should use 6.0mm² green-and-yellow-sheathed cable for the connection to the earth terminal.

Sections of thin plastic will have to be knocked out to admit these cables and a blank will also have to removed at the top of the unit to allow for the entry of the circuit cable. It's a good idea to connect this cable before fitting the unit to the wall. Connect the red core of the circuit cable to the fuseway terminal, the black to the upper neutral terminal and the sleeved earth conductor to the earth terminal. If you are using a fuseway and an MCB, double-check that you have the correct one and then replace the cover. Finally, call the electricity board to connect the meter leads to the mains and test the circuit.

WIRING FOR COOKERS

Installing the wiring for a new electric cooker is not such a daunting task as it seems. The mains circuitry is similar for freestanding and built-in cookers, and the final connection is simplicity itself to make.

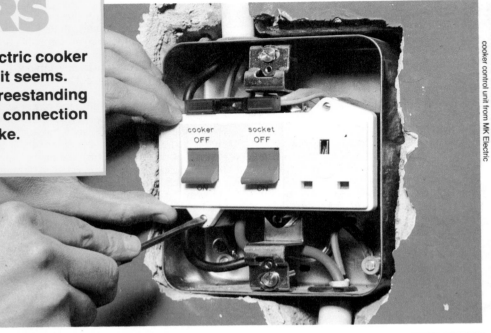

cooker control unit from MK Electric

There are two main types of electric cooker which you will come across in the showrooms. The first is the traditional, freestanding electric cooker which consists of an oven, a hob with three or four boiling rings or hot plates, and a grill that is either at eye-level or else just above the oven. This type is self-contained and usually stands against a wall in the kitchen. The second type is the split-level cooker, and a separate hob and oven are normally built into the kitchen units. In addition to these two there are smaller, table-top models which have only two hot plates, and the increasingly popular microwave ovens.

Cooker circuits

Because cookers are heavy current consuming appliances, they require a radial circuit for their exclusive use. This will run from the consumer unit, provided there is a spare MCB or fuseway, or else from a separate switch fuse unit. A circuit like this may already exist, but it is more likely you will have to install it.

Small cookers that can rest on the top of a kitchen unit, and micro-wave ovens, can be run without a special circuit. This is because they have an electrical loading of 3kW or less and when that is converted into current rating (see below) you will find that they can safely get their power supply from a 13A socket outlet. But before you install a new radial circuit (see pages 266-269 for further details) you will have to make sure that it is of the correct rating.

Circuit current rating

A small electric cooker with, say two boiling rings, a grill and an oven, is likely to have an electrical loading of around 10kW, while a fully equipped cooker with a double oven will probably have a rating of 14kW or more. A cooker that rates up to 11kW is usually supplied by a circuit controlled by a 30A fuse, while one with a higher rating is supplied by a 45A circuit. The current rating of the circuit is determined by the maximum current demand from the cooker. To determine that, the total wattage is divided by the voltage of the mains electricity

CHOOSING CABLE RUNS

The cable and switching arrangements for cookers differ depending on whether you have a freestanding cooker or separate hob and oven sections.

1 Freestanding cooker

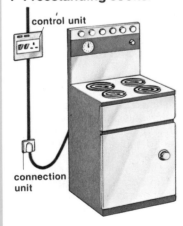

Above: A connection unit allows the trailing cable to join the chased cable, protects the connections and allows the cooker to be easily disconnected for repairs.

2 Separate hob and oven

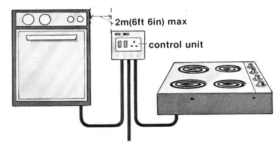

If you want the control unit centred between the sections, run two cables from the control unit, using 6mm² cable; the circuit must originate at a cartridge fuse or MCB.

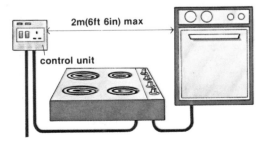

Another method is to run just one cable from the control unit and loop it in and out of one section and then run it onto the second section.

INSTALLING A COOKER CONTROL UNIT

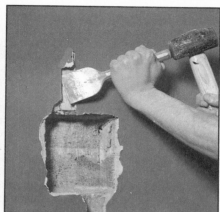

1 Using a club hammer and cold chisel, chop a recess for the mounting box and chases for the circuit cable and the cable to the connection unit.

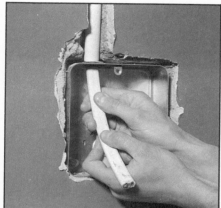

2 Drill and plug holes in the wall before fitting the box. Remember to put grommets on the knockout holes and run the cable inside conduit.

3 Detach the unit from its faceplate to make the connections on the mains side. Earth the box by linking its earth screw with the earth terminal.

4 Then make the connections on the cooker side. Remember to sleeve all the earth cores in green/yellow PVC before connecting them.

5 When you've made all the connections, make sure the unit is square to the wall and then screw it securely onto the mounting box.

6 You can now fix the centre part of the face plate. Before fixing the rest, make good and redecorate the surface of the wall.

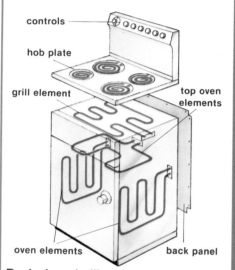

THE CONNECTION UNIT

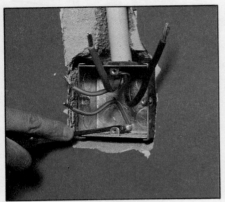

1 *Chop the recess for the box and the chase for the cable. Then run in the cable and earth the box to give it extra protection.*

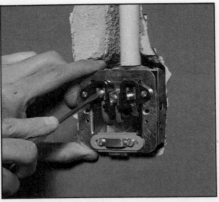

2 *Connect the earths to the centre terminals and other cores to the outer two. If you aren't connecting the cooker yet, fit the unit's cover.*

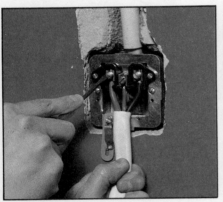

3 *Undo the clamp and hold in place the trailing cooker cable while you connect it. Remember, it should be the same size as the circuit cable.*

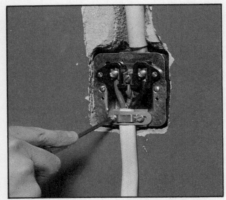

4 *Screw up the clamp plate to hold the cable and protect the connections. Make good before fitting the cover, which should cover any ragged edges.*

supply. So, if you have a 12kW cooker, dividing 12,000 by 240 indicates that, in theory at least, the cooker should be supplied by a 50A circuit. In addition, if the cooker control unit incorporates a 13A socket outlet, the total current demand reaches 63A. However, in practice allowance is made for the fact that the boiling rings, the oven, and the grill will rarely be used all at the same time. And, even if they are, the current demand will still be less than 63A because peak demand is reduced by thermostatic devices incorporated in the cooker.

In fact, when calculations are being made for the current demand of a domestic electric cooker, the wiring regulations take account of this. Therefore, the 12kW cooker, theoretically rated at 63A, is actually reckoned to have a current demand of 27A. That means it can be supplied safely by a circuit controlled by a 30A fuse or MCB.

The new circuit

Cooker circuits are normally run in two-core and earth PVC-sheathed cable. It's best to use 6mm² cable for a 30A circuit and 10mm² for a 45A one. The circuit cable runs from the consumer unit to a cooker control unit or control switch, taking the shortest possible route. This could be under the floorboards or in the ceiling void. You could either run the cable in a chase chopped in the wall or else surface mount it by using either mini-trunking or cable clips. Obviously it looks much neater to have your cable concealed within conduit beneath the surface of the wall. For more detailed information on running cable see pages 274-277.

Do remember that this larger size cable can be quite expensive and before buying it, it's a good idea to measure fairly precisely the length you will require, and to aim for the most economical cable run in your planning.

However, you ought to allow a surplus for contingency purposes should you encounter obstacles when you run the circuit.

Cooker control units and switches

You will be able to control the power for your electric cooker from a cooker control unit or a cooker switch. A control unit has two switches, one of which controls the power to the cooker, while the other controls the power supply to a 13A socket outlet that is incorporated in the unit. A cooker control switch is an alternative to this sort of unit and is merely a double-pole switch marked 'cooker'. While it's more convenient to fit a control unit with an extra socket, there is the danger of having the kettle flex trailing across a switched on boiling ring and so risking fire. If you're planning to install a free-standing cooker, a special connector unit is fitted at the end of the chased cable run and from it cable is run on to the cooker. The advantage of this is that if you want to repair or replace your cooker all you have to do is disconnect it at the unit after switching off at the control unit or cooker switch. A connector like this also provides special clamps to prevent any unnecessary strain being put on the terminals when the cooker is moved out from the wall.

An alternative is to use a cable outlet unit which clamps the cable and allows it to run to the cooker without a break.

Position of the control unit

The traditional height for a cooker control unit is about 1.5m (5ft) above the floor so that it can be reached easily. It shouldn't be any closer than 300mm (1ft) to the cooker but mustn't be more than 2m (6ft) away from it. One control unit or switch may supply both sections of a split-level cooker, provided that both of them are within 2m (6ft) of the unit. As the control unit is usually sited midway between the two sections it means that they can be up to 4m (13ft) apart – which allows for considerable scope in kitchen planning. When the control unit is fixed between the two cooker sections, two cables can be run from the unit supplying the oven and hob sections respectively. But if the unit is fixed at the side of one of the sections then one cable is used to connect that and another links into it to provide power for the second section. However, the same size cable is used throughout. Another alternative is to install both a cooker control unit and a cooker switch. The main cooker circuit will still run from the consumer unit or switchfuse unit to the cooker control unit, and from there a cable of the same size will run to one of the sections. Another cable will loop out of the control unit and link the cooker switch into the circuit. Finally, a cable from the switch will then run to the second section.

If you are installing an island hob unit,

CONNECTING UP THE COOKER

1 After removing the cooker's back plate, sleeve the earth core in green/yellow PVC and then connect the cores to their respective terminals.

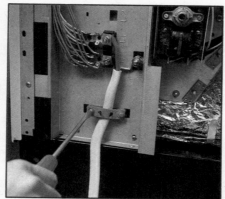

2 Fix the cable under the clamp plate to give the connections extra protection. Then put on the back plate and switch on at the mains.

then this is obviously a more convenient circuit arrangement than running two new radial circuits.

Connecting to the control unit

If you are fitting a flush-mounted unit you will have to sink a metal mounting box into a chase chopped into the plaster and masonry. Obviously the size and depth of the box depends on the type and model of unit you decide to use. Because the mounting boxes are quite deep, chop the recess out carefully on internal walls, or consider using a surface-mounted box instead. Before finally fixing the box into the wall, do remember to remove the necessary knockout blanks to allow in the various cables – usually two for a freestanding cooker and three for a split-level one – and to fix with plastic grommets into the holes to protect those cables.

For surface mounting a control unit, a plastic mounting box has to be fixed to the wall with wood screws. The circuit cable should run down from the ceiling or up from the floor and should be chased into the wall. Take it into the box and strip off the sheathing, leaving about 25mm (1in) within the box. If you're fitting a surface-mounted box unit it's easier to take the unit out of its box to make the connection. Trim the wires to about 18mm (¾in) and strip 12mm (½in) of insulation from the end of each core. The earth cores should be enclosed in green/yellow PVC sleeving and connected to the earth terminal. The two insulated cores are connected to the terminals marked MAINS, with the red going to L and black to N. The cores of the cable, or cables, running to the cooker are connected to the equivalent terminals, marked COOKER, on the lower side of the control unit. These cables should be

secured under the clamp (ie, incorporated in the unit). After you've connected the cables to the control unit, refit it in its box and fit the cover.

Wiring up the connector unit

The cable from the cooker control unit should be chased into the wall and run to the connector unit. Insert both the cable from the control unit and that leading to the cooker itself into the box. After preparing the ends, connect the sleeved earth cores to the centre terminal, the red insulated cores to one of the outer terminals, and the black insulated cores to the other. Then tighten the clamp screws that secure the trailing cable and replace the unit's cover. Double check this because if the clamp is on the individual cores and not the sheathing it could damage the connections.

Connecting to the cooker

At the back of a freestanding cooker there is a panel which must be removed to allow entry for the cable through the grommetted entry hole. Prepare the cable as you did when you connected to the cooker control unit, not forgetting to add an extra sleeve of green/yellow PVC to insulate the earth core. Then connect the red core to the terminal marked L, the black to the one marked N, and the earth core to the terminal marked E. Again, remember to secure the cable under the cable clamp before refitting the panel as this gives vital protection to the connections if the cooker is moved away from the wall at any time. If you are installing a split-level cooker the connections are basically the same as for a freestanding model, although the position of the terminal blocks may well vary from model to model.

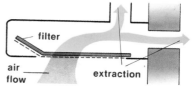
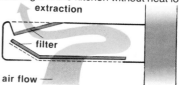

LAYING CABLE

The hardest part of the average electrical job is running the cables: it takes up a lot of time and a lot of effort. But there are certain techniques used by experts which can make it much easier.

Before you get involved in the details of how to install the wiring, there's one simple question you must answer. Does it matter if the cable runs show? This is because there are only two approaches to the job of running cable. Either you fix the cable to the surface of the wall, or you conceal it. The first option is far quicker and easier but doesn't look particularly attractive; it's good enough for use in, say, an understairs cupboard. For a neater finish, using this method, you can smarten up the cable runs by boxing them in with some trunking. Many people, however, prefer to conceal the wiring completely by taking it under the floor, over the ceiling, or in walls.

TYPICAL CABLE RUNS

More and more electrical equipment is now being used in the home. And the chances are that sooner or later you will want to install a new power point, wall or ceiling light, or another switch. In which case you will have to get power to your new accessory. To do that will involve running cable from an existing circuit or installing a completely new one. Running cable to a new appliance can be the hardest part of any job and, as the illustration on the right shows, you will be involved in trailing cable across the roof space or ceiling void, channelling it down walls and threading it behind partitions as well as taking it under floorboards. But it's much easier than it seems. There are a number of tricks of the trade that will make any electrical job simpler and less time consuming. For example, once you can 'fish' cable, the daunting task of running it under a floor is simple.

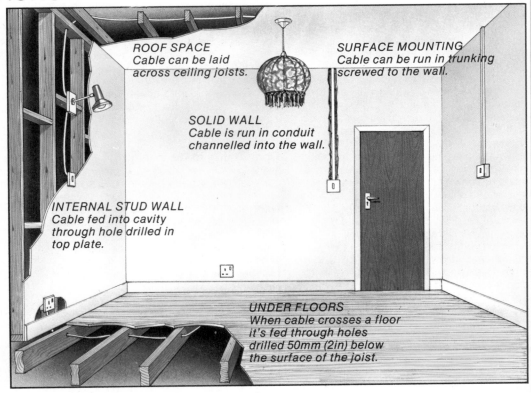

ROOF SPACE
Cable can be laid across ceiling joists.

SURFACE MOUNTING
Cable can be run in trunking screwed to the wall.

SOLID WALL
Cable is run in conduit channelled into the wall.

INTERNAL STUD WALL
Cable fed into cavity through hole drilled in top plate.

UNDER FLOORS
When cable crosses a floor it's fed through holes drilled 50mm (2in) below the surface of the joist.

SURFACE MOUNTING CABLE

1 *To run cable in trunking, cut the trunking to length and fix the channel half to the wall with screws and wall plugs at 450mm (18in) centres.*

2 *Run the cable and press it firmly into the channel as far as it will go, carefully smoothing it out to avoid kinks and twists.*

3 *Next, snap the trunking's capping piece over the channelling, tapping it firmly along its length with your hand to lock it into place.*

4 *If the cable is to be on show, merely secure it every 225mm (9in) with cable clips. Fit them over the cable and drive home the fixing pins.*

Planning the route

Having made your decision you must now work out a suitable route for the cable to follow.

If it is to be surface-mounted – with or without trunking – run the cable around window and door frames, just above skirting boards and picture rails, down the corners of the room, or along the angle between wall and ceiling. This not only helps conceal the cable's presence, but also protects it against accidental damage. This last point is most important, and is the reason why you must never run cable over a floor.

With concealed wiring, the position is more complicated. When running cable under a floor or above a ceiling, you must allow for the direction in which the joists run – normally at right angles to the floorboards – and use an indirect route, taking it parallel to the joists and/or at right angles to them.

When running cable within a wall, the cable should *always* run vertically or horizontally from whatever it supplies, *never* diagonally.

Surface-mounting techniques

If you are leaving the cable on show, all you need do is cut it to length, and fix it to the surface with a cable clip about every 225mm (9in), making sure it is free from kinks and twists. With modern cable clips, simply fit the groove in the plastic block over the cable and drive home the small pin provided.

Surface mounting cable within trunking involves a bit more work. Having obtained the right size of PVC trunking, build up the run a section at a time, cutting the trunking to length with a hacksaw. Once each piece is cut, separate it into its two parts – the

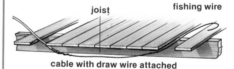

channelling and capping – and fix the channel to the wall with screws and wall plugs at roughly 450mm (18in) intervals (you may have to drill screw clearance holes in the channelling yourself).

Continue in this way until the run is complete. Turn corners by using proprietary fittings or by angling the ends of two pieces of trunking to form a neatly mitred joint, then run the cable. Press this firmly into the channel, and finish off by snapping the capping pieces firmly into place.

Concealing cables in walls

There are two ways to conceal cable in a wall. With a solid wall, chop a channel (called a 'chase') out of the plaster using a club hammer and bolster chisel, carefully continuing this behind any skirting boards, picture rails, and coverings. You could now run the cable in this chase and plaster over it. However, to give the cable some protection, it is better to fit a length of PVC conduit into the chase and run the cable through this before replastering.

To continue the run either above the ceiling or through the floor before you position the conduit, use a long drill bit so you can drill through the floor behind the skirting board. If a joist blocks the hole, angle the drill sufficiently to avoid it.

With a hollow internal partition wall, the job is rather easier, because you can run the cable within the cavity.

First drill a hole in the wall where the cable is to emerge, making sure you go right through into the cavity. Your next step is to gain access to the timber 'plate' at the very top of the wall, either by going up into the loft, or by lifting floorboards in the room above. Drill a 19mm (3⁄4in) hole through the plate, at a point vertically above the first hole, or as near vertically above it as possible.

All that remains is to tie the cable you wish to run to a length of stout 'draw' wire – single-core earth cable is often used – and then to tie the free end of this wire to a length of string. To the free end of the string, tie a small weight, and drop the weight through the hole at the top of the wall. Then all you do is make a hook in a piece of stout wire, insert it in the cavity, catch hold of the string and pull it (and in turn the draw wire and cable) through the hole in the room below.

What are the snags? There are two. You may find that, at some point between the two holes, the cavity is blocked by a horizontal timber called a noggin. If this happens, try to reach the noggin from above with a long auger bit (you should be able to hire one) and drill through it. Failing that, chisel through the wall surface, cut a notch in the side of the noggin, pass the cable through the notch, and then make good.

The second snag is that you may not be

CHASING OUT SOLID WALLS

1 *Mark out the cable run using a length of conduit, and chop a channel ('chase') in the wall to receive it, using a club hammer and a bolster chisel.*

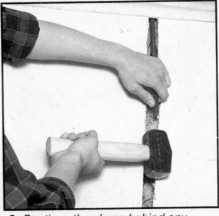

2 *Continue the chase behind any coving, skirting board, or picture rail by chipping out the plaster there with a long, narrow cold chisel.*

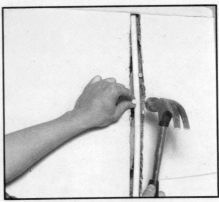

3 *Cut a length of PVC conduit to fit, and lay it in the chase, securing it temporarily with clout nails driven into the wall's mortar joints.*

4 *Pull the cable through the conduit, then make good the wall by filling in over the conduit with plaster or cellulose filler.*

able to reach the top plate to drill it. In which case, either give up the ideas of having concealed wiring, or try a variation on the second method used to run cable into the cavity from below the floor.

Here, it is sometimes possible to lift a couple of floorboards and drill up through the plate forming the bottom of the wall. Failing that you have to take a very long drill bit, drill through the wall into the cavity, then continue drilling through into the timber plate. You can now use the weighted string trick to feed the cable in through the hole in the wall, and out under the floor.

Running cable beneath a floor

The technique for running cable beneath a suspended timber floor depends on whether the floor is on an upper storey and so has a ceiling underneath, or is on a ground floor

with empty space below. If it's a ground floor, it may be possible to crawl underneath and secure the cable to the sides of the joists with cable clips, or to pass it through 19mm (3⁄4in) diameter holes drilled in the joists at least 50mm (2in) below their top edge. This prevents anyone nailing into the floor and hitting the cable.

If you cannot crawl underneath, then the cable can be left loose in the void. But how do you run it without lifting the entire floor? The answer is you use another trick, called 'fishing'.

For this, you need a piece of stiff but reasonably flexible galvanised wire, say 14 standard wire gauge (swg), rather longer than the intended cable run, and a piece of thicker, more rigid wire, about 1m in length. Each piece should have one end bent to form a hook.

Lift a floorboard at each end of the

COPING WITH STUD WALLS

1 Drill a hole in the wall where the cable is to emerge, then bore a second hole in the wooden plate forming the top of the wall.

2 Tie a weight to a length of string and lower this through the hole in the wall plate. Tie the free end of the string to a stout 'draw' wire.

3 If the weight gets blocked on its way to the hole in the wall, use a long auger bit to drill through the noggin obstructing it.

4 Fish out the weighted string through the hole in the wall, using a piece of wire bent to form a hook. Now, pull through the draw wire.

5 Tie the draw wire to the cable you wish to run, then return to the hole in the wall's top plate, and use the string to pull up the draw wire.

6 Then use the draw wire to pull the length of cable through. Remember, do this smoothly and don't use force if there's an obstruction.

proposed cable run and feed the longer piece of wire, hook end first, into the void through one of the resulting gaps in the floor. Hook it out through the second gap using the shorter piece of wire, and use it to pull through the cable in the same way as the draw wire used to pull cable through a hollow wall.

This technique is also used where there is a ceiling below the floor, and where you wish to run cable parallel to the joists, but in this case, check for any ribs and struts between the joists which might stop the fish wire getting through. Do this with the aid of a small mirror and a torch. If there is an obstruction, lift the floorboard above it, and drill a hole through which the cable can pass.

If the cable is to run at right angles to the joists, lift the floorboard above the line of the cable run, and feed the cable through holes drilled in the joists, 50mm (2in) below their top edge.

And what about solid floors? Obviously there is no way to run cable beneath these. Instead run the cable around the walls of the room, surface-mounting it just above the skirting board.

Running cable above a ceiling

Running cable above a ceiling is essentially the same as running it below a suspended timber floor. In fact, if there is a floor above the ceiling, it is generally easier to tackle the job from there, rather than from the room below.

If running the cable above the ceiling means taking it into the loft, then you can tackle it in much the same way as if you were running it below a suspended ground floor. If you cannot gain access to the loft, fish the cable through. If you can get into the loft, run the cable by hand, clipping it to the sides of the joists where it runs parallel to them.

You can run the cable at right angles to the joists by passing it through holes as already described, but this is frowned on by many electricians. Instead, they prefer to run it parallel to the joists as far as the 'binder' – the large timber cross-member linking the joists. They then clip the cable to the binder to traverse the ceiling, before running it to the desired position, again working parallel to the joists.

Unfortunately, there are situations in which running cable above a ceiling is almost impossible. The main ones are where the ceiling is solid concrete, as in many modern flats; where the ceiling is below a flat roof; and where, although there is a floor above the ceiling, you can't get at it (again this applies mainly to flats).

In the last two instances, if you intend the cable to run parallel to the joists, you may be able to fish it through. If not, you will have to treat the ceiling as if it were solid, and that means surface mounting the cable.

RUNNING CABLE UNDERGROUND

The most important part of taking power outside to a garden, a detached garage, or a workshop is running the electricity supply. An overhead cable run is a possibility, but taking it underground is the safer and more secure solution.

There are all sorts of reasons for taking a power supply out of doors. You may want to provide power to a garage so you can work on your car in light and warmth, or to transform your shed into an efficient workshop; you may require power sockets so you can use electrical power appliances in the garden, or a circuit to light your pool or garden fountain. Whatever you do involves running cable out of doors and this is bound to be the major part of any outside installation. There are three ways of running cable: overhead (for further details of overhead cable runs see pages 282-286), along a wall or underground. Running the cable underground is probably best, even if it involves the most installation work. That way it is concealed, cannot be disturbed and presents no danger whatsoever. But before you run the power supply, you'll have to decide which type of cable you want to use.

Underground cables

Three sorts of cable are suitable for running underground, and two of them can be laid directly in the ground without the need for further protection. PVC-covered mineral-insulated copper-covered cable (MICC) has a very small diameter and will pass conveniently through an airbrick, so avoiding the necessity of chopping a hole through the house wall. However, as the mineral insulation tends to absorb moisture, the ends of the cable have to be fitted with a special seal to prevent this. It is a complicated job for the do-it yourselfer to fit these seals and several special tools are required. The easiest thing to do is measure the cable run and ask your local electrical contractor for the length of cable with seals already fitted. This cable is usually two-core, as the copper sheathing provides adequate earth bonding and, as the cable run starts and ends in a metal conversion box (see below) which allows you to switch to ordinary PVC two-core and earth cable for indoor sections or for connection to accessories, each end should also be fitted with a screwed compression gland. These glands attach the cable to the box and provide the necessary earth continuity,. The cable usually has an outer

CABLE TYPES AND CONNECTIONS

Only PVC cable run in conduit (1) can be taken directly from the consumer unit to the switchfuse unit. If you use either PVC armoured cable (2) or mineral insulated copper cased cable (3) they must both be fitted with a gland and MICC with a seal and then run from a conversion box to another in the garage.

1 PVC cable

conduit

2 PVC armoured cable

armouring
gland
back-nut
coupler

3 MICC cable

copper casing
gland

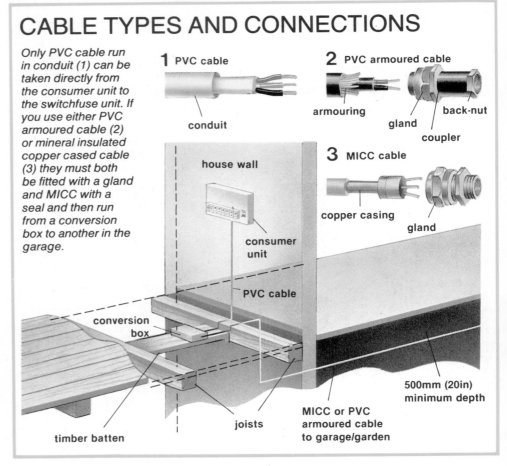

house wall

consumer unit

PVC cable

conversion box

timber batten

joists

MICC or PVC armoured cable to garage/garden

500mm (20in) minimum depth

covering of PVC, often orange in colour, and is slim enough to be fairly unobtrusive – if run on the surface to wall-mounted light fittings, for example.

PVC-covered wire-armoured insulated and sheathed cable needs no seals, but has to have glands fitted at each end where it, too, enters the conversion box. This cable often comes with only two cores, in which case the armouring serves as an earth, but it may well be better to run three-core armoured cable. If you are using the three-core version, you'll find that the insulation colours will be slightly different to ordinary cable. Live is red, neutral blue, and earth yellow. The cable itself is usually black.

Both these types of cable are protected enough to allow them to be laid directly in the ground. But if you use PVC-sheathed two-core and earth cable then you'll have to run it in either heavy gauge galvanised steel or high impact rigid plastic conduit. You'll undoubtedly find it easier to use the plastic conduit as the steel sort requires stocks, dies and bending equipment that is not normally available to the householder. When using plastic conduit, however, do remember that it's likely to fracture in temperatures of −5°C or below, and also that fairly substantial holes will have to be cut in both the exterior wall and the garage wall to admit the cable.

The indoor section

All power supplies that are run outside are classified as sub-main cables and must originate from a spare fuseway in the consumer unit, or else from a new switchfuse unit. For further details on this and on the size of cable to use see page 269.

The section inside the home will normally be run in ordinary PVC-sheathed two-core and earth cable which will be taken to the exit point. Obstructions inside the home can alter the route of the indoor cable but there are a number of straightforward methods (for example, fishing cable through a ceiling void) which can be employed if you don't have access from above.

For further details on running cable inside the house see pages 274-277.

When the cable is being taken underground, the exit point is likely to be where the ditch in which it will run starts against the house wall. However, the presence of a concrete terrace or some other obstruction may mean you'll have to change the proposed exit point (although it may be possible to take other measures, such as chopping a chase to protect the cable). It is important to note that only if you're running the outdoor section in PVC two-core and earth cable will it run directly from the switchfuse unit to the outside installation. Otherwise the indoor section must be taken right inside the conversion box.

Laying cable underground

Having drilled the exit point in the house wall, if you are running the power to a garage in the outbuilding, you'll have to dig a ditch in which to lay the cable. This should be at least 500mm (20in) deep, and digging it will probably be the most tiring part of the job! Try to avoid taking the cable under vegetable plots and flower beds where it could be disturbed; and obviously you won't want to dig up your lawn. Probably the best place for a ditch is at the side of a concrete or gravel path; but if you're forced to run it at the edge of a flower bed, dig the ditch somewhat deeper to give the cable extra protection. If you're using either PVC-armoured cable or MICC cable, it's a good idea to place the cable on a layer of sand at the bottom of the trench and also to sift the soil before filling it in; that way you can avoid the slight risk of sharp stones damaging the cable. It's also wise to place a line of slates on top of the cable to give it extra protection, when you fill in the trench. If you're using PVC-sheathed two-core and earth cable, you should first lay the conduit in the trench and cut it to fit. You'll have to buy couplers for lengths that need to be joined; for vertical runs you'll have to fit elbows and you'll need a further elbow to take a short length of conduit into the wall so that the cable has complete protection. Do not use solvent-weld adhesive to assemble the conduit run at this stage, as you'll have to dismantle the fittings to thread in the cable. Start at the house end and, working in sections, thread through enough of the PVC cable to reach the mains switch in the garage to wherever you're running it. An alternative method is to attach the cable to a drawstring; thread it through the conduit and then pull the cable through after it. You can then start fixing the elbows and couplers permanently. Smear the solvent-weld adhesive over the end of the conduit and inside the elbows and couplers with the special brush provided before joining the sections together. Then place the assembled run into the trench, making sure that each elbow is correctly positioned. At the garage end push the end of the cable and the short length of conduit into the hole in the wall and then carefully fill in the trench. If you're using PVC-covered wire-armoured cable it should be laid directly in the trench and the ends passed directly into the house and garage. It will then be taken into a conversion box at each end.

Fitting a conversion box

Extending either PVC-armoured or MICC cable beyond the entry point to the house or garage is pointless. They are both relatively expensive cables, cannot usually be connected to a switchfuse unit and can be awkward to run. That is why you should fit what is called a conversion box. This allows

RUNNING CABLE UNDERGROUND

1 After digging a ditch that is a minimum of 500mm (20in) deep, lay the conduit in it to give you an idea of what length you'll need.

2 Use a hacksaw to cut the conduit to length where necessary, and link it with special couplers; don't weld the joints yet.

3 Use an elbow fitting to join the vertical (above-ground) section of the conduit to the horizontal (underground) part next to the wall.

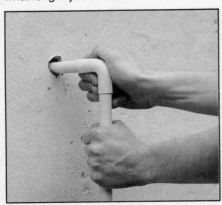

4 Fix a short section of conduit to the top elbow and check that it's long enough to take the cable completely through the garage wall.

5 Thread through the cable from the consumer unit. You can either dismantle the conduit or use a drawstring to pull through the cable.

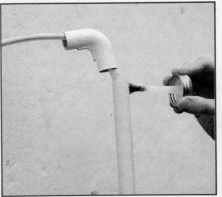

6 With the cable in place, you should use special conduit adhesive to fix the couplers and elbows firmly in position. Then bury the conduit.

you to change the type of cable in your sub-main circuit to ordinary PVC two-core and earth cable.

All that is required is a box containing three terminals and two entry holes. The correct one to use is an adaptable conversion box and lid or alternatively a standard one-gang metal mounting box fitted with a blanking-off plate as a cover. You can use a special three-way terminal block to make the connections, or else ordinary cable connectors. However, if you do use the cable connectors, you must make sure they are large enough for the current.

At the house end, the conversion box should either be fixed with wood screws to a timber batten fitted between the joists beneath the floor, or alternatively to the wall near the entry point of the cable. If you're running power to a garage or shed, the box at that end should be fitted to the wall near the cable entry point. You should remove two knockout holes, one of which must be fitted with a PVC grommet while the other should be large enough to accommodate the PVC-armoured cable. Strip away the outer layer of PVC and slide a PVC sheath and gland nut onto the armoured cable. You should put a back-nut in the knockout hole without a grommet and then prepare the cable by clipping away the excess armouring, leaving enough to carry up to the end of the gland's thread. You can now slide on the gland which will screw into the gland nut and keep the armouring in place. It's a good idea to attach a coupler to the gland as this will allow you more room in the box for the connections. Then feed the cable into the box and attach the back-nut to the coupler. If you are using two-core cable the armouring will serve as the earth so the back-nut must be tightened by a spanner to provide good metal-to-metal contact. Then pull the PVC protective hood over the whole assembly and remove the remaining PVC insulation to expose the red and black cores. If you are using two-core cable you'll now have to earth the box; it's a good idea to do this even if you're using three-core cable. You should link the earth screw on the box (which holds the earth connector) with a length of core that you have sleeved in green/yellow PVC. Feed in the PVC two-core and earth cable, which must be the same size as the sub-main cable, through the knockout hole previously fitted with a grommet, and prepare the ends of the cable in the usual way before joining the cores of the two cables together. From here the PVC cable will run to whatever appliance you want to supply. If it is a garage or workshop, it's likely to go to a switchfuse unit; if in the garden, it might be to well-protected sockets for lawnmowers, hedge trimmers, or lighting for an ornamental fountain.

FITTING A CONVERSION BOX

1 Use an adaptable mounting box to serve as a conversion box. Remove two opposite knockouts and fit a grommet to just one of them.

2 Remove two small knockouts at the back for the screws. Drill and plug holes in the corresponding spots on the wall, and position the box.

3 Fit a back-nut in the knockout hole. without a grommet, and then slide the PVC hood and gland nut onto the armoured cable.

4 Put on the gland and coupler and trim the armouring of the cable so that it ends at the bottom of the thread on the gland.

5 Feed the cable into the box and attach the back-nut to the coupler. Using a coupler allows you more room in the box for the connections.

6 The armouring serves as an earth but you should earth the box too by fitting an extra core to the box and connecting it to the terminal block.

7 Feed in the PVC two-core and earth cable that is to run to the switchfuse unit. Remember, this must be the same size as the armoured sub-main cable to which it is connected.

8 Using a block of three connectors, join the two cores of the armoured cable to their equivalents in the two-core and earth PVC cable and then connect the earth cores.

9 Finally screw on the lid of the conversion box. At the house end, the conversion box can be fitted safely to a timber batten that is fixed under the floorboards.

PROVIDING POWER IN THE GARAGE

If you add power and lighting to a garage, you can make it more than mere storage space for your car: your garage becomes a workshop. Connecting up the electricity supply is not difficult and sturdy accessories are produced specially.

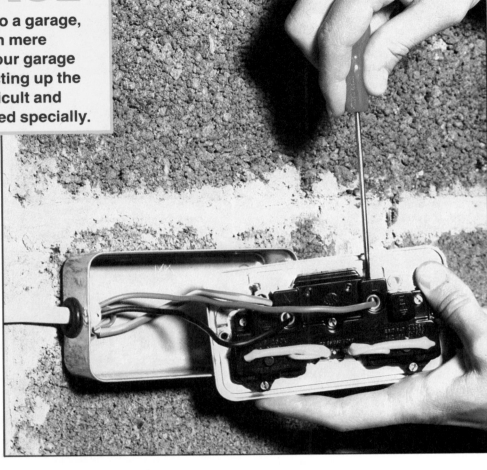

Installing electricity in a garage can completely transform it. No more fumbling in the dark for car keys; or flat batteries on a winter's morning; and car repairs will be carried out in the relative comfort of a well-lit and pleasantly heated garage. Indeed, a garage equipped with a number of power sockets, some lights and a couple of work surfaces can double as an extremely efficient workshop. If your garage is attached to your home, it is likely that it will already have a power supply; if it's detached, it's possible you'll have to install the supply yourself. But running electricity to a garage, or indeed to any other outside building, is not that difficult. It should be done in three stages: work inside the house; work outdoors, and finally the new circuitry in the garage itself.

Inside the home

If you're going to run a power supply to your garage you should remember that the electricity supply to any outbuilding, even if only for a lighting circuit, must be independent of the house circuits. Tempting though it may be, you're not allowed to run the supply in the form of a spur from a ring circuit in the house. The basic requirments are: a separate mains switch and fuse unit in the home, and an isolating switch and fuse unit in the garage. The mains switch at the house end will usually be a switchfuse unit that should be linked to the mains by the electricity board. If there is a spare fuseway in the main consumer unit obviously you can make use of it. However, it's probably better to leave the spare fuseway unit for another circuit within the house and install a new switchfuse unit for the circuit to the garage or outhouse. This must also contain a high-sensitivity RCD to protect socket outlets in the garage that will power outdoor electrical appliances.

The cable running from the new switch-fuse unit in the house to the garage is technically not a circuit cable and is classed as a sub-main cable. This is because it supplies a complete installation which has its own mains switch and fuse.

The section inside the house will normally be run in ordinary two-core and earth PVC sheathed cable, the size of which depends upon the circuit requirements in the garage.

The 2.5mm² size is suitable for a 20A supply; use 4mm² for a 30A supply, and 6mm² for a 45A supply. Do remember that if you are using the 4mm² cable for a 30A supply you must make sure that both switchfuse units are fitted with either a cartridge type fuse or MCB so that the circuit is uprated by one third. This is because 4mm² cable controlled by a rewirable fuse has a current-carrying capacity of only 27A and would consequently be a safety risk.

The outdoor section will either be in the same type of cable or else in special cable; which sort you use is determined by whether you run it overhead or underground, and if run underground, whether or not it is to be in conduit. More details about the underground cable runs can be found on pages 278-281.

It's best to make the outdoor section as short as possible, so the point at which the cable emerges from the house should be as near as practicable to the garage. This will obviously affect the section run in the home, as will obstructions inside. For further information on running cable procedure, take a look at pages 274-277.

Installing an overhead cable

Where the distance between the house and garage is no more than 5m (about 17ft), an overhead cable attached to a catenary wire is a practical alternative to an underground cable run. A catenary wire is merely a length of galvanised steel-stranded cable similar to that sometimes used for fencing and should be secured to an eye bolt or eye screw fixed into the wall of the house and of the garage. For spans larger than 5m, intermediate supports such as poles are required to prevent sagging. Apart from looking unattractive, there is always the risk of damage in high winds so you may find it better to take the cable underground for long runs.

In theory a span of less than 3.5m (11ft) need not be supported by a catenary wire. If you're running an overhead cable to your garage, you'll have to make sure that there is no danger of it being hit by anything passing underneath. For that very reason the regulation minimum height of an overhead cable run is 3.5m (11ft). However, when the cable is suspended across a driveway the minimum height is increased to 5.2m (17ft).

RUNNING CABLE OVERHEAD

Running power overhead keeps the cable out of harm's way provided you have the catenary wire at a minimum height of 3.5m (11ft). The cable should be taped and clipped and the catenary wire itself should be bonded to earth. To gain extra height at the garage end use a length of 100x50mm (4x2in) timber which should be bolted securely to the wall with 150mm (6in) coach screws.

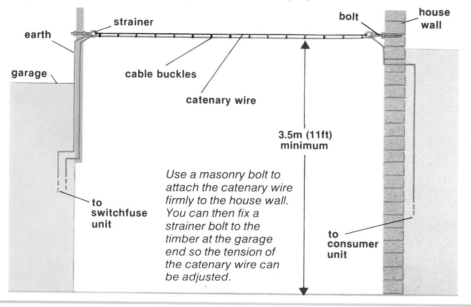

Use a masonry bolt to attach the catenary wire firmly to the house wall. You can then fix a strainer bolt to the timber at the garage end so the tension of the catenary wire can be adjusted.

THE GARAGE CIRCUITS

The lighting circuit can be either a loop-in or junction box system; the power circuit is wired as a radial circuit. Metal-clad sockets and switches are more robust than plastic ones. Cable should be taken on the surface with vertical runs being clipped every 400mm (16in) and horizontal runs over 250mm (10in).

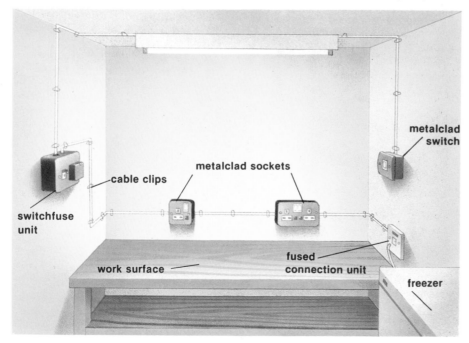

ATTACHED GARAGES
If your garage is attached to your home you can safely run the power as a spur from a ring circuit.

DETACHED GARAGES
If your garage is detached from your home then it is deemed a separate building and must be:
● supplied by a sub-main cable
● controlled by an isolating switch and fuse unit at each end.

TEMPORARY POWER SUPPLY
The only other form of power supply allowed to a detached garage, other than a sub-main cable, is an extension cable. This can be linked up temporarily while the actual appliance that it supplies is in use.

PERMANENT POWER SUPPLY
Power can be supplied permanently to a detached garage in three ways:
● by an overhead cable
● by an underground cable
● by a cable fixed along a wall. Cable should never be taken along a fence for reasons of safety.

OVERHEAD CABLE RUNS
Points to note:
● the minimum height for an overhead cable run is 3.5m (about 11ft)
● if the cable crosses a driveway the minimum height is increased to 5.2m (17ft)
● with a span of under 3.5m (11ft) the cable need not be supported
● if the span is between 3.5m (11ft) and 5m (about 17ft) the cable should be attached to a catenary wire
● for spans over 5m (17ft) there should be intermediate supports in addition to a catenary wire.

TIP: TAPE THE CABLE

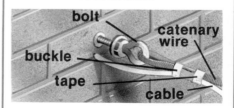

Attach the cable to the catenary wire with tape before fitting the buckle clips. That way the buckles will neither cut into the cable nor slide along it. It's also a good idea to leave a loop in the cable at each end to ease the strain and prevent water from entering the wall.

FITTING THE SWITCHFUSE UNIT

1 If your garage is situated away from the house, it will need its own mains switch and fuses. Fix the unit to a sheet of treated chipboard.

2 Thread in the circuit cable and feed the red and black cores behind the switch so that they can connect to the unit's terminals.

3 Strip off some of the insulation from each core and make the connections. Sleeve the earth core in green/yellow PVC.

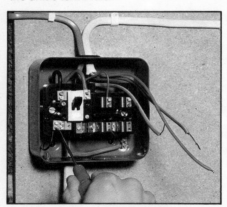

4 Then feed in the cables for the two circuits to provide power in the garage. Connect the lighting circuit to the fuseway nearest the switch.

5 When you have made all the connections fit the fuseway covers in the correct rating sequence, with the highest nearest the switch.

6 Finally fit the cover and shield and slot in the two MCB's. You can then turn on the power in both the house and garage.

Running the cable

It's a good idea to insert an adjusting device at one end so that the catenary wire can be tightened once the cable has been attached to it. You'll probably have to fix a length of 100x50mm (4x2in) timber to the garage wall to obtain the necessary minimum height at that end. To fix the timber to the garage wall you'll have to drill and plug two holes and use 150mm (6in) coach screws. You should drill a hole in the house wall to serve as an exit point for the cable. This should be at about first floor level in a two-storey house and at eaves level in a bungalow.

You'll also have to drill a hole in the garage wall to enable the cable to enter and run to the mains switch. In addition, it's wise to run a length of green/yellow PVC insulated cable from the catenary wire to the mains switch to bond the catenary to earth. Measure the length of cable required to run from the switchfuse unit in the house to the mains switch in the garage. Having fixed and tightened the catenary wire to the two eye bolts, pass the end of the cable through the hole in the house and then pull through sufficient to reach the mains switch in the garage. You should connect the bared end of the catenary wire to the bonding earth core by using a cable connector. After temporarily attaching the cable to the catenary wire (so you can make sure that there is sufficient to reach the garage) you can make a permanent attachment by using cable buckles every 250mm (10in). Both the supply and the earth cable should be fixed to the post with plastic cable clips that should be no more than 400mm (16in) apart. Alternatively, you can run the vertical section in metal or plastic conduit that is attached to the timber. You can now make the connections to the switchfuse unit in the house and in the garage.

An alternative method of running cable overhead is to carry it in an unjointed length of heavy gauge steel conduit; in this case the minimum height is reduced to 3m (10ft). You could also run it in rigid plastic conduit, but this will sag and is also likely to fracture at temperatures below −5°C. If you don't want to run the cable either overhead or underground then you may be able to take it along a boundary wall to the garage. Under no circumstances, however, may the outdoor section be fixed to a fence.

Inside the garage

Running cable to the garage is probably the most important and also the most difficult part of installing electricity there. There are, to begin with, certain precautions you must take with the work inside the garage. Remember that a detached garage is classed as a completely separate building and therefore must be fitted with a double-pole isolating switch, enabling the electricity to all circuits

FITTING POWER POINTS IN A GARAGE

1 To provide current for a garage power point you should use 2.5mm² two-core and earth cable clipped firmly to the wall every 150mm (6in).

2 Fit a grommet on a knockout hole and fix to the wall the special metal box for surface mounting in garages and workshops.

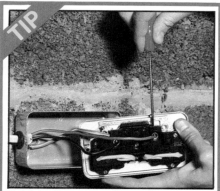

3 Make the connections after sleeving the earth core in green/yellow PVC. It's a good idea to add an extra earth to protect the box.

4 Fit the faceplate with great care. This is necessary because its screws link the box into the earthing of the socket.

Ready Reference

GARAGE ACCESSORIES

It's best to fit metal-clad switches and socket outlets in a garage or workshop. They are tougher than the plastic variety and last longer.

It's a good idea to choose versions which incorporate a neon indicator light. That way you can see at a glance if the power is on or off.

FIXING THE ACCESSORIES

These accessories are usually surface mounted. To install them:
- drill and plug the holes in the wall
- feed the cable into the surface mounting box
- fix the box to the wall with No 8 wood screws
- make the connections in the usual way
- attach the faceplate.

TIP: EARTH THE BOX

The circuit cable earth core protects the socket itself but it's wise to add extra protection for the mounting box. You can do this in two ways:

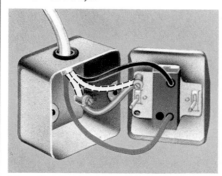

- loop the circuit earth core into the earth screw on the box and then take it onto the socket, or
- add an extra green/yellow sleeved earth core linking the box earth screw to the socket earth terminal.

---

and equipment to be completely cut off at the flick of a switch. If you're going to run more than one circuit within your garage, it's best to fit a switchfuse unit and the mains switch on this will serve as an isolating switch.

When you fit the new switchfuse unit, it's best to fix it as near as possible to the point where the incoming cable enters. It should be installed in the same way as inside the home and it's important to fit a sheet of fire-resistant material such as treated chipboard or asbestos to the wall beforehand.

You can obviously install as many circuits as you like, but for most garages two – one for power and one for lighting – should prove ample. Generally, you should fit the new switchfuse unit with a 5A and 15A MCB. If, however, you plan to have a number of power sockets, heaters and appliances, it is wise to fit a 30A fuse for the power socket. Cartridge fuses will also suffice but it's not advisable to

use rewirable fuses. You should run the lighting circuit in 1.0mm² or 1.5mm² two-core and earth PVC cable, fixed to the wall and roof surfaces, and you can install a loop-in or junction box system. The power circuit will have to be run in 2.5mm² two-core and earth cable and horizontal runs should be clipped every 250mm (10in), while vertical runs need to be clipped every 400mm (16in).

Although the standard plastic fittings can be used safely in a garage, it's probably best to use the special metal-clad versions. Although these are slightly more expensive, they are more robust and therefore safer in an environment where they could be subjected to the occasional knock or blow. It's also wise to choose versions with neon-indicators to show, at a glance, whether the socket is on or off. They are designed specifically for surface mounting and come complete with mounting boxes.

INSTALLING A LAMP AND SWITCH

1 If you're fitting a lamp to a beam, clip the cable along the middle of the beam so it runs to the centre of the battenholder.

2 You'll have to nibble out some plastic knockouts on the pattress block before offering it up to the beam or ceiling.

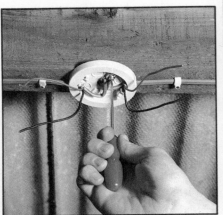

3 Clip the power and switch cables to the beam and run them into the pattress. Then sleeve and connect up the earth cores.

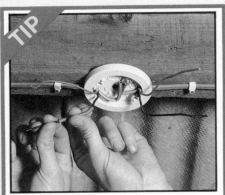

4 Before going any further make sure that you have flagged the black core of the switch cable with red PVC tape: this indicates that it's live.

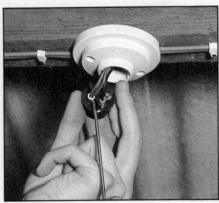

5 Make the connections. The two red cores go to one terminal; the flagged black core to another and the neutral to the third.

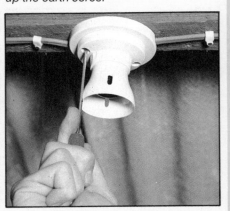

6 Finally screw the battenholder and pattress block to the beam after making holes with a bradawl. You can then connect up the switch.

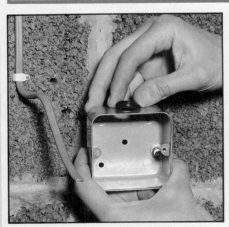

7 Clip the switch cable onto the wall and run it to the point where you'll mount the switch. Fit a grommet to the knockout hole.

8 Feed the cable into the box and make the connections. Remember to sleeve the earth in green/yellow PVC and also to earth the box itself.

9 Replace the switch in the mounting box and fit the faceplate. You can now switch on the power in the house and in the garage itself.

DIMMER SWITCHES AND TIMERS

You can make your life more comfortable and your home that much more secure by installing a variety of special controls for your lighting and electrical appliances.

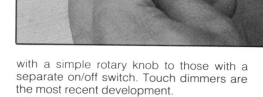

Special controls for electric appliances can be a real boon to the householder. They can make life much more comfortable by automatically switching appliances on and off, and more economic by preventing appliances from being left on to consume costly electricity. They can also help to make the home more secure by controlling lights, radios and curtains to give would-be burglars the impression that there's someone in.

But before you dash off to your local electrical supplies shop, pause for a moment's reflection. Are you being tempted by the sheer novelty of automatic controls? Remember, all automation is expensive, so it pays to take a slightly more hard-headed attitude towards making the decision. First of all, make sure that the equipment will actually do the job you have in mind. Read all the technical specifications carefully. You don't want to discover that your new dimmer light switch won't allow two-way switching or won't work on fluorescent lights. Secondly, do make sure that you know exactly what you're getting for your money. You may find out that the price quoted in the sales leaflet is just a basic 'starter kit' and that you'll have to spend more money to achieve the full performance suggested by the advertisement. Thirdly, consider whether it's actually worth automating a particular appliance; after all, many of the currently available devices perform only fairly menial tasks. Finally, remember that the development of home technology is advancing rapidly; buy now and you may well find that next year you can buy something that does more and does it cheaper.

Dimmer switches

Although dimmer switches offer no automatic form of control, they are considerably more versatile than the conventional rocker switch – allowing you greater flexibility in controlling the level of artificial lighting in the room where they are installed. They're usually used to control tungsten filament lights and spotlights. However, you can dim even a fluorescent lamp provided you have a special choke for the fitting. Various types of dimmer switches are available, ranging from those

with a simple rotary knob to those with a separate on/off switch. Touch dimmers are the most recent development.

Connecting a dimmer switch into your existing circuit is perfectly straightforward. Switch off at the mains and remove the fuse for the particular circuit you're working on; then you can switch the mains back on and have some light to work by. Unscrew the faceplate of your existing switch and pull it carefully away from the mounting box. This will give you enough room in which to disconnect the cable cores. Then simply connect up the cores to the dimmer switch according to the manufacturer's instructions and screw the faceplate to the box. If you want to put a dimmer into a two-way system then remember you can only replace one of the switches with a dimmer. Most one-gang dimmers will fit a standard plaster-depth or surface-mounted box, but some need a deeper box. Two-gang and multi-gang dimmers may need a double box.

Automatic light controls

The most basic automatic light switch is the time delay switch designed primarily for use on communal landings and stairwells. When you want light, all you do is switch on and leave the device to turn the light off again after a pre-set interval – usually anything from five to twenty minutes, depending on the model. Most versions allow you to adjust the timing to suit your needs. The most simple type works by means of a large spring-loaded button, while more sophisticated models use electronic timers and touch plate controls.

Time delay faders are a sort of cross between a dimmer and a time delay switch. They fade out the light gradually over a pre-set delay time and so are extremely handy for a child's bedroom, say. These are normally fitted with dual touch plate controls; the upper plate allows the switch to work like a conventional touch dimmer, the lower one triggers the dimming sequence. Time delay faders can be simply installed in the place of ordinary rocker switches, but, as a rule, they are not suitable for use with fluorescent lights.

Security switches

These switches are useful from a security point of view because lights are thereby turned on and off automatically to convince would-be burglars that you're at home. The basic switch incorporates a light-sensing device that will turn on the light at dusk and then off after a certain period of time (usually between two and ten hours). The faceplate carries a dial for selecting the time the light is on, and two switches, one to allow the switch to function as an ordinary on/off switch and the other to activate the light sensing device. It's not a good idea to fit this type of switch in unusually light or dark situations where the light-sensing device could get confused; avoid fixing it in a corner where there is little natural light or close to a window by a street light.

Photoelectric security switches don't, as a rule, incorporate on/off switches, so, if necessary, manual override will have to be provided separately. However, these switches are usually designed to be installed outside to control lights in exposed conditions. They

INSTALLING A DIMMER SWITCH

1 Switch off at the mains and remove the lighting circuit fuse; then switch the power back on and unscrew the existing faceplate from its mounting box.

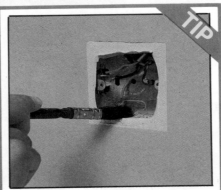

2 Disconnect the old switch. Before fitting the dimmer switch brush away any plaster or debris that's fallen into the mounting box.

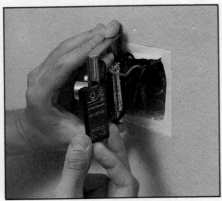

3 Make the connections to the new switch following the manufacturer's instructions. You may have to remove covers to get access to the terminals.

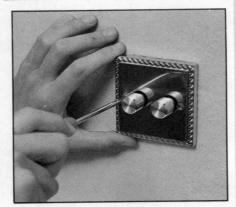

4 If you're installing a metal switch, make sure the faceplate is earthed by linking it with the box earth terminal. Then screw the faceplate in place.

USING A PLUG-IN DIMMER

1 Plug-in dimmers can be easily moved, allowing you to dim any table lamps. They are not suitable for lamps below 40W or above 400W.

2 Simply plug the lamp into the dimmer socket. You'll then be able to control the brightness by moving the dial on the dimmer face.

INSTALLING A TIME-DELAY SWITCH

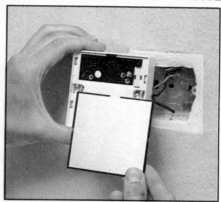

1 Switch off at the mains and remove the existing switch. Take off the front cover of the switch to gain access to the terminal screws.

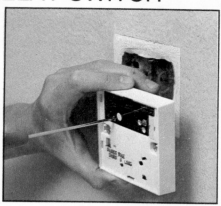

2 Connect the cores to the terminals as indicated on the switch. You can then fix the switch to the mounting box with the screws provided.

3 You can set the switch so the light will be switched off up to twenty minutes after being turned on. Use the special screwdriver to adjust the delay.

4 Finally, fit the touch plate back in position. Switch on at the mains and test the time setting. If necessary, adjust the setting again.

FITTING A SECURITY SWITCH

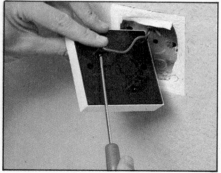

1 Switch off at the mains and remove your old switch. Make the connections to the security switch and screw it to the mounting box.

2 You can programme the light switch to turn interior and exterior lights on or off automatically. Programmes can be easily cleared and overidden.

can usually be mounted within plastic conduit systems and will switch outside lights on at dusk and off at dawn, so giving your home extra security when no one's in. And, of course, you'll have the lights on for you when you return from an evening out. Most exterior switches incorporate a designed time delay of 1 to 2 minutes so that car headlights won't cause the light to go off.

Automatic power control

Plug-in timers are merely a sort of sophisticated plug-in adaptor for ordinary power sockets. Once you have one in place, all you do is plug in whatever device you want the timer to control. This can be just about anything that can be powered from your home's ring circuit – standard lamps, radiators, blankets and radios. You programme the timer by using small pegs fixed in special holes on the dials or by moving small spring-loaded lugs; the timer will automatically turn the power on and off at these pre-set times.

The minimum period the power can be on for is thirty minutes, although you can control the timer to the nearest fifteen minutes. The on/off pegs are usually protected by a clear dust cover and spare pegs are normally provided with each timer so that more than one operation can be made in each cycle. Most basic versions will operate on a twenty-four hour cycle, although timers programmable for up to seven days are available. With these the setting intervals tend to be quite long – up to two hours in some cases. However, the timer with a longer cycle will obviously be more useful from a security point of view, since you can set it to turn lights on and off at different times each day.

Other control gear

Other devices on the market perform more specific tasks. An electric curtain controller, for example, will both open and close corded curtains provided the weight of pull on the cord required to do so is no greater than 8kg (17½lbs). The motor is controlled by a two-position switch and is simply plugged into the mains. As a safety precaution it will only operate for a period of five minutes before cutting out; that way any accidents in the event of a cord failure will be prevented.

Fan controllers are suitable for use with most electric extractor fans. They are basically specialised dimmer switches that allow you to vary the speed of the fan. They're normally fitted with a separate on/off switch and in some cases a switch for opening and closing the shutters found on very large fans. Other models also have reversing switches. Finally, immersion heater timers work in much the same way as plug-in timers, allowing a number of switching operations per day or per seven days.

SECTION 8

PLUMBING

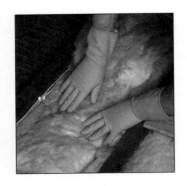

TECHNIQUES

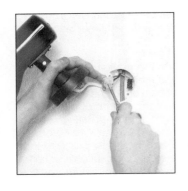

UNDERSTANDING WATER SUPPLY

Each one of us uses about 160 litres (35 gallons) of water a day, and takes it for granted. Only in a long spell of dry weather comes an awareness that we should use it carefully. Our use is controlled by the supply system – this is how it works.

In the last 50 years the consumption of water has almost doubled. Rising standards of living have given rise to increased consumption, and a greater awareness of the need for hygiene has also played a large role in increasing the demand. Faced with this high demand, supply sources have been hard pressed to keep up.

Where it comes from

Water is supplied by the local water authority (or the 'Undertaking' as it is known in the plumbing trade). After falling as rain it is collected in reservoirs which are fed by streams and rivers, or is pumped from underground wells. Water varies a lot in its chemical makeup since it picks up minerals and gases as it flows. If it picks up calcium, magnesium and sodium salts it will be 'hard' – the menace of pipe systems. Before being distributed it is usually filtered through sand and pebble beds to remove solids and organisms, and may have chlorine added to it to ensure that it is 'potable' – drinkable. Fluoride is also sometimes added for the protection of teeth.

Distribution is carried out by a network of pipes starting with 'trunk mains' which may be as much as 610mm (24in) in diameter. These split into mains and sub-mains which run underneath streets and side streets. It is these sub-mains which are tapped by individual houses for their supply.

The house system may be 'direct' in which all cold water supplies are piped direct from the rising main, with the cistern only being used to supply the hot water tank. Or it may be an 'indirect' system in which all cold-water supplies are taken from the cistern, with the exception of a direct supply to the kitchen sink for drinking purposes.

For water to flow through the trunk mains – and eventually into your house – it must be under a certain amount of pressure. This pressure is assisted by pumps but it is vital that somewhere in the mains system the water should reach a height in a reservoir or water tower, higher than any domestic system it has to supply. The vertical distance through which the water 'falls' is known as the 'pressure head' and without it our

cisterns would never fill up without a lot of expensive additional pumping. The storage cistern also provides a pressure head inside the house, which is why it's preferable to have it in the roof space.

The house system

The sub-main underneath the road is tapped by the 'communication pipe' which ends at the authority's stop-valve. This is usually situated under the pavement about 300mm (1ft) outside the boundary of your property. The stop-valve is located at the bottom of a vertical 'guard' pipe – about 1 metre (39in) deep – which is covered at the surface by a hinged metal cover. It should only be operated by the water authority and requires a special key to turn it. But in a real emergency you may be able to turn it yourself. In old houses it may be the only way of turning off the water supply. After this stop-valve the water enters the service pipe and from then on all pipes become your responsibility.

The service pipe continues under the wall of the property at a depth of at least 750mm (2ft 6in) to protect it from frost – though some water authorities insist that it should be 900mm (3ft) deep. As it travels under the house wall or foundation it usually goes through an earthenware pipe to protect it

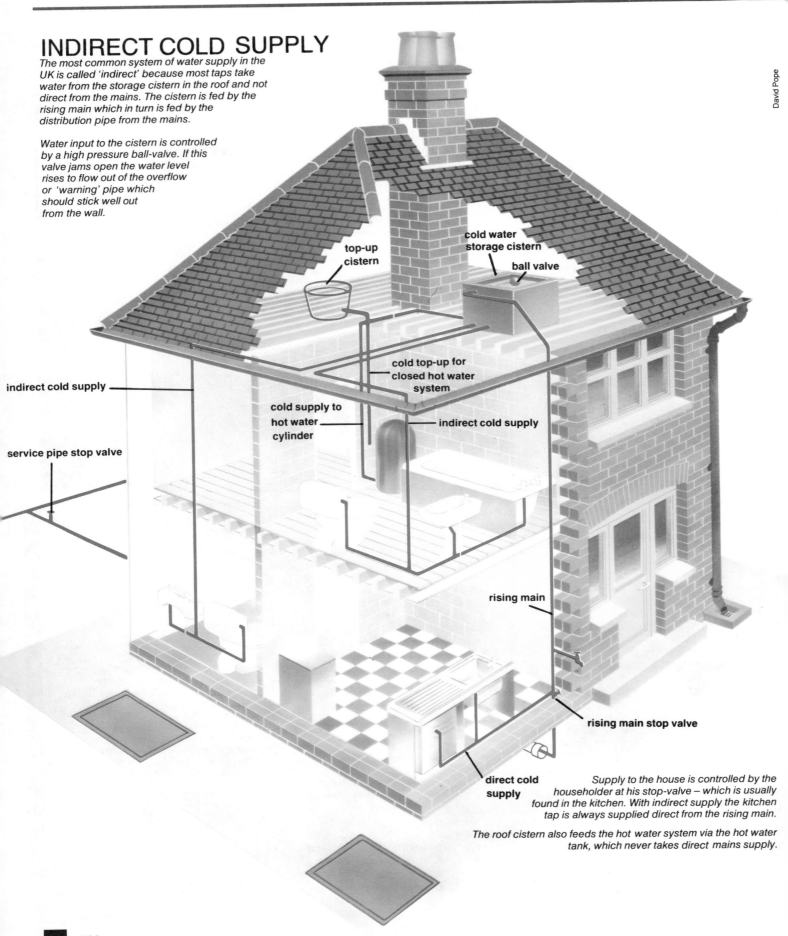

INDIRECT COLD SUPPLY

The most common system of water supply in the UK is called 'indirect' because most taps take water from the storage cistern in the roof and not direct from the mains. The cistern is fed by the rising main which in turn is fed by the distribution pipe from the mains.

Water input to the cistern is controlled by a high pressure ball-valve. If this valve jams open the water level rises to flow out of the overflow or 'warning' pipe which should stick well out from the wall.

David Pope

top-up cistern

cold water storage cistern

ball valve

cold top-up for closed hot water system

indirect cold supply

cold supply to hot water cylinder

indirect cold supply

service pipe stop valve

rising main

rising main stop valve

direct cold supply

Supply to the house is controlled by the householder at his stop-valve – which is usually found in the kitchen. With indirect supply the kitchen tap is always supplied direct from the rising main.

The roof cistern also feeds the hot water system via the hot water tank, which never takes direct mains supply.

from possible settlement which might cause it to fracture. To prevent any risk of freezing in cold weather the service pipe should not emerge above ground level until it is at least 600mm (2ft) inside the inside wall surface.

Up to about 40 years ago, service pipes were usually made of lead (in fact the word plumbing originally stemmed from the Latin word for lead – *plumbum*). Today copper and polythene are used instead. The latter is particularly good as it is a poor conductor of heat and is less prone to freezing and fracture.

The service pipe

The service pipe continues under the wall near the kitchen sink, which means that it is often attached to the inner face of the outside wall. This is contrary to the recommendation that it should be attached to an inside wall, and so such a pipe should be lagged with insulation material. The pipe should also be insulated if it comes through any sub-ground floor cavity where it would be subjected to the icy blasts of winter from under-floor ventilation. Again these precautions are both intended to minimise the risk of frost damage.

When the service pipe rises above the ground floor it is called the 'rising main' and it eventually terminates in the supply cistern, which is usually in the roof cavity. The householder's main stop-valve is usually found on the rising main a little way above floor level. This is the most important 'tap' in the house. In any plumbing emergency – when bursts or leaks occur, for example, your first action should be to turn this tap off, thus isolating the house system from the mains water supply. The stop-valve should always be turned off when you go away if the house is going to be empty. In old houses the location of the stop-valve may vary considerably, it may be in the cellar, under the stairs, or even under a cover beneath the front path – or it may not exist at all, in which case the authority's stop-valve is the only control.

Branch supply pipes

At least one 'branch' supply pipe leaves the rising main close above the stop-valve and drain tap – this is to the tap over the kitchen sink. This tap must be supplied direct from the main supply as it is supposed to provide all drinking and cooking water. Water which has been in a storage cistern is no longer considered drinkable, sometimes termed 'potable', as it may be slightly contaminated by debris in the storage cistern.

Other branches may be taken at this point to an outside tap, or to a washing machine or dishwasher.

The rising main continues upwards and while its ultimate destination is the cold water storage cistern the pipework in between will vary from house to house, depending on

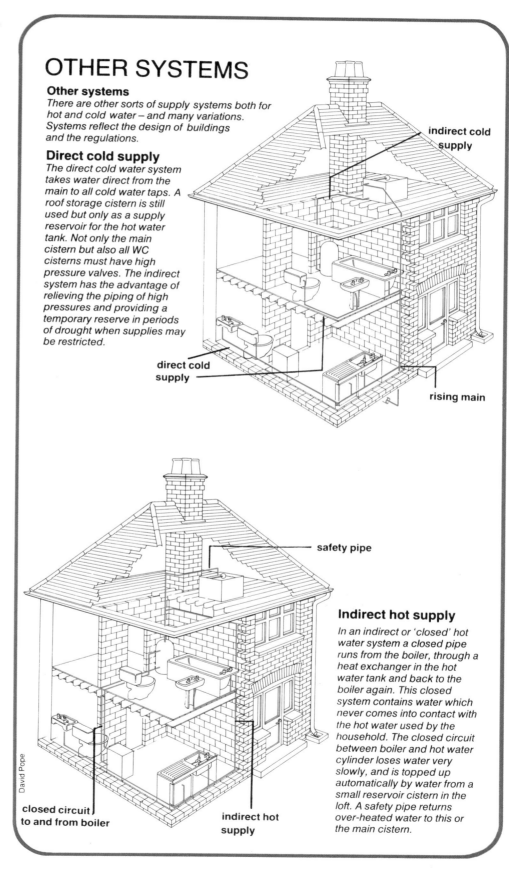

OTHER SYSTEMS

Other systems
There are other sorts of supply systems both for hot and cold water – and many variations. Systems reflect the design of buildings and the regulations.

Direct cold supply
The direct cold water system takes water direct from the main to all cold water taps. A roof storage cistern is still used but only as a supply reservoir for the hot water tank. Not only the main cistern but also all WC cisterns must have high pressure valves. The indirect system has the advantage of relieving the piping of high pressures and providing a temporary reserve in periods of drought when supplies may be restricted.

indirect cold supply

direct cold supply

rising main

safety pipe

Indirect hot supply
In an indirect or 'closed' hot water system a closed pipe runs from the boiler, through a heat exchanger in the hot water tank and back to the boiler again. This closed system contains water which never comes into contact with the hot water used by the household. The closed circuit between boiler and hot water cylinder loses water very slowly, and is topped up automatically by water from a small reservoir cistern in the loft. A safety pipe returns over-heated water to this or the main cistern.

closed circuit to and from boiler

indirect hot supply

David Pope

DIRECT HOT WATER SUPPLY

The direct or 'open' system of hot water supply is based on the water being supplied to the hot water tank from the cold water cistern, passed to the boiler for heating, returned to the tank for storage and then piped to the supply taps.

The cold water cistern is always used to supply water to the hot water cistern. Direct feed from the mains supply should never be used as the pressure would be too great.

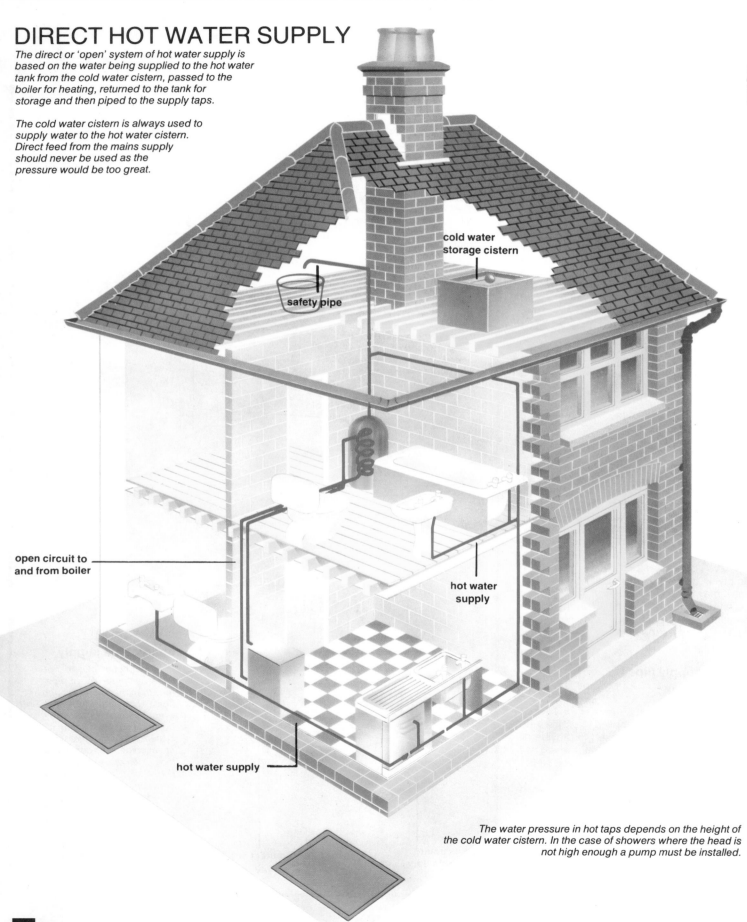

cold water storage cistern

safety pipe

open circuit to and from boiler

hot water supply

hot water supply

The water pressure in hot taps depends on the height of the cold water cistern. In the case of showers where the head is not high enough a pump must be installed.

whether a 'direct' or 'indirect' system has been installed.

In many areas indirect systems must be installed in new buildings, yet in Western Europe direct systems are the rule. Indirect systems have been encouraged because of the difficulty in maintaining constant mains pressure particularly at times of peak demand. Routing of most supplies through the storage cistern evens out fluctuations, and it also rules out the risk of 'back siphonage' whereby dirty water could be sucked back into the mains supply – though this rarely occurs. The 1976 drought in the UK provided good reason for indirect systems, since each house had an emergency supply in the storage cistern if the mains water had to be shut off.

Cisterns

The 'tank' in your loft or attic is in fact a 'cistern'. Cisterns are not sealed – though they should be covered – and so are subject to atmospheric pressure. Tanks are completely sealed – as with a hot water storage tank – and are not subject to atmospheric pressure.

Cold water cisterns have traditionally been made of galvanised mild steel and it is quite likely that you will find one like this in your loft. They are still available, but are not usually installed in new houses. Other materials used have been asbestos, cement, copper and glass fibre, but today the most common material is plastic, of which glass fibre reinforced polyester (GRP), polythene and polypropylene are the most common varieties.

The advantages plastics have over all other cistern materials are their lightness in weight, resistance to corrosion and flexibility. Galvanised steel is heavy and liable to corrode, while asbestos and cement are not only heavy but can become porous and are prone to accidental damage. Don't forget the capacity of a typical cistern is 227 litres (50 gallons), and this water alone weighs nearly 0.25 tonne (¼ ton), so all cisterns must be fully supported on the joists. With rigid materials such as steel the cistern can rest across the joists, but with plastic and glass fibre a platform should be installed to support the whole area of the bottom, otherwise the material may develop local weaknesses.

Cisterns should be covered to prevent any contamination of the water. Where the underside of the roof is exposed dust and dirt are liable to fall in. The top and sides should also be insulated to minimise the risk of freezing. The bottom is left uncovered to allow rising warm air from rooms below to keep the water above freezing point, and so you shouldn't insulate the roof space under the cistern.

Cisterns were often installed before the roof was put on and if you want to replace yours, perhaps because it's made of steel and is corroding, you may not be able to get it through the trap door. While it is sometimes suggested that a cistern should be cut up to get it out this is in fact a very heavy and arduous job in such a confined space and it would be better to manoeuvre it to one side and leave it in the loft, installing a new cistern alongside. Modern plastic cisterns can literally be folded up so they can be passed through small loft hatches.

Pipes and taps

Water leaves the storage cistern in distribution pipes which are usually 22mm (¾in) or 15mm (½in) in diameter. In a direct system, supply from the cistern will usually only be to the hot water tank, and in an indirect system this link must also be direct – but other distribution pipes are used with branches to supply the other appliances – basins, baths and WC cisterns. Distribution pipes usually end in taps but in the case of a WC a low pressure ball-valve controls the flow.

The WC in an indirect system has a low pressure ball-valve because when the water leaves the storage cistern it is no longer at mains pressure but at normal atmospheric pressure which is pressing down on the surface of the stored water. This means that the higher up the house a tap or other outlet is situated the lower will be the water pressure. In practice this means that you can't have a tap in an indirect system which is above the level of its distribution outlet from the cistern. Showers are particularly affected by this difference of pressure, and if there is not sufficient 'head' to 'drive' the shower a special pump may have to be installed.

Cold water supplied to the hot water tank is heated in two different ways again called indirect and direct systems – or, respectively, closed and open. In the latter the cold water is circulated through the boiler, where it is heated, and returned to the tank from where it flows to tapped outlets. In the indirect system the cold water supplied never actually goes to the boiler, instead it is heated in the tank by a coiled pipe or jacket containing hot water which is continuously circulating through the boiler. In either case a pump often helps the water flow through the boiler, and supplementary or alternative heat may come from an immersion heater. If there is no boiler but only an immersion heater in the tank the system is essentially direct with the heating of the water taking place in the tank rather than in the boiler.

Draining the system

Just above the rising main stop-valve should be a drain cock. With the stop-valve turned off the drain cock can be used to drain part of the cold water system when repairs are necessary – the hot water system has its own drain cock.

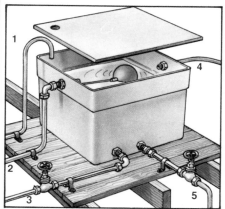
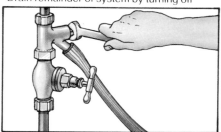

WASTE WATER SYSTEMS

Each day every one of us uses an average of 160 litres (35 gallons) of water from the mains supply. When it's used it has to be got rid of – something we tend to take for granted. Here's how it's done.

The supply of hot and cold water to the taps in your house is really only half the domestic plumbing story. You also need a waste system to remove what you've used or don't want. And besides coping with the dirty water from the bath, basin and sink and the waste from the WC, the system also has to deal with the rainwater which falls on the roof.

The drainage system therefore has to be efficient and durable, and for obvious reasons of hygiene, self-cleansing. Waste matter mustn't be allowed to remain in the pipes and if blockages occur it should be possible to remove them easily.

How the drainage system works

There are several domestic drainage systems but each of them can be broken down into five separate sections. When waste water leaves an appliance of any sort, it will go immediately through a 'waste trap' – a 180° bend containing a water seal which fills the trap whenever the waste pipe empties. This keeps drain smells out of the room and prevents insects and the like from entering the home. With WCs it also makes self-cleansing easier. WC traps are cast as an integral part of the WC pan, but on other appliances they are separate, and are attached to the outlet pipe by a large retaining nut.

From the trap, waste water enters a branch pipe which leads to the main vertical drainage 'stack'. This takes it below ground level to the first underground section of the drainage system where it flows through at least one inspection chamber (covered with a manhole cover) and into the public sewer, which is usually situated underneath the road. The sewer is provided by the public health authority and it is their responsibility to remove all waste running into it.

Often rainwater from the roof is fed into the drainage system to flow into the public sewer. But some authorities provide a separate street drain for it or insist on the provision of soak-aways (pits filled with rubble and gravel which allow the water to soak into the surrounding earth) near the house. Tanks and cisterns rarely overflow, but when they do they discharge clean water, so it's not necessary for the overflow pipes to be located over a drain.

The water can fall directly onto the ground.

The cost of laying public sewers in rural areas means that the waste from many houses in these parts flows into a cess pool or septic tank. These are specially constructed pits for storing effluent (and in the case of a septic tank, for breaking it down into harmless matter). Both of these require periodic pumping out, cess pools much more often as they store all the waste. If you're buying a house with one of these systems, check how often this has to be done, who does it and how much you may have to pay.

How it all began

Proper plumbing systems have only been around for about 100 years. The large urban expansion which took place during the Industrial Revolution lead to squalid housing conditions, and disease was rife. Eventually, enclosed sewers were introduced along with piped water supplies and pottery WC pans. By the 1870s many homes were equipped with a basin, a WC and a sink; but an acute shortage of qualified plumbers lead to ridiculous installations which often produced as great a health threat as before. The London County Council took the lead in sorting things out by laying out a set of rules in 1900, establishing the 'two-pipe' system – one stack for waste water from basins and sinks, another for 'soil water' from WCs.

The amount of pipework needed with the two-pipe system, and the increased siphonage problems on tall buildings, led to the introduction of the 'one-pipe' system. This system was the forerunner of the modern 'single stack' system and abandoned the distinction between the soil and the waste pipe stacks. It was only used extensively on multi-storey buildings.

On the one-pipe system all discharges flowed into a single stack which had an open-ended outlet at roof level. All traps had deep seals and each branch pipe was also connected to a vent pipe which rose to eaves level.

The single stack system was developed in the UK in the late 1940s to overcome the drawbacks and complications of the two-pipe systems, and to simplify the installation – everyone must be familiar with the untidy cluster of pipes on the outside walls of houses with these systems.

The advent of light plastic piping helped in this development, as it made the production of accurate mouldings easier, and cut down the installation time because plastic was quicker to join than the old metal piping.

The single stack system

This consists of a single waste stack into which all the branch pipes discharge. However, ground floor waste doesn't have to go

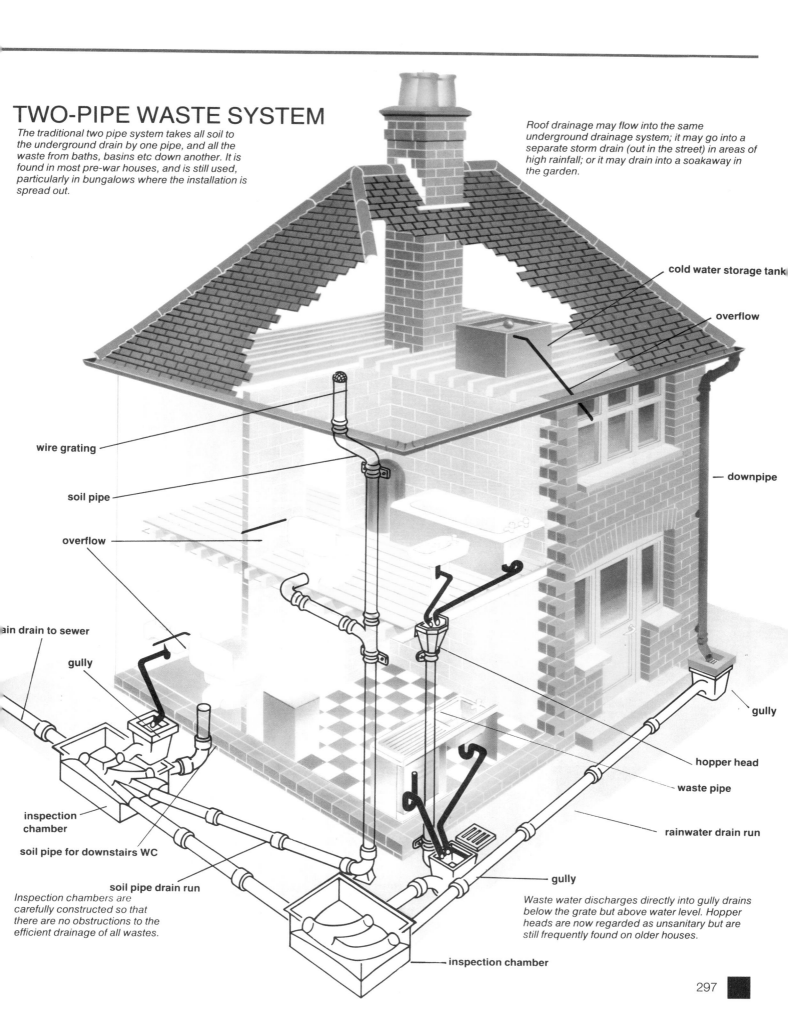

TWO-PIPE WASTE SYSTEM

The traditional two pipe system takes all soil to the underground drain by one pipe, and all the waste from baths, basins etc down another. It is found in most pre-war houses, and is still used, particularly in bungalows where the installation is spread out.

Roof drainage may flow into the same underground drainage system; it may go into a separate storm drain (out in the street) in areas of high rainfall; or it may drain into a soakaway in the garden.

cold water storage tank

overflow

wire grating

soil pipe

overflow

downpipe

ain drain to sewer

gully

gully

hopper head

waste pipe

inspection chamber

soil pipe for downstairs WC

rainwater drain run

gully

soil pipe drain run

Inspection chambers are carefully constructed so that there are no obstructions to the efficient drainage of all wastes.

Waste water discharges directly into gully drains below the grate but above water level. Hopper heads are now regarded as unsanitary but are still frequently found on older houses.

inspection chamber

297

SINGLE STACK WASTE SYSTEM

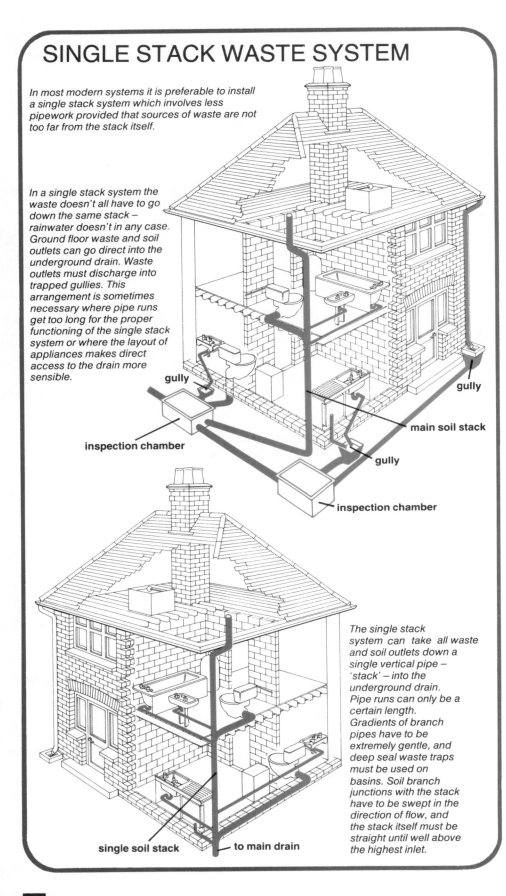

In most modern systems it is preferable to install a single stack system which involves less pipework provided that sources of waste are not too far from the stack itself.

In a single stack system the waste doesn't all have to go down the same stack – rainwater doesn't in any case. Ground floor waste and soil outlets can go direct into the underground drain. Waste outlets must discharge into trapped gullies. This arrangement is sometimes necessary where pipe runs get too long for the proper functioning of the single stack system or where the layout of appliances makes direct access to the drain more sensible.

gully

inspection chamber

gully

main soil stack

gully

inspection chamber

The single stack system can take all waste and soil outlets down a single vertical pipe – 'stack' – into the underground drain. Pipe runs can only be a certain length. Gradients of branch pipes have to be extremely gentle, and deep seal waste traps must be used on basins. Soil branch junctions with the stack have to be swept in the direction of flow, and the stack itself must be straight until well above the highest inlet.

single soil stack   to main drain

---

into the stack. Sink waste water may flow into a trapped gully and ground-floor WCs may be connected directly into the underground drain. This avoids any risk that a blockage at the base of the stack (where it bends to join the underground drain) could lead to waste water being forced back along the waste pipes to ground-floor appliances.

In appearance the single-stack system is the simplest waste system of all and the most economical to install. As a result it is incorporated in the majority of new houses. But because the branches have to be comparatively short, the system is less useful in bungalows where appliances are likely to be spread out. Usually all the pipework is sited indoors, which means a neater appearance for the house exterior; it also reduces the possibility of frost damage. All you'll see of the system is a tell-tale vent pipe poking up through the roof.

In order to make the system work properly a number of technical regulations have to be taken into account when it's being installed. These relate to the length, diameter, bend radii and angles of bend of the branch pipes, the use of P-traps and S-traps on waste pipes other than WCs (see *Traps for each appliance),* the positioning of the stack connectors, and the dimensions of the stack itself. While the system may look simple, considerable research has been done to ensure that problems of siphonage aren't likely to occur.

The two-pipe system
The principles of the two-pipe system were based on a belief that all kinds of disease were caused by the 'bad air' in drains, and the system aimed to keep this out of homes. The basic principle was that the 'soil' discharge from WCs went directly down one stack into the underground drain. All other discharges, termed 'waste', went down another stack which led into a trapped gully (a cast drain incorporating a water trap) at ground level and from there joined the soil discharge under-ground. Sometimes waste had to fall into a channel at ground level before running into the drain.

All waste and soil pipework had to be fixed to the outside of the building. The soil pipe was continued upwards to eaves level where it terminated open-ended in a wire cover to keep nesting birds from causing a blockage. This allowed free passage of air from the underground drain.

When the two-pipe system came into existence, most homes only had an outside WC (quite often shared) and a kitchen sink, so discharge was entirely at ground level, but when upstairs bathrooms became popular waste was directed into hoppers attached to stand-pipes, which caused new problems. Hoppers were not self-cleansing and soapy water drying on the inside could start to smell; draughts could also blow up the pipe to the hopper, bringing smells from the drain at the bottom. This led to some authorities banning hoppers and insisting on discharge direct into another stack which meant installing an eaves-level vent as with the soil stack.

On buildings over two storeys high this created another problem known as 'induced siphonage'. When water flowing down the waste stack from one outlet passed another outlet where it joined the stack, it could cause a partial vacuum in the second pipe which could suck out the contents of the water trap. To cure this problem the upper part of each trap had to be connected to a branch vent pipe which either connected to a separate vertical stack to eaves level, or joined the vented waste stack at least 900mm (3ft) above the level of the highest waste connection. If you live in a tall house you may have this system, and any repairs to vent pipes should follow the existing system. The alternative is to take out the entire system and replace it with a single stack arrangement.

Traps for each appliance
The traditional trap was a simple U-shaped bend attached to a horizontal branch outlet – today called a 'P' trap. If the branch outlet is vertical this trap bends round again into a double 'U' or 'S' outlet. In systems with lead pipes, the traps were often formed from lengths of pipe, while with modern plastic waste systems the traps are separate and easily detachable. The plastic bottle trap, which performs the same function, is also now widely used, and this is more compact and neater in appearance.

The depth of the water-filled part of the trap is known as the 'depth of seal'. Shallow traps have a seal depth of around 50mm (2in), 38mm (1½in) or 19mm (¾in), while 'deep-seal' traps have a 75mm (3in) seal.

Lead traps usually allow access for clearing blockages, and this is obtained by unscrewing an access cap or 'eye'. Modern plastic traps are connected by screwed collars at both ends and can be completely removed for cleaning if blocked. The lower part of bottle traps likewise completely unscrews. Adjustable plastic traps are available for fixing to existing pipework where access is difficult and special adaptors are used to link to copper and iron pipes.

Traps must remain filled with water and it is against the bye-laws if they don't. This is the most important and lasting principle handed down from the waste disposal thinking of the last century.

The water seal can be lost from traps for lots of reasons. Siphonage is the worst problem and where it occurs it's usually due

to a badly designed system. Simply, if the air pressure beyond the trap is slightly less than the normal atmospheric pressure acting on the surface of the water in the trap, the water will drain away. This is more likely with 'S' traps than 'P' traps, and with shallow rather than deep traps. The problem of siphonage led to the introduction of venting systems and dictated the dimensions in the single stack system (and also excluded the use of 'S' traps).

Overflow pipes
There are two sorts of overflow pipes – those which are connected to storage cisterns and WC cisterns, and those which are attached to or form a part of appliances such as basins and baths. They are known in the trade as warning pipes. Both sorts should be fitted to avoid the risk of overflows damaging your home. This may be caused when you forget to turn off the bath, or by mechanical failure when the ball-valve on the water storage tank jams open.

In sinks, basins and baths the overflow must discharge into the branch waste pipe between the trap and the appliance, or into the trap above the water level of the seal, and must be able to cope with the flow of water from one tap turned full on.

Sink and basin overflows are usually built into the design of the appliance, while those for baths are supplied as part of the plumbing and connect to a slot in the waste outlet casting.

Overflows from tanks and cisterns consist of a length of pipe of a minimum 22mm (⅞in) internal diameter, capable of discharging water as quickly as any incoming flow. They usually emerge through the outside wall and stick out far enough to avoid any water flow sluicing down the wall surface, which could be a potential source of damp.

Pipe and trap materials
All waste and soil pipes are today mainly manufactured in plastic. Branch pipes were made of lead or copper, stack pipes of cast iron, traps of lead or brass and underground pipes of vitrified clay. Only the latter still predominantly utilize the traditional material.

Your legal position
Drainage regulations fall under the Public Health Acts as well as the Building Regulations, so it's important to know where you stand. The householder is responsible for the entire drainage system until it enters the public sewer – even though this is usually beyond the boundary of the property. While blockages beyond the lowest inspection chamber are rare, any clearance work can be very expensive – particularly if you use a '24-hour' plumbing service. The public

sewer is provided by the public health authority and is their responsibility.

If your house was built as one of a group of houses, then it's quite possible that you'll have shared drainage facilities. This means there is one drainage pipe collecting the waste of several homes before it discharges into the public sewer. The system was adopted because it saved installation costs. If your house was built before 1937, it's still the responsibility of the local authorities to cleanse the shared drainage runs, although you're responsible for clearing blockages and for maintenance. But if you live in a post-1937 house then the responsibility for the shared drains rests collectively on all the owners concerned and if a blockage is caused by someone else you will have to pay a proportion of the bill. It is therefore important when moving house to check out the exact position. If this is difficult to ascertain, try the Environmental Health Officer for advice; he should also be consulted if you want to change the system.

PLASTIC WASTE TRAPS

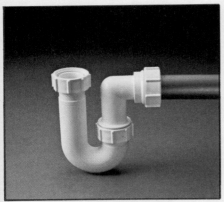

The modern U-bend *is made from one of several plastic materials.*

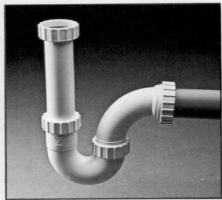

A U-bend with telescopic extension *can be adjusted to existing appliances.*

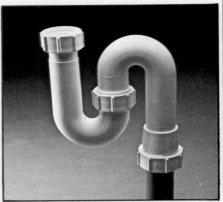

An S-bend *is designed for use where the outlet is vertical.*

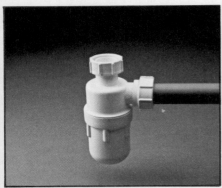

A bottle trap *gives a neater appearance, but is less efficient.*

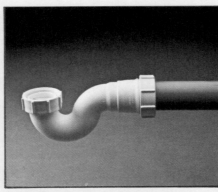

A shallow trap *is used beneath a bath or shower where space is crucial.*

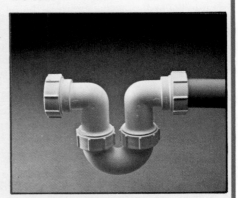

A running U-trap *handles two or more untrapped appliances piped together.*

A dip partition bottle trap *has a base which unscrews.*

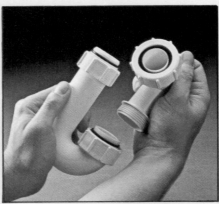

All modern traps come apart for easy cleaning and installation.

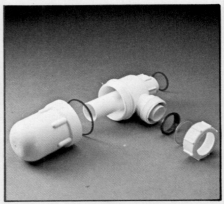

A dip tube trap taken apart to show the O rings and washers.

CUTTING & BENDING COPPER PIPE

One of the advantages of domestic copper pipe is that it's easy to cut and bend. Few tools are required and even if you've only a few bends to make in a pipe run, it makes sense to know how it's done. Making accurate bends may need some practice, but it's cheaper than buying specially-shaped fittings.

In all plumbing water has to be carried from a source to a fixture and often then to some type of exit where it can disperse as waste. Basic to all of this is that water must run smoothly with nothing causing resistance to the flow — an important factor when the pressure is low.

Generally the best plumbing practice is to make pipe runs as straight and direct as possible. But sometimes bends are unavoidable (like, for example, when pipe has to go around a room or to turn down into an area below) and if available fittings are neither right for the angle nor attractive to look at, then you'll have to bend the pipe to suit.

Copper piping, because it is both light and resistant to corrosion, is a popular choice for home plumbing work. It can be joined with either capillary or compression fittings (see pages 304-308 for more details) and when bends are needed you can create the angles in several ways.

The first essential is to accurately work out the pipe lengths you require. Once you've made the measurement double check it — it's quite easy to forget to allow for the pipe that will fit into the socket ends of the joints. You can make the actual marks on the pipe with pencil as this is clearly visible on copper and is a good guide when you come to cutting.

Cutting pipe accurately

For smaller pipe sizes, a sharp-bladed hacksaw is the best tool to use to make the cut. You'll need to hold the pipe firmly, but if you use a vice be careful not to over-tighten the jaws and crush the bore of the pipe (see *Ready Reference, page 303*).

It's important to cut the pipe square so that it butts up exactly to the pipe stop in the joint. This will ensure the pipe is seated squarely in the fitting which is essential for making a watertight seal. It will also help to make that seal. It's surprising how near to square you can get the end just cutting by eye. But the best way to make a really accurate cut is to use a saw guide. This can be made very easily by placing a small rectangle of paper round the pipe with one long edge against the cut mark. By bringing the two short edges of the paper together and aligning them you effectively make a template that's square to the pipe. All you then have to do is hold the paper in place and keep the saw blade against it as you cut. Any burr that's left on the cut edges can be removed with a file.

If you intend to carry out a lot of plumbing, or are working mainly in the larger pipe sizes, it may be worthwhile buying (or hiring) a wheel tube cutter. Of course using one of these is never absolutely essential, but it does save time if you've more than, say, half a dozen cuts to make. And once you have one you'll use it for even the smallest jobs. It's quick to use and will ensure a square cut without trouble every time. You simply place the pipe in the cutter and tighten the control knob to hold it in place. The cutter is then rotated round the pipe and as it revolves it cuts cleanly into the copper. This circular action automatically removes burr from the outside of the pipe, but burr on the inside can be taken away with the reamer (a scraping edge) which is usually incorporated in the tool.

Bending copper pipe

If a lot of changes of direction are necessary in a pipe run it's cheaper and quicker to bend the pipe rather than use fittings. This also makes the neatest finish particularly if the pipework is going to be exposed. Under a pedestal wash-basin, for example, the hot and cold supply pipes rise parallel to each other in the pedestal before bending outwards and upwards to connect to the two tap tails.

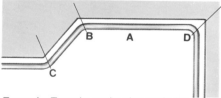

and upwards to connect to the two tap tails. Using fittings in this situation would be costly while the cheaper alternative, making bends, means the pipework is less conspicuous. The pipe can also be bent to the exact angle required so this method of changing direction is not limited by the angles of the fittings. And with fewer fittings in a pipe system there are fewer places where leaks can occur.

The smaller sizes of copper pipe, those most commonly used in domestic plumbing, can be bent quite easily by hand. The technique of annealing — heating the pipe to red heat in the vicinity of the bend to reduce its temper (strength) and so make bending easier — is unnecessary when working in these pipe sizes. But the pipe will need support, either internally or externally, as the bend is made otherwise the profile will be flattened and this would cause a reduction in the flow of water at the outlet point.

For small jobs a bending spring is the ideal tool, supporting the pipe internally. It is a long hardened steel coil which you push into the pipe to the point where the bend will be made. It's best used for bends near the end of the pipe, since the spring can be easily pulled out after the bend is made. However, it can be used further down the pipe if it is attached to a length of stout wire (which helps to push it into place, and is vital for retrieving it afterwards).

Bending techniques

You actually bend the pipe over your knee, overbending slightly and bringing back to the required angle. The spring will now be fixed tightly in the pipe and you won't be able simply to pull it out. However, its removal is quite easy. All you have to do is insert a bar – a screwdriver will do – through the ring at the end of the spring and twist it. This reduces the spring's diameter and will enable you to withdraw it. It's a good idea to grease the spring before you insert it as this will make pulling it out that much easier (also see *Ready Reference*, page 303).

Slight wrinkles may be found on the inside of the bend, but these can be tapped out by gentle hammering. It's wise not to attempt this before taking out the spring. If you do you'll never be able to remove it.

Bending springs are suitable for 15mm and 22mm diameter pipe. But although it is possible to bend 28mm pipe as well, it's advisable to use a bending machine instead. This is also preferable if you have a lot of bends to make. And if you don't want to go to the expense of buying one, you can probably hire a machine from a tool hire shop quite easily.

A bending machine consists of a semi-circular former that supports the pipe externally during the bending operation and a roller that forces the pipe round the curve when the levers of the machine are brought together. The degree of bend depends on how far you move the handles.

Flexible pipe

Although not yet available in Australia, this is a kind of corrugated copper pipe which can be bent easily by hand without any tools. It has either two plain ends for connection to compression joints, or has one end plain and one with a swivel tap connector for connection to a tap or ball-valve.

As it's the most expensive way of making a bend, it's not cost effective to use it when you have to make a number of changes of direction in a pipe run. It's not particularly attractive to look at so it is best used in places where it won't be seen — like, for example, when connecting the water supply pipes to bath taps in the very confined space at the head of the bath. This kind of pipe can make the job of fitting kitchen sink taps easier, particularly when the base unit has a back which restricts access to the supply pipes.

CUTTING COPPER PIPE

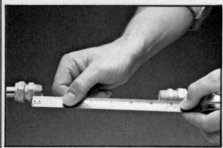

1 *Make an accurate measurement of the proposed pipe run. It is important to allow for the pipe that will fit into the joints.*

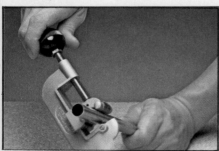

4 *When using a wheel tube cutter, the cutting mark on the pipe is put against the edge of the cutting wheel and the control knob is tightened.*

2 *Use a simple paper template to help you cut pipe squarely. Wrap the paper round the pipe and align the edges.*

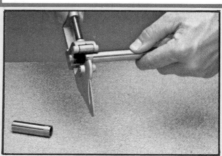

5 *Once the pipe is clamped in place, the cutter rotates to make an even cut. The rollers on the tool will keep the blade square to the pipe.*

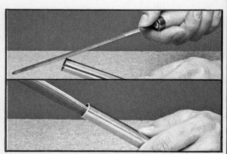

3 *Any burr on the outside of the pipe can be removed with the flat side of a file. The curved side can be used to clean the inside of the pipe.*

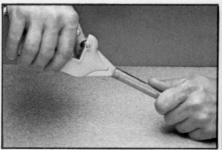

6 *A wheel tube cutter leaves a clean cut on the outside of the pipe, but any burr on the inside can be removed with the reamer (an attachment to the tool).*

BENDING COPPER PIPE

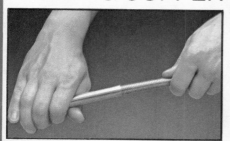

1 The bending spring must be compatible in size with the pipe. Smear it with petroleum jelly.

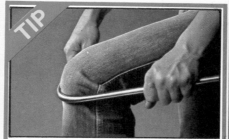

2 Overbend the pipe slightly, and then bend it back to the required angle.

3 Put a screwdriver through the ring at the end of the spring. Twist it, then pull the spring out.

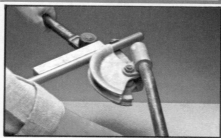

4 To use a bending machine, open the levers, place the pipe with the straight former on top.

5 Raise the levers so the wheel runs along the straight edge and the pipe is forced round the circular former.

6 Bend the pipe to the required angle, then remove by opening the levers, taking out the straight former.

FLEXIBLE COPPER PIPE

1 Flexible pipe is frequently used in Europe for making awkward bends in the pipe run when connecting to taps.

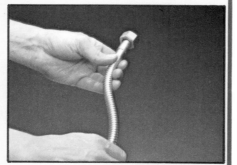

2 It's easy to hand bend the pipe to the required shape, but don't continually flex it or the thin wall will split.

Jem Grischotti

Ready Reference

PIPE LENGTHS

On your sketch plan (see *Ready Reference* page 81) measure the length of the run then work out
- how many 2 metre lengths you'll need
- where to join them in on the straight (not at a bend)
- how many fittings you'll need to connect the pipes to each other.

TIP: CUTTING PIPE

Copper pipe can be crushed in the jaws of a vice so use a bench hook when cutting with a hacksaw. Pin a scrap of wood beside it to hold the pipe snugly.

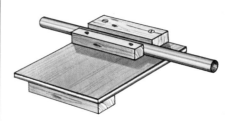

BENDING AIDS

For small diameter pipe use a *bending spring* to match the pipe size. It's a flexible coil of hardened steel about 600mm (2ft) long.

For pipe over 25mm diameter hire a *pipe bending machine* which supports the outside of the pipe wall as it bends.

TIP: REMOVING BENDING SPRINGS

For bends over 600mm (2ft) from the pipe end use a wire coathanger with a hooked end to turn and withdraw the spring.

JOINTS FOR COPPER PIPE

Joining copper pipe is one of the basic plumbing skills. Compression and capillary joints are easy to make and once you've mastered the techniques, you'll be prepared for a whole range of plumbing projects.

Connecting pipes effectively is the basis of all good plumbing as most leaks result from poorly constructed joints. For virtually all domestic plumbing purposes you will only have to use compression or capillary joints. Compression joints are easy to use but expensive, while capillary joints are cheap but need some care in fitting.

If you are making a join into an existing pipe system remember to make sure the water supply has been turned off at the relevant stoptap or gatevalve (see pages 291-295 and 319-321 for more details), and the pipe itself completely drained of water.

Preparing the pipes
Before joining the pipes together, check that the ends are circular and have not been distorted. If they have been dented, cut back to an undamaged section using a hacksaw with a sharp blade or a wheel tube cutter (see pages 301-303).

The ends should also be square and a simple way of checking this is shown overleaf (see *Ready Reference*). Use a file to make any correction and remove ragged burrs of metal. If you're using a capillary joint clean up the sides of the pipe with abrasive paper or steel wool.

Compression joints (friction joints)
A compression joint, as its name implies, is made by compressing two brass or copper rings (known as olives or thimbles) round the ends of the pipes to be joined, so forming a watertight seal. There are two main types of compression joint – the non-manipulative fitting and the manipulative fitting.

Although not the cheapest means of joining a pipe, a non-manipulative joint is the easiest to use and requires only the minimum of tools. It comprises a central body made of brass or gunmetal with a cap-nut at each end which, when rotated, squeezes the olive tightly between the pipe end and the casing. This is the most commonly used type of compression joint suitable for most internal domestic plumbing purposes.

A manipulative joint is now rarely used in indoor domestic water systems. Because it

cannot be pulled apart it is sometimes used for underground pipework, but capillary joints will do equally well in these situations.

The joint usually comprises a male and a female union nut. These are slipped over the pipe ends which are then flared ('manipulated') using a special steel tool called a *drift*. Jointing compound is smeared on the inside of the flares and a copper cone is inserted between them. The nuts are then screwed together to complete the seal.

How a compression joint works
The olive (thimble) is the key part of a non-manipulative compression joint. When the cap-nut is rotated clockwise the olive is forced between the casing and the pipe and is considerably deformed in the process.

A watertight seal is dependent upon the pipe ends having been well prepared so they butt up exactly to the pipe stop in the casing. This forms a primary seal and ensures that the pipe is parallel to the movement of the rotating cap-nut. An even pressure is then

applied to the olive so that it does not buckle under the strain of tightening.

What size of pipework and fittings?
Pipework is now sold in metric dimensions, but plumbing in your home may be in imperial sizes. The metric sizes are not exactly the same as their imperial equivalents – check the table *(Ready Reference, right)* which shows the different ways pipe can be bought.

These differences can cause problems. With capillary joints you have to use adaptors when converting pipe from one system to another. Adaptors are also needed for some compression joints although the 12mm, 15mm, 28mm and 54mm sizes are compatible with their imperial equivalents. This means if you already have imperial compression joints you can connect in new metric pipework, without replacing the joints.

Adaptors are made with different combinations of metric and imperial outlets to fit most requirements. A supplier will advise on what replacements to use.

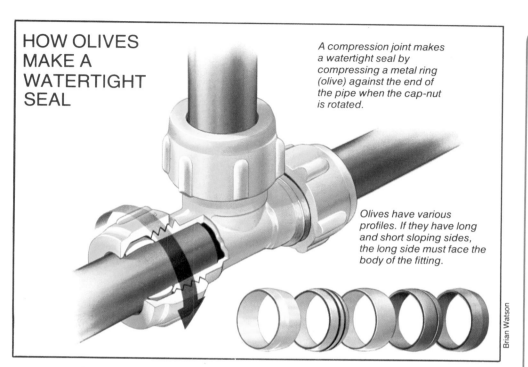

HOW OLIVES MAKE A WATERTIGHT SEAL

A compression joint makes a watertight seal by compressing a metal ring (olive) against the end of the pipe when the cap-nut is rotated.

Olives have various profiles. If they have long and short sloping sides, the long side must face the body of the fitting.

Brian Watson

Capillary joints

A capillary joint is simply a copper sleeve with socket outlets info which the pipe ends are soldered. It is neater and smaller than a compression joint and forms a robust connection that will not readily pull apart.

Because it is considerably cheaper than a compression joint it is frequently used when a number of joints have to be made and is particularly useful in awkward positions where it is impossible to use wrenches.

Some people are put off using capillary fittings because of the need to use a blow-torch. But modern gas-canister torches have put paid to the fears associated with

paraffin lamps and are not dangerous.

How a capillary joint works

If two pipes to be joined together were just soldered end to end the join would be very weak because the contact area between solder and copper would be small. A capillary fitting makes a secure join because the sleeve increases this contact area and also acts as a brace to strengthen the connection.

Molten solder is sucked into the space between the pipe and fitting by capillary action, and combines with a thin layer of copper at the contact surface thus bonding the pipe to the fitting. To help the solder to

What happens when solder melts

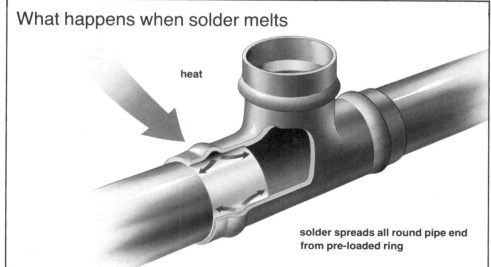

heat

solder spreads all round pipe end
from pre-loaded ring

Brian Watson

MAKING A COMPRESSION JOINT

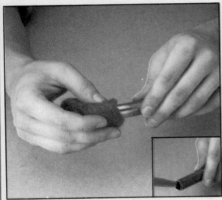

1   Check that the end of the pipe is square using a file to make any correction and to remove burr. Clean pipe end and olive with steel wool.

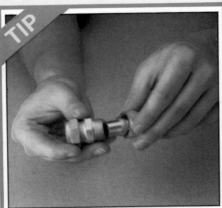

2   The olive goes on after the cap-nut. If it has both long and short sloping sides, make sure the long side faces the main body of the compression fitting.

3   Push pipe end firmly into body of fitting so that it rests squarely against pipe stop. Screw up cap-nut tightly with your fingers.

4   Make pencil mark on cap-nut and another aligning on body of fitting to act as guide when tightening cap-nut with wrench.

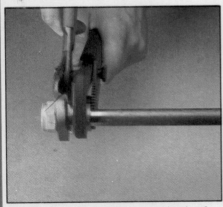

5   Use one wrench to secure body of fitting and the other to rotate the cap-nut clockwise. About 1½ turns is sufficient to give a watertight seal.

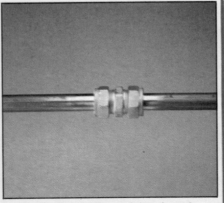

6   Repeat operation to join other pipe to fitting. If water seeps through when supply is turned on, tighten cap-nut further by half a turn.

'take' the copper needs to be clean and shining. Therefore flux is applied to prevent oxides forming which would impair the solder-copper bond.

Types of capillary joint
The most common type of capillary joint has a ring of solder pre-loaded into the sleeve. It is known as an integral ring or 'Yorkshire' fitting – the name of a leading brand.

The 'end feed' type of capillary joint is virtually the same as an integral ring fitting, but you have to add the solder in a separate operation. The sleeve is slightly larger than the pipe and liquid solder is drawn into the space between by capillary action.

Flux and solder
Essential in the soldering operation, flux is a chemical paste or liquid which cleans the metal surfaces and then protects them from the oxides produced when the blow-torch heats the copper so a good metal-solder bond is formed. Mild non-corrosive flux is easy to use as it can be smeared onto the pipe and fitting with a clean brush or even a finger. Although it is best to remove any residue this will not corrode the metal. There is an acid-corrosive flux which dissolves oxides quickly, but this is mostly used with stainless steel. The corrosive residue must be scrubbed off with soapy water.

Solder is an alloy of tin and lead or silver and is bought as a reel of wire. Its advantage in making capillary joints is that it melts at relatively low temperatures and quickly hardens as it cools. Lead-free solder must now be used on pipes carrying drinking water.

Blow-torches
A blow-torch is an essential piece of equipment when making capillary joints. It is easy, clean and safe to use providing you handle it with care. Most modern torches operate off a gas canister which can be unscrewed and inexpensively replaced (larger cans are relatively cheaper than small). Sometimes a range of nozzles can be fitted to give different types of flames, but the standard nozzle is perfectly acceptable for capillary joint work.

Using a blow-torch
When using a blow-torch it's most convenient to work at a bench, but you'll find most jointing work has to be carried out where the pipes are to run. Pipework is usually concealed so this may mean working in an awkward place, such as a roof space, or stretching under floorboards. However, always make sure you are in a comfortable position and there's no danger of you dropping a lighted blow-torch.

Jem Grischotti

MAKING A CAPILLARY FITTING

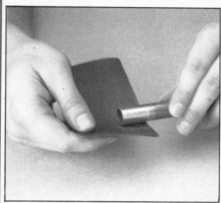

1   Make sure the pipe end is square, then clean it and the inner rim of the fitting with steel wool or abrasive paper until shining.

2   Flux can be in liquid or paste form. Use a brush, rather than your finger, to smear it over the end of the pipe and the inner rim of the fitting.

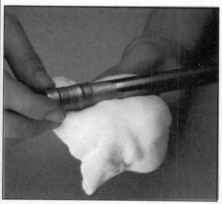

3   Push pipe into fitting so that it rests against pipe stop, twisting a little to help spread the flux. Remove excess flux with a cloth.

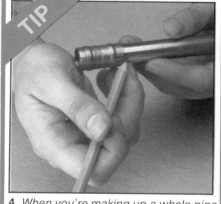

TIP

4   When you're making up a whole pipe-run, it helps to make corresponding pencil marks on pipe ends and fittings as a guide for correct lining up.

5   Make other side of joint in same way, then apply blow-torch. Seal is complete when bright ring of solder is visible at ends of fitting.

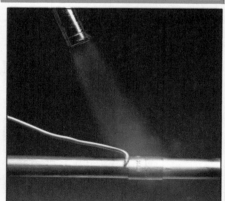

6   For an end feed fitting, heat the pipe, then hold the solder to mouth of joint. A bright ring all the way round signifies a seal.

Jem Grischotti

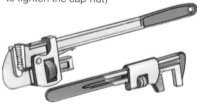

When working near to joists and floor-boards, glass, paintwork and other pipework with capillary joints it is important to shield these areas with glass fibre matting or a piece of asbestos.

Applying the heat

When making a capillary joint gradually build up the temperature of the copper by playing the flame up and down and round the pipe and then to the fitting. When the metal is hot enough the solder will melt and you can then take away the flame. The joint is complete when a bright ring of solder appears all round the mouth of the fitting. Stand the torch on a firm level surface and turn it off as soon as you have finished. Where two or more capillary joints are to be made with one fitting, for example the three ends of a tee, they should all be made at the same time. If this is not possible wrap a damp rag round any joints already made.

Repairing a compression joint

If a compression joint is leaking and tighten-ing of the cap-nut doesn't produce a watertight seal you'll have to disconnect the fitting and look inside – after turning off the water supply. If a cap-nut is impossible to move, run a few drops of penetrating oil onto the thread. If that doesn't do the trick, you'll have to cut it out and replace the fitting and some piping.

Once you have unscrewed one of the cap-nuts there will be enough flexibility in the pipe run to pull the pipe from the casing. Usually the olive will be compressed against the pipe. First check that it is the right way round (see page 56) and if it isn't replace it with a new one making sure that it is correctly set.

Sometimes the olive is impossible to remove and needs to be cut off with a hacksaw – make the cut diagonally. Reas-semble the joint following the procedure on page 306 and repeat the operation for the other end of the pipe. Turn on the water supply to check that the repair is watertight.

Repairing a capillary joint

Poor initial soldering is usually the reason why a capillary fitting leaks. You can try and rectify this by 'sweating' in some more solder but if this doesn't work you'll have to remake the joint.

Play the flame of the blow-torch over the fitting and pipe until the solder begins to run from the joint. At this stage you can pull the pipe ends out of the sockets with gloved hands. You can now reuse the fitting as an end feed joint or replace it with a new integral ring capillary connection.

If you reuse the fitting clean the interior surface and the pipe ends with abrasive paper or steel wool and smear them with flux. Then follow the procedure for making an end feed capillary joint.

REPAIRING A COMPRESSION JOINT

1   Unscrew cap-nut using wrenches. There's enough flexibility in pipe run to pull pipe from casing. Check that olive fits, and isn't damaged.

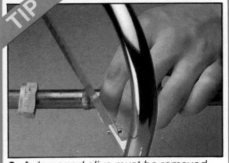

2   A damaged olive must be removed. Use a hacksaw and to make it easier make the cut on the diagonal – but take care not to cut into the pipe itself.

3   Prepare end of pipe with steel wool or abrasive paper. Slip on new olive and finger tighten cap-nut. Rotate cap-nut 1½ turns using wrenches.

REPAIRING A CAPILLARY JOINT

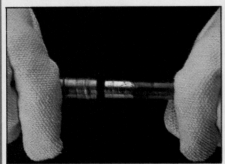

1   Drain pipe and wrap a damp cloth round nearby joints. Play flame on fitting and pull pipe from rim using gloved hands.

2   If you remake both sides of joint use a new fitting. A spent integral ring fitting, thoroughly cleaned, can be used as an end feed joint.

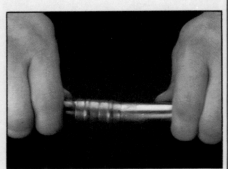

3   Use steel wool to clean end of pipe and inside of fitting. Brush with flux and push pipe into socket. Apply blow-torch to melt solder.

USING PLASTIC PIPE AND FITTINGS

Plastic pipe and fittings can now be used for hot water supplies and central heating. They are easy to work with and allow the DIY plumber to tackle a wide range of jobs.

Over the last twenty years plastic has become the most popular plumbing material for above and below ground drainage, for rainwater collection and disposal, and for subsoil drainage. In the form of black polythene tubing it has also become a material widely used for water transportation on camping sites and farms. In the home, however, it has not proved popular. Although this lack of interest can partly be attributed to the conservatism of plumbers and householders, the main reason has been that up until now the plastic pipes that have been available have been suitable for cold water supplies only. This has meant that plumbers, who have had no choice but to use copper or some other metal for the hot water or central heating system, have almost always tended to use the same material when dealing with the cold water system. Householders have doubted the ability of plastic pipework to do a good, life-long job, and have also tended to resist its use on grounds of taste: quite simply, in places where pipework is exposed to view the combination of plastic and copper (or stainless steel or iron) is not one that is very pleasing to the eye.

Now, however, all this has changed. Recently the National Water Council (NWC) gave its approval to two proprietary systems of plastic plumbing, one made out of polybutylene and the other of chlorinated polyvinyl chloride (CPVC), both of which can now be used for cold *and* hot water supply as well as for wet central heating systems. These two rival plumbing systems should hold a special appeal for the DIY enthusiast and – now that they have gained the NWC's approval – there is nothing to prevent them gaining widespread acceptance.

The advantages of plastic pipework

The most obvious advantage is the lightness of the pipework, which makes for ease of handling, but the most important benefit is the ease with which plastic can be cut and joined. This means that the level of skill you require to undertake a particular plumbing task is greatly reduced, as is the amount of time you require to carry it out. Both systems are also strong and durable, more resistant

to frost than a traditional plumbing system and, unlike the latter, not subject to corrosion. Last but not least, they are competitively priced.

Plastic pipes are less vulnerable to frost because plastic is a poor conductor of heat compared to metal (which means that, unlike metal, it provides a certain amount of insulation), and because it has greater elasticity. This means that plastic pipes are not only less likely to freeze than metal ones, but also that in the event of their doing so they are much less likely to burst. The greater degree of insulation that plastic provides also brings other benefits: it results in less heat being lost from pipe runs between radiators (or between the hot water cylinder and the hot taps), as well as meaning that less insulation is necessary for pipework that needs to be protected against the cold.

Plastic pipes aren't subject to corrosion for the simple reason that plastic isn't attacked by the water supply. Electrolytic corrosion, which results in the build up of hydrogen gas and black iron oxide sludge (magnetite) and can ultimately lead to leaky radiators and early pump failure, is therefore far less of a problem when a central heating system is fitted with plastic pipes.

This also means that plastic is a safer material to use for your drinking water supply pipes than metal, the use of which can, under some circumstances, present a health risk.

One final point to be borne in mind before you replace metal pipes with plastic ones is that plastic is a non-conductor of electricity. This means that all-plastic plumbing systems cannot be used to earth a domestic electricity supply (see *Ready Reference*, page 312.)

You can obtain both polybutylene and CPVC tubing in the 15mm (½in), 22mm (¾in) and 28mm (1in) diameters commonly used in domestic hot and cold water supply and in small-bore central heating. However, in other respects – particularly as regards the flexibility of the two different types of tubing and methods of cutting and jointing – the two systems differ. So, before you undertake a plumbing task using plastic pipes and fittings, you'd do well to consider which system best suits your particular application.

Polybutylene tubing

Polybutylene tubing is brown in colour and naturally flexible; in this respect it differs from CPVC tubing, which is rigid. As well as being available in 3m (10ft) lengths in all three diameters, it is also obtainable as a 100m (390ft) coil in the 15mm (½in) size, and as a 50m (195ft) coil in the 22mm (¾in) size. This flexibility, and the long lengths in which the tubing is available, is particularly useful as it cuts down the time you need to spend on installation, and reduces the number of fittings necessary (which means less cost). You can thread polybutylene pipes under floors and between joists with minimal disturbance, their flexibility also allowing you to take them through apertures and round obstacles that would otherwise present serious difficulties. You can bend the tubing cold to easy bends with a minimum radius of eight times the pipe diameter; 15mm (½in) tube can therefore be bent to a minimum radius of 120mm (4¾in) and 22mm (¾in) to a minimum radius of 176mm (7in). You must, however, provide a clip on either side of the bend to secure it. The flexibility of polybutylene tubing means that

POLYBUTYLENE PIPE AND FITTINGS

1 The best way to cut polybutylene pipe is with the manufacturer's shears. These are easy to use and ensure that you get a square-cut pipe end every time.

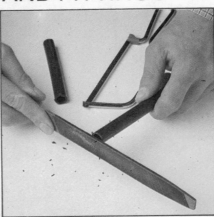

2 Alternatively, you can cut polybutylene pipe with a hacksaw or a sharp knife. If you use this method don't forget to clean off any burr or swarf with a file.

3 Before jointing the pipe, insert a stainless steel support sleeve into the pipe end. This prevents the tube end getting crushed within the fitting.

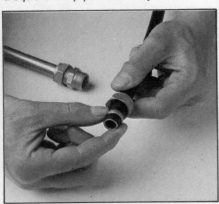

4 Polybutylene pipe can be used with ordinary compression fittings. The joint is made in exactly the same way as one made using ordinary copper pipe.

5 Within a polybutylene fitting a grab ring holds the pipe in place, while an 'O' ring ensures a watertight seal. The two are separated by a spacer washer.

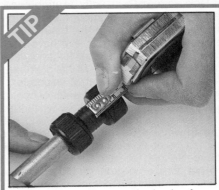

6 The witness lines on the body of the fitting indicate the length of pipe hidden within it when the joint is assembled. Remember to allow for this.

7 Before inserting polybutylene pipe into a polybutylene fitting, apply a special lubricant to both the pipe end and the interior of the socket.

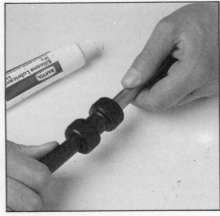

8 Make the joint without unscrewing or even loosening the cap-nuts. Simply thrust the pipe end into the socket until it meets the pipe stop inside.

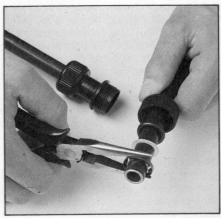

9 The pipe can be withdrawn only if you unscrew the cap-nut. To re-use the joint, crush and discard the grab ring, and then replace it with a new one.

CPVC PIPE AND FITTINGS

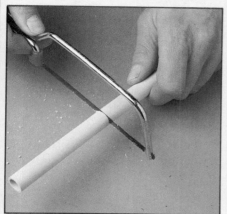

1 You can cut CPVC pipe with either a fine-toothed saw or an ordinary pipe cutter. If using a saw, make sure that you hold it at right-angles to the pipe.

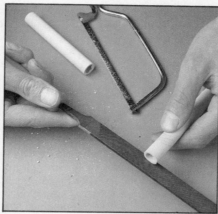

2 Use a file or a knife to remove the swarf from the pipe end. Check that the pipe fits snugly in the socket, and that the fitting is free from imperfections.

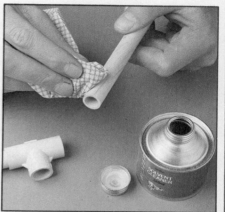

3 Before making a joint with CPVC the surfaces to be solvent-welded must first be cleaned. Use the manufacturer's special solvent cleaner for this purpose.

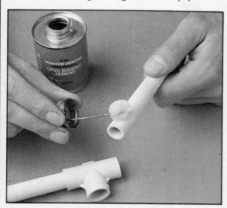

4 Immediately afterwards, apply the solvent weld cement, brushing this liberally on the tube end and only sparingly in the interior of the fitting socket.

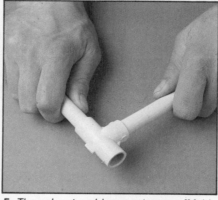

5 The solvent-weld cement goes off fairly rapidly, so you must make the joint as soon as you've applied it. Push the pipe home with a slight twisting motion.

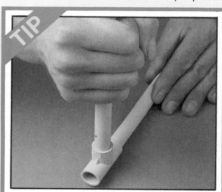

6 The solvent-weld cement's rapid setting time also means you must make adjustment for alignment immediately. Do not remove surplus cement.

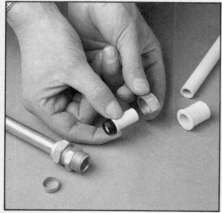

7 You can join CPVC pipe to copper using a compression fitting and a two-part adaptor. Discard the olive as the first part of the adaptor is self-sealing.

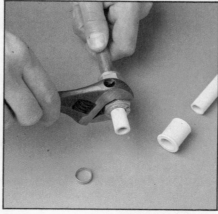

8 Tighten up the compression fitting in the usual way. Use a second spanner to hold the body of the fitting before giving the coupling nut a final turn.

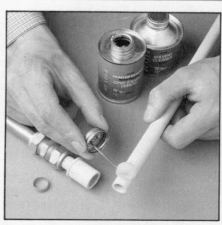

9 Having solvent-welded the two parts of the adaptor together, complete the fitting by solvent-welding the CPVC pipe to the second part of the adaptor.

311

you will have to give continuous support to any visible horizontal pipe runs in order to eliminate the possibility of unsightly sagging (see *Ready Reference*).

You can cut polybutylene tube with a sharp knife or a hacksaw. However, for speed of operation and to ensure an absolutely square cut pipe end every time, the manufacturers recommend that you use their specially designed pipe shears. It would certainly be worthwhile investing in a pair of these shears before embarking on a major project that involved the marking of a large number of joints.

You can join polybutylene tubing by using either non-manipulative (Type 'A') compression joints (as used with copper), or else the manufacturer's own patent push-fit connectors. One of the advantages of being able to use Type 'A' compression joints with tubing is that it enables you to replace a length of copper pipe with polybutylene tubing using the existing compression tee or coupling.

When using polybutylene tubing with this type of joint the procedure you follow is identical to that which you adopt with copper pipe. But in order to prevent the collapse of the tube end when the cap-nut is tightened, you must insert a purpose-made stainless steel support sleeve into the tube end. And if you use jointing compound to complete a threaded fitting connected to polybutylene pipe, make sure none comes into contact with the polybutylene.

The patent polybutylene joints and fittings are available in the usual range of straight couplings, tees, elbows, reducing fittings and tap and tank connectors, and in appearance they resemble their brass compression counterparts. But there is one important difference – you don't have to loosen or unscrew the cap-nuts to make a joint.

To make a connection you simply have to push the prepared pipe end into the fitting (see step-by-step photographs). Polybutylene fittings have one further advantage in that they allow you to rotate a pipe that has been inserted into one of them, even when it is filled with water. This means, for example, that a polybutylene stop-valve can rest neatly against a wall until you need to use it. You then pull the handle away from the wall so you can open and close it easily.

CPVC tubing
CPVC tubing differs from the polybutylene type in two basic ways. First, it is rigid rather than flexible, which means that it is only available in relatively short lengths of 2m (6ft 6in) or 3m (9ft 9in). Secondly, it is joined by a process known as solvent welding, a slightly more involved procedure than making a push-fit or compression connection (see

step-by-step photographs). Superficially, CPVC tubing can be distinguished from polybutylene by its off-white colour. An hour after the last joint has been made you can flush through the system and fill it with cold water; before filling with hot water you need to wait at least four hours.

CPVC pipe does expand when hot water passes through it, but this won't cause a problem in most domestic systems unless one of the pipe runs exceeds 10m (33ft), which is unlikely. In this case you will have to create an expansion loop using four 90° elbows and three 150mm (6in) lengths of pipe.

The manufacturers of CPVC tubing provide an exceptionally wide range of fittings to meet every eventuality. There are 90° and 45° elbows, equal and unequal tees, reducing pieces, tap and ball-valve connectors, stop-valves and gate-valves, and provision for connection to existing copper or screwed iron fittings. The connectors for copper tubing have a solvent-weld socket at one end and a conventional Type 'A' compression joint at the other. Those for iron fittings have a solvent-weld fitting at one end and either a male or female threaded joint at the other. If you are connecting a fitting to an existing iron socket, make sure that you render the screwed connection watertight by binding plastic PTFE tape round the male thread before screwing home.

What system to use
Neither system is 'better' than the other, and each has its merits and its drawbacks. The polybutylene tubing is flexible and available in extremely long lengths which reduce the number of joints you will have to use, as well as enabling you to get through or round obstacles that might prove difficult were you using the CPVC system. On the other hand the push-fit polybutylene joints are bulkier and more obtrusive than those used with the CPVC system.

Bearing in mind this, and the fact that the rigid CPVC pipes will be less prone to sagging than the flexible polybutylene tubing, the CPVC system is probably the more acceptable one in situations where plumbing is exposed to view. The more complex construction of the polybutylene joints – the cause of their bulkiness – also makes them relatively expensive: which means that the smaller number necessary for carrying out a given plumbing task won't always cost you less than the greater number necessary with CPVC. However, polybutylene joints, unlike CPVC ones, can be used more than once.

Lastly, in case your decision to opt for one system or the other is influenced by the colour of the material out of which it is made (dark brown for polybutylene and off-white for CPVC), you can paint both systems with ordinary household paints.

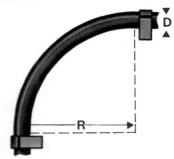

Ready Reference

TIP: CHECK EARTHING
Metal plumbing systems were often used to earth the domestic electricity supply. Since plastic pipework doesn't conduct electricity, it's vital that the house's earthing arrangements are checked by an electrician if you replace any part of the plumbing system with plastic.

BENDING POLYBUTYLENE PIPE
You can form bends in polybutylene pipe to a minimum radius of eight times the pipe diameter.

CONNECTING POLYBUTYLENE TO IMPERIAL COPPER PIPES
You can use 15mm (½in) polybutylene fittings with ½in imperial-sized copper pipe without adaptation. If you wish to use 22mm (¾in) fittings with ¾in imperial-sized copper pipe, you have to replace the sealing ring with a purpose-made one of larger size.

SUPPORTING PIPE RUNS
With CPVC pipe, space pipe brackets at 500mm (20in) intervals on horizontal pipe runs, at 1m (39in) intervals on vertical ones. With polybutylene pipe, use the following spacings:

Pipe size	Horizontal run	Vertical run
15mm (½in)	400mm (16in)	800mm (31in)
22mm (¾in)	600mm (24in)	1m (39in)

Reduce these by 25 per cent for pipes carrying water over 60°C (140°F), increase them by 25 per cent for cold pipe runs.

CONNECTIONS TO BOILERS
Although polybutylene and CPVC pipes are suitable for all other applications, you can't connect them directly to a boiler. Instead you should
● connect short lengths of copper pipe to the boiler flow and return tappings
● link the plastic pipe to the copper using the appropriate type of fitting. The copper pipe tails should be
● 380mm (15in) long with CPVC pipe
● 1m (39in) long with polybutylene pipe.

COMPARING THE SYSTEMS

To show how the two plastic systems look
in use, here is the pipe run involved in
teeing off a spur to a washing machine,
assembled using the appropriate fittings
in each case. For comparison the
same run has been assembled
using copper pipe with capillary
and compression fittings too.

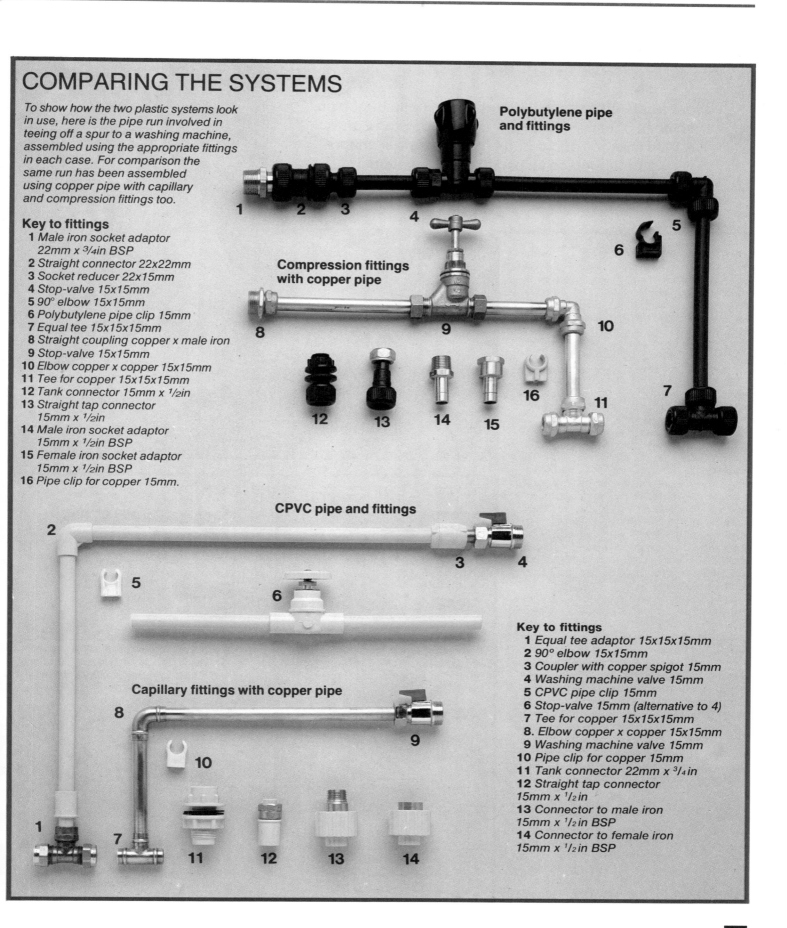

**Polybutylene pipe
and fittings**

**Compression fittings
with copper pipe**

Key to fittings
 1 *Male iron socket adaptor
   22mm x ³/₄in BSP*
 2 *Straight connector 22x22mm*
 3 *Socket reducer 22x15mm*
 4 *Stop-valve 15x15mm*
 5 *90° elbow 15x15mm*
 6 *Polybutylene pipe clip 15mm*
 7 *Equal tee 15x15x15mm*
 8 *Straight coupling copper x male iron*
 9 *Stop-valve 15x15mm*
10 *Elbow copper x copper 15x15mm*
11 *Tee for copper 15x15x15mm*
12 *Tank connector 15mm x ¹/₂in*
13 *Straight tap connector
   15mm x ¹/₂in*
14 *Male iron socket adaptor
   15mm x ¹/₂in BSP*
15 *Female iron socket adaptor
   15mm x ¹/₂in BSP*
16 *Pipe clip for copper 15mm.*

CPVC pipe and fittings

Capillary fittings with copper pipe

Key to fittings
 1 *Equal tee adaptor 15x15x15mm*
 2 *90° elbow 15x15mm*
 3 *Coupler with copper spigot 15mm*
 4 *Washing machine valve 15mm*
 5 *CPVC pipe clip 15mm*
 6 *Stop-valve 15mm (alternative to 4)*
 7 *Tee for copper 15x15x15mm*
 8. *Elbow copper x copper 15x15mm*
 9 *Washing machine valve 15mm*
10 *Pipe clip for copper 15mm*
11 *Tank connector 22mm x ³/₄in*
12 *Straight tap connector
   15mm x ¹/₂in*
13 *Connector to male iron
   15mm x ¹/₂in BSP*
14 *Connector to female iron
   15mm x ¹/₂in BSP*

JOINING PLASTIC PIPING

Most waste pipes installed today are made of plastic, which is cheap, lightweight and easy to work with. A little practice and careful measuring will enable you to replace all parts of your system. Here's how to join them together.

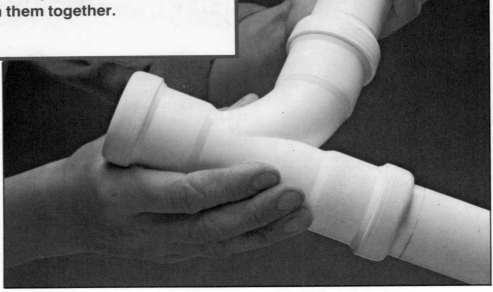

Waste systems draining baths, basins and sinks used to be made of lead, heavy galvanised steel with screwed joints, or copper. Soil pipes from WCs were traditionally cast iron, as was all the outside pipework for both waste and soil disposal. Nowadays waste and soil pipes are made of one or other of a variety of plastic materials, which may be used for repairs, extension work or complete replacement of an existing system.

These plastic pipes are lightweight and easily cut, handled and joined. They are made of materials usually known by the initials of their chemical names – UPVC (unplasticised polyvinyl chloride), MPVC (modified polyvinyl chloride), ABS (acrylonitrile butadiene styrene) and PP (polypropylene). CPVC (chlorinated polyvinyl chloride) is usually used for hot and cold water supply pipes. Pipes and fittings are available in white, grey or a copper colour, depending on type and manufacture.

All these materials are satisfactory for domestic waste systems and – with one exception – can all be joined in the same way: either by push-fit (ring-seal) jointing or by solvent welding.

The exception is PP pipe. This was first developed because of its good resistance to very hot water and chemical wastes, and was therefore extensively used in industry. Nowadays, however, it is frequently used in the home for waste or rainwater drainage. The big difference between PP and other plastic pipes used in waste drainage is that it cannot be solvent-welded. All joints must be push-fit. In most situations this is no great disadvantage but it does make it important to be able to distinguish PP from other plastics. It has a slightly greasy feel and, when cut with a fine toothed saw, leaves fine strands of fibrous material round the cut edges.

Sizes

When buying plastic pipe and components it is wise to stick to one brand only. Pipes and fittings from different makers, though of the same size, are not necessarily interchangeable. Most suppliers stock the systems of only one manufacturer, although the same

PREPARING THE PIPE ENDS

1 To make sure that you cut the pipe squarely, hold a sheet of paper around it so that the edges meet and overlap each other. This is your cutting line.

2 Hold the pipe firmly and cut it with a hacksaw, using gentle strokes. You may find it easier to use a junior hacksaw, which gives a finer cut.

3 When you've cut the pipe, use a piece of fine glass paper to clean off the burr left by sawing.

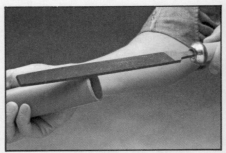

4 Now take a file and chamfer the end of the pipe all round the edge to a 45° angle. Try to keep the chamfer even.

SOLVENT-WELD JOINTING

1 *Push the end of the pipe into the socket of the fitting as far as it will go. Mark the pipe at this point with a pencil as a guide to the length within the joint.*

2 *Take the pipe out of the fitting and, with a file, roughen the whole of the end surface that will be inside the fitting up to the pencil mark.*

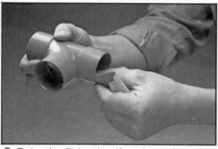

3 *Take the fitting itself and roughen the inside of the socket with fine glass paper. This will provide a key for the solvent cement.*

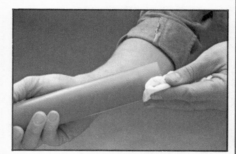

4 *Now clean off the roughened surface of the pipe and socket with spirit as recommended by the manufacturer to remove all dust and debris.*

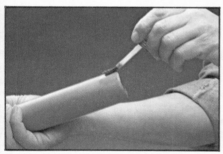

5 *Apply the solvent cement to the roughened end of the pipe, making sure that the whole roughened area is covered. Try and keep it off your fingers.*

6 *Also apply solvent cement to the socket of the fitting. Try to use brush strokes along the line of the pipe.*

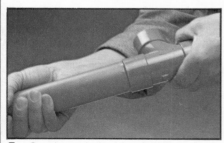

7 *Gently push the pipe fully home into the socket. Some manufacturers suggest a slight twisting action in doing this but check their instructions first.*

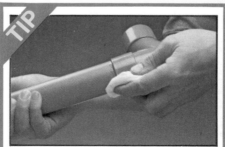

8 *Remove any excess solvent at the edge of the socket with a clean cloth, hold the joint in position for 15 seconds.*

PUSH-FIT JOINTING

1 *Cut the pipe squarely as in solvent-weld jointing and remove the burr, then take the fitting and clean the socket out with the recommended cleaner.*

2 *Check that the rubber seal is properly seated in the socket. You may find seals are supplied separately and you will have to insert them.*

3 *Now chamfer the end of the pipe to an angle of 45°, and smooth off the chamfer carefully with fine glass paper so that no rough edges remain.*

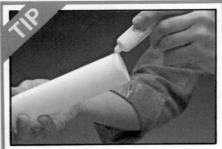

4 *Lubricate the end of the pipe with petroleum jelly over a length of about 5mm (3/16in).*

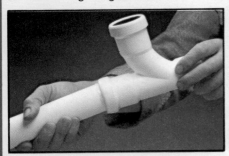

5 *Push the pipe into the socket gently but firmly. Then push it fully home and check that all is square, otherwise you may damage the sealing ring.*

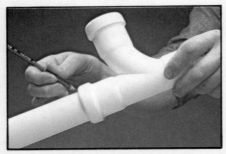

6 *Now make a pencil mark on the pipe at the edge of the socket – you can easily rub it off later if you want to – to act as a guide in setting the expansion gap.*

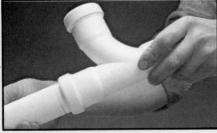

7 *Gently pull the pipe out from the fitting so that your pencil mark is about 10mm (3/8in) away from the fitting to allow for expansion when hot water is flowing.*

8 *The joint is now complete. Wipe off any excess petroleum jelly. Don't lose the expansion allowance when joining the other side of the fitting.*

manufacturer may make both PP and either PVC or ABS systems.

It is worth asking the supplier if there is an instruction leaflet supplied by the maker. There are slight variations in the methods of using each particular make of pipe and fitting. The manufacturer's instructions, if available, should be followed to the letter.

Buying new pipe

Existing waste pipe is likely to be imperial in size – 1½in internal diameter for a sink or bath and 1¼in internal diameter for a wash basin.

Metric sized plastic pipes are normally described – like thin-walled copper tubes – by their external diameter, though at least one well-known manufacturer adds to the confusion by using the internal diameter. Both internal and external diameters may vary slightly – usually by less than one millimetre between makes. This is yet another reason for sticking to one make of pipe for any single project.

The outside diameter of a plastic tube that is the equivalent of a 1¼in imperial sized metal tube is likely to be 36mm and the inside diameter 32mm. The outside diameter of the equivalent of a 1½in pipe is likely to be 43mm and the inside diameter 39mm. If in doubt, it is usually sufficient to ask the supplier for waste pipe fittings for a basin waste or – as the case may be – a bath or sink waste. Plain-ended plastic pipe is usually supplied in 3m (10ft) lengths, though a supplier will probably cut you off a shorter piece.

Joining solvent-weld types

Solvent-weld fittings are neater and less obtrusive than push-fit ones and they offer the facility of pre-fabrication before installation. However, making them does demand a little more skill and care and – unlike push-fit joints – they cannot accommodate the expansion (thermal movement) that takes place as hot wastes run through the pipe. A 4m length of PVC pipe will expand by about 13mm (just over ½in) when its temperature is raised above 20°C (70°F). For this reason, where a straight length of waste pipe exceeds 1.8m (6ft) in length, expansion couplings must be introduced at 1.8m intervals if other joints are to be solvent-welded. This rarely occurs in domestic design, however, and use of push-fit or solvent-weld is a matter of personal preference.

Although the instructions given by the different manufacturers vary slightly, the steps to making solvent-weld joints follow very similar lines. Of course, the first rule is to measure up all your pipe lengths carefully. Remember to allow for the end of the pipe overlapping the joint. When you've worked out pipe lengths cutting can start.

JOINING SOIL PIPES

These pipes are joined in the same way as plastic waste pipes but are much bigger – about 100mm (4in) in diameter – so they take longer to fit. They also have some different fittings, such as a soil branch for use where the outlet pipe joins the stack, and access fittings with bolted removable plates for inspection. There are also special connectors to link to the WC pan, via a special gasket, and to link to the underground drainage system which is traditionally made of vitrified clay.

The accurate moulding of the fittings and the ease of assembly means that you can confidently tackle complete replacement of a soil system.

1 Soil pipes are joined in the same way as their narrower waste counterparts, but as they're bigger take special care with cutting and chamfering.

2 You have got a lot more area to cover with the solvent cement so you must work speedily – but don't neglect accurate application.

3 The soil branch pipe has a swept entry into the main stack fitting. This is one of the most important joints in the system, so make sure you get it right.

4 When you finally push the pipe into the fitting socket make quite sure that it goes right home against the pipe stop inside the fitting.

Cut the pipe clean and square with a hacksaw or other fine-toothed saw. A useful tip to ensure a square cut is to fold a piece of newspaper over the pipe and join the edges beneath it. The paper will then act as a template.

Remove all internal and external 'burr' or roughness at the end of the pipe, then use a file to chamfer the outside of the pipe end to about 45°. Not all manufacturers recommend this, but it does provide an extra key for the solvent.

Insert the pipe end into the fitting and mark the depth of insertion with a pencil. Using medium grade abrasive paper, or a light file, lightly roughen the end of the pipe, as far as the pencil mark, and also roughen the interior of the socket. Thoroughly clean the roughened surfaces of the socket and the pipe end using a clean rag moistened with a spirit cleaner recommended by the manufacturer of the fittings.

Select the correct solvent cement (PVC pipes need a different solvent cement from ABS ones; once again, buy all the materials needed at the same time from the same supplier). Read the label on the tin and stir only if instructed.

Using a clean paintbrush apply the solvent cement to the pipe end and to the

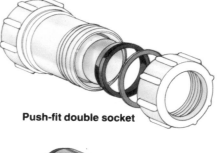

inside of the fittings, brushing in the direction of the pipe. It is usually necessary to apply two coats to ABS pipes and fittings. The second coat should be brushed on quickly before the first has dried.

Push the pipe fully home into the fitting (some, but not all, manufacturers suggest that this should be done with a slight twisting action). Remove excess solvent cement and hold the assembled joint securely in position for about 30 seconds. If hot water will be flowing through the pipe, don't use it for 24 hours to give time for the joint to set completely.

Joining ring-seal types
Preparation for ring-seal or push-fit jointing is similar to that for solvent welding. The pipe end must be cut absolutely squarely and all the burr removed. You should draw a line round the cut end of the pipe 10mm from its end and chamfer back to this line with a rasp or shaping tool, then clean the recess within the push-fit connector's socket and check that the sealing ring is evenly seated. One manufacturer supplies sealing rings separately, and they should be inserted at this point. The pipe end should now be lubricated with a small amount of petroleum jelly and pushed firmly into the socket past the joint ring. Push it fully home and mark the insertion depth on the pipe with a pencil. Then withdraw it by 10mm (which is the allowance made for expansion). The expansion joint that is inserted into long straight lengths of solvent-welded waste pipe consists of a coupling with a solvent-weld joint at one end and a push-fit joint at the other.

As with solvent-weld jointing, individual manufacturers may give varying instructions. Some, for instance, advise the use of their own silicone lubricating jelly. Where the manufacturer supplies instructions it is best to follow these exactly.

Fittings
PVC pipe can be bent by the application of gentle heat from a blow-torch, but this technique needs practice and it is best to rely on purpose-made fittings. Sockets are used for joining straight lengths of pipe, tees for right-angled branches, and both 90° and 45° elbows are usually available. If you need to reduce the diameters from one pipe to another you can use reducing sockets. These are really sockets within sockets which can be welded together, one taking the smaller diameter pipe and the other the larger. Soil outlet pipes from WCs are joined in the same way; they are merely bigger — usually 100mm (4in) — in diameter. Sockets work in the same way, but the branch-junction with the main soil stack must be of a specially 'swept' design.

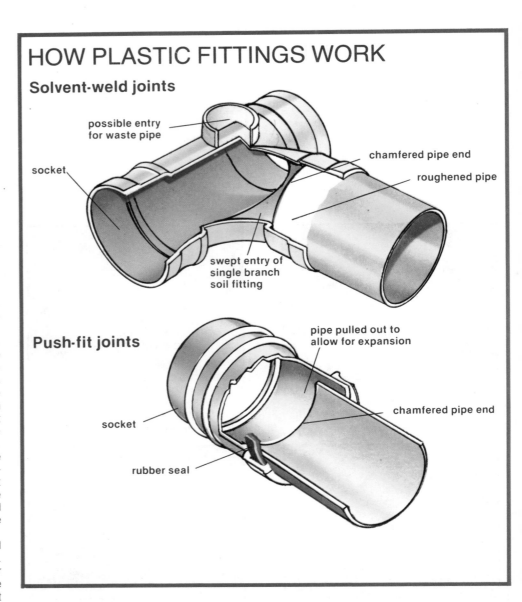

HOW PLASTIC FITTINGS WORK

Solvent-weld joints

possible entry for waste pipe

socket

chamfered pipe end

roughened pipe

swept entry of single branch soil fitting

Push-fit joints

pipe pulled out to allow for expansion

chamfered pipe end

socket

rubber seal

SPECIAL FITTINGS

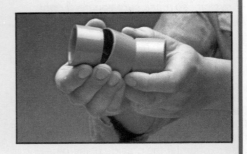

Special fittings are available when pipe fitting is not straightforward. This is a reducing adaptor for push-fit fittings where you need to join a

32mm pipe to a 40mm pipe. You join the relevant pipe to the mating part of the adaptor and then join the two adaptor parts together.

DRAINING PLUMBING SYSTEMS

When you are carrying out repairs or alterations to your plumbing or wet central heating system, you will usually have to drain water from the parts you are working on. Here's what you'll have to do.

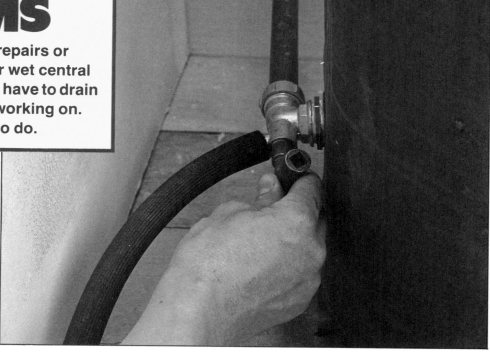

Virtually all major and many minor plumbing operations demand the partial or total drainage of either the domestic hot or cold water supply. If you have a 'wet' central heating system you'll also have to drain that before carrying out repairs or alterations. Before attempting this – long before the need for drainage arises, in fact – you should make yourself thoroughly familiar with the design and layout of these systems in your home. Here are some questions to which you should know the answers:

● Are all cold water draw-off points supplied direct from the rising main, or are the bathroom cold taps and the WC cistern supplied with water from a main cold water storage cistern (probably situated in the roof space)?
● Is the hot water system 'direct' or 'indirect' (see pages 291-295)?
● If the system is direct, is the domestic hot water heated solely by means of an electric immersion heater, solely by means of a domestic boiler (gas, oil or solid fuel), or are both means of heating available?
● If hot water is provided solely by means of an immersion heater, is there a drain-valve at the base of the cold supply pipe from the storage cistern to the hot water cylinder?
● If hot water is provided by means of a boiler, is there a drain-valve on the pipework beside the boiler, or possibly incorporated into the boiler itself?
● If the system is indirect, is it a conventional indirect system (indicated by the presence of a small feed-and-expansion tank in the roof space, feeding the primary circuit) or is it a self-priming indirect system such as the Primatic?
● Is there a 'wet' central heating system provided in conjunction with hot water supply?
● Where is the main stop-valve, and are there any other stop-valves or gate-valves fitted into distribution or circulating pipes in the system?
● Are there drain-valves at low points in the central heating circuit?

Draining down for simple repairs
Once you are thoroughly familiar with the contents and layout of your own plumbing and central heating systems, you will be able to work out for yourself how much draining-down will be necessary before you undertake any particular item of maintenance or any particular project. If, for instance, you wish to rewasher the cold tap over the kitchen sink (this is supplied direct from the rising main) or to tee into the rising main to provide a garden water supply, all that you need to do is to turn off the main stop-valve and to turn on the kitchen cold tap until water ceases to flow from it. You will then have drained the rising main to the level of the cold tap. In many modern homes a drain-valve is provided immediately above the main stop-valve to permit the rising main to be completely drained.

Rather more drainage is necessary when you wish to renew the washer on a hot tap, or on a cold tap supplied from a storage cistern, or to renew a ball-valve in a WC cistern that is supplied with water from a storage cistern. First of all, see if there are any stop-valves or gate-valves on the distribution pipes leading to the particular tap or ball-valve. There could be gate-valves on the main hot and cold distribution pipes just below the level of the main cold water storage cistern. There could even be a mini-stop-valve on the distribution pipe immediately before its connection to the tail of the tap or ball-valve.

In either of these circumstances you're in luck! All you have to do is to turn off the appropriate gate-valve or mini-stop-valve and then to turn on the tap or flush the lavatory cistern. You can then carry out the necessary repairs.

Avoiding unnecessary drainage
The chances are, though, that the main stop-valve will be the only one in the system, and that you'll have to contemplate draining the main cold water storage cistern and the appropriate distribution pipes before you can get on with your task, by turning off the main stop-valve and draining the cistern and pipes from the taps supplied by the cistern. This, however, will mean that the whole of the plumbing system is out of action for as long as it takes you to complete the job. It is generally better to go up into the roof space and lay a slat of wood across the top of the cold water storage cistern. You can then tie the float arm of the ball-valve up to it, so that water cannot flow into the cistern. Then drain the cistern by opening the bathroom taps. In this way the cold tap over the sink will not be put out of action.

Here's another useful money-saving tip: even if you are draining down to rewasher a hot tap, there is no need to run to waste all that hot water stored in the hot water cylinder, *provided that your bathroom cold taps are supplied from the cold water storage cistern.* Having tied up the ball-valve, run the bathroom *cold* taps until they cease to flow and only then turn on the hot tap you want to work on. Because the hot water distribution pipe is taken from above the hot water storage cylinder, only a little hot water – from the pipe itself – will flow away to waste and the cylinder will remain full of hot water.

For the same reason, unless you expect to have the hot water system out of action for a

WHERE TO DRAIN THE SYSTEM

On a well-designed plumbing system you should find that drain-valves have been installed at several points, so that partial draining-down is possible.

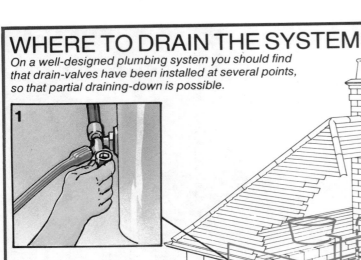

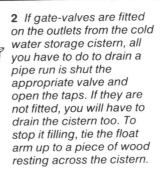

1 *A drain-valve at the point where the cold feed from the storage cistern in the loft enters the hot water cylinder means that you can empty the main body of the cylinder (at least, down to the level of the inlet pipe) in the event of it springing a leak. Here a T-shaped drain-valve spanner is being used to open the valve.*

3 *Drain-valves fitted beside the boiler allow you to drain the primary circuit and the central heating system.*

2 *If gate-valves are fitted on the outlets from the cold water storage cistern, all you have to do to drain a pipe run is shut the appropriate valve and open the taps. If they are not fitted, you will have to drain the cistern too. To stop it filling, tie the float arm up to a piece of wood resting across the cistern.*

4 *A drain-valve fitted above the rising main stop-valve allows you to drain the main and connect tees to it. The stop-valve saves you from having to tie up the storage cistern ball-valve when draining the cold supply pipes.*

Action checklist
Which part of the system you drain, and how you go about it, depends on the job you're doing. Here's a brief checklist of the sequence of operations in each case.

Job: *to rewasher/replace kitchen cold tap, tee off rising main for new supply pipe;*
● *turn off rising main stop-valve and drain rising main via drain-valve*
● *if no drain-valve fitted, open kitchen cold tap to drain main down to level of tee to kitchen sink.*

Job: *to rewasher/replace other cold tap, renew WC ball-valve, extend cold supply;*
● *if gate-valve fitted to outlet at cold cistern, close valve and open lowest appropriate cold tap; otherwise*
● *tie up arm of cold cistern ball-valve and drain cistern by opening cold taps.*

Job: *to rewasher/replace hot tap, extend existing hot supply;*
● *close gate-valve on outlet at cistern or tie up cistern ball-valve*
● *open cold tap until flow stops*
● *only then open hot tap.*

Job: *to replace hot cylinder;*
● *close gate-valve or tie up ball-valve arm*
● *turn off boiler or immersion heater*
● *empty cylinder via cylinder drain-valve*
● *close gate-valve on outlet from feed/expansion tank, or tie up ball-valve*
● *drain primary circuit via drain-valve at boiler.*

Job: *to replace cold cistern;*
● *close rising main stop-valve*
● *drain cistern by opening cold taps (hot water will still run from cylinder).*

Job: *to replace boiler;*
● *on **direct systems,** turn off boiler or immersion heater and also heating system*
● *close rising main stop-valve*
● *open all taps, and drain boiler from drain-valve nearby*
● *on **indirect systems,** turn off boiler*
● *close feed/expansion tank gate-valve*
● *drain primary and central heating systems from drain-valves at boiler.*

prolonged period there is no need to switch off the immersion heater or to let out the boiler when carrying out a maintenance operation on the bathroom hot tap.

Problems with air locks

If your hot and cold water distribution systems are properly designed – with 'horizontal' runs of pipe actually having a slight fall away from the storage cistern or the vent pipe to permit air to escape – then the system should fill up with little or no trouble when you untie the ball-valve and permit water to flow into the cistern again. Should an air-lock prevent complete filling, try connecting one end of a length of hose to the cold tap over the kitchen sink and the other end to one of the taps giving trouble. Turn on first the tap giving trouble and then the one over the kitchen sink. Mains pressure from this cold tap should blow the air bubble out of the system.

Draining the whole system

Very occasionally – perhaps because of a major reconstruction of the system or because of that most traumatic of all plumbing emergencies, a leaking boiler – it may be necessary to drain the whole system. Let's assume, first of all, that you have either a direct hot water system or a self-priming indirect one.

Switch off the immersion heater and let out or switch off the boiler. Turn off the central heating system if this is operated from the self-priming cylinder. Close the main stop-valve and open up every tap in the house – hot as well as cold. Connect one end of a length of hose to the drain-valve beside the boiler or, if the cylinder is heated by an immersion heater only, at the base of the cold supply pipe entering the cylinder, and take the other end of the hose to an outside gully. Open up the drain-valve and allow the system to drain.

If you have an indirect system you should again turn off the boiler and central heating system. Then close the gate-valve leading from the feed-and-expansion tank, or tie up it's ball-valve, and drain the system from the boiler drain-valves.

How you proceed depends upon the reason for which you have carried out the draining-down. Your aim should be to get as much of the plumbing system as possible back into operation quickly.

Restoring partial supplies

The first step is to go up into the roof space and tie up the ball-valve on the main storage cistern as already described. Open up the main stop-valve and water supply will be restored to the cold tap over the kitchen sink.

It should also be possible to restore the bathroom cold water supplies. Trace the distribution pipe that takes water from the cold water storage cistern to the hot water cylinder.

COPING WITH AIRLOCKS

Clear supply-pipe airlocks by linking the affected tap to the kitchen cold tap with hose secured by worm-drive clips. Open the affected tap first, then the kitchen tap.

Avoid airlocks in primary or heating circuits by filling them upwards via a hose linking the kitchen cold tap and the boiler drain-valve. Close vents as radiators fill.

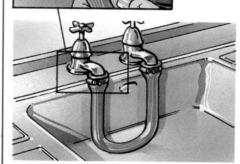
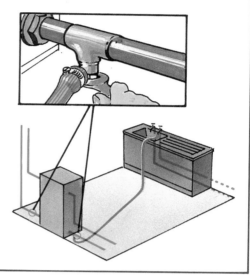

Find a cork of the correct size, lean into the cistern and push it into the pipe's inlet. Before doing so, it is a good idea to screw a substantial woodscrew part of the way into the cork to facilitate removal. You can then untie the ball-valve and allow the cistern to refill; no water will flow to the hot cylinder.

Draining heating systems

If you have a conventional indirect hot water system – perhaps installed in conjunction with a central heating system – you can drain the primary circuit, together with the radiator circuit if there is one, without draining the water from the outer part of the storage cylinder. Because of the increased risk of corrosion that arises from water and air coming into contact with steel surfaces, a radiator circuit should be drained only when absolutely essential. When this has to be done – to add additional radiators, perhaps – you should tie up the ball-valve serving the feed-and-expansion tank and drain from both the drain-valve beside the boiler and from any drain-valves provided at low points of the system. You must, of course, let out or switch off the boiler before attempting this.

When refilling the primary circuit (or when refilling a direct system with boiler) it may help to prevent the formation of air-locks if you connect one end of your garden hose to the boiler drain-valve and the other end to the cold tap over the kitchen sink. Open them both up and the system will fill upwards, with air being driven out in front of the rising water. As the central heating circuit refills,

open up all the radiator vents – and any other air vents that there may be in the system – and leave them open until water begins to flow through them. It is a good idea, when refilling a central heating system, to introduce a reliable corrosion-proofer into the feed-and-expansion tank to prevent future internal corrosion, but you can do this only if you fill the system from the top, not from the bottom.

Winter precautions

One final point: if you are leaving your home empty during the winter months, you should drain the main cold water storage cistern and, if you have a direct hot water system and will be away for more than two or three days, you should drain the hot cylinder, the boiler and its circulation pipes as well. Human memory is fallible. Having done so, leave a conspicuous notice on the boiler and by the immersion heater switch saying 'SYSTEM DRAINED – DO NOT LIGHT BOILER OR SWITCH ON HEATER UNTIL IT HAS BEEN REFILLED'.

Because of the risk of corrosion already referred to, the primary circuit and any central heating system connected to it should not be drained in these circumstances. If you have a central heating system that is capable of automatic control, leave it switched on under the control of a frost-stat. This is a thermostatic control, usually positioned in a garage or in the roof space, that will bring the heating into operation when a predetermined, near-freezing-point temperature, is reached.

INSTALLING A SINK UNIT

The sink is a highly important item of kitchen equipment, and replacing an old model is usually one of the first priorities for anyone modernising their kitchen. In this article we consider the range available and how to fit them.

If your house was built in the 1930s or 1940s, and the kitchen has never been modernised, the chances are that it contains the original deep white glazed stoneware 'Belfast pattern' sink, supported by heavy cast-iron brackets built into the wall. It will incorporate a weir overflow and will probably have a detachable wooden draining board. A deep sink of this kind was regarded as the height of domestic luxury in the pre-war and early post-war years. An even older property might have a shallow yellow 'London pattern' sink, probably supported by brick pillars. In either case the water will very likely come from brass bib-taps (taps with horizontal inlets) projecting from a tiled splash-back fixed to the wall behind the sink. Old London pattern sinks were sometimes installed with an untrapped waste that passed through the kitchen wall to discharge over an outside gully drain. More recent sinks would have a lead or brass U-trap screwed to the waste outlet from which a branch waste pipe would discharge over the gully.

Sink units

Because these old stoneware sinks were certain death to crockery dropped into them, and looked increasingly dated, they were gradually replaced by sink units with one-piece sink tops. The sink tops were made of enamelled pressed steel or stainless steel, and the units into which they were fixed became the starting point for complete kitchen ranges incorporating continuous work surfaces. The early enamelled pressed steel sink tops had the disadvantage that the enamel was vulnerable to accidental damage. Dropping any hard object onto them could easily chip or crack the enamel. The stainless steel sink therefore became the most important innovation.

Taps and traps

It was usual, when replacing an old stoneware sink with a stainless steel or an enamelled pressed-steel sink, to get rid of the old bib-taps projecting from the wall, and to replace them with chromium-plated brass pillar taps or a mixer fitted into the holes provided at the back of the sink and connected to the hot and cold water distribution pipes concealed within the unit.

Early sinks of this kind were provided with traps, also concealed within the unit. The trap might still be of brass with a copper waste pipe, but plastic was soon introduced, connected to a plastic waste pipe by means of ring-seal push-fit connectors. Bottle traps, as distinct from the traditional U-traps, became increasingly popular. They were neater in appearance, space saving and easy to dismantle in case of a blockage, although their discharge rate was not as great. Modern ground floor sinks often still discharge over a yard gully, but the waste pipe outlet should be taken to below the gully grid either through a slotted grid or by the use of a back or side-inlet gully.

Overflows

Early sink tops had a built-in overflow consisting of a unit welded to the back of the sink. But these inevitably leaked after a time, and nowadays they have been replaced by a flexible overflow pipe. This is like the overflow pipe from a bath which is taken from the sink's overflow outlet to connect, by means of a sleeve or 'banjo' fitting, to the slotted waste pipe, before its connection to the trap. Householders who possess a sink of the older pattern with a leaking built-in overflow, will find that if the sink is dismounted and turned upside down, the overflow unit can be sawn off and replaced with one of the more modern waste and overflow fittings. But, of course, it may be better to replace the the sink.

New developments

Nowadays, there is no question of being restricted to a single sink with either right or left-hand drainer. Double sinks, one for washing the crockery and cutlery and the other for a hot rinse before air drying, have become more and more popular. The two sinks may be of equal size, around 450mm (18in) in width, or one may be smaller than the other for use in food preparation. A second sink like this might be only 240mm (10in) in width. There are also sinks with double drainers, though these are rather less in demand as they take up a lot of space; they are usually around 2m (6ft 8in) long. Overall sizes of rectangular sinks and drainer units range from about 900mm (3ft) to 1500mm (5ft) in length, and usually measure 500 or 600mm (20 to 24in) deep, to fit metric base units. Some sink tops are still available in the 21in (533mm) size to match old imperial base units. There are also many intermediate sizes, and bowl depths may range between 130 and 180mm (5 and 7in).

Early glass-reinforced plastic sink tops and drainers proved to be a complete disaster. They were incapable of standing up to the very heavy use to which sinks are subjected, their colours faded and they cracked, and crazed. Considerable advances have since been made, and modern plastic sinks and sink tops seem well able to stand up to everything that is required of them.

Ceramic sinks are making a come back, though they are very different from the old Belfast and London pattern sinks. Modern ranges include tough inset sinks and tops in an attractive range of colours. There are inset round bowls 450mm (18in) in diameter with an accompanying but separate round drainer 380mm (14in) in diameter. Then there is a conventional rectangular double sink and drainer – all of ceramic ware – an overall size of 1125 x 505mm (45 x 20in). There is also a conventional rectangular single sink and drainer and round double sinks and drainer in one unit. A feature of these new ceramic units is their extreme toughness.

The waste and overflow of the new ceramic sinks are arranged in exactly the same way as those of the old Belfast models. A built-in overflow connects to the slot in a slotted waste outlet that is bedded on mastic in the outlet hole. Stainless steel sinks are provided with the flexible overflow already referred to, which connects to the slotted waste below the sink but above the trap. Double sinks have only one trap. This is fitted into the outlet of the sink nearest to the drain outlet, the waste from the other sink being connected to it above the level of the single trap.

Mixers

Individual sink pillar taps are still freely available, but the choice nowadays is more likely to be a sink mixer. A mixer with a swivel spout is an essential where a double sink is installed.

Sink mixers differ from bath and basin mixers in one important respect. The latter are simply two taps with a single spout. The hot and cold streams of water mix within the body of the mixer unit. Sink mixers have separate channels for the hot and cold streams of water which mix in the air as they leave the spout. The reason for this is that the cold water supply to the kitchen sink (the household's supply of water for drinking and cooking) comes direct from the rising main. The hot supply usually comes from a cylinder storage hot water system, fed with water from a main cold water storage cistern. It is illegal to mix, in one fitting, water from the main and water from a storage cistern.

Everybody is familiar with the conventional sink mixer, made of chromium-plated brass with 'shrouded' cross-top handles of plastic and a long swivel spout. Nowadays, though, there are some exciting new designs available. With some the mixer unit is fitted into just one hole at the back of the sink. The other hole may be blanked off or may be used to accommodate a rinsing brush, supplied with hot water by a flexible tube connected to the hot water supply pipe.

Putting in the sink top

When you come to install your new sink it's a good idea to make the first job fitting the taps or mixer, waste and overflow to it. This will avoid unnecessary interruption to the rest of the plumbing services. Start by putting in the combined waste and overflow unit, then attach the taps or mixer. If the sink is made of stainless steel the shanks of the taps will protrude through the holes so you won't be able to screw up the back-nuts tight. Use 'top hat' or spaces to accommodate the shanks.

When the sink is in position the tap tails will usually be fairly inaccessible, so it may be a

good idea to attach purpose-made extension pieces to bring them to a level below the sink basin where they will be accessible.

When you've got the new sink top ready, you'll have to turn off the main stop-valve and drain the hot and cold water pipes which supply the existing sink. Then you can disconnect the waste outlet, and use a cold chisel and hammer to chip away any seal between the back of the sink and the wall. You can remove the old sink (remember, it's going to be very heavy) and saw off the heavy cantilevered brackets that supported the old sink flush with the wall.

The hot and cold water supply pipes to the bib-taps over the old sink will probably be chased (inset) into the wall, so you'll have to unscrew and remove the old taps, excavate the pipes from the wall and pull them forward so that they can be connected to the tails of new taps.

With the new sink unit in position, the next job is to cut the water supply pipes to the correct length to connect to the tails of the taps. The sink top simply rests on the sink unit, so the tails of the taps can now be connected to the water supply pipes. If the trap of the old sink will connect to the new waste it can be reused.

THE PLUMBING CONNECTIONS

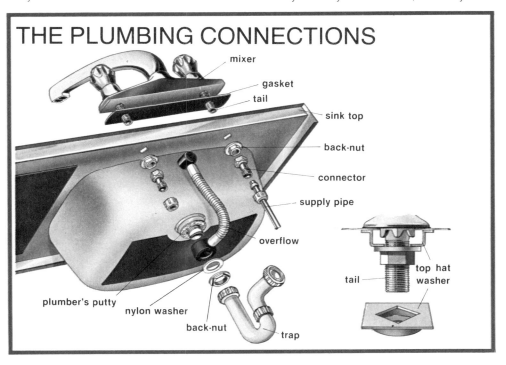

mixer
gasket
tail
sink top
back-nut
connector
supply pipe
overflow
plumber's putty
nylon washer
back-nut
trap
tail
top hat
washer

INSTALLING A SINK TOP

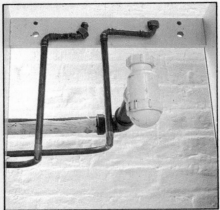

1 Take out your old sink top and check that the existing plumbing connections are undamaged. Replace as necessary.

2 Place your new sink top downwards on the floor. Take the waste outlet and press plumber's putty around the top of the screw.

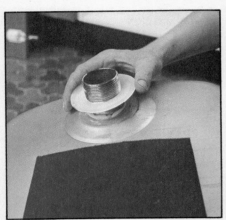

3 Press the outlet firmly into position in the sink outlet aperture, at the same time squeezing out excess putty. Then put on the plastic washer.

6 Place the outlet collar of the banjo unit firmly on top of the plastic washer and support it with one hand before putting on the back-nut.

7 Put on the back-nut and screw it up tightly against the banjo unit collar, making sure it runs straight towards the sink outlet hole.

8 Screw up the overflow rose to the banjo unit overflow pipe. To help get it tight, hold the back of the outlet with a pair of pliers.

11 Take the mixer unit and ensure that the rubber gasket has no grit on it; then place the inlet tails into the holes and press the unit into position.

12 Screw on the inlet tail back-nuts and tighten them making sure the gasket remains flat. You don't need to use any plumber's putty.

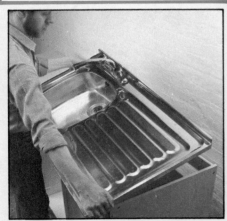

13 When the outlet and mixer installation is complete, lift the sink top into its correct position and screw it to the kitchen unit.

4 With the plastic washer pushed firmly home, take a roll of PTFE tape and run it around the thread right up to the end of the outlet.

5 Before putting on the banjo unit run a thick film of pipe-jointing compound around the uppermost surface of the plastic washer.

9 Run a knife around the edge of the plumber's putty squeezed out from around the outlet flange. Be careful not to score the metal.

10 Peel away the surplus putty and check that the outlet flange is tightly held into the sink. If not, tighten the back-nut further.

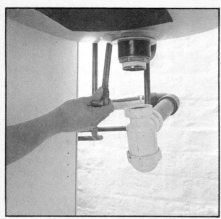

14 Attach the inlet pipes to the mixer tails and tighten the nuts with a crowsfoot spanner, which helps you reach them.

15 Check that the old trap is clear and screw it up tightly to the outlet pipe; then turn on the taps to check that there are no leaks.

SINK DESIGNS

Sink designs come in several different variations particularly in the inset range. Think carefully about what you use your sink for, and what space you have available before deciding on size and design.

TYPICAL SINK SIZES

S=single, D=double, Si=sink, Dr=drainer

	Tops	Inset
SDrSSi	42x31in	37x19in
	1000x500mm	940x485mm
	1000x600mm	
	1200x600mm	
DDrSSi	63x21in	55x19in
	1500x500mm	1395x485mm
	1500x600mm	
SDrDSi	63x21in	55x19in
	1500x600mm	1395x485mm
DDrDSi	84x21in	74x19in
	2000x600mm	1850x485mm

TYPICAL DESIGNS

If you don't have a dishwasher a double bowl is useful – one for washing and one for rinsing.

double bowl

A double drainer will give you a greater working area at the sink but will cut down on the remainder of your work surface.

double drainer

If you're short of space you may dispense with the drainer altogether and use an inset bowl only. There are also units with small subsidiary bowls specially incorporated to house a waste disposal unit. These may also be supplied with trays which fit in or over the bowl, facilitating such tasks as salad preparation.

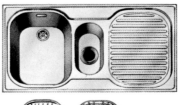

disposal sink and trays

INSTALLING AN INSET SINK

If you're fitting a new kitchen, or modernising an old one, one job you'll almost certainly have to carry out is to install an inset sink into a worktop.

N ot so long ago, an assortment of cupboards, work surfaces and a kitchen sink unit formed the framework of the average kitchen. It was not a particularly efficient arrangement, but because few appliances had to be fitted in it didn't matter too much if a little space was wasted. However, as more and more homes acquired washing machines, tumble dryers, refrigerators and the like, some way had to be found of fitting these appliances into what was often a relatively small area.

What resulted from this was the 'integral' kitchen which housed all this equipment under roomy and well-lit worktops. And hand in hand with this development went the introduction of the inset sink.

The old enamelled and stainless steel sit-on sinks, with their single or double drainers, completely covered their base units. From a functional point of view they were ideal because the one-piece top meant that it was virtually impossible for water to seep into the cupboard below. Yet the kitchen sink remained a conspicuous, and somewhat unattractive, feature, divorced from other kitchen surfaces. And because of the space it took up, the unit was restricted to only one or two positions in the room. Consequently, many kitchens had to be planned around it, which naturally limited the ways in which they could be made more labour-saving and pleasant to work in.

However, once the move to creating uninterrupted work surfaces took hold, the benefits of installing a 'built-into-the-worktop' sink became readily apparent. For the first time it meant that a sink could be fitted into an overall design, which could still retain a clean, streamlined look. It didn't have to be fitted directly over a base unit, which gave far more flexibility as to where it could be positioned. However, there still had to be sufficient clearance under the worktop to take the bowl, and the plumbing supply and waste runs still had to make sense.

In fact, the idea for inset sinks stemmed from bathroom and bedroom vanity units, where a washbasin was let into the surface of a small cupboard. The surrounding melamine-finished surface was easy to clean and provided a standing area for bottles, cosmetics and the like. It was only a matter of time before the idea was adopted in the kitchen.

Choosing an inset sink

Whether you're revamping your kitchen, or just modernising the existing sink, there are a number of points to take into account before buying a new inset model.

The first is to decide what exactly the sink has to handle, because this will give you a fair guide as to the size you'll need, and whether two bowls would be better instead of just one. Indeed, there are a number of advantages in installing two or even two-and-a-half bowls (the 'half' being specifically for cutlery) not the least being that you'll still have access to the taps even if one bowl is occupied. And the amount of extra plumbing you'll have to carry out is quite small. All it entails is slightly extending the waste run. If you install a mixer tap with a swivel spout this can be used to fill both bowls so there's no additional work on the water supply side.

As with sit-on sinks, there is a wide range of bowl/drainer combinations. There are also individual round bowls which don't have an attached drainer, although there are separate drainers available that you have to let into the worktop nearby.

Round bowls do look attractive and they are increasing in popularity, but they have a couple of disadvantages. They tend to be shallower than the traditional rectangular shape – generally, the deeper the bowl the better – and their shape sometimes makes it awkward to submerge large pans and grill trays when they're being washed.

Which material to go for?

The other main consideration when choosing a sink is the material it's made of. Nowadays there is a far wider choice than ever before.

Stainless steel has retained its popularity, principally because it is relatively cheap and there is a wide range of styles available. Yet while it is heat-resistant and hard wearing, it can suffer at the hands of scourers and abrasive cleaners which leave minute surface scratches. You may also find this material somewhat clinical in appearance. However, if you do there are alternatives.

Don't shy away from plastic, for example. Admittedly the early glass-reinforced plastic tops proved to be a disaster: they simply weren't sturdy enough to cope with the use – and misuse – a kitchen sink is subjected to. But the ones on sale now are vastly different. These are made of impact-resistant modified polycarbonate in a range of attractive colours that extend right through the material. You can buy double as well as single sinks with round or rectangular bowls. As far as temperature resistance is concerned these sinks are very tough, and to prove it they are put through some remarkably nasty tests. One manufacturer, for example, has tested such sinks in hot water at up to 95°C for 40 days, in boiling water at five different levels of water hardness for 50 hours and by placing hot

THE PLUMBING CONNECTIONS

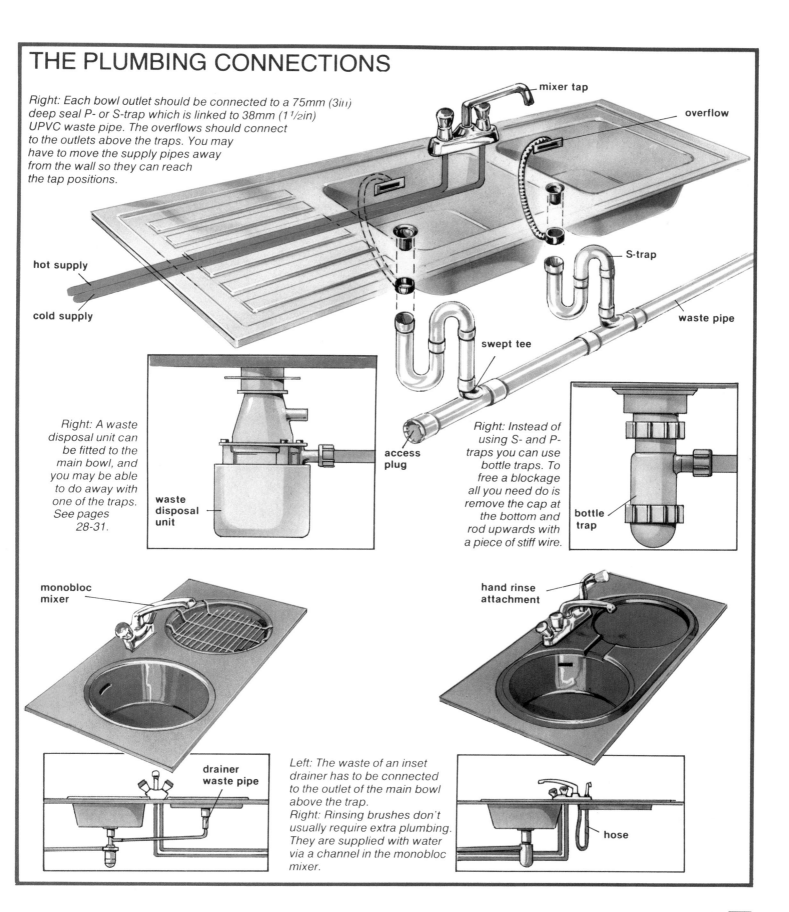

Right: Each bowl outlet should be connected to a 75mm (3in) deep seal P- or S-trap which is linked to 38mm (1½in) UPVC waste pipe. The overflows should connect to the outlets above the traps. You may have to move the supply pipes away from the wall so they can reach the tap positions.

mixer tap

overflow

hot supply

cold supply

S-trap

waste pipe

swept tee

access plug

Right: A waste disposal unit can be fitted to the main bowl, and you may be able to do away with one of the traps. See pages 28-31.

waste disposal unit

Right: Instead of using S- and P-traps you can use bottle traps. To free a blockage all you need do is remove the cap at the bottom and rod upwards with a piece of stiff wire.

bottle trap

monobloc mixer

hand rinse attachment

drainer waste pipe

Left: The waste of an inset drainer has to be connected to the outlet of the main bowl above the trap.
Right: Rinsing brushes don't usually require extra plumbing. They are supplied with water via a channel in the monobloc mixer.

hose

327

INSTALLING AN INSET SINK

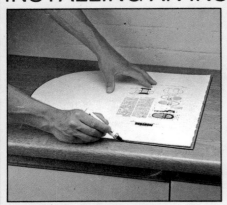

1 If space is limited and the worktop is fixed in position, check underneath that there is clearance for the bowls and then mark round the template.

2 Drill a hole through the worktop on the waste side of the cut-out. Insert the jigsaw and cut out the hole, supporting the waste on the underside.

3 Test fit the sink in the hole, wriggling it a little to get it to drop down flush with the top. If it sticks, file back the area where it catches.

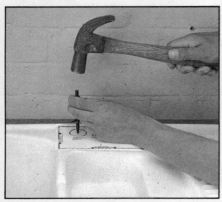

6 If the sink doesn't have a tap hole punched, place the special template over the knockout and gently use a hammer and punch to make one.

7 Insert the monobloc mixer, making sure that it sits on a rubber gasket. Then use a spanner to tighten the back-nut underneath the sink.

8 Make up the outlets for the main and half bowls and the overflow. Some outlets are bedded on plumbers' putty while others sit on a special plastic washer.

saucepans on them for short periods at temperatures up to 180°C. No domestic sink is likely to experience anything like that amount of misuse; even so the sinks weathered the punishment.

Ceramic sinks are once more on the market and are becoming increasingly popular. Again, they are very different from their early counterparts, but one thing hasn't changed. They spell certain death to any piece of crockery dropped into them. It's a point that should perhaps be borne in mind when choosing a sink top. Having said this, these sinks are available in an attractive range of colours (you can even get a mixer tap to match), and as with plastic and stainless steel models some versions have integral drainers. Once installed these sinks are highly resistant to being damaged. However, if you do plump for a ceramic sink and you want to install a waste disposal unit check

that the two are compatible, because it's impossible to widen the outlet as you can do with a stainless steel top.

Choosing the taps
Apart from all the other considerations it's important to choose an inset sink with the taps in mind.

If you go for a two or two-and-a-half bowl top then you're going to need some form of swivel mixer. Some sinks will only take a monobloc mixer because there is only one access hole for the hot and cold supply pipes. Others take conventional mixers. Alternatively, you could use separate pillar taps.

Some sink tops are reversible, in that depending on which way round you fit them they can have a left-hand or right-hand drainer. Obviously you can't have tap holes on both sides of the bowl, so to get round the problem usually there are knockouts in the

potential tap sites and you just remove those you want to use.

Sometimes no provision is made for taps. In this case you'll have to install bib taps coming out of the wall or drill holes through the worktop itself and fit the taps to these.

How to install an inset sink
Installing an inset sink presents no special difficulties. As with conventional sinks, and indeed most other plumbing fittings, it's best to carry out as much work as possible before putting the worktop in position. But if the worktop is fixed, rather than remove it work in situ instead. First, fit the taps. With a mixer you'll need a flat washer between the base and the sink top. And for a plastic or stainless steel sink, you'll probably need to use top hat or spacer washers over the tap tails to accommodate the protruding shanks before screwing on the back-nuts.

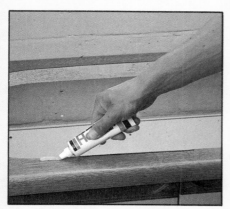

4 Some sinks are bedded on a rubber or plastic seal. If not, run silicone rubber or non-setting mastic round the edge of the hole before sitting the sink.

5 Lower the inset sink into the hole and then fasten it in position underneath using the clips provided. Clean away any filler that oozes from the edges.

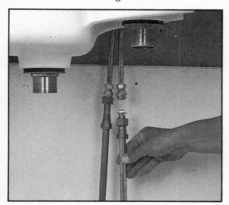

9 Use tap connectors and special reducers to connect the 15mm (1/2in) hot and cold supply runs to the tap tails which on this model are slightly narrower.

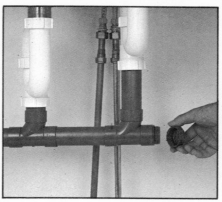

10 Use S-traps and swept tees to connect the 38mm (1 1/2in) wastes to a common waste run. An inspection eye at the end of the run aids blockage removal.

CHECK UNDERSURFACE CLEARANCE

You've got considerable flexibility as to where you position an inset sink – it need not necessarily be directly over a base unit. But wherever you propose to site it make sure there is sufficient depth under the worktop to accommodate the bowls.

WHICH SINK TO CHOOSE

Inset sinks can have one, two or two and a half bowls. Some incorporate drainers, but with individual bowls separate drainers have to be installed alongside.

Many inset sinks are made of stainless steel, but if you choose a plastic or ceramic sink you have the added option of a wide range of colours.

TIP: CARE WITH HOT PANS

Whatever material your sink is made of it will withstand all likely treatment. If you've a plastic sink it's advisable not to put frying pans that have just been used for frying hot meat, dry cooked foods and hot oil directly in the sink. First allow the pan to cool briefly.

TIP: FITTING A WASTE DISPOSER

If you're installing a ceramic sink and you also want a waste disposal unit, make sure the outlet of the sink is compatible with the inlet on the disposer. Ceramic sinks can't be cut, so the two must match exactly.

BOWL ACCESSORIES

There are various accessories you can fit over the bowl of the sink such as a draining tray (A) and a chopping board (B). Ideally, use the chopping board over the sink with a waste disposer so that any vegetable matter can be hygienically flushed away.

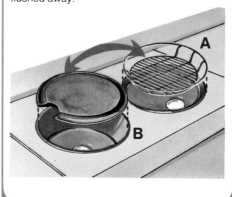

The tap tails will be difficult to get to once the sink is in position, particularly if the unit you are fitting over has a back to it. Therefore it's best to fit a small run of pipe, or lengths of corrugated flexible pipe, to each of the tap tails at this stage.

The waste and overflow unit is usually supplied with the sink. Don't forget to bed the outlet on a layer of mastic, and as you tighten up the back-nut make sure the slot in the shank points in the direction of the overflow. Next, screw the overflow to the outlet point at the top of the sink bowl and then slip the 'banjo' connector at the other end of the flexible hose over the slotted waste. This is held in place by another back-nut.

As far as marking out the work surface is concerned, most sink manufacturers supply a template indicating the area of worktop to be removed. Needless to say this must be done with care and accuracy, and for this reason it's best to work on the top surface and not the underside so there's no risk of getting the sink in the wrong place.

Drill a hole through the waste side of the cut-out and then use a jigsaw to cut the hole. You can then fit the retaining brackets or rim round the underside edge. The fixing clips on the sink are secured to these when it's set in its final position.

Usually, inset sinks are provided with a rubber seal or gasket so that when fitted there's a watertight seal between the bowl and drainer and the worktop. If there isn't one, run a continuous bead of non-setting mastic round the perimeter and bed the top firmly onto this.

Once you've lowered the sink into position and clipped it in place all that then remains is to set the worktop in position on top of the unit and to connect the waste pipe and the hot and cold supply runs.

PLUMBING IN KITCHEN APPLIANCES

Washing machines and dishwashers can be a great boon in the house. They are best plumbed into a water supply and the waste outlet, otherwise you'll find they don't save as much time as they should.

These days you'll probably opt for an automatic washing machine that fills and empties itself according to a pre-set programme, and so can be left unattended. There is a choice between top loaders and front loaders, although the latter are by far the more common. Obviously top loaders can't fit under a work surface, but drum-type top loaders tend to be narrower and this may suit your particular space requirements.

Dishwashers are almost always automatic, except for some small, cheaper sink-top models. They, too, are available as top or front loaders, though again front loaders are by far the more popular. They are also easier to load and unload, as with top loaders it's easy for crockery and cutlery to slip to the bottom of the machines.

Washing machines have become almost a necessity in busy family homes, especially where there are young children. Dishwashers are far less common, but sales are developing rapidly as more and more people wake up to their advantages. It's a simple matter to stack a dishwasher with dirty crockery direct from the meal table and then turn it on before going to bed at night. Again, for a family the labour saving is considerable.

Some washing machines don't have to be plumbed in. The inlets can be attached to the kitchen taps when the sink isn't being used, and the outlet can be hooked over the edge of the sink. The same goes for dishwashers, which usually require only a cold water feed. But to keep things really neat and tidy as well as more practical, it is best to create permanent connections for both the water supply and the waste outlet. In most kitchens this should be a fairly easy task, provided you have room for the machines in the first place.

As far as the capacities of washing machines and dishwashers go, you don't really have much choice. Washing machines have a capacity of about 4-5kg (9-11lb) and dishwashers will function quite happily provided you stack them up within the obvious tray limitations. It's important to follow the manufacturers' instructions for day-to-day maintenance. Many washing machines need their outlet filter cleaned regularly, as

do dishwashers. They may also need regular doses of salts, not to mention rinse aids.

Water supply

There are a number of ways in which you can arrange the water supply. One of them is sure to suit your plumbing system or the layout of your kitchen or utility room. A washing machine may need a hot and cold supply; dishwashers and some cheaper washing machines need only a cold supply.

Let's first consider the conventional means of plumbing in – the means that a professional plumber would almost certainly adopt if you called him in to do the job for you. It is likely to be most satisfactory where the machine is to be positioned in the immediate vicinity of the kitchen sink and the 15mm (1/2in) hot and cold supply pipes to the sink taps are readily accessible and in close proximity to each other.

The technique is to cut into these two pipes

at a convenient level, after cutting off the water supply and draining the pipes, and to insert into them 15mm compression tees. From the outlets of the tees lengths of 15mm (1/2in) copper tube are run to terminate, against the wall, in a position immediately adjacent to the machine. Onto the ends of these lengths of pipe are fitted purpose-made stop-cocks. These are usually provided with back-plates that can be screwed to the wall after it has been drilled and plugged. The outlets of the stop-cocks are designed for connection to the machine's inlet hose or hoses.

As an alternative, which is best used where the hot and cold water pipes in the kitchen are in close proximity to the position of the machine, you can use a special patent valve. This is a 'tee' with a valve outlet designed for direct connection to the washing machine hose. There are compression joints at each end of the tee and the valve is particularly

PLUMBING IN A WASHING MACHINE

Plumbing in a washing machine shouldn't present too many problems. Normally it's sited next to an existing sink, so you'll know that the water supply pipes and drainage facilities are close at hand.

Most machines are run off separate 15mm (½in) hot and cold supplies (1 & 2) taken from tees (3) inserted in the pipe runs to the sink. You should also insert some form of stop-valve (4) into the pipes so the machine can be isolated for repairs. You'll have to use female/male connections (5) to join the copper pipes to the machine's rubber inlet hoses (6).

When the water has been used, it's fed into a rubber drain hose (7) which should be loosely inserted into the top of the stand-pipe (8). This in turn connects to a 75mm (3in) trap (9) and from here the waste water is taken in 38mm (1½in) pipe to discharge in the gully outside below the grille.

Dealing with single-stack drainage

From the trap at the bottom of the stand-pipe (11) the waste water is conducted to the main drainage stack (12) where the pipe is connected via a fitting known as a strap boss (13).

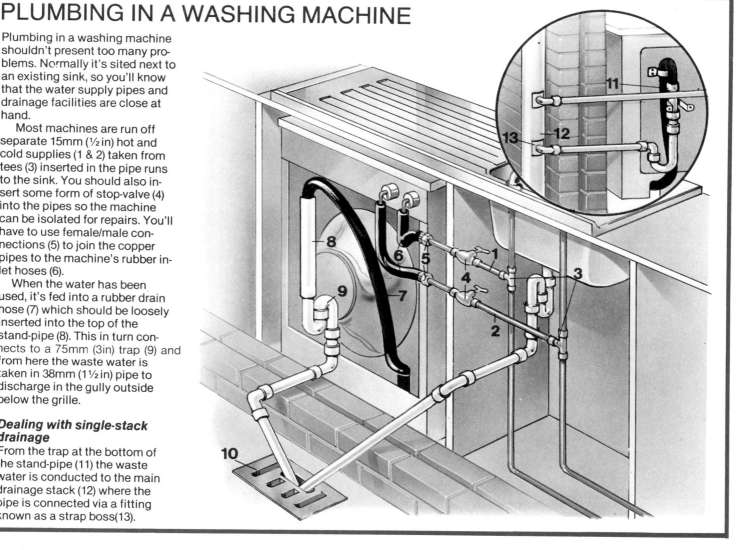

easily fitted because there is no tube-stop in one of these joints. This cuts out the difficult business of 'springing' the cut ends of the pipe into the tee.

Then there are valves which can be connected without cutting a section out of the water supply pipes. With one such valve the pipe is drained and is then drilled with a 8mm (⁵⁄₁₆in) bit. A back-plate is then fitted to the wall behind it and a front-plate, with a short projecting pipe and a rubber seal that fits into the hole in the pipe, is clamped to it. The washing machine valve then screws into this front-plate.

Yet another valve is self-tapping and screws its own hole in the water pipe. This, so the makers claim, can be done without cutting off the water supply and draining the pipe.

A valve which depends upon drilling the water supply pipe will not permit the same flow of water as one in which the pipe is cut and a tee inserted. It must be said, though,

that this seems to make very little difference in practice, but obviously in the former case the tightening of the connection must be more than sufficient for it to work properly.

Putting in drainage

The simplest method is undoubtedly to hook the machine's outlet hose over the rim of the kitchen or utility room sink when required. However, this method isn't always convenient and is certainly untidy. An alternative is to provide an open-ended stand-pipe fixed to the kitchen wall into which the outlet hose of the machine can be permanently hooked. The open end of the stand-pipe should be at least 600mm (24in) above floor level and should have an internal diameter of at least 35mm (1⅜in). A deep seal (75mm or 3in) trap should be provided at its base and a branch waste pipe taken from its outlet to an exterior gully, if on the ground floor, or to the main soil and waste stack of a single stack

system if on an upper floor. As with all connections to a single soil and waste stack this should be done only under the supervision of the district or borough council's Building Control Officer. Manufacturers of plastic drainage systems include suitable drainage stand-pipes and accessories in their range of equipment (the trap and pipe being sold as one unit).

It is sometimes possible to deal with washing machine or dishwasher drainage by taking the waste pipe to connect directly to the trap of the kitchen sink and this course of action may be suggested at DIY centres and by builders' merchants staff. But it must be stressed that this is not recommended by the manufacturers of washing machines, who consider that it involves a considerable risk of back-siphonage. This could lead to waste water from the sink siphoning back into the machine. In the case of a washing machine this could mean considerable problems.

PLUMBING IN A DISHWASHER

1 Start by working out how to run the waste outlet. This will often mean making a hole in the wall using a club hammer and cold chisel.

2 Measure up the run on the inside, then cut a suitable length of 38mm (1½in) PVC plastic waste pipe and push it through the hole you have made.

3 Make up the outside pipe run dry, to ensure it all fits, then solvent weld it. It's useful to put in an inspection elbow in case of blockages.

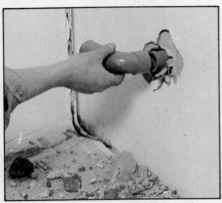

6 Carry on assembling the run on the inside using standard waste pipe fittings. Try to keep the run close to the wall for a neat appearance.

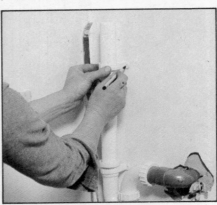

7 Take the trap and stand-pipe, which you can buy as a standard fitting or make up yourself, and mark the bracket positions on the wall.

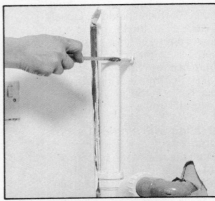

8 Drill and plug the wall, and fix the stand-pipe in position. Make sure that it is fully supported and vertical and the trap is screwed tight.

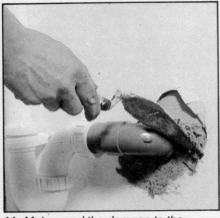

11 Make good the damage to the wall both on the inside and out; the plastic pipe will be held firmly in place by the mortar and plaster.

12 You can now move the machine into position and connect it up. The inlet hose has a female screwed connector, which must have a washer in it.

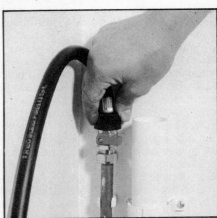

13 With the washer in place, screw up the connector to the tap on the inlet pipe; it's enough to hand-tighten this connection.

4 If the run terminates in a gully drain, then make sure that you fit the pipe so that the end is situated below the level of the water.

5 When you have completed the outside waste run, replace the grid. Cut away as much of it as necessary to fit round the pipe, using a hacksaw.

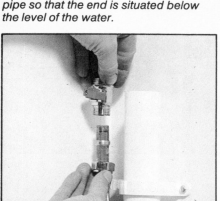

9 Run the cold water supply using 15mm (¹/₂in) pipe via a tee cut into the domestic cold supply, and attach a running tap to the end.

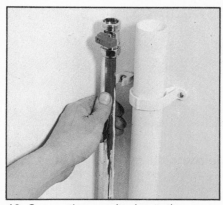

10 Secure the supply pipe to the wall using pipe brackets, then go back and make sure that all your connections are sound.

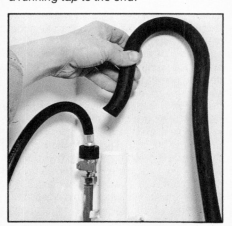

14 Take the outlet hose from the machine and place it in the top of the stand-pipe.You should not attempt to make the connection airtight.

15 Move the machine exactly into position and check that it is level; if not, adjust the feet. Then turn on the water and test the machine.

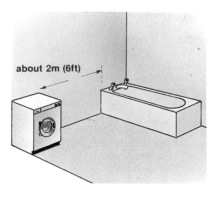
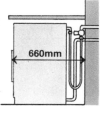
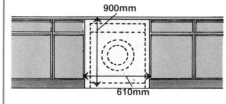

PLUMBING IN A BATH

Replacing a bath may seem to be an ambitious do-it-yourself project but it is well within the capabilities of the determined home handyman prepared to tackle the job carefully and logically. Here is what is involved.

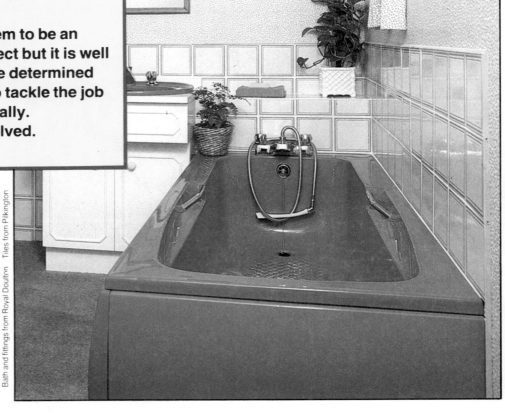

Bath and fittings from Royal Doulton   Tiles from Pilkington

As with many other plumbing projects the most difficult part is likely to be the removal of the old fitting rather than the installation of the new one.

The old bath will almost certainly be made of enamelled cast iron. The once-white enamel may be discoloured and wearing away, and may even reveal rusting bare metal underneath. Green or brown coloured stains beneath the taps indicate a long-neglected need for rewashering. The taps may look out of date and have worn chromium plating. The finish of the bath may be old and unattractive and the bath itself not panelled in.

Checking it out

First have a look at the existing bath. If there are side or end panels, strip them off and examine, with the aid of an electric torch, the water supply pipes and the waste and the overflow arrangements in the cramped and badly lit space between the foot of the bath and the wall. You will see that the water supply pipes connect the threaded tails of the taps by means of brass 'swivel tap connectors' or 'cap and lining joints'.

Check whether the water supply pipes are made of copper or lead by scraping their surface with a blade of a pocket knife. If this reveals the characteristic grey sheen of lead you should think of replacing the piping. If you do not think you are capable of carrying out this replacement work, ask a plumber – it's not an easy task. If the pipes are of copper you should be able to tackle the entire project without professional aid.

The overflow from a modern bath is taken, by means of a flexible pipe, to the waste trap. In the past, the overflow pipe often simply led through the external wall, and was the source of incurable bathroom draughts. If your bath's overflow is like this, you'll have to cut it off flush with the wall.

If the bath has adjustable feet, apply some penetrating oil to the screws. Once they begin to move, lowering the level of the bath before you attempt to remove it can help to prevent damage to the wall tiling.

The alternatives

It is possible to replace your cast iron bath with a new one made of the same material, but more modern in styling. However, these baths are expensive and very heavy indeed. Carrying one into the bathroom and fitting it requires considerable strength (you'd need at least one strong helper) as well as care. There are other snags about enamelled cast iron baths. They normally have a slippery base that can make them dangerous to use – particularly by the very young and the elderly, though some are available with a non-slip surface. Furthermore, the material of which they are made rapidly conducts the heat away from the water and while this didn't matter too much in the days when energy was plentiful and cheap, large amounts of hot water cost rather more today.

One economical alternative is an enamelled pressed steel bath. This is lighter and cheaper than enamelled cast iron but can be more easily damaged in storage or installation.

For do-it-yourself installation a plastic bath is the obvious choice. These are made of acrylic plastic sheet, sometimes reinforced with glass fibre. They are available in a number of attractive colours and, as the colour extends right through the material of which they are made, any surface scratches can be easily polished out. They are light in weight and one

man can quite easily carry one upstairs for installation. The plastic of which they are made is a poor conductor of heat which means that they are both comfortable and economical to use. Many of them have a non-slip base to make them safe.

But plastic baths do have their snags. They are easily damaged by extreme heat. You should beware of using a blow torch in close proximity to one and a lighted cigarette should never be rested, even momentarily, on the rim. A fault of early plastic baths was their tendency to creak and sag when filled with hot water and, sometimes, when you got into them. This has now been overcome by the manufacturers who provide substantial frames or cradles for support; but these frames must be assembled and fixed exactly as recommended. Some come already attached to the bath.

A combined plastic waste and overflow assembly is likely to be the choice nowadays for any bath, and is obligatory with a plastic bath. If a rigid metal trap is used with a plastic bath, the material of the bath could be damaged as hot water causes unequal expansion.

You obviously won't want to re-use the old bath taps and will probably opt for either individual modern ¾in bath pillar taps or a bath mixer. A mixer should be chosen only if the cold water supply is taken from the same cold

REPOSITIONING A BATH

In many bathrooms, a new bath simply takes the place of an existing one; there's no room for manoeuvre. But in some cases moving the bath to another position in the room can lead to a more practical arrangement and better use of the available space. In this bathroom the new bath was installed at the other side of the room, so that the space it had formerly occupied could house a shower cubicle and a WC. Moving the bath to this position involved extending the existing hot and cold water supply pipes, but brought it nearer the soil stack on the outside wall and meant that the waste pipe was short and simple to connect up outside.

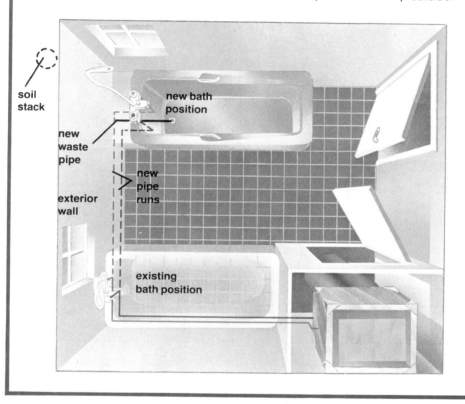

soil stack

new waste pipe

exterior wall

new bath position

new pipe runs

existing bath position

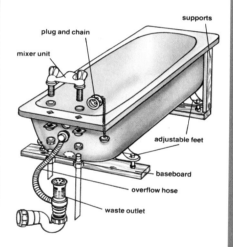

EQUIPMENT ROUND-UP

To replace a bath, you're likely to need the following tools:
● crowsfoot wrench
● adjustable spanner
● adjustable wrench
● hacksaw (possibly)
● spirit level

You'll also need:
● new bath — measure up carefully before you buy it to make sure it fits. It should come complete with supports, carcase and side panels, otherwise you'll need these as well
● new overflow connection, waste outlet and PVC trap
● taps/mixer and new inlet pipe if you are replacing them
● plumber's putty

KNOW YOUR BATH

plug and chain — supports

mixer unit

adjustable feet

baseboard

overflow hose

waste outlet

THE SPACE YOU NEED

You need a minimum amount of space around a bath (below) and also a minimum ceiling height above it (right).

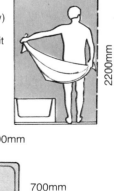

2200mm

1100mm

700mm

700mm

1700mm

water storage cistern that supplies the hot water system. It should not be used where the cold water supply to the bathroom comes directly from the mains supply.

How to proceed

To avoid too long a disruption of the domestic hot and cold water supplies you can fit the taps, waste and trap into the new bath before removing the old one.

Slip a flat plastic washer over the tail of each tap and insert the tails through the holes provided for them. A mixer usually has one large flat washer or gasket with two holes – one for each tap tail. Beneath the rim of the bath, slip 'top hat' or 'spacer' washers over the tails to accomodate the protruding shanks of the taps. Screw on the back-nuts and tighten them. For details see pages 344-346.

Bed the waste flange onto plumber's putty or non-setting mastic, secure the back-nut

and connect up the trap. Then connect up the overflow pipe.

Removing the old bath may well be the most difficult part of the procedure. Turn off the hot and cold water supplies and drain the distribution pipes from the bath taps. If you haven't done so already, remove the bath panel to give access to the plumbing at the foot of the bath. You can try to unscrew the back-nuts holding the taps in position, but it's generally easier to undo the nuts that connect the distribution pipes to the tails of the taps. In order to reach the one nearest the wall you may have to dismantle the overflow, either by unscrewing it or, if it is taken through the wall, by cutting it off flush with the wall. Then undo the waste connection.

The bath is now disconnected from the water supply pipes and from the branch waste pipe and can be pulled away from the wall. Unless you particularly want to save the old bath and have some strong helpers, do not attempt to remove it from the room or the house in one piece. It is very heavy. The best course of action is to break it into manageable pieces. Drape an old blanket over it to prevent flying chips of enamel and wear goggles to protect the eyes. Then, with a club hammer, break the bath up into pieces that you can easily carry away.

Place the new plastic bath in position and assemble the cradle or other support exactly as recommended by the manufacturer. It is most unlikely that the tails of the new taps will coincide with the position of the tap connectors of the old distribution pipes. If they don't, the easiest way of making the connections is by means of bendable copper pipe. This is 'corrugated' copper tubing — easily bent by hand. It is obtainable in 15mm and 22mm sizes and either with two plain ends for connection to soldered capillary or compression joints, or with one plain end and a swivel tap connector at the other. For this particular job two lengths of 22mm corrugated copper pipe will be required, each with one end plain and one end fitted with a swivel tap connector.

Offer the corrugated pipe lengths up to the tap tails and cut back the distribution pipes to the length required for connection to the plain ends. Leave these pipes slightly too long rather than too short. The corrugated pipe can be bent to accommodate a little extra length. Now connect the plain ends to the cut distribution pipes using either soldered capillary or Type 'A' compression couplings.

The chances are that the distribution pipes will be ¾in imperial size. If you use compression fittings an adaptor — probably simply a larger olive — will be needed for connection to a 22mm coupling. If you use soldered capillary fittings, special ¾in to 22mm couplings must be used. Remember to keep the blowtorch flame well away from the plastic of the bath. Connect up the swivel tap connectors of the corrugated pipe and the overflow of the bath. Do this in a logical order. First connect the tap connector to the further tap. A fibre washer inside the nut of the tap connector will ensure a watertight joint. Then connect up the flexible overflow pipe of the combined waste-and-overflow fitting to the bath's overflow outlet. Finally connect the nearer tap to the nearer tap connector.

If you have installed new pipework then you can install the entire trap, waste and water supply pipe spurs before moving the bath into position. Whatever you have decided upon, finish making all the connections, then reinstate the water supply and check for leaks.

The level of the positioned bath should now be checked using a spirit level, and adjustments made (you'll need a spanner to adjust the adjustable feet). When all is level, fit the side and end panels in position and the job is finished.

TAKING OUT THE OLD BATH

1 Think about how you're going to get the old bath out before you begin. The connections are likely to be inaccessible, old and corroded.

2 Start by trying to detach the waste trap using an adjustable wrench and, if necessary, penetrating oil.

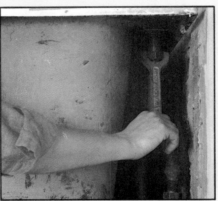

3 Undo the back-nuts underneath the taps or mixer. These are likely to be more difficult to undo than the trap; use a crowsfoot wrench.

4 If the back-nuts won't undo you may have to detach the supply pipes at another joint. Use an adjustable spanner to undo the nut.

5 Unscrew the old overflow pipe. Alternatively you can simply saw off both supply and overflow pipes — but you'll need to install new ones.

6 When the bath is free, drag it out of position. You'll need at least one other person to help you get a cast iron bath out unless you break it up first.

ATTACHING THE NEW FITTINGS

1 Start to assemble the new plumbing. Wind PTFE tape around the screw thread of the waste outlet and spread some plumber's putty underneath the rim.

2 Put the waste outlet in position and make sure that it is firmly seated. These days the overflow will be made of plastic and connects to the waste outlet.

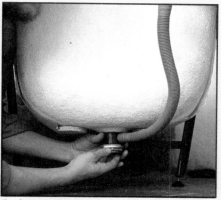

3 Attach the overflow to the outlet with a locking nut and a plastic O ring, which is inserted between. Screw up the nut and tighten gently.

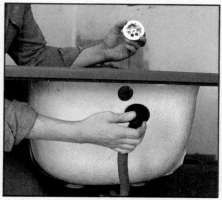

4 Attach the inlet end of the overflow which will have the plug and chain attached to it. Screw it into the pipe connector and tighten it up.

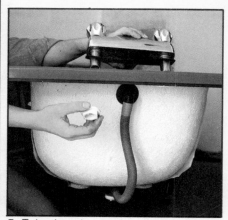

5 Take the mixer and check that the rubber gasket is in position between the unit and the bath, and also that it is clean and free from bits of grit.

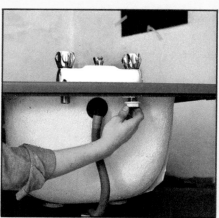

6 Screw the back-nuts up onto the trap and tighten them. Insert a flat plastic washer or top hat washer between the nut and the bath.

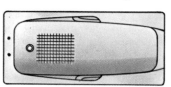
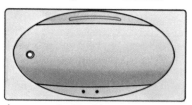

INSTALLING THE NEW BATH

1 *If you have installed new pipework, you should attach inlet spurs to the taps before you have to install the bath in its final position.*

2 *Put the bath into position. You may want to stand it away from the wall at the front end so that you can build in a shelf. Connect the inlet pipes.*

3 *Fit the waste trap and attach it to the waste pipe. When all the pipework is connected up, turn on the water and check for leaks.*

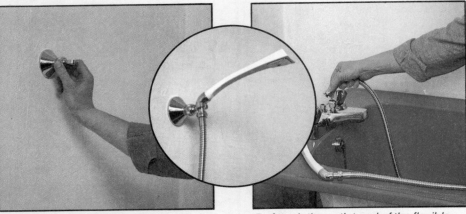
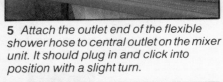

4 *When installing a mixer with a shower attachment, fix the shower head bracket to the wall and fit the shower head into the bracket (inset).*

5 *Attach the outlet end of the flexible shower hose to central outlet on the mixer unit. It should plug in and click into position with a slight turn.*

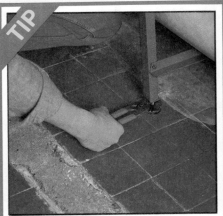

6 *Check that the bath is level both lengthways and widthways with a spirit level. Adjust the screwed-on feet to get the level right.*

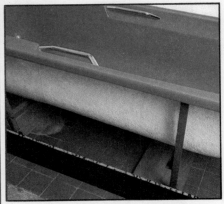

7 *Fix the bath panels in position by screwing them to the wooden carcase which surrounds the bath and is supplied by the manufacturer.*

8 *Screw the panels on carefully. They will usually be made of moulded high impact polystyrene which is easily chipped around the screw holes.*

9 *When all the bath work is complete you will have to make good the décor. If possible tile around the bath and box in the pipe work.*

REPLACING A WASHBASIN

Replacing a washbasin is fairly straightforward. It's a job you'll have to undertake if the basin is cracked – but you may also want to change the basin if you're redesigning your bathroom and adding some up-to-date fittings.

A part from replacing a cracked basin, which you should do immediately, the most common time to install a new basin is when you're improving a bathroom or decorating a separate WC. The chances are that the basin you'll be removing will be one of the older ceramic types, wall-hung, a pedestal model or built into a vanity unit.

The main advantage of a wall-hung basin is that it doesn't take up any floor space and because of this it is very useful in a small bathroom, WC or cloakroom. You can also set the basin at a comfortable height, unlike a pedestal basin whose height is fixed by the height of the pedestal. However, it's usual to fit a wall-hung basin with the rim 800mm (32in) above the floor.

Vanity units are now increasing in popularity. In fact they're the descendents of the Edwardian wash-stand, with its marble top, bowl and large water jug. The unit is simply a storage cupboard with a ceramic, enamelled pressed steel or plastic basin set flush in the top. The advantage of vanity units is that you have a counter surface round the basin on which to stand toiletries. There is rarely, if ever, sufficient room for these items behind or above conventional wall-hung or pedestal basins. Usually the top has some form of plastic covering or can be tiled for easy cleaning.

Fittings for basins

It's a good idea to choose the taps and waste fittings at the same time you select the basin, so everything matches. You could perhaps re-use the taps from the old basin, but it's doubtful if these will be in keeping with the design of the new appliance. As an alternative to shrouded head or pillar taps, you could fit a mixer, provided the holes at the back of the basin are suitably spaced to take the tap tails. But remember that because of the design of most basin mixers, you shouldn't use them if the cold water supply is directly from the mains.

Ceramic basins normally have a built-in overflow channel which in most appliances connects into the main outlet above the trap. So if you accidentally let the basin overfill you reduce the risk of water spillage.

PUTTING IN A NEW BASIN

You should have little trouble installing a new washbasin in the same place as the old one. It's also a good opportunity to check the pipe runs. If they're made of lead it's a good idea to replace them.

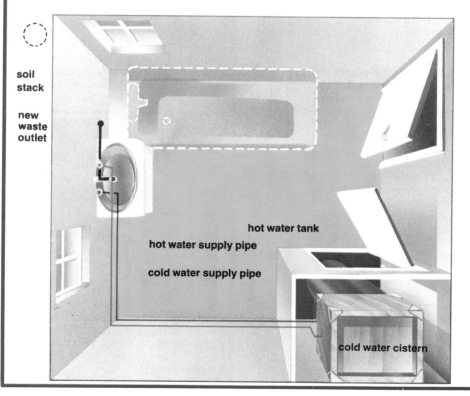

soil stack

new waste outlet

hot water tank
hot water supply pipe
cold water supply pipe
cold water cistern

Vanity unit basins are usually sold complete with a waste and overflow unit which resembles that of a modern stainless steel sink. A flexible tube connects the overflow outlet of the basin with a sleeve or 'banjo' unit which fits tightly round a slotted waste fitting.

With both types of basin the flange of the waste outlet has to be bedded into the hole provided for it in the basin on a layer of plumber's putty. The thread of the screwed waste must also be smeared with jointing compound to ensure a watertight seal where the 'banjo' connects to it.

Traps

The outlet of the waste must, of course, connect to a trap and branch waste pipe. At one time it was the practice to use 'shallow seal' traps with a 50mm (2in) depth of seal for two-pipe drainage systems, and 'deep seal' traps with a 75mm (3in) depth of seal for single stack systems. Today, however, deep seal traps are always fitted.

Of course, the modern bottle trap is one of the most common types used. It's neater looking and requires less space than a traditional U-trap. Where it's concealed behind a pedestal or in a vanity unit you can use one made of plastic, but there are chromium-plated and brass types if you have a wall-hung basin where trap and waste will be clearly visible. The one drawback with bottle traps is that they discharge water more slowly then a U-trap. You can now also buy traps with telescopic inlets that make it easy to provide a push-fit connection to an existing copper or plastic branch waste pipe (see pages 296-300).

Connecting up the water supply

It's unlikely that you'll be able to take out the old basin and install a new one without making some modification to the pipework. It's almost certain that the tap holes will be in a different position. To complicate matters further, taps are now made with shorter tails so you'll probably have to extend the supply pipes by a short length.

If you're installing new supply pipes, how you run them will depend on the type of basin you're putting in. With a wall-hung basin or the pedestal type, the hot and cold pipes are usually run neatly together up the back wall and then bent round to the tap tails. But as a vanity unit will conceal the plumbing there's no need to run the pipes together.

You might find it difficult to bend the required angles, so an easy way round the problem is to use flexible corrugated copper pipe which you can bend by hand to the shape you need. You can buy the pipe with a swivel tap connector at one end and a plain connector, on which you can use capillary or

FITTING A VANITY UNIT

1 Cut a hole in the vanity unit with the help of the template provided or, if the hole is precut, check the measurement against that of the sink.

2 Prop the basin up while you install the mixer unit. Start with the outlet spout which is fixed with a brass nut and packing washers.

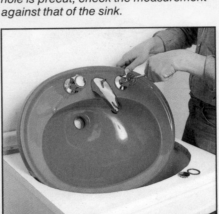

5 Now complete the tap heads by first sliding on the flange which covers up the securing nut; next put on the headwork and tighten the retaining nut.

6 Finish off the tap assembly by fitting the coloured markers into place (red for hot is usually on the left), and gently pressing home the chrome cap.

9 Before you put the basin into its final position put a strip of mastic around the opening in the vanity unit to ensure a watertight seal.

10 Press the basin gently into position and fix it to the underside of the top of the vanity unit. Attach the waste plug to its keeper.

3 Now take the water inlet assembly and check that the hot and cold spur pipes are the right length so that the tap sub-assemblies are correctly positioned.

4 Fix the assembly in position with the brass nuts supplied by the manufacturer. Make sure that all the washers are included otherwise the fitting won't be secure.

7 Now insert the waste outlet. Make sure the rubber flange is fitted properly and seats comfortably into the basin surround.

8 Turn the basin over; secure the outlet and the pop-up waste control rods. These may need shortening depending on clearance inside the vanity unit.

11 Now fix the inlet pipes to the two mixer connections and screw on the waste trap. Take the doors off the vanity unit to make access easier.

12 Turn the water back on and check for leaks. Check the pop-up waste system works, then put the doors of the vanity unit back on.

BASIN SIZES

On basins, the dimension from side to side is specified as the length, and that from back to front as the width.

Most standard sized basins are between 550 and 700mm (22 and 28in) long, and 450 to 500mm (18 to 20in) wide.

BASIN COMPONENTS

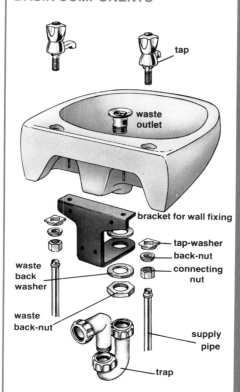

tap

waste outlet

bracket for wall fixing

tap-washer

back-nut

connecting nut

waste back washer

waste back-nut

supply pipe

trap

THE SPACE YOU'LL NEED

2200mm

1000mm

400mm   700mm

Think about the space around your basin particularly if you are installing a new one. You not only need elbow room when you are bending over it, such as when you are washing your hair, but also room in front to stand back — especially if you put a mirror above it. Here are the recommended dimensions for the area around your basin.

341

When fitting the taps all you have to do is to remove the back-nuts and slip flat plastic washers over the tails (if they aren't there already). The taps can then be positioned in the holes in the basin. When this has been done more plastic washers (or top hat washers) have to be slipped over the tails before the back-nuts are replaced. It's important not to overtighten these as it's quite easy to damage a ceramic basin.

Because some vanity unit basins are made of a thinner material, you may find that the shanks of the taps fitted into them will protrude below the under-surface of the basin. The result is that when the back-nut is fully tightened, it still isn't tight against the underside of the basin. To get round the problem you have to fit a top hat washer over the shank so the back-nut can be screwed up against it.

Mixers usually have one large washer or gasket between the base of the mixer and the top of the basin and you fix them in exactly the same way.

When you've fitted the taps you can then fit the waste. With a ceramic basin you'll have to use a slotted waste to enable water from the overflow to escape into the drainage pipe. Getting this in place means first removing the back-nut so you can slip it through the outlet hole in the basin – which itself should be coated with a generous layer of plumber's putty. It's essential to make sure that the slot in the waste fitting coincides with the outlet of the basin's built-in overflow. You'll then have to smear jointing compound on the protruding screw thread of the tail, slip on a plastic washer and replace and tighten the back-nut. As you do this the waste flange will probably try to turn on its seating, but you can prevent this by holding the grid with pliers as you tighten the back-nut.

Finally, any excess putty that is squeezed out as the flange is tightened against the basin should be wiped away.

A vanity unit will probably be supplied with a combined waste and overflow unit. This is a flexible hose that has to be fitted (unlike a ceramic basin, where it's an integral part of the appliance). The slotted waste is bedded in in exactly the same way as a waste on a ceramic basin. You then have to fit one end of the overflow to the basin outlet and slip the 'banjo' outlet on the other end over the tail of the waste to cover the slot. It's held in position by a washer and back-nut.

Fitting the basin
Once the taps and waste have been fixed in position on the new basin, you should be ready to remove the old basin and fit the new one in its place. First you need to cut off the water supply to the basin, either by turning off the main stop-valve (or any gate valve on

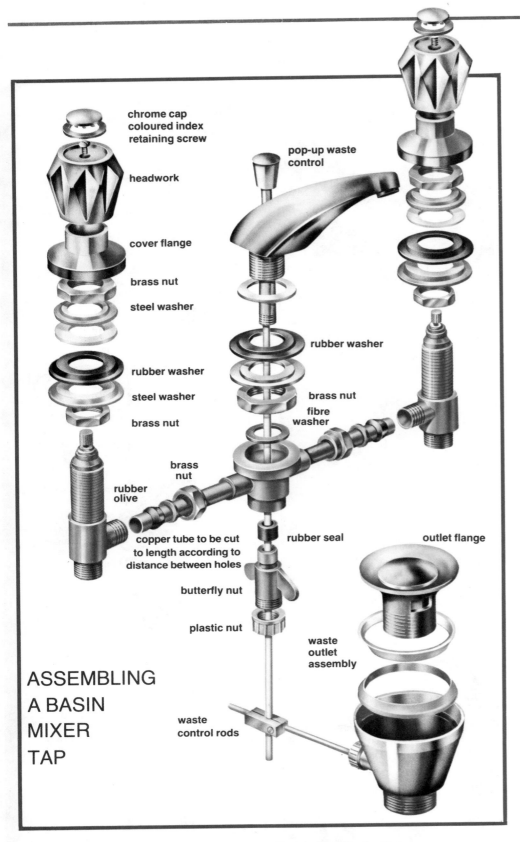

chrome cap
coloured index
retaining screw

headwork

pop-up waste
control

cover flange

brass nut

steel washer

rubber washer

rubber washer

steel washer

brass nut
fibre
washer

brass nut

brass
nut

rubber
olive

copper tube to be cut
to length according to
distance between holes

rubber seal

outlet flange

butterfly nut

plastic nut

waste
outlet
assembly

ASSEMBLING A BASIN MIXER TAP

waste
control rods

compression fittings at the other. If you're using ordinary copper pipe, the easiest way to start is by bending the pipe to the correct angle first, and then cutting the pipe to the right length at each end afterwards. See pages 301-303 for more details.

Preparing the basin
Before you fix the basin in position, you'll need to fit the taps (or mixer) and the waste. It's much easier to do this at this stage than later when the basin is against the wall because you will have more room to manoeuvre in.

the distribution pipes) or by tying up the ball-valve supplying the main cold water storage cistern. Then open the taps and leave them until the water ceases to flow. If the existing basin is a pedestal model you'll have to remove the pedestal which may be screwed to the floor. Take off the nut that connects the basin trap to the threaded waste outlet and unscrew the nuts that connect the water supply pipes to the tails of the taps. These will either be swivel tap connectors or cap and lining joints. You'll need to be able to lift the basin clear and then remove the brackets or hangers on which it rests.

You'll probably need some help when installing the new basin as it's much easier to mark the fixing holes if someone else is holding the basin against the wall. With a pedestal basin, the pedestal will determine the level of the basin. The same applies with a vanity unit. But if the basin is set on hangers or brackets, you can adjust the height for convenience.

Once the fixing holes have been drilled and plugged, the basin can be screwed into position and you can deal with the plumbing. Before you make the connections to the water supply pipes you may have to cut or lengthen them to meet the tap tails. If you need to lengthen them you'll find it easier to use corrugated copper pipe. The actual connection between pipe and tail is made with a swivel tap connector – a form of compression fitting.

Finally you have to connect the trap. You may be able to re-use the old one, but it's more likely you'll want to fit a new one. And if its position doesn't coincide with the old one, you can use a bottle trap with an adjustable telescopic inlet.

FITTING A PEDESTAL BASIN

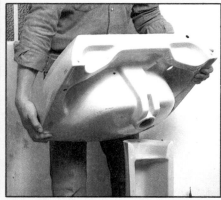

1 *Stand the basin on the pedestal to check the height of the water supply pipe runs and the outlet. Measure the height of the wall fixing points.*

2 *When you're making up the pipe run to connect to the tap tails, plan it so the pipes are neatly concealed within the body of the pedestal.*

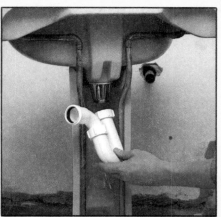

3 *Line up the piped waste outlet and fix the trap to the basin outlet. A telescopic trap may be useful here to adjust for a varying level.*

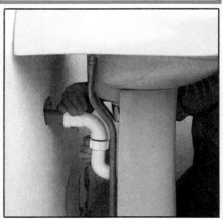

4 *Move the whole unit into its final position, screw the basin to the wall, connect the waste trap to the outlet, and connect up the supply pipes.*

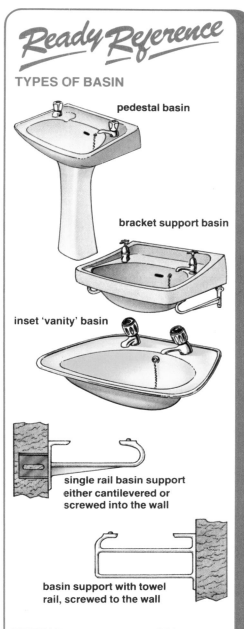

TYPES OF BASIN

pedestal basin

bracket support basin

inset 'vanity' basin

single rail basin support either cantilevered or screwed into the wall

basin support with towel rail, screwed to the wall

FITTING A VANITY BASIN

When you buy a vanity basin it should be supplied with a template to guide you in cutting your work surface or vanity unit. This should also include fitting instructions, and necessary fixing screws and mastic strip. It may look like this.

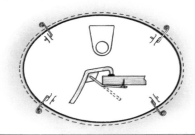

REPLACING TAPS

Changing the old taps on your basin is a bright and practical way of making your bathroom more attractive. It may also be a good idea if they are old and inefficient. Here's what is involved.

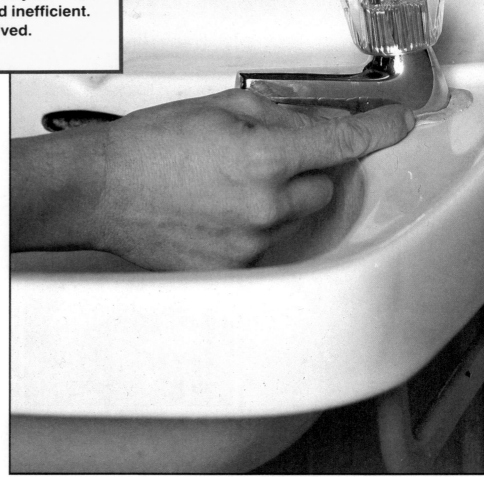

There may be a number of reasons why you wish to replace the taps supplying your sink, basin or bath. They may continually drip or leak, where new taps would give efficient, trouble-free service. Perhaps you want the advantages that mixers have over individual taps or perhaps it is simply that the chromium plating has worn off leaving the taps looking incurably shabby.

It is more likely, however, that appearance, rather than malfunction, will be your reason for changing. There are fashions in plumbing fittings as in clothing and furniture. Taps of the 1950s or 60s are instantly recognisable as out-of-date in a bathroom or kitchen of the 1980s. Fortunately, fashions in sinks, basins and baths have changed rather less dramatically over the past three decades. There is probably no more cost-effective way of improving bathroom and kitchen appearance than by the provision of sparkling new taps or mixers.

Choosing taps

When you come to select your new taps you may feel that you are faced with a bewildering choice. Tap size, appearance, the material of which the tap is made, whether to choose individual taps or mixers and – for the bath – whether to provide for an over-bath shower by fitting a bath/shower mixer: all these things need to be considered.

Size is easily enough dealt with. Taps and mixers are still in imperial sizes. Bath tap tails are ¾in in diameter, and basin and sink taps ½in in diameter. There are, however, a few suppliers who are beginning to designate taps by the metric size, not of the taps themselves, but of the copper supply pipes to which they will probably be connected. Such a supplier might refer to bath taps as 22mm and sink and basin taps as 15mm.

Most taps are made of chromium-plated brass, though there are also ranges of enamelled and even gold-plated taps and mixers. Although taps and mixers are still manufactured with conventional crutch or capstan handles, most people nowadays prefer to choose taps with 'shrouded' heads made of acrylic or other plastic. In effect, these combine the functions of handle and easy-clean cover, completely concealing the tap's headgear. A still popular alternative is the functional 'Supatap', nowadays provided with plastic rather than metal 'ears' for quick and comfortable turning on and off.

There is also a very competitively priced range of all-plastic taps. These usually give satisfactory enough service in the home, but they cannot be regarded as being as sturdy as conventional metal taps, and they can be damaged by very hot water.

So far as design is concerned the big difference is between 'bib taps' and 'pillar taps'. Bib taps have a horizontal inlet and are usually wall-mounted while pillar taps have a vertical inlet and are mounted on the bath, basin or sink they serve.

Taking out old basin taps

When replacing old taps with new ones the most difficult part of the job is likely to be – as with so many plumbing operations – removing the old fittings. Let's first consider wash basin taps.

You must, of course, cut off the hot and cold water supplies to the basin. The best way of doing this will usually be to tie up the float arm of the ball valve supplying the cold water storage cistern so as to prevent water flowing in. Then run the bathroom cold taps until water ceases to flow. Only then open up the hot taps. This will conserve most of the expensively heated water in the hot water storage cylinder.

If you look under the basin you will find that the tails of the taps are connected to the water supply pipes with small, fairly accessible nuts, and that a larger – often

REMOVING OLD TAPS

1 *It's best to change taps by removing the basin completely. Loosen the two tap connectors carefully with an adjustable spanner.*

3 *Undo any screws holding the basin to its brackets on the wall, and lift it clear of the brackets before lowering it carefully to the floor.*

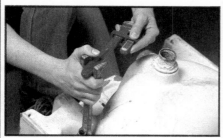

5 *Use the crowsfoot (with extra leverage if necessary) to undo the back-nut. If more force is needed, grip the tap itself with a wrench to stop it turning.*

2 *Disconnect the waste trap connector using an adjustable wrench. Take care not to damage the trap, particularly if it is lead or copper.*

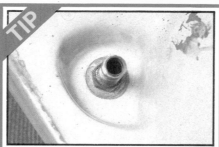

4 *Check the condition of the back-nuts, which may be badly corroded. It's a good idea to apply penetrating oil and leave this to work for a while.*

6 *Remove the back-nut and any washers beneath it and the basin. Old washers like these should always be replaced with new washers.*

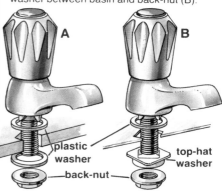
inaccessible – back-nut secures the tap to the basin. The nuts of the swivel tap connectors joining the pipes to the taps are usually easily undone with a wrench or spanner of the appropriate size. The back-nuts can be extremely difficult – even for professional plumbers!

There are special wrenches and basin or 'crows foot' spanners that may help, but they won't perform miracles and ceramic basins can be very easily damaged by heavy handedness. The best course of action is to disconnect the swivel tap connectors and to disconnect the trap from the waste outlet. These are secured by nuts and are easily

undone. Then lift the basin off its brackets or hanger and place it upside down on the floor. Apply some penetrating oil to the tap tails and, after allowing a few minutes for it to soak in, tackle the nuts with your wrench or crowsfoot spanner. You'll find they are much more accessible. Hold the tap while you do this to stop it swivelling and damaging the basin.

Fitting the new taps
When fitting the new taps or mixer, unscrew the back-nuts, press some plumber's putty round the tail directly below the tap body or fit a plastic washer onto the top tail.

FITTING NEW TAPS

1 *Remove the tap and clean up the basin surround, chipping away scale and any old putty remaining from when the tap was originally installed.*

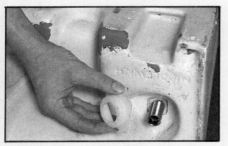

3 *Twist the tap so that it's at the correct angle to the basin and is firmly bedded on the putty. Then push a top-hat washer onto the tail.*

5 *Tighten up the back-nut until the tap assembly is completely firm, using the crowsfoot or an adjustable spanner. Repeat the process for the other tap.*

7 *When all is secure, remove any surplus putty from around the base of the taps, wiping it over with a finger to leave a smooth, neat finish.*

2 *Now take one of the new taps and fit a washer or plumber's putty around the top of the tail before pushing it into the hole in the basin.*

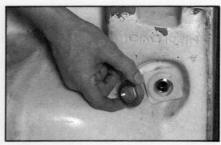

4 *With the top-hat washer firmly in place, take the new back-nut and screw it up the tail of the tap by hand.*

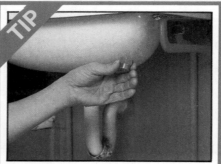

6 *Reconnect all the pipework. Use tap-tail adaptors if the new taps have shorter tails than the old ones.*

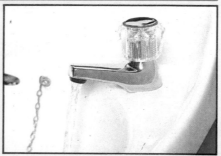

8 *Turn the water back on. Check that the flow from the taps is regular and that the waste trap is not leaking. If it is, tighten up its connectors slightly.*

Push the tails through the holes in the basin. Slip flat plastic washers over the tails where they protrude from beneath the basin, screw on the back-nuts and tighten them up. Make sure that the taps or mixer are secure, but don't overtighten them. To make tightening easier, (and undoing, if ever necessary) use top-hat washers.

All that remains to be done is to connect the swivel tap connectors to the tails of the new taps or mixer. You will see that a tap connector consists of a lining – with a flange – that is inserted into the tap tail and is then secured by the coupling nut. This nut is provided with a washer to ensure a watertight connection. When renewing taps you may well need to renew this small washer.

It is possible that when you come to connect the water supply pipes to the taps you will get an unpleasant surprise. The tails of modern taps are slightly shorter than those of older ones and the tap connectors may not reach. If the water supply pipes are of lead or of copper it is quite likely that they will have enough 'give' to enable you to make the connection but, if not, there are extension pieces specially made to bridge the gap.

Bib taps

If you're replacing existing bib taps with those of a more modern design, it's a relatively simple matter of disconnecting and unscrewing the old ones and fitting the new taps in their place. However, it's quite possible that you'll want to remove the bib taps altogether and fit a new sink with some pillar taps. This will involve a little more plumbing work. To start with, turn off the water supply and remove the taps and old sink. If the pipework comes up from the floor, you'll need to uncover the run in the wall to below where the new sink will go. You should then be able to ease the pipes away from the wall and cut off the exposed sections. This will allow you to join short lengths of new pipe, bent slightly if necessary, to link the pipe ends and the tap tails. Alternatively, if the pipes come down the wall you'll have to extend the run to below the level of the new sink and use elbow fittings to link the pipe to the tap tails. In either case it's a good idea to fit the taps to the new sink first and to make up the pipework runs slightly overlong, so that when the new sink is offered up to the wall you can measure up accurately and avoid the risk of cutting off too much pipe. Rather than having to make difficult bends you can use lengths of corrugated copper pipe. One end of the pipe is plain so that it can be fitted to the 15mm supply pipes with either a soldered capillary or compression fitting; the other end has a swivel tap connector.

REPLACING A WC

Replacing your WC need not be a frightening prospect provided you follow a few basic rules. It also gives you the opportunity to install a quieter and more efficient piece of equipment.

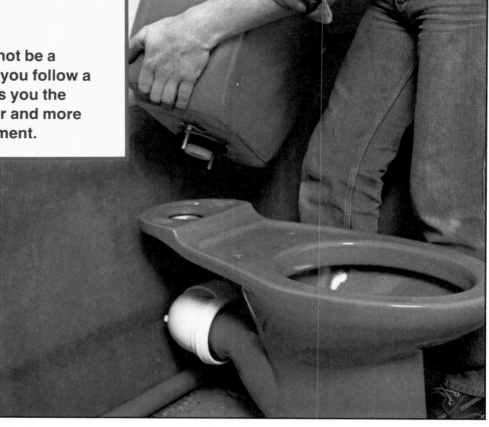

There are several reasons why you may wish to remove and replace your WC suite. The existing pan may be cracked, in which case replacement must not be delayed, and no attempt should be made to repair it. Or the porcelain may be crazed making it unsightly, and difficult to keep clean. Most likely, however, the reason will be that your existing WC is simply old fashioned and due for replacement as part of an overall improvement plan.

Pan or cistern?
If it's just the pan you find fault with then that's all you need to replace. Colours for sanitary-ware, as WCs are usually called by the manufacturers, are fairly standardised, and you should have no difficulty in obtaining a pan to match the existing cistern.

If, on the other hand, you want to convert an old-fashioned lavatory suite with a high-level cistern, it may be possible to replace only the flushing cistern and flush pipe (or 'flush bend' as it is often called) with a low level one, while keeping the existing pan.

However, in order to accommodate the flushing cistern, the pans of low level suites are usually positioned 25 to 50mm (1 to 2in) further from the wall behind the suite than are those of high level ones. If you overlook this point you are likely to find that the seat and cover of the pan cannot be raised properly when the new cistern is fitted.

Slim-line cisterns
In recent years manufacturers have developed slim-line flushing cisterns or 'flush panels' only about 115mm (4¼in) deep. These can, in most cases, be used to convert a WC from high level to low level operation without moving the pan. With such a cistern the flushing inlet to the pan can be as little as 130mm (5¼in) from the wall behind, instead of the 200 to 230 (8 to 9in) required by an ordinary low level cistern. To make room for the full 9 litres (2 gal) of water needed for an adequate flush, these slimline cisterns are rather wider from side to side than conventional ones. So make sure that there is sufficient unobstructed width of wall behind the suite to accommodate it.

PLANNING THE MOVE
The biggest problem concerns the position of the soil stack. In this bathroom the old soil pipe was disconnected, and a new soil pipe run was installed on the outside of the bathroom wall to link the new WC to the existing soil stack. This was much neater than running the new pipe inside the bathroom, where it would have had to be boxed in.

The other alteration to existing pipework involved cutting the cold feed to the cistern part-way along its run, and re-connecting it to the new cistern.

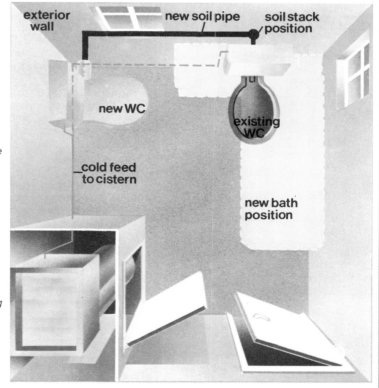

exterior wall   new soil pipe   soil stack position

new WC

existing WC

cold feed to cistern

new bath position

PAN AND CISTERN POSITIONS

There are various WC suite arrangements you're likely to come across. The position of the pan in relation to the cistern is crucial, and if you're changing one without the other you must measure up carefully, to ensure that major changes of position can be avoided.

1 High level cistern

To convert this to a low-level cistern without replacing or moving the pan you will probably have to use a slim panel cistern.

2 Medium-level cistern

3 Low-level cistern

4 Close-coupled suite

5 Wall-mounted pan

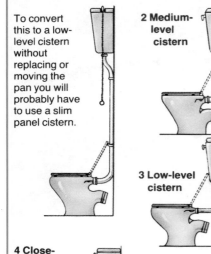

HOW MUCH SPACE

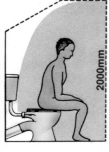

You need a minimum amount of space around a WC in order to be able to use it comfortably – above it, to each side of it and in front of it.

2000mm

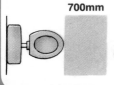

700mm

800mm

Siphonic suites

Close-coupled lavatory suites, in which the pan and cistern form one unit without even the short flush bend of a low level cistern, are neater in appearance than the other kinds. They are particularly silent and effective where they are flushed and cleansed by siphonic action, as distinct from the 'wash down' action in which flushing simply releases the full contents of the cistern into the pan, and the weight of water carries away its contents. They also provide a larger water surface area than older pans, an important factor in maintaining the cleanliness of the pan.

There are two kinds of siphonic suite, single-trap and double-trap. The single-trap pattern is the simpler and cheaper. The outlet is first constricted and then widened to connect to the branch drain or soil pipe. When the suite is flushed, water completely fills the restricted section of the outlet and passes on, taking air with it, to create a partial vacuum. Atmospheric pressure then pushes the contents of the pan into the drain. The siphonic action is broken, often with a gurgle, as air passes under the bend of the trap.

With a double-trap siphonic suite a specially designed air pipe or 'pressure reducer' connects the air space between the two traps to the channel through which the flushing water passes. As this water flows past the pressure reducer it sucks up air from the space between the two traps, in the same way that the wind passing over the top of a chimney sucks up air from a room below. It's this that creates the partial vacuum on which siphonic action depends. Where a double-trap siphonic suite is working properly, you'll see the water level in the pan fall before the 'flush' water flows in. Although more expensive than other kinds, these suites are valuable where, as in an entrance lobby cloakroom for instance, silent operation is a prime consideration.

Just as low level WC suites normally project further from the wall behind them than high level ones, close-coupled suites project further than either. Don't forget this when considering the provision of such a suite in a small bathroom or cloakroom. You may have to change the position of the washbasin and this, in turn, could obstruct the door.

Pan fixings

Moving an existing WC pan isn't always easy. It's likely to depend largely upon whether it is installed upstairs or on the ground floor. Upstairs WCs usually have a P-trap outlet, which is almost horizontal and is connected to a branch soil pipe by means of a putty or mortar joint. This can easily be broken with a club hammer and cold chisel

once you have disconnected the pan from the floor.

Downstairs WCs usually have their bases firmly cemented to a solid floor and usually have an S-trap outlet which is vertical. This connects via a cement joint to an earthenware drain socket protruding above floor level. To remove such a pan it's necessary to break the outlet. Use a cold chisel to detach the front part of the pan from the floor, then use a cold chisel and hammer again to clear the pan outlet and the joining material from the drain socket.

Nowadays it is usual to connect both ground floor and upstairs WCs to the soil pipe using a flexible joint, usually a patent plastic push-fit joint with a spigot that is inserted into the drain and a 'finned' socket that fits over the WC pan outlet.

Such patent joins are nowadays manufactured in a range that covers virtually any WC installation. Not only are they easy to use but they help reduce the noise of a flushing lavatory. It's not considered to be good practice today to cement the base of a WC to a solid floor, as the setting of the cement can create stresses resulting in a cracked pan. It is best to remove every trace of cement from the floor and, having achieved a dead-level base, to secure the WC pan with screws driven into plugs pushed into holes drilled in the floor.

How to start

After you have turned off the water supply and flushed the cistern to empty it, the next step is to disconnect the cistern's water supply, overflow and outlet pipes. So begin by unscrewing the cap-nut connecting the water-supply pipe to the cistern's ball-valve inlet. Then undo the back-nut retaining the cistern's overflow or warning pipe. Finally undo the large nut which secures the threaded outlet of the cistern to the flush pipe. It should now be possible to lift the old cistern off its supporting bracket or brackets.

If the WC suite is a very old one and screwed to a timber floor, unscrew and remove the pan's fixing screws. Then, taking the pan in both hands, pull it from side to side and away from the wall. If the connection to the soil pipe is made with a mastic or putty joint, the pan outlet should come easily out of its socket (which will have to be cleaned of all jointing material before the new unit is fitted). If a rigid cement joint has been used then there's usually no alternative but to use a bit of force. This means deliberately breaking the pan outlet, just behind the trap and above the drain socket, with a club hammer. You can then prise the front part of the pan away from the floor using a cold chisel and hammer. This will separate the pan outlet from the drain. At this point it's a

REMOVING THE OLD PAN

1 Locate the water pipe which supplies the WC cistern and completely shut off the stop valve which controls it. If no valve exists, block the cistern outlet.

2 Lift the top off the cistern and then press the flush handle to empty it. No more fresh water should flow in as the ball float falls.

3 Disconnect the overflow pipe. If it is made of lead you should replace it with a PVC pipe run. Saw it off if you are repositioning the WC elsewhere.

4 Disconnect the supply pipe in the same way as the overflow. If you are replacing the piping altogether, you can cut through it with a hacksaw.

5 Disconnect the cistern from the pan. A close-coupled one is lifted off; with other suites you may have to disconnect the flush pipe between cistern and pan.

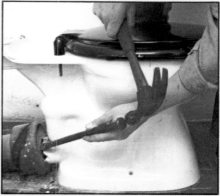

6 Unscrew the pan from the floor, and then use a hammer and cold chisel to break the joint between the pan and the outlet, tapping gently but firmly.

7 When you have fractured the joint, ease the pan away from the pipe. Even if it is bedded on mortar it should come away easily. Chip away the old mortar.

8 Dispose of the pan and extract any loose bits of debris from the socket. Stuff newspaper into the opening to stop bits falling into the soil pipe.

9 If you are going to use the pipe again clean it out carefully, ready to be connected up to the new WC pan with a proprietary connector.

Ready Reference

CISTERN MECHANISMS

There are two sorts of flushing mechanism the bell type in well-bottom cisterns and the piston type found otherwise. The latter is by far the more popular today.

well-bottom cistern for replacement of high-level arrangements

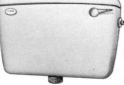

lever flush cistern for low-level suite

slim-line flush panel where depth is restricted – usually when a high-level arrangement is converted to a low-level one

THE FLUSH MECHANISM

You'll find you have to assemble the mechanism which is bagged up inside the new cistern. Lay out the components (A) and check them against the enclosed instruction leaflet before assembling them correctly (B).

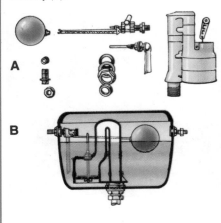

INSTALLING THE NEW PAN

1 *Offer up the pan to the outlet (note that here a new PVC soil pipe has been installed). When it fits snugly, mark down the positions for the fixing screws.*

3 *Secure the cistern to the wall with screws and plugs. Then attach the new overflow pipe, finally tightening up the lock-nut with an adjustable spanner.*

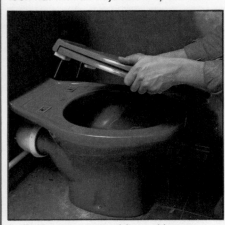

5 *Fit the seat assembly, making sure that the gaskets are correctly in place between the seat and the pan; screw up the nuts tightly.*

2 *Drill the holes (inset) and reposition the pan and cistern. Fit the pan outlet into the white push-fit adaptor so that it is firmly in position.*

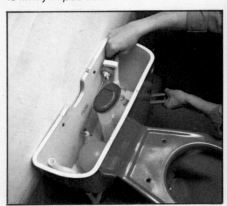

4 *Assemble the internal flushing mechanism, see Ready Reference. Attach the water supply pipe and the flushing handle.*

6 *Restore the water supply. Check that the cistern fills to the correct level and adjust the ball-valve if it does not. Finally flush to fill the pan trap.*

THREE TYPES OF WC

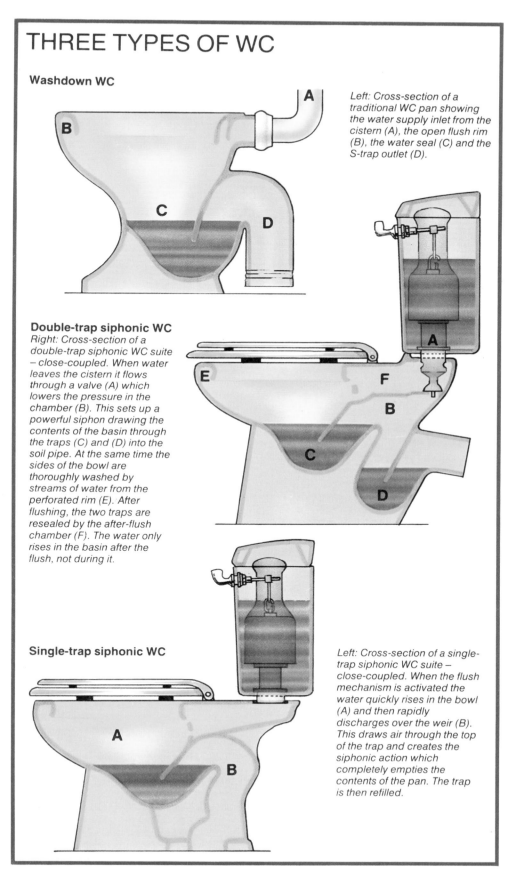

Washdown WC

Left: Cross-section of a traditional WC pan showing the water supply inlet from the cistern (A), the open flush rim (B), the water seal (C) and the S-trap outlet (D).

Double-trap siphonic WC

Right: Cross-section of a double-trap siphonic WC suite – close-coupled. When water leaves the cistern it flows through a valve (A) which lowers the pressure in the chamber (B). This sets up a powerful siphon drawing the contents of the basin through the traps (C) and (D) into the soil pipe. At the same time the sides of the bowl are thoroughly washed by streams of water from the perforated rim (E). After flushing, the two traps are resealed by the after-flush chamber (F). The water only rises in the basin after the flush, not during it.

Single-trap siphonic WC

Left: Cross-section of a single-trap siphonic WC suite – close-coupled. When the flush mechanism is activated the water quickly rises in the bowl (A) and then rapidly discharges over the weir (B). This draws air through the top of the trap and creates the siphonic action which completely empties the contents of the pan. The trap is then refilled.

good idea to stuff a bundle of rags or screwed-up newspaper into the drain socket to prevent any debris getting into the soil pipe. Next attack the socket to remove the remains of the pan's outlet. For this, use a small cold chisel and hammer but do it carefully to avoid damaging the drain socket itself – this will be used again. It's best to keep the point of the chisel pointing towards the centre of the pipe. Try to break it right down to the shoulder of the socket at one point and the rest will then come out fairly easily. Repeat the chipping process to remove all the old jointing material. Remove the bundle of rags or newspaper with the fragments of pipe and jointing material. Then with your cold chisel, remove every trace of the cement base that secured the old pan to the floor.

Installing the new pan

Don't set the pan on a cement base – just use screws and plugs to fix it to the floor. But first you've got to get the connection to the drain socket right. Start by positioning the patent push-fit joint in the drain socket. Then offer up the new pan to the patent push-fit socket and move the pan around until it fits snugly. To fix the pan, mark the screw positions on the floor by tapping a nail through the screw-holes, and draw round the base on the floor so that you can replace it in exactly the same position. Drill holes in the floor at the points marked and finally fit the screws. If it's a solid floor, of course, it's essential to use plastic or fibre plugs in the screw holes.

For fixing the pan, it's advisable to use brass non-corroding screws with a lead washer slipped over each one so you won't crack the pan as you tighten the screws. Screw the pan down, checking that it is exactly horizontal with the aid of a spirit level laid across the top of the bowl. If it is not dead-level, pack the lower side with thin wood or plastic strips. The latter are more suitable because thin wood rots too easily. Finally check that the outlet of the pan is firmly pushed into the connector and that you've followed any specific fitting instructions from the manufacturer.

Fitting the cistern

Fix the new cistern to the wall at the level above the pan recommended by the manufacturer. In the case of a separate cistern, secure the upper end of the flush pipe to the cistern, usually by means of a large nut, and the lower end to the pan's flushing horn with a rubber cone connector. With a close-coupled suite, follow the manufacturer's instructions. You will now quite likely have to extend or cut back the water supply pipe to connect it to the new cistern. Complete the job by cutting and fitting a new overflow.

INSTALLING A SHOWER

Showers have become a part of the modern home, whether fitted over the bath or in a separate cubicle. They save time, space and energy and are quite easy to install once the design is right.

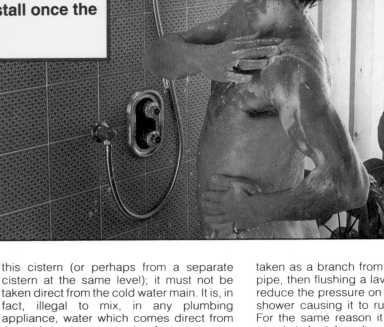

It is possible for four or five members of a family to have showers in the same time – and with the same amount of hot water – that would be needed for just one of them to have a bath. Showers, if properly installed, are safer for use by the elderly and the very young than a sit-down bath and need less cleaning. They are also more hygienic to use than a bath, as the bather isn't sitting in his own soapy and dirty water, and can rinse thoroughly in fresh water.

Where a shower is provided in its own cubicle, as distinct from over a bath, it takes up very little extra space. One can be provided in any space which is at least 900mm (36in) square, and can be put in a variety of locations such as a bedroom, on a landing, in a lobby or even in the cupboard under the stairs.

Yet shower installation can all too often prove to be a disappointment. Poorly designed systems may provide only a trickle of water at the sprinkler, or may run icy cold until the cold tap is almost turned off, and will then run scalding hot.

So, although it is possible to provide a shower in virtually any household, it is important that you match the shower equipment and your existing hot and cold water systems. If you have a cylinder storage hot water system, which is by far the commonest kind of hot water supply to be found in British homes, a conventional shower connected to the household's hot and cold water supplies is likely to be the most satisfactory and the easiest to install. But the hot and cold water systems must comply with certain quite definite design requirements if the shower is to operate safely and satisfactorily.

Pressure

The most important requirement is that the hot and cold supply pipes to the shower must be under equal water pressure. With a cylinder storage hot water system, whether direct or indirect (see pages 291-295 for the distinction), hot water pressure comes from the cold water storage cistern supplying the cylinder with water. The cold water supply to the shower must therefore also come from

this cistern (or perhaps from a separate cistern at the same level); it must not be taken direct from the cold water main. It is, in fact, illegal to mix, in any plumbing appliance, water which comes direct from the main and water coming from a storage cistern. However, quite apart from the question of legality, it is impossible to mix streams of water satisfactorily under such differing pressures. The shower will inevitably run either very hot or very cold, depending on which stream is the high-pressure one.

The cold water storage cistern must also be high enough above the shower sprinkler to provide a satisfactory operating pressure. Best results will be obtained if the base of the cold water storage cistern is 1.5m (5ft) or more above the sprinkler. However, provided that pipe runs are short and have only slight changes of direction, a reasonable shower can be obtained when the vertical distance between the base of the cistern and the shower sprinkler is as little as 1m (39in). The level of the hot water storage tank in relation to the shower doesn't matter in the least. It can be above, below or at the same level as the shower. It is the level of the cold water storage cistern that matters.

There is yet another design requirement for conventional shower installation which sometimes applies. This is that the cold water supply to the shower should be a separate 15mm (½in) branch direct from the cold water storage cistern, and not taken from the main bathroom distribution pipe. This is a safety precaution. If the cold supply were

taken as a branch from a main distribution pipe, then flushing a lavatory cistern would reduce the pressure on the cold side of the shower causing it to run dangerously hot. For the same reason it is best for the hot supply to be taken direct from the vent pipe immediately above the hot water storage cylinder and not as a branch from another distribution pipe, though this is rather less important. A reduction in the hot water pressure would result in the shower running cold. This would be highly unpleasant, although not dangerous.

Mixers

Showers must have some kind of mixing valve to mix the streams of hot and cold water and thus to produce a shower at the required temperature. The two handles of the bath taps provide the very simplest mixing valve, and push-on shower attachments can be cheaply obtained. Opening the bath taps then mixes the two streams of water and diverts them upwards to a wall-hung shower rose. These very simple attachments work quite satisfactorily – provided that the design requirements already referred to are met. However, it isn't always easy to adjust the tap handles to provide water at exactly the temperature required.

A bath/shower mixer provides a slightly more sophisticated alternative operating on the same principle. With one of these, the tap handles are adjusted until water is flowing through the mixer spout into the bath at the required temperature. The water is then

CHOOSING THE RIGHT SHOWER TYPE

The type of shower you can install depends on the sort of water supply you have in your home. This chart will help you make the right selection.

```
┌──────────────────────┐   ┌──────────────────────┐   ┌──────────────────────┐
│ Hot and cold water   │   │ Cold taps from mains │   │ No water storage     │
│ stored               │   │ hot water stored     │   │                      │
└──────────────────────┘   └──────────────────────┘   └──────────────────────┘
           │                          │                          │
           ▼                          ▼                          ▼
┌──────────────────────┐   ┌──────────────────────┐   ┌──────────────────────┐
│ Is there 1m (3ft)    │◄──┤ Can new cold water   │   │ Consider instantaneous│
│ between cistern base │YES│ cistern be installed?│NO▶│ water heater shower  │
│ and shower rose?     │   └──────────────────────┘   └──────────────────────┘
└──────────────────────┘            │                          │
    │          │NO                   │                          ▼
    │          ▼                     NO              ┌──────────────────────┐
    YES  ┌──────────────────────┐                   │ How is domestic      │
    │    │ Can cistern be raised│                    │ hot water heated?    │
    │    │ or a pump be fitted? │                    └──────────────────────┘
    ▼    └──────────────────────┘            ┌───────────────┴───────────────┐
┌──────────────────┐   │YES                  ▼                               ▼
│ Consider mixer-  │   │           ┌──────────────────────┐   ┌──────────────────────┐
│ type shower      │   │           │ Instantaneous gas    │   │ Non-storage electric │
└──────────────────┘   │           │ water heater         │   │ water heater         │
        │              │           └──────────────────────┘   └──────────────────────┘
        ▼              │                      │           YES            │
┌──────────────────┐   │           ┌──────────────────────┐   ┌──────────────────────┐
│ Will children or │   │           │ Mixer-type shower can│◄──│ Is there a gas       │
│ the old use the  │   │           │ be used with some gas│   │ supply in the house? │
│ shower?          │   │           │ water heaters        │   └──────────────────────┘
└──────────────────┘   │           └──────────────────────┘            │ NO
   │YES      │NO                              │                         ▼
   ▼         ▼                                ▼            ┌──────────────────────┐
┌──────────┐┌──────────┐         ┌──────────────────────┐ │ Install instantaneous│
│ Use       ││ Use manual│        │ If heater suitable,  │ │ electric shower      │
│ thermostatic││ or therm-│       │ use mixer-type       │ └──────────────────────┘
│ mixer-type││ ostatic   │        │ shower               │
│ shower    ││ mixer-type│        └──────────────────────┘
└──────────┘│ shower    │
            └──────────┘
```

diverted up to the head by turning a valve.

Then there are manual shower mixers. These are standard equipment in independent shower cubicles and may also be used over a bath. With a manual mixer the hot and cold streams of water are mixed in a single valve. Temperature, and sometimes flow control, are obtained by turning large knurled control knobs.

Finally, there are thermostatic shower mixing valves. These may resemble manual mixers in appearance but are designed to accommodate small pressure fluctuations in either the hot or cold water supplies to the shower. They are thus very useful safety devices. But thermostatic valves cannot, even if it were legal, compensate for the very great difference of pressure between mains supply and a supply from a cold water storage cistern. Nor can they add pressure to either the hot or cold supply. If pressure falls on one side of the valve the thermostatic device will reduce flow on the other side to match it.

Thermostatic valves are more expensive but they eliminate the need to take an independent cold water supply pipe from the storage cistern to the shower and can possibly reduce the total cost of installation.

Where a shower is provided over an existing bath, steps must be taken to protect the bathroom floor from splashed water. A plastic shower curtain provides the cheapest means of doing this but a folding, glass shower screen has a much more attractive appearance and is more effective.

Electric showers

You can run your shower independently of the existing domestic hot water system by fitting an instantaneously heated electric one. There are a number of these on the market nowadays. They need only to be connected to the rising main and to a suitable source of electricity to provide an 'instant shower'. You'll find more information about these on pages 83–87.

Installing a bath/shower mixer

To install a shower above a bath, first disconnect the water supply, and drain the cistern if no gate-valve is fitted to its outlet. Remove the bath panel, if there is one, and disconnect the tap tails from the supply pipes. Then unscrew and remove the tap back-nuts and take the taps off.

You can now fix the new mixer in place. Finally, decide on the position for the shower spray bracket and fix it in place on •the bathroom wall.

WHY HAVE A SHOWER?

Showers have many advantages over baths:
● they are hygienic as you don't sit in dirty, soapy water and you get continually rinsed
● they are pleasant to use. Standing under jets of water can be immensely stimulating, especially first thing in the morning
● they use a lot less water per 'wash' than a bath, which saves energy and is also an advantage where water softeners are in use
● economy of hot water usage means that at peak traffic times there is more water to go round
● showers take less time, they don't have to be 'run', and users can't lay back and bask, monopolizing the bathroom
● easy temperature adjustment of a shower gives greater comfort for the user and lessens the risk of catching cold in a cold bathroom.

SHOWER LOCATION

You don't have to install a shower over a bath or even in the bathroom. A bedroom is one alternative site, but landings and utility rooms are another possibility. Provided a supply of water is available, the pressure head satisfactory, and the disposal of waste water possible, a shower can provide a compact and very useful house improvement in many parts of the home.

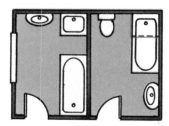

In a bathroom a shower will usually go over a bath, which is the easiest and most popular position. In a larger bathroom a cubicle is a good idea.

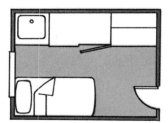

In a bedroom a shower can be easily fitted at the end of built-in wardrobes.

HOW TO ADAPT YOUR SYSTEM

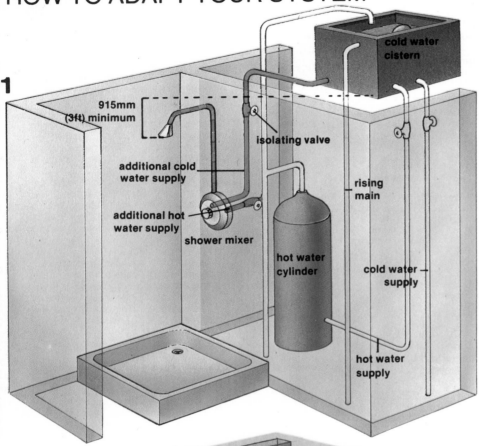

1

915mm (3ft) minimum

isolating valve

additional cold water supply

additional hot water supply

shower mixer

hot water cylinder

rising main

cold water supply

hot water supply

cold water cistern

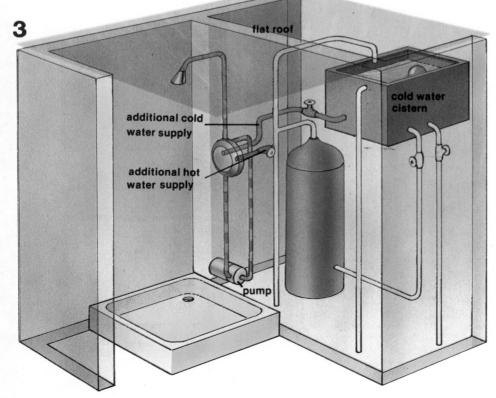

3

flat roof

additional cold water supply

additional hot water supply

pump

cold water cistern

1 : Just add pipework

◁ *The most common domestic plumbing system has a cold water cistern in the loft which feeds a hot water tank. In this case you must check that the vertical distance from the bottom of the cold cistern to the shower outlet head is at least 915mm (3ft). To install a shower you must take a 15mm cold water supply direct from the cistern to the cold inlet of the mixer, and a 15mm hot water supply from the vent and draw-off pipe, which emerges from the hot water tank, to the hot water inlet of the mixer.*

2 : Raise the cistern

▷ *In many older houses the cold water cistern may be in the airing cupboard immediately above the hot water tank, or in another position but still beneath ceiling height. This will usually mean that there is insufficient pressure for a mixer-type shower on the same floor. To get round this problem the cistern can be raised into the loft by extending the pipework upwards. Moving an old galvanised cistern will be rather arduous so this is a good opportunity to replace it with a modern plastic one, (see a future issue).*

3 : Install a pump

◁ *In some homes which have flat roofs it is impossible to raise the cistern indoors to provide a sufficient pressure head for a shower on the same floor. While you could consider putting the cistern on top of the roof this would involve providing extensive insulation and is an unsatisfactory solution. Pump-assisted mixer showers are available which will artificially increase the pressure head when the shower is turned on and these are fairly simple to install. As they are electrically operated they should be situated outside the bathroom area.*

4 : Add a new cistern

▷ *Many modern houses have combination hot and cold water storage units which are supplied and installed as one unit. They have a disadvantage in that cold water capacity is about one-third of the hot water cylinder and would provide an insufficient supply for a shower. This problem can be overcome by installing a pump and a supplementary cold water storage cistern. To ensure similar hot and cold pressures at the shower the supplementary cistern must be at a comparable level with the combination unit's cold water storage .*

2

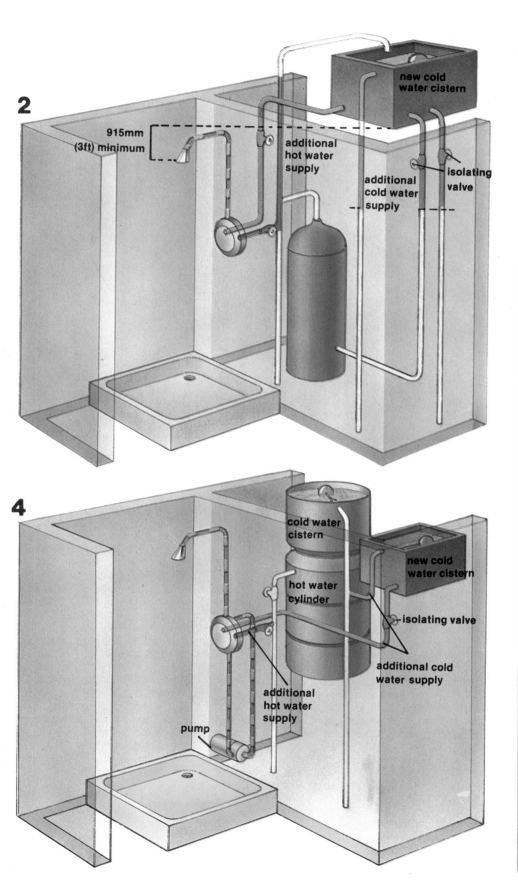

915mm
(3ft) minimum

new cold
water cistern

additional
hot water
supply

additional
cold water
supply

isolating
valve

4

cold water
cistern

new cold
water cistern

hot water
cylinder

isolating valve

additional cold
water supply

additional
hot water
supply

pump

Ready Reference

TYPES OF SHOWER

There are two basic types of shower:
● those attached to a mixer on a bath
● those independent of the bath, discharging over their own bases, in their own cubicles.

Bath showers may be attached to a mixer head on which you have to adjust both taps, or they may simply fit over the tap outlets. The shower head in either case is detachable and may be mounted at whatever height you require.

Independent showers have fixed position heads or are adjustable. They may have a single control mixer, or a dual control which means that you can adjust the flow as well as the temperature. Thermostatic mixing valves are also available which can cope with small pressure fluctuations in the hot and cold water supply. These only reduce pressure on one side of the valve if that on the other side falls; they cannot increase the pressure unless they have already decreased it.

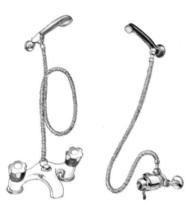

bath/shower mixer   **single control mixer**

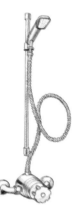

**dual control
mixer with fixed head**

**thermostatic mixer
with adjustable head**

BUILDING A SHOWER CUBICLE

The simplest way to add showering facilities to your bathroom is to install the shower over the bath. However, building a separate cubicle is a better solution.

When you come to install a shower in your home, the most obvious place for it is over the bath because you can make use of the bath's water supply and waste facilities. But this isn't the most advantageous site: putting a shower there does not increase your bathing facilities, it merely improves the existing ones. It's far better to have your shower as a separate cubicle, even if the cubicle is in the bathroom itself. If you can put the cubicle in another part of the home, you have as good as provided an extra bathroom.

You may think that you have no room in your home for a shower outside the bathroom, but that is not necessarily true. A shower does not require all that much space and you can make do with an area about 750mm (2ft 6in) square. But you've got to think about how much space you need to get into and out of the shower. It isn't usually that easy or efficient to dry off inside, so you need some space to dry off at the point of exit. You will also have to take into consideration the relationship of the drying area with bathroom fittings.

You can buy a ready-made shower cubicle, or build your own from scratch. The latter course will save a lot of money, and is easier than you might think, but you've got to take care to ensure that it is properly waterproofed.

Putting in the tray

To build a shower cubicle you start with the shower tray. Many people attempt to make one of these themselves by building a box that they cover with some impervious material – usually tiles. However, the construction is not easy because making the box absolutely waterproof can present problems, and then it is difficult to get the right gradient from every part of the tray to carry water to the waste outlet. On the whole, you would do better to buy a tray.

Normally, trays are made in acrylic plastic or glazed ceramics. The latter are dearer, but much longer-lasting, as acrylics can crack. Both types are available in standard sanitary-ware colours, so if you have a modern coloured bathroom suite, you should be able to match it. Trays come in a range of sizes, so be sure to choose one to fit the space you have, since obviously the size of tray governs the area your installation will take up. Ceramic trays can also be very heavy so it's likely you'll need help to get one into position.

The tray will have a waste outlet, and this may be in one corner, or in the middle of one side. It must be sited so that its waste pipe can discharge conveniently into a hopper of a two-pipe system, or be connected up to an existing waste pipe, or to the main stack of a single-pipe system. The waste pipe must slope downwards all the way, and it is important to get the fall right in order to drain water away efficiently. In general, the fall should be between 6 and 50mm per 300mm run of pipe (¼ to 2in per ft) depending on the length of the run (measured from the actual waste outlet). Too steep a run can produce a siphonage effect that will drain the water out of the trap, thus depriving your home of its protection from drain smells (see pages 296-300 for more details). It's a good idea to set a fall of 25mm (1in) per 300mm for a short run of say 600 to 900mm (2 to 3ft), but only a 12mm (½in) fall where the run will be 3 to 4.5m (10 to 15ft).

Most shower trays are square, and obviously these can be turned round to place the outlet in the most convenient position. However, for installation in a corner, triangular shaped trays, or quadrants – with two straight sides at right angles and a curved front – are on sale, but they're quite expensive.

The outlet does not have a plug, because it is never the intention that the tray should be filled up. Since there is no plug, no overflow is required. However, like all your bathroom fittings, it must have a trap. This should be 38mm (1½in) in diameter but, like a bath, does not have to be of the deep-seal variety.

Some trays are designed to have enough depth to enable the trap to be installed above floor level. Others are quite shallow, and the trap must go under the floor, a point to bear in mind if you have a concrete floor. Yet another possibility is to mount the tray on supports, to raise its height, and some manufacturers sell special supports to raise the tray off the ground. Otherwise you can use bricks or timber, suitably disguised by a plinth. It's a good idea to provide an inspection panel should you ever want to get access to the plumbing. Whatever the case, you will never have good access to the outlet plumbing after it's been installed – so be sure to make a good job of it.

Providing a cubicle

A shower tray is best positioned in a corner, so that two sides of the shower enclosure are already provided by the shower tray itself; you can bridge the gap with timber covered with tiles set flush with the top of the tray.

INSTALLING THE SHOWER TRAY

1 Press a sausage of plumber's putty around the underside of the outlet flange, then wind PTFE tape along the length of the thread.

2 Push the flange into the waste hole in the tray, press it home until the putty squeezes out round the edge, and put on the metal washer.

3 Screw on the back-nut by hand and tighten it with an adjustabale wrench. This will squeeze more putty out; remove the excess neatly.

4 Take the special low-seal shower trap and screw it onto the outlet flange, after first making sure that the O ring is in place.

5 Measure up the position needed for the waste run, and install the plastic waste pipe in position ready to be connected up to the trap.

6 Lower the tray into place and connect up the trap to the waste pipe. Check that it is level on your prepared base.

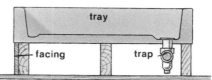
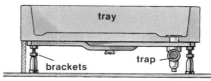
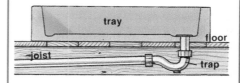
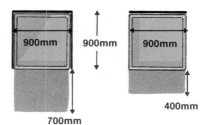

PUTTING UP A SURROUND KIT

1 Mark the position of the wall uprights; use a spirit level to make sure that they will be truly vertical when fixed in position.

2 Drill holes for the upright fixings, then plug them with plastic wall plugs and screw on the uprights with the screws supplied.

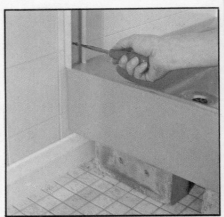

3 Slide the first panel into position on the wall upright and fix it; again check that the structure is in a properly vertical position.

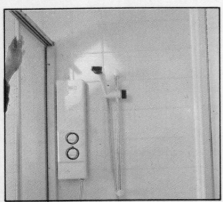

4 Adjust the length of the panel to fit the size of the shower tray and tighten up the screws carefully. Attach the corner bracket.

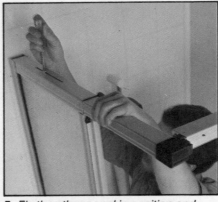

5 Fix the other panel in position and adjust its length so that it mates up accurately and squarely with the corner bracket.

6 Adjust the bottom runners to the correct size so that they match up with the bottom corner bracket; check they are square to the tray.

7 Screw up the bottom corner bracket, then check that the whole structure is firm and square and that the door opens and closes smoothly.

8 Loosen the wall upright fixings and wedge up each side in turn. Squeeze sealant between the frame and the tray and refix the frame.

9 Check again for alignment, then finish off the base by firmly fixing the supports in position and finally boarding in the sides of the shower.

Existing walls forming part of the cubicle will also need tiling or covering with some laminated material – commonly waterproofed decorative wallboard, or even glass or sheet plastic over paint or wallpaper. It is obviously very important to make sure that all gaps are sealed, otherwise gradual water seepage will occur which will damage the fabric of your house.

The sides of the cubicle you have to install can be home-made or bought as kits. The simplest way to fill one or two sides is with a curtain rail and shower curtain. This works quite well with a shower in the bath, but the sides of a shower tray are much shallower than those of a bath and water is therefore quite likely to splash onto the floor. This means that curtains are really only at all suitable for the entry side of the cubicle where you might protect the floor with a bath mat, or where the floor of your bathroom is tiled and fully sealed.

You can construct any solid sides of the cubicle using a timber framework, but you will have to buy a suitable proprietary door unless you use a curtain. These doors are usually made of aluminium frames with opaque safety glass or plastic panels. They come in a wide variety of designs and colours. You can have, for example, a plain aluminium frame with clear glass, or a gold satin frame with dark smoked glass. If you plan to buy a door, check that you have calculated the size of your cubicle to fit it, and that the door comes with suitable rust-proof fittings to hang it.

The easiest (though most expensive) solution is to buy the complete surround, including a sliding or ordinary door, which will be supplied in kit form. These surrounds are made by the same manufacturers as shower doors and usually come complete with fixing instructions. They are usually adjustable to fit different shower tray sizes, and are simply fitted to the wall at each end to provide a rigid frame. Before finishing they have to be sealed where they meet the tray using a proprietary sealant, to ensure a waterproof joint. If this isn't done perfectly, water will gradually seep in and cause damp on the floor and walls of your bathroom.

Home-made surrounds

Making your own surround will save money, and it has the advantage that you can tailor it exactly to your needs. You might, for example, want a surround which is larger than the tray itself; in which case you can install a shelf or seat next to the tray.

Begin by making a framework of 50mm (2in) square timber. You need a length on every edge, plus extra horizontal ones at 450mm (18in) centres. All should be joined with halving joints. In addition, fit any extra length needed to provide a fixing point (for

the shower rose, for instance). The inside face of the partition should then be clad with 6mm (¼in) plywood. Use an exterior-grade board if the cubicle is to be tiled.

Another possibility is to use 10mm (⅜in) thick plasterboard. The framework for this should consist of a 50mm (2in) sq batten on every edge, plus one extra vertical and horizontal in the middle, and any additional member needed to provide a fixing point. Fix the board with galvanised plasterboard nails driven in until the head slightly dimples the surface of the board, but without fracturing the paper liner. You can use 3mm (⅛in) hardboard to cover the outside of the cubicle framework.

Do not fix the exterior cladding for the time being. You should first clad the inside face, then fix the half-completed partition in place by driving screws through the frame members into the floor below, the wall behind and the ceiling too if it is to be a room height job.

The interior of this partition is a good place in which to conceal the supply pipes to the shower. You would then need an inspection panel, held by screws (not glued and nailed) to allow easy access to the pipework should maintenance ever be needed.

If the cubicle is not a floor-to-ceiling one, you will also need extra support at the top as you cannot leave the front top edge flapping free. This can take the form of a 75x25mm (3x1in) batten, decoratively moulded if you wish, spanning the two sides of the cubicle or fixed at one end to a block screwed to the wall, should there be only one side.

The whole interior of the shower cubicle needs to be clad with an impervious material to make sure it is waterproof. The most obvious choice is tiles, and these can be fixed to both the plywood or plasterboard cladding and the plaster of a wall. Make sure that the latter is clean and sound before tiling. Do not, however, fix the tiles direct to the timber part of the framing.

As an alternative to tiles you could use a special plastic-faced hardboard, with a tile pattern and a backing of plain hardboard. Fix the plastic-faced board by glueing and pinning with rustproof nails (if these can be lost somewhere in the pattern). Otherwise use a contact adhesive. This does not need to be spread all over the meeting surfaces. Apply it in a pattern similar to that detailed for the framework of the partitions. Adhesives applied by gun are available for this sort of work. The board on the back wall should be fixed in a similar manner.

Whatever material you use, all joins – where partitions meet the wall, or the tray – should be sealed with a silicone bath sealant. Any parts not clad with impervious material should be well painted with a three-coat system of primer, undercoat and one or two top coats.

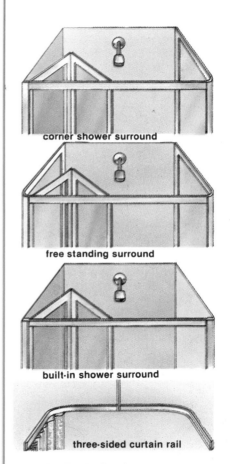
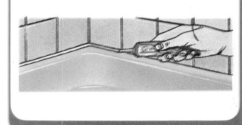

REPLACING A RADIATOR

If one of your existing radiators is malfunctioning in some way, or else just out of character with the decor of your home why not replace it with a brand new one? You'll find this job straightforward if you follow our instructions.

There are a number of reasons why you may want to replace an existing radiator in your home's central heating system. These can range from the aesthetic to the purely practical. At one time radiators were ugly and cumbersome, and if you have any still in use like this it's quite likely that they'll clash with the decor of your home. On the practical side, you may well find that a radiator in your system has developed leaks. This will mean both water and heat loss, as well as the inconvenience of cleaning up the mess. And, of course, you may simply feel that a modern radiator would produce more heat, and so improve the comfort in your home. Whatever your reasons for replacing a radiator, you'll have to choose a new one to go in its place, before actually removing the existing one.

Choosing a new radiator

Modern radiators are usually made of 1.25mm (about 1⁄16in) thick pressed steel, and are designed to be space-saving, neat and attractive. For a simple replacement job, size will be among the most important considerations. If the new radiator can be successfully connected to the existing fittings, you won't need to alter or modify the circulating pipes. Consequently, the job will be that much easier. Radiators are available in a wide variety of sizes, ranging in height from 300mm (12in) to 800mm (30in) and in length from 480mm (19in) to 3200mm (10ft 6in) – so you shouldn't have too much difficulty in finding one that will fit into the space left by the old one. Special low, finned radiators are also available. These are usually fitted along the skirting and are both neat and unobtrusive – yet can be turned into decorative features in their own right.

But size isn't the only important consideration. After all, a radiator's job is to provide heat, so you'll have to shop around and find the one which, for its size, will produce most heat. A radiator's heat output is measured in Btu – British Thermal units – so you should look for the one with the highest Btu rating for its size. Remember, it's always possible to turn off a radiator that makes a room too warm; it's far less easy to increase heat output in a room which, with the radiator

THE FITTINGS

A typical panel radiator is fitted with a flow control valve (below), a lock-shield valve (bottom right), an air-bleed valve (right) and a blanking-off plate (far right).

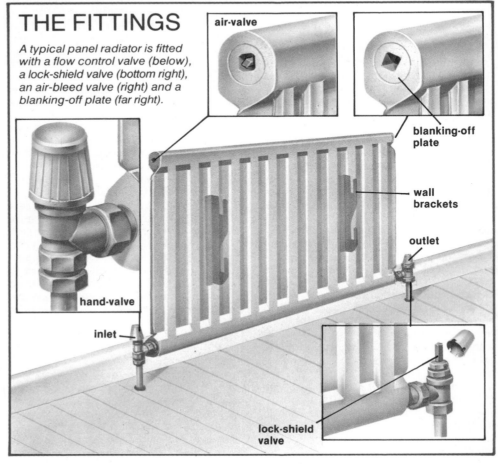

REMOVING THE OLD RADIATOR

1 *Turn off the flow control valve by hand, and the lock-shield valve by turning its spindle with pliers. Note how many turns are needed to close it completely.*

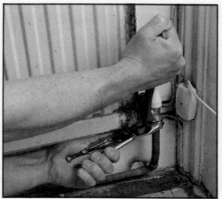

2 *Hold the lock-shield valve body with a wrench so you don't bend the pipework, and undo the valve coupling carefully with an adjustable spanner.*

3 *Open the air-bleed valve, pull the coupling away and allow the radiator to drain into a convenient container. Have rags and a larger bowl handy too.*

4 *Having drained most of the water, undo the other coupling, lift the radiator off its brackets and drain out the dregs. Then remove the old brackets.*

turned fully on, remains uncomfortably chilly.

However, one way of increasing heat output, while retaining the same sized radiator, is to install a double-panel radiator. This is, literally, an ordinary radiator with two panels for the hot water to fill instead of the usual one and therefore has virtually double the heat output. So, while a single panel radiator 685mm x 1150mm (27in x 45in) will have a heat output of 3575Btu, a double panel one of the same size will be rated at 5990Btu.

Although modern radiators are likely to provide more heat than the older variety, they do have one drawback. Because of the thinness of their metal, they are more prone to internal corrosion and this will ultimately produce leaks.

Dealing with internal corrosion

Internal corrosion in modern radiators arises from an electrolytic reaction between the steel of the radiators and the copper circulating pipes of the central heating system. This results in the production of a corrosive black iron oxide sludge (magnetite) and hydrogen gas. In a similar fashion, if the original installation of your heating system was somewhat messily done, then copper swarf, produced when the pipes were cut, could have been retained within the circulating pipes. This will also corrode the steel at any point where the two come in contact – usually within a radiator. Because the raw material from which the sludge is produced is the metal of the radiators, eventually they will leak and need to be replaced. And as the sludge is also attracted by the magnetic field of the circulating pump, its abrasive qualities are a common cause of early pump failure.

Early indications of serious internal corrosion are a need to vent one or more radiators at regular intervals, and cold spots on their

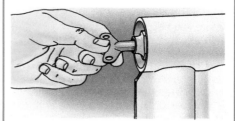

surfaces. If in doubt, the diagnosis can be confirmed by applying a flame to the escaping gas when the radiator is being vented. If it burns with a blue and yellow flame, you can be sure that hydrogen is in the system and will have been produced by the chemical reaction of the two metals.

Once you've confirmed that corrosion is present within the system, you'll have to flush it through and introduce a reliable corrosion preventative chemical into the feed and expansion tank. By doing this, you should be able to prevent further corrosion and so save your system.

Removing the old radiator

One of the great deterrents to anyone wanting to remove a radiator is the prospect of having to drain the whole system. However, this won't be necessary provided the radiator to be replaced has a valve at both the hot water inlet and the outlet. Once these are closed, you'll be able to keep virtually all the system's water isolated in other parts.

At the inlet end you're likely to find the hand-valve which is the control by which you open and close the radiator. At the outlet end you'll find what is termed the lock-shield valve. When you come to inspect your radiator, don't worry if their positions are reversed – they will still be equally effective.

The first thing to do when removing a radiator is to close these valves. The hand-valve is straightforward, but you'll have to remove the cover to get at the lock-shield valve. You'll be able to close this valve using a spanner or an adjustable wrench with which to grip its spindle.

As you turn it, it's a good idea to note carefully how many turns it takes to close. And you'll find this task slightly easier if you mark the turning nut with a piece of chalk before you begin. The reason for all this is to maintain the balance of the system. After it was first installed, your system would have been balanced. The lock-shield valves of all the radiators were adjusted to give an equal level of water through-flow so that they were all heating up equally. So, by noting the number of turns taken to close the lock-shield, when you come to fit the new radiator you can simply open it up by the same amount – so avoiding the somewhat tedious task of re-balancing the whole system.

Once you've closed both valves, you can unscrew the nuts which connect the valves to the radiator inlet and outlet. Do these one at a time after having placed a low dish under each end to collect the water and protect the floor. Use an adjustable wrench to undo the coupling nuts. It's wise to hold the circulating pipe securely in place with another wrench. Otherwise, if you apply too much pressure to the coupling nut you risk fracturing the flowpipe, and this would cause

FITTING THE NEW RADIATOR

1 *To ensure watertight connections to the new radiator, wrap PTFE tape round all threaded fittings and then smear on some jointing compound.*

2 *Screw in the valve couplings with a hexagonal radiator spanner. Use extension pieces if the new radiator is slightly narrower than the old one.*

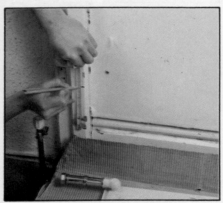

5 *Mark the height taken in **4** on the wall above each valve, and join up the marks at each end with a pencil line. This marks the level of the new brackets.*

6 *Transfer the measurements taken in **3** to the wall to indicate the vertical position of each bracket. Accuracy is not so vital here as in **5**.*

9 *Lift the radiator into place on its brackets. You can move it slightly from side to side to align the valve couplings with the inlet and outlet valves.*

10 *Wrap the coupling threads in PTFE tape and jointing compound, and do up the couplings. Again, use a wrench to support the valve body and prevent strain.*

3 Lay the radiator down in line with the two valves, and measure the distance from each valve coupling to the centre of the nearest bracket mounting.

4 Next, measure the height of the base of the radiator brackets from a line joining the centres of the inlet and outlet valves.

7 Hold the bracket against the wall in line with the vertical and horizontal marks you've made, and draw in the positions for the fixing screws.

8 Drill and plug the four holes – two to each bracket – and fix the brackets in position. Make sure the wallplug is well below the plaster to avoid cracking.

11 After connecting up the couplings, use a bleed key to open the air-bleed valve slightly so that air can escape as the radiator fills with water.

12 Open the inlet valve, allow the radiator to fill and then close the air-bleed valve. Finally open the lock-shield valve by as many turns as you took to close it.

you a lot of extra work and expense to mend – as well as causing quite a mess. As you unscrew each nut, the water from the radiator will flow out. If the system has been previously treated with corrosion proofer, it's well worth saving the water. That way you can pour it back into the feed-and-expansion tank when the job is complete.

Once the water has drained out, remove the tail pieces and coupling nuts from each end. Then block up each hole with a rag and lift the radiator from the brackets that hold it to the wall. It's a good idea to get the radiator out of your home as soon as possible – just in case it leaks any remaining dirty water on to your carpet.

Fitting a new radiator

Your new radiator will probably have four holes or tappings – one at each corner – and each one will have a female screwed thread. How you connect the radiator up to your system depends on the way in which the old one was fitted. Nowadays it is usual for the flow and return connections to be made to the bottom two holes but, of course, if your system had the flow pipe at a higher level then you'll have to reconnect it in the same way.

Fit an air-valve into one of the top tappings. First wrap PTFE thread sealing tape anti-clockwise round the male thread of the valve and then use a radiator key that grips inside the body of the valve to screw it home. Unless your radiator has a top inlet the other top tapping must be plugged with a blanking off plate. This should also be wrapped with PTFE tape and screwed home in the same way as the air vent.

You'll then have to fit tail pieces and coupling screws (either new ones, or the ones from the original radiator if you can remove them) on to the new one. Again wrap each thread with PTFE tape before fitting them. It's a good idea to buy new wall brackets for your replacement radiator. After all, you can't be sure the old ones will be suitable. You should drill and plug the wall and then fix the brackets in place. Fit the radiator so that the inlet end is a few millimetres higher than the outlet valve. This will make venting easier. You can now fix the radiator in place and connect the coupling nuts to the hand-valve and lock-shield valve and screw them up tightly.

You'll have to open the air-valve at the top of the radiator so that the air in it can be displaced as it fills with water. All you do is slowly open the hand-valve and allow the radiator to fill. When water starts to flow from the air-valve you'll know all the air has been displaced and you should immediately close the valve. Finally, open the lock-shield valve by the same number of turns and part turns it took originally to close it.

SECTION 9

DAMP-PROOFING, VENTILATING & INSULATING TECHNIQUES

CONDENSATION Causes and Cures

Condensation in buildings is a bigger problem now than ever before – the result of changes in building methods and our way of life. To tackle it, you need to know what it is and why it happens.

The air around us contains water vapour, and the amount it can carry depends on the temperature – the higher the temperature, the greater the amount of water vapour. If the air becomes cooler it cannot carry as much vapour, and the excess may be released in the form of water droplets. In the atmosphere this produces clouds and rainfall; in confined spaces like the home it produces condensation.

You can see this happening quite easily in a kitchen when you're cooking. A lot of water vapour is created by boiling pans, and this remains suspended in the air in the kitchen as long as the temperature is high. But if the air meets a cold surface – a window, for example – its temperature drops, and the excess water vapour turns back into water, or condenses. Condensation occurs particularly in bathrooms, but can be found throughout your home at some time or another.

Condensation is always a menace, and can lead to corrosion and rot as can any unwanted water. If it forms only a thin film of moisture, this may quickly evaporate when the room heats up, but too often the water seeps into cracks and crevices in the house's structure and starts to cause problems.

The problem of moisture
Dense materials, like glass and glazed tiles, are not harmed by moisture and can be easily wiped off. But if it runs off the surface it can carry with it dirt, which can stain nearby materials. Metal surfaces do not absorb moisture, but moisture combined with oxygen in the air will cause iron to rust. If mineral salts are present, or if dissimilar metals are in contact, corrosion may take place.

Some materials, like fibreboard and plaster-board, lose their strength when wet and may swell and sag. But more damaging is the risk of mould and rot. Mould spores are almost always present in the air, and on the surface of many materials. To flourish, they need moisture, and food which is supplied by general dirt. Condensation provides the moisture. Textured surfaces collect more dirt than smooth surfaces, and are more likely to develop mould growth.

Mould first appears in spots or small patches and spreads to form a furry layer – usually grey-green, black or brown in colour. Though unsightly it can easily be cleaned off in the early stages. It may do little harm, but will reappear unless a fungicide is used.

Fungal attack on timber, particularly dry rot, is more serious, causing lasting damage. Once established, dry rot can actually produce the moisture needed for further growth and it can spread extensively through other materials such as brick.

Moisture has another unwanted effect. Many materials, such as sheeps' wool and plastic foam, gain heat insulating qualities through the small pockets of air in them. If this air is replaced by water, then this insulating power is lost. If this happens within a brick wall – so-called 'interstitial' condensation – the wall's resistance to heat flow is decreased and the wall gets colder, producing still more condensation.

How water vapour is created
We can't avoid producing water vapour indoors. For example, during eight hours of sleep, every human body gives off a quarter litre (½ pint) of water. When we are active we make much more. One of the worst offenders in the home is the flueless room heater, which gives out one litre (1¾ pints) of water vapour for every litre of oil burnt.

TYPES OF CONDENSATION
There are two types of condensation – surface (or superficial) and interstitial. The first is where water vapour condenses on the inside surface of a wall or window, the second where it starts to condense inside the wall itself.

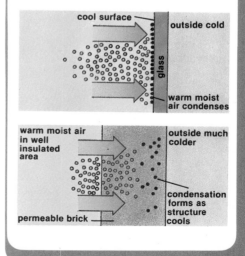

cool surface — outside cold — glass — warm moist air condenses

warm moist air in well insulated area — outside much colder — permeable brick — condensation forms as structure cools

WHAT CAUSES CONDENSATION

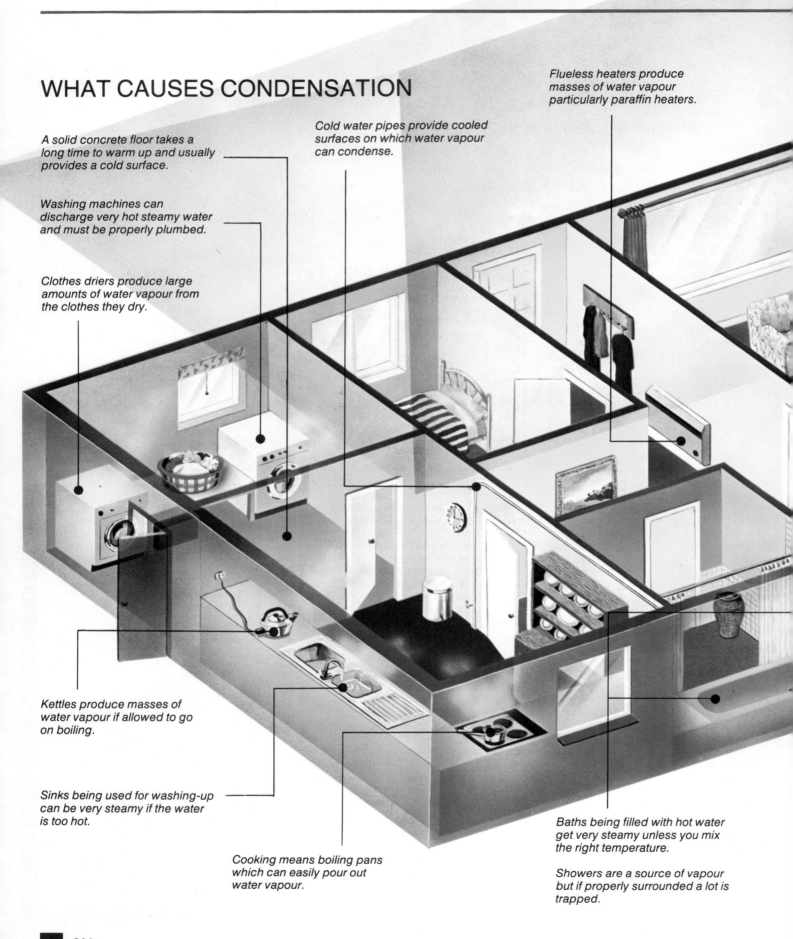

A solid concrete floor takes a long time to warm up and usually provides a cold surface.

Washing machines can discharge very hot steamy water and must be properly plumbed.

Clothes driers produce large amounts of water vapour from the clothes they dry.

Cold water pipes provide cooled surfaces on which water vapour can condense.

Flueless heaters produce masses of water vapour particularly paraffin heaters.

Kettles produce masses of water vapour if allowed to go on boiling.

Sinks being used for washing-up can be very steamy if the water is too hot.

Cooking means boiling pans which can easily pour out water vapour.

Baths being filled with hot water get very steamy unless you mix the right temperature.

Showers are a source of vapour but if properly surrounded a lot is trapped.

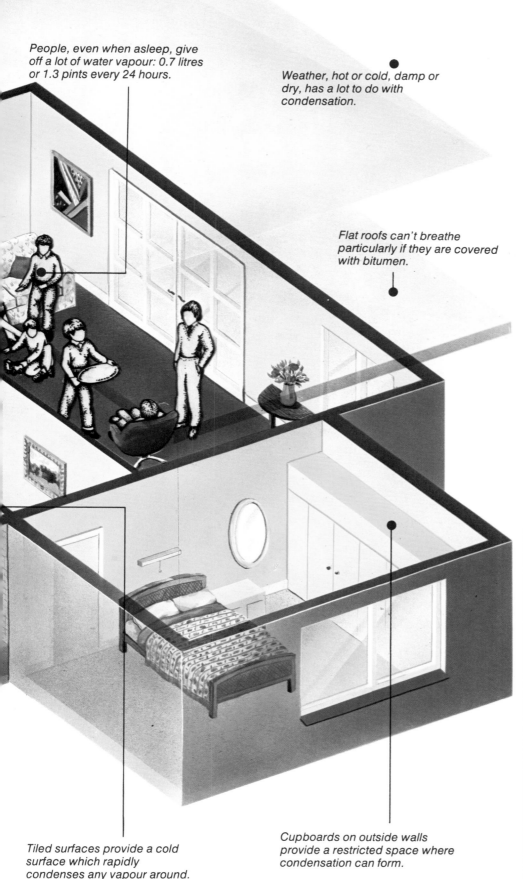

People, even when asleep, give off a lot of water vapour: 0.7 litres or 1.3 pints every 24 hours.

Weather, hot or cold, damp or dry, has a lot to do with condensation.

Flat roofs can't breathe particularly if they are covered with bitumen.

Tiled surfaces provide a cold surface which rapidly condenses any vapour around.

Cupboards on outside walls provide a restricted space where condensation can form.

HOW TO CURE CONDENSATION

Mechanical ventilators
Powered by an electric motor, these are the sophisticated development of wind-operated vents and obviously much more efficient. If one is installed in a room where there is a central heating or hot water boiler there should be a vent in the inside door to ensure that noxious gases are not drawn into the room.

Inner wall insulation
Lining rooms with polystyrene sheet is a cheap form of wall insulation and reduces heat loss. It also reduces the condensation threat but can lead to interstitial condensation inside the cavity itself.

Cavity wall insulation
This reduces heat loss from the house and therefore your heating bills. It also cuts down the incidence of cold outside walls, reducing the likelihood of condensation.

Vented clothes driers
Clothes driers produce masses of water vapour and should always be vented direct to the outside of the house. This can be done via a flexible hose put out of a window, but ideally should be through a vent pipe placed in the wall exiting via a protective cowl.

Self-closing doors
Where there are heavy sources of water vapour, as in the kitchen, it is best to contain them rather than let the vapour spread to other rooms where quite often they are likely to condense. A self-closing door is the answer here.

Cooker hoods
These are designed to vent hot air and gases coming up from the cooker. Those which simply filter the air are really only good for getting rid of kitchen smells, but those which can be vented to the outside air, either directly through the wall or via a fan controlled duct, can cut down condensation risk.

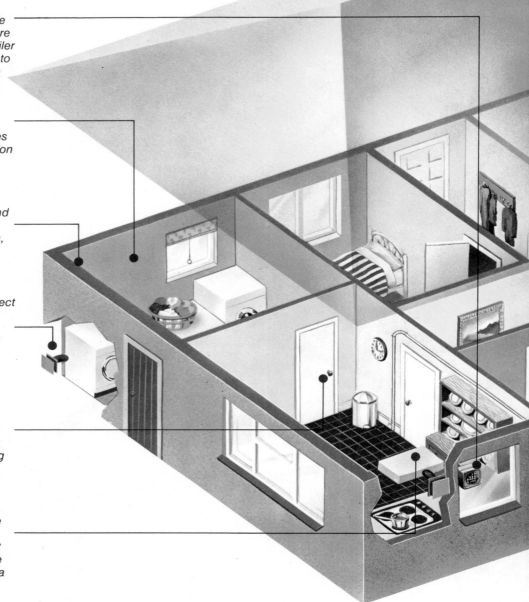

Having a bath or shower can produce two litres (3½ pints) of water vapour. Another offender is damp. This can penetrate an outside wall or a solid ground floor lacking damp-proofing and later evaporate because of indoor warmth, so adding more water vapour to the air.

Because it is impossible to prevent the creation of water vapour, the main aim then becomes to get rid of it before it can give trouble by forming condensation. Ventilation is the answer. This can be done by opening windows, installing extractor fans, venting exhaust air from clothes driers to the outside air and the use of balanced flue gas heaters.

Water vapour moves about. It doesn't only condense on cold surfaces in the room where it is produced; it can penetrate all parts of the home, and is likely to condense in any colder area it reaches. It also rises by convection to cooler bedrooms and the space under the roof.

Warm, moist air gets into the roof space through ceiling cracks, holes used by pipes and electric wiring and gaps around the trap door. It doesn't matter how small the gap – it can still get through as it's a gas. It also passes through porous plaster or plasterboard ceilings unless they incorporate a moisture barrier.

Unless there is sufficient ventilation for it to escape to the outside air, it will condense on the roof covering and roof timbers. The severity of the condensation depends on the roof construction, how well the loft is insulated and ventilated, and how easily moist house air can get into it. However, it can very quickly build up in a poorly ventilated loft, saturating the insulation and

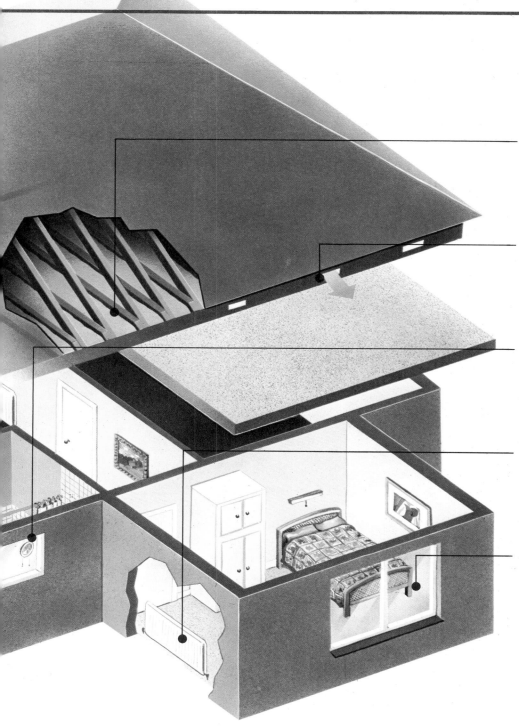

Loft insulation
Loft insulation is yet another way of retaining heat inside the main part of the house and also contains the risk of condensation, but it must be coupled with the provision of proper loft ventilation, or condensation may become a problem in the loft.

Loft ventilation
This is vital to protect the timbers in your roof from rot attack. The better the loft insulation the greater the temperature contrast between the loft and rooms below, and the greater the risk of condensation.

Wind-operated vents
These small plastic vents set into the window frame usually blow round in the wind, and even a small breeze can make them work. They simply provide ventilation which disposes of unwanted water vapour. While not that effective they are very cheap to install.

Central heating
Usually installed as the source of heat, central heating will also reduce the risk of condensation as the water vapour is not allowed to cool and the temperature differential between different parts of the house is reduced. But effective central heating is rather expensive to run for long periods these days.

Double glazing
This is a highly effective way of retaining heat as 20% is lost through windows which are single glazed. It also ensures that the inner pane of glass is not cold, which is usually the case with single glazing, and thus eliminates a major source of condensation.

making it quite useless. In the end it can soak through the ceiling too.

Loft insulation certainly makes a house warmer, but means that the roof structure will be colder. This exaggerated difference in temperature enables the water vapour to pass more easily from the house itself to the roof space. Tiles on loosely laid felt will 'breathe' and allow the moisture to disperse, but fully lined roofs tend to trap moist air. Even worse are flat roofs, having a lead, bituminous felt or asphalt covering: these cannot breathe at all.

Vapour inside the walls
The better draught-proofed, and more airtight a house, the more likely it is that moist air will force its way into the structure during the winter, possibly leading to condensation.

While 'superficial' condensation is a nuisance and can spoil decoration, it is visible, and serves as a warning to the householder to provide better ventilation. But interstitial condensation can cause serious and lasting damage to a building and, unless it is so severe that damp shows through on a ceiling or outside wall, it can go

unnoticed for many years. In older draughty houses, risk of 'interstitial' condensation is slight, though superficial condensation will sometimes occur in unheated rooms. Risks increase when fireplaces are blocked up, windows double-glazed, external doors draught-proofed, and lofts and external walls better insulated. Builders of new, well-insulated air-tight houses should guard against moist air getting into walls and the loft by using air barriers, called vapour checks, and by ensuring that any air leaking through is easily vented to the outside.

IDENTIFYING AND CURING DAMP

Dampness will ruin your home, your possessions and your health, unless you eradicate it. Here's how to identify the menace and its cause.

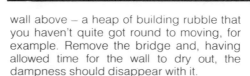

Dampness in the home is a problem that's not only evident by its classic symptoms – stained, peeling decorations, mould forming on your clothes and other possessions, and an accompanying musty smell – but also it can be unhealthy and extremely destructive. If it's left to take hold it can rust metal fittings, cause masonry to crumble and even rot the structural timbers of your house.

Only rarely will you get away with merely treating the more obvious effects of dampness; in most cases you'd merely be concealing the problem cosmetically, and it would almost certainly return. You must, therefore, seek out the root of the problem and effect a permanent cure.

There are basically three types of damp; rising damp, penetrating damp and dampness due to condensation. Dampness due to mechanical failure (a burst pipe, for example), and abnormal weather conditions (such as floods and tidal waves) usually appears as penetrating damp. In some situations, it's only too obvious which type applies, but dampness has a knack of appearing to be what it is not.

Rising damp
Rising damp is moisture absorbed by the building from the ground, which means that trouble tends to begin at or below ground and work its way up the walls and floors.

Modern homes have built-in protection against this, in the form of a damp-proof course (dpc) set into the walls just above ground level, and a damp-proof membrane (dpm) set into any solid floors. However, occasionally these do fail – a crack in the concrete can cause the membrane to split – resulting in rising damp. If this happens the best thing to do is to repair or replace the damaged dpc or dpm (see pages 376-379). It's worth checking first, though, that the dpc has not merely been by-passed in some way.

Bridging the dpc
The classic example of a by-passed dpc is where something has been piled against the house in such a way that dampness can use it as a 'bridge' to cross the dpc and reach the

wall above – a heap of building rubble that you haven't quite got round to moving, for example. Remove the bridge and, having allowed time for the wall to dry out, the dampness should disappear with it.

A more costly variation on this theme is where the bridge is something you've deliberately built against the wall, such as a new step leading to a door, a raised patio, or even an extension if this was built so that its own dpc didn't tie in with the dpc in the house.

A dpc can also be bridged indirectly if you build a patio or a path next to the wall and raise the ground-level to within 150mm (6in) of the dpc. Here, heavy rain bounces off the paving, strikes the wall above the dpc.

Atmospheric changes
Each of these examples have one thing in common – they will all produce cases of rising damp shortly after you've done some sort of work on the house or its surroundings. It is, however, worth making a point about the relationship between rising damp and the weather. True rising damp – where the dpc is either faulty or has been bridged – is, droughts excluded, more or less a year-round problem. It simply gets markedly worse in winter because of the higher level of moisture in the soil. It doesn't come and go depending on whether or not it has been raining. The

exception is where the dampness is due to the dpc having been indirectly by-passed (see Bridging the dpc).

Houses without dpcs
But if your house doesn't have built-in protection against rising damp, and it's been free from damp for hundreds of years, you're faced with the problem of whether to bother installing damp-proofing.

There are two main reasons why rising damp may not have showed itself before. The first is that the materials used in construction may have lost some of their waterproofing properties with age. The more likely explanation is that the buildings in question have actually had rising damp all along, but have never had it so badly as to be noticeable. In older homes it's not uncommon for the moisture to evaporate almost as soon as it appears on the surface. However, this obviously involves quite a fine balancing act, and like all balancing acts it's easily upset. It may take something as major as settlement of the building's foundations to do the trick. On the other hand, it could be something as simple as laying a new floor.

Penetrating damp
Penetrating damp occurs where the weather finds its way into your home through parts of

CAUSES OF PENETRATING DAMP

The main points where damp penetrates the structure of your house are:
1 cracked concrete fillet or flashing
2 rain penetrating cracked flaunching which creates damp patches on an unvented chimney breast in room below
3 torn or porous chimney flashing
4 cracked or missing slates or tiles
5 loose or crumbling putty on windows
6 sagging or leaking gutters
7 dripping overflow pipe
8 gaps round door and window frames
9 cracked or 'blown' rendering
10 cracked or leaking downpipes
11 gutter blocked and overflowing
12 clogged drip groove under sill
13 cavity wall ties bridged with debris
14 debris in cavity bridging dpc.

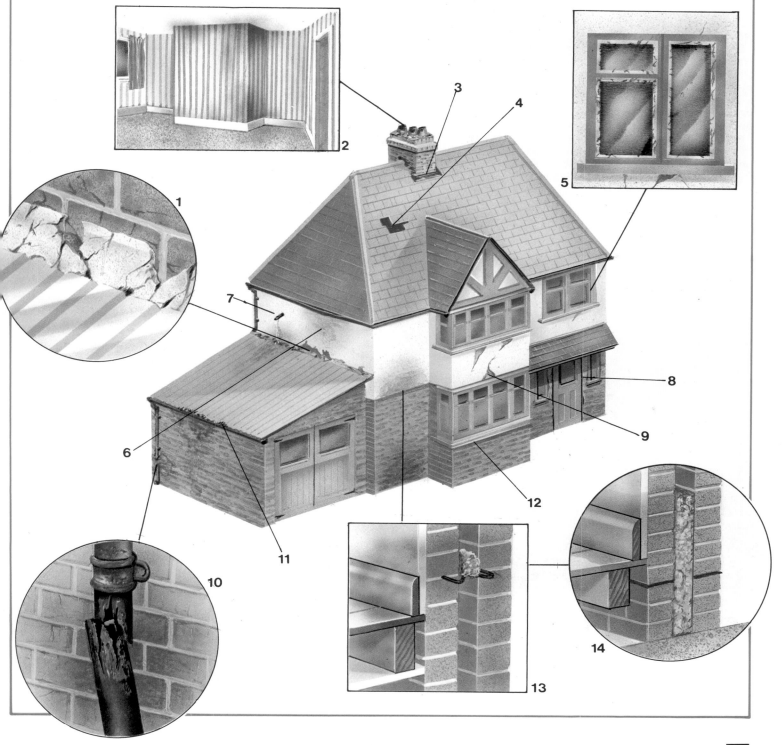

the structure that should, in theory, keep it out — notably the walls.

Where the walls of your home are solid, this is generally due to old age and the consequent reduction of the waterproofing properties of the material or a breakdown of the mortar pointing, or cracked rendering. However, in some situations, it may simply be due to the use of inferior materials in the first place, or to a faulty design: substandard, porous bricks may have been used, for instance.

If you do find evidence of rising damp, examine the general condition of your wall, just as if you were preparing to redecorate, paying particular attention to any pointing or rendering. Make necessary repairs, filling cracks or making good areas of blown render or repoint the mortar joints, then clean off all traces of algae and mould and treat the affected areas with a proprietary fungicide/algicide to inhibit regrowth. Finally, paint the wall using a good quality weather-proofing exterior paint or, if you prefer to retain the natural look of the masonry, treat it with a silicone-based, exterior grade water repellent. This may be brushed or sprayed on to give the wall a reasonable soaking. Very porous surfaces may require a second coat of water repellent to provide sufficient protection.

With the waterproofing completed, wait for the walls to dry out before making good any damp damage indoors. This is very important and therefore the treatment is best carried out during a longish dry spell in the summer.

Most exterior paints and water repellents give better results when applied to walls that have had at least a week to dry out, although some will work if applied to a wall that's a little damp.

Cavity walls

With modern homes the problem shouldn't occur at all because modern buildings are usually built with cavity walls — that is with an inner and outer skin of masonry separated by an air gap — the idea being that moisture can't jump across the cavity. But in practice, cavity walls do have their weak spots.

To begin with, the two leaves of masonry are held together at intervals by metal ties, and if mortar or some other porous material was dropped on to these during the construction of the wall, or has collected there since, it could form a bridge for damp across the cavity.

On the other hand, the cavity may have been purposely filled in order to reduce heat loss. If this was not done properly, it too could bridge the cavity and allow damp to reach the inner skin. In this instance, though, any dampness tends to be overall,

CAUSES OF RISING DAMP

Rising damp occurs when moisture is absorbed from the ground by the walls and solid floors of your house. However, most houses built since about 1880 should have a water-resistant barrier called a damp-proof course (dpc) set in the walls and more recently-built houses will also have a damp-proof membrane (dpm) in solid floors to prevent the passage of the moisture. Without this protection dampness can attack the timbers supporting your floors, ruin your decorations, and even rot the masonry. It can also be a health hazzard, causing a cold, wet atmosphere. There are several routes along which dampness can travel to gain entry, as illustrated here.

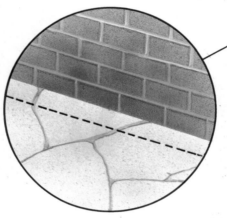

A path, flight of steps or extension base built too high against a wall bridges the damp-proof course.

If the dpc is less than 150mm (6in) from ground level, heavy rain is likely to splash above it, creating a temporary damp patch on the wall.

Cellars and basements present a special problem: damp from the ground is under terrific pressure to seep through the walls.

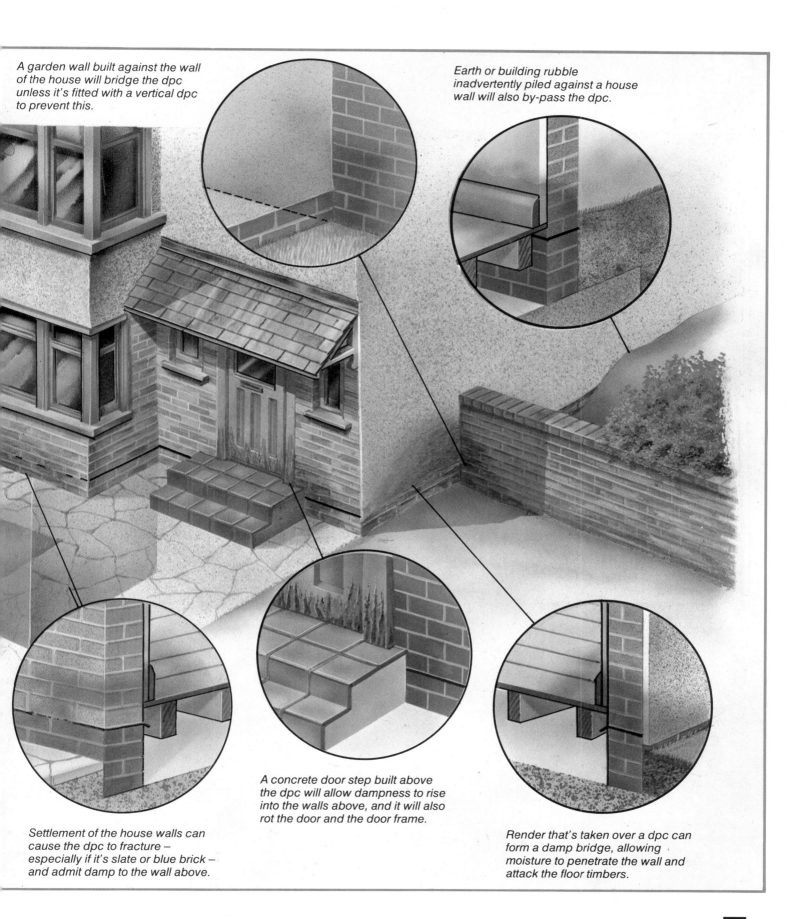

A garden wall built against the wall of the house will bridge the dpc unless it's fitted with a vertical dpc to prevent this.

Earth or building rubble inadvertently piled against a house wall will also by-pass the dpc.

Settlement of the house walls can cause the dpc to fracture – especially if it's slate or blue brick – and admit damp to the wall above.

A concrete door step built above the dpc will allow dampness to rise into the walls above, and it will also rot the door and the door frame.

Render that's taken over a dpc can form a damp bridge, allowing moisture to penetrate the wall and attack the floor timbers.

CHECKING FOR DAMP

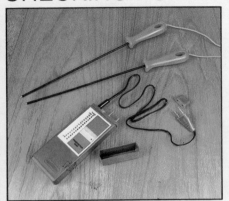

1 *You can test for damp in timber and masonry using a battery-powered moisture meter, which comes with plug-in contact pins and deep-wall probes.*

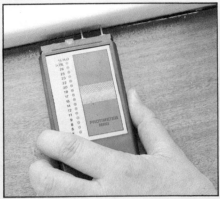

2 *The meter features a scale of moisture content in wood from 6 to 28 per cent — fibre saturation. Simply pressing the pins in the wood gives a reading.*

3 *You can trace accurately round a suspect area of wall using the meter in the same way, to outline the extent of the dampness. Mark it with pencil.*

4 *A colour-coded table (green; shaded; red) next to the indicator lights indicates respectively 'safe', 'investigate' or 'remedial action needed'.*

5 *Surface moisture readings can be misleading, so the meter features deep-wall probes for monitoring in depth. Drill two holes in the wall for the probes.*

6 *Insert the probes. They're insulated except for their tips. So if the wall's wet inside there's probably rising damp; if it's dry it may be condensation.*

though it may simply affect the area of the wall ties.

Rain penetration

The weather, of course, plays a vitally important role in the severity of penetrating damp — because for dampness to penetrate a structure there has to be dampness in the atmosphere outside. Penetrating damp is therefore only likely to occur during, or shortly after, rain.

The time lag varies from a few hours, to a few days, according to the nature of the wall. If it is penetrating damp in the true sense, you'll also probably find that those walls facing the prevailing wind are affected worst of all, and are affected before the rest of the house. What's more, the damp should disappear during dry spells, though if the wall has been thoroughly soaked, this could take months.

Doors and windows

If rainwater appears to penetrate the joints between door and window frames and the wall, it's likely that the material used to fill the gap has deteriorated with age. Rake out the joint using a cold chisel and seal the gap with a bead of flexible, non-setting mastic.

You can fill smaller cracks with an exterior filler, which can be primed and painted when set.

You should also inspect the drip groove under the front edge of the windowsill — if it's clogged with dirt or successive layers of paint, rainwater can trickle back underneath the sill and cause dampness on the wall outside. Clear the blockage and the problem should cease, once the wall has dried out thoroughly.

You may also find that the putty retaining and sealing the panes of glass in your

windows has become crumbly and cracked, admitting moisture. If the frame hasn't become too badly rotted, simply apply new putty — forming bevelled rebates with a putty knife — to the rebate and redecorate the frame when the putty is set.

In cavity walls, the join between windows and the two leaves of the wall are sealed with a vertical dpc, usually of bituminous felt, which slots into the perimeter of the frame and is located within the cavity. This type of dpc is unlikely to fail; however, if for some reason it should fail, in older houses for example, you can usually seal the gaps around the frame with mastic.

Faulty roof

Loose or missing roof tiles or slates, for example, should be replaced immediately: they offer easy access for rain, and the effects may not even become visible until a few days later, when the moisture seeps downwards and penetrates the upstairs ceiling. While you're on the roof, inspect the flashings around the chimney stack and the mortar flaunching in which the pots are set.

If the flashings have come adrift, or they're damaged, moisture may be able to trickle behind them and down the chimney breast to appear on the walls, or ceilings in the rooms below. If the damage is slight you may be able to seal the gaps with mastic. Badly damaged flashings must be replaced with self-adhesive strips.

So that the new flashing will stick firmly, brush a wide band of bituminous primer onto the angle between the masonry and the roof — do this all around the chimney.

To ensure a perfect seal, press the flashing strip firmly onto the primed areas. Eliminate gaps or air pockets by using a wallpaper seam roller.

Cracks in the flaunching could allow rain to seep into the flue, and you may have to remove the old mortar and re-set the pots in new mortar.

If the dampness is lower down the chimney breast wall, then the problem could be due to the flue and the fireplace having been completely sealed. In cases like this, you should introduce a gentle supply of air into the flue; the usual way is to fit an air-brick or ventilator grille in the blocked-off fireplace and a chimney pot cap.

Plumbing and drainage
Likewise, leaking gutters and downpipes or faulty plumbing can gradually wear down the defences of your house and open the way for widespread damp to enter. Isolate and remedy these faults first and deal with their effects later, when the walls have dried out thoroughly.

Dampness in cellars
Finally, there's the special case of the basement room or cellar. Because it's below ground level — and therefore doesn't allow you access to the outside of the wall — this is one of the few situations in which a cover-up is acceptable. It's unlikely, though, that damp-proofing the inside of the wall with special paints or chemicals will do the trick (although you could try this if the dampness doesn't seem too severe). The pressure on the moisture to get through is usually too great for this to offer sufficient protection. For more widespread dampness in cellars you'll need to fit a more substantial barrier, such as a waterproof lining.

The easiest barrier to install is a brush-on bituminous membrane of the sort used on solid floors. If the existing plaster is in poor condition, remove it and apply a skim coat of mortar to provide a smooth surface for the membrane. Once this is dry, apply the first coat of the membrane, leave it to dry, then apply a second coat, brushing at right angles to the first to ensure complete coverage. While still wet, throw handfuls of clean sharp sand at the wall so that it sticks to the bitumen to provide a key for replastering.

Of course, dampness coming through walls in not necessarily penetrating damp. In a newly-built home, damp walls could simply be a sign that the mortar and plaster making up the wall are drying out — the water put in during the mixing has to go somewhere, and it can take well over six months to disappear. This is why you shouldn't paint newly plastered walls, or cover them with anything other than the thinnest, cheapest wallpaper.

Lining damp walls
If for any reason it's not possible or practical for you to install a dpc in your walls, you can at least cover up the effects of damp, by lining the affected wall with special vapour-check plasterboard fixed to battens. Alternatively you could use corrugated bitumen lathing, which can be plastered or clad with plasterboard, then decorated.

Although these treatments — which are ideal for cellars and basements — hide the damp, they don't cure it, and so in the long term, damage to saturated masonry and structural timbers will result.

To install the corrugated lathing, all you have to do is strip the wall to bare brick, clad it with the sheets fixed in place with clout nails driven in at roughly 300mm (1ft) centres.

You can then apply a plaster finish or clad the sheets with plasterboard. In the latter case, the plasterboard must be stuck on using a special adhesive — usually available from the manufacturers of the corrugated lathing.

There are, however, a few points to watch if damp is not to get around the barrier. Vertical joins should overlap by one corrugation, and horizontal joins should be backed up with a strip of bituminous felt as an extra precaution against damp seeping through.

Dampness may also find its way over and under your barrier and so, here too, care is needed. At ceilings you should carry the lining up as far as the joists allow. With suspended timber floors, it is necessary to carry the lining down at least 150mm (6in) below floor level.

Solid floors should be damp-proofed at the same time, in which case the dpm should link up with the wall lining — leave the lining fractionally short of the floor. This small gap, which may be hidden behind the skirting board, will prevent dampness transferring from the floor to the new plast-erwork; just make sure the plaster doesn't bridge the gap.

Condensation dampness
Condensation can, in severe cases, be a serious source of dampness. The problems of recognising condenstion and how to deal with it are discussed in detail on pages 365-369, but there are a few points worth highlighting here, because condensation may hamper your diagnosis of the other forms of dampness.

Firstly, condensation often looks a bit like penetrating or rising damp. If the dampness occurs in kitchens, bathrooms, or upstairs rooms and is at its worst in corners, or in poorly ventilated areas, then condensation is the more likely explanation.

Also, if the penetrating damp is anywhere near a chimney breast, you should suspect condensation in the flue. This is more probable where the flue is disused and has been blocked up without providing adequate ventilation, but it can occur in flues that are in use if these are faulty, or if they're used only occasionally.

Rising damp in suspended timber floors may also be due to condensation; check that the air bricks in the outside walls below floor level have not become blocked, cutting off ventilation. A full discussion on fitting air-bricks and ventilators can be found on pages 380-383.

Secondly, condensation can often masquerade as a plumbing leak, particularly a leak in a cold water pipe or cistern; plumbing leaks don't stop and start, whereas condensation will be at its worst on warm, muggy days, and will disappear on cold, dry days.

Disaster dampness
Finally, dampness can be caused by abnormal weather conditions such as floods, or a combination of gales and torrential rain. There is, of course, nothing you can do to prevent it, but once the weather improves, the dampness should dry out naturally.

Drying out
Once you've cured your house's damp problem you must allow sufficient time for the structure to dry out completely before you redecorate with materials that are likely to retain moisture in the walls and floors.

A damp wall takes about one month per 25mm (1in) of wall thickness to dry out. One way around this is to clad internal walls with waterproof render, which can be decorated sooner.

As an added precaution, you should also provide efficient heating and ventilation to the affected rooms in order to avoid dampness caused by condensation.

INJECTING A NEW DPC

A chemical damp-proof course will provide your walls with a durable, long-lasting barrier against rising damp. It's easy to install using injecting equipment which you can readily hire and chemicals that are readily available.

D amp can affect your home in a variety of ways: through faulty guttering or plumbing, weak or missing pointing between bricks, or even by seeping straight through the walls if they're old or in poor condition. Most of these problems, however, known as penetrating damp, can be remedied by thorough maintenance of the house: you should, for instance, regularly inspect chimney flashings and flaunchings for damage, and replace missing or loose slates or tiles from your roof. Check also that rendered or painted wall surfaces are sound and waterproof.

For full details on how to identify and cure penetrating damp, see pages 370-375.

Preventing rising damp
The worst effects of rising damp, which passes up and through the walls from the ground, can be concealed with a special dry lining. But this isn't a practical solution in the long term: the damp is still likely to cause damage to the walls and any structural woodwork that's connected to them. The only totally effective cure is to install an impervious barrier — a damp-proof course (dpc) — low down in the wall, below the inside floor level.

If your house is more than 100 years old then the chances are that it won't have a dpc. Even if there's no sign of damp most local authorities now agree that it's better to be safe than sorry, and to install a dpc. In fact, if you ever have an old house surveyed you'll probably find that this is one of the first suggestions the surveyor will make.

Even if your house has a dpc it's possible that this may have been damaged by settlement of the walls; this is especially likely in older houses, which have dpcs made of slate, bituminous felt, lead or copper.

Types of damp-proof course
There are basically four different methods of providing a dpc, however, they are not all suitable for do-it-yourself installation and some are expensive.

Electro-osmosis, for example, uses a metal conductor to prevent the dampness rising; another method involves cutting a channel in the wall and setting a physical barrier between the brick courses; the third method places porous ceramic tubes in the wall to increase the evaporation rate.

The fourth method, however, is both relatively cheap and simple enough for you to tackle in a day. It involves impregnating a layer of the wall with a chemical that repels liquid moisture, yet lets moisture vapour pass through, allowing the wall to 'breathe'.

The chemical is usually a silicone-based material similar to the brush-on water repellents that you can apply to the surface of a wall as a cure for penetrating damp.

Installing a chemical dpc
There are two main methods of getting the chemical into the wall: by gravity-feed or pressure injection.

With the gravity-feed system, all you do is drill holes into the wall at intervals and connect to each hole a container full of the damp-proofing fluid, which is usually water-based. The containers are supported so that the fluid simply runs into the holes under the force of gravity, over a period of two or three days. By that time the masonry should have soaked up as much fluid as it can take.

Although in practice the procedure is simple, because the only factor inducing the chemical to penetrate the masonry is gravity, if the bricks are quite hard (and therefore relatively impervious) not much damp-proofing fluid will be absorbed. The result is that you don't get such a durable dpc.

Pressure injection
Pressure injection, therefore, is in many respects the more efficient method of getting the liquid into the wall. You still have to introduce the chemical into holes drilled in the wall in order to saturate the masonry, but what makes this system so much better is the pressure used, supplied by a special pump.

The bricks would have to be very impervious indeed to resist the force, in which case they probably wouldn't need damp-proofing anyway. Also, the job can be completed in a matter of hours instead of days, and the walls tend to become more evenly saturated, resulting in a more resilient and effective dpc.

Both the pressure injection machine and its injection nozzles, along with the masonry drill and bit you'll need to make the holes can be hired, accompanied by detailed instructions on how to operate the equipment. All you need to buy is the damp-proofing fluid.

Types of wall
Most types of wall are suitable for injection with a chemical dpc, although exceptionally thick walls, rubble-filled random flint walls or

DRILLING THE INJECTION HOLES

1 *Prepare the wall for damp-proofing by removing the visibly damp plaster indoors about 450mm (18in) above the affected area; mark this area on the wall.*

2 *Hack off the damp plaster below your guideline using a club hammer and cold chisel to expose the brickwork, then remove the skirting board.*

3 *If you're injecting the dpc from outside only, first drill 10mm (³⁄₈in) diameter holes along the wall 150mm (6in) below floor level and above ground level.*

4 *Drill the holes 75mm (3in) deep at a slight downward angle into the bricks. Wind masking tape around the bit to indicate the depth you want to drill.*

Ready Reference

AMOUNTS OF CHEMICAL

The amount of damp-proofing chemical you'll need depends on the porosity of the bricks. The liquid is sold in 25 litre (6 gal) drums, and as a guide you'll need:
● 27 to 45 litres (6 to 10 gal) per 30m (100ft) of 112mm (4½in) thick solid wall
● 67 to 90 litres (15 to 20 gal) per 30m (100ft) of 225mm (9in) thick solid wall.

HOW MANY HOLES?

In most cases you'll need to inject only one course of brickwork. The number of holes you'll need to drill depends on the type of bricks. On a standard 225mm (9in) solid brick wall:
● drill two holes per stretcher, one per header – overall about 112mm (4½in) apart.
If the bricks are exceptionally dense:
● drill two or three holes per brick.

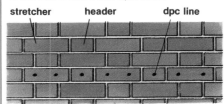

TIP: INJECTING HARD BRICKS

If your wall consists of hard, non-porous engineering or 'blue' quality bricks damp may rise through the mortar joints and you'll need to treat these with damp-proofing chemical.

INJECTING THE FLUID

There are various ways to carry out the drilling. To treat a 112mm (4½in) thick wall:
● drill 75mm (3in) deep holes and inject from one side only (A).
To treat a 225mm (9in) thick wall:
● drill 75mm (3in) deep holes and inject from both sides (B), or
● drill 75mm (3in) deep holes and inject (C); then drill to 190mm (7½in) in the same holes and inject again (D).

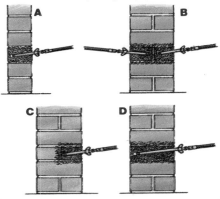

similar impermeable materials bonded by an irregular mortar course pose difficult problems. Newer brickwork with a failed dpc, for example, may have an alkaline mortar which might prevent effective treatment. It's not possible to treat walls below ground level – in a basement, for example – with a chemical dpc.

Cavity walls that contain insulation such as urea formaldehyde or mineral wool, won't normally be adversely affected by the dpc fluid, although if your cavity is filled with polystyrene granules it shouldn't be treated. Likewise the fluid may damage an existing dpc membrane of polythene or bitumen; check with your supplier.

On solid walls the job is straightforward, (see *Ready Reference*) and although it is best to treat the wall from both sides, satisfactory results can still be achieved when the drilling and the injection is tackled from the outside only. This, of course, involves the minimum amount of disturbance to your home. Only if the wall is visibly very wet need you remove the internal skirting boards, together with a band of plaster about 450mm (18in) wide above the floor level, in order to help the wall to dry out more quickly when you've injected your dpc.

Cavity walls present more of a problem. A chemical dpc can still be installed, but here you must drill and saturate each leaf of brickwork separately, which means some of the drilling must be carried out from indoors. If your home has cavity walls, it should have a dpc already, and if this has merely broken down in places, you may well be able to effect a cheaper, simpler cure than installing a completely new dpc. You can, however, install a new chemical dpc just above an original one, but avoid puncturing it when drilling the injection holes.

INJECTING THE FLUID

1 When you've drilled all of the holes, you can make your initial injection. First insert the filtered suction hose into the drum of silicone fluid.

2 Plug the pump into the mains and insert two of the three 75mm (3in) long injection nozzles into the holes at your starting point, with their valves closed.

3 Secure the nozzles with two or three turns of their wing nuts to form a seal. Don't overtighten them or you'll damage the expansion nipples at their tips.

5 Turn on the control valve of the third nozzle and 'bleed off' some fluid to expel air from the system, then switch it off when it flows freely.

6 Insert the third nozzle into the next free hole, tighten its nut and turn on the valve again, so that all three nozzles are injecting fluid into the bricks.

7 When each brick becomes saturated the fluid will wet the surface, and you should switch off the valves, remove the nozzles and insert them in the next holes.

9 As soon as you've completed the first injection return to the starting point and drill through the same holes to a depth of 190mm (7½in).

10 Undo the nuts securing each of the short nozzles, remove the nozzles and connect the longer 190mm (7½in) long ones using PTFE tape to seal the threads.

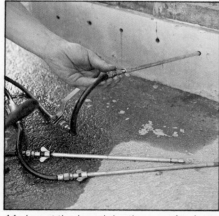

11 Insert the long injection nozzles into the wall and form a seal by tightening the wing nuts. Turn on the valves and inject the bricks as before.

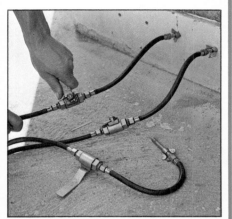

4 *Turn on the control valves of the two injection nozzles you've inserted in the wall and switch on the pump to start the fluid circulating through the system.*

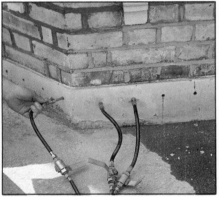

8 *Carry on injecting in this way until you've completed the length of wall. Keep the pressure maintained at 90 to 100 psi by adjusting the pump's valve.*

12 *Move along the wall, making the second injection. When you've finished, clean the pump by flushing it through with white spirit, turps or paraffin.*

Damp-proof course height

Another consideration when planning your new dpc is its position in the wall, and here it's important to remember the reason for having a dpc in the first place. It's not so much to stop rising damp ruining your wallpaper, though it should certainly do this; rather it's to stop rising damp attacking the timberwork in your home, and this means that it must be at least 150mm (6in) below the level of the floor joists.

What's more, in order to prevent heavy rain from indirectly bridging the new dpc on the outside of the house, the dpc must also be at least 150mm (6in) above ground level.

Most older houses have a rendered plinth surrounding the walls at ground level, concealing the brickwork. It's often at this level that you want to inject your dpc. Although it does help when drilling to be able to see the individual bricks, you need only hack off the plinth to expose the masonry if it's especially high; in this case it's possible for the plinth to bridge the dpc. Unfortunately, once you've removed the plinth you can't replace it when you've completed your dpc, and you may consider that this ruins the character of the house.

Drilling the injection holes

Use a masonry drill with a 10mm (⅜in) bit to make the injection holes. Wind a length of tape around the bit to act as a depth guide, and withdraw the bit two or three times during drilling to clear out the dust. If the holes aren't drilled perfectly straight you'll risk distorting the injection nozzles when you insert them in the wall.

If you're going to treat a 225mm (9in) thick solid brick wall from both sides, drill 75mm (3in) deep holes the diameter of the nozzles – either angled downwards or horizontally – along the brick course which is to form the dpc, on each side of the wall. Drill two holes per stretcher and one per header (see *Ready Reference*); overall this is about 112mm (4½in) apart.

To treat this type of wall from one side only, follow the same procedure on one side and then inject the fluid. Next, drill through the same holes to a depth of 190mm (7½in) and inject the fluid again, using the longer nozzles supplied with the machine, to saturate the inner section of the wall. You can treat a 112mm (4½in) thick wall from one side only by drilling and injecting once only with the short nozzles.

To treat a cavity wall saturate each leaf separately (one by working indoors with a margin of plaster removed, the other from the outside) using the appropriate length of nozzle for the thickness of the wall.

If you're treating walls of hard or dense brick you should drill deeper into the brick than with standard bricks, or increase the number of holes, by spacing them at 65mm (2½in) centres, so you can thoroughly saturate the masonry.

Injecting the chemical

To inject the damp-proof fluid into your pre-drilled holes, first insert the filtered suction hose connected to the pump into the drum containing the chemical. Ensure that the valves controlling the nozzles are closed, and connect the pump to the mains electricity supply.

Insert two of the three nozzles into the holes at your starting point – at one end of the wall – and secure them by tightening their wing nuts. Turn on their control valves, switch on the pump, then open the third control valve to 'bleed' the fluid and disperse any trapped air in the system. When the fluid flows freely, turn off the valve, insert the nozzle in the wall and turn on its valve again.

The pump includes a pressure gauge, and this should be maintained at 90 to 100 psi (pounds per square inch) if the liquid is to be fed into the wall at the correct rate. The valve controlling this should be closed at this stage but, if the pressure's too high (denoted by a high-pitched noise from the relief valve) you'll have to open the gauge valve slightly to reduce the pressure.

As each brick becomes saturated the fluid will soak its face, and you should turn off the nozzle control valve and remove the nozzle from the wall. Slot it into the next hole and switch on again. Work along the wall with this step-by-step procedure until you've completed the dpc.

When you're treating a very damp wall, liquid water may be displaced by the dpc fluid and water droplets may emerge on the face of the wall. Continue to inject until the droplets cease to show.

If you're making a second, deeper drilling from the same side of the wall, do this straight away and then make the injection with the longer nozzles.

Flush the machine after use by pumping through white spirit, turps or paraffin, which act as a solvent for the fluid. Never use water to clean the pump: it won't prevent the dpc fluid from 'curing' in the machine, and may even damage the system.

Finishing off

You can plug the drilled holes outside with mortar that's been coloured to match the brick, when the dpc fluid has 'cured'.

A damp wall actually takes a long time to dry cut – about one month per 25mm (1in) of wall thickness – but if you've had to remove the internal plaster you won't want to leave the bricks exposed for long. You can, therefore, apply a proprietary waterproofing render or use waterproofing additives, after about two days.

FITTING AIRBRICKS & VENTILATORS

Houses need a supply of fresh air just as much as their occupants do if they are to stay healthy. Airbricks and ventilators fitted in the right places ensure they get it.

Good ventilation is essential for a number of reasons. If the structure of the house is well ventilated this will ensure that dampness cannot take a hold, and any moisture that does get inside the building will soon dry out before any harm is done. This applies not only to walls and ceilings, but in particular to structural timbers which must be kept dry if they are to stay in good condition. Dampness not only encourages timber to rot, but damp timber is also prone to woodworm attack.

Good ventilation, combined with an efficient heating system, will also minimise condensation, which is another major cause of dampness getting into the fabric of the building. Finally, good ventilation is vital to ensure efficient and safe combustion of any conventionally-flued, fuel-burning heating appliances, and so to guarantee the health and comfort of the occupants of the house.

Underfloor ventilators
Wherever there is a timber ground floor, it is essential to have good underfloor ventilation to keep the flooring timbers in good condition. To achieve this, airbricks are built into the outer walls of the house to give an airflow under the floor. Usually the airbricks are found just above the damp-proof course (dpc), but in some houses the airbricks may be below it, particularly when the dpc is well above ground level, as is sometimes found when a house is built on sloping ground. The actual siting of the bricks is not critical, although if the airbricks are below the dpc they are more likely to become damp, and therefore may be damaged by frost. What is critical is that the airbricks are unobstructed and that there are sufficient of them.

Make sure that soil is pulled away from the airbricks, use an old screwdriver to ensure the holes are not blocked and most important of all, remove any covers that may have been fitted over airbricks in a foolish attempt to cure underfloor draughts. The best way of curing draughts that may come up between floors and skirting boards, and between floorboards, is to cover boards with stout paper or hardboard, to use thick underlays and to pin quadrant moulding into the angle between floorboards and skirtings.

Damaged airbricks
When the existing airbricks are examined, it may be found that some of them are damaged. If the grille is broken, this can allow vermin to get under the floors of the house where they can multiply.

To remove a damaged airbrick, use a hammer and cold chisel to break out the pieces and clear mortar from around the opening in the brickwork. Buy a new airbrick of the same style and size as the old one – see 'fitting air bricks' below. Modern airbricks are now produced in metric sizes and rather than have an airbrick that is considerably smaller than the existing opening, it is better to choose the next size up and enlarge the opening, if necessary; it is better to have too much rather than too little ventilation under a floor.

In a solid wall it is unlikely that the opening in the wall will be lined, but in a more modern house with cavity walls, the cavity between the inner and outer skins of the brickwork should be sealed to prevent dissipation of the airflow into the cavity instead of beneath the floor. This is done with pre-formed clay ducts or by lining the opening with slates. If the cavity is found not to be sealed when the old airbrick is removed, a duct should ideally be formed in the opening before the new airbrick is fixed in place.

Replacement airbricks will be of clay, cast iron or cast aluminium, and in all cases they fit flush with the surface of the wall, being bedded on cement mortar. The mix to use is 1 part cement to 6 parts sharp sand, with a little plasticiser to improve workability.

Assuming that your replacement airbrick is the same size as the old one, just dampen the opening, spread some of the mortar in the bottom of the hole, ease the airbrick into place, and press more mortar in around the brick. Finally, strike off excess mortar level with the wall surface.

Fitting extra airbricks
A common problem in older houses is insufficient underfloor ventilation – there aren't enough airbricks, and those fitted are probably too small or have gradually got blocked up. Ideally, airbricks on each side of the house will be opposite each other and spaced not more than 1.8m (6ft) apart, which will ensure an adequate flow of air through the underfloor void. The airbricks should be of a size that allows 32sq cm (about 5sq in) of open vent per metre run of wall.

Various sizes and types of airbricks are available, each type differing in the amount of free air space available from a given size of brick. The most common airbricks are made from red terra-cotta or buff fireclay. There is also a large range of sandfaced and textured finishes that will match the commonly available facing bricks. More expensive and less widely used these days are plain cast iron, galvanised cast iron and cast aluminium grilles. Commonly available brick designs are square-hole, louvre and rectangular-hole. The latter has a greater area of free air space than the other patterns. For example, a 220 x 70mm (9 x 3in) rectangular-hole clay airbrick has about 27sq cm (4sq in) of free air space compared with 15sq cm (2½sq in) for a

REMOVING AN OLD AIRBRICK

1 Start by using a bolster and club hammer to chop away the rendering and mortar round the airbrick. Take care not to damage the dpc above it.

2 Lever out the old airbrick with a cold chisel – easy with this cast iron version, but more difficult with a clay one, which you may have to break up.

3 Remove all the debris from within the cavity, especially if an old slate lining has disintegrated. Clear the opening in the inner leaf too.

4 Soak the brickwork round the opening with water so that the moisture from the mortar round the new airbrick will not be sucked out too quickly.

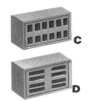
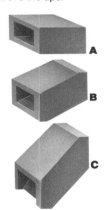
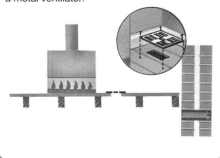
square-hole airbrick, and 13sq cm (2sq in) for a louvre-type.

If the airbricks are being fitted in cavity walls, then terra-cotta cavity liners should be purchased at the same time as the airbricks. These are available in sizes to match the airbrick sizes and in lengths from 100mm to 300mm (4 to 12in) in 25mm (1in) progressions to suit the thickness of the wall. Generally, for underfloor ventilation the horizontal pattern ducts, which are the easiest to fit, will be suitable. However, with this type there is a danger that inblown rain will enter the duct and trickle down the inside wall. To prevent this, inclined ducts are used (see *Ready Reference*), but these are not very easy to fit in replacement work.

If you calculate that extra airbricks are necessary, holes must be knocked through the walls to allow them to be fitted. Insert the new airbricks so they line up where possible

with the existing airbricks. To make removal of the bricks easier, drill them repeatedly with a masonry drill and then break out the bricks using a hammer and sharp bolster chisel, taking care not to let debris drop into the cavity. Once the outer skin of the wall has been penetrated, rags can be pushed into the cavity to catch the rubble.

Maintaining air to airbricks

If an extension is built on to a house with suspended timber floors, it is essential that an air supply is maintained to the existing airbricks, especially if the extension has a solid floor, which is likely. In this case, you have to lay clay, pitch fibre, or plastic ventilating pipes under the solid floor of the extension to take air to each of the existing airbrick positions. The airbricks should be knocked out so as not to hinder the airflow, and new airbricks should be fitted in the extension

FITTING A NEW AIRBRICK

1 *Bridge the cavity within the opening using pieces of slate, or fit a cavity liner (see* Ready Reference*) if space permits. Then trowel in a mortar bed.*

2 *Push the new airbrick carefully into place on the mortar bed so its face is flush with the outside wall surface and there is an even gap all round it.*

3 *Use an old knife or a pointing trowel to force 'slices' of mortar deep into the gap between the airbrick and the surrounding brickwork.*

4 *Add more mortar all round the airbrick to leave the surface of the pointing flush with the surrounding wall surface, and trowel it to a neat finish.*

5 *Where a path or patio surface is immediately below an airbrick opening, chop away the concrete and form a sloping airway with mortar.*

6 *To stop water draining into the airbrick opening from the path surface, form a low mortar kerb round it. Smooth it over with a sponge as the mortar sets.*

wall to prevent vermin from entering the air ducts. Set the airbricks and ducts in mortar as described for airbrick renewal.

Roof ventilation
In the past, when roofs were steeply pitched and there were many air gaps between slates and tiles, roof ventilation was more than adequate and it was very rare for roof timbers to decay as long as the roof covering was properly maintained. However, in modern houses where the roofs are made with low-pitched trussed rafters, the roof is lined with felt under the tiles, and there is thick insulation on the floor of the loft, then lack of ventilation can lead to decay of the roof timbers.

The trouble can be obviated by ventilating the roof space. One method is to fit large air-bricks in gable end walls, where these exist. The other method is to install ventilators at the eaves. In both cases the ventilators are

needed at opposite sides of the roof space to give a through draught. The area of the ventilators should not be less than 0.3% of the roof plan area, or the area of the vents should be equivalent to that of a continuous gap along the sides of the roof of width not less than 10mm where the roof pitch exceeds 15°, or 25mm where the roof pitch is 15° or less.

If airbricks are being set in opposite gable walls, use rectangular-hole airbricks with inclined ducts to bridge the cavity and to ensure that rain cannot blow into the loft. This will mean cutting the hole in the outer leaf of the wall first, then cutting the inner one two courses higher.

Eaves ventilation
It is often easier to provide ventilation at the eaves. If these have been packed with loft insulation material, this should be pulled back slightly so that proprietary ventilation

strips can be inserted – see *Ready Reference.* These hold the insulating blanket away from the roof slope and allow a flow of air to enter at each side. To be fully effective, 19mm (¾in) diameter ventilation holes should be drilled in the soffit board at about 75mm (3in) intervals. Where there is no soffit board, upward-sloping holes should be drilled in the fascia board at the same spacing; they can be made fairly inconspicuous if drilled up behind the gutter.

Chimney ventilation
Disused chimneys are frequently sealed to stop rain penetration, but this can lead to problems of dampness coming through the chimney breast walls due to the formation of condensation in the flue. This can be prevented by ventilating the chimney. If the fireplace opening has been sealed, ensure that there is a hole at least 100 x 50mm (4 x 2in)

SITING VENTS

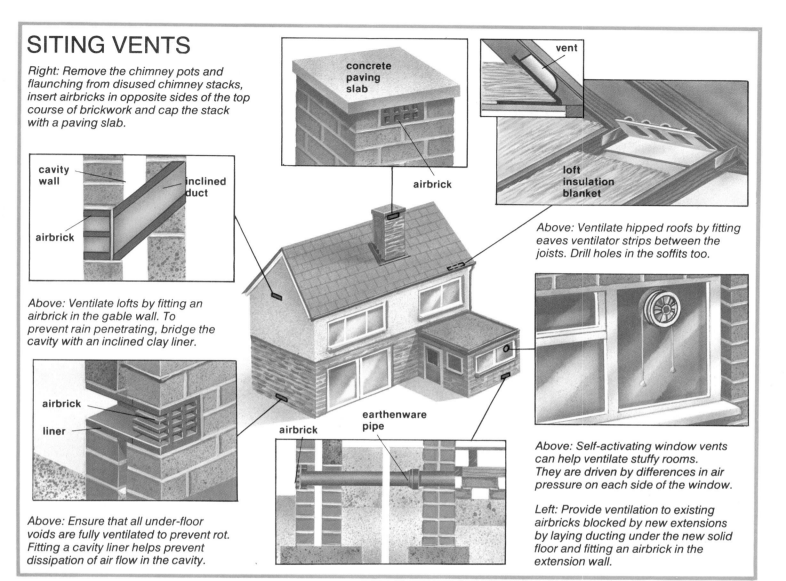

Right: Remove the chimney pots and flaunching from disused chimney stacks, insert airbricks in opposite sides of the top course of brickwork and cap the stack with a paving slab.

concrete paving slab

airbrick

vent

loft insulation blanket

Above: Ventilate hipped roofs by fitting eaves ventilator strips between the joists. Drill holes in the soffits too.

cavity wall

inclined duct

airbrick

Above: Ventilate lofts by fitting an airbrick in the gable wall. To prevent rain penetrating, bridge the cavity with an inclined clay liner.

airbrick

liner

Above: Ensure that all under-floor voids are fully ventilated to prevent rot. Fitting a cavity liner helps prevent dissipation of air flow in the cavity.

airbrick

earthenware pipe

Above: Self-activating window vents can help ventilate stuffy rooms. They are driven by differences in air pressure on each side of the window.

Left: Provide ventilation to existing airbricks blocked by new extensions by laying ducting under the new solid floor and fitting an airbrick in the extension wall.

---

in the plate or wall sealing the flue. For neatness cover this hole with a plastic, plaster or metal ventilator plate, but do *not* use a type that can be closed. The chimney itself can be kept dry and ventilated by fitting a clay or metal capping pot to the chimney stack covered with cement flaunching in which a half-round clay tile is bedded. Alternatively, airbricks can be placed on opposite sides of the chimney stack and the chimney sealed with paving slabs bedded over the flues.

Room ventilation

In kitchens and bathrooms, where condensation is generally a serious problem, an electric extractor fan is generally the best solution. But in other rooms an airbrick and interior grille fitted near ceiling level, or an adjustable non-mechanical window ventilator, will give controlled ventilation without the necessity to open a door or window.

Heater ventilation

For efficient combustion a fuel-burning appliance must have an adequate air supply. The only exceptions to this are balanced-flue heaters, as these appliances draw their air from outside through the balanced-flue terminal, and discharge the waste gases at the same point.

With conventionally flued heating appliances, air is needed to carry the products of combustion up the flue, and it is also needed to carry away some of the heat given off by the appliance and distribute it around the house. When the air for the appliance is taken from outdoors, either direct or from under a suspended floor, approximately 6.5sq cm (1sq in) of ventilator opening at low level is needed for every 2,000 BTU/hour of boiler output. If the air is taken from an adjoining room the free ventilation opening should be doubled in size. Air starvation to

solid fuel appliances is fairly easy to detect because the chimney smokes. This can be confirmed by opening a door or window, when the smoking into the room should cease. A closed solid fuel room heater may need only 15 to 23cu m of air per hour, while an inset open fire with a large fire opening and chimney flue may take an extra 260cu m or more – equivalent to around ten typical rooms-ful of air – per hour. To reduce this air requirement to a reasonable level of about 140cu m of air per hour, a proprietary throat restrictor can be fitted into the flue.

To give additional ventilation for the appliance, air vents can be fitted close to the heater. Ideally with a suspended timber floor air can be taken from under the floor by drilling large holes in the floorboards close to the appliance and covering them with ventilator plates; or from an air vent in an outside wall (see *Ready Reference*).

FITTING AN EXTRACTOR FAN

Stale air, poor ventilation and the build-up of condensation are potential problems in the modern home, particularly in the kitchen and bathroom. Extractor fans can help; they're easy to install, cheap to run and, most important, extremely efficient.

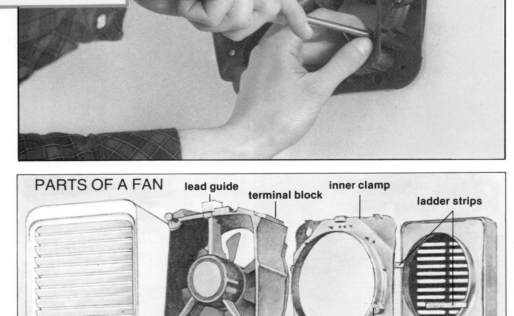

Every home experiences the unpleasantness of lingering cooking smells and poor ventilation. With draught-proofing, double glazing and central heating, the result, in the long term, is likely to be the constant presence of condensation which can eventually damage both the decor and the structure of the home. And in the kitchen persistent condensation is not only unsightly but also unhygienic.

There are a number of measures that can temporarily relieve the problem, but in the long run the only way to deal with it is to get rid of the stale air completely and replace it with fresh. To do this you need to install an extractor fan.

Types of fans
There are three types of extractor fan commonly used in the home and all are comparatively easy to install.

Perhaps the most common is the window fan which is fitted in a hole cut in a fixed pane of glass. These fans can be controlled by an integral switch, usually cord-operated, or else by a separate wall-mounted, rocker switch. The installation involves no structural work; just ask your glazier to replace the pane with one in which a hole has already been cut.

A wall fan, controlled by similar switches, is fitted in a hole made in an external wall or in an air brick vent. This sort of fan takes a little longer to install, as a hole has to be made in the external wall. However, by installing a wall fan in preference to a window-mounted fan you avoid restricting the view from a window and the inconvenience of having to have that window permanently closed.

There's one other common kind of extractor fan and that's the self-actuating, window-mounted plastic ventilator. But although the easiest to install and cheapest to run – no further expenses after installation – this type is also the least effective.

There are other, more specialised, types of extractor fans such as cooker hoods and timed fans for the bathroom or toilet which are variations on the three main types already described. Cooker hoods either

PARTS OF A FAN — lead guide, terminal block, inner clamp, ladder strips, internal grille and shutter, motor assembly unit, worm screw, external clamp and grille

recirculate the air in a kitchen after filtering it, or else extract it. Timed fans in the bathroom or toilet are activated by the lightswitch and are particularly useful when these rooms don't have external walls. Obviously, they will require ducting to enable the air to be expelled outside, but the timed switch poses no extra problems as it's connected up to the light switch when the fan is linked to the lighting circuit. Ceiling-fitted extractor fans are also available. They require an unobstructed space of 300mm (12in) between ceiling joists, and may also require ducting to an external wall if you have glass fibre roof insulation.

Calculating your needs
Which type of fan you install is obviously determined by the size of the room but also by whether there is an accessible external wall available.

It's simple to work out the size of fan required for a particular room. All you do is work out the volume of the room in cubic metres or feet by multiplying the length by the breadth by the height. Then multiply that volume by the number of air changes (see *Ready Reference*).

Siting your fan
If your home has already been fitted with an extractor fan, and it has proved to be less than satisfactory, the chances are that it has been sited in the wrong place.

The most common sign of that is poor ventilation – the result of the short circuiting of air movements between the fan and the air inlet. The extractor fan should be sited as far away from and, if possible, opposite the main source of air replacement.

In a kitchen, fans should always be fitted as high up as possible on a wall or window,

CHOPPING THE HOLE

1 *Drill a hole through the wall and, using a length of string and the drill bit as a compass, accurately mark out the hole to be cut.*

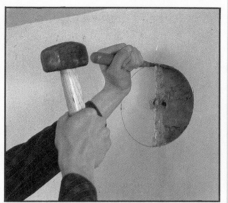

2 *With a cold chisel and club hammer chop round the circle perimeter and then move inwards to dislodge the surface layer of plaster.*

3 *Once you've done this you can use the same chisel to chop away the bricks. Try to leave a brick in the middle of the hole for leverage.*

4 *.The hole should be trued up outside. It doesn't matter if it's slightly inaccurate as the clamp plates will cover and seal any rough edges.*

Ready Reference

TYPES OF FAN
There are three main types of extractor fan:

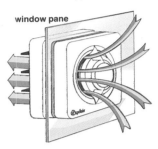
window pane

● the window fan fitted to a window with a hole cut in it

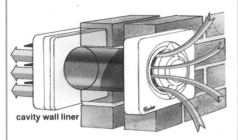
cavity wall liner

● the wall fan fitted in a similar way to a wall with a hole chopped through it

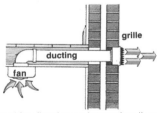
grille
ducting
fan

● the ducted fan fitted to an internal wall or ceiling, with ducting to carry the stale air outside.

CALCULATING YOUR NEEDS
To calculate the size of fan you require, multiply the volume of your room by the number of air changes needed per hour. Therefore, length x breadth x height x changes per hour = capacity.

Examples of air changes. Manufacturers recommend the following number of air changes per hour:
bathroom 15 – 20
kitchen 10 – 15
toilet 10 – 15
living room 4 – 6
Remember, always use the higher of these two figures to avoid any possibility of unsatisfactory ventilation.

but it is advisable not to install one immediately above a cooker or grill where temperatures are likely to exceed 40°C. So, the best place for it to be located would be on the wall or window adjacent to the cooker and opposite the door or main air inlet.

It is vital to make sure there is an adequate source of fresh air. If you have natural gas or smokeless fuel heating and your house is well sealed, but with no air inlet, an efficient extractor fan might cause a reversal of flow in the flue gases, which would prove extremely dangerous.

In addition, without an adequate inlet, the air pressure might drop and so impair the efficiency of your fan.

If you intend to fit a wall fan, it shouldn't be placed any closer than two brick lengths to a wall edge for fear of causing structural weakness. So, working out where to fit the fan is crucial to its ultimate success in ventilating your home. If you have any doubt about the supply of fresh air it might be an idea to fit an air brick.

Installing a wall fan
As only the very high capacity extractor fans rate over 100W, your fan can take its power from the lighting circuit. However, you should check that, including the wattage of the fan, the light circuit does not exceed the safety level of 1200 watts. Otherwise you must connect to a power circuit.

Before breaking into the lighting circuit for power a hole must be made in the wall to accommodate the fan. If you have to go through a cavity wall, it must be sealed with a special sleeve that can be obtained from the manufacturer. This will prevent unpleasant air leaking into the room from the cavity. The fan is connected to the circuit wiring by 1.0mm^2 two-core and earth PVC –

INSTALLING THE FAN

1 Attach the ladder strips to the outer clamp and position it in the hole. The ladder strips should run inside any cavity liner.

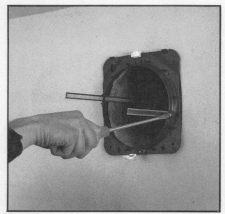

2 Slide the inner clamp plate over the ladder strips and tighten the worm screws to secure the two plates. Then trim the ladder strips to size.

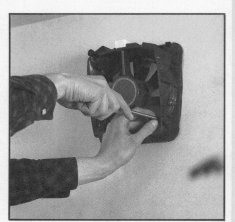

3 Attach the motor assembly unit by screwing it to the inner clamp plate. Make sure that any exposed ladder strip is left outside the unit.

4 Thread the flex through the lead guide hole and connect it to the terminal block (see diagram), which can be temporarily removed for fitting.

5 Clip on and secure the external grille to the outer clamp plate making sure you tighten the holding screw on the underside.

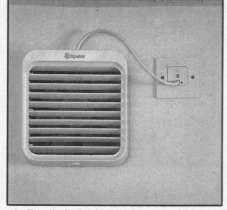

6 Finally fit the inner clamp and connect the flex to the fuse unit of the clock connector, which is linked directly to the power supply.

sheathed house wiring cable; the connecting point should be a fused clock connection unit. This makes isolating the fan for repairs easy: all you do is remove the fuse section.

There are three options for obtaining power for the new fan. You can connect into the circuit at an existing loop-in ceiling rose, run the cable to an existing junction box (always present if you have strip lighting in your kitchen), or install a new junction box in the lighting circuit feed cable and run the new cable to that.

At the fan end of the new cable connect it to the fixed section of the fused clock connector unit. With the main switch turned off connect the new cable to the appropriate terminals of the ceiling rose or junction box.

Then connect one end of a length of 1.0mm² three-core circular sheathed flex to

the fan and the other end to the plug part of the connection unit. If your fan is double insulated, as in most cases, you need use only two-core flex.

A wall fan is fixed to the wall in almost exactly the same way as a window fan is fitted to a window, the assembly being straightforward and simply a matter of following the manufacturer's instructions. In some cases ladder strips are used to secure the inner and outer clamp plates, and these may need cutting to length to match the wall depth. Otherwise the two plates are mounted independently of each other on either the wall or a panel that must be at least 35mm (1½in) thick. The rubber gaskets on both inner and outer clamp plates are retained in both cases. All fans have shutters which close automatically when the fan is

switched off and so prevent any draughts.

If your fan doesn't have an integral switch then a separate switch will have to be fitted. A mounting box should be fixed to the wall at a convenient height below the clock connector. From the connection unit run a length of the 1.0mm sq two-core and earth PVC flat-sheathed cable to the switch. Remember that as one of the wires is the live feed this must be joined at the connection unit end to the circuit live conductor with a plastic cable connector. The connector should be placed in the box behind the clock connector.

If you want to fit a speed controller in conjunction with a fan that has an integral cord-switch there is no essential difference in the wiring. It should be located at the same height as the new switch.

MAKING THE CONNECTIONS

Making the connections for a wall-mounted fan is the easiest part of the installation. Cable can be channelled in or run on the surface.

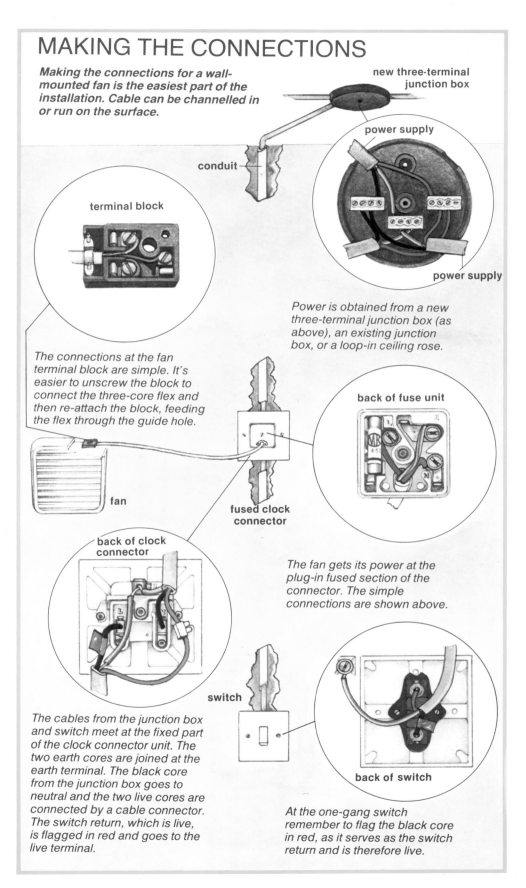

new three-terminal junction box

power supply

conduit

terminal block

power supply

Power is obtained from a new three-terminal junction box (as above), an existing junction box, or a loop-in ceiling rose.

The connections at the fan terminal block are simple. It's easier to unscrew the block to connect the three-core flex and then re-attach the block, feeding the flex through the guide hole.

fan

back of fuse unit

fused clock connector

The fan gets its power at the plug-in fused section of the connector. The simple connections are shown above.

back of clock connector

switch

The cables from the junction box and switch meet at the fixed part of the clock connector unit. The two earth cores are joined at the earth terminal. The black core from the junction box goes to neutral and the two live cores are connected by a cable connector. The switch return, which is live, is flagged in red and goes to the live terminal.

back of switch

At the one-gang switch remember to flag the black core in red, as it serves as the switch return and is therefore live.

SITING YOUR FAN

Correct siting is crucial to a fan's efficiency. Fans should be installed in the window or wall furthest away from the door or source of fresh air.

In a kitchen, the fan should be located on the wall or window next to the cooker – the main source of smells – but not immediately above it.

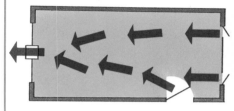

A SOURCE OF AIR

A good supply of fresh air is equally important. If you feel the supply is inadequate, fit an ventilator in the wall opposite the fan if possible.

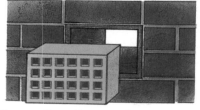

For a cavity wall, you need a cavity liner or an air brick that will extend through the wall. You should:
● chop a hole with a cold chisel and club hammer
● insert the liner, or line the hole with mortar.
● fit the brick and repoint external wall.

solid wall

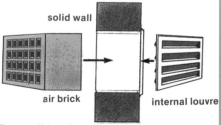

air brick

internal louvre

For a solid wall you should:
● cut the hole in a similar way and line it with mortar
● fit the brick as above
● plaster round the edges of the hole on the inside of the wall
● apply impact adhesive when the plaster is dry and hold the internal louvre in place until a good bond is established, or fit it with screws and wallplugs.

INSULATING YOUR ROOF

About a quarter of the heat lost from an uninsulated house goes through the roof, and so some kind of roof insulation should be your first priority for saving money on heating bills.

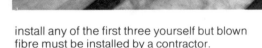

Houses leak heat like a sieve. Up to 75 per cent of the warmth generated within the house finds its way to the outside world through the roof, walls, windows and doors, and this represents an enormous waste of energy and money.

Insulation reduces the rate at which heat passes through the various parts of your house's structure, by trapping 'still' air within the insulating material itself. Still air doesn't conduct heat much and so wrapping your house in suitable insulation serves the same purpose as putting a tea-cosy on a tea pot: the tea stays hot for far longer. The converse is true during the summer: the insulation bars the heat of the sun.

About a quarter of all the heat lost from an average house goes through the roof, and this is a particularly easy area to insulate effectively. What you do is to put your insulation in one of three places: on the highest ceiling; on the loft floor; or on the inside of the roof itself. Insulating the loft floor is the simplest and most effective of these: you should insulate the ceiling where there's no loft or the roof slope where the loft space has been converted into living accommodation.

Why you should insulate

The savings you can make by insulating your loft depend on whether there's any insulation there already (it's the first layer that's most effective), how much you put in, and whether you can control or alter your heating system to take advantage of the insulation. The last point is particularly important: if you install loft insulation and leave central heating controls as they are with a thermostat in, say, the living room, the most noticeable effect will be warmer rooms upstairs rather than dramatically decreased fuel bills. If, however, you can lower the tempertures in upstairs rooms, or keep them the same as before, by fitting thermostatic radiator valves or by turning radiators down (or off), your house will lose less heat and your fuel bills will be lower.

Types of insulation

There are four main types of loft insulation you can use: blanket, loose-fill, sheet (see *Ready Reference*) and blown fibre. You can install any of the first three yourself but blown fibre must be installed by a contractor.

The most extensively used loft insulation material is rolls of glass fibre or mineral fibre blanket, which you lay between the joists of the loft floor. You can choose from either of two thicknesses: 100mm (4in) and 150mm (6in).

Although you'll benefit in terms of warmer rooms by installing thicker insulation, the more you put in, the less cost effective it becomes. From a practical point of view thicknesses greater than 125mm (5in) will probably take the insulation over the top of the joists, making walking about or storing things in the loft rather difficult.

To save storage and transportation space the material is compressed when rolled up and packaged but it regains its original thickness quite quickly when unwrapped. The most common width of roll is 400mm (16in). Lengths vary from brand to brand, but they're usually about 6 to 8m (20 to 25ft) long. Some glass fibre insulation is available in 600mm (2ft) wide rolls for use in lofts with wider-than-usual joist spacings.

The 400mm (16in) width is the most suitable size for most houses and allows a little to turn up where it meets the joists. Joists are usually 400mm (16in) apart but they might be as much as 450mm (18in) or as little as 300mm (1ft). If you have narrow-spaced joists the 600mm (2ft) width is probably the best to use: you can cut a roll in half with a panel saw while it's still in its wrapper.

Working out how much insulation you'll need is simply a matter of multiplying the length of the loft floor by the width to calculate how many square metres there are, and then checking the chart in *Ready Reference*.

Remember that the 150mm (6in) thickness of blanket insulation comes in shorter length rolls than the 100mm (4in) thickness. An 8m (26ft) roll, 400mm (16in) wide, covers 3.2 sq m (35 sq ft). For blanket insulation, ignore the joists in your calculation; for loose-fill and sheet insulation, include the joist size, otherwise you could end up with 10 to 15 per cent too much. Loose-fill insulation comes in bags, typically containing 110 litres (4 cu ft). This is enough for 1.1 sq m (12 sq ft) laid 100mm (4in) deep. By far the most effective material is called vermiculite, which is made from a mineral called mica, though you might also find expanded polystyrene granules, loose mineral wool or cellulose fibre being sold as loose-fill insulation.

Thickness for thickness, vermiculite is more than twice the price of glass fibre blanket and it's not as effective. To get the same insulating effect as 80mm (3in) of glass fibre, you'd need 130mm (about 5in) of vermiculite, which might well come over the top of the ceiling joists.

Another disadvantage of loose-fill insulation is that it can blow about in a draughty loft:

WHERE TO INSULATE

Use blanket insulation between the joists (1) or lay loose-fill or sheet materials; insulate the loft hatch (2) by sticking on a sheet of polystyrene; clad the rafters (3) with plasterboard or fix blanket insulation between them; lag the cold water tank (4) with a proprietary jacket or tie blanket or sheet insulation around it; lag pipes (5) with foam tubes or mineral fibre rolls.

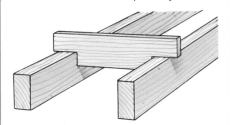
even if your loft isn't draughty now, it might well be after you've ventilated it properly (see pages 380-383). However, it's ideal if you have unevenly-spaced joists where one of the other types of insulation material might leave gaps.

To lay loose-fill insulation, you simply empty out the bags between the joists and spread it to an even thickness.

Sheet insulation isn't used much for loft insulation, though it's sometimes used for insulating between rafters, over solid walls and on flat roofs. The best type of rigid sheet for loft insulation is expanded polystyrene. It comes in various thicknesses in sheets from 1200 × 2400mm (4 × 8ft). You'll have to cut it up to get it through the loft hatch, and then cut each strip to the precise width required to match the joist spacing.

Other sheet materials such as fibreboard or chipboard can be laid across the joists, with loose-fill or blanket insulation sandwiched underneath. You can walk on chipboard, so it's also suitable for use as a floor, but fibreboard won't support your weight.

Blown fibre insulation costs little more than installing glass fibre blanket but it must be installed by a contractor. The three common materials are mineral fibre, pelleted glass fibre and cellulose fibre. It's easy and quick to put in, and will cover all the nooks and crannies that are difficult to reach by other methods.

Preparation
Lofts are usually dark, dirty places, so it's advisable to wear some really old clothes, preferably ones you can throw away afterwards.

Blanket insulation, especially glass fibre, can cause irritation to the skin, so you must wear rubber gloves when handling it. Remove your wrist-watch and roll up your sleeves. It's

LAYING BLANKET INSULATION

1 *Clean up any dust and dirt from the loft floor. Use a cylinder vacuum cleaner with a nozzle attachment so that you avoid disturbing the dust.*

2 *Starting from the eaves, unroll the insulation between the joists. Leave a small gap at the eaves to allow air to circulate in the loft space.*

3 *If the headroom at the eaves is limited, unroll the blanket and push the end gently into the eaves with a broom. Take care not to tear the insulation material.*

6 *Once you've unrolled the blanket, return to the other end and press it down. Where you're joining one roll to another, butt the ends together.*

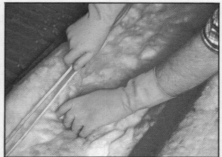

7 *The electric cables serving your lighting system are probably lying loose on the loft floor. Never cover them with insulation: lay them on top instead.*

8 *An even better solution is to attach loose cables to the side of a joist, if there's enough slack. Use cable clips to hold them in place.*

also sensible to wear a simple mask to cover your nose and mouth as the insulation material is not only unpleasant but dangerous to inhale. Loose-fill is a dusty material and you'd be wise to wear a pair of protective goggles — as well as a mask — when laying this. You can buy a mask, with replacement lint filters, and the goggles, all of which are available from most DIY stores.

You'll need a good light to work by; a fixed loft light is best, but if there isn't one, you could rig up an inspection lamp or even a table lamp. Don't, however, use a torch: you'll have enough to contend with without having to carry and aim a light. Don't use a naked flame because the risk of fire is high in the enclosed space of the loft.

Be careful where you tread. The space between the joists — the ceiling of the floor below — is only plasterboard or, in older houses, lath and plaster, and neither will support your weight. Rather than balancing on the joists — especially when you're carrying rolls or bags of insulation — it's better to have a short plank or piece of chipboard to stand on, but make sure that both ends are resting on a joist without overlapping, or it could tip up under

your weight, with disastrous consequences.

Before you start to lay the insulation you should remove any boxes or other items you have stored in the loft to give you plenty of room to manoeuvre: if there's too much to take down from the loft you can shift it up to one end of the loft, lay the insulation in the free area, then move the boxes back again and lay the other half.

Clean up the spaces between the joists using a vacuum cleaner with a nozzle attachment to enable you to reach awkward corners. If you don't have one you can use a soft-bristled broom or a hand-brush and a dust-pan, but you'll stir up a lot of dust in the process.

Use small pieces of the insulation material to block up any holes made in the ceiling for pipework to and from storage tanks.

Laying the insulation

Laying the blanket type of insulation is simplicity itself: all you do is to start at the eaves and unroll the blanket between the joists. On widely-spaced joists it'll just lie flat on the loft floor but if the joist spacing is narrow, or irregular, you can tuck it down and allow it to curve up the sides of the joists. Cut or tear

LAYING LOOSE-FILL

Right: Stop the loose-fill insulation from falling into the wall cavity at the eaves by placing a few bricks or a chipboard panel between the joists.

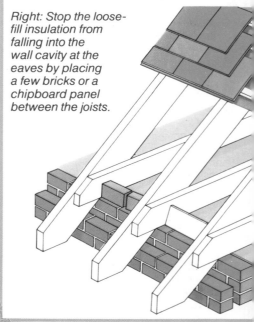

4 The blanket can either lie flat between the joists or, if the joist spacing is narrow or irregular, you can allow it to curve a little way up the sides.

5 Continue to unroll the blanket between the joists. As the loft floor won't support your weight, work from a plank or board placed across the joists.

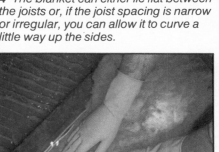

9 When you've secured the cables to the side of a joist you can lay your blanket in the usual way; if it still covers the cable, you should cut it away.

10 Where there are cross beams, lay the blanket over the top, cut it with a sharp knife and push the ends under the obstruction. Butt the ends together.

INSULATION

Left: Empty out the bags of loose-fill between the joists; stand on the footboard across the joists.
Right: Use a timber spreader to even out the insulation to the correct level.

small pieces of blanket from the roll to fit very small nooks and crannies.

Butt up new rolls and allow for extra material at beams and pipes that are set at right angles to the joists. Cut the insulation and tuck it under the obstruction, then butt up the next piece to it.

Don't insulate under the cold water tank, which will be mounted on timber bearers at right angles to the joists: heat rising through the ceiling immediately beneath the tank will help to prevent the water freezing in very cold weather. The tank itself should be insulated (see *Ready Reference*), with glass fibre blanket or expanded polystyrene sheets all round and on top, or you can use a proprietary tank lagging kit, available from DIY stores.

If your tank is mounted high above the loft floor — usually to enable you to get a sufficient head of water for a shower unit – you can insulate underneath it. The whole tank should, in this case, be lagged.

Cut a square of blanket to cover the top of the loft hatch cover and tack it in place, leaving an overlap to stop draughts getting into the loft space.

If you're laying one of the loose-fill materials you'll have to stop it from falling into the wall cavity at the eaves. Place a few bricks on edge, or a panel of chipboard, between the joists near the eaves, to contain the granules.

Empty out the bags between the joists, starting at the eaves, and use a specially shaped timber spreader (see *Ready Reference*) to spread it to the correct thickness.

The loft space will be much colder after you've insulated it, so it's particularly important that you lag any water pipes that pass through the loft (see *Ready Reference*).

Insulating pipework

If the pipes lie within your loose-fill or under your blanket insulation there's no need to lag them separately, but if they're positioned above you'll need to wrap them with pieces of blanket insulation, ready-made mineral fibre rolls, or proprietary pre-formed pipe insulation.

To prevent electric cables overheating you shouldn't cover them with insulation. Attach them to the side of a joist or, if you're using blanket material, lay them on top. If your wiring is the old rubber-insulated sort you'd be wise to replace it.

Another point to watch now that the loft will be much colder is the greater risk of condensation in the loft space. This can be a serious problem, which can rot the roof timbers and soak the insulation, making it useless.

The way to avoid this is to ensure there's sufficient ventilation in the loft space by leaving gaps at the eaves equivalent to 10mm (¾in) all the way round. Don't fill the gaps with insulation. At the same time, made sure that the gaps around pipes and the loft hatch are well sealed to keep moisture out.

INSULATING TANKS AND PIPEWORK

Worried by the thought of your next heating bill? Concerned by the prospect of your pipes freezing in winter? Proper insulation could well be the answer – and what's more it's cheap and easy to install.

Insulation is important because it reduces heat loss, and when properly applied to your water system it benefits you in a number of ways. Firstly, it saves you money by slowing down the rate at which heat is lost from the pipes and tanks of your hot water system. Secondly, by reducing the heat loss from your cold water system (and even the coldest water contains *some* heat) it tends to keep your cold water warmer in winter, thereby minimising the risk of frozen pipes. Warmer cold water in winter also means that it takes less energy to heat it up to the desired temperature when it enters your hot water tank. In this respect too insulation saves you money.

So for all the above reasons you should consider properly insulating your pipes and tanks. The cost of the materials you will need is small and the potential savings great. And if you have already insulated your loft floor then this is one job you really must attend to. It has to be done because the temperature of your loft in winter will now be only marginally higher than that of the air outside, which means that the danger of any exposed pipework freezing in cold weather is greatly increased. Ideally you should therefore insulate your pipes and tanks before you tackle the loft floor. And don't forget that the risk of frozen pipes also applies to pipes in the cellar, and anywhere else where they might be subject to extremes of cold.

Before purchasing the insulation material for your pipes and tanks, work out how much you are likely to need. Most tanks will have their capacity and/or their dimensions marked on them somewhere – if yours don't then measure them yourself. You will also need to calculate the combined length of the pipes you intend insulating and establish what their diameter is – though this last measurement is only important if you plan to use split sleeve insulation (see below). As you'll want the insulation on your tanks to overlap that which you fit to any pipes that run into them, it's best to start by insulating your pipework.

Insulating pipes

Two types of pipe insulation are commonly available. The first is made out of a glass fibre or mineral wool material similar to that used for insulating loft floors, but supplied in bandage form (75 to 100mm/3 to 4in wide and 10mm/⅜in thick) generally with a flimsy plastic backing. The second type comes in the form of split sleeves which are made from some sort of foamed material – usually plastic. Both types of pipe insulation have their advantages and disadvantages (see below) and both types are cheap. And since there is no reason why they can't be used side by side on the same pipe system, you'll almost certainly find that the easiest way to insulate your pipework is by using lengths of both.

Fitting bandage insulation

The bandage type is fitted by wrapping it around the pipe in a spiral, with each turn overlapping the previous one by at least 10mm (⅜in). It doesn't matter which way round the plastic backing goes. Make sure that the bandage is sufficiently tight to prevent air circulating between the turns, but don't pull it too tight or you will reduce its effectiveness. When starting or finishing each roll, and at regular intervals in between, hold it in place using plastic adhesive tape or string. Tape or tie the bandage, too, on vertical pipe runs and on bends as these are places where the turns are likely to separate. And don't forget to lag any stop-valves properly – only the handle should be left visible.

Apart from being rather more time consuming to install than split-sleeve insulation the main drawback with the bandage type is that it is difficult to wrap round pipes in awkward places, such as those that run under floorboards. For pipes like these you will generally find that sleeves are more suitable since once fitted they can be pushed into position.

Fitting split-sleeve insulation

Split-sleeve insulation normally comes in 1m (3ft 3in) or 2m (6ft 6in) lengths. It is available in a variety of sizes to fit piping from 15mm (½in) to 35mm (1½in) in diameter. The thickness of the insulating foam is generally around 12mm (½in). Make sure that you buy the right size sleeve for your pipes – if the sleeves don't fit snugly round your pipework they won't provide satisfactory insulation.

INSULATING PIPEWORK

1 Start by wrapping the bandage twice round the end of the pipe next to the tank. Hold the turns in place securely with string or tape.

2 Wrap the bandage round the pipe in a spiral. Make sure that each turn overlaps the previous one by at least 10mm (³/₈in). Don't pull the bandage too tight.

3 Whenever you finish a roll of bandage and start a new one allow a generous overlap to prevent air circulating between the turns of the join.

4 Finish off the pipe in the same way that you started, with an extra turn of bandage. Lastly, check the pipe to make sure all the insulation is secure.

5 Fitting split-sleeve insulation is simple. You simply prise apart the split and slip the sleeve over the pipe. Use tape to keep the sleeve in place.

6 At bends, where the sleeve tends to come apart, tape the split lengthways. Tape the sleeves, too, whenever you join one to another.

7 At tees, first cut a 'notch' from the main pipe sleeve. Then shape the end of the branch pipe sleeve to fit and slot it into place. Tape the join.

8 Use split sleeve insulation on pipes that would be hard – or impossible – to fit with bandage. Slip the sleeve over the pipe and slide it into position.

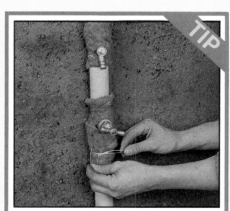

TIP

9 Sleeve and bandage insulation can – and sometimes must – be used together. A stop-valve, for example, can only be properly lagged with bandage.

INSULATING COLD TANKS

1 *Proprietary jackets will fit most cold water tanks. Start by flopping the jacket over the tank and pulling it roughly into position.*

2 *Rather than cut into the jacket's 'envelopes', try to accommodate a pipe by parting the seam between them. All cuts must be sealed with tape.*

3 *When installing blanket insulation start with the side of the tank. If you're using glass fibre blanket wear gloves and a face mask.*

5 *The tank must have a firm lid to prevent the water inside being polluted. Don't tie the lagging to the lid in such a way that it is impossible to undo.*

6 *Expansion tanks need insulating too. If using sheet polystyrene, remember to cut the panels so that they overlap when fitted to the tank.*

7 *Use tape, string, or glue to hold the side panels together. Fill the gaps left as a result of making cut-outs with wedges of waste polystyrene.*

Both flexible and rigid sleeves are available, but as the rigid type isn't much use for pipework that bends frequently, you'd probably be better off using the flexible variety.

Fitting the sleeves is very straightforward. You simply prise apart the slit that runs along the length of the sleeve and slip the insulation over the pipe. It's advisable to tape the sleeve at intervals, and you must do so at joins. At bends, where the sleeves will tend to come apart, you should tape the split lengthways.

Once sleeve insulation has been fitted, it can easily be slid along a length of pipe to protect a part of it that may be hard to get at. However, you should bear in mind that it won't be able to get beyond any pipe clips, very sharp bends or bulky joints it may encounter. You'll find that most flexible sleeves will readily slide round curves and even 90° bends made using soldered fittings, but whenever you run up against problems in the form of bulky compression elbows or

tee connectors the sleeves will have to be cut accordingly. However, in some circumstances you might well find that bandage insulation provides the better solution.

To fit round a 90° elbow the sleeve should be cut in two and the sleeve ends then cut at an angle of 45° before being slipped over the pipe. You should then tape over the resulting join. For the most convenient method of dealing with a tee fitting see the step-by-step photographs.

Insulating cold water storage tanks

When it comes to insulating your cold water storage tank and central heating expansion tank (if you have one), there are a number of options open to you. If your tank is circular you could cover it with a proprietary jacket consisting of a number of polythene or plastic 'envelopes' filled with insulant; or you could simply wrap it up in a layer of mineral wool or glass fibre blanket similar to – or even the

same as – that which is used to insulate loft floors. If, on the other hand, your cold water tank happens to be rectangular then you could construct a 'box' for it yourself out of expanded polystyrene, or buy a proprietary one ready-made.

A proprietary jacket couldn't be easier to fit: you simply pull it into position and then tie it in place – tapes are sometimes provided by the manufacturer. If you have to cut into the jacket to accommodate a pipe, make sure that you seal it up again with plastic adhesive tape to prevent moisture getting in and the insulating material from escaping.

Expanded polystyrene kits are also extremely easy to fit. Apart from having to fix the pieces of polystyrene together with tape, string or polystyrene cement, the only work you will have to do is to make cut-outs for the pipework. More work will be required should you decide to make your tank kit out of sheet polystyrene (see step-by-step photographs)

4 If the blanket isn't as wide as the tank is deep, a second layer, which should overlap the first, will be necessary. Use string to hold the blanket in place.

8 Make a lid for your tank by gluing together two panels of polystyrene. The smaller (inner) panel should just fit inside the tank.

HOT TANKS

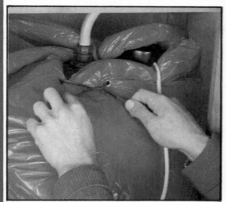

1 When using a proprietary jacket to insulate a hot water cylinder, start by securing the polythene 'envelopes' round the hot water supply pipe.

2 The sides of the jacket are held in place with straps. Take care not to cover the capping and wiring of any immersion heater.

SLEEVING SIZES

To be effective, split-sleeve insulation must be the right size for your pipes. If they are modern – which usually means copper – most of your pipes will be 15mm (½in), though the main distribution ones are likely to be 22mm (¾in). Check any pipes that you aren't sure of.

TIP: PROBLEM PIPES

There are two areas where you must take extra care:
● when insulating a pipe that runs close to a wall – especially an outside wall – make sure that you protect the *whole* surface. To insulate only the more accessible side of the pipe would be worse than useless: the pipe would still be exposed to the cold wall but denied the heat of your house
● if the expansion pipe of the cold water tank you are insulating stops short of the lid then you'll have to devise some means of catching any outflow. The easiest way to do this is to use a plastic funnel. Bore a hole to accommodate the funnel through the lid and the insulation material, and fix it in place with plastic adhesive tape.

TIP: GOING AWAY

Insulation alone may not be sufficient to protect your pipes and tanks from the cold if you leave your house unoccupied for more than a few days in winter. So in your absence make sure that the heating is switched on briefly each day. If you can't trust your thermostat, ask a neighbour.

– but it would of course be a lot cheaper.

If you decide to use insulation blanket to lag your tank then try to buy the sort that is bonded with paper as you will find it much easier to handle. Buy a roll that is as wide as your tank is deep if you can, as this will save you the trouble of having to go round the side of your tank twice. The thickness of the blanket isn't critical, but blanket 50mm (2in) thick will give your tank adequate insulation and be easier to work with than a thicker one. However, it could well be that you have an odd roll or two of blanket left over from some previous insulation job; if you do, then use that rather than going to the expense of buying additional rolls.

The top of the tank to be insulated must have a firm covering to prevent the water inside being contaminated by fibres from the blanket you are fitting. So if it doesn't already have a lid, cut one out of hardboard, polystyrene or some other sheet material.

Lagging a tank with blanket insulation is simply a matter of common sense. You cut the blanket to size, drape it round the side of the tank, and having cut slits to enable the blanket to fit round the pipes, secure it with string. The lagging on the lid should overlap the side lagging by about 150mm (6in); and as you'll need to inspect the inside of your tank from time to time make sure it's easily removable.

Under normal circumstances the bottom of your tank should not be insulated, nor should the loft floor directly below. The reason for this is that it allows heat from the house to rise up through the floor and slightly increase the temperature of your cold water. The only circumstance in which you do insulate these places (and this applies regardless of what form of insulation you are using) is when, in order to increase the water pressure for a shower on the floor below, the tank has been raised more than a foot or so above the joists.

Insulating hot water tanks

Although you could in theory lag your hot water tank by adapting any of the methods that are used for cold water tanks, in practice you will nearly always find that you have no choice but to use a proprietary jacket. The fact that most hot water tanks are situated in airing cupboards means that blanket insulation is out of the question, and unless your tank is a rectangular one (which these days are very rare) you won't be able to use polystyrene.

Proprietary jackets for hot water tanks are made of the same materials as those used on cold water tanks and are just as easy to fit. The system used to fasten the jacket to the tank varies, but basically at the top you secure the 'envelopes' round the hot water supply pipe with a loop of cord, while further down you hold them in place with straps. The base of the tank is left uninsulated, as is the capping and wiring of any immersion heater.

FITTING DOUBLE GLAZING

Secondary double glazing – the fitting of fixed, hinged or sliding panes to the inside of existing windows – cuts heat loss and draughts dramatically. If you install it yourself, it need not be prohibitively expensive either.

There are two basic types of double glazing available to the homeowner. Primary double glazing involves the fitting of a sealed glazing unit – two linked panes of glass separated only by a hermetically sealed gap – into an existing or replacement window frame. These sealed units are factory-made, but can be installed by the do-it-yourselfer (see pages 400-403).

Secondary double glazing is the term used to describe the installation of a completely independent second layer of glass (or other glazing material) some distance away from the existing single glazing, either to the inside of the window frame or to the window reveal surrounding it.

The fitting of this form of double glazing is well within the scope of the do-it-yourselfer and offers some advantages over primary double glazing. It is cheaper and quicker to install, since instead of having to order sealed units from a specialist manufacturing company you need only visit your local DIY shop and collect the necessary kit of component parts.

Sealed units have no draughtproofing abilities when installed in old badly-fitting opening windows, whereas secondary double glazing seals the entire frame, acting as both a thermal barrier and draught-proofer.

It is worth noting, however, that primary double glazing is more effective as a thermal barrier and is also less obtrusive, being no more visible than a single pane of glass.

Types of secondary double glazing

An extremely wide variety of secondary double glazing systems exist to cater for virtually all situations (and pockets). Glass is by no means the only material used for glazing. Other products used are clear polythene film in varying degrees of strength and clarity, or other transparent rigid plastics.

Methods of framing the glazing also vary enormously, with just double-sided adhesive tape being used for some systems and rigid or flexible PVC or aluminium extrusions for others.

Yet more choice comes with installation methods, where there are fixed, hinged or sliding systems (vertical or horizontal).

Which type to choose

When deciding on a secondary double glazing system, several factors should be considered carefully. Cost naturally plays an important part. If you live in rented accommodation and don't expect to stay for long, or simply want the cheapest form of double glazing for financial reasons, then the chances are that you will find clear polythene sheeting will serve your purposes. Attached to the existing window frame with double-sided adhesive tape, the polythene will prevent draughts very successfully, but in its most basic form it is not totally clear, is easily damaged, and seldom looks very tidy.

This type of double glazing, although inexpensive and effective, does have one major disadvantage; once fixed, it is there for good – or at least until completely removed and discarded at the end of the winter.

Double glazing of this nature is classed as fixed, but there is another 'fixed' variety which is less permanent and which can be temporarily removed and later replaced successfully. This type generally consists of a sheet of glass or rigid plastic sheet fitted into either a plastic or aluminium frame and then secured to the existing window frame

using turnbuttons or shaped studs which hold it firmly in place.

One drawback with fixed systems is that they do not allow for ventilation, and this can be very important. In situations where ventilation is necessary or you simply want easily openable windows, you will have to decide whether to purchase a double glazing system which incorporates sliding panels or hinged ones. And one factor which could help you make this choice is the sort of existing window you have.

Sliding double glazing systems need to have their outer tracks or channels secured to the sides, top and bottom of the window reveal. If your window has no reveal, or this is less than about 40mm (1½in) deep, then you will be unable to fit a sliding system unless you choose a type that is attached to the window frame itself.

Hinged systems are fixed to the existing window's surrounding wooden frame. In some cases, notably on metal windows, catches and stays project into the room past the frame and could prevent a hinged panel closing. The space between old and new panes can, however, be increased to allow for such projections by fitting an additional

FITTING SLIDING TRACK

1 Measure the height and width of the opening at each side, and write down the smaller measurement in each case if the figures differ.

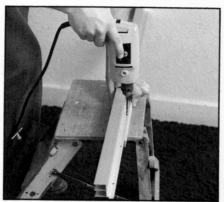

2 Mark the length required on each of the track sections, cut them with a hacksaw, and file the ends smooth. Then drill holes for the fixing screws.

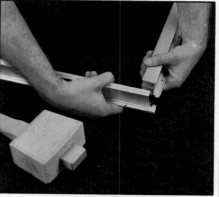

3 Assemble the track sections on a flat surface. Insert the corner pieces and use a mallet to tap the sections together gently but firmly.

4 Lift the assembled frame into place against the window frame, offering up the top track first. Then secure it with just one screw at top and bottom.

5 Check that the frame is square by measuring diagonals, and that the top and bottom tracks are level. Add more screws to secure the frame.

6 Where screws have to be driven into inaccessible corners, use a short piece of clear plastic tubing to hold the screw on the blade as you drive it.

timber framework to the face of the existing one, or within the reveal itself.

The width of the frame, whether old or newly-installed, must be sufficient to accommodate the hinge posts and panel surround of the hinged system you have chosen. It is therefore essential, before buying the materials for a hinged system, to check the minimum window frame dimensions recommended by the makers of that system. It is not uncommon for wooden window frames, particularly those around metal windows, to be too narrow for face fixing. Here again the problem can be overcome by fitting a new frame of sufficient width inside the reveal.

An additional inner frame can also be used to increase the gap between panes, as would be necessary if the double glazing were being installed for sound insulation. Where the aim is to reduce noise penetration the ideal gap between panes should be about 200mm (8in). A gap of around 25mm (1in) is the optimum for good thermal insulation when installing secondary double glazing.

Preparing for installation

Once you have chosen the basic variety of double glazing which suits your home and taste, you must study the manufacturers' literature with great care. This will tell you what thickness of glass should be used, the most common being 4mm (32oz). It will also detail existing frame size requirements, and indicate the maximum size that any one glazing panel should be. Information will also be provided, particularly with hinged or sliding systems, on how to measure the required sizes for each pane of glass so that this can be ordered in advance.

Some preparatory work may well be needed on the existing window frames. An additional sub-frame may have to be fitted,

if, as described earlier, the present frame is not wide enough or has window fittings projecting past it. Use prepared timber painted to match the existing frame. Either secure it directly to the old frame with screws, or fix it to the window reveal with screws driven into wallplugs.

Clean and make good any defects on the old frame. Use draught excluders on badly-fitting opening windows to prevent as much air as possible from outside entering the space between the two glazing panes. It is the movement of air in the cavity that transfers warm air from the inner pane to the outer, and cold air from the outside pane to the inside one. Although the secondary double glazing will stop the draughts, it will be no more use than a single pane of glass at preventing heat loss if there is a howling gale blowing between the panes.

Plan your double glazing so that new

MAKING UP SLIDING PANELS

1 Follow the instructions for measuring and ordering the glass. Then mark each length of edge section to the correct dimension.

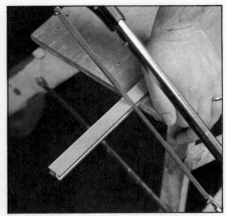

2 Carefully cut each edge section to length with a hacksaw, making the cut as square as possible and filing away any burr that's left.

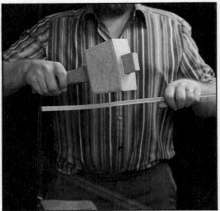

3 Measure and cut the lengths of glazing gasket using a fine-toothed saw. Then tap them into place along the appropriate edges of the glass with a mallet.

4 Tap the top and bottom edge sections into place over the gaskets, add the handle to one of the side sections and then tap the side sections into place.

5 With the pane completely framed by the four edge sections and their gaskets, drive in small self-tapping screws to lock the corner blocks in position.

6 Move the handle along the groove in the side section to the desired position and then use a screwdriver blade to form a notch in the aluminium.

7 Now use a mallet to tap the handle along the groove and over the burr formed by the screwdriver to lock it in place. Repeat on the other panel.

8 Tap the small PTFE slides into the recesses in the two bottom corner blocks of each panel. These help the panels to slide smoothly in the tracks.

9 Offer up first the inner and then the outer sliding panels to their respective tracks, and check that they slide from side to side without binding.

panels match as closely as possible the layout of your existing windows, with vertical divisions kept in line with mullions and opening sections (whether hinged or sliding) aligned with opening windows.

Measure your window opening carefully before ordering any glass. Problems can arise, particularly with sliding systems, if the window opening or frame is not square. If the two diagonal measurements of the opening are not equal, then the opening is definitely out of true, so for all calculations use the shortest width and height measurements.

Fitting the systems

1: Clear plastic film. To fit this very basic form of fixed double glazing you will need a roll of the special film, some double-sided adhesive tape, a tape measure, a sharp knife and a hair drier to remove creases from the film.

Stick the tape, without removing the backing paper, to the face of the outer window frame all around the perimeter. Measure the size of the opening and cut a piece of the plastic over-size. Remove the backing paper from the top piece of tape and attach the edge of the plastic film to it. Hold the film clear of the window while you remove the rest of the backing paper from the other lengths of tape and stick the film to it. Pull it taut, then play a hair drier over it to remove the creases and trim it to size all round.

Strong, less creasable polythene, classed as semi-rigid, can be fixed in a different way by cutting it to the exact size first, then attaching the sticky tape to it rather than the window frame. With the backing paper removed from the top edge only, the sheet is aligned to the head of the window frame, then stuck in place, followed by the other three edges.

2: Non-opening removable panels The most recent version of this form of double glazing uses a PVC extrusion stuck to the window frame, with a second extrusion holding the plastic sheeting in place. The work required involves cutting the PVC extrusion to size and fitting it around the existing frame. Either butt or mitred joints can be made at the corners. The plastic sheeting is then cut to size to fit in the profile. The clip-on extrusion is finally cut to size and snapped into place.

Other variations of this non-opening type of double glazing usually consist of plastic 'U' channelling fitted around pre-cut panes of glass. The glass, now with protected edges, is secured to the window frame with turnbuttons or clips spaced every 300mm (12in) around the perimeter to press the panel firmly against the frame and so exclude draughts. The glass for this type must be cut to size, allowing for the space taken up by the fixing clips on the frame. The panels can be removed and stored elsewhere at the end of the winter season.

Rather stronger non-opening panels can be made using aluminium framing instead of plastic 'U' channel, but these are generally a fixed version of hinged panels described next.

3: Hinged panels The most common hinged secondary double glazing systems are constructed using glass with an aluminium extrusion frame. The frame incorporates one channel with a plastic glazing gasket for the glass, a draught-proofing insert of either plastic or nylon fibre bristles which press against the window frame, and a second channel into which hinge fittings, turn-buttons and corner joins are fitted. Glass of the specified thickness is cut to size. Some makes can be fitted with more than one thickness of glass, this being determined by the overall panel size. A different size of glazing gasket is used for each thickness.

Once the glass is cut, the glazing gasket can be fitted to it, and the aluminium extrusions cut to length using a hacksaw. Straight cuts are made since the special corner joins eliminate the need for mitred corners.

The panel is then assembled, special care being needed to ensure that the glazing gasket is correctly seated in its channel and that all hinge fittings are properly inserted in the outer edge of the aluminium frame.

Hinge posts are then screwed to the window frame and the panel is lifted into place. Turnbuttons are finally fixed round the other three edges of the hinged panel to ensure that the panel is held tightly against the window frame when closed.

4: Sliding panels Made from either aluminium or PVC extrusions, sliding double glazing units are generally quick and easy to assemble and fit. Normally sold in two-part kit form with everything but the glass provided, the biggest problem is often deciding which part belongs where, so the first step is to identify the different sections. One part of the kit will contain all the vertical sections – the frame uprights and glass edging – and the other, the horizontal sections – the top and bottom sliding tracks and more glass edging.

The outer frame is fitted to the window reveal. This will usually involve drilling holes into the reveal sides, top and bottom and plugging the holes to take screws. Great care must be taken to ensure that the top double channel (the deeper one) is fitted directly above and in line with the bottom channel.

With the frame secured, the panes of glass can be fitted with their edge profiles, and the panels are then lifted into position in the sliding channels.

Provided that you have measured the glass correctly according to the instructions given by the double glazing manufacturer, you should find that the panels slide easily and that all nylon fibre draught excluders built into the system align perfectly.

window frame

aluminium sub-frame

beading

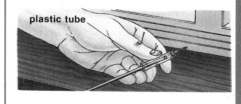

plastic tube

FITTING SEALED GLAZING UNITS

Fitting sealed double glazing units will provide good heat and sound insulation as well as reducing draughts. They are easy to install in either existing or replacement window frames.

It is well known that double glazing offers considerable benefits for the homeowner. It can considerably reduce draughts from around the window area, not only those which enter through badly fitting frames but also down-draughts caused by warm air close to a cold, single pane of glass being quickly cooled and so falling. Eliminating these down-draughts makes for a more comfortable environment and prevents that 'chilly' feeling even though the room is heated. Some forms of double glazing can, to some extent, also reduce the penetration of noise from outside the building, but the major advantage is that the use of two panes instead of one can help reduce heat losses through glazed areas, providing a potential for saving energy and, hence, cutting fuel costs.

By far the most efficient method of achieving such thermal insulation is by the fitting of sealed double glazing units in place of single panes of glass in the window frame. This is known as primary double glazing.

Each sealed unit comprises two sheets of glass separated by a metal, glass or rigid plastic spacer which is fitted around the edges. The air between the two panes is dehydrated so that it contains no moisture, and the entire unit is sealed hermetically so that none can enter. As long as the seal remains unbroken condensation cannot form between the two sheets of glass.

The space between the panes normally varies between 6 and 12mm (¼ and ½in), the wider gap providing the best thermal insulation properties. The glass itself will vary in thickness from 3mm (⅛in) upwards depending on the size of the pane and the position of the window, many different types being available including float, laminated, toughened, standard sheet, tinted and obscured.

All sealed double glazing units are factory made by specialist companies and cannot be assembled at home. However, they can be fitted by the non-professional glazier in much the same way as normal replacement panes of glass either to existing window frames or into completely new replacement windows.

Local glass merchants are becoming increasingly involved in the supply of sealed double glazing units in a wide range of standard sizes or in made-to-measure form to suit individual requirements, and it is now common practice for complete replacement windows, made from wood, aluminium or UPVC, to be supplied with sealed glazing units fitted as standard.

Fitting to existing frames

There are several factors you should consider in deciding whether or not to replace single panes of glass with sealed double glazing units.

Your existing window frames must be in excellent condition as there is little point in fitting sealed units into frames which may themselves have to be replaced within a few years. If the frames are more than 30 years old they are not likely to be of a standard size and so they would need specially-made sealed units. These would not be reusable in a new standard replacement frame and so this would have to be made specially, too.

Standard size sealed units are, in effect, mass-produced and so are cheaper than specially made ones. They are obtainable virtually 'off the shelf' from many suppliers, particularly for use in wooden-frame windows.

The rebate in the existing frames must be deep enough to accommodate the thickness of the sealed units and still allow them to be puttied in place or fixed with a glazing bead. You are likely to be changing from a single glazing thickness of 3 or 4mm (about ⅛in) to at least 12mm (½in), rising to 18mm (¾in) if you want units with a 12mm gap. For the latter, therefore, you would need a rebate measuring some 30mm (1¼in) from front to back, and not all old frames have this.

It is possible, however, to overcome the problem of too narrow a glazing rebate by using what are known as 'stepped' sealed units. These have one sheet of glass smaller than the other, the larger pane being fitted exactly in the same position as the original single pane with the smaller one on the inside, overlapping the back of the glazing rebate. Such stepped units are readily available to fit standard modern window sizes, or they can be made specially. They can be used in wooden frames but not in steel, which are generally unsuitable for sealed unit double glazing.

The same can be said of any windows incorporating a large number of small panes, such as Georgian styles. The cost of replacing all the individual panes with sealed units

PREPARING THE FRAME

1 *Chop out all the old putty with a glazier's hacking knife or an old chisel. Take care not to damage the wooden window frame.*

2 *The glass will be held in place by small sprigs driven into the glazing rebate. Remove them with pincers or pliers. If straight they can be reused.*

3 *Have a helper tap around the edge of the window inside to free it. Wear gloves, or use a towel, to hold the glass and to avoid cuts.*

4 *With the old glass removed, chop away all remaining traces of putty from the rebate, being careful not to damage it in the process.*

5 *Brush all the dust and debris from the rebate and then prime any areas of exposed wood, allowing the primer to dry thoroughly.*

6 *When the primer has dried, apply a layer of bedding putty to the glazing rebate, working it well into the angle with your thumb.*

would be extremely high, even if the glazing bars were of a suitable size. However, if you wish to keep this appearance, complete sealed units are available that reproduce the Georgian or leaded-light look quite effectively.

If you are quite satisfied that sealed units can be fitted to your existing frames, the first step is to measure the rebate so you can order the correct size. Take great care to get the correct dimensions because, once made, the size of the sealed unit cannot be altered. With standard sizes this is not so much of a problem, but if you are having the units specially made it could prove to be an expensive mistake if you get it wrong. The height and width of the rebate should each be measured in at least two places. If there is a difference between any of the measurements, work with the smaller size. Deduct a further 3mm (⅛in) from both the selected height and width to allow for clearance

around the unit, and this will be the size you should order.

Once you have the new sealed units, remove the putty from the window frame using an old chisel or similar tool and taking care not to damage the wood. Pull out the glazing sprigs with a pair of pincers and carefully lever the glass from the frame. Wear thick gloves or wrap a towel round the edge of the pane to prevent cuts as you lift it clear. If the glass is stuck fast to the old bedding putty, you may find that it can be tapped out from inside by a helper. Only gentle taps should be used to avoid breaking the glass accidentally. If all else fails, break the glass from the inside with a hammer (making sure there is no-one outside who might be injured by the flying fragments) and pull out any remaining glass with a gloved hand or pair of pliers. Clean out the remains of the putty and brush any dust or dirt from

the rebate. Reprime any areas of exposed wood and allow the primer to dry before fitting the new unit.

Line the rebate with a bedding layer of fresh putty, inserting rubber spacing blocks at intervals along the bottom and at each side. These should be cut to a thickness that will centralise and square the double glazing unit in the frame.

Offer up the new unit bottom edge first and gently press it into place with the palms of your hands so that the bedding putty oozes out round the inside edges of the sealed unit. Apply pressure only to the edges of the unit to prevent the glass breaking where it is unsupported in the middle. Check inside that there is about 3mm (⅛in) of putty between the inner face of the glazing unit and the rebate.

Next, very carefully tap in the glazing sprigs, using a cross-pein hammer. Use at least two sprigs per side and slide the head of the hammer across the glass to avoid breaking it. Drive each sprig in squarely so that it does not pinch the glass until only 6mm (¼in) remains visible. If you can't obtain proper glazing sprigs, you can use 19mm (¾in) panel pins with their heads nipped off.

Apply a finishing fillet of putty all round the rebate, pressing it into place with your thumb so that it covers all the edges of the glass. Smooth this off to an angle with a putty knife, making sure it does not project above the level of the rebate otherwise it will be visible from inside the room. Mitre the corners carefully and clean off any excess putty from both inner and outer panes of the unit. Leave the putty to harden for two weeks before applying a coat of primer and finally a finishing coat of paint. The latter should overlap onto the glass by 3mm (⅛in) to ensure a watertight seal.

If stepped double glazing units are to be fitted, a rebate for the stepped portion of the unit can be made by pinning lengths of beading around the inside of the window frame. Extra putty will be needed around this stepped rebate to provide a bed and surround for the inner pane of glass.

New wooden window frames
The increasing use of sealed double glazing units has led to most manufacturers supplying new wooden frames with glazing rebates of sufficient depth to take standard sealed units up to a maximum thickness of about 20mm (⅞in). By choosing your supplier carefully you will be able to order both frames and glazed units at the same time. You won't need to measure for the glass if the frame is one of the many standard sizes available.

If you need to have frames made, you should make it clear to the supplier that you will be fitting sealed double glazing units. He will then make allowance for this when making up the frames.

Normally, the glass is fitted using wooden glazing beads to hold it in place and putty or a similar glazing mastic to provide a seal between the unit and the frame. Acrylic putty is coming into use now and is ideal for double glazing units.

Aluminium and UPVC replacement windows
Although they are still available, it would be difficult to find either aluminium or UPVC replacement windows which are intended for use with single pane glazing. Invariably, such windows are designed to be fitted with sealed units having a 6 or 12mm (¼ or ½in) gap. It is common for companies specialising in these windows to operate a supply-and-fit service. However, most will also work on a

FITTING THE UNIT

1 Rubber spacing blocks should be set into the putty to centralise the unit in the frame. These can be cut from an ordinary hard pencil eraser.

2 Offer up the sealed double glazing unit, positioning the bottom edge first by setting it on the rubber blocks. Then push the unit into place.

5 Apply a fillet of putty to cover the sprigs and edge of the glazing unit, trimming it off with a putty knife. Remove excess putty from the glass.

6 Carefully mitre the putty at the corners of the glazing rebate with the putty knife. Alternatively, a straight-bladed filling knife could be used.

supply-only basis. This means that they will provide you with all the component parts ready for you to install yourself.

When doing your own fitting, the only measurements you need to give the supplier are the height and width of the opening into which the window is to be fitted. If the existing outer wood frame is in excellent condition, particularly at the bottom of the jambs and along the sill, you can normally fit the new window in exactly the same place as the old one, with no trouble at all.

If the outer frame is in poor condition and a new one is required, then the window supplier will be able to provide this as well. In this case, the only dimensions he needs are those of the opening in the wall. From these he will be able to calculate all the other sizes. You will, of course, need to specify the style of window, the type of glass, whether or not the glass has to be leaded or fitted with a grille to

simulate a Georgian style window, or be made non-standard in any other way.

The sealed double glazing units fitted in replacement aluminium or UPVC windows are the same as those used in wooden framed windows but the installation method is somewhat different. The glazing unit is always fitted 'dry', rubber or PVC gaskets being used to provide a seal to the frame. No mastics or sealants are required at the glazing stage. There are two basic glazing methods in common use. One of them involves making up the frame around the glazing unit. Each frame section, complete with gaskets on either side, is pushed over the sealed unit and then the four corners are screwed together tightly to hold it in place.

The other method is to make up the frame, which has an integral glazing rebate, insert the glazed unit and secure it in place with a 'snap-in' glazing bead. Provided that the

3 Once the unit is in place in the rebate, use firm hand pressure around the edges to bed it properly in the putty. Don't apply pressure to the centre.

4 If the old glazing sprigs are in good condition, re-use them; use new ones otherwise. Slide the hammer across the glass to prevent breakage.

7 Trim the putty which oozes out of the back of the rebate (when the glazing unit is pressed in place) flush with the edge of the frame.

8 Allow the putty to dry for 14 days before applying the first undercoat of paint. The final top coat should lap onto the glass by 3mm (¹/₈in).

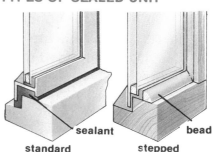

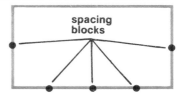
glazing bead is on the inside (which is becoming standard practice) the sealed unit can be replaced easily if damaged, and the glazing is secure. No potential intruder can prise off the bead and remove the glass from the outside. Gaskets are incorporated in the glazing rebate and glazing bead to ensure a watertight and airtight seal.

Condensation and safety

Obviously, the fitting of sealed double glazing units to old window frames can only be of value if those old frames are in good condition and are not so badly fitting that they let in draughts. This should be checked very carefully beforehand and, if necessary, the frames should be replaced.

Condensation will never appear in the space between the two panes of glass as long as the hermetic seal remains undamaged. Consequently, care should be taken during installation to ensure that the seal is not broken accidentally. Sealed units, may, however, develop condensation on the room side of the inner pane, although this is likely to be far less troublesome than on single glazed windows. The units should never be considered as a complete cure for a condensation problem. Their value lies in their thermal insulation properties and the elimination of down-draughts.

When ordering sealed double glazing units seek the advice of your local glass merchant. He will be able to tell you what thickness of glass should be used and, even more important, the type of glass. New regulations concerning glass for use in particular situations, such as in windows at low level and in doors, have come into force. They are intended to ensure your safety and so should be followed carefully, hence the need for expert guidance.

REGLAZING A WINDOW

Windows may be a vital barrier against the elements but they're also quite fragile and can be broken easily. When this happens the glass has to be replaced. It's not a complicated job and few specialist tools are required – it does, however, need a degree of care.

Windows may be all shapes and sizes but basically all have a main frame containing one or more fixed or opening frames. The glass is held in a rebate – a narrow 'shelf' – on the outer face of the window, and is kept in place with either angular metal nails called sprigs (on wooden frames) or wire clips (on metal frames). These are then covered with putty, a pliable material which hardens when exposed to the air and provides a water-proof bedding for the glass (see *Ready Reference*).

The technique for reglazing a window depends mainly on what the window frame is made from – and wooden ones are by far the most common.

Removing the glass

Obviously, this has to be done carefully. If necessary, tap the old pane with a hammer until it is sufficiently broken to let you pull out most of the pieces by hand – you should wear thick gloves for protection. Any tiny fragments embedded in the putty can be tugged out with pincers, but don't worry if they refuse to budge. They can wait until the putty is removed.

Preparing the frame

The professional glazier uses a tool called a hacking knife to chop out the old putty. It's an inexpensive tool to buy. If you have an old chisel, you could use this in conjunction with a mallet. If the putty is very old it can be quite stubborn, so take care not to damage the window frame. On multi-paned windows, you should also avoid using so much force that surrounding panes crack.

As soon as the rebate is clear, brush it out. Rub it down with medium grade glasspaper until it is clean and smooth, then give it a coat of ordinary wood primer – not paint because this will prevent the putty drying.

Jem Grischotti

PREPARING A WOODEN FRAME

1 Tap out most of the broken glass with a hammer, then remove the remaining splinters by hand – but wear thick gloves for protection.

2 Chop out the old putty from the rebate using a hacking knife. Tap it with a hammer if necessary. Be careful not to damage the window frame.

3 Pull out the old glazing sprigs with a pair of pincers. If the sprigs aren't damaged you can re-use when fitting the new pane of glass.

Jem Grischotti

Buying new glass

It's important to choose the right type of glass, but don't try to cut it to size yourself. Your local glazier will do a much better job, and is less likely to break the pane in the process. There's also no financial advantage to doing the job yourself for you'll be left with unusable off-cuts. And don't think you can use up that odd piece of glass you may have lying about. Old glass does not cut well at all, and tends to break in the wrong place even when you've scored it with a carbide-tipped glasscutter.

So measure the width and height of the rebate into which the glass must fit; double check the measurements to be sure, and order the glass to be cut 3mm (⅛in) smaller on each dimension. This allows for any slight inaccuracy in your measurements, and avoids the risk of the glass cracking due to expansion or contraction of the frame. If you need patterned glass, make a note of which way the pattern runs.

The fixing process

First you must line the rebate with putty. You can either take a ball of putty in the palm of your hand and squeeze it out between thumb and forefinger using your thumb to press it in; or you can roll the putty into finger-thick sausages and press these into place. Wet your hands before handling putty to prevent it sticking to your fingers, and knead it until it is pliable and any surface oils are thoroughly mixed in.

Next, press the pane into the puttied rebate with the palms of your hands, so that putty oozes out, around and behind the glass. Apply pressure around the edges rather than in the centre of the pane and check that, when you've finished, the glass is separated from the frame on the inside by a bed of putty which is 2mm to 3mm (up to ⅛in) thick.

Now for the unnerving part – nailing the glass in place. It's best to use glazing sprigs,

but you could make do with 19mm (¾in) panel pins that have had their heads nipped off with pliers. You'll need at least two per side, spaced no more than 230mm (9in) apart, and you must be sure to drive them squarely into the wood so they don't pinch and crack the glass. When you've finished, just over 6mm (¼in) of pin should be showing.

The final stage is to fill the rest of the rebate with a triangular fillet of putty that neatly covers the pins. Apply the putty in the same way as when lining the rebate, and use a putty knife or an ordinary filling knife to do the shaping, mitring the corners of the fillet as neatly as possible. Wet the knife blade to prevent the putty sticking to it as you draw it over the fillet.

Clean off the excess putty – including any that oozed out inside the pane earlier – and allow to dry hard before painting.

When you need to reglaze a window that isn't at ground level, you'll have to work from a ladder. Obviously you'll have to be organised when working at a height. Tap out most of the glass first from inside – and make sure there's no one standing below as you do so. Put all the tools and equipment in a bucket which you can hang on a hook attached to the ladder at the top. Don't try to carry the glass – it's best to get someone to pass it through the window.

Modern windows

Conventional steel-framed windows are reglazed in almost the same way as wooden ones, except that the glass is fixed with wire clips fitting into holes in the frame, rather than with glazing sprigs. Remove these and re-use them to fix the new pane – along with the right type of putty – after priming with a metal primer.

Because putty needs paint to protect it, and because modern aluminium and plastic windows aren't meant to be painted, a different method is used to hold the glass. Normally, it's a variation on the rubber gasket system used to keep the windows fixed in a car.

Just how easy these windows are to reglaze depends on the design; different manufacturers have their own systems and unless it is obvious how the glass fits in, all you can do is ask the window manufacturer for his advice. In some cases, he will prefer to do the repair himself.

Replacing double glazing

There are few problems where secondary double glazing is involved. This system uses a completely separate window frame to hold the extra pane of glass. All you do is treat each element of the system as a single glazed window. One complication you may come up against is where a do-it-yourself

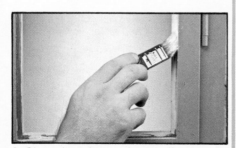

4 *Clean the rebate using medium-grade glasspaper, then remove any dust and prime the rebate with a narrow paintbrush.*

PUTTING IN NEW GLASS

1 When the primer is dry line the rebate with putty. Hold the putty in the palm of your hand and squeeze it out between your forefinger and thumb.

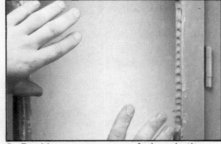

2 Position a new pane of glass in the rebate. Press it in place gently from the sides to avoid pressure on the centre, which could shatter the glass.

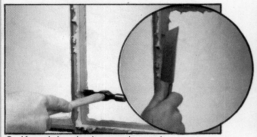

3 Knock in glazing sprigs using a cross-pein hammer or (inset) the back of a hacking knife. Slide the tool across the surface of the glass.

4 When all the glazing sprigs have been inserted, apply putty to the rebate to cover the edges of the glass. Press it into the angle with your thumb.

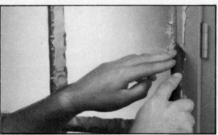

5 Shape the putty fillet into a slope using the straight edge of a putty knife. The slope shouldn't extend beyond the rebate line on the inside of the frame.

6 When you've shaped the putty into a slope, mitre each corner with the square edge of a filling knife, laying the blade on lightly to smooth out any ridges.

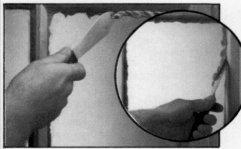

7 Trim off any surplus putty – from the surface of the glass and (inset) from the inside face of the pane – by running the putty knife along the rebate.

8 Leave the putty to dry for about a fortnight, then prime, undercoat and top coat. Allow the paint to extend 2 or 3mm (1/8in) onto the glass surface.

double glazing kit has been used. In this case the extra 'frame' may be no more than plastic channelling clipped over the edge of the glass, so it's more a case of remaking this frame than reglazing it.

Replacing double glazing where both panes are mounted in the same frame is more involved, and how you approach it depends on whether factory-made sealed units or two ordinary panes of glass have been used.

In the latter case, you merely fix two new panes in the same way as if reglazing an ordinary window. Just be sure you don't get marks on the panes facing into the double glazing's air gap – you can't clean them off once the second pane is in place.

Factory-made sealed units are also sometimes fitted like a single pane of glass but, more often, you'll have a modern gasket system to contend with. In any case, the most important thing is to order the new sealed units to exactly the right size. They cannot be trimmed if you make a mistake.

Dealing with leaded lights

Strictly speaking, to reglaze a leaded light, you must remove the putty and glazing sprigs from the main window frame and lift out the entire glass and lead latticework, so it can be worked on flat. You may, however, get away with working in situ if you get a helper to hold a sheet of hardboard or something similar against the other side of the pane, to keep it flat while you carry out the repair.

Whichever approach you adopt, you must lever away the lip of lead (called the 'came') holding the glass in place by using an old chisel. Cut the lead near the corners of the pane with a knife to make this easier. Remove the broken glass, clean out the putty from the channel in the lead, apply new putty and then fit the new pane – this should be cut to fit the dimensions of the rebate exactly. Finally, smooth back the lead with the handle of the chisel to hold it in place. To finish, make good the knife cuts with solder, or with a proprietary plastic repair compound.

If the pane is in very poor condition, it will be better to remove it and replace it completely.

Why glass?

You may be wondering why nobody has come up with a glass or glass substitute that never breaks. Well, they have. Leaving aside bullet-proof glass and the like, there are a host of plastic glazing materials on the market ranging from the familiar Perspex to compounds with complicated chemical names. But they all have two major drawbacks – they are comparatively expensive to buy, and they scratch so easily that they lose their transparency.

INDEX